AUTHORITY AND TRADITION IN ANCIENT HISTORIOGRAPHY

This book is a study of the various claims to authority made by the ancient Greek and Roman historians throughout their histories and is the first to examine all aspects of the historian's self-presentation. It shows how each historian claimed veracity by imitating, modifying, and manipulating the traditions established by his predecessors. Beginning with a discussion of the tension between individuality and imitation, it then categorises and analyses the recurring *topoi* used to establish the historian's authority: how he came to write history; the qualifications he brought to the task; the inquiries and efforts he made in his research; and his claims to possess a reliable character. By detailing how each historian used the tradition to claim and maintain his own authority, the book contributes to a better understanding of the complex nature of ancient historiography.

AUTHORITY AND TRADITION IN ANCIENT HISTORIOGRAPHY

JOHN MARINCOLA

*Associate Professor in the Department of Classics,
Union College, Schenectady, New York*

PUBLISHED BY THE PRESS SYNDICATE OF THE UNIVERSITY OF CAMBRIDGE
The Pitt Building, Trumpington Street, Cambridge, United Kingdom

CAMBRIDGE UNIVERSITY PRESS
The Edinburgh Building, Cambridge CB2 2RU, UK
40 West 20th Street, New York NY 10011–4211, USA
477 Williamstown Road, Port Melbourne, VIC 3207, Australia
Ruiz de Alarcón 13, 28014 Madrid, Spain
Dock House, The Waterfront, Cape Town 8001, South Africa

http://www.cambridge.org

© Cambridge University Press 1997

This book is in copyright. Subject to statutory exception
and to the provisions of relevant collective licensing agreements,
no reproduction of any part may take place without
the written permission of Cambridge University Press.

First published 1997
Reprinted 1999
First paperback edition 2004

A catalogue record for this book is available from the British Library

Library of Congress cataloguing in publication data
Marincola, John
Authority and tradition in ancient historiography / John
Marincola.
p. cm.
Includes bibliographical references and index.
ISBN 0 521 48019 1 (hardback)
1. History, Ancient – Historiography.   I. Title.
n56.M37   1997
930.072–dc20   96-18630 CIP

ISBN 0 521 48019 1 hardback
ISBN 0 521 54578 1 paperback

Transferred to digital printing 2004

TO MICHELE

animae dimidio meae

Contents

Preface	*page xi*
List of abbreviations	*xiv*
INTRODUCTION	1
1 The scope and subject of the book	1
2 Authority	3
3 Tradition	12
4 History's place and audience	19
I **THE CALL TO HISTORY**	34
1 The greatness of the subject	34
2 Decisions and dreams	43
3 Dedications and the desires of friends	52
4 Glory and renown	57
II **THE HISTORIAN'S INQUIRY**	63
1 Eyes, ears and contemporary history	63
2 Closed societies and privileged access	86
3 Improving the past	95
4 Myth and history	117
III **THE HISTORIAN'S CHARACTER**	128
1 The importance of character	128
2 Experience	133
3 Effort	148
4 Impartiality	158
IV **THE HISTORIAN'S DEEDS**	175
1 Praise and self-praise	175
2 Person and perspective	182
3 Strategies of self-presentation	205

v THE 'LONELY' HISTORIAN: CONTRAST AND CONTINUITY   217

1 The uses of polemic   218
2 Polemic and self-definition   225
3 Continuity and culmination   237

CONCLUSION   258

Appendices   267

I Table of historians   267
II Name and nationality   271
III Isocrates on autopsy and inquiry?   276
IV Variant versions   280
V The Roman convention of 'nos' and 'nostri'   287
VI Greek continuators   289
VII Roman continuators   291

Bibliography   293
Index locorum   316
Index of Greek words   335
General index   336

Preface

I began this work with a simple question: what do ancient historians tell us about themselves? Like many simple questions, it proved rather difficult to answer. Ancient historians give us a great deal of information about themselves, whether in their choice of subject, or their language of implied judgement, or what incidents they choose for elaboration, or how they see human actions and motivation. Indeed, it is only a slight exaggeration to say that for most ancient historians almost every sentence in their work tells us something about its creator. As I further refined the topic, I saw that I wanted to examine the *Selbstdarstellung*, the self-presentation or self-display, of the ancient historian, that is, how he claimed to be a trustworthy and authoritative narrator. When I saw that the same or similar claims reappeared so often, I realised that I also needed to consider the importance of tradition in ancient literary criticism and creation. And I began to see, moreover, how the two issues were closely related.

My goal in this book has been to examine the creation of authority as an aspect of the ancient historiographical tradition, as it developed from Herodotus and Thucydides. In doing this, I have treated many topics in ancient historiography that have been intensively studied for over a century. Many of the passages will be readily familiar, even to those who have only a passing acquaintance with ancient historians. I felt there was still work to be done, even though several studies of the tradition as a whole already exist, because previous scholars have been mostly interested in establishing the similarity of what ancient historians say, without looking at the individual adaptations made by specific historians over time. On the other hand, the numerous excellent studies of individual historians emphasise their own man (as one would expect), and are, as a rule, less concerned with seeing their subject as one person working within a tradition. Naturally, there are excellent studies of historians in which the individual is placed within the tradition, but I know of no work that tries to look at the individual within the continuity and development of the tradition.

I have chosen to treat only explicit remarks by historians, and in doing so I am aware of taking only a first step. I do not suggest by any means that the conventions here studied are the only, or indeed even the primary, means by which an historian commands assent in his audience. Ultimately, it is the narrative itself that will persuade the reader, and no number of protestations of accuracy, honesty, or care can rescue what a reader believes is a fundamentally mendacious account; similarly, we do not fail to trust an historian's account, simply because such claims are absent. If an historian compels belief, this will frequently depend on more things than what historians say about themselves. Nevertheless, the prevalence of such remarks in the ancient histories that have come down to us suggests that the ancients saw them as fulfilling an important or ancillary role in establishing the narrator's credibility and authority. It is not, in any case, the purpose here to determine the truth or falsity of the claims of individual historians. Rather, we want to trace in detail this literary tradition, and to draw from it some conclusions on how the ancient historians saw their role.

I must emphasise as well that although I have tried to be comprehensive, I cannot claim that every section is exhaustive and treats all the relevant material. Almost every ancient historian would have some place in the various categories by which I have organised this work, but I have not treated every historian in every section. Rather, I have tried to indicate the general outline of the issues, while concentrating attention on those historians who most clearly lend themselves to an examination of the specific conventions under study.

This book has been several years in the making, and I have incurred many debts during its writing. My chief intellectual debt is to Charles Fornara, who first encouraged me to look at what historians said about themselves, and who, more importantly, opened up for me the world of ancient historiography, and revealed how its study could give valuable insights into the intellectual world of Greco-Roman antiquity. I wrote the first draft of this work at Ludwig-Maximilians-Universität in Munich during the academic year 1989-90, and I am grateful to Christian Meier, my sponsor there, and to the staff and librarians in the Institut für Alte Geschichte and the Institut für Klassische Philologie for their unfailing courtesy and helpfulness.

I have been fortunate to have at Union College three colleagues, Mark Toher, Christina Sorum, and Scott Scullion, who have been uncommonly generous with their time and advice. They have created a wonderful intellectual environment, in which I felt free to pester them for information and subject them again and again to my ideas. In addition, they have often acted beyond the call of duty or friendship in rearranging their own schedules so that I could have leave time for this project. My secretary, Mrs Marianne Snowden, has been invaluable, typing many drafts of this book cheerfully and efficiently, as well as seeing to the daily details that would otherwise have overwhelmed me. I thank the staff of Schaffer Library for their assistance in obtaining many inter-library loan items. And for financial support I am grateful to the College's Humanities Faculty Development Fund.

My readers for the Press have saved me from many errors and obscurities of expression. Dr R. B. Rutherford helped me particularly to focus more clearly on several issues, and to clarify my lines of exposition and argument. Tony Woodman has put me further in his debt by his wealth of comments and corrections. I owe him a great deal, not only for the stimulation of his published work, and for the enthusiastic support he has given me in this (and other) projects, but also for the encouragement and kindness he has shown me since our first meeting.

Several friends have made the task more pleasurable, and been generous with their time and advice. I thank especially Deborah Boedeker, Harriet Flower, Michael Flower, Nina Klebanoff, and Kurt Raaflaub. To my parents, Margaret and John, my first and best teachers, I can only acknowledge all that they have done, rather than in any way repay it.

I am most grateful to the Cambridge University Press, and especially to Pauline Hire and Glennis Foote, for their patience, assistance, and constructive advice, to say nothing of their indulgence of the author in some of his more fanciful requests. I thank also Alan Finch and Caroline Murray for their help in the latter stages of the book's production.

It is not to be expected that any of the people mentioned here necessarily agrees with what I have written, and it goes without saying (so I shall say it) that I alone am responsible for all errors of omission and commission that remain.

Even with the support and help of these people, the task may have come to nothing, were it not for my wife Michele. The dedication of this volume to her is but a small repayment for the true generosity of spirit and love that she has given me over many years.

J.M.

Abbreviations

For ancient authors I follow the traditional abbreviations, as found in H. G. Liddell and R. Scott, *A Greek-English Lexicon* and P. G. Glare, ed., *Oxford Latin Dictionary*. Lucian's *How to Write History*, because of the frequency of citation, is abbreviated *h.c.* All translations of ancient authors are my own.

Journals are abbreviated as in *L' Année Philologique*, with the conventional modifications in English. I use the following abbreviations for frequently cited modern works:

ANRW	*Aufstieg und Niedergang der römischen Welt*, edd. H. Temporini and W. Haase (Berlin 1972–).
Avenarius, *LS*	G. Avenarius, *Lukians Schrift zur Geschichtsschreibung* (Meisenheim am Glan 1957).
Bosworth, *HCA*	A. B. Bosworth, *A Historical Commentary on Arrian's History of Alexander* (Oxford 1980–).
DK	H. Diels and W. Kranz, *Die Fragmente der Vorsokratiker*, 3 vols. (Berlin ^{6}1951).
FGrHist	F. Jacoby *et al.*, *Die Fragmente der griechischen Historiker* (Berlin and Leiden 1922–56; Leiden 1994–). Jacoby's (and his continuators') commentary is cited as *Komm.* with volume, page, and (occasionally) line number.
FHG	C. and F. Müller, *Fragmenta Historicorum Graecorum*, 5 vols. (Paris 1841–7).
Fornara, *Nature*	C. W. Fornara, *The Nature of History in Ancient Greece and Rome* (Berkeley, Los Angeles, and London 1983).
Gelzer, *KS*	M. Gelzer, *Kleine Schriften*, 3 vols., edd. H. Strasburger and C. Meier (Wiesbaden 1964).

GGM	C. Müller, *Geographi Graeci Minores*, 2 vols. (Paris 1855, 1861).
HCT	A. W. Gomme, A. Andrewes, and K. J. Dover, *A Historical Commentary on Thucydides*, 5 vols. (Oxford 1941-79).
Herkommer, *Topoi*	E. Herkommer, *Die topoi in den Proömien der römischen Geschichtswerke* (Tübingen 1968).
Herzog-Schmidt	R. Herzog and P. L. Schmidt, *Handbuch der lateinischen Literatur der Antike* (Munich 1989-).
Homeyer, *Lukian*	H. Homeyer, *Lukian: wie man Geschichte schreiben soll* (Munich 1965).
Hornblower, *CT*	S. Hornblower, *A Commentary on Thucydides* (Oxford 1991-).
Jacoby, *Abhandlungen*	F. Jacoby, *Abhandlungen zur griechischen Geschichtsschreibung*, ed. H. Bloch (Leiden 1956).
HRR	H. Peter, *Historicorum Romanorum Reliquiae*, 2 vols. (Stuttgart ²1914, 1906).
L&F	C. Gill and T. P. Wiseman, edd., *Lies and Fiction in the Ancient World* (Exeter and Austin, Texas 1993).
Lloyd, *MRE*	G. E. R. Lloyd, *Magic, Reason and Experience* (Cambridge 1979).
ORF	H. Malcovati, *Oratorum Romanorum Fragmenta Liberae Rei Publicae* (Turin ⁴1976).
Past Persp.	I. S. Moxon, J. D. Smart, and A. J. Woodman, edd., *Past Perspectives. Studies in Greek and Roman Historical Writing* (Cambridge 1986).
Peter, *GL*	H. Peter, *Die geschichtliche Literatur über die römische Kaiserzeit*, 2 vols. (Leipzig 1897).
PoH	H. Verdin, G. Schepens, and E. deKeyser, edd., *Purposes of History. Studies in Greek Historiography from the 4th to the 2nd centuries BC*, Studia Hellenistica 30 (Leuven 1990).
Rawson, *RCS*	E. Rawson, *Roman Culture and Society: Collected Papers* (Oxford 1991).
RE	A. von Pauly, G. Wissowa and W. Kroll,

	Real-encyclopädie der classischen Altertumswissenschaft (Stuttgart 1894-1978).
Schanz-Hosius	M. Schanz, C. Hosius, and G. Krüger, *Geschichte der römischen Literatur*, 4 vols. (Munich 1914-35).
Schwartz, *GG*	E. Schwartz, *Griechische Geschichtschreiber* (Leipzig 1959).
Syme, *RP*	R. Syme, *Roman Papers*, 7 vols. (Oxford 1979-91).
Walbank, *HCP*	F. W. Walbank, *A Historical Commentary on Polybius*, 3 vols. (Oxford 1957-78).
Walbank, *SP*	F. W. Walbank, *Selected Papers. Studies in Greek and Roman History and Historiography* (Cambridge 1985).
Wiseman, *CC*	T. P. Wiseman, *Clio's Cosmetics. Three Studies in Greco-Roman Literature* (Leicester and Totowa, New Jersey 1979).
Wiseman, *RS*	T. P. Wiseman, *Roman Studies. Literary and Historical* (Liverpool 1987).
Woodman, *RICH*	A. J. Woodman, *Rhetoric in Classical Historiography* (London, Sydney, and Portland 1988).
Woodman, *VP* I, II	A. J. Woodman, ed., *Velleius Paterculus.* I = *The Tiberian Narrative* (2.94-131); II = *The Caesarian and Augustan Narrative* (2.41-93) (Cambridge 1977, 1983).

Introduction

I. THE SCOPE AND SUBJECT OF THE BOOK

This book is a study of the explicit attempts by which the ancient Greek and Roman historians claim the authority to narrate the deeds encompassed in their works. The term 'authority' has many meanings over a range of disciplines, but in this book it is used to refer to literary authority, the rhetorical means by which the ancient historian claims the competence to narrate and explain the past, and simultaneously constructs a persona that the audience will find persuasive and believable.[1] The work is thus a study of certain forms and conventions of persuasion employed by the historians. No attempt is made to evaluate the truth or falsity of historians' claims; rather, I try to set out the various claims which are part of the construction of the author's historiographical persona; to see how and why these claims are made; to explain how the tradition of such claims developed; and to show how the tradition moulded the way in which writers claimed historiographical authority.

The writers treated range from Herodotus in the fifth century BC to Ammianus Marcellinus in the fourth century AD. Included in this study are both the surviving (either whole or in part) historians and those whose works have come down to us only in fragments.[2] By the standard classification, the historical writing of the Greeks and Romans is usually divided into five types or genres: (i) mythography or genealogy, concerned mostly with establishing lines of descent, and oftentimes going

---

[1] Except for brief treatment at Ch. II §2, I do not discuss authority in the sense of an established political, religious, or social power, something external to the history itself, which impinges, either beneficially or harmfully, upon the literary work; for the ancient historian's relation to power see Meissner, *Historiker zwischen Polis und Koenigshof*, *passim*. For an overview of the various meanings and forms of 'authority' see Scanlon, *Narrative, Authority, and Power* 37–45.
[2] When using fragmentary historians I have tried to apply the cautions suggested by Brunt, *CQ* 30 (1980) 477–94.

back to the mythical period; (ii) ethnography, the study of a people's customs and way of life; (iii) chronography, attempts to establish timetables of events, sometimes even written in a tabular form; (iv) history, the narrative of deeds, whether it be a contemporary history, a work that mixes contemporary and non-contemporary history, an historical monograph, a memoir, or a universal history; and (v) horography, or local history, told from the point of view of a single city-state and sometimes in a bare annalistic form.[3] In this work I treat all those who wrote narrative or largely narrative histories, so that my material comes mainly from section (iv) above. Material from geographers, biographers, epitomators, and writers of chronicles is occasionally adduced as evidence, but no systematic study of these genres has been made.[4] Works of ancient literary criticism, when they have a bearing on the writing of history, have also been used, but I have not made a special study of them. Lucian's second-century AD work, *How to Write History*, is, of course, included throughout, although I have avoided the tendency, sometimes seen, to begin with Lucian and then seek confirmation in the historians before and after him. My own procedure has been to include him either at the end of a section after the historians themselves have been examined, or in his proper chronological place.[5]

I have not chosen certain historians as representatives or spokesmen for ancient historiography as a whole. It has long been common to separate historians into two camps, and to posit, on the one hand, an events-oriented, largely political history that counts as its practitioners Thucydides, Polybius, Tacitus, and Ammianus, to name a few; and on the other hand, a pleasure-oriented, highly artificial 'rhetorical'

---

[3] The fundamental exposition of the development of historiographical genres is Jacoby, *Abhandlungen* 16-64; followed in large measure but with modifications by Fornara, *Nature* 1-46. Both arrangements are somewhat constrictive and leave too little room for innovation; some works (Xenophon's *Anabasis*, Velleius' history, Tacitus' *Agricola*) are problematic and do not fit well into any of the categories. See also the survey of the development of Greek historiography by Hornblower in id., ed., *Greek Historiography* 7-54.

[4] I do include Agatharchides of Cnidus' *On the Red Sea*, because Verdin, in *Egypt and the Hellenistic World* 407-20, and Burstein, *Agatharchides* 21-4 argue convincingly that it is a history, not a geography.

[5] The tract was written in AD 166: Jones, *Culture and Society* 59-60. There are several studies of Lucian's work, the most useful being Avenarius, *LS* and Homeyer, *Lukian*; for bibliography see Georgiadou and Larmour, *ANRW* II. 34. 2, 1448-78. I treat the historians satirised by Lucian as actual historians, although this is contested: see Jones, ibid. 63-4, 161-6.

historiography, whose founder or patron saint was Isocrates and whose members include Ephorus, Duris, Dionysius, Livy and many others. In my opinion, such a schematic approach, quite apart from the rather useless designation as 'rhetorical', belies the number of approaches to history in antiquity and the various reasons why both good and bad writers turned to the past. Since there was great variety in the writing of narrative history, I have tried to represent that variety in this work, believing that only with a consideration of all types of Greek and Roman historical writing will we be able to come to a better understanding of the nature of ancient historiography.[6]

2. AUTHORITY

When we look at our earliest examples of Greek literature, the narrators of Homer's epics, we see that the poet's claims of authority, which are neither explicit nor lengthy, rest on his invocation of the Muse. She is portrayed as the inspiration of the poet, who supplies that which the mortal poet cannot, and who (in some sense) guarantees the truth or reliability (however this is to be interpreted) of the account that follows.[7] Having made the opening invocation, the poet will only occasionally thereafter break the mimetic pane of the narrative.[8] It has been suggested that the poet of the *Odyssey* shows a greater self-awareness of his poetic authority, moving away from dependence on the Muse, and expressing pride in his own ability.[9] Such a view has much to recommend it; one sees in the *Odyssey* both the Muse's inspiration and an acknowledgement of the poet's technique or craft, as, for example, when the bard Phemius says that he is both self-taught and inspired by

---

[6] For various views on the nature of ancient historiography, see Wiseman, *CC*; Fornara, *Nature*; Woodman, *RICH*; Meister, *Griechische Geschichtsschreibung*.

[7] I have here simplified greatly, since the exact nature of poetic inspiration and its importance for and relation to the truth-claims of the poet are much discussed topics that have been interpreted quite differently: see Kirk, *The Iliad: A Commentary* 1.51, 167; Heubeck *et al.*, *Commentary on the Odyssey* 1.68 and references there; P. Murray, *JHS* 101 (1981) 87-100; Slings, *LF* 112 (1989) 72-80; Bowie, *L&F* 8-20.

[8] According to de Jong, *Narrators and Focalizers* 46, Homer refers to his activity as narrator six times in the *Iliad* (1.1-7; II.484-93; 761-2; XI.218-20; XIV.508-9; XVI. 112-13), and invocations of the Muse are common before narratives requiring enumeration; cf. P. Murray, op. cit. (n.7) 90-2; see the latter's distinction (89-90) between the general inspiration that the poet possesses and his need at times for specific assistance.   [9] Maehler, *Auffassung des Dichterberufs* 33ff.

the Muse, and by so doing recognises his own role in the composition of his songs.[10] Yet as in the *Iliad* so in the *Odyssey*, the narrator's authority is absolute, and the poet expresses no uncertainty when reporting actions, intentions, or motivations.[11] The human characters, on the other hand, behave differently from the narrator. Speakers in Homer (as we would expect in real life) will sometimes claim to be speaking truth by appealing in oaths to the gods as guarantors of their credibility, by offering wagers, and by other forms of bargaining.[12] Moreover, unlike the narrator, humans in the epic are not omniscient, a condition best seen in Odysseus' narrative of his own adventures where he frequently expresses ignorance of the workings of the gods, or even of some aspects of his own experience.[13]

In the *Theogony* Hesiod speaks more explicitly of his authority, but the source of his knowledge is the same: it is the Muses who visit him and give him the poet's staff and their ambiguous message that they can speak both truth and falsehood that sounds like truth.[14] In archaic lyric poetry, the invocation of the Muses remains common, although one can also see traces of new validations interspersed amongst the traditional ones: Theognis invokes the gods at the outset of his poems, yet speaks of some of the content of his poem as derived from 'the experience of my elders'; Mimnermus appeals to eyewitnesses as validators for his description of a fighter's prowess in battle; Solon calls the Earth to witness for his political actions.[15]

Similarly, and perhaps in imitation of the poets, the early philosophers invoke Muses or gods as a validation for the truth of their tales or explanations: Parmenides speaks of δαίμονες, Empedocles of the Muse who directs him.[16] But here too there is a movement away from the divine apparatus. Part of the philosophers' claim to authority is an

---

[10] *Od.* xxii.347-9, with P. Murray, op. cit. (n.7) 96-7.
[11] Booth, *Rhetoric of Fiction* 4-6.   [12] See Bowie, *L&F* 1-2.
[13] For a full treatment see de Jong, *CQ* 42 (1992) 1-11. The narrator is careful to portray the hero as knowing no more than he should; Odysseus even cites sources when relating events in heaven: ταῦτα δ' ἐγὼν ἤκουσα Καλυψοῦς ἠϋκόμοιο. | ἡ δ' ἔφη Ἑρμαίαο διακτόρου αὐτὴ ἀκοῦσαι (*Od.* xii.389-90). (The lines have been considered spurious; for a defence of their genuineness see H. Erbse, *Beiträge zum Verständnis der Odyssee* (Berlin and New York 1972) 12-15.)   [14] *Theog.* 22-32, with West's commentary ad loc.
[15] Theognis 1-18; 769-72, esp. 769-70; Mimnermus F 13; Solon F 13. 1-2; F 36. 3-5. On the more pronounced use of the first-person among the poets see App. II n.3.   [16] DK 28 B 1; 31 B 3, 4.

emphasis on their own knowledge and innovation, as can be seen partly in their more pronounced use of the first person,[17] and partly in the attacks on their predecessors and contemporaries.[18] It is this pattern which the early historians follow. Greek historiography opens with a striking and individual claim:

> Hecataeus of Miletus speaks thus: I write what follows as it seems to me to be true; for the stories of the Greeks are varied, and, as is manifest to me, ludicrous.[19]

The historian here seems to claim only his own intellectual gifts – 'as it seems to me to be true' – for the narrative to follow in his work. He has no recourse to oaths, he calls no one as witness, he stands unsupported by god or Muse. We do not know, of course, that this is the sole validation used by Hecataeus, nor whether at various points in his narrative he supported his presentation by other means. But the claim at the outset is nonetheless striking, and introduces a fundamentally new direction.

The ancient historian did not, like the epic or didactic poet, profess inspiration or omniscience, nor did he swear an oath to the truth of his words.[20] In place of these he used a variety of claims, promises, 'proofs', and advertisements. The earliest and most common was the assurance that the work before the reader rested on the author's personal inquiry and investigation. Although the claim was to take many forms, from actual participation in events to the more sedentary perusal of previous histories, it was nevertheless a persistent feature of ancient historiography and can be found in nearly every historian from Herodotus to Ammianus. As the historical consciousness of the Greeks grew, and as more areas of exploration seized their interest, the historians were forced to confront new challenges to their authority and new ways of asserting it. Without abandoning the original means of validation, they superimposed new types on existing models. Claims are piled upon claims, not only because of the omnipresent influence of rhetoric, but also because, as more and more assayed the task of history, it became correspondingly more difficult to distinguish oneself, in Livy's phrase, 'in such a crowd of writers'.[21] Add to this that the Romans, although

---

[17] See Lloyd, *MRE* 59-70; id., *Revolutions of Wisdom* 83-108; id., *PCPhS* 40 (1994) 28-9. [18] For polemic as an element in winning authority, see Ch. V §1.

[19] Hecataeus, *FGrHist* 1 F 1a.

[20] Cf. Sen. *Apocol.* 1. 2: 'quis umquam ab historico iuratores exegit?'

[21] Livy, *praef.* 3: 'in tanta scriptorum turba'.

influenced by the Greeks, had social and literary traditions of their own which affected how they claimed authority, and that many types of Roman validation co-existed with the ones inherited from the classical and Hellenistic Greek worlds. Some of these claims – rather a large number of them – have to do with the non-epistemic basis of the historian's account, and revolve around issues of character. This is not surprising given the importance in antiquity of character in rhetoric and real life: the highly stratified societies of Greece and Rome cared a great deal about the status of the speaker. The proof that things are as the historian says they are depended not a little on the audience's perception of the narrator's character: to believe an historical account, it was necessary to believe the historian himself.

Now historical narrative, as it first appears in Herodotus and continues to Ammianus (and beyond), is a largely third-person account that employs some element of creative imitation or representation (*mimesis*) to portray the actions, thoughts, intentions, and words of characters who are presumed, with more or less certainty, to have really existed and acted so.[22] This is historiography's legacy from Homer, who, as the writer of the most 'authoritative' third-person narrative, provided a model not only for later poets epic and otherwise, but also for the prose historians who, by way of Herodotus, saw him as their model and rival. Homeric epic provided historiography with many of its distinctive and long-lived features: its predominantly third-person narrative; its subject matter of great deeds and great words, of λόγοι and ἔργα; its concern to articulate a sequence of events and to discuss their causes and effects; and (not least of all) its concern with praise and rescue from oblivion.[23] Historiography differs from epic, however, in that it also contains commentary on the narrative by the historian himself: here the narrator employs an 'artificial authority' by which he interprets the events in his work for the reader, and explicitly directs the reader to

---

[22] For ancient categories of narrative, divided according to narrator, see Plato, *Rep.* III.392d–394d, with de Jong, *Narrators and Focalizers* 3ff.; Arist. *Poet.* 3, 1448a 19–25, with Lucas' commentary ad loc.; Halliwell, *Aristotle's Poetics* 128 with n. 34; Else, *Aristotle's Poetics* 97ff. For narratives divided by subject see below, p. 118.

[23] Strasburger, *Studien zur alten Geschichte* II.1057–97 remains the fundamental treatment; see also Fornara, *Nature* 62–3, 76–7; Woodman, *RICH* ch. I, *passim*; for the influence of Homer on Herodotus see Hüber, in *Synusia: Festgabe . . . Schadewaldt* 29–52; Huxley, *Herodotus and the Epic* 5–7, 21–2; Erbse, *Studien zum Verständnis Herodots* 122–32.

think in a certain manner.[24] Whereas the Homeric narrator is largely unintrusive, Herodotus, frequently, in his own person, calls attention to his role as the organiser and expositor of his history, reminding his audience of the travels, investigative work, and comparison of accounts that went into the making of his history, while oftentimes commenting explicitly on the quality of the material he includes.[25]

Whether this owes something to Hecataeus cannot be determined: like Dionysius, we can say very little about the styles of the earliest historians.[26] To what extent their narrative methods originated in traditional story-telling methods[27] or earlier non-historical prose works is impossible to say. We do know, however, that Herodotus' activity coincides with other investigative and 'historical' works, that Ionian rationalism in general and the works of Hecataeus (and, less certainly, Xanthus of Lydia[28]) in particular provided the spur to and (at least at the beginning) the intellectual framework of his investigations. Had we more prose literature of Herodotus' time we would have a clearer sense of the tradition and his place in it, of the conventions of prose narrative and the accepted ways of telling and validating stories. Yet all we have is Herodotus, emerging with a massive work at the beginning of a tradition:[29]

---

[24] On intrusive narration see Booth, op. cit. (n.11) 40-2, 67-86. Historians could also intrude into their narratives in less explicit ways, for example, oblique characterisation, ascription of motives, language of judgement, and so on; for an analysis of some of these techniques in Thucydides see Hornblower, *Greek Historiography* 131-66.

[25] On the Herodotean narrator see Beltrametti, *Erodoto*; Darbo-Peschanski, *Le discours du particulier*; Dewald, *Arethusa* 20 (1987) 147-70, who records 1,087 explicit or implicit intrusions.

[26] D. Hal. *Thuc.* 23, though he is here speaking of historians before Hecataeus, a category not recognised by moderns: for Hecataeus as the first historian, see Jacoby, *Abhandlungen* 20-1. For Dionysius' stylistic evaluations of early historians see Toye, *AJPh* 116 (1995) 298-9 with reff.

[27] O. Murray, in *Achaemenid History* II.93-115.

[28] On Xanthus' influence on Herodotus, *FGrHist* 765 T 5; discussion in Pearson, *Early Ionian Historians* 109-16; at 134, he places Xanthus between Hecataeus and Herodotus, an advance over the former and (accepting Ephorus) a spur to the latter. Von Fritz, *Griech. Geschichtsschreibung* I.88, II.72 n. 49 says 'etwa mit Herodot gleichzeitig', but notes that influence on Herodotus from Xanthus' fragments is not demonstrable. Jacoby in the *Fragmente* dates Xanthus 'nach 425'.

[29] Or could it possibly be the end of a tradition (like the *Iliad*) with a long history behind it, of which only faint traces remain? That, at least, is how it seemed to Dionysius (*Thuc.* 5).

> Herodotus of Halicarnassus here displays his inquiry, in order that human action may not become obliterated in time, and in order that great and marvellous deeds, some displayed by Greeks, some by barbarians, may not lack their renown; and most especially why they made war on each other.

The work is a display of inquiry (ἱστορίης ἀπόδεξις) in the sense that it both publishes the results of the author's inquiries, and shows the narrator himself in the act of discovery.[30] Herodotus is the first to have written a mainly third-person narrative that wished to commemorate deeds and bestow fame upon them, yet at the same time he was working in a new tradition – no longer the poetic with its guarantees of validity from the Muse.[31] His solution was a constant stream of comment that represents a pervasive concern with obviating any doubts that might arise: Herodotus seems to assume that the question, 'How do you know?', is constantly on his audience's mind.[32] His solution was to place himself, if not front and centre, then in a constant and direct relationship with his material, ensuring that he, the narrator, was recognised as the medium, the authority, through which the deeds became known and celebrated. Such self-display does, however, find parallels in the contemporary milieu of performance known from other genres, particularly by the sophists and the medical writers. Here authors performed before citizens in wisdom contests, and it is possible to see something of Herodotus' persona in their pronounced use of the first-person pronoun, in their claims of truth telling, and in their polemic with predecessors and contemporaries.[33]

A different method, and the one that was to become standard, is revealed by Thucydides. This narrator, although like Herodotus' a controlling intelligence, intrudes only briefly upon the narrative, and even these intrusions are nearly exclusively in digressions. Unlike Herodotus, who gives his methodological procedures piece-

---

[30] Dewald, op. cit. (n.25).

[31] Hüber, op. cit. (n.23) 52 n. 74 points out that still in Herodotus' time epic poems about the Persian Wars could begin with an appeal to the Muses. For earlier examples from historical epic see Mimnermus F 13 (probably from his *History of Smyrna*) and Simonides F 11.21 (from his *Battle of Plataea*).

[32] For the importance of avoiding this question in narrative see Dowden, *CQ* 32 (1982) 420.

[33] See Lloyd in the works cited above, n. 17; for Herodotus' similarity in method and narrative manner to the medical writers see Lateiner, *Antichthon* 20 (1986) 1-20; Thomas, in *Vermittlung und Tradierung von Wissen* 234-43.

meal and throughout the history, Thucydides reveals the type of mind to be expected in his work all at the beginning: his extended preface plays a crucial role in the establishment of the historian's authority.[34] In a move away from Herodotus, Thucydides de-emphasises the first person, even in non-contemporary history, using an impersonal or third-person language of investigation and conjecture.[35] What few first-person remarks exist are reinforced by the constant stream of reasoning, with its whole host of words emphasising mental activity; and the analytical mind behind them is producing simultaneously a 'history' of early Greece and a justification of the claim at the outset that the Peloponnesian War was greater than any that had gone before. The narrator is just as present in Thucydides; but he is not as intrusive as in Herodotus. All seems assured (within human limits, of course), and the entire dynamic is presented as impersonal and irrefragable. Plato was fond of stating that he and his interlocutors must follow an argument to whatever place the *logos* led,[36] and in the opening chapters of Thucydides, the reasoning is so effectively made that he seems almost to be that Platonic servant of *logos*.[37] No doubt part of the purpose of such assuredness is that the author wishes to avoid questions about the source of his knowledge – whether autopsy, inquiry, hearsay, or even written sources – which seems to have been constantly on Herodotus' mind. The narrative homogeneity of Thucydides is meant to inspire confidence; he does not, like Herodotus, want the emphasis to be on his tracking down of sources, but on the finished product: the reader is to be concerned not with the process of research, but rather with the result.

To the extent that Thucydides omitted the constant authorial comment in Herodotus, and in his contemporary narrative attempted to win authority by producing an account that shows little or no uncertainty, to this extent we may say that he fashioned an alternative persona to that of

---

[34] See Connor, in *The Greek Historians* 1–17 for intelligence as a factor in the author's credibility; *contra*, Robinson, ibid. 19–23; Moles, *L&F* 98–106 shows that in many ways Thucydides modelled his preface on Herodotus'.
[35] See Connor, *Thucydides* 27–32.
[36] See R. Robinson, *Plato's Earlier Dialectic* (Oxford ²1953) 7–15.
[37] Parry, *Language of Achilles and other Papers* 287 argues that this is one of Thucydides' most subjective aspects; Woodman, *RICH* 23 speaks of 'an essentially rhetorical procedure'.

Herodotus.[38] The constant first-person comment was not to be repeated,[39] nor was the frequent injection of the narrator himself revived, except for conscious (but limited) imitation of Herodotus in non-contemporary history.[40] In Xenophon we see an extreme application of the Thucydidean model. The narrator in Xenophon (both *Hellenica* and *Anabasis*) is not only unintrusive: he is practically anonymous.[41] His works recognise the value of a mostly impersonal narrative told in a style largely free of rhetorical adornment, in achieving credibility.[42] It is no coincidence that for the ancients and (until recently) moderns, his work was considered very reliable.[43]

Another method of narration, that of Polybius, is not unrelated to the question of authority, and should here be mentioned. The Polybian narrator combines a largely unobtrusive narrative of the deeds with a highly intrusive explicator of that narrative. Many major (and not a few minor) episodes are explained, analysed, commended,

[38] Thucydides' authority is helped by the fact that he is our sole source for most of what he reports and we cannot compare his account with another: see Dover, *HCT* v.403-5; id., *Thucydides* 4-5.

[39] For the long but different first-person accounts of Dio and Ammianus, see below, pp. 199ff.

[40] As, for example, by Dionysius: see Ek, *Herodotismen*; id., *Eranos* 43 (1945) 198-214.

[41] On Xenophon's anonymity in the *Anabasis* see Ch. IV n. 135; in the *Hellenica*, note the extreme effacement of the author in the incident where the Spartan government has reprimanded the troops under Dercylidas for their previous behaviour but commended them for their present actions; they are defended, says the narrator, by 'the one who was in charge of the partisans of Cyrus' (ὁ τῶν Κυρείων προεστηκώς, *Hell.* III.2.7), i. e. Xenophon – whose name is strikingly omitted.

[42] As style is not an explicit means of claiming authority, I do not treat it in this book (but see below, pp. 116ff.). For some indications that an unadorned style could be a mark of authoritativeness, see Sall. *Jug.* 85. 31; Livy, III.56.3; for a soldier's 'plain' (and therefore trustworthy) style, see Cic. *Brut.* 262 (on Caesar's *Commentarii*); Livy, x.24.4; Luc. *h. c.* 8; 16.

[43] Only the recovery of a contemporary account of the same events (the Oxyrhynchus historian) has shown the obvious shortcomings of Xenophon's *Hellenica*. The unintrusiveness of the narrator had seemed to guarantee a type of veracity: see Cawkwell, introduction to the Penguin *Hellenica* 16. Imitating only the outward feature of Thucydides' narrative, Xenophon nevertheless compelled belief. There is a difference in the narrator's voice from the first part of the history to the second: see *Hell.* II.3.56; IV.3.16; 8.1; VI.2.32; 2.39; VII.2.1. Yet even with such examples acknowledged, Xenophon's narrator remains basically that of Thucydides, unintrusive except for occasional passages where the narrator's voice becomes emphatic.

or reproved by the historian in his own person, in digressions placed without fail throughout the entire work. Morals are frequently drawn and interpretations consistently re-emphasised.[44] Thus a Thucydidean component, more or less faithfully followed, has had grafted upon it a method much closer to the demonstrative method of Herodotus. But Polybius goes beyond even Herodotus in interpreting his own narrative: where Herodotus could be dramatic and subtle, Polybius allows nearly nothing to pass without drawing his own moral from it for the benefit of his audience, almost as if he were afraid that they might overlook an incident's importance, or draw the wrong lesson or moral from what he has so carefully constructed.[45] If this were not enough, he also at times even explains his explanations.[46] Whether this was the method of the Hellenistic historians (who may have begun a more explicit tradition of explaining the use or benefit of their histories[47]) cannot be known.

How the early Roman historians claimed authority we can only suggest, since their narrative manner can hardly be recovered from the meagre fragments. When we can finally examine the tradition, with Sallust's *Catiline*, Greek influences on Roman literature had been present for more than a century. Narrative styles among the Romans differ, yet it is only rarely (comparatively speaking) that Sallust, Tacitus, and Ammianus comment explicitly in their own person on events, characters, digressions, or problems with the tradition. Indeed, as we shall see, the Roman historians use far fewer explicit methods to create an authoritative persona than do the Greeks. Livy, however, is a significant exception, since he presents himself in a Herodotean manner, sifting through the tradition, comparing accounts and sources, marvelling, or addressing the reader.[48] His use of the first person is more pronounced than in

---

[44] On the Polybian persona see Ibendorff, *Unters. z. darstellerischen Persönlichkeit des Polybios*, who speaks of 'sein schulmeisterliches Temperament' (24); cf. Davidson, *JRS* 81 (1991) 15, that Polybius provides us 'with a paradigmatic gaze and exemplary responses'.

[45] The method has been called 'apodeictic': see Pédech, *Méthode* 43-53; Petzold, *Studien* 3-20; Sacks, *Polybius* 171-8. In the nineteenth century it was common for historians to combine a narrative and a dissertative mode, in the latter of which they gave their views and opinions on the matters they had narrated, much as in Polybius: see White, *Content of the Form* 27-8 with nn.

[46] See, e.g., VII.11.1.

[47] Polybius says (I.1.1) that nearly all historians before him had spoken of history's utility and benefit.   [48] See below, pp. 248f.

any of the other Roman historians.⁴⁹ On the whole, however, the Romans, like the Greeks, maintain a narrative with few interruptions; when expressing comment, however, they do so, unlike the Greeks, in an indirect and oblique manner.⁵⁰

3. TRADITION

When Thucydides said that his history would have value because it showed the sort of things that had happened and would, given human nature, happen again in the same or similar ways, he was probably not expecting that a later writer would take him literally. Crepereius Calpurnianus, an historian of the second century AD writing on Rome's wars with Parthia, took whole incidents and speeches from Thucydides; he even included a plague falling on the Romans, describing it in the same way as the one that attacked Athens.⁵¹ Crepereius' error, however, was not in trying to imitate Thucydides, but rather in the approach he took to his imitation; for he appropriated rather than imitated.

Between Herodotus and Ammianus lie a millennium and a myriad of Greek and Roman writers who sought to preserve, exalt, defend, or decry some area of the historical past in a predominantly third-person narrative prose account. It might seem foolish even to suggest that we may speak of a 'tradition' that could embrace so many writers over so vast a time. Yet the literary tradition of classical antiquity – including the writing of history – was conservative and, for many centuries, consciously classicising, with appeal made to a few unchanging models of acknowledged mastery. It had as its central technique the employment of *mimesis*, the creative imitation of one's predecessors.⁵² The idea that one should imitate one's great predecessors, and look to them for the proper way to treat almost any task is a fundamental aspect of

---

⁴⁹ Although one finds in him a paradoxical alternation between assurance and diffidence: Kraus, *Livy: Ab Urbe Condita Book VI*, 13–15. It is possible that Livy, not possessing the *auctoritas* that came with political experience, needed to justify his narrative far more than his predecessors did: see below, pp. 140ff.

⁵⁰ See below, pp. 93ff. and 246ff.

⁵¹ Thuc. 1.22.4; Luc. *h.c.* 15; for the references to Thucydides see Homeyer, *Lukian* ad loc.

⁵² For the dual sense of *mimesis* as both the representation of reality by narrative and the imitation of previous models, see McKeon, in *Critics and Criticism* 147–75.

ancient literary creation and criticism.[53] Already established by the fourth century BC,[54] imitation of one's predecessors never ceased to exert an influence on ancient writers of both poetry and prose. Quintilian speaks for the entire tradition when he says that 'a great part of art lies in imitation'.[55]

Historiography, as a branch of rhetoric in the ancient world, was subject to the same types of literary analysis as poetry or oratory. The historian's terrain might be different and he might have a different relationship to his subject matter, but it was expected that he would give care and attention to the arrangement, language, and presentation of his material; that his finished product would be 'artistic' and appealing; and that he would write with a real sense of what his predecessors had done, especially those who had done well and were worthy of imitation.[56] 'Longinus' in *On the Sublime* provides the clearest prescriptive: when composing with an eye towards sublimity, he says, one should imagine how the masters – Homer, Plato, Demosthenes, or Thucydides – would have said the same thing, and one should even imagine that those great models were present and would be the critics of what one had written.[57] Good imitation was not, however, a literal copying,[58] but rather an understanding both of the general spirit of the original and of

[53] On imitation see Kroll, *Studien* 139-84; id., *RE* Suppl. VII, 1113-17; McKeon, op. cit. (n.52); Bompaire, *Lucien écrivain* 13-154; Russell, in *Creative Imitation* 1-16; Fantham, *CPh* 73 (1978) 1-16, 102-16.   [54] Kroll, *RE* Suppl. VII, 1113.

[55] Quint. x.2.1: 'neque enim dubitari potest quin artis pars magna contineatur imitatione'.

[56] Cf. Cameron, in *History as Text* 8: '[W]e had better stop condemning as mere plagiarism or "empty rhetoric" the deep-seated ancient tendencies to embody in their work reminiscences of earlier authors and to follow literary precedents set years, or even centuries before.'

[57] [Long.] *Subl.* 13. 2-14. 1. The ancient critics, however, were not so naïve as to think that imitation was all that was necessary, or that everyone had the same possibilities of success. Dionysius, for one, separated imitation into two types, that which was natural to some, and that which could be learned through precepts, the second of which was always inferior to the first and could always be detected by the expert eye (*Dinarch.* 7=II.268-70 Usher). Quintilian too makes clear that one's success or failure depended as much on native talent as on any propensity or capacity for imitation (x.2.12 et al.).

[58] The critics are, in fact, quite clear on what constitutes bad imitation (κακοζηλία): Lucian cites as examples both Crepereius and an unnamed historian who modelled his phrases on Herodotus, taking over slavishly his dialect and phraseology (*h.c.* 15: 18). On the importance of a model, see *h.c.* 34-54 *passim*; for excessive imitation or imitation of others' faults see below, n. 76 and Fantham, op. cit. (n.53) 106-7.

those things that were admirable in previous writers, whether they be choice of language, arrangement, attitude, or even the subject matter itself. The imitator does not seek a one-to-one correspondence with a single previous model, nor is his imitation to be slavish (this is mere copying) but rather creative:[59] the writer must appropriate the spirit of his model or models and breathe new life into them, to show how something could be better done, or, if not better done, then well done in a different way.[60]

Thus the goal of ancient composition was not to strike out boldly in a radical departure from one's predecessors, but rather to be incrementally innovative within a tradition, by embracing the best in previous performers and adding something of one's own marked with an individual stamp.[61] For the historian, the genre was both an 'enabling condition' and a 'restraint upon his inventiveness'.[62] Those historians whom antiquity considered great (and they are, for the most part, those whom we consider great[63]) were all seen to have accomplished, by imitation of their predecessors, that delicate balancing act whereby they could at once remind the listener of their great predecessors and display to that same audience something yet different from those time-honoured models. For the writer was to see himself not just as an imitator, but also as a competitor.[64] Critics often explain a writer's achievement by his conscious efforts to rival his predecessors: both Herodotus and Thucydides are characterised as imitators *and* rivals of Homer, as later historians were seen as imitators and rivals of the two great fifth-century historians. Dionysius says that Herodotus was 'not deterred' by writers

---

[59] Cf. [Dionysius] *Art. Rhet.* 19 (U-R II.373): 'he imitates Demosthenes who speaks not the words of Demosthenes but in the spirit of Demosthenes' (μιμεῖται τὸν Δημοσθένην οὐχ ὁ τὸ ⟨Δημοσθένους λέγων ἀλλ' ὁ⟩ Δημοσθενικῶς).   [60] Russell, op. cit. (n.53) 5-16; Quint. x.2.27-8.

[61] See Russell, op. cit. (n.53) 5; cf. Peter, *Wahrheit* 417: 'Im allgemeinen hat selbst die öffentlich gesprochene Rede sich an die von der Kunst aufgestellten Regeln gehalten und von den Griechen ist dies nicht als eine Beschränkung der Freiheit empfunden worden.' Even the use of accepted *topoi* did not prevent innovation: cf. Cairns, *Generic Composition*, ch. 4; and next note.

[62] E. Said, *Beginnings: Intention and Method* (New York 1985) 83 (of the novel); cf. DuQuesnay, *PLLS* 3 (1981) 56 (of Virgil in the *Eclogues*): 'exploiting, manipulating and defeating the expectations of his readers which they shared with him as a result of their common cultural, literary and educational background'. It is precisely their relationship to conventions that allows writers to do something new, when they wish.   [63] Momigliano, *Quinto Contributo* 13-31.

[64] See Lefkowitz, *First-Person Fictions* 161-8; Wiseman, *CC* 27-9.

who had treated the subject before him, but 'trusted in his own ability to produce something better', and the same critic says that Thucydides sought a new direction different from both the local history of Hellanicus and the universal history of Herodotus.[65]

Ancient critics see the possibility of success differently. 'Longinus', for example, in what he saw as an age of decline, thought that it was impossible to surpass writers such as Plato or Demosthenes.[66] Quintilian, however, envisions an incremental increase in the materials available to the writer, and maintains an abiding belief in the movement towards the 'perfect' practitioner, even if, as both he and Cicero admit, this perfectability remains only an ideal.[67] If improvement were not possible, Quintilian says, we should still be living in caves and sailing on rafts, and we would have nothing better in literature than Livius Andronicus, or in history than the annals of the Pontifex Maximus.[68] Quintilian's view provides a balance to the often expressed belief by ancient critics in the inevitability of decline, and his approach represents the most optimistic viewpoint in regard to imitation, which finds its best expression in Seneca's comment that 'the one who comes last has the best position'.[69]

Historiographical imitation might take many forms, and only a summary is possible here. The most common type is verbal imitation, which can range from a single word[70] to a phrase to the appropriation of an entire style. The employment of the same or slightly altered phrases from predecessors, especially the great masters, is a feature of almost every ancient history. Sometimes it is the placing of a familiar element into a new context where it is striking because it is appropriate in a

---

[65] D. Hal. *Pomp.* 3 (II.374 Usher); *Thuc.* 6; on Thucydides as rival of Homer and Pindar, see Marc. *Vita Thuc.* 35-7. On *aemulatio* see Heldmann, *Antike Theorien* 35-42.   [66] Russell, op. cit. (n.53) 11.

[67] Cic. *Orat.* 100-1 (among many). On Cicero's belief in incremental progress by imitation see Fantham, op. cit. (n.53) 3-14; see also Heldmann, op. cit. (n.65) 40-2.   [68] Quint. x.2.4-8.

[69] Sen. *ep.* 79. 6: 'condicio optima est ultimi'. This notion appealed to many historians, who sought to portray their works as the culmination of an earlier tradition and approach: see Ch. V §3. Quintilian did write a work *On the Causes of Corrupted Eloquence*, but this seems to have been confined to exposing dangerous trends in his contemporaries: see Kennedy, *Art of Rhetoric* 494-6; Fantham, op. cit. (n.53) 111-15

[70] See Demetrius' praise (*Eloc.* 113) of Thucydides' description of Sicily as 'sea-girt' (περίρρυτος, IV.64.3), taking the word from Homer (*Od.* XIX.173) where it is used of Crete.

different way,[71] while at other times it can be merely verbal ornament.[72] Often it is difficult to determine whether there is any larger meaning in verbal echoes of a predecessor, or whether the ancient audience, with its keen ear for language, simply took pleasure in the echoes and adaptations themselves, without any assumption thereby of the aims and intentions of the author.[73] An historian might also employ a certain dialect or style as an aspect of imitation. When a Greek historian chose the Ionic dialect, it was natural to assume some imitation of Herodotus or other early writers.[74] At its worst, as Lucian details it above, phrases were simply taken out wholesale from the masters' works. In Rome, Sallust's use of an older Latin style has been seen both as an attempt to link

---

[71] A famous example can be found in Sallust's *Catiline*, in which the younger Cato echoes Thucydides' description of the breakdown in language in civil war (*Cat.* 52.10-11 ~ Thuc. III.82.4-7). At least two things make this a successful imitation: first, Thucydides' original analysis pertains to a social conflict, a civil war in which citizens' various interpretations of words match their own actions; so too Sallust's *Catiline* is throughout emphatic on the internecine conflict that reveals the tensions and fault-lines in Roman society (Earl, *Political Thought* 53-5). Second, the observation is not an isolated datum; rather, the entire *Catiline* is concerned with the tension between appearance and reality, and with the adaptation and appropriation by individuals of a common core of beliefs: Catiline can speak (in heavily ironic tones) of *fides, amicitia,* and *uirtus*, while ruthlessly advancing his own ambitions and counselling his followers to vicious and heinous crimes (Earl, ibid. 93-6; cf. Syme, *Sallust* 255-6). Cato's invocation of Thucydides therefore crystallises a whole spectrum of issues that Sallust has explored. For other appropriations of the passage see next note and Vretska's commentary, II.578 with n. 1257, although none of the examples there cited shows anything like Sallust's appreciation.

[72] See, e. g., D. Hal. *A.R.* IX.53.6 (speech of Appius Claudius), an imitation of the same Thucydides passage. On imitation in antiquity as nothing more than the use of specific phrases and words devoid of their context, see Peter, *Wahrheit* 416.

[73] The ancient critics sometimes counsel the use of a predecessor's language to invest a narrative with certain formal virtues, and in this case, of course, no additional meaning may be present. See Woodman, in *Hommages à M. Renard*, I. 798-9 for warnings that the use of language does not necessarily entail a similar 'programme'. One must assume this, particularly when the verbal echoes are not of earlier historians, but of poets or prose writers in different genres. So, for example, Sallust has echoes of Aeschylus, Plato, and Cicero in some of his works (Renehan, *CPh* 71 (1976) 97-105), and Ammianus most often cites not an historian, but Cicero (Fornara, *Historia* 41 (1992) 420-38).

[74] The main models for stylistic imitation were, not surprisingly, Herodotus, Thucydides, and Xenophon; perhaps the most thorough-going verbal imitation is Dionysius' imitation of Herodotus in his *Roman Antiquities*: see the works of Ek, cited n. 40; Usher, *ANRW* II. 30. 1, 819-37.

himself with the archaic rectitude of the elder Cato, and as a rejection of the Ciceronian call for a full, ample style in the writing of history – and of the entire notion of history that goes along with that style.[75] Sallust himself spawned a host of imitators, and Quintilian several generations later singled out for criticism those who tried to out-Sallust Sallust.[76]

Certain types of incidents common in war, such as the capture of a city, or the speech of a commander before battle, were particularly subject to imitation.[77] An historian might also take the type of history practised by a predecessor, and do the same for his own subject. Popular for the writers of contemporary history was the imitation or adaptation of Thucydides' monographic treatment of the Peloponnesian War, examples of which can be found in Josephus' *Jewish War*, and the histories of Dexippus and Herodian. Sallust followed Coelius Antipater (who wrote an independent work on the Hannibalic War) by writing historical monographs. And there were a whole series of continuators, both Greek and Latin, who joined their history to a predecessor's and 'continued' his work.[78] For generic imitation, the title is frequently an indication: Josephus' *Jewish Antiquities* try to do for early Jewish history what Dionysius' *Roman Antiquities* had done for early Rome.[79] Arrian's *Anabasis* is both homage and challenge to Xenophon's *Anabasis*. Pompeius Trogus' *Philippic History* is meant to be seen in the tradition of Theopompus' *Philippica*, a universal history with many digressions.[80]

Historians might imitate the arrangement of predecessors. This can be an internal arrangement, as for example, when the Oxyrhynchus historian, perhaps alone in antiquity, imitated Thucydides' division of the year into summers and winters.[81] Arrian arranged and constructed his preface with those of Herodotus and Thucydides in mind.[82] Among the Romans, many historians adopted the annalistic form, and within this structure arranged the events of the year.[83] In the tradition-bound

---

[75] See Woodman, *RICH* 117–59 (with reff. to earlier discussions).

[76] Quint. x.2.17.

[77] On the former see Paul, *Phoenix* 36 (1982) 144–55; on the latter, Keitel, *CW* 80 (1986/7) 153–62; Hansen, *Historia* 42 (1993) 161–80.   [78] See below, pp. 237ff.

[79] On Josephus' debt to Dionysius, see Shutt, *Studies in Josephus* 94–101.

[80] Trogus' choice of title has been variously interpreted; see Alonso-Núñez, *G&R* 34 (1987) 58–9 for other possibilities.

[81] See D. Hal. *Thuc.* 9 for the statement that no one followed Thucydides' arrangement.   [82] Stadter, *ICS* 6 (1981) 157–71.

[83] For the usual annalistic structure see McDonald, *JRS* 47 (1957) 155–9; for Tacitus' adaptations see Ginsburg, *Tradition and Theme in the Annals of Tacitus*.

society of Rome, the decision to write 'annalistically' might indicate something of one's view of history.[84] Or the historian might imitate external structure, as indicated particularly by book numbers. Herodotus' nine and Thucydides' eight (neither one the author's own division) proved popular for many. Arrian's *Anabasis*, like Xenophon's, has seven books; Diodorus' universal history, like his predecessor Polybius', has forty books;[85] Josephus in his *Antiquities* matched Dionysius' twenty; and Kephalion imitated Herodotus' nine.

Finally, an author might imitate the attitude or disposition (διάθεσις, *dispositio*) of a predecessor.[86] One could, for example, see oneself in the Herodotean role of dispenser of praise, taking delight in the glorious deeds that one narrated, as did Dionysius and Arrian. Or a somewhat harsher attitude, critical of the events might be taken, as we find in the works of Theopompus and Tacitus. Here too the choice of a disposition might mirror fundamental beliefs about the nature and purpose of one's history.[87]

When and how these theories of imitation and emulation came into existence cannot be determined with precision. Imitation, no doubt, was an obvious result of the codification of rhetorical and sophistical technique, an ancillary tool in the study of speaking well, but no less serviceable across a variety of genres. Naturally, the establishment of the 'canon' of great authors, perhaps in Pergamum in the second century BC, codified yet further the procedures for literary imitation, if in no other way than by limiting those writers who were acceptable models for imitation.[88] More transient, but no less influential, would be variations in current taste, such as the Atticising movement, which derogated the authors of the entire Hellenistic period, and influenced both Greek and Latin historians; the Palatine library at Rome which enshrined

---

[84] See Ginsburg, op. cit. (n.83) 96; cf. 103 n. 11, where she emphasises that to write annalistically was a choice. See also below, n. 131.

[85] Alonso-Núñez, op. cit. (n.80) 58 suggests that Trogus' first forty books were an imitation of Polybius and Diodorus.

[86] Or, like Arrian, he might imitate all aspects of his model (Xenophon): see Stadter, *GRBS* 8 (1967) 155-61; id., *Arrian* 27-8; 53-4; Bosworth, *ANRW* II. 34. 1, 272-5. An author could also imitate himself: see Woodman, in *Creative Imitation and Latin Literature* 143-55.

[87] On the historian's attitude see D. Hal. *Pomp.* 3 (II.380-2 Usher); Scheller, *De hell. hist. conscr. arte* 34-7; Woodman, *RICH* 40-7.

[88] On the canon see Radermacher, *RE* X.2, 1873-8; Marrou, *Histoire de l'éducation* 1.243-4; Nicolai, *La storiografia nell'educazione antica* 250-339.

those writers of whom the ruling emperor especially approved; and archaising movements, which resurrected little-read historians and poets.[89] But these were at most occasional changes; more remarkable is that over a thousand year period the great historians remained fixed and few, such that it is no exaggeration to say that the appeal to tradition is itself a part of the historian's authority, for it is a shorthand used by the historian to identify his interests, approach, and alliances.

4. HISTORY'S PLACE AND AUDIENCE

There is something paradoxical about the status of history in antiquity: the writing of history was attempted by many men, and its popularity, if we are to believe the ancients themselves, extended across social lines. Yet historians were never a defined group in antiquity, nor did they have a fixed position: there were no professors of history.[90] Many of the historians who wrote in antiquity were not exclusively historians, nor could that be described as their 'occupation'. History was only one of several genres that an individual might attempt. From Xenophon (who also wrote biography, philosophy and even political science) to Duris of Samos (who wrote Homeric criticism) to Polybius (biography, military tactics) to Livy (rhetorical criticism) to Tacitus (biography, ethnography, dialogue) and beyond, the ancient historian was more a man of letters than specifically an historian. Such a situation would not have been surprising two centuries ago when similar circumstances obtained in western Europe during and after the Enlightenment.[91] The modern world is different because it both maintains some of the nineteenth-century approach to history, and employs a restricted (and largely poetic) concept of literature.[92]

---

[89] On Atticism see the brief survey of Kennedy, *Art of Persuasion* 241-6; 351-4, with further references; Reardon, *Courants littéraires* 81-96. Its effect on historiography can be seen in Dionysius, below, pp. 245f.; on the influence of the library at Rome, Marshall, *Phoenix* 30 (1976) 261-4; for an example of an emperor's taste, *SHA Hadrian* 16.1-6; on archaising, R. Marache, *La critique littéraire de langue latine et le développement du goût archaïsant au IIe siècle de notre ère* (Rennes 1952).

[90] Malitz, *PoH* 326: 'Ein regelrechtes Fachstudium war in der Antike unbekannt'; cf. also Meissner, *Historiker* 191-3; 208-14; on the audience for historiography in general see Momigliano, *Sesto Contributo* 361-76.

[91] Gossman, *Between History and Literature* 227.

[92] Ibid. 228-9; White, *Tropics of Discourse* 27-50.

Each historian must envision his audience before deciding how to establish his authority, and the detailed study of the implicit and explicit assumptions that each makes would reveal a great deal about the writer and his times. Here, however, it will be possible to give only an overview, based largely on the explicit remarks made by the historians themselves. Although concentrating on the audience for narrative history, it is salutary to remember also that this was hardly the sole source of knowledge about the past for the ancients: there were oral traditions, family traditions, pictorial representations of the past, the words of orators and panegyricists, and monuments commemorating (or purporting to commemorate) great historical actions.[93] We cannot say, unfortunately, how many people learned their history of Marathon from Herodotus and how many from Micon's painting of the battle in the Painted Stoa; or how many in Augustan Rome learned their history from Livy and how many from the portrait busts of great Romans in Augustus' Forum – not to mention the interaction of the different forms of commemoration upon each other.[94]

Of the fifth-century audience for Herodotus we know very little.[95] Whereas we could perhaps postulate for Hecataeus' *Circuit of the Earth* some practical purpose for travellers around the Mediterranean, no 'practical' aspect of a similar sort attaches itself to Herodotus' work. There is little in his work of that type of genealogy that seems always to have appealed to the Greeks and Romans from the time of the sophist Hippias onward, and which could be used to enhance the status of individuals, families, or states.[96] A desire to preserve great deeds and search out causes of human events puts Herodotus into a category different from that of his Ionian predecessors. Herodotus is distinguished by the monumentality of his work (which is longer than either Homeric poem) and by his universality (his treatment of the deeds of Greeks and non-Greeks). If such a work were performed in public,[97] it would require

---

[93] Both paintings and monuments would have had oral traditions associated with them. On the use of monuments in writing non-contemporary history see below, pp. 101ff.; on oral and family tradition see below, pp. 99ff.

[94] On the Marathon painting see Paus. 1.15.1-3; on the Forum, Peter, *GL* 1.54, 60-1; Luce, in *Between Republic and Empire* 123-38.

[95] As Malitz, *PoH* 327-8 points out, Herodotus nowhere comments on the audience he expected for his work.

[96] Hippias, *FGrHist* 6 T 3 = Plato, *Hipp. Mai.* 285d; Wiseman, *RS* 207-18.

[97] The testimonia about Herodotus' recitations at Olympia are late and unreliable: see Flory, *AJPh* 101 (1980) 14-15, and Lefkowitz, *Lives of the Greek Poets* on the unreliability of the biographical tradition in general.

several recitations over many days. Perhaps this was the case, or perhaps the author recited selected excerpts on different occasions.[98]

It has been suggested that Thucydides' criticism of 'performance to be heard in the present' (ἀγώνισμα ἐς τὸ παραχρῆμα ἀκούειν, 1.22.4) refers to the specifically oral, agonistic milieu in which Herodotus and his contemporaries worked, whereas Thucydides saw his own work as meant for future readers and considered it an independent and permanent 'possession for all time' (κτῆμα ἐς ἀεί).[99] This does not necessarily mean that he was the first to distinguish a written work from an oral presentation, nor that his work required thoughtful seclusion, whereas previous works (such as Herodotus') were less serious and more oriented towards the audience's entertainment than truth.[100] It is equally invalid to claim that Thucydides' work was meant for political men exclusively or primarily. Thucydides says that his work was meant for 'all those who want to know' and we must not retroject the ideas of political and military usefulness known from Polybius onto Thucydides.[101] It is true, however, that what is learned in Thucydides is most meaningful within the framework of the Greek city-state, which expected participation from a majority of its citizens.[102]

The generations after Thucydides took history further and in a different direction from either fifth-century historian, and Xenophon,

---

[98] In the middle of the second century BC Aristotheos of Troezen gave a reading of his work at Delphi that lasted several days (*FGrHist* 835 T 1). On Herodotus' audience see above, p. 8.

[99] So Havelock, *Preface to Plato* 53-4 n. 8; Hunter, *Past and Process* 287-96; on the problems presented by a written text in addressing an audience see Ong, *Orality and Literacy* 78ff.; against excessive reliance on theories of orality, Thomas, *Literacy and Orality* ch. 2.

[100] Flory, op. cit. (n.97) 16-18, 27-8; Thucydides in 1.20.3-21.1 is clearly attacking Herodotus (Hornblower, *CT* 1.56-8), other prose writers (Gomme, *HCT* 1.138-9, 148), encomiastic orators (Loraux, *Invention of Athens* 288-98), and poets writing historical epics, such as Simonides (Boedeker, *ZPE* 107 (1995) 226-9) – all of whom he saw as caring more for bestowing glory than establishing what actually happened. On Thucydides and ἀκρίβεια, see below, p. 68.

[101] Against this idea, Fornara, *Nature* 106, who sees it as a nineteenth-century prejudice; see also below, pp. 71f. For Thucydides' intended audience see specifically 1.22.4.

[102] Malitz, *PoH* 333 suggests that Herodotus and Thucydides imagine as their audience citizens of fifth-century city-states, who could draw practical lessons from history; for a different (less political and more intellectual) interpretation of what Thucydides expected his audience to gain, see Farrar, *Origins of Democratic Thinking* 131-7.

interested in ethical questions, seems to chafe at the restrictions of political history.[103] In Thucydides the primary focus seems to be the individual in the context of his political relationships, within the structures of the polis as a whole, whereas in Xenophon and the later historians by contrast, ethical behaviour is individualistic and can be applied, *mutatis mutandis*, to any political system, be it democracy, oligarchy, or monarchy.[104] An alternative reaction may be seen in Ctesias, who brought the fabulous worlds of the East before his Greek audience's eyes.[105] The *Persica*, an historical narrative, contained much palace intrigue, and seems to have frequently shaded into romance; the *Indica* was an account of a fabulous land, complete with marvels of all types. Both works suggest that the audience cared little for practical political lessons.[106] A generation or two later, the conquests of Alexander introduced yet more innovations, since that conqueror's deeds furnished material on a scale never seen before. But what was the point of such history? If it was to marvel at great deeds, there was ample precedent for that in Herodotus. But such history could not fit into the Thucydidean tradition, since only a very limited idea of human nature (τὸ ἀνθρώπινον) could come from this.

These developments are the reaction of history, like other genres, to the changed political world of the fourth century, where the rise of Macedon destroyed the framework in which political participation had up to that time defined itself for the Greeks.[107] Whereas Athens and Sparta had been in Thucydides 'characters' at the centre of the work, in the fourth century the history of Greece becomes the history of rulers, a progression mirrored quite nicely in the career of Theopompus who went from writing an epitome of Herodotus to a *Greek History* (*Hellenica*) to a *History of Philip* (*Philippica*).[108] As the reader became

---

[103] See Breitenbach, *Historiographische Anschauungsformen Xenophons* 47-104; Rahn, *TAPA* 102 (1971) 507-8 suggests that the fall of Athens and Sparta, and the important leaders that Xenophon had seen in the East, made him turn more to character and away from politics.

[104] For Xenophon's lack of interest in political systems and his focus on morality see Gray, *Character of Xenophon's Hellenica, passim*, esp. 178-82.

[105] On Ctesias' *Indica* and *Persica* see Jacoby, *RE* XI. 2, 2037-47; Drews, *Greek Accounts of Eastern History* 103-16 (*Persica* only).

[106] Drews, op. cit. (n.105) 107ff. Ctesias' work prefigures the court intrigue so familiar when history is written under an autocracy: see Ch. II §2. See Bigwood, *Phoenix* 43 (1989) 302-16 for some cautions in judging the *Indica* by Photius' summary.   [107] Malitz, *PoH* 333-4.

[108] Christ, *CQ* 43 (1993) 47-52 suggests that the epitome of Herodotus was part of the *Hellenica*.

less and less a participant and more and more an observer, his relationship to history had to change. The utility of history could no longer be practical lessons for participation in the polis, or even that foreknowledge that might help public men make intelligent decisions. The loss of political autonomy was perhaps mirrored in the loss of personal autonomy as seen in the growing importance to historians of fortune (τύχη) as an inescapable, at times irresistible, force at work in history.[109] It was individual reversals of fortune that became more and more the stuff of history. We cannot enter here into the vexed question of what goes by the name of 'tragic' history in which, supposedly, a vivid narrative of reversals of fortune was the dominant element that produced an historiography strongly at odds with the political history that had been pioneered by Thucydides.[110] Tragic history is supposed to have been the reading material of a different class from that which enjoyed political and military history.[111] But if the rate of literacy in antiquity was low,[112] we would only be talking about various distinctions among the elite, not upper- and lower-class audiences.[113] This should make us hesitant to postulate many classes of readers, each with a desired type of history. It is quite possible that the same reader could turn to several types of history for different experiences.[114]

During the fourth and third century, history was vigorously practised and differently adapted, ranging from Ephorus' universal history

---

[109] On *tyche*, Walbank, *HCP* 1.16–26. Malitz, *PoH* 334–5 points out the paradox that historians, beginning with Ephorus, talk more and more about the use of their history, just as actual participation was becoming less and less a real possibility.

[110] On 'tragic' history see Fornara, *Nature* 131–4; Walbank, *BICS* 2 (1955) 4–14; id., *SP* 224–41; Meister, *Griechische Geschichtsschreibung* 95–102; Zegers, *Wesen und Ursprung*. Malitz, *PoH* 335–6 notes that dramatic historiography is not just the result of a change in taste but also in circumstances; he compares the loss of political content in comedy, and notes that where Aristophanes addressed political issues, Menander shows the private and personal life on stage.

[111] See, e.g., Gabba, *JRS* 71 (1981) 50–62.

[112] For the minimalist view of literacy, see Harris, *Ancient Literacy, passim*; cf. *Literacy in the Roman World, JRA* Suppl. Ser. 1 (1991) for counter-arguments.

[113] The notion of a lower-class audience for tragic history is reminiscent of the same postulation for the ancient novel; but cf. Stephens, in *The Search for the Ancient Novel* 405–18; Dowden, ibid. 419–34; Bowie, ibid. 435–59 for the evidence that novels (like everything else in the ancient world) were addressed to and read by the upper class.

[114] Just as, no doubt, those exclusively interested in military matters would devote themselves to Polybius and others like him, or to the vast body of technical works on tactics and sieges and the like.

of the Mediterranean to the local histories of Manetho and Berossus in the service of Alexander's Successors.[115] New types of history may well have brought about new audiences for history, and the diminished political participation hinted at in the fourth century became the established way of life in the third and second. There can be no doubt that history began to be closely allied with the courts of great kings, first Alexander and then his successors employing historians to entrust their deeds to memory. This had far-reaching effects on the orientation of historiography.[116] Even under these conditions, history may well have maintained some of its value for the elite, and public readings of histories of their kings may have made subjects proud. From the Hellenistic period we know of several historians honoured for their works.[117]

When we come to Polybius who in this, as in so many other matters, speaks explicitly about issues relating to his history, we find that he envisions three groups of readers, each with a corresponding type of history: genealogy appeals to the 'casual reader' (ὁ φιλήκοος); accounts of foundations and colonies are enjoyed by the 'curious and lovers of recondite material' (ὁ πολυπράγμων καὶ περιττός); the deeds of nations and rulers appeal to the 'political man' (ὁ πολιτικός).[118] Now Polybius claims that his work contains only the last of these three types, what he sometimes calls 'pragmatic history'.[119] Yet he also suggests elsewhere that his work will be useful, above all, to those who love to learn (οἱ φιλομαθοῦντες) as opposed to those who simply like a good story (οἱ ἀκούοντες, or, as in the passage above, ὁ φιλήκοος). Polybius, it is true, seems to limit what is useful in history to military and political matters (and to those things such as geography that are of value to polit-

---

[115] For an overview see Will, in *Geschichtsbild und Geschichtsdenken* 113-35; on the use of history by the successors of Alexander see Murray, *CQ* 22 (1972) 200-13; Mendels, *SCI* 10 (1989/90) 78-86.

[116] Meissner, *Historiker* 362ff.; Rosen, *Hermes* 107 (1979) 460-77; Schepens, in *Egypt and the Hellenistic World* 351-68.

[117] Mnesiptolemus of Cyme read his history to Antiochus the Great and was rewarded for it: *FGrHist* 164 TT 2-3; additional examples at Chaniotis, *Historie und Historiker* 290-325; Meissner, op.cit. (n.116) 205-7.

[118] Pol. IX.1.2-5, with Walbank, *HCP* II.116-17. It is worthwhile to note that Polybius does not mention any class that resembles putative lovers of 'tragic' history, and he, if any, would be the one to do so, given his harsh criticism of Phylarchus who, he says, confuses the purposes of tragedy and history (II.56).

[119] On what Polybius means by 'pragmatic history' see Gelzer, *KS* III.155-60; Pédech, *Méthode* 21-32; Walbank, *HCP* I.6-11; id., *Polybius* ch. III; Fornara, *Nature* 112 n. 31; Meissner, *Saeculum* 37 (1986) 313-51.

ical men). Yet a more universal audience is envisioned, when he states at the outset of the work that one of the benefits of history is that it teaches men how to bear the vicissitudes of fortune by examining reversals experienced by others.[120] Since this is something that all can appreciate, and since even in other places Polybius suggests that the lessons of history are open to everyone, it is safe to conclude that although his primary audience is political men (for they will most benefit from his type of history), he nevertheless envisions that many who are not statesmen and generals will also derive benefit, and at times pleasure, from his work.[121]

When Polybius wrote, the states of Greece were only coming to know their Roman master, and there was still a role for political men to play, even under a Roman hegemony, as Polybius' own later career made plain. A century later, however, the Mediterranean had more or less passed entire into the control of Rome, and the Greek states became only so many observers of the expansion of Rome and its subsequent internecine struggles. As earlier in the fourth century, so now in the first century BC, the prospects of meaningful political participation were slim for those outside the ruling Roman elite. The element of political utility is, not surprisingly, absent from Diodorus, who substitutes for it a more general concept of utility which includes, but is not limited to, men in public life. All types seem to be comprehended by his terms 'readers' (οἱ ἀναγινώσκοντες) and 'lovers of reading' (οἱ φιλαναγινώσκοντες): young and old,[122] speakers, leaders, soldiers and even those who belong to none of these categories. History's appeal is universal:

> It gives the young the intelligence of the old, to the old it increases the experience that they already have; it makes private citizens worthy of leadership, and leaders it encourages, by the immortal renown that it gives, to attempt the finest of actions; in addition, because of the praises it brings after death, it makes soldiers more prepared for dangers on behalf of their country; and wicked men it turns from the impulse for evil by the fear of everlasting shame.[123]

---

[120] Pol. 1.1.2; Meissner, op. cit. (n.119) 334ff., demonstrates that the scope of Polybius' history is much wider than simply political affairs, and the lessons Polybius envisions can be applied to many readers, not just political or military men.   [121] See Walbank, *PoH* 253–66.
[122] This category had also been one about which Polybius had thought: see Pol. XXXI.30.1.   [123] Diod. 1.1.5.

Diodorus' work, however imperfectly constructed, is just the sort that Polybius had in mind of writers who combined all the different types of history to command as large an audience as possible. As Diodorus' words demonstrate, one who wrote history with an avowedly moralistic purpose could claim to be all things to all people, since his history's benefit was not dependent on a specific time or type of government.

With Diodorus we have moved to the late Republic and we should here make mention of the Romans. Roman historiography was a comparatively late development; for the first five hundred years of their existence, the Romans had no narrative history which recorded their deeds. What was known of their early history was contained in family records and traditions, and in a chronicle kept by the Pontifex Maximus which recorded those events that called for some priestly intervention or activity, such as declarations of war, famines, eclipses, and the like.[124] Paradoxically, the first Roman historical work is not a prose history but an epic poem by C. Naevius on the First Punic War (in which Naevius himself participated), which began with Rome's origins and the background to the war itself.[125] Q. Ennius, claiming to be both poet and historian, carried on this tradition of historical epic by writing a narrative poem, entitled *Annals*, which began with Rome's foundations and ended with events of the middle of the second century.[126] His coeval Q. Fabius Pictor wrote the first prose history of Rome, and he wrote it in Greek, primarily for the Mediterranean world, to whom he introduced the newly important Rome, but also for his compatriots and the Senatorial order in

---

[124] There is an enormous bibliography on the Pontifical Chronicle; most of the earlier discussions are summarised by Frier, *Libri Annales* 9–25; for the physical makeup of the Chronicle and the probable ways that records were kept in Rome, see Bucher, *AJAH* 12 (1987 [1995]) 2–61. The Pontifical Chronicle (the *tabula apud pontificem*) must be kept separate from the *Annales Maximi*, which were published in eighty books, and which (no doubt) contained some authentic material from the Pontifex's Chronicle: Frier, ibid. 64–7, who has also (179–200) cast doubt that the *Annales* were published c. 130 BC by P. Mucius Scaevola. What else the *Annales* contained, what role literary invention played in them, and what traces they have left in surviving historians are issues still very much debated.

[125] On Naevius' *Bellum Punicum*, written in the last years of the third century, see Schanz-Hosius I.53.

[126] On its scope and structure, see Skutsch, *Annals of Ennius* 5–6; on Ennius as poet and historian (*scriptor rerum*), ibid. 168, 371.

general.[127] Once this occurred, Roman historiography became, even more so than among the Greeks, the province of the upper class. All of the early Roman historians were men of political and military affairs, and it is only reasonable to suppose that their histories emphasised exactly these things. Indeed, from the *ius imaginum* to the *laudatio funebris* (the latter an important historical source), the nobility at Rome controlled the portrait of the past in a way unimaginable for the Greeks.[128] After Pictor, the tradition of contemporary historical writing maintained itself, and Cato's decision to write his *Origins* in Latin widened the possible audience for Roman prose history.[129] It is generally agreed that the Roman historians up to and including Cato, whether employing Greek or Latin, wrote history of a Polybian or pragmatic type, that is, concentrating on the deeds of cities and rulers.[130] Beginning, however, just around the time of Cato's death in 149 BC, a new type of historical writing was attempted, which tried to fill out the early years of the Roman Republic that had been overlooked or treated only summarily by previous historians. The earliest of these writers, known as 'Annalists' (because they wrote year-by-year history) were L. Cassius Hemina, L. Calpurnius Piso, and Cn. Gellius.[131] Their works were on a scale previously unseen, and since it is assumed that they did not base their expansive works on actual historical material, they are frequently derided as rhetorical practitioners, who contaminated the entire historical tradition of early Rome.[132]

[127] On Pictor's probable audience see Gelzer, *KS* III.96–7, cf. ibid. 51 n. 1, 105; Badian, in *Latin Historians* 3–6.

[128] Peter, *GL* I.54–5; bibliography at Lewis, *ANRW* II. 34. 1, 658 n. 97, 659 n. 100. Wiseman, *Historiography and Imagination* 1–22 argues that Roman drama (especially the *fabula praetexta*) was an important source for Roman history, but the evidence does not lend itself to this interpretation: see H. I. Flower, *CQ* 45 (1995) 170–90.

[129] Such a trend may also be reflected in a translation of Fabius Pictor's history into Latin, on which see Peter, *HRR* I. LXXV–LXXXI.

[130] See Gelzer, *KS* III.93–103; Walbank, *SP* 94–8; Fornara, *Nature* 25–6.

[131] On the earliest Annalists see the detailed treatment of Rawson, *RCS* 245–71. Most Roman historians, except for those who composed monographs, wrote 'annalistically', that is, following a year-by-year pattern. The term 'Annalist', however, even though inexact, distinguishes those historians who wrote year-by-year histories from Roman origins to their own day: this series may be said to begin with Cassius Hemina and end with Livy.

[132] Again, there is disagreement over the level, extent, and nature of annalistic invention and contamination; for representative views see Wiseman, *CC* 9–26 ('voluminous, and largely imaginary, histories', 26); Cornell, in *Past Persp.* 76–86 ('limited scope for tampering', 82).

Their methods were continued in the next century by Claudius Quadrigarius, Valerius Antias, and Licinius Macer, whose works, because of their inventions and brazen patriotic bias, are sometimes supposed to represent the nadir of Roman historiography.[133] We do not know, unfortunately, what provided the spur to annalistic writing nor whether these writers, some of whom were not political men, represent the movement of history to a different audience.[134] By the late first century, however, Cicero could claim that history's appeal was universal. He remarks that men of the lowest station, men with no hope of a public career, and even men who are mere craftsmen take pleasure in history.[135] It is fair to interpret such a passage as implying a mass audience for history,[136] at least in late republican Rome and it is possible that the audience for history was larger than merely the literate, since the Romans, like the Greeks, performed their histories in public places: the Forum, the baths, and the theatre.[137]

We find as well in the late Republic further indications of a wide audience for history in the appearance of the brief compendium. Short works of history were written by Varro (*Annals* in three books), Atticus (a single *Liber Annalis*), and Cornelius Nepos (*Chronicles* in three books).[138] Nepos also wrote a series of short *Lives*, almost certainly

---

[133] On these later annalists see Timpe, *A&A* 25 (1979) 97-119, who cautions against judgements of them as a group.

[134] Timpe, ibid. 113-14 believes Quadrigarius and Antias were members of the Italian municipal aristocracy (as was Livy later) and that this was their primary audience.

[135] Cic. *Fin.* v.52: 'quid, quod homines infima fortuna, nulla spe rerum gerendarum, opifices denique delectantur historia?'

[136] This passage does not tell us that the audience necessarily preferred written history, but speaks rather to a general interest in the past by people, and, as we mentioned above, that appetite for the past might be satisfied by various historical and quasi-historical means.

[137] Wiseman, *RS* 253-6. Cf. Schultze, in *Past Persp.* 133: 'If supply indeed reflects an actual demand, there clearly was a reading public for history in the Augustan age, as in the preceding generation'. She names a dozen historians known just from Cicero's generation.

[138] On these works see Schanz-Hosius 1.567; 329-31; 352-3 (resp.); Starr, *CQ* 31 (1981) 166-8. Somewhat in a different category, if not a different spirit, is the *Breuiarium rerum omnium Romanarum* that L. Ateius Philologus is supposed to have compiled for Sallust (Suet. *gramm.* 10). Despite the sometimes inexact terminology, one should distinguish between an epitome and a *breuiarium*; the former is a résumé or précis of a single work, whereas the latter is a (usually) short work of history that is composed from more than one source. In the

meant for a general audience.[139] This may indeed represent a 'down-marketing' of history, in a sense, as histories began to appear for people who could not make their way through Livy's 142- or Nicolaus' 144-book histories.[140] This type of writing continues into the Empire and Velleius Paterculus, Granius Licinianus, Florus, and Eutropius (in different ways) are heirs to this tradition.[141]

Yet for many of the Romans the late Republic and early Empire resembled the fourth century BC with its diminished political participation and a world out of control. First Sallust and then Livy, like Xenophon and Theopompus before them, emphasised the moral component of history. The new political world meant that the figures and examples of Roman history no longer had practical value, but rather moral force. Good citizens exhibit universally valid virtues, whatever the form of government, and the individual citizen can learn, even from the lives of the great. This is not to suggest a wholly apolitical world for Livy and his contemporary audience. But as an apolitical man himself, Livy wrote history to admire and to enshrine the great deeds of the men who had made Rome mistress of the Mediterranean, and any practical political lessons would have had little meaning for him and his intended audience.

Other historians continued to claim their histories as valuable for the political man, even if the possible arena for such activity was circumscribed by Greece's position as a Roman province.[142] Dionysius of

---

former category should be counted Justin, who made an epitome of Pompeius Trogus (although Goodyear, *Papers on Latin Literature* 210-12, argues that it is an anthology), Brutus, who made an epitome of Polybius (Plut. *Brutus* 4), and Dionysius of Halicarnassus, who made a six-book epitome of his own *Roman Antiquities* (Phot. *Bibl.* 84; see Schwartz, *GG* 359 = *RE* V, 961); in the latter group, in addition to those named above, are Florus, Granius Licinianus (whose *breuiarium* was at least thirty-six books long – brief only in comparison to Livy), Festus, and Eutropius.

[139] Wiseman, *CC* 157: a 'crash course to help the ordinary reader in a literary world where ignorance of things Greek was no longer tolerable'. Malitz, *PoH* 352 (cf. 339 with n. 65) notes that papyrus finds indicate that the number of epitomes was already growing in the third and second centuries BC.

[140] On 'down-marketing' see Schultze, op. cit. (n.137) 133; Wiseman, *RS* 254; Starr, op. cit. (n.138) 173-4.

[141] Velleius, however, has made something yet different, since his work, short as it is, broadens into a contemporary account of Tiberius' campaigns; Woodman, *CQ* 25 (1975) 282-7 calls it a summary universal history.

[142] For a sense of the restricted area of competence by a Greek magistrate, see Plutarch's *Political Precepts*.

Halicarnassus, though addressing his own political work to upper-class Greeks who would have to learn to live with Rome,[143] sees members of both the upper and lower classes as the audience for history: in his essay on Thucydides he had noted that although each group would not take the same pleasure in that historian's work, those who said that Thucydides wrote only for philosophers and students of rhetoric were 'removing from ordinary men's lives a necessary and universally useful subject of study'.[144] In the preface of his *Roman Antiquities*, he (like Polybius) envisions three (somewhat different) classes of readers: those interested in political debate (οἱ πολιτικοί) who will appreciate the forensic aspect of his history; philosophers (οἱ φιλόσοφοι) who will like the theoretical aspect; and any who wish undisturbed instruction (οἱ ἀοχλήτου διαγωγῆς δέοντες) who will enjoy the pleasurable[145] aspect.[146] Dionysius later joins the first two groups by defining philosophers as those 'who regard philosophy as the practice not of fine words but of fine deeds'.[147] The primary audience envisioned by Dionysius seems to be men in positions of responsibility, since they can put the lessons of history to practical use, and in this he shows himself very much a man of the Augustan age: Strabo composed his *Geography* for a similar group, and Nicolaus of Damascus, in encouraging King Herod towards history, said that it was most fitting for a statesman and most beneficial to a king to investigate the deeds of previous kings and statesmen.[148] In the next century, Appian, choosing Rome as a subject, could still speak of the pleasure and utility to be won from history.[149]

In the Empire of the second and third centuries AD we see both the attempt to come to grips with the rule of a single man, and an interest in a more antiquarian history, concerned with a distant and glorious past. In the former category are Tacitus and Dio, who, in different ways, address the Senatorial order. Tacitus, who portrays himself as the lone voice of a lost tradition,[150] was concerned with the performance of service to the state under an autocratic regime.[151] Like Cato a provincial

---

[143] On Dionysius' audience see Schultze, op. cit. (n.137); Gabba, *Dionysius* ch. II.
[144] *Thuc.* 50-1.
[145] Reading the addition of Stephanus, followed by C. Jacoby, ⟨καὶ ἡδείας⟩. The Loeb editor Cary reads ⟨καὶ διηγηματικῆς⟩, which would mean that the last group enjoys the 'narrative' aspect.   [146] *A. R.* I.8.3.   [147] *A. R.* XI.1.4.
[148] Gabba, op cit. (n.143) 49-51 shows the important parallels between Strabo and Dionysius; for Nicolaus see *FGrHist* 90 F 135, quoted below, p. 52.
[149] Brodersen, *ANRW* II. 34. 1, 359-60, citing App. *Syr.* 207; cf. *B. Ciu.* 1.24.
[150] Below, pp. 250ff.   [151] A brief survey in Goodyear, *Tacitus* 6-8.

and a new man, he was the defender of an old and individual *uirtus*. The hope (or façade) that Trajan raised of an actual working partnership with the Senate made real again the lessons of history for those who would once more have a share in rule. Instances of senatorial subservience, as seen under earlier emperors, could thus serve as useful *exempla* to the new nobility governing with an enlightened *princeps*. This nobility suggests itself as Tacitus' primary audience, especially as his remark on Senatorial opinions indicates:

> I in no way intended to go through [Senatorial] opinions in detail, unless they were distinguished for their honesty or were of notable disgrace (which I think a chief task of history), so that virtues not be passed over and so that depraved words and deeds would have the fear of posterity and infamy.[152]

In the next century Cassius Dio wrote a history that in its contemporary portions is largely centred around the Senate's dealings with the Emperor. For all his differences with Tacitus, Dio too reveals a 'pragmatic' approach between Senate and Emperor, a display of survival tactics for those who, like Dio, would in the future need to work with emperors both good and bad. And he too, like Tacitus, shows concern for the maintenance of Senatorial dignity and privilege.[153]

Yet other Greek writers, especially in the second-century literary renaissance known as the Second Sophistic, turned to the glorious, and more distant, Greek past.[154] Several historians wrote histories of the classical Greek era of the fifth and fourth centuries BC, emphasising the campaigns of the Persian Wars; others treated the career and conquests of Alexander himself, as we can see from a variety of genres, including history. Not only would these topics have a natural excitement of their own; in addition, they could be important contributions to the authors' current world, since the past could be used to address issues such as the nature of the just monarch or Roman-barbarian relations, which were

---

[152] Tac. *Ann.* III.65.1-2. This is a much discussed passage; on the nobility as Tacitus' audience see Luce, *ANRW* II. 33. 4, 2904-27, with references to earlier discussions; on the translation see Woodman, *MH* 52 (1995) 111-26.

[153] See Millar, *Cassius Dio* 73-118.

[154] See the survey of historical topics in Anderson, *Second Sophistic* 101-18. That the use of the Greek past was not anti-Roman (as were the Greek historians mentioned by D. Hal. *A. R.* 1.4.3), is shown by the figure of the thoroughly Romanised Arrian: see Gabba, op. cit. (n.143) 57; Stadter, *Arrian* 167-9.

important to contemporaries, without the danger of confronting one's own times directly.[155]

Between Tacitus' death in the early second century and Ammianus' history in the late fourth century, we know of no narrative history written in Latin.[156] The rhetor Fronto considered writing a history of Lucius Verus' wars, but the work, so far as we can tell, was never written.[157] In place of narrative history we have only epitomes and breviaria, or, in a different genre, imperial biography.[158] An indication of the low esteem in which history was held during these years is provided by the actions of the Emperor Tacitus (AD 275-6), who claimed descent from the historian, and ordered that each year ten copies of his ancestor's works be made, 'lest they perish from the neglect by readers'.[159] When Ammianus again takes up history from where Tacitus had left off, he has harsh words for the gossipy and sensationalistic biographies of emperors that had replaced his type of serious history.[160]

This was not the case, however, among the Greeks. In their tradition we can follow a continuous line of historians who chronicled their own and the Empire's affairs: Herodian, Dio, Dexippus, through to Eunapius and beyond. Some of these works, it is true, display a restricted focus, sometimes centring largely around the events that the historian himself knew well.[161] Nevertheless, the Greek tradition of continuous history showed no signs of abating, and despite the vagaries

[155] On Alexander in the Empire see Heuss, *A&A* 4 (1954) 85-97; Bowie, in *Studies in Ancient Society* 170-1; Anderson, op. cit. (n.154) 113-17 gives examples of the popularity of Alexander from outside of historiography. Even the Romans could turn to Alexander, as seen by Curtius Rufus' *History of Alexander the Great*, written in the middle of the first century AD (on the controversy about Curtius' date see the full summation of evidence by Atkinson, *Commentary* 19-57). Because the preface to this work is lost, we do not know why Curtius chose Alexander, nor whether he gave it some relationship to his own era, but it is likely that he did. On the Persian Wars and their cultural importance, see Spawforth, in *Greek Historiography* 233-47.
[156] Schanz-Hosius III. 234-5; Syme, *Emperors and Biography* 34-6.
[157] Champlin, *Fronto* 55; Cova, *I principia historiae, passim* argues that Fronto never intended to write the history of this war; contra, Steinmetz, *Untersuchungen zur römischen Literatur* 152-3.
[158] For the fourth-century writers of *breuiaria*, Festus and Eutropius, see Herzog-Schmidt v.201-11. In biography there was Marius Maximus (who wrote twelve lives in imitation of Suetonius, going from Nerva to Elagabalus) and an unknown writer who ended with Caracalla (Syme, op. cit. (n.156) 49-51). [159] *SHA Tac.* 10.3.
[160] See, e.g., XXVI.1.1-2; XXXI.5.10 and below, p. 217. [161] See below, pp. 92f.

of government and their political position towards outside powers, their devotion to the writing of history remained constant. They could assume that an audience to read and appreciate it was always at hand. When it no longer was, this was not because history itself perished, but rather that the success of Christianity had brought with it a new and different approach to the past.

I
The call to history

Most of the ancient historians give some indication to their audience why they embarked upon writing their history. These remarks sometimes concern themselves with the unique nature of the historian's subject matter; in addition to the greatness of the deeds, historians will frequently explain other circumstances that led them to the composition of their histories. There is, in general, a tendency as time goes on for authors, while not abandoning the magnification of their theme, to present a more 'personal' call to history, that is, to say something of themselves and the personal experiences that underlay their writing of history.

1. THE GREATNESS OF THE SUBJECT

The most common call to history, as the historians present it, is the subject matter itself.[1] The magnification (αὔξησις, *amplificatio*) of events will depend on the type of history being written, since not all magnifications are the same, and the type employed for universal history is not that favoured by the writer of an historical monograph. Even for universal history, the type of magnification favoured by Polybius, who writes a contemporary history, will not be the same as that taken by Diodorus, whose history embraces events already treated by others.

For contemporary historians the ultimate model is Herodotus' introduction to the campaigns of Xerxes against Greece. Here Herodotus notes that Xerxes' expedition was the greatest 'of all those we know', and that it dwarfed Darius' expedition against Scythia, or the Scythian expedition to Asia, or even the campaign of the Greeks against Troy (VII.20.2-21.1). The primary elements that Herodotus

---

[1] See Herkommer, *Topoi* 165-71 on the greatness of the subject.

bequeathed to later historians were the use of superlatives, mostly of size and magnitude, and a comparison with previous events or deeds by which the unique greatness of the present history is brought out in relief. Herodotus himself, as his mention of Troy makes clear, vies with Homer, and the historian's amplification of his subject portrays the deeds as worthy of the same renown (κλέος) that Homer had given to his.[2] For Herodotus, as for his successors, the greatness of the deeds themselves demands that they be recounted.

Thucydides placed himself in a direct line with Herodotus and Homer in his own amplification, where, in keeping with Herodotus' example, he compares his theme with his immediate predecessor's and uses the same superlatives of size and power. The Peloponnesian War exceeded all previous wars in its length, sufferings, sackings, exiles, and civil strife. The Persian Wars, which Herodotus had needed five books to treat, are disposed of in a single sentence as being nothing more than three battles in two campaigns (1.23.1-2). The armament of the Persian King, epically and lovingly described by Herodotus, had already been deflated in Thucydides' preface by the demonstration that it was in his own time that the Greek world was at the height of its power and material prosperity, and that what passed for greatness in previous eras could not be compared with the present day.[3] Thucydides, again like Herodotus, does not simply allow one or two introductory passages to persuade the reader of the truth of his assertions. Rather, he finds in many events something exceptional and unique: Delos was shaken, which had never happened before; Archidamus reminds the Spartans that 'we have never gone out with a greater force than this'; the plague of the war's second year was the greatest ever known; Pericles reminds the Athenians that they rule over more Greeks than any Greeks before them had; and so on. Within the war narrative itself, attention is called

---

[2] For Herodotus' echoes of the *Iliad* and *Odyssey* in his prefaces see Krischer, *Hermes* 93 (1965) 159-67; Strasburger, *Studien z. alten Geschichte* II.1066-7; Moles in *L&F* 92-4. Amplification was developed for epideictic: see Caplan's note on [Cic.] *Herenn.* II.47; see also V. Buchheit, *Untersuchungen zur Theorie des Genos Epideiktikon* (Munich 1960) 15-26.

[3] Thucydides deliberately shies away from treating the non-Greek world in the 'Archaeology', so as to focus on the two combatants, and to avoid a comparison with the East, which even Thucydides would have had to admit dwarfed Greece in its wealth and power. This - and not any deficiency of historical judgement - is, I think, the reason why Thucydides consistently downplayed the importance of Persia, of which he can have been only too well aware.

again and again to something that was greatest, most disastrous, most unexpected.[4]

Whether Thucydides' continuators, Cratippus, the Oxyrhynchus historian, and Theopompus in the *Hellenica*, emphasised the unique greatness of their subject is uncertain; Xenophon did not, and nowhere in the *Hellenica* does he suggest anything of the sort that Thucydides had done; on the contrary, his remarks at the end of the history – 'up to this point let it be written by me; the affairs after this will perhaps be of interest to someone else' – indicate quite clearly that Xenophon, while thinking the deeds he has narrated as worthy of account, believes events other than his own to be equally worthy of record.[5]

The focus, but not the principle, changed in the fourth century. Theopompus decided to centre his history around Philip, arguing for that individual's unique greatness: Europe, he said, had never before brought forth such a man as Philip.[6] This trend, no doubt, became standard practice under the Alexander historians, and some sense of this survives even in Arrian's *Anabasis*, where the historian says that no one achieved so great or so many deeds among Greeks or barbarians as did Alexander.[7] Such an arrangement had many benefits when writing under a monarch, since individual rulers were no doubt pleased to see their deeds marked out as unique and greater than any before. So Velleius begins the narrative of the campaigns under Tiberius with similar emphasis on the unprecedented deeds accomplished by the commander and his soldiers: all Germany sees Roman arms; nations barely known by name are brought beneath Roman rule; and a Roman army marches to the Elbe, a feat not only previously untried, but even undreamed of.[8]

---

[4] Thuc. II.8.3; 11.1, cf. 20.2; 47.3; 64.3; 77.4; V.14.3; 60.3; 64.2; 74.1; VI.31.1, cf. 31.6; VII.66.2; 70.2; 71.2; 71.7; 87.5, cf. 87.6; VIII.41.2; 68.2; for unique events see II.94.1; III.98.4; IV.40.1; VII.30.3; 85.4; 86.5; VIII.96.1; 106.1. On the purpose of such remarks, cf. Woodman, *RICH* 28–32; Hornblower, *CT* I.371 sees superlatives as a favourite Thucydidean way of making an emphatic point.

[5] *Hell.* VII. 5.27; for more on this see below, pp. 237ff.   [6] *FGrHist* 115 F 27.

[7] Arr. *Anab.* I.12.4; on the echoes of Herodotus in Arrian see Moles, *JHS* 105 (1985) 163; for Arrian and Theopompus see below pp. 253f.

[8] Vell. II.106.1–2. For the sort of pressure an historian might be subjected to, see Fronto, *ad Verum* 1.2.2, where the Emperor Lucius Verus encourages Fronto to dwell on the greatness of the Parthians, so that the monarch's achievements may seem all the more distinguished ('ut quantum nos egerimus appareat').

After Theopompus, it is thus likely that the amplification consisted of praise of deeds, but deeds closely allied with whatever monarch formed the main subject of one's history.[9] Polybius rejected this orientation,[10] and based the uniqueness of his subject both on the greatness of the deeds themselves, and on the number of theatres his work embraced. Although Ephorus was probably the first to praise universal history,[11] Polybius' treatment is the first that survives in full, and we can see, even with an imperfect knowledge of Ephorus, that Polybius was moving beyond his predecessor, for he emphasises not only the number of events but also their unique conjunction, which had in his lifetime united the entire Greco-Roman world. Polybius' amplification is both historical and historiographical, since, as Rome exceeds all empires ever known, so universal history surpasses history written on single subjects, such as *Hellenica*, monographs, and individual-centred history. We are first told that Rome has subjected nearly the whole world to herself, 'a thing which is found formerly never to have occurred' (1.1.5), and Polybius then provides a comparison with previous empires, adapting what had been applied by Herodotus to expeditions and by Thucydides to wars. In this comparison, reference is made both to geographical extent and temporal duration, and the Romans emerge as clearly superior in both (1.2.2–7). Praise of fortune's unique conjunction of events then follows, a set of circumstances described as 'finest and most beneficial', and her achievement is personified as if she herself were an historical actor (1.4.5). Then comes the praise of universal history which alone has vividity,[12] imparts true knowledge, and allows the reader to derive both benefit and pleasure (1.4.8–11). Superior, therefore, are both the deeds and the account of those deeds.

Despite Polybius' scorn for single histories, historians did follow in

---

[9] One can see this still in the fourth century AD: Praxagoras of Athens wrote a history of Constantine the Great, saying that this Emperor had by his excellence overshadowed every ruler before him: *FGrHist* 219 T 1 (§8); on the possible circumstances of composition, Jacoby, *Komm.* II. B. 632.

[10] He criticises Theopompus for arranging his history around Philip: VIII.13.3–4 = *FGrHist* 115 T 19.

[11] Pol. v.33.1 states that other writers boasted of writing universal history (τὰ καθόλου), and it is inconceivable that Ephorus, adopting a new arrangement, would not have explained and lauded it.

[12] It differs as much from separate parts of history as a living creature does from a dead one: see 1.4.7 where, it is said, individual histories can give no sense 'of the liveliness or beauty of a living creature'.

Thucydides' footsteps, emphasising the unique greatness of an event – a war, usually – or the time period that they chose to write up. Josephus speaks of the war of the Jews against the Romans as 'the greatest, not only of those in our time, but of all those we know from report' (*B. J.* 1.1). Just as Thucydides' war had involved all the Hellenic and nearly all of the non-Greek world, so the Jewish War affected Rome and all of the East (4–5). Turbulence, motion, confusion – all echo Thucydides' description of the Peloponnesian War as the greatest upheaval ever, as does the remark that the Jewish revolutionaries were at the height of their powers.[13] The same conjunction of turbulence and an entire world in upheaval can be seen at the beginning of Tacitus' *Histories*, where his subject is described as 'rich in crises, brutal in battles, and discordant with revolutions' (1.2.1). East and West are embraced, the latter by Britain which was conquered and immediately lost, while the former saw such troubles that the Parthians were almost[14] roused to war. Tacitus suggests world-wide sufferings, exactly as Thucydides had done. Even the heart of the Empire saw things never seen before: conquered cities, decimated shores, Rome itself afire, and the Capitol burned by the hands of citizens; slaves set against their masters and freedmen against their patrons (1.2.2–3). Here Tacitus has employed a liberal use of superlatives, painting the vivid images of seas full of exiles and isles running blood, and summing his topic up as a world in which all things (*cuncta*) were overturned by hatred and terror.[15]

Civil wars attendant upon the deaths of emperors provided fine fuel for the historians of the Empire. Dio when he arrives at the contemporary portions of his history speaks of the 'greatest wars and civil strife' that befell the Empire after the death of Commodus (LXXII.23). Herodian is yet more explicit, stating that no comparable period had seen such civil and foreign wars, such disruptions in the provinces, so many destructions by natural and man-made causes, or such reversals of fortune (1.1.4–5). The two basic elements appear here as they have from the beginning, the unique nature of the deeds to be treated, and the deprecation of events before the author's chosen time period. An even

---

[13] Jos. *B. J.* 1.4 ἀκμάζον ~ Thuc. 1.1.1: ἀκμάζοντές τε ἦσαν ἐς αὐτὸν ἀμφότεροι παρασκευῇ τῇ πάσῃ, κ.τ.λ. Cf. 1.11, where Jerusalem is said to have reached the peak of prosperity and in turn to have fallen to the depths of misfortune.

[14] Note that they were 'almost' (*prope*) roused to war, a mention that clearly serves the purpose of amplification.   [15] Woodman, *RICH* 166–7.

more explicit comparison with the great events of the past can be found later in Herodian after Severus defeats Albinus, the last of the contenders for power. Severus' victories are marked as unique in the size of the forces and the number of battles, and no previous internal struggle for power – not that of Sulla and Marius, Caesar and Pompey, or Augustus and Antony – can compare with them (III.7.8). The great names of earlier Roman conquerors appear to lend magnitude both to the importance of the event itself, and to the author's subject, whose unique achievement was that he defeated three reigning emperors.

How Ammianus handled these matters in his preface is unfortunately lost.[16] Some sense of his amplification may, however, remain in the remarks made by the historian throughout his work. Julian's deeds, in particular, are described as surpassing many valiant achievements of the ancients, and elsewhere that Emperor's war against the Alemanni is said to be comparable to those the Romans waged against the Carthaginians and the Teutones.[17]

The writer of the historical monograph in Latin emphasises the uniqueness or importance of his theme, but he is less likely to play up its greatness in superlatives or to suggest that the events contained therein are beyond all others in importance. Sallust, for example, will write of Catiline's conspiracy which was memorable because of the novelty of the crime and the danger that it offered.[18] This is a brief notice compared to the ones we examined above, and Sallust allows himself a little fuller treatment when he describes the enrolment of troops by Antonius before the final act of the tragedy (*Cat.* 36.4–37.1). Here there is a clever reversal of what we had seen earlier: whereas in large-scale histories there is an emphasis on a world in turmoil, in the *Catiline*, by contrast, the outer world is peaceful from one end to the other (*ad occasum ab ortu solis*), and serves as the framing device to concentrate attention on what is within, the civil strife and division of the Roman state: this in turn would lead to the destruction of the very nation that had conquered the

---

[16] In writing of Roman affairs from where Tacitus left off (AD 96), Ammianus could have spoken, like Herodian, of more revolutions and more emperors raised and ruined than at any other time in Roman history. The anarchy of the third century alone saw more than fifty emperors and pretenders, and the near impoverishment of the Empire.   [17] Amm. XVI.1.2; XVII.1.14.
[18] *Cat.* 4. 4: 'nam id facinus in primis ego memorabile existumo sceleris atque periculi nouitate'.

world. The extreme danger to the state mentioned only generally in the preface is concretely portrayed at the end of the work, where the ferocity and bravery of Catiline's army is brought out in a series of superlatives: nearly every man had died at his place; all fell with their wounds in front; no freeborn citizen was taken alive; and all had been as sparing of their own lives as of the enemy's (61.1-6). A similar concern with civil strife informs the *Jugurtha*.[19] Sallust says that he chose this war because it was great and brutal and of fickle fortune, and because during it the arrogance of the nobility first became clear (*Jug.* 5.1). This strife is then described as confounding all things human and divine, and as ending only with the destruction of Italy (5.2). The war is magnified thus by association, because it began a series of events that was to culminate in the greatest destruction and sufferings. It should be noted that Sallust's *amplificatio* here, as in the *Catiline*, is not that of a Thucydides or Josephus or Tacitus; in neither case does he say that his subject was the greatest of all, nor the deeds of a magnitude not seen before.[20]

The writers of non-contemporary, or largely non-contemporary, history, such as Diodorus, Dionysius, and Livy, have a rather different manner of amplification. Neither the Thucydidean nor the Polybian type, in which the author emphasises that the present age is the culmination of all previous eras, is suited for a large-scale history that embraces hundreds of years. For Dionysius and Livy, the 'greatness' of their history is its expansiveness and comprehensiveness, perhaps as Ephorus had once argued. By this reasoning, a history which included, let us say, the Hannibalic War and the Marsic War, would surpass a history of either war by itself. Not surprisingly, then, the author of a universal history of this type calls attention to the vastness and variety of his topic: more is better, most is best, and the more events comprehended, the greater the variety of human experiences and deeds that can be com-

---

[19] See Paul, *Commentary* 21-3.
[20] Sallust, as we shall see, does not present his call to history as motivated exclusively by the deeds themselves, however worthy they may be of remembrance. Paul, op. cit. (n.19) 18ff. is at times critical of Sallust's claims; he notes, e.g., s. v. 'atrox' (p. 20) that 'the Jugurthine War did not provoke greater displays of ferocity than any other': but Sallust does not say it did. In fact it is a reference to suffering (πάθος), and is in the direct line from Thucydides 1.23.1-4 (on which see Woodman, *RICH* 28-40). Paul's comparison of Livy, xxi.1.2 (see below) does not bring out the different nature of Livy's claims with its superlatives and emphases.

mended to the reader. The model for this type of amplification may be the opening of Herodotus' history which is a universal history, of a sort,[21] and promises to treat, in general terms, 'great and marvellous deeds' (ἔργα μεγάλα τε καὶ θωμαστά). Whereas in Thucydides and his followers the amplification demonstrated and verified the importance of the historian's theme and 'his' war, Diodorus' (and Livy's) amplifications are those of what we might call an historical observer who surveys history's panorama and calls our attention to the highlights among the many things worth our observation.[22] The most elaborate amplification in Diodorus, however, is that of the Marsic War, where the two elements of unique greatness and comparison of previous actions are combined in a novel way. Roman greatness is asserted, even for those lands that the Romans did not conquer. The Greeks defeated the Persians, but the Romans defeated the Greeks, so they must be superior to Persia. Alexander defeated Persia, but Rome conquered Macedon. Then Fortune set Rome and Italy against each other, and kindled a war surpassing all others (XXXVII.1.1-6). This amplification has been adapted to circumstances: the Marsic War was not particularly long, so that avenue is closed to Diodorus; nor was it a conflict of east and west but rather narrowly restricted to the Italian peninsula. So Diodorus makes it as if Rome *and Italy* conquered the world together and then turned on each other. And since the nations of Italy had been accounted the bravest, the war that ensued had to reach the very peak of greatness.[23]

In Livy, similarly, the vast scale of the work precludes any single sustained amplification. As the Romans rule the world, so their deeds must be the greatest, and any work that contained the greatest number of their deeds must *ipso facto* be the greatest history. This does not preclude the author from availing himself of the traditional amplification of individual events, as Diodorus had done for the Marsic War. At the beginning of his treatment of the Second Punic War, Livy states that what for other

---

[21] Jacoby, *Abhandlungen* 42-5.
[22] See, e.g., in Diod. XV.48.1-4 (earthquakes in the Peloponnese in 373/2 BC which saw the greatest disaster and sufferings); XX.72.2, a massacre 'most elaborately planned' of all those that had gone before. Such a procedure is visible in the early books of Herodotus where he often calls attention, frequently with superlatives, to marvellous achievements of every sort.
[23] Although Diodorus' account of the Marsic War comes from Posidonius, the amplification is considered his own: see Malitz, *Historien des Poseidonios* 385 with reff.

historians would be their entire work is for him only a part, albeit a great part,[24] of the enormous deeds of the Roman people. Both Romans and Carthaginians were at the height of their power, both were skilled in the ways of war, and the changes of fortune were so great that little separated victor from vanquished (XXI.1.1-2).

Appian begins with a description of all the nations over whom the Romans hold sway, beginning with Britain, going all the way to the East and coming back again to the Pillars of Heracles (*praef.* 1-15). The Romans rule the world, and what they do not rule, says Appian, is by choice, since it would bring them little benefit, and they have already chosen the best areas of the globe to rule; they have even refused to accept some who offer themselves as subjects.[25] This amplification serves a dual purpose: the traditional one of magnification of the theme, but also to convince the reader of what will be Appian's unique contribution to the problem of Roman history. Since he is going to arrange his history by theatre of action, it is worth his while to emphasise how great in extent the Empire is, and how difficult it would be to narrate events occurring simultaneously throughout so great a realm. He then proceeds with the comparison of previous empires, his individual approach being the duration of Roman rule which exceeds all of the Greek hegemonies (Spartan, Athenian, Theban) put together and equalling that of the three great Eastern empires of the past, Assyrian, Median, and Persian (*praef.* 29-42).

Dionysius, like Polybius and Appian, has the usual amplification of Rome, comparing her favourably with previous empires, again both in extent of land and duration of time (*A. R.* 1.3.1-5). Yet this is not Dionysius' theme, and his amplification, even if true, would not explain his choice of topic, which is the history of *early* Rome. He is aware that some will find fault with his choice (4.1), but his justification[26] is that he will show the Greeks who complain of Roman rule that the Romans are in fact truly Greek.[27] Rome from its founding, he says, displayed all the virtues, and 'no city, either Greek or barbarian showed greater piety,

[24] See his remarks on the magnitude of the Hannibalic War at XXXI.1.1-5. (quoted below, p. 154), although even there he emphasises how much remains to be done.

[25] See *praef.* 18 where they hold that part of Britain that is of use; cf. *praef.* 26 where their decision not to extend their empire is attributed to their prudence, since they do not want troublesome and useless foreign nations.

[26] Aside from previously incompetent treatments, for which see below, pp. 113ff.

[27] For the importance of this to Dionysius, see Gabba, *Dionysius* 107-18.

justice, moderation, or bravery' (5. 3). The promise of great deeds, therefore, will be kept even for this early history, and the continuity of past and present, so important for Dionysius' justification, means that in writing the history of the early Romans, he *is* writing about the men and deeds of the greatest empire ever known.

We have seen, therefore, several types of amplification to which an historian could appeal, based on the deeds, the individual who performed them, or the number and variety of events embraced by one's history. While the deeds must always be considered great and worthy of record, this is not the sole justification advanced by many historians. Several tell us in even more detail or more personally why they chose their topic, sometimes when others were also available. Benefit to one's readers is often emphasised,[28] but some claim dreams, the requests of friends, and even the desire for glory.[29]

2. DECISIONS AND DREAMS

Beginning in the late Republic we can trace a tradition whereby the author explains how he came to write the history he is presenting to the audience. Nearly every historian, as we said above, gives some indication that he thinks the deeds to be narrated by him are most worthy of account. As time went on, historians began to give the details of their life that caused them to turn to history. It is not only that what had before been easily inferred in Herodotus or Thucydides should now be explicitly stated; this is, after all, nothing more than we would expect in a rhetorical genre. It is rather that the historian orients himself differently with respect to the deeds he chronicles and to history in general.[30]

---

[28] Although it is common for historians to praise the utility of their subject and of history in general, they do not, as a rule, present the reader's benefit as a main reason why they took up history. Even Polybius, who has the most to say about history's utility (see Walbank, *PoH* 253-66), presents Rome's rise to power as the most important spur to his work. For explicit remarks on benefiting the reader see Pol. I.1.2; IX.2.5; Diod. I.1.4-5; D. Hal. *Pomp.* 6 (II.392-6 Usher); *A. R.* I.1.2; 2.1; 6.4; Sempronius Asellio, *HRR* F 2; Sall. *Jug.* 4.1-7; Livy, *praef.* 10; Strabo, *FGrHist* 91 F 2; Tac. *Ann.* IV.32.2-33.2 (with Martin and Woodman's commentary ad loc.); Arr. *Anab.* VII.30.3; Philip of Pergamum, *FGrHist* 95 F 1. For general discussions of utility in history see Avenarius, *LS* 22-6; Herkommer, *Topoi* 128-36; Fornara, *Nature* 104-20.

[29] For the correction of predecessors as a reason for re-doing a non-contemporary history see below, pp. 113ff.

[30] Cf. Fornara, *Nature* 54: 'In Herodotus's time, the work was all and the writer little.'

Amplification coexists with a description (almost purely autobiographical) of how the author came to write this particular history. This is the historian in search of a theme, as seen clearly in Sallust and Dionysius, but also in Livy, Appian, and Dio.

In the *Catiline* Sallust gives a description of the events that led him to his new field of historiography. He attempts to justify his choice of occupation and to suggest that it is as valuable as the traditional types of *uirtus*, a concept that dominates the introduction to this particular work.[31] The details that Sallust gives about his life are intelligible only within this framework. To the old Roman concept of *uirtus* as 'benefiting the state' (*bene facere rei publicae*, 3.1) Sallust adds (or better, emphasises, since it too was a recognised part of *uirtus*) that of 'speaking well' (*bene dicere* recalling a connection between speech and action that he had already made at 1.6); and he adds that one may become renowned in both military and civic achievements (3.1). His own career is now introduced as the specific example of the previous generalisations. As a youth, he too was led to the realm of public service but contemporary politics, he found, led not to *uirtus* but rather to *mores mali* (3.3-5). And so, abandoning such a wretched and dangerous existence, Sallust resolved[32] to spend the rest of his life away from the Republic, and his choice of occupations was the writing of history. This scenario, as is well known, is based both on Plato, who in the seventh letter explained his reasons for abandoning a corrupt state after the death of Socrates, and on Isocrates' defence of his own retreat from public life, and his decision to use his oratory to the benefit of the state.[33] As it is presented, then, the choice of history is an attempt by the author to display his *uirtus* for the benefit of the state, but it is a second choice since the first is no

---

[31] On *uirtus* in Sallust see Earl, *Political Thought* ch. II; on *uirtus* as the prerogative of the nobility, K.-J. Hölkeskamp, *Die Entstehung der Nobilität* (Stuttgart 1987) 209ff.

[32] Sallust is careful to portray his abandonment of politics as his own choice: *Cat.* 4.1 (*decreui*); *Jug.* 4.3 (*decreui*); for the details of his political career, Syme, *Sallust* 29-42.

[33] Plato, *ep.* 7.324b-326b; Isoc. *Panath.* 11; the passages are conveniently tabulated side by side in Vretska's commentary, 1.96 and Egermann, *Die Proömien zu den Werken des Sallust* 27ff. Posidonius and Plato are the favourite candidates for the origin of Sallust's prologues (see Leeman, *Systematical Bibliography to Sallust* 28-33), but Earl, op. cit. (n.31) chh. I-II sees most of the motifs as arising from Roman thought and traditions.

longer possible.³⁴ Sallust's portrayal of his decision is thus categorically different from the series of early Greek historians from Herodotus through Polybius who portrayed their decision as one demanded by the events themselves. Of course, Sallust believed his choice of subjects was worthy.³⁵ But in the prefaces he is a man sitting back in retirement, deciding on a career,³⁶ and then surveying all of Roman history to choose from it edifying and important incidents (*Cat.* 4.2). He thus presents himself as one who first resolved to write history *and then* looked for a suitable subject. To what extent this was a traditional persona of a Roman historian we cannot say, although Cato's *Origins* may suggest it. For in that preface Cato clearly stated the difference between *negotium* and *otium*, and made the writing of history a suitable occupation for the latter. First comes the leisure and the opportunity, then the question, 'how may I benefit the state even in my free time?', then the decision to write history. Sallust's political situation is slightly different from Cato's, but the historian in search of a theme fits in easily with Roman relegation of history to the position of a serious pastime.³⁷

Livy, a man without a political career, does not proceed like Sallust. Indeed, Livy's uniqueness is that, while not minimising the greatness or importance of Roman deeds or their utility, he presents the history as undertaken mainly for his personal pleasure. In contrasting himself with those readers who may be less pleased with the early history of Rome and would prefer to read about more recent events (*praef.* 4), Livy boldly asserts that the reward for his effort will be the ability to turn his eyes from the ills of the present.³⁸ Thus the impetus for writing, to the extent that Livy presents any, is exclusively personal, the desire to lose

---

[34] Cicero had similarly portrayed his enforced exile from the Republic as something he would turn to the benefit of the Roman state: *Brut.* 7-9, cf. *Rep.* 1.7-8; *Tusc. Disp.* 1.1.

[35] But as we saw above (n. 20) he did not claim that they were 'worthiest of all'.

[36] *Cat.* 4.1: 'igitur ubi ... mihi relicuam aetatem a re publica procul habendam decreui, non fuit consilium socordia atque desidia bonum otium conterere, neque uero agrum colundo aut uenando, seruilibus officiis, intentum aetatem agere.'

[37] Cato, *HRR* F 2. For more on Sallust's relation with Cato, see below, pp. 138ff. There is no indication from the fragments of the *Histories* that Sallust spoke similarly of himself there.

[38] *praef.* 5: 'ut me a conspectu malorum quae nostra tot per annos uidit aetas ... auertam'. Livy's escapism in a time of civil war can be paralleled from other writers: see Fraenkel, *Horace* 52ff.; Gabba, *JRS* 71 (1981) 59.

himself in his work. And lest we conclude that this was merely a pose adopted at the beginning of the work, we have some evidence that Livy continued to portray his efforts in personal terms (if in a less diffident spirit), since in the preface to a later (now lost) book, he claimed to have won enough glory for himself and to have been able to cease writing, except that his restless spirit fed on work.[39] Naturally, personal renown is not Livy's sole purpose in writing nor are we meant to take these remarks simply at face value.[40] Livy does make the traditional claims for the importance of Roman history itself (*praef.* 9-10) and he clearly intended to instruct as well as present a superior account. But it must be noted that the emphasis on the personal solace the author receives is unique.[41]

Among the Greeks there is the first suggestion of a different orientation of writer to deeds in Diodorus, who begins by speaking of the usefulness of having a truly universal history because of its wealth of moral and ethical *exempla*, and then suggests that since such a need exists, he has decided to put together his *Library*, even though it required much work and danger. Diodorus chose the career of historian from a desire to be a benefactor (εὐεργέτης) of mankind, in much the same way that Heracles was.[42] Even more explicit is Dionysius in the *Antiquities* when he remarks that although there were many possible topics for him to treat, he chose the early history of Rome because the Greeks have misguided notions of why Rome rose.[43] Again, he first decides to be a historian, then (like Sallust) looks around for what is worthy of memory. He differs strongly, however, from the Roman historians in his commitment to and emphasis on the effort involved in writing history. As just mentioned, history as a secondary occupation or hobby (πάρεργον) was built, so to speak, into the very nature of Roman historiography, and no Roman apologies for it were necessary. On the other hand, this will not do for Dionysius, who elsewhere expresses strongly the belief that history must be the work of a lifetime, to which one brings the greatest commitment.[44] Yet these four writers – Sallust, Livy, Diodorus, and

---

[39] Livy, F 58, quoted below, p. 57.   [40] Moles, *PCPS* n.s. 39 (1993) 145-9.

[41] I argue below, pp. 140f., that Livy adopts this pose to avoid the question of his qualifications.

[42] Diod. 1.1.1-4.5, esp. 1.4, 2.2, 2.4, 3.1, 4.1; on the importance to Diodorus of Heracles and his εὐεργεσία see below, pp. 149f.

[43] D. Hal. *A. R.* 1.4.1-2; the disdain that some might feel for early history recalls Livy above.   [44] Below, p. 149.

Dionysius – betray the bookishness of their era: each surveys the field from his study and proceeds to choose a suitable theme.[45] It is no longer portrayed as only the events themselves demanding their own recognition. Something similar is to be found later in Appian. Many writers, he says, have described Roman history and he himself took up the subject wishing to examine individually the history of the several nations against whom Rome fought. The result, he hopes, will prove agreeable to those who would like to learn their Roman history this way.[46] The emphasis is on the uniqueness of the approach, a new method whereby one can study different aspects of the Roman conquest. Again it is the writer surveying the field and choosing (and, in this case, arranging) it in a way pleasurable and beneficial to the audience.

Two 'calls to history' are particularly noteworthy for their obvious affinities with poetry. In a letter to Baebius Macer, the younger Pliny provides for his correspondent a bibliography of his uncle's writings, of which one was the *German Wars*. His uncle, he says, began the work 'advised by a dream, while he was serving in Germany; for over him stood the image of Drusus Nero, who had conquered the greater part of Germany, and died there. He entrusted his memory to my uncle, and besought that he should preserve him from the injustice of oblivion.'[47] What we know of Pliny the Elder's work suggests that it began with Rome's wars against the Cimbri and the Teutones in the first century BC, and culminated with Drusus' wars in AD 4-7.[48] Pliny the Younger does not say explicitly that this dream was narrated in his uncle's *German Wars* but there is little reason to doubt it;[49] and if it did, it most likely appeared in the preface[50] as one justification[51] for the author's

---

[45] Dionysius (*Pomp.* 3 = II.372-6 Usher) even retrojects this attitude onto Thucydides, who, he complains, could have *chosen* far better topics than the Peloponnesian War.

[46] *praef.* 45-52. Appian's history thus represents the undoing of Polybius' concept of universal history (1.4.1-11); cf. Walbank, *SP* 318.

[47] Pliny, *ep.* III.5.4; the list, Pliny says, is in chronological order and the *Bella Germaniae* was preceded by a *de uita Pomponi Secundi* and followed by the *Historiae a fine Aufidi Bassi* and the *Historia Naturalis*.

[48] Peter, *HRR* II. cxxxxviii, relying on the implications of 'Germaniae latissime uictor'.

[49] Peter, ibid., assumes that it was; cf. Sallmann, *ANRW* II. 32. 1, 580.

[50] Even here caution is necessary. If we had only a summary of Dio's dream (below) we would assume that it came from the preface; it does not.

[51] Surely not by itself: there will have been some mention of the wars' greatness or vicissitudes or Drusus' exploits.

presentation of the work to the public. Drusus' entrustment of his memory to Pliny, and his desire to be protected from the *iniuria obliuionis* have been considered sufficient to posit a political purpose in the work.[52] Surely the indisputable point is that Drusus' plea in a history will have recalled Herodotus' preface and its similar purpose, 'that human achievement not be forgotten in time, and that great and marvellous deeds not be without their glory'. The concern with one's own memory and renown will have fit in well both with the ethos of Roman political life and the traditions of Roman historiography.[53] Although a vision as poetic inspiration goes back to Hesiod, and has a more immediate Roman inspiration in Ennius' dream of Homer in his *Annals*, there is no ground to assume that Pliny adorned his account with numerous poetic colourings. As it is presented in the younger Pliny's letter, the dream serves only as the motivation to write up the wars; it is concerned with specifically historical matters – *memoria*, *obliuio*, and *fama* – by a specific historical person, and for this we have many precedents, from Gaius Gracchus' dream of his brother Tiberius, to Cicero's dream of Marius.[54]

By far the most elaborate description of the call to history (almost within a tradition of its own, we might say) is Dio's portrayal of the divine (or at any rate supernatural) events that gave birth to an historian. Unlike most of his predecessors, Dio does not portray his decision as motivated by the worthiness and magnificence of the deeds themselves[55] (as Thucydides, Theopompus, Polybius, Dionysius, Josephus, or Herodian had) or as a superior treatment over earlier writers (Dionysius, Diodorus, Arrian), or even as a personal desire and pleasure (Livy). Instead, Dio says, he was encouraged to try history by a

---

[52] Peter, *HRR* II. cxxvi thinks that Drusus may have been left out of Aufidius Bassus' German history; opinions surveyed by Sallmann, op. cit. (n.49) 583, who rejects political interpretation.

[53] See Woodman, *VP* 1.30-45; Sallmann, op. cit. (n.49) 596 says that the work was not 'Polemik gegen ... sondern Enkomiastik für jemanden'. And cf. the same Roman concerns in Pliny's *de uita Pomponi Secundi* which his nephew says he wrote, 'because greatly loved by [Pomponius], he paid this as a debt to his memory' (*ep.* III.5.3).

[54] Cic. *Div.* 1.56 (Gaius' dream); for Cicero's dream, see ibid. 59, with Suerbaum, *Untersuchungen zur Selbstdarstellung älterer römischer Dichter* 317; additional examples at Sallmann, op. cit. (n.49) 585ff. For Ennius' dream see *Annales* I.iii, with Skutsch's commentary, 147-53; cf. Suerbaum, ibid. 94-113 on its function in the poem as a legitimating device.

[55] Indeed at one point he says the opposite: Ch. II n. 136.

Decisions and dreams 49

complimentary letter received from the future Emperor Septimius Severus on a book which he, Dio, had composed on the dreams and portents that had indicated Severus' rise to power.[56] Having received this letter at nightfall, Dio continues, he fell asleep and dreamed that a divine power (τὸ δαιμόνιον) commanded him to write a history of Severus' rise to power. When others, including the Emperor Severus, approved of that work, he became eager to write about all the rest of Roman history, and to put it together with his previous work. And he concludes by saying that he will write to whatever point is pleasing to Fortune (μέχρις ἂν καὶ τῇ Τύχῃ δόξῃ). He then extols the goddess for the beneficent effect she has had upon him and his work.[57]

The passage occurs at the point where Dio has noted the death of Commodus, the last of the genuine Aurelii (LXXII.22.6). It was during the civil wars which followed – wars which saw Severus the ultimate victor – that Dio wrote his book on the portents which he interpreted. Thus the passage, although suitable for a preface (where the author tells how he came to write history), fits organically into the history here and is brought forward at an appropriate point. And if it is true that Dio saw the rule of Septimius as the inauguration of a new and rejuvenated era in Roman history,[58] a second (or third) personal preface would perhaps have been suitable. In fact, we can be certain that we are dealing with a tradition different from that in Pliny because of what follows. Dio mentions two other dreams that also play some part in his decision to write history. After he narrates the death of Caracalla, he explains to the reader that it had been predicted to him that he would write these events too, for after Severus' death Dio had a dream in which he saw Severus surrounded by the armed power of the Romans. When Dio tried to hear

---

[56] Dio, LXXII.23.1. I suspect that the motif of the future historian prophesying the future accession of an Emperor is influenced by ('modelled on' may be too strong a term) Josephus' portrayal of himself as a prisoner before Titus (*B. J.* III.399–408), an incident that became legendary (see Schreckenberg, *Die Flavius-Josephus Tradition in Antike und Mittelalter* 68–75) and was known to Dio, who recounts it at LXVI.1.4.

[57] Dio, LXXII.23.2–5. For a reconstruction of Dio's composition, Millar, *Cassius Dio* 193–4; for the various theories see Barnes, *Phoenix* 38 (1984) 240–55.

[58] Schwartz, *RE* III, 1685 = *GG* 396; *contra*, Bering-Staschewski, *Römische Zeitgeschichte bei Cassius Dio* 51–9; on Dio's attitude to Severus, see also Millar, op. cit. (n.57) 138–50; Barnes, op. cit. (n.57) 253–4 points out the contradictory portrait of Severus in Dio and suggests that the history contains earlier panegyrical material, and a later more hostile opinion. For the panegyrical elements see Rubin, *Civil War Propaganda and Historiography* 41–84.

what was transpiring Severus said, 'Come closer, Dio, so that you may learn accurately and write up all that has been said and done'.[59] It is a curious addition to the first dream and functionally unnecessary since in the earlier passage Dio had said that he would continue his narrative to whatever point was pleasing to Fortune. It can only be here to remind the reader of the continuing presence of the divine as Dio's guide.[60]

A final dream closes out Dio's history. After he left Campania where he had met with the Emperor and was on his way back to his native Bithynia, Dio was reminded of a dream that had once appeared to him. Here the divine power (τὸ δαιμόνιον again) revealed to him how to end his history with words from Homer: 'Zeus led Hector out of the missiles and dust | out of the battle's slaughter and blood and din.'[61] Thus Dio presents the decision to end his work as coming from the same source that had commanded him to begin.

The use of dreams as motivation for the writing of history cannot be considered common. It is true that dreams as legitimating devices are found in rhetorical teaching, but they were problematic.[62] We can, however, point to important parallels with Pliny's and Dio's dreams in other literary figures of the middle and late Empire. Marcus Aurelius in his *Meditations* thanks the gods for giving him good advice in dreams,[63] and Maximus of Tyre speaks of the value of what the gods send in dreams; best known of all are the dreams of Aelius Aristides and Artemidorus: like Dio, Aristides has divine prompting in his literary efforts, and says that at times the divine even gives him the beginnings of works (as Dio's gives him the concluding words).[64] Dio tells us that he

---

[59] Dio, LXXVIII.10.1-2.

[60] Sallmann, op. cit. (n.49) 592 points out that the second dream is a logical consequence of the first with the added benefit for Dio that Septimius, now dead, can appear in the dream.   [61] Dio, LXXX.5.3; the lines are *Il.* XI.163-4.

[62] Men. Rhet. 390. 4-6: χρὴ δὲ καὶ ὀνείρατα πλάττειν καὶ ἀκοήν τινα προσποιεῖσθαι ἀκηκοέναι, καὶ ταύτην βούλεσθαι ἐξαγγέλλειν τοῖς ἀκούουσιν. Cf. Cic. *Top.* 77: 'a dormientibus quoque multa significata uisis. quibus ex locis sumi interdum solent ad fidem faciendam testimonia deorum'; cf. 75 where truth is sometimes found i. a. 'per somnum'. But Seneca (*Contr.* II.1.33) thought otherwise: 'sed ridiculum est adfectari quod falsum probari non possit. non multum interest in causa sua falsum aliquis testem det an se: alteri enim credi non debet, alteri non solet.'   [63] *Med.* 1.17.9.

[64] Sallmann, op. cit. (n.49) 587 points out some of these parallels; for other references and discussion, see Dodds, *Pagan and Christian in an Age of Anxiety* 38-53, esp. his treatment of Aristides (39-45) and the influence of Asclepius on Aristides' work (44 n. 5); cf. M. Nilsson, *Geschichte der griechischen Religion*

had begun with a book on dreams and portents and throughout his history they play an important role.[65] Although there is no need to deny that Dio actually had these dreams, we must not be considered overly suspicious if we feel that something more than a mere recording of actual experience is at stake here. A dream or vision such as Pliny's or Dio's could not but recall the poetic motif that goes back to Hesiod and the Muses. Now the use of Homer to end the history, the comparison with Hector that suggests that Dio too is protected by Zeus, and the presentation of the divine as the determining factor on where to end the history show clearly that Dio's dreams (unlike Pliny's dream) are far closer to the traditional motifs of poetic inspiration. For all this similarity, however, Dio has made something new of it. He has not used this divine inspiration as justification for his knowledge of events or as a replacement of the traditional type of inquiry; rather, he has grafted these primarily poetic motifs onto the usual methods of validation that one finds in historiography.[66] Dio presents his journey to history as motivated by a series of divine incidents; once he has arrived at his task, however, he dons the mantle of the investigator as it had been handed down since Herodotus. The divine, therefore, adds meaning and recalls Homer, while yet coexisting with the more human work of inquiry.[67]

(Munich ²1961) II.520–1; cf. Bowersock, *Greek Sophists* 73 for the dream of Galen's father that determined his son's career, and the dreams of Polemo, Favorinus, Hermocrates, and Lucian.

[65] See Millar, op. cit. (n.57) 179–81, and his index, s. v. 'prodigium'.

[66] On Dio's techniques of inquiry, below, pp. 91ff.

[67] One may contrast this with a wholly poetic persona, that of the Atthidographer Amelesagoras, whom Maximus of Tyre ranks with Aristeas and Epimenides as those who portrayed themselves as divinely inspired historians: Amelesagoras, he says, claimed wisdom not from his craft (τέχνη) but from the divine gift of the nymphs (ἐκ Νυμφῶν κάτοχος θείᾳ μοίρᾳ, *FGrHist* 330 T 2). Even from this brief characterisation, we can see that Pliny's dream belongs in a different class. Amelesagoras' claims are all poetic conceits, for none of which we have any evidence in Pliny. Amelesagoras, it should be mentioned, is a problematic figure: D. Hal. *Thuc.* 5 dates him to the earliest writers (Hecataeus, Acusilaus, etc.), but his name (cited as Ἀμελησαγόρας and Μελησαγόρας), his date, and the genuineness of his work all are disputed. Pearson, *Local Historians of Attica* 89 considered it a 'genuine work written in the fifth or fourth century'. Jacoby (*Komm.* IIIb Suppl. (Text) 598–9) dated him to c. 300 BC and considered the work *Schwindelliteratur* (ibid. 600). Pritchett, *Dionysius of Halicarnassus: On Thucydides* 52–3 defends his genuineness and his early date against Jacoby.

3. DEDICATIONS AND THE DESIRES OF FRIENDS

Two authors of the early Empire present their decision to write history as determined or largely influenced by individuals. The first is Nicolaus who tells in his autobiography how he came to write history:

> [Herod] had an eager interest in rhetoric and he compelled Nicolaus to study with him, and so they practised together. Then a desire for history took Herod, and Nicolaus praised that genre, saying that it was most politic and useful, especially for a king, to investigate the deeds and actions of kings before him. And when Herod had set out upon this, he encouraged Nicolaus also to undertake history. And Nicolaus even more greatly gave himself to the task, [etc.][68]

We cannot be certain how much of this, if any, was presented in the history itself, nor indeed how any or all of this was woven together with the traditional themes of effort and labour which are visible in this quotation. Herod is clearly a pivotal figure, but we cannot be certain that the work was denoted as being exclusively or even partly for the king. Josephus, who knew Nicolaus' work well and had before him the preface entire, may furnish a useful parallel or contrast. In the *Jewish Antiquities* Josephus does not portray the encouragement of his friend Epaphroditus as the sole motivation for attempting a complete history of the Jews. Instead, Epaphroditus appears at a crucial moment in the historian's efforts. Josephus says that while writing his *Jewish War*, he had a desire to write up the entire history of the Jewish people, but he knew that it would be an enormous work. He therefore put it off a long time, until some who loved history directed him to attend to it, chief among them Epaphroditus, a man enamoured of every form of learning.[69] Then, by the combined persuasion of Epaphroditus and his own shame in shirking the effort, Josephus became eager and strengthened in his resolve.[70] Here it is significant that Epaphroditus is a crucial but not the sole motivator of Josephus' actions. It is singularly unfortunate that we do not have Nicolaus' preface as it actually was in the *Histories*, since it would have been

---

[68] *FGrHist* 90 F 135.
[69] *A. J.* 1.8–9: καὶ μάλιστα δὴ πάντων Ἐπαφρόδιτος ἀνὴρ ἅπασαν μὲν ἰδέαν παιδείας ἠγαπηκώς. On his identity see Rajak, *Josephus* 223–4 with n. 1. [70] *A. J.* 1.9.

Dedications

invaluable to know how he placed Herod (if he placed him at all) within the larger aims and claims of his work.[71]

In connection with this, we may here consider dedications and addresses to friends. This is a feature well known from many other genres, where the author presents his work as the fulfilment of a friend's request for information on a topic or theme.[72] Though comfortably ensconced in the other historical genres – biography, memoirs, epitomes – dedications do not seem to have been a common feature of large-scale or 'Great' historiography.[73] The earliest dedications of histories that we know are Hellenistic, and are made to kings: Manetho to Ptolemy II, and Berossus to Antiochus Soter.[74] It is unfortunate that we cannot tell how the dedications were managed, and what role the king in each played, whether he ordered the work, or was an important spur (as with Josephus), or was simply an interested party.

A different type of dedication may be seen in a Greek local history. Arrian, we learn from Photius' summary, dedicated his *Bithynian History* to his homeland, in thanks for the upbringing he had received there.[75] It should not surprise us that local history contains expressions

---

[71] As we know from Josephus, a man could present details about his work in his autobiography rather differently from those in the histories themselves; see Ch. IV n. 135.

[72] On dedications in general see Janson, *Latin Prose Prefaces* 116ff.; Herkommer, *Topoi* 22–34.

[73] The term is used by Jacoby, *Abhandlungen* 34ff. et al. to distinguish narrative political history from ethnography, chronicles, and local history.

[74] Manetho, *FGrHist* 609 T 11b, 11c; Berossus, *FGrHist* 680 T 2. Herkommer, *Topoi* 22ff. (with references) disregards Manetho and Berossus as irrelevant (25 n. 1) because they were non-Greeks. Certainly they were, but they wrote in a developed Greek genre and (like all practitioners) followed its conventions. It has been suggested that Berossus' dedication to Antiochus was an attempt to convince that king, by a description of the greatness of Babylonian culture, to reverse the policies of his father Seleucus I who had transferred the population of Babylon: so Burstein, *Babyloniaca of Berossus* 5, rejected by Kuhrt in ead. and S. Sherwin-White, edd., *Hellenism in the East* 47–8. Manetho's dedication of his work to Ptolemy II seems likewise to have had political, or at least religious and cultural, motivation: see Mendels, *PoH* 91–110. It can also be no accident that these works appeared within a few years of each other, and they may even have been weapons in the propaganda wars of Alexander's successors: see Murray, *CQ* 22 (1972) 200–13.

[75] Arrian, *FGrHist* 156 F 14: τῇ πατρίδι δῶρον ἀναφέρων τὰ πάτρια. Dionysius (*A. R.* 1.6.5) comes as close as possible to an outright dedication when he says that he wishes his work to be seen as a gift to the city of Rome, the land in which he was educated and from which he has received such blessings.

of thanks from adopted or native sons. 'Great' historiography, by contrast, will have avoided expressions of thanks and obligation such as these because they would have interfered with the persona of impartiality, which shows itself to be an ever-present concern among ancient historians.[76] The suggestion that one might write at another's behest, or even with an eye towards another's enjoyment, could easily have led the audience to suspect some form of obligation on the part of the author.[77] The historian, however, had to seem his own man. In local history, by contrast, with its emphasis on cult and antiquities, and its fundamentally favourable disposition towards the city in question,[78] there was less need to present an impartial persona.

An apparent objection to this interpretation might be the large number of Roman writers who seem to have dedicated historical works. We could, of course, solve the problem by calling attention to the bias that is so prominent a feature of Roman historiography, or perhaps consider it as a form of local historiography and thereby avoid further explanation. Yet the major historians of Rome – Sallust, Livy, Tacitus, and Ammianus – do not dedicate their works, and nearly all the Roman historical works dedicated to someone can be understood not to contradict the interpretation given here.

Dedications are common, first of all, in autobiographies and memoirs: C. Gracchus, Aemilius Scaurus, Q. Catulus, Sulla, Cicero on his consulship, and Augustus in his autobiography all dedicated their works.[79] These have in common not form but content: they are all political 'justifications' or, perhaps better, 'displays'. The use of an addressee serves the important function of providing the writer with a motivation to compose his life's story, and is a strategy to present his deeds without apology. The addressee mitigates the envy attendant upon self-disclosure (and self-praise), and provides the author's 'justification' for dwelling at

---

[76] Herkommer, *Topoi* 25, following J. Ruppert, *Quaestiones ad historiam dedicationis librorum pertinentes* (diss. Leipzig 1911), thinks that historiography avoided dedications because they are a feature of parainetic writing, which history was not. This can hardly be correct (although Herkommer qualifies this by saying that history 'in erster Linie' did not have the parainetic function), given the importance of instruction in history. Herkommer's comparison with epic is appropriate, but I would see this more in terms of the impartiality of Homer that historians sought to emulate (below, pp. 158f.). [77] See Ch. III §4.
[78] Jacoby, *Atthis* 55, 141; *Der Kleine Pauly* s. v. 'Lokalchronik'.
[79] Cic. *Div.* II.62; *Brut.* 112; 132; Plut. *Lucull.* 1.4; Cic. *Att.* II.1; Plut. *Comp. Dem. et Cic.* 3.1

length upon his own actions.⁸⁰ Sometimes, as with Catulus, Sulla, or Cicero, the author requests that the work be bettered in style, but once again this is a strategy of *diminutio* that suggests – given the frequent dichotomy between accuracy and a simple style on the one hand, and adornment and falsification on the other – a humble devotion to truth.⁸¹

Scholarly or antiquarian works might have dedications: Atticus dedicated his *Liber Annalis* (to Cicero) and Varro his *Antiquitates* (to Caesar), following in the tradition of dedicating learned works, perhaps begun with Apollodorus' *Chronicle* dedicated to Attalus II.⁸² Since writers of chronicles, like epitomators, do not need to take the sort of stands that narrative historians must, a dedication in such works as these will not suggest a concomitant loss of objectivity.

That leaves us with the Romans Coelius Antipater, Claudius Quadrigarius, and Velleius Paterculus, all writers who clearly composed narrative history, and who dedicated their works.⁸³ Coelius, who seems to have introduced the dedication into Roman historiography,⁸⁴ is a far from typical author. His work on the Hannibalic War, which inaugurated the historical monograph in Latin, was noted for its poetic colourings and great concern with literary polish.⁸⁵ Moreover, since it was dedicated to L. Aelius Stilo, the first Roman grammarian,⁸⁶ it seems likely that

---

⁸⁰ See Herkommer, *Topoi* 27-30; Most, *JHS* 109 (1989) 120-7 is illuminating on this in fiction and in Greek culture in general. On the dangers of self-praise see Ch. IV §1.

⁸¹ On style see Peter, *HRR* I.CCLXX-LXXI; Avenarius, *LS* 100-2; Bömer, *Hermes* 81 (1953) 236ff. (who points out the contradiction in Cicero's request on the one hand for betterment, and, on the other, his claim to have used all of Isocrates' cosmetics in the adornment of his account: Cic. *Att.* II.1.1, and below, pp. 181f.); Herkommer, *Topoi* 29-30; cf. Introduction n. 42.

⁸² Cic. *Brut.* 13; Lact. *Inst.* 1.6.7; *FGrHist* 244 T 2. Herkommer, *Topoi* 25 n. 1 disregards Apollodorus because his *Chronicle*, written in verse, belongs in the tradition of didactic poetry. Yet Apollodorus' importance as a model may well have suggested a similar type of dedication for Apollodorus' followers, whether in prose or verse.

⁸³ Coelius, *HRR* F 1; Quadrigarius, *HRR* F 79; Velleius' work is assumed to be dedicated to M. Vinicius who is frequently apostrophised: see Woodman, *CQ* 25 (1975) 273-82; That Velleius' history is not an epitome, see Introd. n. 141.

⁸⁴ Cato, we are told, wrote a history for his son 'in large letters' (Plut. *C. M.* 20.7) but this is not considered to be the *Origines* (Astin, *Cato the Censor* 182-3) which (so far as we know) was not dedicated to anyone.

⁸⁵ The work seems to have mixed serious research with rhetorical effect: Badian, in *Latin Historians* 15-17 brings out both aspects well.

⁸⁶ On Aelius Stilo see Suet. *gramm.* 3.1-2 with Kaster's commentary, 68-70.

Coelius' literary pretensions were the determining factor. Again, it must be remembered that he was writing a monograph on a war fought two or perhaps even three generations earlier,[87] and a dedication in such an 'antiquarian' history would not have called the author's reliability into question.[88] Quadrigarius' *Annales*, on the other hand, did reach to his own times but our knowledge of his dedication is based on a single fragment without any indication who the dedicatee was, and in such a situation, there is little we can say of its purpose or function.[89] It should be noted that his use of a dedication does not seem to have been imitated by other annalists. It is safe to say, however, that neither man dedicated his history to a person in power, and this is the most important point.

As for Velleius, his work has a strongly panegyrical element to it, like Dionysius' history: it is, in some sense, a praise of Tiberius addressed to a like-minded friend.[90] Though only speculation, it is possible that Velleius, recognising the large element of panegyric in his work and knowing that praise, although a part of history, still needed to be moderate, felt that he could lessen the difficulty brought on by the praise of his commander and his campaigns by presenting the work to a friend. The history could then, by notices of the writer's and dedicatee's family members at appropriate points, be portrayed as a private possession for the two of them.[91]

Dedications can serve different purposes and the mere fact that a work was dedicated will tell us very little about the use the historian made of such dedications. On the whole, both Greek and Roman historians did not present their decision to write history as the result of an individual's

---

[87] On Coelius' dates, see Peter, *HRR* I.CCXI–CCXII.
[88] As Luce, *CPh* 84 (1989) 17 points out, it was contemporary history that was dangerous in terms of partiality. Herkommer, *Topoi* 26 sees the dedication as made 'nach dem Vorbild der didaktischen Werke', but there does not seem to have been anything particularly didactic about Coelius' work.
[89] Quadrigarius, *HRR* F 79; Timpe, *A&A* 25 (1979) 110 believes that Quadrigarius here addresses his patron.
[90] This is not to say that that is all it is. For Velleius' awareness of his partiality see below, pp. 169, 173.
[91] There was real honour for the dedicatee in being named in a history: see Herkommer, *Topoi* 31 who quotes (n. 6) Sidon. Apoll. *epp.* IV.3.2; cf. Woodman, *CQ* 25 (1975) 274-5. Nor is the interpretation above at odds with the thesis that Velleius' work was a mini-history meant for the public and not Vinicius alone (Starr, *CQ* 31 (1981) 170-1 points out that the references to Vinicius could have been inserted after the history was written). I am here only suggesting a strategy of presentation.

request (however that *topos* was understood in antiquity). What seems fairly certain is that, even at Rome, dedications were avoided in large-scale non-antiquarian historical works, because they hindered the persona of the unbiased historian writing not for the present but for posterity, and writing for the benefit of all readers, not at one man's request.

4. GLORY AND RENOWN

When Horace says that he has 'carved out a monument more lasting than bronze' or that he will not 'wholly perish', we are accustomed to seeing this as a poetic *topos* that can be traced back almost to the beginnings of ancient literature.[92] Aper in Tacitus' *Dialogue on Oratory* says that poets are enslaved to fame, whereas Quintilian (with greater honesty, perhaps) thought that a desire for fame was the stimulus to all literary endeavour.[93] Even for philosophers, says Tacitus, a desire for fame is the last thing to depart.[94] For Pliny the Elder, however, writing in the Preface of his *Natural History*, it was quite surprising that an historian should see his work in terms of his own glory:

> And indeed I am amazed that Livy, that most renowned author, should have said in the preface of one of his books in *From the Founding of the City* that he had won glory enough for himself, and that he could have ceased writing, if his restless spirit did not feed on work. In my opinion, it would have been more proper to have persevered from love of the task, not because of his spirit, and to have brought this to accomplishment for the Roman people, not for himself.[95]

Perhaps the professions of *mediocritas* so common in imperial writers[96] made Pliny downplay the element of individual pride that attached to his work. Yet Livy's remark, while unique, has several parallels with other Greek and Roman historians of the late Republic and early Empire, even if it is the most explicit example of the historian reflecting on his own achievement and renown.

---

[92] Hor. *Carm*. III.30.1–6, cf. II.20, with Nisbet and Hubbard's commentary, 332–7 for the earlier parallels.
[93] Tac. *Dial*. 10.1: 'ne opinio quidem et fama, cui soli seruiunt, et quod unum esse pretium omnis laboris sui fatentur, e. q. s.'; cf. Quint. XII.1.8; [Long.] *Subl*. 1.3.
[94] Tac. *Hist*. IV.6.1: 'quando etiam sapientibus cupido gloriae nouissima exuitur.'
[95] Pliny, *n. h. praef*. 16 (=Livy, F 58).
[96] On this *topos* see Janson, *Latin Prose Prefaces* 125.

It is not difficult to imagine that history, with its concern for bestowing fame, should have suggested the analogy between the work and its writer. That the historian as a narrator of deeds is himself involved in their glory is given its clearest expression in Plutarch:

> [Although Xenophon was his own historian,] the rest of the historians wrote of others, like actors in a drama, putting together the deeds of generals and kings and submerging themselves with their characters, so that they might share in their glimmer and light. For the image of another's renown is reflected and shines out from the doers to the writers, when a deed becomes visible through words, as if in a mirror.[97]

It is interesting, nevertheless, how late it takes for this claim to appear openly in histories. We need not doubt that historians from the outset genuinely felt proud of their achievements: Thucydides claimed his work as a possession for all time, even if he was careful to play down the evident pride he felt in his own work.[98] So it is not so much a question of the pride one feels in one's work as it is an issue of whether one should express this feeling (as the poets do), and if so, how much one should say. The earliest claim of renown comes from the preface of Theopompus' *Philippica*. Photius tells us that Theopompus claimed first place among the Hellenes in literary ability, and that there was not a single city or area that he visited where he did not demonstrate this or fail to leave behind great renown (μέγα κλέος) and the memory of his oratorical excellence (ὑπόμνημα τῆς ἐν λόγοις αὐτοῦ κατέλιπεν ἀρετῆς).[99] Yet this is not quite what Plutarch refers to, since Theopompus magnifies his own achievements independently of the *Philippica* and indeed as part of the justification for undertaking that work.[100] His fame is the result of his total achievement in letters. No doubt his earlier history, the *Hellenica*, will have been one of the works that contributed to his renown, but there is no evidence in this fragment that Theopompus gave it a preferential place in his literary output.

---

[97] Plut. *de glor. Ath.* 345E-F. For discussion see F. Frazier's Budé edition of the *Moralia*, Tome V, 1re partie (Paris 1990) 169-71. She sees it as largely critical of historians, because of the comparison to actors, and the phrase 'image of another's renown' (δόξης εἴδωλον ἀλλοτρίας). I find this unconvincing, as is her attempt to link the passage with tragic history.

[98] Thuc. I.22.4, where his work is described in the passive voice – κτῆμα τε ἐς ἀεὶ μᾶλλον ἢ ἀγώνισμα ἐς τὸ παραχρῆμα ἀκούειν ξυγκεῖται – as if it had written itself.   [99] *FGrHist* 115 F 25.   [100] See below, pp. 134ff.

A strong consciousness of and confidence in the historian's fame is detectable in the story of Callisthenes and Alexander told by Arrian:

> I think unseemly the remark of Callisthenes (if the report is true) that Alexander and Alexander's deeds depended on him and his history; and that Callisthenes himself had not come to win fame from Alexander, but that he would make Alexander renowned among men; and that Alexander's share in divinity did not rest on what Olympias had fabricated about his birth, but from the things he himself wrote for Alexander and published among men.[101]

The ability of Callisthenes to immortalise Alexander indicates a strong self-consciousness in the historian, but Arrian's qualification, 'if the report is true', shows that Callisthenes did not say this in his history.

By the time of Polybius, the assumption that an historian desires glory and renown is taken for granted. Zeno and Antisthenes, Polybius says, were serious students of history who took up the subject 'not for gain, but for renown and for the benefit of political men'. So too Agatharchides at the end of his *On the Red Sea* says that those who complete what he has left undone will not hesitate 'to seek fame through toil'.[102] Diodorus has a long and interesting discussion of the historian's fame running throughout his preface. He begins by saying that historians by their labours benefit human society (1.1.1), since history itself incites leaders to perform well because of the immortal renown that it confers (1.5). Indeed, he continues, it is an excellent thing to receive eternal fame in exchange for mortal toils, just as Heracles had done when he undertook toils and dangers in order to benefit the human race, and as previous historians have received a just renown for their efforts.[103] Like Polybius and Agatharchides, there is an assumed relationship between the historian and glory, and yet like them, Diodorus does not address the issue of his own glory explicitly.[104]

---

[101] Arr. *Anab.* IV.10.1-2 = *FGrHist* 124 T 8; as Bosworth, *HCA* II.75 points out, the claims are not all that different from what Arrian himself says in his second preface. See Gray, *JHS* 110 (1990) 183-4 for the historian's submergence of his own renown into that of his subjects.

[102] Pol. XVI.14.3; Agatharchides, *Mar. Rub.* §110 = *GGM* I.194.

[103] Diod. 1.2.4-3.1; for more on toil see Ch. III §3.

[104] The closest Diodorus comes to this is the note in Book XL that his work was circulated before he himself had put the final touches on it (XL. 8), suggesting the renown that his work had achieved.

Dionysius, like Diodorus, avoids any overt claim to fame and says that although he is constrained to say something about himself, he will not dwell on his own praise.[105] Josephus, interestingly enough, twice states that historians enter their task with a desire for glory. In his *Against Apion* he assails those Greek writers who enter upon history simply to gain a reputation, trying to surpass the fame of others by literary skill or attacks on predecessors. And in the preface to the *Jewish Antiquities* he gives four reasons why historians write history, one being the desire 'to display their literary ability and to gain renown from it'.[106] Josephus is careful, however, to distance himself from such a motive.[107] And so we see again the recognition of the desire for glory on the part of historians, and the simultaneous denial that it has played a role in the present historian's call to history.

Our earliest reference among Latin historians that speaks of the historian and his glory is found in Sallust's *Catiline*. The tone is somewhat defensive: 'Even though an equal glory in no way follows the writer and the performer of deeds, nevertheless I think it difficult to write history' (*Cat.* 3.1–2). Now Sallust in his prefaces was concerned to widen the traditional field of *uirtus*, which before him had been limited to public service.[108] He himself had made reference to this when he remarked that in early Rome there was never an abundance of historians, because each man preferred to be himself the doer of deeds rather than the one who records them.[109] Sallust does not associate his task too closely with *gloria*, confining it to a subordinate clause, and then going on to the difficulties of history-writing itself.[110] The same tentativeness that Sallust displayed

---

[105] D. Hal. *A.R.* 1.1.1. For compulsion as a justification for self-praise see below, p. 211. [106] Jos. *c. Ap.* 1.24–5; *A. J.* 1.2.
[107] See Jos. *A. J.* 1.4, where he claims only the desire for truth and the refutation of false works that had already appeared.
[108] See above, p. 44; cf. *Cat.* 2.9, with Earl, *Political Thought* 7ff., who notes that part of Sallust's effort in the prefaces is directed towards extending the *fama* traditionally associated with deeds to the writing of history (35–40). See also Vretska's commentary, 1.82.
[109] *Cat.* 8.5, recalling Plato, *Rep.* x.599a–b where in a discussion of the difference between the real thing and the imitator, Plato assumes that anyone would choose the former over the latter: 'he would rather be praised than compose the praises of others' (b5–7).
[110] We do not know whether Sallust made any reference to glory in the *Histories*, nor whether his remark about being in such an abundance of learned men (*Hist.* 1.3, on which see below, Ch. V n. 152) was the occasion (like Livy's remark below, which was modelled on it) to reflect on the place that he himself hoped to win.

is seen in Livy's opening preface, where, like Sallust, he confines a remark about his *fama* to a subordinate clause. In contrast to the later preface with which we opened this section, Livy at the outset of his work magnanimously suggests that 'if, in so great a crowd of writers, my fame shall be obscured, I would console myself with the nobility and the greatness of those who will overshadow my name' (*praef.* 3). For Pompeius Trogus, who wrote a universal history in the late Republic, we have only the words of Justin, that Trogus set out upon his *Philippic Histories*, 'either in a effort to win glory or because of the variety and uniqueness of the work'.[111] The 'either . . . or' suggests that Trogus did not say that he was striving for glory, and this is as we have come to expect.

From our survey here, it appears that Pliny was justified in his amazement at Livy's remark about the renown that he had won. We have not seen any other historian so openly comment on his own fame. Nevertheless, we must concede in Livy's case that the remark, while explicit, is of a piece with his remarks in the opening preface, where, as we saw above, the motivation for writing history was presented in part as the personal desire to look away from the miseries of the present age. In this sense, Livy was simply continuing to portray his history in personal terms.

Our conclusion in this section overall is thus twofold. That the ancient historian was concerned with his own fame and wrote history to achieve renown is not to be doubted: it is evident in many writers and it is even retrojected onto the earliest historians as a motivation for their writing.[112] On the other hand, no tradition of claiming glory or renown within the history itself (much less putting it forward as a reason to write history) seems to have developed as it had in poetry, where expressions of the consciousness of one's fame may have been sanctioned by the example of the early lyric poets and the conceit (however much it changed over the years) of the influence of the Muse (an 'external' influence to whom the responsibility could be attributed), and in the belief that the poet is a man set apart by the gods for wisdom or talent.[113] By

---

[111] Justin, *praef.* 1: 'seu aemulatione gloriae siue uarietate et nouitate operis delectatus'.

[112] Quint. x.1.31 notes that history is written, among other things, 'ad . . . ingenii famam'; see also Lucian, *Hdt.* 1, where Herodotus decided to read his history at Olympia because he sought the least troublesome path to fame and reputation.

[113] As in, e.g., Plato's *Ion*; see G. Ferrari in *Cambridge History of Literary Criticism. I. Classical Criticism*, ed. G. Kennedy (Cambridge 1989) 92-9; P. Murray, *Plato on Poetry* (Cambridge 1996) 6-12.

contrast, the historian relies not upon inspiration but rather upon effort and inquiry. Moreover, and just as importantly, one writes history, as Pliny the Elder pointed out, because of the greatness of the subject, and we have seen this in a sufficient number of cases above. Yet for all that, many longed to win glory by the writing of history, and perhaps it is the younger Pliny who more accurately portrays the feelings of actual and potential historians:

> You encourage me to write history, and you are not alone in so doing. Many things suggest to me that I want to do it; not that I think it would be easy ... but because it seems to me a fine thing not to allow to die that which is owed to immortality, and to ensure the renown of others as well as one's own (*aliorumque famam cum sua extendere*). Nothing moves me so much as that love and longing for immortality, a thing most worthy of a man.[114]

In conclusion, then, we see that for the most part the ancient historians present their decision to write history using a 'public' face: they most often emphasise the greatness of the deeds and the seriousness of their subject. Although they may say something of the personal circumstances which led to their history's creation, they nevertheless present this 'private' decision as one with benefit to individuals and the state. This largely public persona militated against the historian portraying his work as privately or personally motivated, or as meant to secure his own fame and glory, rather than that of his subject.

---

[114] Pliny, *ep*. v. 8.1-2.

II

The historian's inquiry

At the court of the Phaeacians, Demodocus sings of the quarrel between Odysseus and Achilles and delights his listeners, all except the still-unrevealed Odysseus who covers his head and weeps. During the feast that follows, Odysseus, despite his grief, sends the singer a rich portion of meat and salutes him, praising how well he sang 'all that the Achaeans did and suffered and toiled, as if you were present yourself, or heard it from one who was'.[1] In this simile, Odysseus anticipates the twin methods of validation for contemporary historians: eyewitness (autopsy) and inquiry of the participants in events. In ancient historiography, professions of autopsy and inquiry are found from Herodotus to Ammianus, and they serve as one of the most prominent means of claiming the authority to narrate contemporary and non-contemporary history. In this chapter, we shall survey some of the issues revolving around inquiry for ancient historians, treating the theoretical observations of the historians on the difficulties and problems raised by inquiry, as well as the explicit claims made by historians in the course of their narratives.

1. EYES, EARS AND CONTEMPORARY HISTORY

In Greek historiography, reliance on autopsy and inquiry is first found in developed form in Herodotus but, not surprisingly in view of the Greek capacity for examination, a long tradition of reliance on, and questioning of, the validity of this type of knowledge lies behind the first historian. In Homer, as we have already mentioned, the authority to narrate the story comes from the inspiration of the Muses.[2] Odysseus, in the passage above, equates Demodocus' song inspired by Apollo or the

---

[1] Homer, *Od.* VIII.487–91: ὥς τέ που ἢ αὐτὸς παρεὼν ἢ ἄλλου ἀκούσας.
[2] See above, pp. 3f.

Muses with eyewitness and experience. So too, the poet of the *Iliad* invokes the Muses before enumerating the Greek forces, calling on them as goddesses 'who are present and know all things', and as such are superior to mortals who 'have heard only the rumour of it, and know nothing'.[3] For the poet of the *Iliad*, no natural facility would be sufficient if the influence of the Muses were lacking. The emphasis here is on the gulf between the goddesses' knowledge and mortals' ignorance, between 'knowing' and only 'learning' the report, the latter of which is not knowledge.[4] And the poet suggests that only the Muses can supply that knowledge to the poet.[5]

In the *Odyssey*, where discovery and report play a greater role, one finds more interest in the human sources and reliability of knowledge. When Telemachus visits Nestor, he asks the old man whether he has seen or heard anything of Odysseus, 'whether you saw it perhaps with your own eyes, or heard the tale from another who wandered too'; in the course of his reply Nestor confesses ignorance about the fates of the Achaeans and offers to tell Telemachus 'all that I have learnt by inquiry sitting here in my palace'.[6] This is not to say, of course that the report of another would have equal validity with Nestor's own autopsy: indeed, it is the absence of autopsy that ensures ignorance, just as knowledge is predicated upon seeing for oneself: Eumaeus, when reporting on the ship of the suitors putting in at Ithaca, says, 'There is another thing I know; for I have seen it with my own eyes'.[7] The epistemological hierarchy of the *Odyssey* is that autopsy is the best and most reliable source of knowledge, and the report of an eyewitness is next. After that, it seems, no certainty is possible, especially in the *Odyssey* where travellers are wont to tell inaccurate stories, and the hero himself weaves deception.[8]

With the sixth-century intellectual revolution in Ionia, we begin to see a questioning of the value of sense perception. Here, of course, the evidence is fragmentary and, in the case of the pre-Socratics, subject to the most varied interpretations, yet the outlines seem clear. To simplify,

---

[3] Homer, *Il.* II.484–93; see Introduction nn. 7–8.
[4] Lanata, *Poetica Pre-Platonica* 5–6.   [5] Cf. Hesiod at Introduction n. 14.
[6] *Od.* II.92–5; III.186–7: ὅσσα δ' ἐνὶ μεγάροισι ... πεύθομαι. Gould, *Herodotus* 21 thinks that Telemachus' stay with Menelaus is one model for Herodotus' inquiry.
[7] *Od.* XVI.470: ἄλλο δέ τοι τό γε οἶδα· τὸ γὰρ ἴδον ὀφθαλμοῖσιν.
[8] For autoptic remarks in Homer and the early poets see Nenci, *SCO* 3 (1955) 17–21.

there are two approaches to the problem of sense-perception and knowledge in the pre-Socratic philosophers. In the first, autopsy and oral report, as sensory experiences, are part of the process that leads to knowledge, and the former is always superior. When Thales was asked how far a lie was from the truth, he is said to have remarked, 'as much as eyes from ears'.[9] Together with this, however, there exists among some philosophers a profound distrust of sense-perception and a devaluation of the type of knowledge to be derived from mere inquiry.

In Heraclitus we find both a reliance on sense perception and the belief that this is not sufficient as a means to wisdom. We have indications that might lead us to think that he saw autopsy and oral report as useful and desirable things: one fragment reads, 'of as many things as there are autopsy, report and knowledge, these things I prefer'; Polybius remarks that Heraclitus said eyes to be more trustworthy than ears; and he is also said to have remarked that lovers of wisdom must be inquirers of many things (πολλῶν ἵστορας).[10] But such inquiry by itself is not sufficient, since, 'much learning does not teach one to have intelligence; for it would have taught Hesiod and Pythagoras, and again, Xenophanes and Hecataeus.'[11] Similarly, Heraclitus criticises Pythagoras for following a path of inquiry: 'Pythagoras, son of Mnesarchus, practised research most of all men, and making extracts from these treatises he compiled a wisdom of his own, an accumulation of learning, a harmful craft'.[12] Much learning (πολυμαθίη) is not wisdom (νόον ἔχειν), because sense perception is not consistently unproblematic: 'Bad witnesses for men are the eyes and ears of those whose souls are barbarian'.[13] In the wrong hands and without a guiding principle, sense-perception will simply miss the mark.

In the middle of the fifth century Anaxagoras continued to question

---

[9] Thales ap. Stobaeus, *Florileg.* III.12.14 (not in DK): Θάλης ὁ Μιλήσιος ἐρωτηθεὶς πόσον ἀπέχει τὸ ψεῦδος τοῦ ἀληθούς, "ὅσον" ἔφη "ὀφθαλμοὶ τῶν ὤτων".

[10] Heraclitus, DK 22 B 55; B 101a = Pol. XII.27.1; B 35.

[11] DK 22 B 40 = *FGrHist* 1 T 21. [12] DK 22 B 129.

[13] DK 22 B 107; there are different opinions about what Heraclitus might mean by ψυχαὶ βάρβαροι: see G. S. Kirk, J. E. Raven and M. Schofield, *The Presocratic Philosophers* (Cambridge ²1983) 188 n. 2, who suggest that 'barbarian souls' are misled by appearances; J. Barnes, *The Presocratic Philosophers. I. Thales to Zeno* (London and Boston 1979) 147-9 suggests that only the practised eye can discern truth; see also C. Kahn, *The Art and Thought of Heraclitus* (Cambridge 1979) 106-7. For a similar correlation of sense-perception and νοῦς, see Epicharmus, DK 23 B 12.

the value of sense-perception, even while conceding that it must at times serve as the source of knowledge. He states that the weakness of our senses prevents them from being able to judge the truth, although he also says that the things that are visible (τὰ φαινόμενα) must be the vision (ὄψις) for what is obscure.[14] Democritus continues this somewhat inconsistent viewpoint, returning to the notion that the senses are limited, suggesting in one fragment that they are not part of genuine knowledge, while in another fragment he has the senses say to the mind that it derives its proofs from them.[15] However we construe these many points of view, we can at least point to a vigorous and productive debate among the philosophers on the value, limitations, and weaknesses of sense perception.

Compared with the philosophers, the historians cannot but seem somewhat naïve in their faith in the directness and reliability of sense-perception. For them, the steadfast claim of reliance on their eyes and ears remained from start to finish the chosen 'methodology' for historical inquiry. To be sure, this is not in any way inappropriate, given their task; but what we lack is any sense of the occasionally problematic nature of sense-perception or its inadequacies as a methodology for the writing of history.[16] Modern studies have noted the intense difficulty of reconstructing battles from the reports even of many eyewitnesses,[17] but the ancients, with few exceptions, seem rarely to have imagined such problems, the more surprising in that many of them were themselves participants in a way that modern historians rarely are.

Not much can be said about the methodology of the earliest historians. We would dearly like to know how Hecataeus, who is called a

---

[14] Anaxagoras, DK 59 B 21; B 21a; Lloyd, *Polarity and Analogy* 338-41.

[15] Democritus, DK 68 B 11; B 125. In B 299 he speaks of investigations in the spirit of an historian: 'Of all men of my time I have wandered most extensively, inquiring most widely (ἱστορέων τὰ μήκιστα), and I have seen the most climates and lands, and have heard the greatest number of learned men; and no one has ever bettered me in writing treatises with proofs, not even the so-called Arpedonaptae of Egypt, with whom I passed eighty years on foreign soil.' There is some doubt whether this fragment is genuine.

[16] The claim was so simple (and ultimately so undemonstrable) that it easily led to parody: see Luc. *v. h.* 1.4: γράφω τοίνυν περὶ ὧν μήτε εἶδον μήτε ἔπαθον μήτε παρ' ἄλλων ἐπυθόμην. Cf. *h. c.* 29, the historian who never set foot outside Corinth claimed: γράφω τοίνυν ἃ εἶδον, οὐχ ἃ ἤκουσα. Cf. n. 98 below.

[17] J. Keegan, *The Face of Battle* (London and New York 1976) ch. 1; Woodman, *RICH* 15-23.

'far-wandering man',[18] introduced his *Circuit of the Earth*, since the importance of investigative travels in that work would have been paramount.[19] Perhaps methods of inquiry and its verification existed even before Hecataeus in the form of travellers' reports such as the one undertaken by Scylax of Caryanda.[20] What was perhaps implicit in Hecataeus and early writers becomes manifest in Herodotus. For this historian, eyewitness or autopsy (ὄψις) is the most certain way to knowledge; where this is unavailable, one has recourse to oral report, preferably of eyewitnesses. Confirmation of such reports may be established by one's own autopsy (in the case of a monument, for example); if inquiry is not possible, one may use conjecture and subject the account to the test of probability. Where certainty is impossible, and where sources disagree, one can attempt to disentangle the conflicting strands, but very often one can do no more than state what each side says.[21]

Thucydides' decision to write contemporary history opened new possibilities for the historian. Thucydides makes clear, as Herodotus only at times suggests, that he is basing his war narrative on his own eyewitness and the reports of others who were also eyewitnesses.[22] In Herodotus, the superiority of autopsy over hearsay is clear and consistent: indeed, the opening story of Candaules and Gyges explicitly asserts that 'ears are less trustworthy than eyes'.[23] For Thucydides, the line between autopsy and certain knowledge is not quite so directly drawn. Concerned as he is with underlying realities that are not always apparent or easily perceived,[24] he does not suggest that autopsy is superior to inquiry, and in at least one place casts doubt on autopsy's

---

[18] *FGrHist* 1 T 12a: ἀνὴρ πολυπλανής.

[19] For some thoughts on Hecataeus' methods of inquiry, see Schepens, *Autopsie* 84-90, with reff. there. As he points out (85 n. 178), a similar method of validation would not have been appropriate for the *Genealogies*; but travel and inquiry, especially of local sources, may also have played some part: cf. Jacoby at Appendix IV n. 15.   [20] *FGrHist* 709 T 3 = Hdt. IV.44.

[21] On Herodotus' methodology see Verdin, *De historisch-kritische Methods*, *passim*; Schepens, op. cit. (n.19) ch. II; Müller in *Gnomosyne: Festschrift... Marg* 299-318; Lateiner, *Antichthon* 20 (1986) 1-20; id., *Historical Method of Herodotus, passim*.

[22] Thuc. I.22.2-3; note οἷς [sc. ἔργοις]... αὐτὸς παρῆν and οἱ παρόντες τοῖς ἔργοις ἑκάστοις.

[23] Hdt. 1.8.2, used by the Anonymous historian of L. Verus' wars: see Luc. *h. c.* 29; cf. n. 16; cf. Heraclitus, above n. 10.

[24] As in his belief in the causes of the war: τὴν δ' ἀληθεστάτην πρόφασιν, ἀφανεστάτην δὲ λόγῳ (1.23.6).

validity for non-contemporary history. In the Archaeology (1.2-19) he states that it would be misleading for future generations to judge the power of Athens and Sparta by an examination of their monuments, since the paucity of Spartan, and the abundance of Athenian buildings and adornments would in each case lead to the wrong estimate about the actual power of those states.[25] This is the reason why in his methodological statement in Book I, no advantage is given to autopsy over inquiry, since both alike must be subject to a process of verification (1.22.2):

> Of the things done in the war, the deeds I deemed it worthy to write not by learning them from a chance source, nor how it seemed to me, but by going through with accuracy as much as possible concerning each thing, both for those at which I myself was present, and for those I received from others.

From both grammar and sense it is clear that Thucydides will subject both his own autopsy and his inquiry of others to a process of accuracy (ἀκρίβεια), which must here mean 'in conformance with external reality'.[26] His own autopsy, reliable as it might be, was yet insufficient, or it could be misleading, given what was occurring elsewhere, perhaps without his knowledge.

His contemporary Euripides recognised the problem as well; in the *Suppliant Women* Theseus casts doubt on all reports of participants in battle:

> One thing I shall not ask, lest you laugh: who stood beside each of these in battle, or from which one of the enemy each received a spear-wound. For these accounts are useless (κενοὶ λόγοι), both for the listeners and the speaker, whoever, standing in battle as the lance comes close to his eyes, reported clearly (σαφῶς ἀπήγγειλ') who was brave. I could neither ask these things nor trust those who dare speak them. For when standing opposite the enemy, one can scarcely see what one has to see (τἀναγκαῖ' ὁρᾶν).[27]

---

[25] Thuc. 1.10.1-3, esp. the conclusion of §3: οὔκουν ἀπιστεῖν εἰκός, οὐδὲ τὰς ὄψεις τῶν πόλεων μᾶλλον σκοπεῖν ἢ τὰς δυνάμεις.

[26] See the exhaustive analysis of Schepens, op. cit. (n.19) 113-46 (with nearly all major opinions cited), which I follow here; *contra*, Woodman, *RICH* 52 n. 53. For ἀκρίβεια here as 'external reality', see Schepens, op. cit. (n.19) 135-43; so too Hornblower, *CT* 1.60.

[27] Eur. *Suppl.* 846-56; for additional passages from tragedy and comedy bearing on autopsy see Nenci, op. cit. (n.8) 25-9.

In a similar way Thucydides indicates in his prefatory words to the narrative of the night battle at Epipolae the difficulty of reconstructing not only a night battle, but even one occurring under normal conditions (VII.44.1):

> And here the Athenians were at a loss and in great confusion; it was not easy to learn even from others in which way each matter turned out. For in the daytime things are clearer (σαφέστερα), yet even in these matters, those present scarcely know anything except what each knows is going on around himself. In a night battle – the only substantial one in this war – how could one know anything at all clearly (πῶς ἄν τις σαφῶς τι ᾔδει)?

And yet the description of the battle at Epipolae, where the supposed difficulty of ascertaining what happened ought to have left some sign in the narrative, has the familiar Thucydidean certainty.[28] The point here needs to be emphasised, since it is sometimes held that Thucydides' reliance on autopsy marks a use superior to that found in Herodotus.[29] Thucydides, however, devalues even the value of autopsy by saying that eyewitnesses of the same events do not always tell the same story (1.22.3). Memory and prejudice (in addition to other difficulties) affect one's account, such that even autopsy may not be reliable on occasion, and the historian needs, therefore, to set right contradictory accounts (of which there may have been many, if Herodotus' history is any guide) with ἀκρίβεια. How he did this he does not say. In Thucydides, autopsy and inquiry are guaranteed in a general way in the first section of the work, and a methodology is elaborated which will be valid for the rest of the work. The substructure of inquiry, so prominent in Herodotus, has been taken from view.[30]

Xenophon, as so often, leaves his methodology to be inferred from the text, and we have some reason to think that he accepted without difficulty the belief that eyewitnesses were the most reliable.[31] Ephorus, as the first to write a universal history, was concerned to elaborate a methodology that would explain his different attitude to the various time periods embraced by his work. While we have no claims of

---

[28] Dover, *Thucydides* 28ff. [29] See, e.g., Schepens, op. cit. (n.19) 187–195, 197–8. [30] See above, pp. 8f.

[31] See Xen. *Hell.* IV.3.2 (Agesilaus to Dercylidas): 'since you were present, would you not be the best at reporting this?'

personal autopsy or inquiry in the fragments that survive, we do have two methodological statements, probably from the preface of the entire work, where he also discussed history as a genre:

> Ephorus says that when writing about our own times (καθ' ἡμᾶς), we consider those speaking most accurately (ἀκριβέστατα) to be the most reliable; but concerning things long ago (τῶν παλαιῶν), those who proceed in such a way we consider most untrustworthy, since we assume that it is not probable, given the great distance in time, that all of the deeds or a majority of the speeches would be remembered.[32]

Ephorus here distinguishes between contemporary and non-contemporary history by their level of detail, the former being more trustworthy the greater the detail, whereas for the latter the opposite is the case.[33] His distrust of older accounts that contained very full details suggests a critical approach to written sources that distrusted rhetorical adornment and elaboration. We cannot, of course, be sure exactly what Ephorus meant by ἀκριβέστατα, but when read in conjunction with another fragment it does seem to suggest that accuracy was dependent upon autopsy: 'Ephorus says that if it were possible for those who write histories to be present at all the deeds, this would be a much preferable form of knowledge.' This passage is cited by Polybius in his attack on Timaeus, so we cannot be certain that the words are Ephorus' own.[34] But it does at least show that Ephorus continued the tradition of

---

[32] FGrHist 70 F 9; Lieberich, Studien zu den Proömien in der griechischen und byzantinischen Geschichtsschreibung 15–16 points out that Ephorus is the first to discuss not only his own history but the genre itself. See further Canfora in PoH 353–4.

[33] Avenarius, LS 80 n. 26 thinks τῶν παλαιῶν refers only to mythical times (i.e., before the return of the Heracleidae, with which Ephorus opened his history), but this is unlikely given καθ' ἡμᾶς in the first part; the more likely distinction is contemporary and non-contemporary history. In Thucydides 1.20.1, τὰ παλαιά refers to what occurred before the Peloponnesian War, including the Persian Wars, as his mention of them in the preceding chapter shows; cf. 1.1.3 with Gomme, HCT ad loc.; but cf. 1.73.2, quoted at App. III n. 7.

[34] Pol. xii.27.7 (=FGrHist 70 F 110). An argument that the words are Ephorus' own is that ἐμπειρία in Polybius usually means 'practical experience' while here it seems to be 'knowledge': see Sacks, Polybius 35; cf. Walbank, HCP 1.10; 11.393. Schepens, Anc. Soc. 1 (1970) 163ff. takes the words as Ephorus' own, but Polybius is not so exact when he quotes other historians: Walbank, HCP 11.395–6.

claiming great reliability for autopsy,[35] though the nature of his work forced him to modify the Thucydidean claim.[36]

On the other hand, Timaeus presented a rather different persona, as we can see even through the distorted lens of Polybius' criticism. It is not difficult to perceive his use of autopsy for the history of the past, where we have evidence that he relied on monuments and inscriptions in the Herodotean manner.[37] It is more difficult to know how he used these tools for the contemporary portion of his history, since in this part Timaeus mentioned not participation or eyewitness of events, but his exile from the land whose history he aspired to write. What methodological procedure he enunciated by this is unclear, though it is not impossible that he emphasised certain benefits to be had only in exile.[38] Presumably he relied on eyewitnesses and participants who reported to him during his exile at Athens.

What Timaeus lacked, according to Polybius, was experience, and Polybius – who discusses inquiry more than any predecessor or follower – spends a good portion of his polemical Book XII in advancing his own beliefs on the importance of experience as a fundamental requirement for the historian and as an important guiding principle in the pursuit of inquiry. Several historians come in for criticism in XII, including Callisthenes, who is ridiculed for his naïveté and errors in tactical arrangement and military matters, a direct result, Polybius says, of his lack of experience.[39] Ephorus, although knowledgeable about naval battles, is likewise completely inexperienced in land warfare, which prevents him from correctness in the detailed descriptions of

---

[35] It may very well be that Ephorus went on to suggest that since complete autopsy was impossible, one should then choose sources that had been there, as Polybius was later to do (see Pédech, *Méthode* 400), but we cannot say for sure.

[36] See App. III for two passages of Isocrates sometimes used in analyses of historical methodology.   [37] See below, p. 101.

[38] *FGrHist* 566 F 34; Brown, *Timaeus of Tauromenium* 6 suggests that Timaeus made reference to his return to Sicily in 'looking back' on his fifty-year exile; this interpretation is attractive, but we have no evidence that Timaeus returned to Sicily; cf. Pearson, *Greek Historians of the West* 37–8. It seems inconceivable that Timaeus, given his love of display and his disdain for predecessors (below, pp. 228ff.), would not have portrayed his exile as some sort of advantage.

[39] Pol. XII.22.6: διὰ τὴν ἀπειρίαν οὐδὲ τὸ δυνατὸν καὶ τὸ μὴ ἀδύνατον ἐν τοῖς τοιούτοις δύναται διευκρινεῖν. Walbank, *HCP* II.364 says that this passage 'shows P. at his worst'. For more on Polybian polemic see below, pp. 229ff.

battles.⁴⁰ It is in his criticism of Timaeus, however, that Polybius gives the clearest indications of his beliefs about the importance of experience and participation for the practitioner of inquiry and autopsy.⁴¹

History, he claims, consists of three parts: (i) the study and comparison of literary sources; (ii) the survey (autopsy) of those lands treated in the history; (iii) political experience. The first is the least important, only a part of the writing of history; Timaeus' mistake was that he made it everything. The second, autopsy, is necessary because its lack (ἀορασία) leads to a dependency on others and thereby to exaggeration and omission. Third, only personal experience (αὐτοπάθεια) can produce the vividity (ἔμφασις) needed for a 'pragmatic' history, and the more experiences the writer has, the better equipped he is to deal with the work of history.⁴² Expanding the argument slightly, Polybius then states that an author must take pains (φιλοπόνως) in the compilation of evidence. Eyes (autopsy) are more accurate than ears (the reading of books here, not oral report), since inquiries from books are made without danger and hardship, whereas personal inquiry requires labour and expense.⁴³

Polybius here states the case more clearly than any of the previous authors considered. Autopsy alone, he maintains, can defend against common errors: it is superior to literary sources under whose influence the author cannot decide for himself.⁴⁴ And yet even autopsy is liable to error if the historian lacks the experience that guides the historian in his research by telling him what to look for, and what to ask of others. Perhaps this is only making explicit what had long been assumed; later in Book XII Polybius quotes Theopompus who also praised the usefulness of experience:

---

⁴⁰ Pol. XII.25f.1–7; in 25f.1 Polybius considers him wholly inexperienced in land battles; cf. 25f.3, where he is both totally inexperienced and laughable. In 25f.6–7, Polybius says the same is true of Theopompus and most of all of Timaeus.

⁴¹ There is a certain contradiction in Polybius' analysis, caused perhaps by the desire to attack Timaeus (Walbank, *Polybius* 73–4), but his argument is clear in its outlines.

⁴² Pol. XII.25e.1–25h.4. On 'pragmatic history', see Introduction n. 119.

⁴³ Pol. XII.26d.3–27.6. On the *topos* of pains and dangers, see Ch. III §3.

⁴⁴ Experience is also a requirement if the historian wishes to bring vividity (ἔμφασις) to his narrative, but this is a separate point: see Sacks, *Polybius* 31ff.; Schepens, *RSA* 5 (1975) 185–200.

> Theopompus says that the one who has undergone the greatest number of dangers is the best in war, and the one who is most able in speech is he who has shared in the most political contests; and the same is true for medical or nautical skill.[45]

We do not know the provenance of Theopompus' remarks, nor whether he used them specifically in conjunction with observations about autopsy and inquiry. Polybius' extensive treatment of the topic suggests that the formulation is his own and not entirely familiar to his audience. If this is the case, we have in his work a progression from the theoretic that had been employed up to his time. For Thucydides, the difficulties of ascertaining the truth were the result of prejudice or faulty memory on his informant's part; for Polybius, they are the result of inexperience on the inquirer's part.

Although the statements here seem to be a ringing endorsement of autopsy and inquiry, it should be noted that even these methods have suffered a diminution in importance at Polybius' hands, for they must submit to, and be corrected by, experience, since only this can make a really useful history:

> One who has no experience of warfare cannot write well about those things that happen in war, nor can one inexperienced in political life write of these kinds of events and circumstances ... Whenever they try to write about cities and places, it is necessary, since they are devoid of such experience, that ... they shall omit many things worthy of account, while making much of things which are not worthy of account.[46]

Polybius elaborates this idea further, pointing out the cardinal importance of the inquirer himself in giving shape and direction to the reports of eyewitnesses:

> And yet even in this matter [sc. the questioning of eyewitnesses and of those personally acquainted with the facts] the inexperienced must make great errors... For how can one judge rightly about battle order or a siege or a sea battle, and how can one properly understand those telling the details, if he himself has no conception of such things? For the inquirer contributes to the narrative no less than his informants, since the recollection of the concomitant details leads the narrative on from point to point. So the man who is inexperienced is unsuited to inquire of those who were present, nor, being present, does he know what is happening: even when he's there, he's not there.[47]

---

[45] *FGrHist* 115 F 342 = Pol. XII.27.8–9. [46] Pol. XII.25g.1–3.
[47] Pol. XII.28a.8–10, with Walbank, *HCP* II.412.

Polybius must be given his due: no other ancient historian, not even Thucydides, gave so much thought to the epistemological difficulties inherent in writing up an historical narrative.[48] Later historians, as we shall see, emphasise the main difficulties in inquiry as the prejudice of the informers, but Polybius sees the great complexity in any attempt to find out what actually happened, even to the extent of recognising what moderns have only recently begun to emphasise again, that a fundamental element in an historical narrative is the narrator himself. Polybius does not imagine that an historian has only to question informants to find out what happened: the truth is rather bound up in a complex nexus of inquirer and informer, and is as dependent on the ability of the former as it is on the reliability of the latter.

We may trace this emphasis on experience back through the philosophers and medical men. It is not a coincidence that Polybius had divided medicine, like history, into three parts, one of which, the rational (λογικόν), was exclusively theoretical and more concerned with abstract reasoning than pragmatic performance of actual cures for patients. Polybius allied himself with the empiricists who had, he says, the true habit of mind necessary to make medicine a useful science, even though they sometimes were defeated before the public by the theoreticians' persuasiveness of speech.[49] Polybius then applies to history the practical approach used by men of medicine in the Hellenistic world. This approach can be found in Aristotle too, who in several passages similarly speaks of the need for an experienced eye,[50] and even more significantly, in the *Prior Analytics* notes that experience is necessary in securing the different starting points of inquiry.[51] Polybius therefore is drawing on an old tradition, and one

---

[48] It may be, as Schepens, *Anc. Soc.* 6 (1975) 273 points out, that the importance of the researcher is ultimately rooted in the Greek concept of ἱστορία, but only Polybius has elucidated it clearly and emphatically.

[49] Pol. XII.25d.2-7; the experts are defeated at the hands of the theoreticians 'because of the lack of discernment among the multitude (διὰ τὴν τῶν πολλῶν ἀκρισίαν)'. Polybius is fond of comparisons with medicine: see Wunderer, *Polybios-Forschungen* III.61-5.

[50] In the *Historia Animalium*, Aristotle notes that the distinctness of the sperm-ducts of the male selachi are 'not obvious to a non-expert' (566a 6-8), that to detect menstruation in cows and mares, one must 'be constantly attending to, and thoroughly acquainted with, such animals' (573a 10-16), and that the swelling of a bitch's teats 'is difficult for any but an expert to detect' (574b 15-19). These references are from Lloyd, *MRE* 212 n. 427.

[51] Arist. *A. Pr.* 46a 4ff., cited by Lloyd, *MRE* 137 n. 62.

that we can see also at work in the medical writers who similarly note the importance of experience for the proper practice of medicine.[52] Polybius' requirements for the historian can thus be seen to be an integration of traditional historiographical methods with those of other 'scientific' endeavours in antiquity, as well as a recognition akin to that of the philosophers that undirected sense-perception is not the path towards any valuable ἐπιστήμη. For the historian to have his greatest effect, and to make his history really useful, it is necessary that he himself have been a man of public life and political and military achievements.[53]

Diodorus, perhaps not surprisingly, adds nothing to the methodology of autopsy. He claims to have travelled Europe and Asia with considerable hardships and dangers to correct the errors, he says, even of reputable historians, but there is little evidence of this in the text.[54] Since his work reached to Caesar's conquest of Britain, he could possibly have used eyewitnesses for the latter (contemporary) parts of his history, and since he is fond of methodological insertions, he may have given some indication in the later books of why he chose the sources that he did. But Diodorus already betrays a different spirit when, in the preface, he praises the supply of written materials at Rome,[55] and we are reminded of both the bookish Timaeus and Polybius' criticisms of excessive reliance on written histories.

The later Greek historians add little to the problems of autopsy and inquiry. For many of them, as we shall see in the next section, inquiry became restricted under an autocratic regime. Overcoming this challenge occupied much of their efforts, and it should not surprise us that we find no remarks of the Thucydidean or Polybian sort that face or, at the least, acknowledge the difficulty of inquiry squarely.[56] Typical and quite revealing is the brief remark on this subject to be found in Lucian's *How to Write History* (h. c. 47):

---

[52] Lloyd, *MRE* 88ff.
[53] Polybius speaks also of the importance of eyewitness at xx.12.8, where it is distinctly said to be superior to hearsay. (Pédech, *Méthode* 359–60 thinks the remarks are from the preface of Book XXI; *contra*, Walbank, *HCP* III.2–3.) Note also how at x.11.4 Polybius gives the circumference of New Carthage not just as an eyewitness, but as an eyewitness with professional competence (αὐτόπτης ... μετ' ἐπιστάσεως).   [54] See n. 234.
[55] Diod. 1.4.3–5, on which see Ch. III §2.
[56] I mean here of course the epistemological difficulty; for other types of remarks on the 'difficulty' of composing a history, see Ch. III §3.

The deeds should be assembled not at random (ὡς ἔτυχε), but with repeated laborious and painstaking investigation. Most of all the historian should be present and an eyewitness (παρόντα καὶ ἐφορῶντα), but, if not, he should follow those telling the more impartial story, those whom one would reason least likely to add to or take away from the facts because of favour or hostility. Here let him be skilful in putting together the more credible story.

The material here is all more or less based on Thucydides' methodological chapter,[57] and yet Lucian has made of it something quite different from what Thucydides himself says. What Thucydides said was that people at the same events did not say the same thing because of memory or partiality. Lucian leaves out the first and says only that one should accept the story of the observer who is more impartial and who would be reckoned least likely to speak out of favour or hatred. Lucian has thus conflated what were two things in Thucydides, the necessity of 'going through with accuracy' each thing reported, *and* the difficulty that informants sometimes spoke with partiality. In the equation that the one who speaks without bias is telling the truth, Lucian shows himself to be thinking primarily in terms of the omnipresent danger of flattery or hatred so common among the Roman historians and the historians, both Greek and Roman, of the Empire.[58] And the requirement that the historian use the more credible (τοῦ πιθανωτέρου) story is nothing more than the application to historiography of the common rhetorical practice of ensuring that the *narratio* of a speech is probable.[59] To be sure, this may have been all that Thucydides meant, and it may have been the path that he followed, but his words suggest a more comprehensive understanding of the problem than is to be found in later writers.

As for the Roman historians, it is not unusual to criticise them for a failure to maintain standards of inquiry,[60] although such an attitude

---

[57] Homeyer, *Lukian* 252–3. It is not all that different from Pol. XII.4c.4–5, where Polybius says that an historian must question as many informants as possible (πυνθάνεσθαι ... ὡς παρὰ πλείστων), believe those witnesses that are trustworthy (πιστεύειν ... τοῖς ἀξίοις πίστεως), and be a good judge (κριτὴν ... μὴ κακόν) of the reports he receives. But as we have just seen, there is much more to Polybius' discussion of inquiry.   [58] See Ch. III §4.
[59] For this technique as a way of resolving variant versions, see App. IV §3.
[60] So Fornara, *Nature* 56: '[H]istory would not have acquired its name from any obvious emphasis placed upon that activity [sc. inquiry] by Roman writers.'

overlooks both the deplorable state of our evidence, and the indirect method by which the Romans comment on their investigations. With the exception of Sallust's *Catiline* we possess not one contemporary history from the Republican era. Even for the Empire we have only the work of Velleius (but not the contemporary portions of Tacitus' *Histories*), and our only large-scale contemporary history in Latin is that of Ammianus written six centuries after the first Roman historian. Any analysis, therefore, must reflect this shortcoming. As we know, contemporary history predominated in Rome, as in Greece: even Livy is no exception. Whether claims of autopsy and inquiry played the same role in contemporary Roman historiography as they did in Greek is difficult to determine. That historiography was the province of the Senatorial class for the first two centuries of its existence, and that the writing of history was frequently begun in retirement as a suitable activity for a statesman do not prohibit the author from having based his history on his participation and experience, especially when we recall that Roman historiography is local, and that the theatres of action were usually fewer than in a *Hellenica*.[61] There is evidence that the early writers of Roman history made clear their participation and eyewitness in the wars they recounted.[62] We can plausibly suggest that when Fabius narrated the contemporary portion of his history, he made clear the dependence of that report on autopsy of the events. In the face of little evidence elsewhere, his autopsy must have been the main component of his narrative.[63] What is difficult to determine is whether Roman inquiry extended to the other side. Polybius' claim that Fabius was biased in his presentation of the First Punic War may mean simply that his assignation of blame was faulty or injudiciously applied.[64] Yet the fact that Polybius needed to use both Fabius and Philinus suggests that each narrated the events predominantly from his own side. Pictor may have based himself on Philinus for the Carthaginian viewpoint and merely corrected him in details.[65] Moreover, Plutarch suggests that Fabius followed Diocles of Peparethos in many matters when narrating the founding of Rome.[66]

---

[61] On the local character of Roman history, Fornara, *Nature* 53-4, and below, App. V.
[62] D. Hal. *A. R.* 1.6.2 says that Fabius Pictor and Cincius Alimentus narrated fully (ἀκριβῶς, cf. n. 262) the events at which they themselves were present.
[63] Bung, *Q. Fabius Pictor* 195-6.   [64] *FGrHist* 809 T 6a = Pol. 1.14.2.
[65] See Jacoby, *Komm.* II. B. 598.
[66] *FGrHist* 809 F 4; for more on Fabius' non-contemporary inquiry see below n. 185.

Neither of these is a minor point since Fabius, as the first, may have set the example of what type of inquiry was acceptable for future Roman historians. On the other hand, there is no doubt that L. Cincius Alimentus used the experience as a prisoner in the Second Punic War to emphasise the superior nature of his autopsy and inquiry (of Hannibal himself!).[67] We should likewise not doubt that Cato too spoke, like Polybius, of his participation at events.[68] And Sempronius Asellio, we know from Gellius, wrote up the events of the late second century at which he was present.[69]

For the other Roman historians it becomes more difficult to ascertain their method, but the absence of such remarks in Sallust, for example, should not be seen as evidence for a de-emphasis on inquiry and autopsy. Not only were his prefaces (where one usually finds these remarks) atypical by ancient standards,[70] but he himself was attempting to forge a new persona, distinctly different from the traditional Roman one.[71] Nor is Livy particularly suitable, since he represents a new breed of historians and his preface is much more focused on the early history of Rome where claims of autopsy and inquiry of eyewitnesses would be out of place.[72] In the main, therefore, it should not be doubted that the contemporary historians of Republican Rome would have noted their inquiry and autopsy of the events narrated,[73] and perhaps in the Greek manner (though this is less certain) presented their methodology as a guarantee of the value or accuracy of their work. The Roman recognition of the value of inquiry is suggested by A. Hirtius who, in the preface of Book VIII of the *Gallic War* of Caesar, apologises for daring to complete Caesar's work, since Hirtius himself was not present at the events.[74] More substantially, it is possible to demonstrate the Roman

---

[67] His value as a contemporary source was appreciated by Livy, XXI.38.3 = *FGrHist* 810 F 5 = *HRR* F 7.

[68] He claims (*HRR* F 2) to be a 'clarus uir atque magnus' who needs to account for his *negotium* and *otium*, so it follows that he should have explained each. Cf. Pol. III.4.13, and for Cato's prominence in his narrative, below, p. 195.

[69] Asellio, *HRR* F 6.   [70] Quint. III.8.9, with Earl, *ANRW* I.2, 854–6.

[71] See above, pp. 44f. and below, pp. 138f.

[72] On the preface as designed for the early books, see Dessau, in *Festschrift ... Otto Hirschfeld* 461–6.   [73] Some specific examples below, p. 81.

[74] Hirtius ap. Caes. *B. G.* VIII.*praef.*8: 'mihi ne illud quidem accidit, ut Alexandrino atque Africano bello interessem', who continues that he learned of these matters partly from an eyewitness, Caesar himself: 'quae bella ... ex parte nobis Caesaris sermone sunt nota, e.q.s.'.

concern with inquiry by an examination of the *Gallic War* itself. For throughout the work Caesar is careful to inform the reader of his sources, especially when treating the intentions of other characters, or when narrating the plans of the Gauls. The most common sources are prisoners taken by the Romans. These often inform Caesar of the plans of his opponents, and why at any one time they are or are not fighting him.[75] Sometimes he or his generals learn from deserters (who might be individually named) about the movements and intentions of the enemy; at other times allies of the Romans inform them; not surprisingly, spies are sometimes employed.[76] The narrator himself might seek out information: before describing the custom of the Nervii, Caesar says that he made inquiries about them and learned by that method.[77] There are over two dozen of these remarks in the *Gallic War*, and their presence reveals that Caesar was well aware of the importance of validating events by autopsy or inquiry.[78] It also demonstrates that his audience might expect them and consider them important in guaranteeing the reliability of the narrator. This trend continues into the Empire. Velleius and Ammianus mention their role as participants frequently, and even Eutropius in his brief survey of Roman history finds the occasion to note that he participated in Julian's Persian expedition.[79] In sum, then, there is no reason to think that the Roman historians valued inquiry based on participation any less than did the Greeks.

Where an historian might make specific reference to his own autopsy and inquiry in the narrative should also be considered briefly here.[80] As we noted before, the audience for a history expected a largely third-person narrative relating or extolling deeds and words. 'History required a narrative of events, not an analysis of problems',[81] and since history was a branch of rhetoric, it was the author's task to present the

---

[75] Caes. *B. G.* 1.50.4 ('ex captiuis'); II.16.1; 17.2 ('ut postea ex captiuis cognitum est'); v. 8.6; 18.4; 52.4; VII.18.1.

[76] Deserters: *B. G.* v.18.4 ('a perfugis captiuisque'); VII.44.2; 72.1 ('ex perfugis et captiuis'); individuals named: II.10.1; v.57.2; VII.39.3; 54.1; allies: IV.19.1 (the Ubii tell Caesar what the Suebi intend); spies: II.11.2.

[77] *B. G.* II.15.3: 'quorum de natura moribusque Caesar cum quaereret, sic reperiebat'. See also v.52.4, where Caesar learns of the brave exploits of centurions and military tribunes on the testimony of Q. Cicero.

[78] See also *B. G.* II.32.4; v. 6.7.

[79] Vell. II.101.2–3; 104.4; 106.1; Amm. xv.1.1; XXIX.1.24; Eutr. 10.16.

[80] Only an overview is here possible, since there are hundreds of these remarks in the historians.   [81] Luce, *Livy* 102.

narrative in as felicitous a manner as possible. When Polybius states that the narrative is but a part of history, and not the most important part, he is doing so partly to excuse himself for the constant interruptions in the work.[82] But unless the historian's aim was Polybian instruction, his overriding concern was with the narrative. It was impractical and intrusive for the author to interrupt his narrative constantly with 'I saw' or 'I learned' or 'I conjecture': it would be an impediment to the enjoyment of the narrative's pleasure. In place of a barrage of first-person remarks, historians used an arsenal of techniques implying autopsy or inquiry that contributed to and facilitated the flow of historical narrative and served as a second-level and more or less constant reminder or suggestion of the historian's inquiry.

Thucydides set the precedent for contemporary historiography with the one basic claim made at the outset, and this is the standard (so to speak) form, the claim of autopsy and inquiry from those who know or were eyewitnesses. Nearly all contemporary historians make these claims.[83] Explicit remarks elsewhere are as a rule reserved for two situations, either to underline some special source, or to win credence for something unusual (at times, marvellous). As examples of the first, Thucydides invokes his autopsy to underline his special competence in describing the plague and its effects.[84] Two passages in Polybius show the historian underlining his special source: he tells us that he was present at a conversation between Philopoemen and Archon, a general of the Achaean league; and he claims to have learned details of a secret meeting between Perseus and Eumenes from Perseus' friends

---

[82] See XVI.17.10–11.

[83] See Thuc. I.22.1–3; Ctesias, *FGrHist* 688 T 8; Philistus, 556 F 56 (?); Timonides, 561 F 2 (?); Theopompus, 115 T 20a + F 25; Callisthenes, 124 F 12(a); Ptolemy, 138 T 1 (?); Aristobulus, 139 T 6 (?); Hieronymus of Cardia, 154 T 7 (?); Fabius Pictor, 809 T 2 (?); L. Cincius Alimentus, 810 F 5(3), (5); Silenus, 175 T 2; Sosylus, 176 T 1; Antisthenes of Rhodes, 508 T 1; Zeno of Rhodes, 523 T 3; Pol. III.4.13 et al.; Poseidonius (historian of Perseus), 169 F 1 (?); Sempronius Asellio, *HRR* F 6; Theophanes of Mytilene, *FGrHist* 188 T 2 (?); Q. Dellius, 197 F 1; Olympos, 198 F 1 (?); Jos. *B. J.* 1.3, cf. *c. Ap.* 1.55; Kriton, *FGrHist* 200 T 2 (?); Anonymous of Corinth, 204 F 1; Anonymous historian of L. Verus, 203 F 5; Herodian, 1.2.5; Dio, LXXII.18.4; Magnos of Carrhae, *FGrHist* 225 T 1 (?); Eutychianos of Cappadocia, 226 F 1 (?); Amm. XV.1.1. (A question mark indicates that the testimonia do not unequivocally demonstrate that the historian mentioned autopsy and inquiry in the text.)

[84] Thuc. II.48.3; IV.104.4 is not an autoptic statement, as Norden, *Agnostos Theos* 317 would have it; see below, pp. 182ff.

Eyes and ears

afterwards.⁸⁵ Among the Roman historians of the Republic we have but a few statements: L. Cincius Alimentus reported that he had the exact number of Hannibal's troops from Hannibal himself; C. Fannius emphasised that he himself had seen Tiberius Gracchus as the first to scale the wall at Numantia; Sallust claims to have heard from Crassus himself the opinion that the latter had been maligned by Cicero.⁸⁶ Among the imperial historians, Velleius emphasises his autopsy at the summit conference in AD 1 or so between Gaius Caesar and the king of the Parthians on an island in the Euphrates.⁸⁷ Tacitus mentions that he was a praetor and *quindecimuir* at the *ludi saeculares* in AD 88, and this he says not boastfully (*non iactantia refero*) but only to inform the reader of a certain detail that he knew since the board had charge of the games being held at the time.⁸⁸ Dio cites his time among the Pannonians as validation for his accurate knowledge of them, and invokes his father's testimony for the fact that Trajan's death was concealed for several days.⁸⁹ Ammianus, in his digression on the Eastern abuse of oratory, points to his stay in the East as the time when he became familiar with these practices, and in a passage meant to arouse pathos, Ammianus describes the remains of the whitened bones he himself saw on the fields of Salicus in Scythia.⁹⁰

---

⁸⁵ Pol. XXII.19 (on its possible context, Walbank *HCP* III.209-10); XXIX.5.1-9.13, on which see below, n. 113.

⁸⁶ Cincius, *FGrHist* 810 F 5(3), (5) = *HRR* F 7 (so too the Greek historians Sosylus and Silenus: *FGrHist* 175, 176); Fannius, *HRR* F 4; Sall. *Cat.* 48.9.

⁸⁷ Vell. II.101.2-3. On the date of the conference, see Woodman, *VP* I. ad loc.

⁸⁸ Tac. *Ann.* XI.11.1. Tacitus implies that in the now lost portion of the *Histories* where Domitian's games were treated, he mentioned there too that he was a *quindecimuir*, invoking the privileged information from that office to explain the computations of both emperors. The passage in the *Annals* is something of a parenthesis introduced to inform the reader that the calculations which Augustus (whose reforms are here mentioned) and Domitian used to determine the dates of games were treated in the books which Tacitus composed on Domitian (the books of the *Histories* now lost). Naturally, the mention of the honour played some role (see below, p. 144), but here he emphasises a superior knowledge as a guarantee for his calculations. ⁸⁹ Dio, XLIX.36.4; LXIX.1.2-3.

⁹⁰ Amm. XXX.4.4; XXXI.7.16 (cf. Tac. *Ann.* I.61.2 and on the motif, borrowed from poetry, see Woodman, *RICH* 171); this, of course, is implied autopsy. We should mention one other passage of Ammianus which seems to be the inverse of autopsy-as-validation. Before his long and ornate digression on the horrors consequent on the attempted murder of Valens, Ammianus says that even though all manner of tortures and sufferings occurred, he cannot remember exact details (for he has seen many men tortured since then), and must therefore give a brief (*summatim*)

A second use of an explicit statement of autopsy or inquiry is as voucher for a marvel or wonder. In these, the author steps out of the mimetic narrative to guarantee (in really the only way possible in a historical narrative) that what will seem unbelievable to the reader actually took place. Here the author might have to proceed with caution, lest these marvels strain credulity. This was clearly the case with Ctesias in his *Indica*, where he claimed autopsy of many marvels which his audience disbelieved.[91] Yet other historians did it as well. Aristobulus (not averse to marvels, as we can see even from the fragments[92]) reports the prophecy by Peithagoras about Hephaestion and Alexander and claims to have learned it from Peithagoras himself. He also emphasised that he saw two Brachmanes at Taxila, and he reported their appearance, their customs, and their meeting with Alexander.[93] When Chimara, the daughter of Ortiagos was captured in battle by the Romans, Polybius explained that his description of her extraordinary character and intelligence was based on his own meeting with her in Sardis. And the same author emphasised his presence at the fall of Carthage when Scipio recited the words of Homer.[94] Coelius Antipater claimed that he heard

account (XXIX.1.24). What follows, however, is a fairly exact account with little or no sense of uncertainty or confusion. Since the Latin is unambiguous, we must look elsewhere for the answer, and the passage that suggests itself is Thucydides' description of the night battle of Epipolae noted above. As Thucydides had given an account not demonstrably inferior to his others, so too Ammianus whose virtuosity is thereby highlighted: cf. esp. 'ut in tenebrosis rebus confusione cuncta miscentes'; for the Thucydides passage, above, p. 69. In each case, the interruption calls attention to the skill of the writer in the passage that follows. Additionally in Ammianus, the statement brings out the pathos and deep emotion of the writer, and 'justifies', so to speak, the rhetorical nature of the horrors described.

[91] For explicit statements of autopsy see *FGrHist* 688 F 45b, 45dβ; cf. Photius' remark (F 45 §51: ταῦτα γράφων καὶ μυθολογῶν Κτησίας λέγει τἀληθέστατα γράφειν). Something similar may have been the case in the imperial writer Licinius Mucianus' work about natural curiosities, but this may not have been a history: see Schanz–Hosius II.783-4; Peter was reluctant to include him, *HRR* II. cxxxx, and see FF 7, 10, 12, 13, 18, 20, 24.

[92] We know that his history contained much geographical examination and examination of witnesses (in a Herodotean manner?): *FGrHist* 139 FF 20, 35, 38, 41, 42, 54. See Pearson, *Lost Histories* 174-8; Pédech, *Compagnons* 394-404.

[93] *FGrHist* 139 F 54 = Arr. *Anab.* VII.18.5; F 41 = Str. XV.1.61.

[94] Pol. XXI.38.1-7; XXXVIII.21.1. One could argue that the latter incident belongs with the previous group as emphasising a special source. Yet the quotation of Homer gives it an unreal, dramatic aspect, and there is something of prophecy contained in the remark; it also serves Polybius as the surest proof of Scipio's marvellous nature (cf. esp. ἀνδρὸς μεγάλου καὶ τελείου καὶ συλλήβδην ἀξίου μνήμης).

from Gaius Gracchus himself that Gaius' brother Tiberius appeared in a dream and told Gaius that they would share a similar fate. P. Volumnius, who wrote a monograph on the battle at Philippi, seems to have vouched once for a marvel: before the second engagement, bees appeared on the standards of Brutus, the arm of one of Brutus' men sweated oil, and two eagles fought overhead, with the one closest to Brutus fleeing in defeat.[95] Dio is no less fond of underlining oracles,[96] and Ammianus, in describing the *terrores* on 21 July 365 mentions that he himself saw them.[97] These types of claims were easily parodied, and became favourite authenticating devices for literary forgeries and works of *Schwindelliteratur*.[98]

Splendour and number, particularly high and highly improbable ones, call forth explicit validation. Fabius Pictor said that the Romans and their allies numbered 800,000 men in 225 BC when the Gauls invaded, and averred that he himself had been present at the events; Velleius mentions his presence when he describes the splendour of Tiberius' triumphal parade; Trajan's physician Kriton said in his *Getica* that he himself had seen the extraordinary numbers and spoils from Trajan's conquest of Scythia. A contrary example, no less a marvel, it seems: Cotta who served as under-commander with Caesar averred that he had seen Caesar take but three slaves with him to Britain.[99]

Not surprisingly, claims of eyewitness or inquiry of the natives could be quite valuable in geographical and ethnographical excurses.[100] Strabo tells us that some historians included geographical excurses within their histories, while others placed them in works of physics or mathematics: as examples of the former he gives Ephorus and Polybius,

---

[95] Coelius, *HRR* F 50; Volumnius, *HRR* F 1 = Plut. *Brut.* 48.

[96] Dio, LXVII.18.2, with the interesting comment κἂν μυριάκις τις ἀπιστήσῃ; for other marvels see LXVIII.27.2-3; LXXVIII.8.4.

[97] Amm. XXVI.10.19 (*nos transeundo conspeximus*).

[98] See Speyer, *Die literarische Fälschung* 50-6; Scobie, *RhM* 122 (1979) 244.

[99] Fabius, *FGrHist* 809 F 19b; Vell. II.101.3 (with Woodman, *VP* I. ad loc.); Kriton, *FGrHist* 200 F 1, with Jacoby, *Komm.* II. B. 626. 24-8; Cotta, *HRR* F 1.

[100] Herodotus' work embraced both ethnographical and geographical speculation, since there was a close correlation between a people and their land. Ethnography and geography became separate genres, but some historians continued to incorporate such material into their narratives. On the relation between land and people, see Trüdinger, *Studien zur griechisch-römischen Ethnographie* 37 ff.; on geography and ethnography, van Paassen, *Classical Tradition of Geography* 185-204; on Polybius' belief in the importance of geography to history, see III.36.1-6; 57.2-59. 8; XII.25e. 1-7.

of the latter, Posidonius and Hipparchus.[101] Historians who wrote after a great expansion of the Greco-Roman world were the main beneficiaries, as we see in Onesicritus and Nearchus after Alexander's conquests, or Polybius and Posidonius after Rome's. The primacy of autopsy in geographical discussion could not be questioned, and it remained the best means for improving and correcting one's predecessors. The purpose of the explicit statement of autopsy seems to have been the same as what we noted above: to add details, contradict popular misconceptions, or vouch for unusual customs. Callisthenes, progressing beyond Herodotus' limit of Elephantine, claimed to have superior knowledge on the causes of the Nile's flood; Aristobulus reported a great number of the wonders he saw in Asia; Polybius promised to treat Libya and Spain in order to correct the ignorance of the Greeks about these areas.[102] Posidonius' fragments contain many reflections on geography and natural history but their provenance is uncertain, and the most recent collection has removed many from the *Histories* and assigned them to his geographical works.[103] On the other hand, there is strong evidence that ethnographical speculation was an important, perhaps integral, part of the history.[104] In one fragment,

---

[101] Str. VIII.1.1; we know that Posidonius used geography in his history: see Jacoby, *FGrHist Komm.* II. c. 190.13, and n. 104 below.

[102] Callisthenes, *FGrHist* 124 F 12; for Aristobulus see above, n.92; Pol. III.59. In addition, we have fragments of Polybius' geographical excursus, Book XXXIV. We are told that Polybius cited both eyewitness evidence and theoretical arguments in his geographical book, a procedure similar to Herodotus'. A particularly interesting criticism of Pytheas is made, that he is unreliable because he claimed to have travelled the whole northern area of Europe; far more worthy of trust, Polybius continues, is Euhemerus, who claims to have seen only one country, Panchaia (XXXIV.5.2-9). Cf. XXXIV.10.6-7, where Polybius refutes Pytheas by saying that although the latter makes many statements about Britain, Scipio Aemilianus could get no information about it from the Massaliots. The criticism of Pytheas is influenced by Polybius' desire to be the authoritative historian of the West: see Walbank, *Polybius* 126-7, and for more on Polybian polemic, below, pp. 229-32.

[103] Posidonius, F 244 on the giant serpent, for example, is not assigned by Edelstein and Kidd, *Posidonius: Fragments* to a specific work, while Jacoby (*FGrHist* 87 F 66) assigns it to the *Histories*; similarly F 245 E-K (=87 F 73) on the smiling apes, and F 246 E-K (=87 F 53) on the location of the pillars of Heracles. As Jacoby realised, caution is necessary, and Edelstein and Kidd's arrangement by subject matter (Historical, Scientific, etc.) makes the most sense, given the state of the evidence.

[104] Kidd, *Commentary* 1.309-10 notes that Posidonius wrote ethnographies as an 'aetiological key to explain the behaviour and acts of a nation through its

Posidonius tells of a Ligurian woman who gave birth while digging in the fields, and vouches for the story by saying that he learned it from Charmoleon, his host there; in another, he mentions his autopsy of enemy heads hung up by the Celts on pikes. In each case philosophical conclusions are drawn from the autopsy and inquiry.[105] What Posidonius seems to have done, therefore, is to have adapted a Herodotean persona to the slightly differing demands of a 'philosophical' history, using his investigative work as the evidence upon which to build a theory of human character and its importance. And so in this regard, he used explicit remarks to bolster his own conclusions and interpretations.

As for the Romans, there is little interest in geography evidenced by any of their major historians.[106] Sallust denies any responsibility for his geographical excursus on Africa, and Livy's performance in geography was quite poor.[107] Even Tacitus seems to have acquired most of his geographical knowledge in books,[108] and only in Ammianus do we find a pronounced interest in geography and ethnography: he cites his own autopsy to correct minor errors by previous writers on Thrace; he corrects notions about the number of rivers in the Persian provinces by claiming to have crossed them himself; and he confirms by autopsy his ethnographical observations about the Parthians or Saracens.[109] But in this matter, at least, Ammianus seems to be wholly Greek.[110]

---

character.' Cf. id., in *Philosophia Togata* 38–50, and on Posidonius' aims in general see Malitz, *Historien des Poseidonios* 409–28.

[105] Posidonius, FF 269, 274 (E-K)=*FGrHist* 87 FF 58a, 55.

[106] See Momigliano, *Alien Wisdom* 66ff. on Roman co-operation with Greeks in the matter of geography. The Romans did write independent works on geography, but these seem to have been merely compilations from other works. See Rawson, *Intellectual Life* 257–66; Romm, *Edges of the Earth* 1–7 for the literary tradition of geography.   [107] Sall. *Jug.* 17.7; on Livy see Walsh, *Livy* 153–7.

[108] Syme, *Tacitus* I.126–7.

[109] Amm. XXII.8.1, XXVII.4.2 (Thrace); XXIII.6.21 (rivers in Persia); at XXIII.6.30 he validates the report of *scriptores antiqui* on the special breed of Nisaean horses used by the chiefs of the Parthians who dwell on the west side of Mt Coronus; at XIV.4.6 he emphasises the unusualness of the diet of the Saracens by his claim to have seen that most of them knew nothing about the use of grain and wine.

[110] We should also mention that Cato among the Romans had an interest in geography in the *Origines* (Badian, in *Latin Historians* 8; 30 n. 37) and that Coelius gave an accurate measurement of the Alps and Hannibal's march on Rome (ibid. 16), although the latter cannot really be called an independent interest in geography.

Given the evidence presented here, it is fair to say that the majority of historians, Greek and Roman, believed in the primary value of autopsy and inquiry of eyewitnesses for the writing of contemporary history.[111] The majority explain that their history is based on their own autopsy and inquiry of events, but rarely invoke this in the narrative, preferring to reserve explicit assurance for emphasising special sources and as validation for exceptional events. We must now look briefly to what extent inquiry could be employed under all circumstances and how historiography adapted to autocratic regimes.

2. CLOSED SOCIETIES AND PRIVILEGED ACCESS

Herodotus' history had come to fruition in a period of fervid intellectual activity. Likewise, Thucydides' work was composed under the influence of a society that had encouraged open debate, and had allowed to its citizens at certain times the greatest freedom of speech, even against the leaders of the state.[112] But history was not to retain its freedom in every generation. Not only was the historian's customary freedom of speech (παρρησία, *libertas*) limited, but under autocratic regimes even the practice of autopsy and free inquiry was circumscribed in important ways. The problem, which existed in one way or another for all historians,[113] will have become omnipresent with the historians

---

[111] When the historians wish to emphasise something wholly unbelievable they mark it as something that even eyewitnesses found difficult to believe: see, e.g., Diod. XVII.46.2 (Alexander at the siege of Tyre); Livy, v.42.3 (at the sack of Rome).

[112] On historiography as influenced by democracy see C. Meier, *Die Entstehung des Politischen bei den Griechen* (Frankfurt 1980) 360-434; Farrar, *Origins of Democratic Thinking* 126.

[113] There is an interesting passage in Polybius concerning the intrigues against Rome by Perseus and Eumenes (XXIX.5.1-9.13). These were conducted in secret and Polybius was at a loss to know what had transpired between the two kings. He could not simply pass it over, he says, because it was too important. His solution is to state his own opinion (τὸ δοκοῦν, 5.3) as well as the probabilities and indications that led him to this opinion, since he was living at the time and was more impressed by the affairs than anyone else. He was aided in the task by some facts emerging at the time and learning others from Perseus' friends afterwards (XXIX.8.10). This extraordinarily candid statement is unique, though the problem of secret meetings in one form or another confronted almost every historian before and after Polybius.

of Philip and Alexander. Because decisions were not made openly, traditional inquiry would be of very limited use. One either had access to a circle of power or one did not. Autopsy might be open to any participant in a siege or battle, but the viewpoint of one person would have been of little value. And overarching all of these epistemological problems was the possible hesitation to report anything discovered that was unflattering or harmful to the reigning autocrat. Now Theopompus, for one, did not, in becoming an historian of Philip, cease to practise the traditional means of autopsy and inquiry. Dionysius states his belief that Theopompus travelled widely and incurred great expense in putting together his *Philippica* (and perhaps also his *Hellenica*).[114] But a different form of validation – not evident in Theopompus who perhaps did not wish to compromise his independent judgement – can be found in those who write under autocratic regimes.

This validation consisted of assertions that one was close to the source of power and thus had privileged access. The earliest example of this is Ctesias who claimed that he spent seventeen years as a prisoner of the Persian King at his court, and this was important for the inquiry he practised there, given his treatment in the latter books of his own actions.[115] We ought not to doubt that this form of validation, in which the author portrayed himself as close to those in power, was important for establishing the authority of the historians of Alexander and his successors. It is not to be doubted that the Alexander historians were able to exploit autopsy and inquiry on a grand scale,[116] nor is it unlikely that they gave their presence at events as the guarantee of their reliability. The order in which they wrote may have determined in the first place how they asserted their authority, since they will most likely have attempted to press their own claims by a comparison (either explicit or not) with what previous historians had put forward. Aristobulus, we know, in his preface gave his age as eighty-four when he began to write his work.[117] If it is the case that his history was an attempt to correct the

---

[114] D. Hal. *Pomp.* 6 (II.392 Usher) = *FGrHist* 115 T 20a.

[115] *FGrHist* 688 T 3 + T 8; for Ctesias' sources for the non-contemporary portions of his history, see below, pp. 107f.; for his own actions, see below, pp. 185f.

[116] We can see the use of autopsy among the fragments of Nearchus and Callisthenes in geographical matters (above, p. 84).

[117] *FGrHist* 139 F 1. It is unlikely that his age was given in the same spirit as either Agatharchides (Ch. III n. 96) or Isocrates (*Antid.* 9, apologising for his deficiency of spirit).

effusive histories that appeared after Alexander's death,[118] then he may have mentioned his age to guarantee that he himself had been present with Alexander and was therefore a more qualified witness than those who had not. It should probably not be doubted that the Alexander historians gave some information about their 'special' relationship with Alexander, though certain proof is lacking.[119] And the trend may well have continued with the historians of the Diadochs. Hieronymus of Cardia is designated as one who 'campaigned with Antigonus'; and Mnesiptolemus was closely allied with the court of Antiochus III.[120] Similarly, around the great figures of the late Republic many writers assembled, who could emphasise at crucial points their proximity to their subjects: Posidonius was with Marius at his death; Theophanes accompanied Pompey on his campaigns with the distinct purpose of glorifying his deeds; Olympos and Dellius attended Cleopatra, and wrote of her deeds after her death.[121] We lack the exact words of these historians so it is not clear how they expressed themselves on the issue, but it can hardly be doubted that part of their claims to authority rested largely on their access to the reigning monarch.

Under the Roman Empire, the difficulty of inquiry became unavoidable, and Dio in a well-known passage (LIII.19) gives the clearest expression of this. Whereas under the Republic matters had been referred to the Senate and were public knowledge, and the multiplicity of reports on the same events could be compared to eliminate the prejudice in individual accounts and one could thereby arrive at some notion of the truth,[122] the establishment of the principate in 27 BC imposed greater secrecy upon the government; even material which was made known

---

[118] Schwartz, *GG* 124-5 = *RE* II. 914-15. Recent scholarship supports a late date for Aristobulus: Pearson, *Lost Histories* 150-4, 234-42; Badian, *Studies* 255-6; Bosworth, *HCA* I.27-9; Pédech, *Compagnons* 333-8.

[119] But see Badian, *YCS* 24 (1975) 153-6, for an example of how one writer could exploit this. What might have been just as revealing is how Cleitarchus, who did not partake in the campaigns, tried to validate his history of Alexander; for some possibilities see Pearson, op. cit. (n.118) 229-32.

[120] Hieronymus, *FGrHist* 154 T 2, F 8; 164 T 1; J. Hornblower, *Hieronymus* 184 n. 12 has a list of possible court historians; more detail and fuller treatment in Meissner, *Historiker* 362ff.

[121] See (resp.) *FGrHist* 87 F 37 = F 255 (E-K), with Malitz, *Historien des Poseidonios* 398-405; Plut. *Pomp.* 76. 7 (not in Jacoby: see *Komm.* II. D. 615), with Gold, *Literary Patronage in Greece and Rome* 87-107; for Olympos and Dellius see Plut. *Ant.* 82.3-5 = *FGrHist* 198 F 1.

[122] This is perhaps an echo of Thuc. I.22.3 on comparison of accounts.

was suspect because it was unverifiable. The form of government also affected history because the necessity of referring all things to a single individual meant that material would be arranged with a view towards pleasing the autocrat, not towards the truth. Finally, the expanded boundaries of the Empire made it impossible for any author to be expert in all the important locations.[123] The result for the historian, he concludes, is a greater reliance on hearsay and report. Dio's solution is to give the official version of events, and append his own opinion on those occasions when he can add something to the common report. Dio notes also that it is difficult for those outside to know anything accurate about plots against the Emperor; and that whatever punishment the Emperor metes out is therefore suspect, even if it is just. Here, however, he cannot (or will not) add anything to the official version, contenting himself (one assumes) with the general warning given here that these matters are among the most difficult to investigate, and about which certainty is impossible.[124] As we shall see, Dio was to exercise his inquiry in the sole realm left open to him.[125]

If an historian wished to write the deeds of a society not wholly free, he had but three choices on how to proceed. One solution – the least common among the surviving historians – was to follow in Ctesias' footsteps and to claim a close relationship with the main character of one's history, so as to indicate to the audience that one had privileged access. It may explain why the patronage of a king (be he an Alexander or a Seleucus) was desirable for an historian, since without it he would have scant chance to know secret transactions and the counsels that had led to the deeds.[126] The danger of this form of validation was that such an orientation opened the historian to the charge of bias or favouritism, a

---

[123] App. *Ill.* 16 seems to be a frank confession of ignorance on this score.
[124] Dio, LIII. 19.6 (note that he will give the official reports 'whether true or otherwise'); LIV.15.1–4.   [125] See below, p. 91.
[126] In this regard, it would have been invaluable to know how those historians who were imperial freedmen claimed the authority to write history. We know of several by name: C. Iulius Hyginus, a freedman of Augustus; Phlegon of Tralles, freedman of Hadrian; and Chryserus, freedman of Marcus Aurelius. Did they parade their privileged access and mention their closeness to high power? Did they emphasise deeds at court primarily, or claim a knowledge of machinations behind the scene? The questions may be moot for our narrow purposes here, since none of the preserved book titles for Hyginus and Phlegon sound like narrative histories, and the one testimonium for Chryserus (*FGrHist* 96 T 1) is not conclusive. Some would add to the list of freedmen Herodian, but this is uncertain: see Whittaker, *Herodian* xxi–xxiii.

charge that may well have been the most serious for an historian as it went to the very heart of his reliability and truth, at least as the ancients saw it.[127] An interesting comparison can be made between two passages of Josephus, one in the *Life*, and one in his *Jewish War*. In the *Life*, Josephus suggests precisely the type of information from the sources of action that we have outlined here. Refuting the version of the Jewish War published by Justus of Tiberias, Josephus says that he gave his own version to Vespasian, Titus, and Herod Agrippa, expecting to receive their testimony for his accuracy.[128] Titus, he continues, so approved of the work that he gave orders the books be published with his own seal affixed. And Herod wrote no fewer than sixty-two letters bearing witness to the truth of Josephus' account.[129] In one of these letters Agrippa tells Josephus, 'when you meet me, I shall inform you about many things that are not known'.[130] But in the *Jewish War*, Josephus is careful to make no mention of any special source such as this one, referring only to his own autopsy, inquiry, and participation.[131] So although taking advantage of privileged access, Josephus does not make it known in the history itself.[132]

A second possibility for one who wanted to write history was to compose an account of the military campaigns in which he had served: this comprises the greater part of Velleius' history, and its popularity is attested by the writers on the campaigns of Trajan, Lucius Verus, and Julian, chief among the last Ammianus.[133] It is no coincidence that these

---

[127] On bias see Ch. III §4. The one form of privileged access that seems not to have carried the danger of bias is that of priest: see below, pp. 108ff.

[128] Jos. *Vita* 361-2; the publication referred to here must be that of the circulation among friends, because Josephus mentions the completion of the history after these events (367).   [129] Jos. *Vita* 363-6.

[130] Jos. *Vita* 366: ὅταν μέντοι συντύχῃς μοι, καὶ αὐτός σε πολλὰ κατηχήσω τῶν ἀγνοουμένων.

[131] *B. J.* 1.3 (αὐτός τε Ῥωμαίους πολεμήσας τὰ πρῶτα καὶ τοῖς ὕστερον παρατυχὼν ἐξ ἀνάγκης); cf. 1.18. Here Titus is cited (10) only to bolster the contention that the Jews themselves were responsible for the destruction of the Temple.

[132] Cf. Fronto, *ad Verum* 1.2.1, where the Emperor Lucius Verus promises Fronto all sorts of letters and memoranda for Fronto's history of Verus' campaign against the Parthians.

[133] We know of the following in the Empire: Kriton (*FGrHist* 200 T 2); the historians of Lucius Verus who participated (or claimed to) in the wars (Luc. *h. c.* 18-21); Callimorphus (*FGrHist* 210 F 1); Dexippus of Athens (100 T 3); Magnos of Carrhae (225 T 1); Eutychianos of Cappadocia (226 F 1).

writers appear in fair numbers whenever there is an expansionist Emperor.[134] War, after all, provided the chance to imitate the great masters Herodotus and Thucydides; and as a participant, one could model oneself on Xenophon.

The third possibility was to take up Senatorial history, but this as well had a reduced scope, since, as Dio had noted, one would know only a fraction of what was necessary given that access to the Emperor's decisions would be intermittent and frequently impossible; under the 'bad' emperors it would be completely impossible, and possibly life-threatening. The Greeks, with a longer and more established tradition of individual-centred histories, had less difficulty in adapting their works to the changed circumstances of the Empire.[135] For Dio, the solution appeared along a different line. In an important statement, he explains what appears to be at times a disproportionate emphasis in his history on the Senate's relation to the emperors and the sometimes ludicrous actions of the latter. Having narrated the extravagancies of Commodus in the amphitheatre where the Emperor killed one hundred bears in a single day, Dio notes the incongruity of such activities with the dignity and proper subject matter of history:

> And let no one think that I am sullying the majesty of history when I write such things. I would not have mentioned them otherwise, but since they came from the emperor himself, and I myself was present and took part and saw and heard, and discussed them, I thought it proper to suppress none of them, but to hand down even these things to the memory of those who shall live hereafter, as if they were great and important events. And indeed, all the other events that took place in my lifetime I shall recount in more detail than earlier events, since I was present at them, and know no one else, of those who can write a record worthy of events, who knows so accurately about them as I.[136]

Much of this is certainly familiar from statements by other authors of the value and importance of autopsy for their history, and Dio records a similar statement later.[137] Yet there is something unprecedented in

---

[134] Tacitus, in his famous complaint on the poverty of imperial history, gives as one of the reasons for the tedium of his treatment of Tiberius the fact that the latter was an 'Emperor uninterested in extending the empire' (IV.32.2, 'princeps proferendi imperi incuriosus').

[135] See Toher, in *Between Republic and Empire* 139-54.   [136] Dio, LXXII.18.3-4.

[137] At LXXII.4.2 Dio says that he reports plots against Commodus and others not from other sources but from his own observation (οὐκ ἐξ ἀλλοτρίας παραδόσεως ἀλλ' ἐξ οἰκείας τηρήσεως).

the present remark. To be sure, the increased importance of the Emperor made his character an issue of some importance in history. Even before the Empire, Greek and Roman historiography had had a traditional interest in a man's *mores* and behaviour,[138] and both Sallust and Tacitus proffer the persona of a stern moralist. Dio, however, seems to be saying something else. He admits that certain trivial details are censured by those reading histories, yet he claims that in his history he will record them anyway and pass them on to posterity, and he can only justify this by saying that he was present and best suited to record them.[139] But this is the cart before the horse: deeds are not worthy of record because the historian is present, nor are deeds worthy of record simply because they are the Emperor's, since not everything historical characters do is worthy of history.[140] Dio instead seems to be treading the line between history and biography or, perhaps better, between history and memoirs. Dio will make a claim for the utility of such narratives precisely because they will be an aid to future readers in understanding the relations between Emperor and Senate.[141]

Seen as such, Dio is not so much 'sullying' history, as he is adapting the twin tools of contemporary history to the changed circumstances of the time. A passage from Herodian confirms this approach, and suggests perhaps that Dio was not alone. Herodian notes at the end of his second book that his account of Severus may seem deficient compared with the more detailed accounts written by other historians and poets. But he explains that it is not his aim to write in greater detail, but rather to 'write up the deeds ... which I myself know'.[142] Herodian here must surely be explaining that he is not to be expected to give a history that takes into account all the events of his lifetime. And indeed we notice in many of the imperial Greek historians – Herodian, Dio, Dexippus – that the greater portion of their contemporary histories is taken up with the events that they know of

---

[138] On the interest in character, see Scheller, *De hell. hist. conscr. arte* 23-5.
[139] Should there be any doubt about this, the following passage (LXXII.19.1) shows Dio continuing the narrative of Commodus' performance in the theatre, with the Emperor now as a gladiator.
[140] The interest in details was the business of biography: Plut. *Alex.* 1.2 with Hamilton's commentary ad loc. And note too Ammianus' remark (XXVI.1.1) that history should proceed 'per negotiorum celsitudines'.
[141] For Dio's interest in Senatorial dignity see Millar, *Cassius Dio* 73-118.
[142] Herodian, II.15.6-7: πράξεις ... ἃς αὐτὸς οἶδα.

at first hand.[143] None really writes a universal history in Polybius' old sense. Their reduced goals are revealed in their reduced claims, and this is not a failure on their part to be good Polybians, but a very real achievement in the changed conditions of the Empire.

The procedure of Tacitus represents a different approach to the problems of restricted inquiry in the Empire. Choosing the 'Senatorial' perspective necessitated a certain focus and orientation. In general, military and foreign matters do not suffer from the constriction of domestic affairs, since a military operation cannot be conducted without eyewitnesses and participants whose accounts could later be questioned and compared.[144] It was the domestic scene with its inner court intrigue and endless and fatiguing chronicle of executions that was especially a labour 'in arto et inglorius'.[145] Conspiracies, as Dio notes, were of necessity shrouded in mystery and subject afterwards to the most violent manipulations, especially with an erratic or megalomaniacal Emperor – and no Emperor's reign was completely free of conspiracy. Where Dio could, because of his contemporaneity, re-orient the narrative towards the deeds at which he was actually present, Tacitus (at least in the portions of his work surviving, which are non-contemporary) had no such possibility. The demonstration of his inquiry, his search for the truth, took on a different form in three independent but mutually assisting motifs: the recognition of and commentary on the complexity of disentangling various strands in the tradition; the use of alternative explanations; and the suggestion of a truth beneath what was visible to appearances.

As to the first, Tacitus throughout both *Histories* and *Annals* comments in passing on the difficulties attendant on inquiry. The perversion of truth arises from several causes. Very common is the influence of rumour (*fama*), which by itself is not false, but rather requires discernment, since it mixes false with true.[146] Sometimes rumour is confirmed,[147] but in the majority of cases it is false, because of the human tendency to exaggerate.[148] Whenever details are lacking, people

---

[143] For Herodian see Whittaker, op. cit. (n.126) xix–xxiv; Alföldy, *Anc. Soc.* 2 (1971) 228–30; for Dio, Millar, op. cit. (n.141) 119–73; for Dexippus, Potter, *Prophecy and History* 77–94.

[144] Naturally, publishing the history of a failed campaign is another matter altogether.   [145] Tac. *Ann.* IV.32.2.

[146] Tac. *Hist.* IV.50.1: 'ueraque et falsa more famae in maius innotuere'; cf. Virg. *Aen.* IV.188, where *Fama* is described as 'tam ficti prauique tenax quam nuntia ueri' who 'pariter facta atque infecta canebat' (190).   [147] Tac. *Hist.* II.46.1.

[148] Cf. Livy, XXVIII.24.1: 'insita hominibus libidine alendi de industria rumores'.

simply make them up, either in self-praise or self-defence.[149] Sometimes, particularly where the powerful are involved, the motives for falsification are fear and hatred: Galba's last words are differently reported, depending on whether the individual hated or admired him; so too people interpreted Germanicus' death and Piso's involvement in it based on pity for one or favour for the other.[150] Fear, sometimes of the unknown, is a great hindrance to truth: things far away are always held to be greater than they are, whether it be soldiers approaching a town, or marvels told about far-off places.[151] Frequently, the crowd or the 'unskilled' are faulted for an inability to discern true from false, for their habit of idle exaggeration, and for their love of novelty.[152] Uncertainties are either mistaken for established facts or seen as licence for any interpretation.[153] Finally, the repression of freedom helps falsehood to flourish: Vitellius' attempt to hush up his defeat meant that the rumour of it only increased the more.[154]

The second and third technique are closely allied. The inclusion of variant versions or the giving of several explanations has a long history and is not, of course, new with Tacitus. It had developed as one of several ways that an historian wins credibility by the avoidance of omniscience and was a recognition too that in many matters – especially knowledge of characters' motives – certainty was impossible.[155] Yet in Tacitus' works, alternatives also suggest that the truth is almost always to be found beneath the characters' professions.[156] The last can be

---

[149] See Tac. *Hist.* II.70.3; cf. III.61.2 where soldiers exaggerate the number of the enemy to cover up their loss.   [150] *Hist.* I.29.1; 41. 2 (Galba); *Ann.* II.73.4.

[151] *Hist.* II.83.1 ('maiora credi de absentibus'); *Ann.* II.24.4; 82.1 ('cunctaque ut ex longinquo aucta in deterius adferebantur'); III.44.1.

[152] *Hist.* 1.34.2 where false accusations are accepted by the *incuriosi* but recognised as invented by others; 1.90.3; II.90.2; *Ann.* II.39.3 ('apud inperitissimi cuiusque promptas aures'); XIV.58.3. For the gullibility of the mob towards rumours, see Shatzman, *Latomus* 33 (1974) 575–7.

[153] *Ann.* III.19.2: 'adeo maxima quaeque ambigua sunt, dum alii quoquo modo audita pro compertis habent, alii uera in contrarium uertunt, et gliscit utrumque posteritate.' Cf. Livy, XXI.32.7: 'fama ... qua incerta in maius uero ferri solent'.

[154] *Hist.* III.54.1: 'prohibiti per ciuitatem sermones, eoque plures ac, si liceret, uere narraturi, quia uetabantur, atrociora uulgauerant.' Cf. *Ann.* II.39.3 where suppression assists rumour, especially among the unintelligent.

[155] See App. IV.

[156] In certain parts of his work, for example, the reign of Tiberius in the *Annals*, the contrast between surface and reality is so strong as to be a leitmotif: see Ryberg, *TAPA* 73 (1942) 383–404, esp. 385; she has also demonstrated that

seen, *mutatis mutandis*, as a variation on Thucydides' contrast between surface and reality.[157] Moreover, this type of inquiry has similarities to Dionysius' view of Theopompus who was able 'in every action not only to see and express the things evident to most people, but also to examine even the unseen causes of actions and the emotions of the souls of those committing the actions – a thing not easy for the many to know'.[158] Like that earlier historian who also wrote of autocrats, Tacitus 'inquired' below the surface and into men's hearts. He was careful, however, to maintain the formal distance (as Theopompus may also have[159]) by giving these observations usually as only one possibility, and they are presented – by phrases such as 'it is too little established' or 'it has not been discovered' – as the historian's attempts to get at the facts.[160] They serve as a constant reminder of the historian's attempts to probe beneath the surface, and to inquire into the truth behind the appearances of domestic policies at Rome. One can see that this entire approach is the reaction of history to a society where truth was concealed or unknown: in this way Tacitus' approach, in which uncertainty abounds, and in which truth itself is ambiguous or twisted, mirrors perfectly the closed society it narrates.[161]

3. IMPROVING THE PAST

Although it is true that after Thucydides contemporary history was the dominant form of ancient historiography, Herodotus was by no means forgotten, nor did Thucydides, despite his best efforts and manifest scorn, succeed in preventing later historians from writing

    this conflict is found again in Nero's reign; for a full list of alternatives see Whitehead, *Latomus* 38 (1979) 474-95, and for the concentration of alternative explanations at certain points – the death of Agrippina, the great fire of 64, and the Pisonian conspiracy – see ibid. 495. Develin, *Antichthon* 17 (1983) 87-94 argues that the technique can be found for virtually every character in Tacitus' work.

[157] See n. 25 above.   [158] D. Hal. *Pomp.* 6 (II.394-6 Usher).

[159] M. A. Flower, *Theopompus of Chios* 71-90 shows how Theopompus' moral judgements were built into the narrative.

[160] See, e.g., *Hist.* II.42.1; *Ann.* I.5.3. The formal maintenance was necessary to guard against charges of malice: see below, pp. 173f. See also Pauw, *ActClass* 23 (1980) 83-95 on the use of impersonal expressions.

[161] See Luce, in *Past Persp.* 143-57 on the difficulty of knowing Tacitus' own opinions.

non-contemporary history.[162] Not only did the ancients themselves see the two historians as the founders and the best practitioners of the genre; they also did not completely abandon non-contemporary history simply because one might write contemporary history more accurately.[163] To be sure, the preference seems to have been for the new,[164] but a sufficient number of Greek and Roman historians assayed non-contemporary history to enable it to continue as a viable alternative to contemporary history. Moreover, Ephorus first demonstrated that one need not choose between the two, and although one's reasons for combining the two might have differed, we can nevertheless posit a continuous tradition from Ephorus to Ammianus of writers who chose to combine contemporary and non-contemporary history.

It is difficult to establish whether or not a methodology for non-contemporary history existed or, if it existed, was consistently applied. In his investigation into the past, Herodotus, as we saw, had a hierarchy of epistemological factors such as eyewitness, inquiry, reasoned conjecture and so forth.[165] Thucydides, however, was inconsistent in his attitude towards the more distant past and its discoverability. He begins the Archaeology with the claim that it was 'impossible' to discover clearly events before the Peloponnesian War and things yet more ancient.[166] As he progresses, however, he becomes more confident, and by the end of the Archaeology there is a certain surety in the results achieved.[167] When Thucydides further states that a fundamental problem in

---

[162] It was once popular to emphasise Herodotus' isolation from the tradition (Momigliano, *Secondo Contributo* 32–3; id., *Classical Foundations* 46, where he argues that Herodotus' influence can only be perceived indirectly); against this view see Riemann, *Das herodoteische Geschichtswerk in der Antike*; Murray, *CQ* 22 (1972) 200–13; still valuable is Jacoby, *RE* Suppl. II, 504–20.

[163] Luce, *CPh* 84 (1989) 25–7 points out that non-contemporary history was preferable for some writers because they could be above suspicion of bias, and hence not have their motives called into question.

[164] Livy, *praef.* 4; cf. D. Hal. *A. R.* 1.4.1.   [165] Above, p. 67.

[166] Thuc. 1.1.3: τὰ γὰρ πρὸ αὐτῶν καὶ τὰ ἔτι παλαίτερα σαφῶς μὲν εὑρεῖν διὰ χρόνου πλῆθος ἀδύνατα ἦν. To what affairs the words τὰ πρὸ αὐτῶν and τὰ ἔτι παλαίτερα refer has been the subject of much discussion (Gomme, *HCT* 1. ad loc.; cf. Hornblower, *CT* 1.56 on the τὰ παλαιά of 1.20.1). I think Thucydides wants to say that it was difficult to 'know precisely', not merely 'know', the events of the past. What he means by 'precisely' is clear from 1.22.4, where τὸ σαφές means the way *he* has been able to write a contemporary history. In other words, it is impossible to write of ancient events a history of the sort he will write for the Peloponnesian War.

[167] Connor, *Thucydides* 27–32.

examining non-contemporary history is that men receive accounts of the past without testing them (1.20.1, cf. 20.3), he leaves open the possibility at least that a testing of the sort he has just performed could reveal certain important aspects of the past. Yet when he goes on to say that people always marvel at past events and that the things of the past cannot be tested because of the intervening time (1.21.1), he seems to have returned to the impossibility of discovering the truth about the past. But he there suggests that if one follows the indications (τεκμήρια) in the way that he has done, one will not err in one's calculations (1.21.1). The method in the Archaeology relies on legal and logical terminology, impersonally presented: probability (εἰκός); evidence (σημεῖον, μαρτύριον); reasoning (εἰκάζειν); and examination (σκοπεῖν).[168]

Ephorus, in a passage briefly treated above, claimed in his preface that those who speak in detail about the present are believed, whereas the opposite is true for past affairs, 'since we assume that it is not probable that all of the deeds or a majority of the speeches would be remembered because of the great distance in time.'[169] He seems therefore also to have expressed scant hope in his ability to recover the details of the past. Knowing too little of his method, we cannot say whether he was inconsistent as Thucydides was, but Strabo praised Ephorus for detailed arguments on the foundations of cities, and quotes Ephorus as saying that it is his custom to examine carefully matters which are incorrect or wrongly interpreted.[170] Strabo also informs us that Ephorus, in a discussion of the ideal constitution and what cities may have borrowed what customs from others, noted that one ought not to infer conditions of long ago from what exists now, since societies have been known to change to customs opposite from what they once were.[171] This

[168] Connor, op. cit. (n. 167) 28–9. The caution that seems so much a part of this disquisition about past history is nowhere visible in Thucydides' striking foray into non-contemporary history, the digression in VI.54–9 on the tyrannicides, where even details of past history are given with confidence.

[169] *FGrHist* 70 F 9; as mentioned above (n. 33), Ephorus' καθ' ἡμᾶς must mean 'in our time' and τὰ παλαιά must refer (as in Thucydides) to pre-contemporary affairs. It seems likely that Ephorus is explaining why the non-contemporary portions of his work (Books I–XV) lacked the same fullness of detail as the contemporary parts.

[170] *FGrHist* 70 F 31b, F 122; cf. F 199 for a similar use of inscriptions. On his method in general, Schepens, in *Historiographia Antiqua* 105–12.

[171] *FGrHist* 70 F 149=Str. X.4.17: οὔτε γὰρ ἐκ τῶν νῦν καθεστηκότων τὰ παλαιὰ τεκμηριοῦσθαι δεῖν.

suggests, on the one hand, a far different attitude towards the past from that of Thucydides; yet Ephorus' practice, on the other hand, must have shown no reluctance to argue from the details when he felt he had reliable ones, and no concern that a real gap existed between current times and the distant past.

Polybius elucidates no methodology for the writing of non-contemporary history, and only a few remarks give any idea of his attitude. Based on his discussion of the writing of contemporary history (above), and the obvious disdain he has for Timaeus, it is clear that Polybius had little patience with book learning.[172] He admits that the reading of memoirs forms a part of historiography, but he assigns it the smallest role and gives no elaboration of its methodology, unlike his exposition of autopsy and inquiry.[173] An early remark in the *Histories* seems to confirm this dismissal of non-contemporary history: in the explanation of the starting point of his work, he says that in Greek affairs he has chosen the 140th Olympiad (220 BC), because it follows on the memoirs of Aratus, and it embraced the times in which Polybius himself lived, so that he was present at some affairs and had eyewitness testimony for others. To have gone back beyond this period, he says, would have been 'to write hearsay from hearsay' (ὡς ἀκοὴν ἐξ ἀκοῆς γράφειν), and he would be safe neither in his judgements nor his assertions.[174] Elsewhere Polybius says that if one writes about foundations of colonies and cities (i.e., really ancient events), then one either must repeat what has already been said and treated sufficiently well, or pass another's work off as one's own (IX.2.1–3). Yet Polybius begins his own work by re-writing the history of the First Punic War, and in that account he does not proceed as if it is all hearsay; he seems confident in both judgements and assertions. Even if we limit the intent of Polybius' remark to Greek affairs (which is not the way it reads), and argue that there was no trustworthy equivalent such as Fabius or Philinus, it is evident at once that this is untrue – there were Aratus' memoirs, and Polybius will not accuse them of containing merely ἀκοή.[175] Later, in Book XII, in a spirited defence of Aristotle against Timaeus on the foundation of Epizephyria Locris (a

---

[172] For Polybius' inconsistency, Walbank, *Polybius* 73–4.
[173] Pol. XII.25g.1–28a.10.   [174] Pol. IV.2.1–3, with Walbank, *HCP* I.450.
[175] They were valuable because Aratus was an eyewitness and participant, and himself did not write 'hearsay from hearsay' (cf. II.40.4); so too Fabius and Philinus for the same reasons (I.14). See also XII.4c.3 for the value of eyewitness testimony.

time, of course, much earlier than the First Punic War), Polybius is again confident in judgement and assertion.[176] And Polybius tells his readers not to be surprised if he treats past events in addition to contemporary events, since they are necessary for a proper understanding of the origins of the enmity between Carthage and Rome.[177] It seems, therefore, that the prohibition on non-contemporary history could be ignored when the author believed he had superior information.

Even if we cannot speak of a consistently applied method for non-contemporary history, there are some consistent approaches that can be discerned. As we saw in the treatment of contemporary history, autopsy and inquiry of eyewitnesses was acknowledged to be the most reliable way of ascertaining information. By definition, however, a non-contemporary history lacked eyewitnesses; the historian therefore had to turn to oral tradition or the writings of predecessors.

The inquiry into oral tradition would include family lore and local tradition. The former would be preserved by aristocratic clans in both Greece and Rome, while the latter would be those traditions, stories, legends, aetiologies, and such things as were accepted more or less by the members of the city-state. (Here we would also place monuments without inscriptions, to which some local or national story attached itself.) The inquiry into oral tradition must have been the predominant feature of all the early historians, both Greek and Roman, since there is no evidence that Athens, Sparta, and the other leading city-states of Greece maintained ancient records of their achievements.[178] We can see this best in Herodotus' history, where the narrator presents the work as a record of what the various peoples (both Greek and barbarian) 'say' about their past.[179] These are usually identified with nations

---

[176] Pol. XII.5.1–5.
[177] Pol. I.12.8–9; III.7.4–7. On treatment of early times as background to one's theme, see Avenarius, *LS* 80–1.
[178] *Pace* D. Hal. *Thuc.* 5, written records are not likely to have been available to the early historians: see Jacoby, *Atthis* 178; *contra*, Pritchett, *Dionysius of Halicarnassus: On Thucydides* 54.
[179] The only reference to a written source in Herodotus is the mention of Hecataeus ἐν τοῖσι λόγοισι (VI.137.1); a list of Herodotus' source-citations in Jacoby, *RE* Suppl. II, 398–9. For oral tradition see Murray, in *Achaemenid History* II.93–115; cf. Evans, *Herodotus. Explorer of the Past* 89–146 who postulates Greek 'remembrancers', people whose function it is in an oral society to record what is of value in the community; for some doubts see Thomas, in *Vermittlung und Tradierung von Wissen* 225–6.

(Egyptians, Persians, Libyans) or Greek cities (Athenians, Spartans, Corinthians, Samians), although sometimes it is possible to identify individual family traditions. What these people or nations 'say', together with Herodotus' reaction to it, is itself the validation presented by Herodotus for winning the reader's belief. This, after all, is the 'display of his inquiry' referred to in the preface.[180] Similarly, Herodotus' (perhaps slightly younger) contemporary Antiochus of Syracuse claimed likewise in his *On Italy* to write up from ancient accounts (λόγοι) those that were clearest and most persuasive.[181] We may assume something similar for Pherecydes in his *Genealogies* and Hellanicus in his *Attic History*, who treated events in the early history of Athens, since these early historians simply had nothing other than tradition (familial or local) and the poets on which to base their histories.[182] So too for those historians who wrote of the foundings (κτίσεις) of cities,[183] including Rome, since whatever we presume the Pontifical Chronicle to have looked like and contained, it will not have sufficed by itself for the writing of a history of Rome.[184] Fabius Pictor and the other Hellenophone historians of Rome must have supplemented whatever documentary material they possessed with traditions from noble families and the generally accepted traditions of the Romans themselves.[185] According to Cicero, Cato in his *Origins* made reference to an old Roman custom at banquets of singing the praises and virtues of distinguished men, and he may have cited this procedure as some form of

---

[180] See above, pp. 6–8.
[181] *FGrHist* 555 F 2: Ἀντίοχος Ξενοφάνεος τάδε συνέγραψε περὶ Ἰταλίης ἐκ τῶν ἀρχαίων λόγων τὰ πιστότατα καὶ σαφέστατα. Whether by λόγοι he meant oral or written traditions is uncertain, but the fact that his was the first attempt (Jacoby, *Komm.* IIIb (Text). 486ff.) makes it more likely that he was referring to oral tradition.
[182] Thomas, *Oral Tradition and Written Record* 181–95.
[183] See Timpe, *ANRW* I. 2, 942–4; bibliography at 935–6 n. 18; id. in *Vergangenheit in mündlicher Überlieferung* 278–9.
[184] For the Pontifical Chronicle see Introduction n. 124.
[185] Scholars view Fabius' activity for the early history of Rome, and his influence on the subsequent tradition quite differently, some seeing him as a collector of oral traditions, some doubting that he did anything other than restate and possibly correct only in the details already existing Greek tradition about Rome; some think he shaped all subsequent tradition, others doubt that any one man, even with the *auctoritas* of Fabius, could have done that: for different views with earlier bibliography see Cornell, in *Past Persp.* 68–9; Timpe, *ANRW* I. 2, 932–48; id., in *Vergangenheit in mündlicher Überlieferung* 274–81; von Ungern-Sternberg, ibid., 243–50.

validation for the material on early history that he included.[186] Local tradition must have played an important role in Books II and III of the *Origins* where Cato gave the origins of the Italian city-states.[187] Unfortunately, with the exception of Herodotus' work, we do not have a single history surviving which is a non-contemporary history fashioned from oral tradition, and we cannot thus be certain how early events were validated.[188]

Some historians, we know, used monuments as validation for the oral tradition that they reported. These, of course, might be subject to great freedom in interpretation.[189] Herodotus used the inspection of monuments to validate or expand the account of the Egyptian priests.[190] Thucydides seems to have ignored this type of argumentation, except in the digression on Harmodius and Aristogeiton.[191] Timaeus used monuments just as he had used inscriptions.[192] Even Polybius used monuments for non-contemporary history. He tells his readers not to be surprised by the accuracy of his numbers for Hannibal's forces, because he took the numbers from the stele (erected

---

[186] Cato, *HRR* F 118; as a possible source citation see ref. in Schröder, *Das erste Buch der Origines* 48.

[187] See Timpe, *AAPat* 83 (1970-1) 5-33; Astin, *Cato the Censor* 211-39. See also below at n.195.   [188] For a possibility with Cato see below, n. 195.

[189] On the use of monuments in historiography see Wiseman, *Historiography and Imagination* 37-48; Gabba, *JRS* 71 (1981) 60-1; Rawson, *RCS* 582-98.

[190] Hdt. II.99-146, *passim*. We must note, however, a fundamental difference in the way that Herodotus refers to foreign and native monuments: he does not, as a rule, invoke autopsy for Greek matters as he does for foreign ones. Herodotus claims only once in unmistakable terms to have seen something in Greece, and this is the 'Cadmean letters' in Thebes (V.59), a polemical passage attacking Hecataeus and Dionysius of Miletus (see *FGrHist* 1 F 20; 687 F 1). But in general he does not say 'I went to Delphi' but rather 'this dedication at Delphi is worth seeing'. We may state it almost as a rule that an historian never invokes autopsy for his native country, unless he is claiming to make a substantial improvement in the record: as Herodotus had no one to better in Books VII-IX, there was no need to assume the pose of the earlier books. An excellent example of the difference in procedure between native and non-native writer is the contrast in the way Dionysius and Livy discuss the features of early Rome. The former, writing for Greeks, claims to have seen many things there (see, e.g., *A. R.* 1.32.2; 37.2; 68.1-2; II.23.5; VII.72.12; 72.18) and emphasises his autopsy at appropriate points, whereas Livy, writing for Romans, has no need to do this.

[191] Thuc. VI.54.7 with Dover, *HCT* IV.324-5.

[192] See, for example, *FGrHist* 566 F 26 (=Diod. XIII.82.6), on the luxury of the Acragantines.

by Hannibal himself) that he had seen at Cape Licinium.[193] Dionysius in turn could challenge Polybius' story of the Pallanteum in a vigorous denial that is reminiscent of Herodotus on the moving island of Chemmis. Polybius had said that the Pallanteum was named after Pallas, whose father had built a tomb on the hill, but Dionysius retorts that he saw no such monument nor anything of the sort.[194]

For the Romans, our evidence for their use of monuments in the writing of history is more circumstantial but nevertheless convincing. Cicero tells us that Cato was a great student of tombstones, and it is evident that they, along with inscriptions and other monuments, figured prominently in filling out the history of the Italian city-states in *Origins* II and III.[195] There is also some evidence that the use of monuments was common among the Annalists, who attempted to fill out the past, not (one must add) always with a concern for accuracy. Cassius Hemina had a genuine interest in the topography, cults, and monuments of Rome, Latium, and even Greece.[196] Similarly, L. Calpurnius Piso Frugi discussed monuments and such matters as the location of Romulus' asylum.[197] And the influence of this type of research can still be detected in our surviving histories.[198] In Ammianus we see an interest in monuments when he describes and quotes from the obelisks that he himself had seen in Egyptian Thebes.[199]

---

[193] Pol. III.33.17-18. Livy mentions this monument (XXVIII.46.16), but with no sense that it is somehow a privileged source.

[194] D. Hal. *A. R.* I.32.2, cf. Hdt. II.73.1; 156.2. In a similar way, Dionysius vouches for the fertility of Italy by claiming to have seen three harvests in one year (1.37.2).

[195] Cic. *Sen.* 21; cf. Peter, *HRR* I.CXLIII-IV for other testimonia on Cato's investigations; cf. Chassignet, *Caton* xxviii-xxix.

[196] Rawson, *RCS* 246-54. Hemina may even have criticised armchair historians: ibid. 255-6 where she suggests that Hemina's F 28 'homo mere litterosus' may be 'an attack on a merely bookish man, as opposed to a practical politician or soldier', and offers Timaeus as a possible target.   [197] Rawson, *RCS* 261.

[198] Wiseman, op. cit. (n.189) 39-44; cf. Rawson, *RCS* 582-98; E. Badian, in W. Eder, ed. *Staat und Staatlichkeit in der frühen römischen Republik* (Stuttgart 1990) 216. Though it is an oft-criticised example, we should mention here too Livy's sole statement of autopsy, of the monument of the Scipios at Liternum that had recently been destroyed by a storm (XXXVIII.56.3-4, on which there is a monumental bibliography; I find especially good the discussion in Luce, *Livy* 92-104, 142-4). Atypically, Livy's autopsy does not improve the record; if anything, it is a complaint that autopsy can contribute nothing to the problem.

[199] Amm. XVII.4.6. One must always be careful in evaluating Ammianus because he is a Greek writing with some consciousness of that tradition. On his 'Greekness' as distinguishing, see Ch. V nn. 196-8.

Improving the past

Thus the evidence is not overwhelming, but it may still be suggested that a Herodotean interest in monuments existed also among the Romans and was similarly used to make inferences and observations about the past.

Much more common, of course, is a history based on an already existing written tradition. The ancients themselves recognised that there was a better chance of accuracy if some type of written record was involved. In his polemical essay against Apion, Josephus compares the antiquity of the Eastern tradition with that of the Greeks, and he asserts that the Egyptians, Chaldaeans, and Phoenicians have the oldest and most permanent tradition of memory, whereas by contrast, the Greeks constantly refute one another with alternative versions of events. This is the result, he says, of the Greeks' lack of written records.[200] Livy, at the opening of his Book VI, claims that the events to be treated from here on are 'clearer and more certain' because they are now based on written records, the 'only trustworthy place for the safe-keeping of the memory of history'.[201] The equation which Josephus and Livy make of 'written = reliable' may go back to Ephorus: if an early passage from Diodorus[202] is correctly identified as coming from Ephorus, it will be Ephorus who first gave a methodological defence for the use of written records and their reliability.[203] That historian had treated the invention of letters in his *On Inventions*, and seems to have explored the connection between writing and reliability.[204] Thus it may be Ephorus who suggested that, in the absence of a contemporary written record, accuracy and certainty were impossible.[205]

Yet one thing that is rather strikingly absent from the ancient historians' narrative is the systematic use of documents or archives.[206] To be sure, historians recognised the value of certain types of evidence other than oral report and inquiry of eyewitnesses. By the end of the fifth century the engraving of inscriptions had become, at least at Athens, commonplace.[207] Slightly later, historical documents began to be collected,

---

[200] Jos. *c. Ap.* 1.8–10; 19–23.
[201] Livy, VI.1.2: 'litterae . . . una custodia fidelis memoriae rerum gestarum', with Kraus' commentary, 85–6. [202] Diod. 1.9.5 = *FGrHist* 70 F 105.
[203] Jacoby, *FGrHist Komm*. II. c. 63–4; cf. Schepens, in *Historiographia Antiqua* 106–7. [204] Schepens, ibid. 107.
[205] Note Herodotus' analogous procedure with oral tradition, where he cannot say when no tradition exists: I.49; VII.60.1; VIII.128.1; 133.
[206] Momigliano, *Contributo* 67–106; id., *Classical Foundations* 62–7. Grant, *Greek and Roman Historians* 34–6 claims that historians did not use documents because the archives were poorly organised, but this, if true, is only a partial explanation. [207] See Thomas, op. cit. (n. 182) 34–94.

and constitutions were assembled by Aristotle and his school; Craterus put together a collection of decrees, and Polemon in the second century was fond of collecting inscriptions.[208] Polybius tells us that the investigation of documents was a particular interest of Timaeus, but he claims too that no one really has any interest in this type of history.[209] A polemical statement, to be sure; yet with few exceptions, the ancient historians do not feature documents prominently in their histories. This rarity has several causes. The first is that historiography, as it developed from Herodotus, was about great deeds and the men who performed them. The documentary evidence that existed was of only limited assistance in this matter. Thucydides includes the peace treaties of 421 BC in Book V,[210] but no documentary evidence can have provided him with the material for the narrative of the Sicilian expedition that we possess.[211] Not surprisingly, documents played a larger role among the antiquarians, where a pleasurable and exciting narrative was not expected.[212] Second, documents were not, so far as we can tell, the disembodied witnesses that they sometimes seem to be for moderns. It is true that documents came eventually to be recognised as witnesses of a sort, and written testimony comes to replace oral testimony in the Athenian courts by the time of Demosthenes.[213] But a document's reliability was based on the character of the witness himself,[214] and a witness was for the Athenians an advocate rather than an unbiased party who could be cross-examined and refuted.[215] Documents, therefore,

---

[208] On Aristotle's contribution to history, see Bloch, *HSCP* Suppl. 1 (1940) 355-7; Huxley, *GRBS* 14 (1973) 271-86; Hornblower, *Greek Historiography* 33-4; on Craterus, *FGrHist* 342 T 1; Polemon, *FHG* III.108. On archives see Thomas, op. cit. (n.182) 73-94.

[209] Pol. XII.25d.1-e.7. Polybius is unfair here, since he conceals the crucial fact that the Polybian form of historiography, based on experience and autopsy, is impossible for non-contemporary history (which was a large part of Timaeus' history), and that 'documentary' investigations were the only possible way to improve the record: Walbank, *SP* 273.

[210] Thuc. V.23-4; 47. See further Hornblower, *Thucydides* 88-91.

[211] As Hornblower, op. cit. (n.210) 138-9 notes, there is no evidence to support a prohibition on the inclusion of documents or inscriptions in historical narrative.

[212] Momigliano, *Contributo* 67-106; Rawson, *Intellectual Life* 238-40 on Varro. It is not coincidence that neither the works of Craterus or Polemon (above, n. 208) were narrative histories.   [213] Todd, in *Nomos* 29 n. 15, with reff. there.

[214] Humphreys, *History and Anthropology* 1 (1985) 313-69, esp. 350-6.

[215] Todd, op. cit. (n.213) 23-31, that μαρτύς always has the sense of 'advocate', not just 'witness'.

like all witnesses, would support whoever called them. Third, there were techniques in antiquity for refuting written evidence as we can see already in Aristotle's *Rhetoric*, where several strategies are presented for arguing against even written laws and contracts when defending one's client.[216] Documents and written materials in general were thus not of a quality fundamentally different from any other type of evidence. They were not viewed as a source of information at once immediate and dispassionate. They were, like any witness, to be used to build a case.[217] In that sense, they could be summoned when one was attacking or defending an already existing tradition. Theopompus' famous claim to have disproved the authenticity of the Peace of Callias by exposing its anachronistic writing (perhaps the best known example of this type of citation) was part of a larger polemic against the Athenian claims of their glorious history.[218] Similarly, Timaeus based his refutation of Aristotle's account of the origin of the Epizephyrian Locrians on his own examination of the original treaty between colony and mother-city.[219]

Despite this occasional use of non-literary material, it is fair to say that the 'methodology' of non-contemporary history was to consult the tradition, what previous writers had handed down. We have no indications that a writer concentrating on the past was expected to re-inquire into earlier matters in any way other than reading his predecessors. The younger Pliny distinguishes between contemporary and non-contemporary history solely by the nature of the inquiry and the temptations to bias:

> Shall I write on older topics, those already written up by others? The inquiry has been done, but comparing accounts is burdensome (*parata inquisitio sed onerosa collatio*). Or shall I treat recent times, which no one has treated? In that case, one receives little thanks, and offences are serious.[220]

[216] On arguing against laws, *Rhet.* 1.15, 1375a 22–b25; on contracts ('contracts are credible in so far as the signatories and custodians of them are') see *Rhet.* 1.15, 1376a 33–b 30.
[217] That is why Sallust places responsibility for his African geography on the authors themselves, even though it is based on native records: 'fides eius rei penes auctores erit' (*Jug.* 17.7); on the *topos*, see Paul, *Commentary* 74.
[218] *FGrHist* 115 F 154; W. R. Connor, *Theopompus and Fifth-Century Athens* (Princeton 1968) 78–89.
[219] *FGrHist* 566 F 12, which Polybius tries to refute by the appeal to the *epichorioi*: see App. IV §2. [220] Pliny, *ep.* v.8.12.

In a similar way, Diodorus refers to the effort involved in combing through his sources, and Dio too at the outset of his early history of Rome states that he has read all the relevant material, and made an appropriate selection from it.[221] One writing about older events, then, was expected to make a study of previous works on the subject, and to compare these, no doubt, to discover (by whatever means) what was the more reliable narrative.[222] But his guide, above all, had to be what already existed in the tradition.

The writer of a non-contemporary history, therefore, was not as free as the historian of his own times to shape the tradition (since it was already established),[223] and it is important to note that no ancient historian – not even a Polybius or Thucydides – takes the radical step of tearing the whole edifice down and starting from the beginning.[224] It is true that an historian may reject this or that detail, but he does not abandon the framework already established by his predecessors. This is why, to take one example, Quintus Curtius remarks that he reports more than he believes: he wants to show himself a reliable and knowledgeable recorder of the tradition.[225] The inability to reject or even separate a tradition into its component parts can be seen when Curtius, confronted by the enormous size of the plunder at Alexander's taking of Persepolis, can only say that unless one doubts all the other details, it is necessary to believe this one too.[226] He is not abdicating responsibility, but rather fulfilling the duty of a faithful recorder. At the end of the

---

[221] Diod. 1.3.5-8; Dio, 1.1.2: ⟨'Ἀνέγνων μὲν *uel sim.*⟩ πάντα ὡς εἰπεῖν τὰ περὶ αὐτῶν τισι γεγραμμένα, συνέγραψα δὲ οὐ πάντα ἀλλ' ὅσα ἐξέκρινα. For more on labour see Ch. III §3. Cf. Pol. XII.25f.1 (above, p. 72) where the reading of earlier histories is the least important part of inquiry.

[222] Perhaps applying the yardstick of probability or partiality; Brunt, *Studies in Greek History and Thought* 185-6 has a good brief discussion.

[223] Schwartz, *RE* II, 914 = *GG* 124: 'Wie es für die antike Literatur, ja für das ganze antike Geistesleben gilt, dass das, was einmal geworden und geschaffen ist, auch der Folgezeit die Wege und Formen des Denkens und Produzierens vorschreibt.'

[224] In the Archaeology, Thucydides follows the tradition, rationalising it or changing it only in detail. Nissen, *Kritische Untersuchungen* 80 is interesting as a general evaluation: 'Und dann ist auch daran zu erinnern, dass die Quellenbenutzung im Altertum und Mittelalter... aus dem Grunde allein überhaupt möglich war, weil die Vorgänger in wesentlich denselben politischen religiösen socialen und litterarischen Lebensanschauungen geschrieben hatte wie ihre Nachfolger.' [225] Q. C. IX.1.34; cf. X.10.11.

[226] Q. C. v.6.9: 'ceterum aut de aliis quoque dubitabimus aut crederemus in huius urbis gaza fuisse c et xx milia talentum'.

Anabasis, for example, Arrian gives several versions of Alexander's death, some of which he clearly thinks are wrong, stating, 'I have recorded these things so that I should not appear ignorant of the fact that they are said, rather than that I think they are persuasive in the telling.'[227] The ancient historian does not seek a solution to the discrepancy, nor is he expected to; he need only demonstrate that he has recorded the tradition: that was his investigation.[228]

Written material may be divided into privileged and non-privileged. The former would be writings which are not (or are presented as not) accessible to all, such as sacred writings in temples or royal records, or (in certain societies) archives; the latter would have no sense of exclusivity, and would be accessible to all who could read them: they include documents in public places, inscriptions with or without accompanying monuments, and, most commonly of all, written histories.

The claim to have access to a privileged or secret written tradition seems largely confined to the history of non-Greek lands, where the author presents his account as resting ultimately on a native history or chronicle. Ctesias explicitly adopted this approach, and claimed to base the non-contemporary portion of his *Persica* on 'the royal records in which the Persians had recorded their ancient deeds.'[229] Such a procedure may already have been used by Hecataeus of Miletus or Xanthus of Lydia,[230] and it can be seen clearly in Book II of Herodotus, where the

---

[227] Arr. *Anab.* VII.27.3.

[228] The use of variant versions, sometimes with the addition of the name of the particular author responsible for the account, is far more common in non-contemporary history and is part of this recording of the tradition. See App. IV.

[229] *FGrHist* 688 F 5: ἐκ τῶν βασιλικῶν διφθερῶν, ἐν αἷς οἱ Πέρσαι τὰς παλαιὰς πράξεις ... εἶχον συντεταγμένας. For Ctesias' sources for his contemporary portion, see above p. 87.

[230] For Hecataeus see Hdt. II.143.1 = *FGrHist* 1 F 300. If Herodotus' story of Hecataeus before the priests at Thebes comes from his predecessor's own work, then Hecataeus may have appealed to the priests as his ultimate authority; for some problems with the episode, however, see Fehling, *Herodotus* 77–86; S. West, *JHS* 111 (1991) 145–52. For Xanthus, von Fritz, *Griechische Geschichtsschreibung* I.97 assumes that a phrase in Nicolaus' history (ἐν τοῖς βασιλικοῖς οὐκ ἀναγράφεται, *FGrHist* 90 F 44 §7) comes from Xanthus of Lydia and is evidence 'dass Xanthos solche Aufzeichnungen als Zeugnisse für seine Darstellung angeführt hat'. Caution is necessary when dealing with the fragments of Nicolaus (see Toher, *CA* 8 (1989) 159–72) but if von Fritz is correct, and if Xanthus is earlier than Herodotus (see Introd. n. 28), Xanthus may have introduced this appeal to written sources into Greek historiography of foreign lands.

narrative of Egyptian pharaohs rests on the list read out to him by the 'most learned' priests of Heliopolis.[231] Indeed, there are rather a large number of places where priests play a role as preserver of traditions, and this motif demands a somewhat fuller treatment.

Two types of remarks centred around priests may be distinguished. The first is the Herodotean type where priests are cited for special information, or for the correction of other (usually Herodotus') priests. Hecataeus of Abdera laid claim to the priestly records of Egypt to refute Herodotus, but he used Herodotus extensively, giving only a more rationalised approach to some of the material: most revealingly he follows Herodotus faithfully for the historical section.[232] Diodorus in his account of Egypt, one largely dependent on this same Hecataeus, made clear that his account of Egypt came from his conversations with 'many priests' and 'not a few ambassadors from Ethiopia', with whom he discussed and refuted the accounts of previous historians.[233] This is hardly to be taken literally, since Diodorus' explicit statements of autopsy and inquiry add little of substance to his account, which is quite traditional in its essentials.[234] In the second half of the first century AD,

---

[231] Hdt. II.3.1, where the priests of Heliopolis are called λογιώτατοι. It is nevertheless curious that Herodotus chose the priests as the spokesmen for their Egyptian history, since cult, not history, was the concern of Egyptian priests: see A. B. Lloyd, *Herodotus. Book II. Introduction* (Leiden 1975) 89–113, esp. 95. If it is the case that Egyptian priests were not expert in history, one of two consequences follows: either the invocation of the priests was a *topos* in later authors designed to win credence for an improved narrative; or later accounts of Egypt dwelt more on its cult and culture than on its history. (A third possibility, that the priests became better informed about their history after Herodotus, is not attractive.)

[232] Murray, *JEA* 56 (1970) 150–2; id., *CQ* 22 (1972) 207. On the priestly records see *FGrHist* 264 F 2. A balanced view of Hecataeus of Abdera in Fraser, *Ptolemaic Alexandria* 1.497ff. Fraser says that Hecataeus 'did not necessarily make the best of his opportunities': this seems to be a persistent feature of writers on Egypt. More likely, audience expectations were paramount, and this was a way of placing oneself in a certain tradition; see Momigliano, *Alien Wisdom* 8; cf. Bickerman, *CPh* 47 (1952) 74 on local manufacture of Greek ethnologies; cf. Syme, *Tacitus* 1.126 (a slightly different context): 'A man's own experience might seem less attractive and convincing than what stood in the literary tradition, guaranteed by time and famous names.'

[233] Diod. III.11.3; this is the appeal to numbers (see App. IV §2). In the absence of any methodology about past history, the 'few/many' dichotomy is probably purely rhetorical, a need to explain yet another account of Egypt (could it go back to Hecataeus of Abdera refuting Herodotus?).

[234] Aside from a few monuments with implied autopsy, Diodorus personally vouches for only two things in Egypt: that he saw the Egyptians punish a

Improving the past

Apion of Oasis claimed that the priests pointed out to him the immortal ibis, thereby bettering Herodotus, who had only seen a picture of it.[235] The influence of the priests as authorities is so strong that we can see it even in Tacitus' narrative of Germanicus in Egypt, where an Egyptian priest expounds an inscription to the young general, showing the unbelievable extent of Rameses' army and empire.[236] Indeed the priests seem to have been busy at all times with tourists. We find it reported that Aristotle and Eudoxus said that they learned about the Nile floods from the priests; Heliodorus can cite things written in the 'holy books' (ἱεραὶ βίβλοι); and Aristeides reports that he learned the origin of Canopus' name from the priests themselves in Canopus.[237] The great use of this suggests that it is clearly the way one validates matters about Egypt.

A different use of this *topos* is the identification of the author himself as a priest: this is done always at the beginning of the work, and is, with one exception, confined to local history, either of foreign countries or of Greek city-states.[238] The former seems to be in the same tradition as the examples just given, i.e., to distinguish oneself in terms of reliability towards a Greek audience, in a way that would be immediately understandable given the traditions developed. Again, Egypt furnishes a good example. Manetho announced himself as a priest, perhaps of

---

Roman who had killed a cat, despite their fear of Rome (this to illustrate the renown in which the cat is held), 1.83.9; and he cites οἱ τὰς ἀναγραφὰς ἔχοντες for census figures at Alexandria (which he heard when there) that revealed 300,000 free men and that from this population, the king took more than 6,000 talents in revenue, XVII.52.6. (on the vouching for enormous numbers, see above, p. 83). There are some signs that Diodorus did little more than copy Hecataeus: see, e.g., the indication of time 'around the time of Ptolemy, son of Lagus' (1.46.7, certainly from Hecataeus who wrote then), and the weak tag of autopsy that Diodorus attaches to this, and compare especially the clear 'seventeen' of Hecataeus (1.46.8 = *FGrHist* 264 F 25) with the vague 'many' (ibid.) of Diodorus (so Fraser, op. cit. (n.232) 1.499–500).

[235] *FGrHist* 616 F 12; but as he also vouched for the story of Androcles and the lion (F 5) with his own autopsy, we are perhaps justified in assuming that no one was deceived by such sensationalist history. Apion also saw the shade of Homer and discovered his native country and parents (see App. II n. 20), but was too polite to reveal it.

[236] Tac. *Ann.* 11.60.3–4, again with a special source to vouch for high numbers.

[237] On Aristotle and Eudoxus, *FGrHist* 665 F 60(b); Heliodorus, *Aeth.* 11.28 = *FGrHist* 665 F 60(c); Aristeides, 665 F 68.

[238] The exception is Josephus in the *Jewish War*, discussed below, p. 111. As Meissner, *Historiker* 194 points out, not every priesthood in antiquity was a career; some were simply annual offices.

Heliopolis, who was translating the 'holy writings' (ἱερὰ γράμματα) of the Egyptians. Of course he assailed Herodotus, and of course he followed him.[239] Likewise, a certain Ptolemaios who wrote the deeds of the Egyptian kings mentioned that he was a priest of Mendes. Chairemon of Alexandria in the first century AD identified himself as a sacred scribe (ἱερογραμματεύς) and also cited the priests.[240] We find as well non-Egyptians presenting themselves as priests when introducing their work. The model here seems to have been Berossus of Babylon who wrote *Babylonian Matters* (Βαβυλωνιακά) in three books at the beginning of the third century BC.[241] He introduced himself as a priest of Baal who had access to the writings of many wise men, which embraced cosmogony and history, and which had been preserved with great care.[242] Berossus therefore presented himself in a way familiar to Greek readers: he emphasised his position and his access to ancient (and therefore reliable[243]) writings, now being translated for a Greek public.[244] The claim of priest is additionally justified because Berossus presented an introduction to Babylonian culture, not just history.[245] Here too the

---

[239] *FGrHist* 609 T 7a + FF 1, 10. It is not absolutely certain that he claimed he was from Heliopolis: Fraser, op. cit. (n.232) I.506. It is mentioned in the pseudonymous letter to Ptolemy (F 25) and if it is a fictitious addition, it will have been made, I think, because Herodotus says (II.3.1) that the Heliopolitans are the most reliable preservers of tradition.

[240] *FGrHist* 611 T 1 (Ptolemaios); 618 F 2 + T 6 (Chairemon); citing the priests, F 6.

[241] Berossus, Megasthenes, Hecataeus of Abdera, and Manetho each wrote in the early third century, each perhaps to assert the superiority of the culture they treated as part of the propaganda war of the Diadochs (so Murray, *CQ* 22 (1972) 207-10). Hecataeus wrote c. 320-315 BC (Murray, ibid.), Megasthenes under Seleucus (312-280 BC), Berossus, who identified himself as a contemporary of Alexander (680 T 1 + F1b(1)) c. 281 BC, and Manetho under Ptolemy I (305-283 BC). Murray, ibid. 209 suggests that Manetho is placed so confidently after Berossus that the former may have referred specifically in his work to the latter. Kuhrt, in ead. and Sherwin-White, *Hellenism in the East* 55-6 suggests that Berossus answered Hecataeus of Abdera.   [242] *FGrHist* 680 F 1.

[243] See App. IV §1.

[244] This technique becomes a favourite for literary forgers who claim to be 'translating' earlier works: cf., e.g., Bion of Proconnesus, *FGrHist* 332 T 3; his date is uncertain: Jacoby, *Komm.* IIIb Suppl. (Text) 610-11. For more examples see Speyer, *Die literarische Fälschung* 21-5 and 46-7 (eyewitness accounts of Troy), cf. 75: 'Ob man ... von Fälschung oder eher von Mystifikation und literarischem Spiel zu sprechen hat, lässt sich bei dem mangelhaften Zustand der Überlieferung kaum entscheiden.'

[245] Burstein, *Babyloniaca* 6-7 calls Berossus 'the model for all subsequent attempts by Hellenized non-Greeks to explain their culture to their Greek

Josephus of the *Antiquities* belongs, who claims to be a priest expounding Jewish ancestral custom, law, and history. It is worthwhile to point out that his claim resting on his priesthood would have made no impression on his Jewish audience, since 'priests were not especially renowned in Jewish tradition for their interpretation of the Holy Scriptures'. Rather, the expectations of his Greek audience are the decisive factor.[246]

In local history of Greek city-states there is only a little evidence but it all points in the same direction. The claim of 'priest' here seems to be allied not with that of Herodotus and the Egyptian priests, but rather to be bound up with the general concerns of Greek local history, specifically with matters of local cult and myth.[247] These too can be mysteries of a sort, and thus the priest presents himself as having access to privileged information. Cleidemus, whom Pausanias calls the oldest Atthidographer, was an exegete.[248] The evidence is somewhat more reliable for Philochorus since a verbatim quotation survives in which he refers to the priests as 'we', suggesting that he identified himself as one.[249] Finally, Photius records that Arrian in his *Bithynian History* introduced himself as a priest of Demeter and Kore, the city's protecting deities.[250] Not too much can be built on these scattered pieces of evidence, but it seems fairly likely that Greeks claiming to be priests do not do so for exactly the same reasons as non-Greeks introducing their foreign and frequently fabulous histories and cultures. Both,

---

neighbours', and he emphasises that Berossus, following Babylonian belief, wrote a history of culture, an account of Babylonian history and wisdom, with the former subordinate to the latter. Burstein additionally finds fault with Murray's attempt to place Berossus and Manetho in the Herodotean tradition; but cf. Kuhrt, op. cit. (n.241) 47–8 (for Berossus), and Armayor, *CB* 61 (1985) 7–10 (for Manetho).

[246] Josephus' claims: *c. Ap.* 1.54 (surprisingly not in the preface of the *A. J.*, although he does make reference there to his account of the Jewish war (1.4) where that information was contained). On the claim of translating sacred documents, *A. J.* 1.26. The quotation is from Rajak, *Josephus* 19, who already recognised that the claim 'served to give his non-Jewish readers the impression that their author had some special expertise' (18). Cohen, *Josephus in Galilee and Rome* 27 notes that Josephus' claims to be translating sacred texts should be seen in a line going back to Ctesias; but Ctesias was not promulgating 'wisdom literature' as Berossus and the others did. [247] See Ch. I n. 78.

[248] *FGrHist* 323 F 14. Jacoby at *Komm.* Suppl. iiib. 58 suggests that Cleidemus' *Atthis* was separate from the work that Athenaeus cites as ἐν τῷ ἐπιγραφομένῳ Ἐξηγητικῷ.

[249] *FGrHist* 328 F 67, quoted and discussed below, p. 194 n. 89.

[250] *FGrHist* 156 T 4a.

however, present themselves as having access to privileged information.[251]

This approach, though prevalent for foreign histories, is uncommon with those writing of Greece or Rome. Here, as we said above, an historian usually relies on the writings of predecessors, whether or not they are explicitly acknowledged. In bringing forward a new treatment of an old theme, the historian must nevertheless justify himself. Based on Livy's preface, it is sometimes stated that the historian who re-does a history justifies himself by a promise of greater accuracy or a finer style,[252] but this is not quite correct, since Livy actually says that new historians always *believe* that they will outdo their predecessors in one of these areas, a remark whose subtle irony fits in well with the diffident and undogmatic tone of Livy's unusual preface.[253] Livy was not concerned to give a comprehensive selection of reasons for re-doing an older treatment, and his reduction, however accurate as a summary, overlooks the various justifications put forward by historians for writing their history.

(1) The most obvious reason for writing a non-contemporary history is that it has not been done before. This is perhaps the best claim of all, but it quickly becomes eliminated. Nevertheless, it can be justifiably made by local historians or historians of foreign lands presenting their work for the first time to a Greek or Roman audience. Ctesias in his *Persica* must have in this way justified his Assyrian and Median history, at least the former of which had not been attempted before in Greek.[254] Whether he did the same for his work on India we do not know.[255] Such

---

[251] I should also mention here Charax of Pergamum, about whom the Suda quotes an epigram beginning εἰμὶ Χάραξ ἱερεὺς γεραρῆς ἀπὸ Περγάμου ἄκρης (*FGrHist* 103 T 1). See further Andrei, *A. Claudio Charax* 1-35.

[252] So Syme, *Tacitus* 1.138: 'The justification for a new history, so Livy avers, is greater accuracy or a finer style.'

[253] *praef.* 2; cf. Jos. *A. J.* 1.2; on the diffident tone of Livy's preface see below, pp. 140f.

[254] Unless we believe (as I do not) that the *Assyrian History* promised by Herodotus (1.106.2; 184) was written but has been lost.

[255] Ctesias had been preceded by Scylax (*FGrHist* 709 T 3=Hdt. IV.44) and Herodotus (III.98-105) on India, but as neither treated historical matters, it would still be possible for Ctesias to have said that India's *history* had not been written. An interesting point about the writers on India is that the 'canonical' accounts of Alexander's men (especially Megasthenes) were never improved: see Dihle, *PCPhS* 10 (1964) 15-23, esp. 17ff. For Megasthenes, see Kuhrt, op. cit. (n.241) 95-100.

histories appeared most often as a consequence of the expansion of the Greco-Roman world, most notably after the conquests of Alexander and Rome, and, as we saw above, the historians usually present themselves as someone with special access to a native tradition. In the history of Greece and Rome, of course, it would be more difficult to claim that an entire history had been overlooked or untreated. Nevertheless, an historian might use this motif selectively and on a reduced scale, claiming that this or that epoch or episode has been ignored by his predecessors. Thucydides makes just this claim in the Pentekontaetia, that Athens' history between the Persian Wars and the Peloponnesian War had been overlooked by everyone before him.[256] Arrian, in language that echoes Thucydides, claims (against all the evidence) that the deeds of Alexander had been left out by previous writers. Dionysius argues that the history of early Rome had been ignored by the Greek writers before him. Tacitus says that previous Greek and Roman writers have overlooked the deeds of Ariminius, and he claims elsewhere in the *Annals* that he will treat material passed over by others.[257]

(2) The historian will argue that previous works are not *complete*, and therefore the *entire* history is not known. Dionysius mentions his Greek predecessors in the *Antiquities*, but says they gave only partial information; Josephus likewise in the *Jewish Antiquities* suggests that Ptolemy Philadelphus, who first commissioned a collection of the Jewish law and tradition, did not get *all* of the numerous materials recorded in the sacred writings.[258] Again, the precedent seems to be

---

[256] Thuc. 1.97.2: τὴν ἐκβολὴν τοῦ λόγου ἐποιησάμην διὰ τόδε, ὅτι τοῖς πρὸ ἐμοῦ ἅπασιν ἐκλιπὲς τοῦτο ἦν τὸ χωρίον, κ.τ.λ. The following sentence, naming Hellanicus as an exception (τούτων δὲ ὅσπερ καὶ ἥψατο ἐν τῇ Ἀττικῇ ξυγγραφῇ Ἑλλάνικος) was for Jacoby (*Atthis* 158-9) a later insertion by Thucydides into the manuscript, and evidence that Hellanicus' *Atthis* had been published while Thucydides was finishing his own book; *contra*, Smart, in *Past Persp.* 29-30. It seems that Thucydides has expressed himself unusually ('nobody has treated it - except Hellanicus, etc.'), but the rhetoric is effective and the momentary exception of Hellanicus will not change this; for a similar expression see Aristoxenus, *Harm.* 1.6: τούτου δὲ τοῦ μέρους τῆς πραγματείας ἄλλος μὲν οὐδεὶς πώποθ' ἥψατο· Ἐρατοκλῆς δ' ἐπεχείρησεν ἀναποδείκτως ἐξαριθμεῖν ἐπί τι μέρος· ὅτι δ' οὐδὲν εἴρηκεν ἀλλὰ πάντα ψευδῆ καὶ τῶν φαινομένων τῇ αἰσθήσει διημάρτηκε.

[257] Arr. *Anab.* 1.12.2; D. Hal. *A.R.* 1.4.2; Tac. *Ann.* 11.88.3 (Ariminius); VI.7.5: 'nobis pleraque digna cognitu obuenere, quamquam ab aliis incelebrata.'

[258] D. Hal. *A. R.* 1.4.2; 5.4-6.3; 7.1-2; cf. 1.45.4; Jos. *A. J.* 1.12.

Thucydides, who claims that Hellanicus treated the Pentekontaetia too briefly.[259] Diodorus argues a variation of this for his large-scale work. He claims that his work will be *more* complete than that of his various predecessors, because he will include in it all manner of material from the best historians.[260] In most places Diodorus cites his authorities without in any way suggesting that he has improved on them, other than the implication, already met in the preface, that the use of several accounts makes for a better version: witness his narrative of Cretan affairs where four epichoric authorities are named, from whom Diodorus has taken the more trustworthy details.[261] This procedure is found throughout the first five books where Diodorus is treating early 'foreign' history and events outside of mainland Greece before the Trojan War. Whether this was continued for Books VI–X which went from the Trojan War to Xerxes' invasion of 480 BC cannot, unfortunately, be determined from the fragmentary nature of these books. Indeed, in Diodorus as in Dionysius and Livy, many accounts are brought together, and accuracy (ἀκρίβεια), and thus reliability, is achieved by the very fullness of material.[262] A similar procedure was used by Kephalion in his history, written under Hadrian, of early times to the death of Alexander. He explicitly announced at the outset that he was following Hellanicus, Ctesias, and Herodotus, and according to Photius he cited in each of his nine books the number of accounts and historians he had consulted.[263] For the first five books alone he claimed 140 authors and 2,428 volumes.[264]

(3) He will argue that previous histories are biased, and that he, by contrast, will write without fear or favour. This claim, which appears especially in contemporary histories, is also used by some non-contemporary historians. Polybius' criticism of Fabius' and Philinus' accounts of the First Punic War extends to just this aspect of their work; Arrian mentions the absence of bias in Ptolemy and Aristobulus as that which makes them the best sources for Alexander's reign; Josephus castigates

---

[259] Thuc. I.97.2: βραχέως τε καὶ τοῖς χρόνοις οὐκ ἀκριβῶς ἐπεμνήσθη. The same criticism, of course, is levelled at Thucydides' own treatment of these times: Gomme, *HCT* I.280; Hornblower, *CT* I.148.   [260] Diod. 1.3.2–3.
[261] Diod. v.80.4.
[262] For ἀκρίβεια as fullness, see Schultze, in *Past Persp.* 126; for falsehood as the absence of full details, see Wiseman, *L&F* 144–6.
[263] Kephalion, *FGrHist* 93 F 1b; T 2.
[264] Jacoby, *RE* XI. 1, 191, adding 'purer Schwindel'; he points out the parallel procedure in Pliny's *Natural History*.

previous writers for bias towards Rome in their account of the Jewish rebellion; and Tacitus deprecates an entire generation of historians to justify his own new attempt at the history of the early Empire.[265] What is noteworthy in these types of justification is that the difficulty of writing history is not presented as discovering the facts, but rather in interpreting the facts already known.[266]

(4) He will promise to write with greater accuracy than his predecessors. This claim is already evident in Hecataeus' opening statement in the *Genealogies*, and is often expressed by the historian in details where he is correcting or supplementing the record. We mentioned above that a non-contemporary historian sees himself primarily as a recorder of the tradition. Yet if the historian were only a recorder of tradition, there would be little need for him and his history. And so if he wishes to justify his re-working of an old theme, he must periodically display the improvement of his version, and since the tradition is established in outline (no one has eight kings of Rome, for example), the only place to show superiority is in the details.[267] When promising greater accuracy, the historian will usually bring forward new evidence to justify a new interpretation and add details; or he will invoke his own autopsy to correct predecessors. Herodotus has many examples of this in his account of Egypt, some based on his Egyptian sources, some on his own autopsy.[268] Thucydides justifies his treatment of the Pentekontaetia by claiming that Hellanicus was 'chronologically inaccurate'[269] in his work, and he justifies his other foray into non-contemporary history by saying that the Athenians 'say nothing accurate' about their liberation from tyranny,[270] although in neither case does he explain his own evidence. Polybius justifies his description of Hannibal's crossing of the Alps by his inquiry of the natives, and his own examination of the terrain; and he bases his interpretation of Hannibal's character on the testimony of the Carthaginians themselves.[271] Dionysius, using autopsy, corrects his Greek predecessors on the origins of the Romans.[272] Among the

---

[265] Pol. 1.14.1–9; Arr. *Anab. proem.* 2; Jos. *B. J.* 1.2; Tac. *Ann.* 1.1.2.
[266] For a fuller treatment of bias, see Ch. III §4.
[267] The desire for a pleasurable narrative also militated against continuous or extensive analysis; cf. p. 79.   [268] See below, pp. 225ff.
[269] Thuc. 1.97.2: τοῖς χρόνοις οὐκ ἀκριβῶς.
[270] Thuc. VI.54.1: ἀκριβὲς οὐδὲν λέγοντας.
[271] Pol. III.48; IX.25.   [272] D. Hal. *A. R.* 1.55.1; 68.1–2; II.23.5; VII.72.18.

Romans, Coelius Antipater said he would base his account of the Punic War on 'the writings of those who are judged true', and elsewhere provided through his own inquiry an alternative account of the death of Marcellus.[273] Licinius Macer claimed to have found linen books (*libri lintei*) in the temple of Moneta, and used them as legitimation for his differently detailed list of Roman magistrates.[274] Asinius Pollio faulted Caesar's *Commentarii*, saying that the author had displayed insufficient inquiry and gullibility towards others' reports.[275] Tacitus invokes the testimony of his elders for evidence that implicated Tiberius in the conspiracy of Cn. Calpurnius Piso against Germanicus, and elsewhere he cites the *Memoirs* of the younger Agrippina, for a detail of her mother's relationship with Tiberius, making sure to say that the detail 'has not been recorded by the writers of history'.[276]

(5) Finally, the oft-quoted antithesis of Livy should not mislead us into positing as a justification what Livy claims is only a belief by the historian himself. No surviving historian claims *only* style as a justification for writing a new history, and this is worth noting.[277] Ancient historians, of course, imply that they will write better than their predecessors, and Cicero and others devote much discussion to the proper style for historiography. But no historian presents as a sufficient justification in bringing forward a new work *only* the fact that his language and style will be superior to any that have before attempted it. Arrian comes close in the *Anabasis* by the bold (and, from his point of view, necessary) claim that no one had ever treated Alexander's deeds 'worthily' (ἐπαξίως),[278] and by the challenge to the reader to compare his account with previous ones (*praef.* 3). Yet as his emphasis on reliable sources at the outset (*praef.* 1-2) shows, he saw his work as being superi-

---

[273] Coelius Antipater, *HRR* FF 2 ('ex scriptis eorum qui ueri arbitrantur'); 29.
[274] On Macer and the *libri lintei* see Ogilvie, *JRS* 48 (1958) 40-6.
[275] Pollio, *HRR* F 4 (=Suet. *Div. Iul.* 56.4), perhaps at the point where Pollio narrated in his own history that which Caesar too had treated; presumably, the criticism would be more relevant to the *Civil War* than the *Gallic War*.
[276] Tac. *Ann.* III.16.1: 'audire me memini ex senioribus'; IV.53.2: 'id ego, a scriptoribus annalium non traditum, repperi, e.q.s.'.
[277] Livy's disjunction '*either* greater accuracy *or* a finer style' indicates perhaps that the Annalists of the first century BC (whose prefaces we lack) made just this claim of finer style, but this cannot be certain.
[278] Arr. *Anab.* 1.12.2, with Bosworth, *HCA* I.104, and Moles, *JHS* 105 (1985) 163-4.

or in content as well as in style.²⁷⁹ No doubt, some really offered nothing new except their style, but they do not present it in this way.²⁸⁰

In summation, we may say that the ancient historians did not have what we would call a methodology in their approach to non-contemporary history, at least not one that differed in essentials from their treatment of contemporary history. The first historians in a new tradition must have portrayed their history as based on native sources, either by their own investigations, or by reliance on written traditions and chronicles. As time goes by the tradition becomes more or less fixed, and later historians follow the tradition in all its essentials, changing it only in details here and there, or perhaps placing their own interpretation on a particular era, or adding something from a document or monument to fill out the narrative. Historians who write large-scale works portray their achievement as a full collection of the tradition, and as a work that systematically embodies – and thus supersedes – their predecessors.²⁸¹

4. MYTH AND HISTORY

At the very beginning of non-contemporary history there was myth. Myth presented interesting problems for the writers of non-contemporary history. Either because of audience expectation or simply because one frequently, especially in writing early history, had nothing other than *mythoi* it was rare for historians to avoid them altogether.²⁸² Now there is a general consensus that by the mythic (τὸ μυθῶδες) Thucydides meant the fabulous or storytelling element of his predecessors.²⁸³ He contrasts it with clarity (τὸ σαφές), which seems to be closely bound up with the certainty of contemporary history,²⁸⁴ and this

---

[279] See Bosworth, *HCA* 1.16–31.
[280] Duris of Samos (*FGrHist* 76 F 1) criticises the style of predecessors with the obvious suggestion that his account will be superior; it is hardly likely that this comprised his only reason for writing, but if it did, he will be an exception to the rule above. On this fragment of Duris see Gray, *AJPh* 108 (1987) 467–86.
[281] For more on this last, see Ch. V §3.
[282] On the terminology see Wardman, *Historia* 9 (1960) 403 n. 2.
[283] See Gomme, *HCT* 1.149; *contra*, Flory, *CJ* 85 (1990) 193–208 (accepted by Hornblower, *CT* 1.61) who thinks that it refers to praise and panegyric, that is, stories that satisfied the audience's desire to hear itself praised. Cf. Lucian, below, n. 321, for a similar use of τὸ μυθῶδες.
[284] For a different interpretation of τὸ σαφές see Woodman, *RICH* 23–8.

suggests that 'the mythic' cannot be tested or inquired about, because of both the distance in time from the events, and the essentially fantastic nature of the material.²⁸⁵ It is a tribute to the influence of Thucydides that after him myth could only with difficulty be rescued or redeemed. In later historians we can see only three possibilities: avoid myths altogether; try to 'rationalise' or 'de-mythologise' them; or, as Lucian suggests, include them but leave their credibility to the reader to decide. If one included them, one had to defend oneself. Eventually – we cannot pinpoint exactly when – mythical material was seen as a suitable element in digressions, where the reader might be diverted in *loci amoeni* from the more serious material of history.²⁸⁶ At some time before the second century BC, rhetoricians classified narratives (at first poetic but gradually extending to prose) by their subject matter, and the distinctions are followed with remarkably few (and minor) differences by rhetoricians and grammarians: (i) ἱστορία or *historia* is that which is true and has actually occurred; (ii) πλάσμα or *argumentum* is that which encompasses not real events but those like real events (ὡς ἀληθής or *ueri simile*); (iii) μῦθος or *fabula* is that which is not true and not similar to truth.²⁸⁷ What is noteworthy is that ancient writers were willing to place very little in the realm of the last category; eventually, it comprised only

---

²⁸⁵ Thucydides' use of τὸ μυθῶδες here is consonant with the two uses of μῦθος in Herodotus, both from Book II. Herodotus calls the tradition about the circumambient Ocean a μῦθος, since it is something unseen and unverifiable; and he rejects Heracles' slaughter of the Egyptians when they were preparing to sacrifice him, as a μῦθος, since it was not consonant with what Herodotus knew of the Egyptians' reluctance to sacrifice even animals; and it was improbable that one mortal could kill so many thousands (II.23; 45.1). Herodotus, however, by his *innumerabiles fabulae* elsewhere had left himself open to the charge by later writers of being considered a μυθολόγος. See Ctesias' criticism, quoted below, p. 227; cf. Plut. *Her. Mal.* 854F where one can see (despite the lacuna) that Herodotus is accused not only of partiality in the extreme, but also of lies (ψεύσματα) and fictions (πλάσματα).

²⁸⁶ See Pol. XXXVIII.6 on the reader's need for relief; Plut. *Her. Mal.* 855C-D says that myths, old stories, and praises (μῦθοι, ἀρχαιολογίαι, ἔπαινοι) make up the material of digressions in history; but D. Hal. *Pomp.* 6 (II.396–8 Usher) faults Theopompus for his use of myth in his digressions; see further Wardman, op. cit. (n.282) 406–7.

²⁸⁷ Asclepiades ap. Sex. Emp. *Math.* I.263–4; [Cic.] *Herenn.* I.8.12–13; Quint. II.4. 2; for discussion see Walbank, *SP* 233–6; Nicolai, *La storiographia nell' educazione antica* 124–39 (with additional passages). There is a different set of categories in Isoc. *Panath.* 1; for their relationship to the traditional schema see Pfister, *Hermes* 68 (1933) 457–60.

things impossible by nature.[288] *Horror uacui* and the unwillingness to forego what clearly gave pleasure to some ensured that the mythical continued to have a place in history; but it was required to have the proper look about it.[289] The model of Thucydides might here too be used, since it could be argued that he had 'tamed' myth in the Archaeology, or at least had pointed a way for the rational criticism of poetic and legendary tradition. Polybius had conceded that old myths contained much true and much false, but gave no guidance for determining which was which; this might be part of his general ambivalence we have noted towards non-contemporary history.[290]

The closest we come to an outright challenge to the rejection of myth in history is in Diodorus' *Historical Library*. Diodorus is heir to the Hellenistic tradition where the study of myth 'took on the prestige of the elite knowledge that marks its possessor as belonging to a certain class', and this class began to view myth as a scholarly subject that could be given an 'historical' treatment.[291] In announcing the contents of his work, Diodorus states that the first six books will be devoted to the deeds (πράξεις) and the mythic accounts (μυθολογίαι) of those before the Trojan War; three of these books will be devoted to foreign, three to Hellenic ancient accounts (ἀρχαιολογίαι, 1.4.6). The latter word, more neutral, no doubt comprehends both history and myth. Now it is not surprising, given the daring of this 'transgression' in a serious history, that Diodorus explains himself at greater length, in a passage placed midway between Greek and non-Greek material. Diodorus isolates four difficulties in recounting myths: (i) the antiquity of the material makes recording them difficult; (ii) the fact that the great antiquity of these stories does not allow for refutation or proper testing causes some to look down on the narrative; (iii) the variety or multitude of heroes and semi-heroes makes the narration difficult to apprehend; and (iv) the greatest difficulty: that those who have written on these most ancient deeds and mythic accounts do not agree with one another.

---

[288] Walbank, *SP* 234-5.
[289] As Piérart, *LEC* 51 (1983) 48 points out, the ancients did not concern themselves with the problematic nature of myth itself, but only with individual myths.
[290] See Pédech, *Méthode* 395. Note too that Polybius accepted Homer's geography, provided that it was purified of the mythical element: see XXXIV.2.9-10; 4.1.
[291] Veyne, *Did the Greeks Believe in their Myths?* 45.

For all these reasons, he claims, the greatest writers in the past, such as Ephorus, Callisthenes, and Theopompus avoided this difficult topic.[292] In recounting Heracles' deeds, he says that he expects disbelief because of both the antiquity and the amazing nature of the deeds; but this, he says, is to use an unfair standard[293] in seeking exactness (τὸ ἀκριβές) in such ancient mythical accounts[294] by reckoning according to today's standards. One cannot examine the truth so exactly: for just as in the theatre, even though we know there are no centaurs or Geryones with three bodies, nevertheless we accept these and by our approval increase the god's honour, so also in history it would be strange to fail to honour a god who had done so much for mankind.[295] Now the inclusion of myth, the concern with piety, and the comparison to the theatre[296] all show a different orientation towards events.

Diodorus asserts more strongly than any other historian the value – he might say, the necessity – of including myth in history. On the one hand, a 'universal' history that purported to contain all the things worthy of record would need to include those done by the earliest men. Had not Thucydides himself included references to Agamemnon and Minos? Had not Herodotus discussed the 'historical' Heracles in his account of Egypt? Their presence in a historical narrative was thus justified by tradition. Thucydides, it is true, rejected the earliest times (as had Ephorus and others), but Diodorus tries to suggest that this rejection was merely the result of the difficulty of this earliest material. Where Thucydides had made it a question of accuracy, Diodorus makes it a matter of effort, which, he argues, is necessary and valuable since very many great deeds were performed by these heroes and demigods.

Two things, however, mitigate this abandonment of accepted principles. First, Diodorus claims that his myths serve a useful purpose, and

---

[292] Diod. IV.1.1–4.   [293] Diod. IV.8.3: οὐ δικαίᾳ χρώμενοι κρίσει.
[294] Note the apparent oxymoron ἐν ταῖς μυθολογουμέναις ἱστορίαις at IV.8.4.
[295] For a similar thought see Arr. *Anab.* V.1.2 (with Bosworth, *HCA* II.202), where Arrian says that it is not right to examine τὰ μεμυθευμένα which have a divine element in them.
[296] The comparison to the theatre occurs frequently when speaking of myth. Pol. II.16.13–15 considers myth material for tragedy; D. Hal. *Thuc.* 5 says that the early historians included material that had theatrical reversals of fortune; and Livy (below, at n. 313) adds that a *fabula* about Horatius is more appropriate for the stage than for history.

are not for astonishment or entertainment.[297] Rather, since he sees one of the purposes of history as the incitement of men to just action,[298] so the proper treatment of the gods is a legitimate aspect of his type of historiography. In other words, his inclusion of myths serves a serious purpose. Second, Diodorus maintains a careful narrative manner both in his accounts of the Greek gods in Book IV and more generally in the first six books as a whole: long passages are given in indirect discourse governed by 'they say', 'it is said', 'the myth writers say', and the like.[299] Such a manner shows Diodorus to be maintaining a critical distance (like Herodotus' manner in his Book II) from what he relates; and although he does not usually call into question the material that he narrates, he nevertheless shows himself aware of the different nature of this material by a different and distancing narrative style; no other section of the preserved portions of the *Library* reveals the same narrative manner.

Dionysius of Halicarnassus has a more orthodox approach and a rejection of Diodorus' standards. In his comparison of great empires before that of the Romans, he notes that the Assyrian empire, being the earliest, extends back 'into mythic times',[300] that is, into a time beyond the realm of clarity and exactness (τὸ σαφές and ἀκρίβεια). Then, in the initial summary of the starting-point and end of the history, Dionysius claims that he will begin his history 'from the most ancient myths which historians before me have left out, because they were difficult to discover without great effort.'[301] Like Diodorus who suggested that effort was lacking in his predecessors, Dionysius has tried to turn an obvious disadvantage into a criticism of his predecessors and a praise of his own effort. But unlike Diodorus, Dionysius does not suggest that he investigates myths for their edificatory value; rather, since his purpose is to justify the hegemony of Rome,[302] the truth of the

---

[297] Indeed at one point he censures Herodotus on this score and expressly says that he will pass over those myths about Egypt that Herodotus had included for the sake of entertainment: 1.69.7; cf. x.24.1. So too D. Hal. *Pomp.* 6 (II.392-4 Usher) says that Theopompus' marvels were not for entertainment (ψυχαγωγία) but were useful for philosophic rhetoric.   [298] Diod. I.2.8.

[299] See, e. g., 1.11.1-29.6; 96.2-98.9. Theopompus (*FGrHist* 115 F 381) made his readers aware of the different nature of the μῦθοι he included by stating explicitly that they were myths and not passing them off as anything else. For the proper translation of the fragment see M. A. Flower, *Theopompus* 34-5.

[300] D. Hal. *A. R.* 1.2.2: εἰς τοὺς μυθικοὺς ... χρόνους.   [301] Ibid. I.8.1.

[302] Gabba, *Dionysius* ch. 1.

mythical material will be an ancillary argument for his belief about the Greekness of Rome and thus its justification for ruling the world. In other words, his theme demands that he treat the very earliest times.

By μῦθοι Dionysius almost certainly means early legends which can include exaggerative or impossible stories, the 'mythic material' of Thucydides. In his essay on Thucydides, he remarks that the early writers before Herodotus had collected local traditions from religious and secular records, 'in which there were some myths believed from time long ago, and some dramatic reversals, which seem foolish to people today'. But when Thucydides came along he proceeded differently in every way, first in his choice of topic, and secondly, 'by adding no mythic material to it, nor using his history for deceiving and bewitching the many, as all those before him had done' in stories such as the Lamian women who sprang up from the earth in woods and glades, or the amphibious half-human Naiads coming up from Tartarus, swimming across the ocean and joining up with men to produce a race of demigods, 'and other such stories which seem incredible and very ridiculous to us today'.[303] Dionysius does not, however, find fault with these writers since it was inevitable that they should have come upon fictional stories: the records (μνῆμαι) included them, and generation after generation handed them down. Thus it was inevitable too that these historians 'were obliged to adorn their accounts with mythological digressions'. Thucydides stopped all that, and Dionysius may speak for the standard view (that we have here presented) that Thucydides marks the dividing line between narratives permitting fanciful stories and those forbidding them.[304]

That these stories are specifically to be found in native records can be seen in Dionysius' discussion of early Italy where the Golden Age of Saturn in Italy is called an 'account turned into myth by the inhabitants'.[305] Yet this account can, if one sets aside the fabulous element, reveal that Italy is the best of all countries in the world.[306] Such rationalisation is only one way to ensure that the historian is taming myth. Far more common in Dionysius, however, is the contrast of a 'mythic' and 'historic' account, the two being separate and distinct, with no commerce between them. A particularly good example is Dionysius'

---

[303] D. Hal. *Thuc.* 5–6.
[304] *Thuc.* 7: Θουκυδίδη δέ, emphatically separated from ἐκείνοις μέν.
[305] *A. R.* 1.36.1: λόγος ὑπὸ τῶν ἐπιχωρίων μυθολογούμενος.
[306] Ibid. 1.36.2.

treatment of Heracles in Book I. There is a fairly long and detailed narrative in which Heracles enters Italy with Geryon's cattle, some of which are stolen by Cacus who is then killed by Heracles (the story familiar from *Aeneid* VIII). Dionysius follows it with an account (described as truer, ἀληθέστερος) given by those who have used the 'form of history' (ἐν ἱστορίας σχήματι), which relates that Heracles was a general leading an army of conquest from Spain into Italy.[307] Cacus was an exceedingly barbarous chieftain who troubled his neighbours. Heracles fought him and Cacus died in battle.[308] All of the divine and monstrous elements are gone – the whole account is nothing more than an ordinary run-of-the-mill battle of aggression – and in fact at the end of this latter version Dionysius explicitly casts aspersions on the 'mythical' account by saying that Heracles' passage through Italy had nothing august about it, but his great name was won by the services done for the inhabitants, as those activities were described in the rationalised version.[309]

One may well ask why Dionysius narrated the mythic account at all if it was only going to be dismissed. The answer here is the role expected of a non-contemporary historian, that of a collector of accounts (λόγοι). Just as Dionysius' model, Herodotus, had been forced to rely on native accounts – some of which would contain the fanciful or marvellous – so too Dionysius needed to collect and preserve epichoric traditions. Yet just as Herodotus could demonstrate superior method in giving several accounts, or in asserting occasionally the greater merit of one account over another, so too Dionysius can have it both ways: he can remain faithful to his Herodotean role of collector of traditions but he can also show his Thucydidean side by a rejection of the mythic in favour of a more rational 'historical' narrative.[310]

The Latin historians also show themselves aware of the inappropriateness of *fabula* to history, but since it is not really a Roman characteristic to comment on the quality of the material they relate, there are only

---

[307] A.R. 1.39–40 is the μύθικος λόγος, 41–2 is ὁ δ' ἀληθέστερος. At the outset of the passage Dionysius had noted that of Heracles there existed τὰ μὲν μυθικώτερα, τὰ δ' ἀληθέστερα (39.1).   [308] Ibid. 1.42.1–4.

[309] Ibid. 1.42.4.

[310] For more on Dionysius' attitude towards myth see II.20.1–2, where he speaks of the benefit of myths for those who know how to interpret them correctly. In that passage, the contrast is between the masses unacquainted with philosophy, and the expert who can properly expound their hidden meaning. For Dionysius and Herodotus see the works cited in Introd. n. 40.

a few 'methodological' references among the Latins to the fantastic element which is or is not included in their histories. Perhaps the best known is Livy's in his preface, where he distinguishes between the events to be narrated before the city was founded and those of later times. The former he considers more in the way of 'poetic myths' (*poeticae fabulae*) than 'reliable remnants of historical deeds' (*incorrupta rerum gestarum monumenta*), yet he will neither assent to nor deny the tradition, but leave it to his readers to decide.[311] His remark, coming as it does in the preface, is essential to indicate to his audience that he is well aware of the qualitative difference between the early books and what will follow. Perhaps not by coincidence Livy's distinction tacitly accepts his contemporary Varro's division of time into three eras: the obscure, the mythic, and the historic, the last of which begins only with the first Olympiad (776 BC), approximately the time of Rome's founding (753, according to Varro).[312]

Like Diodorus, Livy reveals a care in the narration as he proceeds; unlike Diodorus, he does not do this by long passages of indirect discourse, but rather by consistent reminders in the early books of the fact that he is reporting tradition. Occasionally he will explicitly call attention to the questionable nature of his material: the story of Horatius at the bridge is described as a deed 'destined to have more fame than credence among posterity'; so too in the narrative of the taking of Veii, Livy prefaces an addition to one of the episodes with the words, 'a *fabula* is introduced in this place' (*inseritur huic loco fabula*). Curiously, there is nothing particularly miraculous about this addition; rather, *fabula* here means 'play' and Livy compares it to what is seen on the stage, a place that delights in marvellous things, and he again states that in such cases it is not even worth the effort to affirm or deny their truth.[313] Livy, however, shows his awareness of the problematic nature of myth by frequently juxtaposing a natural and a supernatural explanation, especially for material in the early books,[314] and this resembles Dionysius' use of both a 'mythic' and 'historic' explanation.

Tacitus, in at least one passage, says that the search for myth and

---

[311] Livy, *praef.* 6: 'ea nec adfirmare nec refellere in animo est'.
[312] Varro apud Censorinus, *die nat.* 21.1-2. The division is very likely based on Eratosthenes: Jacoby, *FGrHist Komm.* II. B. 709.
[313] Livy, II.10.11; V.21. 8-9.
[314] Ogilvie, *Commentary on Livy* 48 has a list of some passages in Book I; he thinks (12) the rationalisations go back to Licinius Macer.

Myth and history

fiction does not accord well with the dignity of history,[315] but this can hardly be taken at face value since he occasionally includes just these things.[316] Naturally, he is cautious: the phoenix's abilities at regeneration are described as 'uncertain and exaggerated by the marvellous',[317] and Tacitus will vouch only for the fact that the bird appears from time to time in Egypt. He brands the story of Nero as an infant being watched over by serpents as 'mythical and similar to foreign marvels'.[318] Ammianus' examples are more interesting. In the course of his amplification of the battle between the Romans and Sapor he gives a description of the many troops the latter led; then strikingly he chides 'Graecia fabulosa' for mentioning Doriscum, a reference to Herodotus' story that Xerxes numbered his troops there by drawing a circle and having the men fill it again and again until they were all counted. This story, along with more Herodotean tales – the Medic hordes led to Greece, the bridging of the Hellespont, and the canal at Mt Athos – are described later as 'fabulosae lectae' to all posterity.[319] Within the narrative itself, however, both Tacitus and Ammianus avoid what might be considered *fabulae*. That which might come closest on a consistent basis to the marvellous or fabulous would be the reporting of portents, a common feature of Greek and Roman historiography. Its acceptance, however, was part of the fabric of Roman historiography and the historian here, as with other fabulous events, gave little indication of assent or acceptance.[320]

In Lucian's *How to Write History*, μῦθοι and τὸ μυθῶδες denote both flattery and tall tales. In the early chapters, Lucian is discussing the ruinous effect in history of flattery, and he attacks those who pass over the events and instead spend their time praising their own generals and vilifying those of the enemy. This leads to further consideration of the distinction between poetry and history, and a series of examples from the *Iliad* of what is appropriate for poetry: not surprisingly, these are impossibilities (ἀδύνατα): winged horses, characters running over

---

[315] *Hist.* II.50.2: 'conquirere fabulosa et ficta oblectare legentium animos procul grauitate coepti operis crediderim'.
[316] See Develin, *Antichthon* 17 (1983) 69.
[317] Tac. *Ann.* VI.28.6: 'incerta et fabulosis aucta'.
[318] Tac. *Ann.* XI.11.3: 'fabulosa et externis miraculis adsimilata'; cf. XII.58.1.
[319] Amm. XVIII.6.23.
[320] On portents in Roman historiography see Rawson, *RCS* 1–15; further bibliography at Briscoe, *Commentary on Livy XXXI–XXXIII* 88.

water or flower tops, and Zeus swinging land and sea by a single cord. Although in poetry one finds humans compared to gods, as when Agamemnon is compared to Zeus or Poseidon or Ares, nevertheless such flattery is inappropriate in history, making it into poetry without metre, and confusing the two genres by failing to observe the established boundaries. Thus, Lucian concludes, it is a great fault if one 'brings into history the embellishments of poetry: myth and encomium, and the excesses in both', which is like dressing an athlete in finery and painting his face.[321] The conjunction of myth (τὸ μυθῶδες) with praise appears again shortly thereafter, when Lucian is answering a hypothetical objection to his earlier remarks, to the effect that eulogy in history gives pleasure: 'it is worthwhile also to say that there is not even pleasure for the listeners in complete myth and praise'. Although eulogy may give pleasure to the many, he concludes, the worthwhile few will see through it, and if one uses eulogy and flattery, one will have made a laughable work lacking all proportion and proper measure.[322]

It is clear in these passages, at least, that Lucian is closely linking myth with praise and encomia, and as his example of Homer's description of Agamemnon suggests, the specifically 'mythic' element that he rejects in history is the exaggerative and inappropriate description of individuals as possessing the attributes of gods. Not only are the gods outside the realm of history; so too are descriptions that smack of exaggeration and that would suggest that humans behaved like gods or achieved more than humanly possible: and here Lucian gives the example of Alexander throwing Aristobulus' book into the Hydaspes because that historian had invented and exaggerated Alexander's deeds.[323] The τὸ μυθῶδες of Thucydides has therefore become for Lucian something quite specific, an exaggeration giving pleasure in the form of flattery: for Lucian the Thucydidean relationship of τὸ μυθῶδες, pleasure, and passing performance is seen essentially in terms of the excessive praise of one's subjects in history, a praise that vitiates history and, as Lucian says elsewhere, assures that the work will indeed give pleasure for the moment (to the one being flattered) but will never be a permanent possession.[324]

Quite in a different spirit is Lucian's later mention of myths, where the historian is advised that if he comes across one, he should include it but not state his belief in it.[325] Here, it is clear, Lucian means by myth

---

[321] Luc. *h. c.* 8.   [322] *h. c.* 10.   [323] On this passage, below p. 160.   [324] *h. c.* 42.
[325] *h. c.* 60.

what Dionysius meant, a local tradition or a story from hearsay, or indeed some story relating to the gods or divine or superhuman activity. It is worthwhile to note, then, that Lucian, like Dionysius, sees the inclusion of myths as not outside the historian's task, but as always requiring an attitude of agnosticism in the Thucydidean spirit.[326]

The inappropriateness of the mythic, then, is due to two factors: it cannot be investigated with the same methods as the material of historical times; and the marvellous or exaggerative nature (often intrinsic) of the material makes it inappropriate to history's pragmatic task or utilitarian pleasure. Let us note finally a passage from Polybius that very clearly delineates the distinction between myth-writers (μυθογράφοι) and historians. In a discussion of the outlying parts of the known world, Polybius distinguishes between suppositions about the matter made before his own time and the knowledge which he and his contemporaries can now enjoy.[327] The cause of this new-found accuracy is the discovery and exploration of all lands and seas. And so, says Polybius, since this is now the case, it is no longer appropriate (πρέπον) to use as witnesses in this discussion poets and mythographers, who had put forward explanations with an unverifiable certainty; instead one can now supply the proper proof which comes from history itself. Here investigative work by travel and inquiry has led to a superior understanding of the phenomenon. It is worthwhile to note that myth has not been validated by such efforts, but rather replaced.[328] One might have thought that this, if anything, would make the ancients aware that rationalised myth was as unreliable as unrationalised myth; but the charms of myth, like those of the Sirens, were simply too great to resist.

---

[326] For Lucian's passage as an indication of the conflict even for serious historians see Homeyer, *Lukian* 280–1.
[327] Pol. III.58–9: the contrast is between the ἄπιστοι βεβαιωταί of poets and mythographers, as opposed to the ἱκανὴ πίστις διὰ αὐτῆς τῆς ἱστορίας.
[328] Note also Pol. III.91.7, where Polybius accepts the story that the gods struggled for the plain of Capua, because it is reasonable (εἰκός) that they would: the area is exceptional for its beauty and fertility. Here, of course, the story does no more than adorn a fact that is obvious to the eyes.

III
The historian's character

Narrative or historical truth must needs be highly estimable... 'Tis itself a part of moral truth. To be a judge in one requires a judgement in the other. The morals, the character, and genius of an author must be thoroughly considered; and the historian or relater of things important to mankind must, whoever he be, approve himself many ways to us, both in respect of his judgement, candour, and disinterestedness, ere we are bound to take anything on his authority.[1]

The historian's task is to narrate, but he must also win credibility for that narrative: his task is therefore also to persuade his audience that he is the proper person to tell the story and, moreover, that his account is one that should be believed. In his capacity as persuader, the historian will often try to shape the audience's perception of his character and to use this as an additional claim to authority; indeed, among the Roman historians, where explicit professions of research are rarer than with the Greeks, the shaping of the narrator's character takes on a correspondingly larger role. But most of the historians, Greek and Roman, try to shape their audience's perception of their character. Nor is this surprising when we consider the teachings of rhetoric.

1. THE IMPORTANCE OF CHARACTER

In the *Rhetoric* Aristotle attempts to separate the elements that contribute to the speaker's persuasion. Certain forms of proof (πίστεις), he says, are atechnic, that is, not invented by the speaker, such as witnesses, testimony, contracts, and so forth; others are entechnic and demand

---

[1] Anthony Cooper, Earl of Shaftesbury, *Characteristicks of Men, Manners, Opinions, Times* (London 1711) I.146.

that the speaker invent or discover (εὑρεῖν) their proper application. Persuasion comes about, Aristotle says, from the character of the speaker; from the disposition of the audience towards what is said; and from the arguments themselves as presented by the speaker. Of character Aristotle writes:

> There is persuasion through character whenever the speech is spoken so as to make the speaker worthy of trust (ἀξιόπιστον); for we believe fair-minded people more and more swiftly on all things in general, and when there is not certainty (ἀκριβές) but doubt (ἀμφιδοξεῖν) we believe them completely.[2]

Aristotle goes on to say that persuasion from character should arise from the speech itself, not from the audience's previous opinion of the speaker (1.2, 1356a 8-13). In other words, the audience should form a mental image of the speaker from his speech, as he is going along. Theoretically, then, it would make no difference whether Pericles was giving the speech or Cleon, for in Aristotle's vision the 'character' he sees as an element of persuasion is not external and previously existent to the speech, but rather only comes into being with the speech.[3]

Aristotle is here thinking of ἠθοποιΐα, the ability of the orator to construct character within the speech. This technique, which was probably modelled on the portrayal of character by the poets,[4] found its acknowledged master in Lysias. Aristotle may indeed be thinking of Lysias when he says that the character of the speaker arises from the speech and is not external to it, since Lysias, when a resident alien at Athens, could only write speeches, not deliver them, and thus his own character was irrelevant to the image of character he needed to form in the minds of his clients' audience.[5] We should also note that Aristotle says character becomes clear by deliberative choice directed towards some end, and it is by this 'indirect' characterisation, not by protestations and direct or explicit claims, that a speaker reveals his character (*Rhet.* 1.8, 1366a 8-16).

---

[2] Arist. *Rhet.* 1.2, 1356a 4-8.
[3] Cf. ibid. II.1, 1377b 20-8: 'for it makes much difference in persuasion ... what sort of person the speaker seems, and how his audience supposes him disposed towards them'.   [4] Kennedy, *Art of Persuasion in Greece* 92.
[5] The usual structure of a Lysianic speech consists of the introduction of direct evidence, a proof or refutation by probability, and a proof or refutation by character: Kennedy, op. cit. (n.4) 91; on Lysias' ἠθοποιΐα see D. Hal. *Lys.* 8.

Later writers, while holding to Aristotle's divisions, were to interpret character differently, seeing it as the actual person who gives the speech and who must, therefore, have a character above reproach. The author of the *Rhetoric to Alexander* writes that the speaker must be concerned not only about his words but about his life, since how he conducts his life contributes both to persuasion and acquiring a good reputation.[6] This will then give the speaker an advantage when he appears before the assembly or in the law courts. Hermagoras, some two centuries later, even reserved a set place in the speech for the construction of the speaker's character, a digression, removed from the main argument, where the speaker might praise himself or castigate his opponent; this procedure was specifically designed, not to convince by argument, but to serve as an ancillary tool in winning credence for one's account.[7]

Roman rhetoric places a greater emphasis than Greek on character. This is, naturally enough, a reflection of Roman society in which a *patronus* relied as much on who he was as on what he said.[8] Despite this, or perhaps because of this, Roman critics do not have a great deal to say about character and its role in persuasion. The early theoretical works, *De Inuentione* and the *Rhetoric to Herennius*, do not recognise character as a form of persuasion like argument.[9] In Cicero's later *De Oratore*, however, the appeal to character finally appears. Cicero says that one means of persuasion is the conciliation of the audience (*de Orat.* II.115), which can be achieved by three things: the speaker's *dignitas*; his deeds; and the opinion which the audience has of his life (II. 182). Aristotle, by contrast, had said that there were three reasons why the character of a speaker would be persuasive: practical wisdom, virtue, and good will (*Rhet.* II.1, 1378a 6–8). The latter's classification appeals to character traits that were open to almost anyone, whereas Cicero's recognise and reflect the much larger role that service to the state and social standing played in Roman life.[10]

---

[6] *Rhet. ad Alex.* 38.2.

[7] Cic. *Inu.* 1.97 thinks this the wrong procedure: 'laudes autem et uituperationes non separatim placet tractari, sed in ipsis argumentationibus esse implicatas.'

[8] Kennedy, *Art of Rhetoric in the Roman World* 42; see also his examination (42–4) of Cato the Elder's speech *de Sumptu suo* (*ORF* 8 F 173) in which the speaker's *auctoritas* plays a large role.

[9] Kennedy, *Art of Rhetoric* 116; the *Rhet. ad Herennium* does have one passage on *notatio* (=ἠθοποιΐα), IV.63.

[10] For differences between Aristotelian and later evaluations of character, see Gill, *CQ* 34 (1984) 151ff.

We can see the importance of character in persuasion by a glance at some of the remarks made by the historians themselves which are not methodological or self-conscious, and thus reflect the preconceptions inherent in Greek and Roman society. In a digression on blaming generals who are foolish, Polybius says that one places trust in adequate pledges, namely oaths, children, wives, and – most important of all – the example of one's previous life. When Scipio is addressing his men before the battle of the Ticinus, Polybius portrays them as eager for battle, because of the trust they put in the speaker and in the truth of what he said. Some years later the son of this Scipio, the future Africanus, quelled a mutiny of his soldiers by inspiring trust in his hearers, 'for since in everything the example of his own life supported his advice, they did not require many words from him'.[11] Not in essence dissimilar are the observations of Livy that directly reflect Roman reality. During the siege of Veii, an old man predicts that the city will fall if the Romans draw off the water of the Alban Lake when it should overflow. But the Senate did not accept the remark, Livy says, because they judged the speaker of low standing and therefore insufficient trustworthiness. At about the same time the Senate rejected a portent that had been reported because of the low social status of the man who reported it. Livy also relates that at the trial of M. Manlius in 384, the tribunes of the plebs stopped the voting which they believed would acquit Manlius (contrary to what they wanted), because Manlius, on trial for sedition, had rehearsed his good deeds and reminded his audience of his role in saving the Capitol from the Gauls six years before. And the tribunes 'clearly saw that unless they could free men's eyes from the memory of such a deed, no charge, even if true, could ever find a place in the people's heart, which had been won over by his service'.[12] The belief that character was far more important than any words spoken can also be seen in Plutarch's *Life* of Phocion, where he says that a word or even a look from an esteemed person is more forceful than numerous enthymemes and periods.[13] Even Polybius says that one must measure the truth by what is known of a person's character.[14]

It was expected that the character most on display in any history was

---

[11] Pol. VIII.36.2-3; III.64.11; XI.10.4-5.   [12] Livy, V.15.12; 32.7; VI.20.10.
[13] Plut. *Phocion* 5; cf. Volkmann, *Rhetorik der Griechen und Römer* 271ff., who notes also in this vein Menander's remark, 'the character, not the word, of the speaker persuades' (τρόπος ἔσθ' ὁ πείθων τοῦ λέγοντος, οὐ λόγος).
[14] Pol. VIII.8.7. Cf. below, p. 281 n.5.

that of the historian himself.[15] Where moderns might speak of a narrator or implied narrator, the ancients spoke of the man himself. This tendency the younger Seneca summed up epigrammatically: 'as are men's lives, so is their speech'.[16] Just as Dionysius in the *Roman Antiquities* says that he will display his character as favourable towards all who are good men and lovers of fine deeds,[17] so he elsewhere reads the characters of his predecessors from their works: Herodotus was fair, being pleased by the good and distressed by the bad, Thucydides outspoken and harsh on account of his exile, Xenophon pious and just, Philistus a flatterer and a tyrant-lover, Theopompus an exacting judge of hidden motives and character.[18] Despite Dionysius' praise, Theopompus was usually seen as bitter and malicious, because of his negative judgements on men and events; similarly Timaeus was criticised for his faultfinding, quarrelsomeness, and maliciousness.[19] It is in terms of character that Plutarch criticises Herodotus, using as his evidence what he inferred about the author from the narrative of the *Histories*.[20] Since the historian's character, for better or worse, was on display in his history, he took care to fashion an appropriate persona for himself in the narrative.

The most common claims made by the historians about their character can be arranged under the topics of experience, effort, and fairmindedness. The last includes both impartiality (by far the most common of these claims) and a generous attitude towards one's predecessors

---

[15] Gray, *AJPh* 108 (1987) 473; Isnardi, *SCO* 3 (1955) 102-10.

[16] Sen. *ep.* 114.1: 'talis hominibus oratio qualis uita'; see Russell, *Criticism* 161ff. Moderns too occasionally read character from the work: see M. I. Finley, 'Thucydides the Moralist', *Aspects of Antiquity* (London and New York 1968) 44-57, who describes Thucydides as 'a humourless, not very lovable man ... superficially cold and reserved, but with strong inner tensions that occasionally break through' (44) – all, of course, derived from his historiographical persona. By contrast, Howald, *Vom Geist antiker Geschichtsschreibung* 225 recognised that Tacitus' 'pessimism' could not be assumed to be part of the historical Tacitus, describing it instead as 'sein historischer Stil, mit dem er seinem Werken Einheit und Geschlossenheit verleiht'. Cf. Syme, *Tacitus* II.541, who follows Howald.

[17] D. Hal. *A. R.* 1.6.5; at 1.1.2 Dionysius calls all literary works 'memorials of the writer's own character' (μνημεῖα τῆς ἑαυτῶν ψυχῆς).

[18] D. Hal. *Pomp.* 3-6 (II.380-2; 386-96 Usher).

[19] On Theopompus see *FGrHist* 115 TT 19, 25, 28b; on Timaeus, see *FGrHist* 566 TT 16-19; Polybius XII.24-26c expends a great deal of energy on Timaeus' disposition (αἵρεσις) and life (βίος); see Schepens, *PoH* 53-6 and esp. 56 n. 48; Isnardi, op. cit. (n.15) 105-9.   [20] Marincola, *AncW* 20 (1994) 191-203.

(which is quite rare). We shall, of course, examine the explicit remarks made by the historians on these topics, but we shall occasionally also look at the implicit methods for establishing these qualities. The usual place for the historian to establish his character is in the preface,[21] but we shall not limit ourselves to examining these alone. Far too many important indications given by an historian about his character come in the course of the history itself, sometimes in digressions, sometimes in small reminders or parenthetical remarks. Our examination, then, will follow an arrangement by topics; occasionally we will need to consider more fully under one or another of these topics an individual historian's efforts to fashion a character appropriate to his history.

2. EXPERIENCE

Since history was largely concerned with deeds in war and politics, it was perhaps only to be expected that historians would emphasise their experience in governing and leading armies and states. Theopompus, as we saw above, expressed the view that experience was closely allied to expertise.[22] But for Herodotus, the first historian, the only experience implied in the narrative is that of inquiry. No special technical expertise is claimed, no knowledge of statecraft or generalship is expressed. It is Thucydides who begins the series of historians who claim experience as an essential element of their authority. His experience, like Herodotus', is expressed in the intellectual terms of inquiring, perceiving, and understanding; this is seen most clearly in his 'second preface' (v.26), where he emphasises that he was of an age to understand the war, and that he was of the right disposition to learn about it, and that his exile worked to his advantage in securing access to both sides (v.26.5). All three points and the second preface in general are an expansion of matters touched on briefly in the preface to the entire work. The assurance earlier of beginning at the war's outbreak (1.1.1) is reinforced and expanded here by the information that he lived through the whole war; the claim that he dedicated himself to finding the truth (1.22.3) is here strengthened by the assurance that throughout the whole war he

---

[21] This follows rhetorical teaching (Arist. *Rhet.* III.16, 1417b 7-8): 'Right away introduce both yourself, what sort of person you are, so that they may see it, and your opponent. And do it inconspicuously.' In the preface, the historians are hardly inconspicuous; they show more subtlety in the narrative of their own deeds: see Ch. IV §3. [22] *FGrHist* 115 F 342, quoted above, Ch. II n. 45.

understood the events unfolding before him and from beginning to end applied himself to the pursuit of accurate information.[23] Some have seen defensiveness in this second preface,[24] but other explanations are possible. Contemporary history was a new province for which conventions and methodology had not yet been discovered or invented; and, unlike Herodotus, Thucydides did not wish to parade his method in the narrative itself. At this point, therefore, where he had to defend his notion that the Peloponnesian War was really one war,[25] it was also appropriate to emphasise again his own qualifications for the task – his experience of the war – in order to demonstrate or guarantee the superior accuracy that he claimed to have achieved as a contemporary of the war.[26]

The historians after Thucydides begin to assert more practical experience, especially that of participation. Xenophon, it is true, as narrator makes no explicit mention of his experience in either *Hellenica* or *Anabasis*. But Ctesias averred that his accuracy was the result of his experience as a war captive, taken prisoner by Artaxerxes, and then given access to reliable information because he was a physician employed by the King.[27] It should also be pointed out that Ctesias appeared in his history and that to some extent his participation was also a qualification, but we do not know whether he called specific attention to it and claimed it as an important element of his credibility.[28] Theopompus, however, spoke of a new sort of experience which he seemed to think qualified him for the writing of history. In the preface of his *Philippica*, he named himself and his contemporaries Isocrates,

---

[23] Thuc. v.26.5: ὅπως ἀκριβές τι εἴσομαι.

[24] Gomme, *HCT* IV.12; rejected by Dover, ibid. v.433 n. 1.

[25] The argument of the length of the war (v.26.2-3) leads to the evidence of the oracle (26.3 *ad fin.*), which is then validated by the historian's recollection (αἰεὶ γὰρ ἔγωγε μέμνημαι, 26.4), and the fact that he lived through it all (26.5). Thucydides is emphatic because his notion went against the general consensus of his time, which saw the Archidamian War as distinct: see G. E. M. de Ste Croix, *The Origins of the Peloponnesian War* (London and Ithaca 1972) 294-5.

[26] See Dover, *HCT* v.433; against the theory of L. Canfora, *Tucidide Continuato* (Padua 1970) that Xenophon put together v.26 and that he is the ἐγώ of 26.4 (as distinguished from ὁ αὐτὸς Θουκυδίδης of 26.1) see Dover, ibid., 431-7, who in addition notes (431, esp. n. 2) that there is no conflict between the use of the first and third person. On first and third person, see Ch. IV §1.

[27] *FGrHist* 688 T 3 = F 5; on the circumstances surrounding his capture, see Brown, *Historia* 27 (1978) 7-10; Eck, *REG* 103 (1990) 428-34.

[28] On his appearances see below, pp. 185f.

Theodectes, and Naucrates as the ones who held first place among the Greeks in rhetorical education; but that he and Naucrates (unlike the other two) did not need to write and teach for pay but, being self-sufficient, could spend their time in philosophy and learning. He extolled his literary prolificness in which he had treated Greek and barbarian affairs, adding that there was no place of importance into which he had not travelled and left behind him a testimony of his excellence; and he concluded by saying that those known in previous generations for rhetorical excellence could not in his lifetime hold even second place, so great an advance had education made in his lifetime.[29] The tone of these remarks is boastful throughout and the experience – rhetorical ability, free time for philosophy and learning, travels, fame – are all given in a spirit alien to that of the earlier historians. The travels which Herodotus and Thucydides put forward as an assistance in achieving superior accuracy were for Theopompus opportunities to display his abilities (it is these, after all, that he emphasises in the preface) and increase his personal repute. Criticism of his predecessors is likewise focused on their inferior literary abilities. The entire passage adduces as the author's qualifications his devotion to learning and his excellence as a writer. He seems to suggest that his literary excellence qualifies him to be Philip's historian. And to the extent that we can tell, his style was indeed epideictic.[30] Is his claim merely the evidence that rhetoric had become an important part of historiography, or was Theopompus suggesting a different approach and purpose to his history? Certain aspects of his work suggest a greater concern with individuals: continuous criticism even of the work's ostensible 'hero'; analysis of character; details of personal life.[31] Seen in this light, the epideictic nature of the history is foreshadowed in the preface, and his rhetorical ability is thus mentioned as a qualification because the techniques of narrative and description will, to no small extent, be used in forming judgement, just as orators in the law courts help the jury to

---

[29] Theopompus, *FGrHist* 115 F 25, partially quoted below, p. 254 n. 189.
[30] This was not lost on ancient critics: D. Chrys. *Or.* XVIII.10 (=*FGrHist* 115 T 45); Quint. x.1.74 (=T 21): 'oratori magis similis'. On the epideictic style, for which he was criticised by Duris, see Gray, *AJPh* 108 (1987) 467–86.
[31] Love of critical judgements: D. Hal. *Pomp.* 6 (II.394–6 Usher); character and personal life: ibid.; individuals criticised: Connor, *GRBS* 8 (1967) 133–54; Shrimpton, *Theopompus the Historian* 127–56; M. A. Flower, *Theopompus* 63–97; Theopompus did praise certain men: see Flower, ibid. 73–5.

reach a verdict on the accused. Put differently, the nature of Theopompus' *Philippica* required oratorical ability, and its mention in the preface can perhaps be seen as functional in the same way that Thucydides' remarks are.[32]

Polybius, as we saw above, spoke at length on the importance of experience for the basic inquiry necessary for any good historian and worthwhile history.[33] Although he mentions his participation often enough,[34] what makes Polybius unique is that more than any other historian he gives many details of his own life and experiences, and consistently emphasises their importance as part of his authority. Polybius is interested not only in the proper method of writing history, but also in the proper training, experience, and outlook of the historian himself, and he portrays his own actions as paradeigmatic for future historians.[35] Just as his narrative technique is 'apodeictic'[36] and provides lessons for the statesman, so the details of the author's experiences and achievements seek to guide the reader into forming an opinion of Polybius as the proper historian. This is seen in remarks on his contribution to the art of fire signalling, his interest in the practical matters of war as demonstrated by his separate work on tactics, his concern with the proper training of generals, and in many incidental remarks made throughout the work.[37] From all of this it becomes clear that Polybius wishes us to appreciate that the practical experience demanded of the historian,[38] is in him admirably achieved.

It will be worthwhile to turn our attention now to the Romans before considering the Greek and Latin historians of the Empire. At the outset we are forced to admit, as before, that our knowledge of the conventions used by pre-Sallustian historians is fragmentary and circumstantial. We simply do not know how Fabius Pictor, Postumius Albinus, or even Cato (let alone the later and more problematic Annalists) presented their experience to their audience. In this particular case, however, the loss is especially great, because of the close relationship in Roman historiography of the political and military man – the man of

---

[32] Lieberich, *Studien zu den Proömien* 16 speaks of this as a 'personal' proem, but the personal information has a purpose.   [33] See above, pp. 71ff.
[34] Pol. III.4.13; IV.2.2; XXIX. 5.1–3.   [35] See Davidson, *JRS* 81 (1991) 10–24.
[36] See Introduction n. 45.
[37] See Pol. x.45.6; IX.12–20; 20.4; see Walbank, *Polybius* 87–9 for more examples.
[38] Pol. II.62.2; XII.25g.-25i.9; Walbank, op. cit. (n.37) 51–2.

experience – and the historian.³⁹ *Auctoritas* seems to have played a greater role in the Roman's establishment of his credibility than in the Greek's.⁴⁰ It is possible – indeed, it is likely – that the early Hellenophone historians of Rome adopted Greek conventions in addressing their Greek audience and that (e. g.) Fabius mentioned his participation and presence at events.⁴¹ It is noteworthy that the poet Naevius, perhaps influenced by historians, mentioned in his *Punic War* that he had served in the war, and it is hardly to be doubted that this served as an important validation for his credibility.⁴² It is certain too, thanks to Livy, that Cincius mentioned his capture by Hannibal and it is not unlikely that his military experience figured in some way as a qualification. Of the history of A. Postumius Albinus, who took part in the war against Perseus and was consul and ambassador to Greece, we again know very little.⁴³

Even for Cato, unfortunately, we can form only an approximate view. Like his contemporary Polybius, he praised history in his preface. He laid claim, either explicitly or tacitly, to be considered one of the *clari* and *magni*; and he made clear (although it is unlikely to have been a point of emphasis) that his history was a work of his *otium*. So much has long been known.⁴⁴ But as the first historian of Rome to write in Latin, Cato will have played a crucial role in the formation of the persona of the Roman historian addressing his fellow Romans. For if it is the case that the Hellenophone historians addressed themselves primarily to the Greeks, the element of the author's personal experience and *auctoritas*, in itself, will for the most part have had little meaning, since the Greek historians cite things such as autopsy, inquiry, and participation to emphasise the possibilities of acquiring reliable information, and, like

---

³⁹ Syme, *Ten Studies in Tacitus* 1–10; La Penna, *Aspetti del pensiero storico latino* 43–104; but cf. Cornell, in *Past Persp.* 78–9.

⁴⁰ When Justin says that 'men of consular standing' ('consularis dignitatis uiri', *praef.* 1) wrote histories of Rome in Greek, does he know this from his own general knowledge or did they mention it in their works?

⁴¹ See above, pp. 77f.; on Pictor's purpose and portrayal of himself see Badian, in *Latin Historians* 2–6.

⁴² Naevius, F 2 with the discussion in Suerbaum, *Untersuchungen zur Selbstdarstellung älterer römischer Dichter* 13–27, who considers the possibility that Naevius was influenced by Hellenistic historiography.

⁴³ Cincius Alimentus, *FGrHist* 810 F 5 = *HRR* F 7 = Livy, XXI.38.3–5; very little is known of Cincius' history; for Albinus, most of what we know of him comes from Polybius who was hostile: see *FGrHist* 812 TT 1–7.

⁴⁴ Cato, *HRR* FF 1–3; discussion in Astin, *Cato the Censor* 221ff.

Polybius, present their experience as an aid in the formation of the proper understanding of the epistemological or heuristic demands of historiography. To be sure, Fabius and his epigoni did not address themselves exclusively to the Greeks. But in the absence of any positive evidence about these early historians, and in view of the positive evidence not only of the accepted methods in Greek historiography for justifying a foreign history,[45] but also of the specific political and perhaps even propagandistic purposes towards which Cato turned history,[46] it is Cato who is most likely the historian who introduced the author's *auctoritas* (that is, his personal standing *vis-à-vis* his Roman colleagues and the Roman people) as an important (certainly not the sole) qualification in the writing of history. Naturally, it was possible for the historians before Cato to exalt their families and their policies, either by inclusion of family history or manipulation of the actual events treated; and to this extent the historian could have raised his family and himself.[47] What I am arguing here is that Cato was the first one who put forward the belief that history was a suitable occupation for the *clari* and *magni* and in thus doing (and perhaps in connection with his moralistic interest in history[48]) made explicit the belief that it was the statesman's prerogative to write history. If we assume that Fabius was the first to do this, we must posit the introduction of a foreign means of justification into the highly developed Greek genre of histories of non-Greek lands. The audience of a Greek 'foreign' history might expect the narrator to be a priest (here Fabius would fit in well) or an investigator or a participator. But the assertion of social standing would have been without precedent and (within the genre) largely meaningless.

After Cato there is yet greater uncertainty. The preface of Sempronius Asellio contained his ringing defence of history against annals (expanding on Cato's), and it is not unlikely that the discussion of motivation, causes, and so forth allowed him to speak of his qualifications as well, since he too had a public career and may have invoked it in writing his contemporary history.[49] Sallust's prefaces, though atypical, may provide some useful perspective, since in both prefaces there is a constant concern with the relation of history-writing to public life, that

---

[45] See above, pp. 107ff. [46] See below, pp. 193f.
[47] Badian, op. cit. (n.41) 3 points to Pictor's F 18 (=*FGrHist* 809 F 15) as an example of the 'family lore' intended for the nobility.
[48] On this see Astin, op. cit. (n.44) 221–2.
[49] *HRR*, FF 1, 2 (see below, pp. 246f.); F 6; cf. Badian, op. cit. (n.41) 17–18.

is, of *otium* to *negotium*, and whatever Greek influence we allow on these prefaces, this particular concern is not in evidence among any Greek historians.[50] Sallust is here making reference to Roman expectations, since unlike most of his predecessors, he was not writing a history at the close of a successful career of service in which he had earned a justifiable *otium*. He was in a sense attempting at mid-life what was not usually earned until later life. To justify his abandonment of the *res publica* he must portray it as a corrupt and dangerous arena in which ignoble men harm the common good by appealing to private interests – an arena in short in which it is impossible any longer to benefit the republic. And so this calls for a reassessment of traditional evaluations: it is not *industria* to court the mob, nor *inertia* to incite men to virtue. Employing Cato's dictum in a new way, he claims that his *otium* will be of greater service to his country than the *negotium* of contemporary politicians. Thus in accordance with Cato (F 2) he gives an account of his *otium* but he differs from Cato specifically in setting his *otium* in contrast with (and not complementary to) *negotium*, which he portrays as having degenerated in his time into disruptive behaviour damaging to the Republic.[51] The novelty and unusual nature of the claim may have persuaded Sallust in the later *Jugurtha* to reiterate and extend the relationship he first propounded in the *Catiline*. He there defends his chosen occupation against the charge of *inertia* (*Jug.* 4.3) by first deriding what in the politics of his day passed for *industria* – gratification of the mob – and then mentioning that he himself held magistracies when (we are to assume) other worthy men did not. Moreover, the reader will realise the utter hopelessness of any benefit to be won by public service when he considers what type of unworthy men now inhabit the Senate (4.3-4). Sallust boldly claims that his *otium* will be of greater service to the state than the *negotium* of others, for he, like the fashioners of portrait busts, will serve to incite others to virtue by the *memoria rerum gestarum* (4.5-8).

Forced thus by circumstance onto the sidelines, Sallust begins to move historiography from its previous place among the Latin historians as a complement to a political career. While not denying his experience, Sallust suggests that there is no longer any place for principled men in

---

[50] What I mean is that the Greeks did not care about the specific Roman need for explaining their use of *otium*; for possible criticisms of the Romans in treating history as the work of retirement, see §3.

[51] For more on Cato and Sallust see Paul, *Commentary* 11; below, pp. 246f.

the state. Because he is interested in the morality, not the practicality, of action – like Plato, on whom the passage is modelled[52] – the importance of political experience recedes into the background. And this separation of practical experience from the writing of history, already begun in Sallust, reaches its culmination in Livy.

Sallust's influence is demonstrable in Livy's preface but the persona is entirely Livy's own. Unlike Sallust, however, Livy in his preface says nothing of his life and experiences, instead exalting the subject and its enormity, much like Polybius in his preface. Livy manages, however, by a skillful and unique construction to pass over completely the issue of his experience and qualifications in the preface. The diffidence that seems so puzzling has a purpose. Having noted that writers of new histories believe that they bring either greater accuracy or superior literary style to their new work, Livy strangely (but characteristically) refuses to say which it is that he offers.[53] He suggests only that if his own fame is lost among the many who have already attempted the task, 'I would console myself with the nobility and greatness of those who will overshadow my name.'[54] It can hardly be doubted that the characterisation of Livy's predecessors – those who possess *magnitudo* and *nobilitas* – is a discreet nod towards Cato's *magni*, and to the nobility who until recently had been the only ones to write history at Rome. Livy treads as an outsider.[55] And because he is not the first to write *ab urbe condita* he cannot state directly that he is uniquely qualified for the task; instead, he questions the very effort, and conceals whatever it is that he feels about his own qualifications. Similarly, the *labor* to which he repeatedly refers[56] is undercut by the hesitancy[57] towards the value of a new attempt, such that the prospect seems simultaneously hubristic and foolish. Now Livy, of course, could not follow in the tradition of Cato or even Sallust, both of whom had had public careers. But in adopting this 'personal' stance and in suggesting that his choice for writing history is strictly a refuge from present ills, Livy has constructed an elaborate *diminutio* that allows him to avoid

---

[52] See Ch. I n. 33.
[53] Livy, *praef.* 2; it is instructive to compare the opinions of moderns on what Livy promised for his history: Luce, *Livy* 184.
[54] Livy, *praef.* 3: 'nobilitate ac magnitudine eorum me qui nomini officient meo consoler'. [55] Moles, *PCPhS* 39 (1993) 144; cf. below, pp. 248ff; 288 n. 16.
[56] *praef.* 1, on which see below, pp. 153f.
[57] Ruch, *Didactica Classica Gandensia* 7 (1967) 77 speaks of a 'hésitation douloureuse ... qui est ensuite progressivement surmontée'.

completely the question of his own qualifications and experience which his audience might reasonably expect. The rhetorical lessening of expectations (Livy seems to question whether it is really even worth it) is thus closely allied to the presentation of the work as the author's personal pleasure. When he admits that he may even be unrecognised in his attempt, he shows more clearly than ever a spirit different from other historians, whose claim to write is founded on confidence in their interpretations and abilities.[58]

Livy excepted, it may fairly be stated that the Roman historians assert not so much their experience as their social status, and even the experience that they do assert is different from that of the Greeks, for whom it is closely tied to the investigative work of history. It is true that certain Greek historians do not assert experience at all, but this is rare.[59] For the Romans, however, it is common to mention offices held as an indication of one's rank. Two reasons may account for the Roman phenomenon: character and *dignitas* played a larger role in persuasion in Roman life than they did in Greek; and since mostly Senators had written history, the correlation of achievement and status was easily made.

In the late Republic and early Empire, we find historians who assert their *dignitas* by mentioning their and their ancestors' advancement. Livy's contemporary, Pompeius Trogus, did exactly that:

> At the end of this book [XLIII], Trogus writes that his ancestors traced their descent to the Vocontii; that his grandfather Trogus Pompeius obtained the citizenship from Cn. Pompey in the war with Sertorius; that his uncle led a squadron of cavalry in the Mithridatic war under this same Pompey; and that his father served under C. Caesar and was in charge of correspondence and legates and served as his private secretary.[60]

---

[58] Funaioli, *Die Antike* 19 (1943) 228ff. notes that Livy's personal preface had no predecessors, and that Sallust's preface was an attempt to convince Sallust himself that writing history was, in its own way, *negotium*. But Sallust is also trying to persuade his audience. The qualifications that the Annalists of the first century BC put forth would perhaps have shed light on Livy's persona here, for some of them were also non-political men. It should also be noted that the preface is suitable for the early part of Rome. What Livy did when he came to contemporary history we do not know, but see n. 198 below.

[59] Diodorus and Dionysius do not, perhaps because both are writing non-contemporary history; both, of course, do speak of their inquiry.

[60] Trogus, F 165 = Justin, XLIII. 5.11-12.

We cannot be certain of Trogus' purpose here, since we do not even know how he portrayed himself in his preface.[61] According to Justin, Trogus at the beginning of Book XLIII said that he would have been an ungrateful citizen indeed if, when he had treated the affairs of all people, he remained silent about his country alone.[62] He then treated Rome from its origins to Tarquinius Priscus, then the history of Liguria and Massilia. Trogus was from the Vocontii, a people around Massilia, so this may have been a suitable place to mention his ancestors, since the benefits given by Rome to Massilia would have blended nicely with the remarks about the benefits to Trogus' ancestors. Since we have no evidence that Trogus took part in public life,[63] and since this information had no bearing on the business of history, we are justified in assuming that this was a way for the author to assert his own *dignitas* and social standing to the reader. Naturally the tone of the remarks is lost and we do not know whether Trogus presented these details proudly and at length, or (like Tacitus later) quickly and reticently.

One sees something similar in Velleius, who mentions his ancestors not in one place, like Trogus, but at whatever point in the narrative he feels is appropriate: his great-grandfather Minatius Magius, his uncle Capito, and his grandfather Gaius Velleius.[64] Two of the passages contain a brief apology for mentioning members of his own family. Velleius recognises the discrepancy in praising one's family in a history, but he suggests that it would be excess modesty to avoid notice of his great-grandfather, and he notes the proof of his meritorious service, a special grant of citizenship by the Romans. In the second passage, he states simply that his uncle Capito assisted Agrippa in the case against Caesar's murderer Cassius. The third passage on his grandfather C. Velleius is a brief death notice for a man who was a partisan of Ti.

---

[61] Given the unusualness of a Latin universal history, he almost certainly explained why he was composing one (as Justin, *praef.* 1 notes), what sources (generally if not specifically) he used, and what material he deemed worthy of record. What he said of himself must remain uncertain. Despite the attempts of Seel in his edition of Trogus to assume that large portions of Justin's preface are taken from Trogus himself (his arguments are invalidated by Janson, *Latin Prose Prefaces* 77–83), we cannot assume that Justin's preface accurately reflects Trogus' own. Justin wrote later, and he wrote an epitome, a genre with different conventions. Cf. below, n.118.

[62] Justin, XLIII.1.1–2; see Vell. 1.7.1; see below, p. 273.

[63] A. Klotz, *RE* XXI. 2, 2300–1.

[64] He mentions his brother too, but this is in a different spirit: II.121.3; 124. 3–4.

Claudius Nero (the emperor's father, it should be noted) in the civil wars of 40 BC and who committed suicide nobly when the latter escaped from Campania to Sicily. Velleius introduces the notice with the remark that he will not deprive his grandfather of the mention (*testimonium*) which he would give a stranger.[65] Naturally we must reckon with the possibility that since Velleius' work is dedicated to Marcus Vinicius, the consul of AD 30 and the possible patron of Velleius, it is not inappropriate to have these brief mentions of family. Yet Velleius' history was not a wholly private work, and he well knew (or hoped) that others would read it too.[66]

What we see in both Trogus' and Velleius' mention of their ancestors, then, is on one level the attempt to assert social status, as that status could be won in the late Republic and early Empire. For these writers no shame attached to benefits conferred: they were most likely proud to be members of the classes from which Caesar and Augustus fashioned a new order at Rome, and they did not seek to hide their dependence for advancement on the Emperor or the army.[67] The unapologetic mention in Trogus and Velleius of *beneficia* conferred earned Tacitus' disapproval, both because it betokened servility and dependence on external powers, and because it cast doubt on the independence that an historian needed to claim. And when it was (as in Velleius) joined to unmeasured praise of Tiberius, the whole narrative took on an air of unreliability, motivated (as it seemed) by a *libido adsentandi* and far from the independence of the Senatorial historian. Tacitus' remarks on *beneficia* in the preface of the *Histories* furnish a useful contrast with those of Trogus and Velleius:

> At the same time [i. e., after Actium] truth was shattered by many means, first by an ignorance of the republic as if foreign, then by a lust for adulation or conversely hatred towards rulers. [...] Galba, Otho, Vitellius were known to me neither for benefit nor injury. I would not deny that my advancement was begun by Vespasian, increased by Titus, and carried farther by Domitian. But for those who have professed an uncorrupted trustworthiness, no one is to be described with affection or hatred.[68]

---

[65] Vell. II.16.2; 69.5; 76.1, respectively.
[66] On Velleius' history, Introduction n. 141; Ch. I n. 91; on the question of Velleius' relationship to Vinicius, see Woodman, *VP* I.126-7.
[67] For this group of *noui homines* see Gabba, in *Caesar Augustus: Seven Aspects* 80-1. [68] Tac. *Hist.* I.1.1, 3.

Tacitus' situation is complicated: he wishes to demonstrate that he is not to be confused with historians who do not have the proper experience,[69] and so he mentions his advancement by Vespasian, Titus, and Domitian. Yet his acknowledgement that he owed his advancement to certain Emperors might seem to compromise him, because the conferral of *beneficia* on an author was seen as the primary cause for flattery and obsequiousness;[70] for this reason Tacitus must immediately assert impartiality. We shall come back to this in the last section; here it must suffice to note that Tacitus' remarks about his own *dignitas* fit in well with the precedent set by Cato and show him to be a member of that distinguished company of Senator-historians, and by implication, that long line of *magna ingenia*. It is evident that Tacitus in the *Histories* is attempting to weave promises of impartiality with details of his social status: being a Senator, of course, he did not need to parade it.[71] So too in the *Annals*, Tacitus informs the reader that he was a praetor and *quindecimuir* at the *ludi saeculares* in AD 88. Although he is careful to disown vainglory and presents the remark as validation for his superior knowledge, the honour was no minor one and the fact of the author's experience and status will have been made there too.[72]

The Greek historians of the Empire have various approaches to the claims of experience. Like the Romans, they at times mention their social status, and although there is not as much evidence as we would like, all indications are that this is a feature of Roman republican historiography that is then picked up and used by both Greek imperial historians (for whom it was a novelty) and Roman. It may be objected that many Greek historians were political men and that the tradition is thus quite old and independent of the Romans. But in fact not a single Greek historian before the Empire gives his offices and social status as

---

[69] He may be here thinking of Aufidius Bassus who was not a Senator. His other predecessors, such as Servilius Nonianus and even the elder Pliny (on whom see Jal, *Helmantica* 38 (1987) 172), were men of public experience.

[70] See Luce, *CPh* 84 (1989) 18–21 for the correlation between *beneficia* and partiality; more below, §4. [71] Fornara, *Nature* 55 n. 8.

[72] Tac. *Ann.* XI.11.1 ('non iactantia refero'); on the honour, Syme, *Tacitus* 1.65-6. Since Syme notes that the interpretation of this college's archives 'called for scholarship and good sense', there is no reason why the mention of it here cannot have done double duty. Syme, ibid. II.540 claims that Tacitus had 'an almost morbid fear of ostentation and "iactantia"', but he is only being careful in the matter of self-praise: see Ch. IV §1.

an independent element of his qualifications: Polybius' requirement of political experience for the historian is no exception because he there says that this experience will then teach the historian what questions to ask, that is, help him in his role as investigator.[73] We are talking here about the mention of one's offices as an indication of status, that is, a component with no formal relationship to the actual writing of the history.

Josephus at the opening of the *Jewish War* gives his experience as a participant and eyewitness of the events as the guarantee of his reliability. This obviously has a direct relationship to the investigative task, and is in keeping with the Greek tradition as we have traced it. He also, however, identifies himself as a priest, and it is fairly certain that this is stated for different reasons.[74] He may, of course, be using the claim of priest in the way we see them as reliable preservers of traditions in foreign lands,[75] but the *Jewish War* is a contemporary, not an antiquarian, history. The explanation is perhaps rather to be found in Josephus' *Life* where he notes that among the Jews the priesthood is a mark of nobility.[76] If this is the reason that he mentions it in the *War*, then we have a clear example of an attempt to assert one's social status in what I would call the Roman tradition.

In this category as well should be placed Appian's claims at the beginning of his history. It is curious that Appian provides in the preface no remarks whatsoever on his qualifications: a passing reference to the geographical areas that his history comprehends perhaps suggests some inquiry, but it is just as likely to be a way of saying, 'my history will treat such and such areas' (*praef.* 46–8). Where he chooses to present himself to the reader he mentions his honours and social status:

> Who I am who have written these things, many know, and I myself have given an indication.[77] To speak more clearly, I am Appian of Alexandria, who have reached the first ranks in my country, and have pleaded causes in Rome before the emperors, until they deemed me worthy to be procurator. And if anyone has a great desire to learn all the rest about me, there is a treatise by me on this subject too.[78]

---

[73] Pol. xii.25g–i, and above, pp. 71ff.   [74] Jos. *B. J.* 1.3.   [75] Above, pp. 107ff.
[76] Jos. *Vita* 1: παρ' ἡμῖν ἡ τῆς ἱερωσύνης μετουσία τεκμήριόν ἐστιν γένους λαμπρότητος.
[77] This is most likely a reference to *praef.* 26 (the narrator has seen ambassadors at Rome) and especially 39, where he referred to Egyptian kings as 'my kings'.
[78] App. *praef.* 62. The treatise referred to does not survive.

In the absence of other evidence, it is difficult to escape the conclusion that in Appian's preface, at least, the offices are in some way put forward as a qualification for writing history, but they are clearly ornamental. When, for example, he notes that he rose to the first ranks, pleaded causes before the Emperors, and became a procurator, it seems clear that Appian has been influenced by the Roman tradition, since these remarks in the preface have little or nothing to do with the experience of a Polybius, and very much to do with the types of remarks found in Trogus and Velleius. Since the mention of offices – and even more of honours – has no bearing on the investigative work demanded by history (as those by Herodian and Dio do, below), it serves only to advance the social status of the narrator.

If this interpretation is correct, we may approach the second preface of Arrian's *Anabasis* with a somewhat wider frame of reference.[79] Here the narrator explicitly refuses to reveal anything about himself:[80]

> As for who I am who make this judgement in my favour, I do not need to write my name, for it is not unknown among men, nor what my country is, nor my family, nor any office I held in my native country; but I do write this: that my country and race and offices are these writings, and they have been from my youth. And on account of this I do not deem myself unworthy of the first place in the Greek language, just as Alexander was first in arms.[81]

The echoes with Appian are clear, as is the direct contrast. There seems little doubt that Arrian, in adopting this stance, wishes to assert the irrelevance of offices as such for a history of Alexander,[82] and to disown here in a work about the greatest Greek historical hero what can only be (from the evidence presented above) a Roman convention. It is not so much that Arrian would see offices *per se* as unimportant in a history. But as is evident in Appian, the offices mentioned are irrelevant to the work of the historian in the same way that Trogus' or Velleius' are, and it

---

[79] Appian's priority is contested: the arguments for the dating of each man's work in Bosworth, *HCA* 1.8–11.

[80] His anonymity is modelled on Xenophon's, but different in spirit; as Moles, *JHS* 105 (1985) 164 n. 13 observes, Arrian's is an 'ostentatious *recusatio*'.

[81] Arr. *Anab.* 1.12.5, following Moles, op. cit. (n.80) 163 in the translation.

[82] Breebaart, *Enige historiografische aspecten van Arrianus' Anabasis Alexandri* 17; Schepens, *Anc. Soc.* 2 (1971) 265–6.

is this motif – the assertion of office as an ornament to indicate social status – that Arrian slyly undercuts in his second preface.[83]

Different in tone and intention are the remarks of Herodian and Dio on their experience. For each of them, the mention of offices held, while certainly conveying some notion of their status, has a practical purpose, usually in the access that their office provided to certain information or people. In Herodian's preface, the mention of offices is brief and part of that connection with inquiry that we saw in the earlier Greek historians: 'things I saw and heard and in which I had a share in my imperial and public services, these I have written up'.[84] Dio also frequently mentions offices: sometimes these directly benefit the work of his history; at other times, the line between inquiry and social status is not clear at all. An example of the latter is his description of the manners of life and customs of the Pannonians, which he follows with the remarks:

> These things I know not only by hearsay and reading, but learning them by action, in as much as I ruled over them. For after my command in Africa and Dalmatia (the latter of which my father also once held) I was assigned to what is called Upper Pannonia; whence I write everything about them with exact knowledge.[85]

The main point, of course, is that as governor he was able to learn of the Pannonians' manners and customs; there remains, however, a secondary function in establishing status, since his previous offices and the mention of his father have no functions in inquiry here.[86]

As for Ammianus, we do not know whether he asserted his social status explicitly in the preface as a qualification. The simple ending of his book – 'ut miles quondam et Graecus' – reveals, in some measure, what he considered important, and recalls the tradition of soldier-historian going back to Xenophon.[87] But we ought not to overlook the delightful aside within the exciting narrative of his escape after the fall of Amida, when he tells us that because of his free birth he was unaccustomed to excessive walking.[88] This is almost certainly an oblique

---

[83] Marincola, *JHS* 109 (1989) 188-9, misrepresented by Gray, *JHS* 110 (1990) 186 n. 25.
[84] Herodian, 1.2.5; a survey of opinions on his actual services in Whittaker, *Herodian* xix-xxiv.   [85] Dio, XLIX.36.4.
[86] As does the citation of his father at LXIX.1.2-3, for the information that Trajan's death was not revealed for several days.   [87] See below, pp. 256f.
[88] Amm. XIX.8.6: 'et incedendi nimietate iam superarer, ut insuetus ingenuus'.

reference (like Tacitus' above) that is meant to indicate something of the author's social status, and it may have been included so that Ammianus might separate himself from those historians (common under the Empire), such as Phlegon and Chryserus, who were imperial freedmen.[89]

We may conclude this section with certain historians mentioned by Lucian, who may serve again to recall the variety of the historiographical tradition in antiquity. A certain Antiochianus mentioned that he was an Olympic victor, an assertion of status, to be sure, even if of a particularly ludicrous kind for history; and a certain Callimorphus explained that as a physician he was the right man for history since Asclepius was son of Apollo and Apollo was leader of the Muses and ruler of all learning.[90] Yet Lucian's ridicule of what these brought forward as their 'experience' reminds us of the restricted circle of acceptable conventions in which ancient historiography actually moved.

3. EFFORT

Claims of efforts made in the research and composition of one's history are common among both Greek and Latin historians in all eras of antiquity. Although Herodotus seems to refer to effort only once, and Thucydides limits himself to saying that it was a 'toilsome' task to discover the truth of conflicting accounts,[91] later historians spoke of the practical efforts they made in compiling their histories. Practical difficulties then replace or coexist with epistemological ones. Claims of effort, however, are of two types. The first emphasises the practical work of travel, inquiry, and expense made in the compilation of the history; the second seems rather to refer to the effort involved in writing up the history and may be subsumed under the larger rubric of the effort or care expected of all who wrote literature in antiquity.

It is in Theopompus' *Philippica* that we find the first explicit claim to have made a great effort in the composition of history.[92] Dionysius says of him:

---

[89] On these see above, Ch. II n. 126.
[90] Luc. *h.c.* 30 (=*FGrHist* 207 F 1); 16 (=210 FF 1-2). Can the latter be a satire of Trajan's physician Kriton, who wrote a *Getica* (*FGrHist* 200 T 3)? Callimorphus' remarks about learning (παιδεία) recall Theopompus' above, p. 135.
[91] Hdt. III.115.2; Thuc. 1.22.3; cf. 20.1 on the difficulty of discovering past events.
[92] For Ephorus see below, n. 109.

For it is evident, even if he had written nothing about it, that he made very great preparation for his task and incurred the greatest expense in gathering material, and that in addition he was an eyewitness of many things and spoke with many men and generals prominent at the time, leaders of the people, and philosophers for the sake of his history. For he did not, like some, think the writing of history a part-time task (πάρεργον), but rather the most necessary of all things.[93]

The effort is related to the historian's care and industry and also to the travels undergone in order to research the material of the history. This tradition of actual labour, the effort of travelling to interview witnesses and examine sights (and sites), continued and expanded in the Hellenistic world, where we find more remarks about efforts made in the fashioning of a history. No longer is it enough merely to suggest a passion for accuracy. As histories became larger, the historian laid greater emphasis on travel and expense or on dangers undergone. Timaeus, for example, said that the expense and difficulty that he incurred in gathering materials on the Tyrians was so great as to justify the distrust of his readers.[94] Polybius also speaks of dangers and hardships undergone for the geographical portion of his history.[95] Some of this expectation of effort and toil, particularly where travel was concerned, may also be seen at the conclusion of Agatharchides' *On the Red Sea*, where the narrator says that he cannot continue beyond what he has already done, but he encourages others, saying that 'whoever has ... decided to win fame from toil will not hold off from this'.[96]

The idea of fame through toil is picked up by Diodorus, who goes further than any of his predecessors by making the historian's efforts a recurring theme of his preface. At the outset he claims both that historians benefit humanity by their individual labours, and that one learns from the experience of others. He summons up the figure of Odysseus, the man who was both the greatest sufferer and the most experienced of men (1.1.1–2), and then the example of Heracles:

> It is a fine thing, I think, for wise men to exchange mortal toils for an immortal renown. Heracles, it is agreed, during the entire time he was among mankind, endured great and continuous toils and dangers

---

[93] D. Hal. *Pomp.* 6 (II.392 Usher) = *FGrHist* 115 T 20a.
[94] Pol. XII.28a.3 = *FGrHist* 566 F 7; on the reading 'Tyrians', Walbank, *HCP* II.411–12.   [95] Pol. III.59.7.
[96] Agatharchides, *Mar. Rubr.* §110 = *GGM* I.194 = *FGrHist* 86 T 3 (abridged).

willingly, so that he might attain immortality by benefiting the race of mankind. And of other good men, some have attained the honour of heroes, some honours equal to the gods', but all have been deemed worthy of great praise, their virtues being immortalised by history.[97]

Here a new idea, only suggested in Agatharchides, is integrated into the motif of labours and dangers: the prospect of honour and fame to be won from such endeavours. This is not evident in Polybius who makes the connection between benefit (not fame) and danger or toil. Like heroes, historians too undergo efforts: Diodorus speaks of the labour (πόνος) of writing a continuous work and then claims that he endured much hardship and danger in order to travel and correct the errors of even distinguished historians.[98] However we interpret such remarks,[99] Diodorus wishes his audience to see him as following in Heracles' footsteps, since, just as Heracles undertook his labours in the hope of winning eternal fame, so too Diodorus was led to the consideration of the writing of history by seeing the renown accorded historians.[100] Like Heracles, Diodorus sees himself primarily as a benefactor (εὐεργέτης) of mankind who will thereby win for himself immortality.[101]

Whence this emphasis on danger and toil arose cannot be determined with certainty, though its genesis can perhaps be explained. We have already seen the germ of it in Thucydides, and the word πόνος is used of wars, the hardships of war, and the struggles of those in them, while the conjunction of toil, expense, and danger is a very common one in the ancient historians.[102] This assurance of hardship undergone for

---

[97] Diod. 1.2.4. For the close connection between πόνος and the labours of Heracles, see Loraux, *AION* (Arch.) 4 (1982) 171-92.
[98] Diod. 1.3.6; 4.1: μετὰ πολλῆς κακοπαθείας καὶ κινδύνων.
[99] Many scholars, beginning with C. Wachsmuth, *Einleitung in das Studium der alten Geschichte* (Leipzig 1895) 82, believe Diodorus' remarks to be merely a repetition of Polybius' and not to be taken seriously; others concede his travels to him.
[100] Diod. 1.3.1; for more on the historian's renown see above, Ch. I §4.
[101] On the importance of εὐεργεσία in Diodorus, see Sacks, *Diodorus* ch. 3. For Lucceius' identification with Heracles see below, p. 165; for an historian greater than Heracles see Nicolaus cited at p. 155 below.
[102] Several passages in Xenophon show this, the best perhaps in the *Anabasis* (III.1.12) where Xenophon falls asleep after being chosen leader by the Greeks and dreams: 'He woke up immediately, feeling very frightened, and considered that in some respects the dream was a good one, because in the midst of his toils

the sake of one's history is also allied to the belief that history instructs vicariously: the historian assures his audience that he has taken pains, incurred expense, and undergone difficulty, and from his efforts the reader may learn effortlessly. The idea, first clearly expressed by Polybius,[103] is perhaps most felicitously expressed by Diodorus who calls history 'instruction in what is beneficial without the accompanying dangers'.[104] This emphasis on labour has a long history: even in the third century AD, Philip of Pergamum insisted on its value, and made the same correlation between the historian's effort and his reader's benefit that Polybius and Diodorus had.[105]

The Greek historians of the late Republic and early Empire continue the trend of adding details about their effort. Exact numbers of the time spent on one's history begin to appear: Diodorus says that he spent thirty years in working on his history, Dionysius claims twenty-two. Since all historians claimed care, the general statement of effort may have come to be considered less effective, so it then became useful to distinguish oneself by an exact reckoning of the time in order to demonstrate one's seriousness at the task. Dio goes yet further and gives the exact figures as ten years in collecting materials, twelve years in writing

---

and dangers (ἐν πόνοις ... καὶ κινδύνοις) he had dreamed of a great light from Zeus.' Similarly, in the *Hellenica* (v.1.4) Xenophon speaks of the usual subject matter of a history as expense, danger, and contrivance (δαπάνημα, κίνδυνος, μηχάνημα). For the conjunction of toil, danger, and/or expense see (to name only a few) Thuc. 1.33.2; 70.8; VI.16.6 (all in speeches); Xen. *Hell.* III.5.12; Pol. VIII.10.9; XII.5.3; 27.4–6; XVIII.46.14; XXVIII.13.5; Diod. 1.36.4–5; XV.1.3; XVII.56.4; 94.1; Sall. *Cat.* 10.2; *Hist.* II.98; Livy, 1.54.4; XXIX.1.4; Vell. II.79.1; 122.2.

[103] Pol. I.1.2; cf. III.59.7. One wonders whether Ephorus said anything about it.

[104] Diod. I.1.1: ἀκίνδυνον ... διδασκαλίαν τοῦ συμφέροντος. It seems best to attribute this commonplace to Diodorus, not to the lost preface of Posidonius: Nock, *Essays on Religion and the Ancient World* II.859–60. Malitz, *Historien des Poseidonios* 38 and 413 with nn. 25–8 would reserve the sentence about the historian's task as preserver of ἀρετή (1.1.3) for Posidonius.

[105] FGrHist 95 F 1: ἐγὼ παντοίων παθέων καὶ ξυνεχέος ἀλληλοφονίας ἀνά τε τὴν Ἀσίην καὶ τὴν Εὐρώπην καὶ τὰ Λιβύων ἔθνεα ἱστορίαν ἐξήνεγκα ... ὅκως καὶ δι' ἡμέων μανθάνοντες, ... ἀπευθήτους ποιέονται τὰς τοῦ βίου διορθωσίας. Cf. App. *B. Civ.* 1.24 for a similar sentiment. Cf. Cicero's claim that thanks to the *labor* which Atticus expended on his *liber annalis*, those who in the future will wish to know the history of Rome will find it far easier (*Orat.* 120). Cicero speaks of his own *labor* and a similar benefit for his countrymen in translating the speeches of Demosthenes and Aeschines at *Opt. Gen.* 15 (if that work is genuine).

them up into a polished work, a total that agrees, perhaps significantly, with Dionysius' twenty-two.[106] In remarking that he spent twelve years in working his materials up, Dio is referring to the second type of effort mentioned above: the literary effort involved in bringing an historical work to final form. This type of literary labour is familiar from Isocrates who frequently extols his own rhetorical abilities.[107] Dionysius mentions the tradition that Isocrates needed ten years to write a single speech, the *Panegyricus,*[108] and this is most likely the ultimate model for Diodorus, Dionysius, and Dio, a guarantee to the audience that, like the master, they had put great effort and care into the making of their history. In historiography, the first example seems to be Ephorus' remarks in the preface of his Book VI where he spoke of the talent and preparation that history required.[109]

This emphasis on literary effort – on *labor* in composition as the mark of a good historian – finds several parallels in Latin historiography. For Sallust the difficulty or *labor* of historiography is given in terms of style and impartiality: 'it seems especially difficult to write history: first, because the deeds must be made equal with the words'.[110] This *topos*, as has long been recognised, goes back to Thucydides (Pericles' funeral oration) and Isocrates, and often is invoked in epideictic rhetoric; it is found in other historians besides Sallust.[111] In the *Jugurtha* he also emphasises the work of history by defending himself against those who 'will call my useful labour laziness',[112] but there is little sense that this is meant in the same way as Diodorus or Polybius meant this. On the contrary, the labour and effort are seen in terms of finding the appropriate words. The dangers, which for the Greek historians had been the practical ones attendant on inquiry, become for Sallust the risks of not being believed should he transgress the limits of his audience's credulity.

---

[106] Diod. 1.4.1; D. Hal. *A. R.* 1.7.2; Dio, LXXII.23.5.
[107] See, e.g., Isoc. *Paneg.* 13–14; *Panath.* 8.
[108] See D. Hal. *Comp.* 25 (II.224 Usher); [Long.] *Subl.* 4.2. Theopompus too, as we saw (above, p. 135), emphasised his literary ability.
[109] Ephorus, *FGrHist* 70 F 111; as Ephorus seems not to have undertaken travels (Jacoby, *FGrHist Komm.* II. c. 25), I assume that he here refers to literary ability.
[110] Sall. *Cat.* 3.2: 'in primis arduom uidetur res gestas scribere: primum quod facta dictis exaequanda sunt'.
[111] Thuc. II.35.2: χαλεπὸν μὲν τὸ μετρίως εἰπεῖν; Isoc. *Paneg.* 13: ὡς χαλεπόν ἐστιν ἴσους τοὺς λόγους τῷ μεγέθει τῶν ἔργων ἐξευρεῖν. See Vretska's commentary, 90–1 for more examples.
[112] Sall. *Jug.* 4.3: 'tanto tamque utili labori meo nomen inertiae imponant'.

Effort

These statements about effort also distinguish the author as one who has taken his work seriously and sees it as a demanding task, exactly as Dionysius had said of Theopompus, in words that echo Polybius' criticism of Timaeus, and his summation of the necessary qualities of a historian:

> And I would say that history will fare well either when men of affairs attempt to write it, not (as now) like a part-time task (παρέργως), but considering it among the most necessary and finest things, and uninterruptedly holding themselves to the task their whole life; or when those who attempt to write history shall consider that the experience to be gotten from affairs is necessary.[113]

Amongst the Roman writers of large-scale histories, there is a similar emphasis on effort. Livy makes constant reference to this in his preface:

> Whether it shall be worth while (lit., a return on the work, *operae pretium*)[114] if I write up the affairs of the Roman people, I do not really know, nor if I knew would I dare to say ...
>
> in addition, the matter is of immense work (*immensi operis*) in as much as it goes back beyond seven hundred years, and, having started from small beginnings, has grown to such a point that it now labours under its own weight (*iam magnitudine laboret sua*).
>
> I on the other hand shall seek this reward also for my labour (*hoc quoque laboris praemium petam*) ...
>
> if it were the custom for us, as for poets, we would more freely begin with omens and vows and prayers to the gods that they give a successful outcome to so great a work as we have begun (*nobis orsis tantum operis*).[115]

There is a clever intermingling here of the historian's labour and an enormous Rome now labouring under its own weight, and by

---

[113] Pol. XII.28.3–5. See also Polybius' criticisms of Phylarchus who made remarks in his history εἰκῆ καὶ ὡς ἔτυχεν (II.56.3); cf. Dionysius' statement that a fine theme wins no praise if the author has compiled his evidence at random and from chance informants (εἰκῆ καὶ ῥαθύμως, *A. R.* 1.1.4), which is an imitation of Thuc. I.22.2 (ἐκ τοῦ παρατυχόντος πυνθανόμενος), discussed at length by Dionysius at *Thuc.* 6; for Dionysius on Theopompus, see above, n. 18.

[114] Livy says literally, 'whether I shall make a return on the work'. I use the impersonal 'it' above because, as Moles, *PCPhS* 39 (1993) 141–2 shows, there are two questions here: will it be worth Livy's while and will it be worth the reader's while?   [115] Livy, *praef.* 1, 4–5, 13.

extension, the historian who must work at sorting it all out. There is a similar play later in the second pentad when Livy sums up a series of seemingly endless wars with the Samnites, Pyrrhus, and the Carthaginians (VII.29.1-2):

> From here we must speak of wars greater in terms of the enemy's manpower, of the remoteness of the locations, and of the duration of fighting... What a mass of events! (*Quanta rerum moles!*) How often it came to the extremity of danger so that empire could be built to this vast extent which can scarcely be supported.

Livy is surely laying claim here to the tradition seen in earlier universal historians that the business of history demands toil and effort,[116] and he elsewhere reminds his audience of the ongoing *labor* of the project, as he does after his narration of the Hannibalic War (XXXI.1.1-5):

> I too am pleased, as if I myself had taken part in the toil and danger,[117] to have come to the end of the Punic War. For although it is least appropriate for one who dared to assert that he would write all of Roman history that he grow weary in the individual parts of such a work (*in partibus singulis tanti operis fatigari*), nevertheless ... I see in my mind that I – like men led on by the shallow water near the shore who wade out into the sea – am being carried away into vaster depths, as if into the deep, whatever progress I make, and the work, which seemed to be growing smaller as I finished each of the earlier pieces, increases (*crescere paene opus*).

There are a few indications (for that is all we can call them) that other Greek and Latin historians writing large-scale histories also emphasised their efforts. Justin, in his preface to his epitome of Pompeius Trogus compares Trogus' *labor* in writing his universal history with Hercules' *audacia*:

> For although to many authors who write the history of individual kings or people, their own work seems to be one of arduous labour, ought not Pompeius to seem to us to have approached the entire world with

---

[116] Ogilvie's view that Livy's emphasis on labour was unique (*Commentary on Livy*, 26) is emended in the Addenda (775), where the commonplace is recognised.

[117] Livy, XXXI.1.1: 'uelut ipse in parte laboris ac periculi [= πόνων καὶ κινδύνων] fuerim'.

Herculean courage, since in his books the events of all the ages, kings, nations, and peoples are contained?[118]

Nicolaus of Damascus emphasised the great labour involved in writing up his history, and took Diodorus' use of Heracles a step further:

> Nicolaus even more greatly gave himself to the task, gathering together every history and undergoing labour such as no other had done. Engaged in this labour of love for a long time, he completed his history, and he said that if Eurystheus had offered this task to Heracles, it would have exhausted him.[119]

Heracles naturally enough suggests himself as an appropriate model because of his benefits towards mankind, as well as the fact that he, more than any other hero, traversed the known and unknown world.

We should also mention the dedication by Catullus of his book of poems to Cornelius Nepos in which the poet compares his own *nugae* with Nepos' historical chronical, *cartae* that the poet calls both *doctae* and *laboriosae*.[120] It has been suggested that Catullus may in fact be referring to Alexandrian poetic theory that saw *labor* as the distinguishing mark of the good poet, and that the poet is claiming that Nepos has written an Alexandrian neoteric history.[121] More likely, I think, is that Catullus has appropriated the *topos* of *labor*, described above, and common to large-scale (not necessarily lengthy) histories, and has used it in conjunction with the notion of *labor* that is inherent in all careful and learned artistic creation.[122] Catullus may have both in

---

[118] Justin, *praef.* 2. Justin continues, (4) 'From these forty-four volumes (for so many did he publish), I have excerpted, while enjoying my leisure in the city (*otium, quo in urbe uersabamur*), those things that were most worthy, etc.' Seel in his edition of the fragments of Trogus believed the words 'otium, quo in urbe uersabamur' to be Trogus' own and printed them as F 14a. I think it extremely unlikely - even for a Latin historian - to claim that his 44-book universal history was a work of *otium*. The sentiment is much more appropriate to an epitomator, and Justin himself is here comparing the work of his *otium* with Trogus' *labor* (*praef.* 2).

[119] Nicolaus, *FGrHist* 90 F 135, from Nicolaus' autobiography. We do not know whether it appeared in the preface of the history.

[120] Catullus, 1.3-7 = Nepos, *Chronica, HRR* F 7.

[121] So F. Cairns, 'Catullus I', *Mnemosyne*, 4th ser. 22 (1969) 153-8 at 154; cf. L. Ferrero, *Un' introduzione a Catullo* (Turin 1955) 52 n. 20; Wiseman, *CC* 170-1 on the appropriateness of the dedication and its unironic character; Kroll, *Studien zum Verständnis der römischen Literatur* 38-9 for the relationship between *doctus* and *labor*.

[122] See Kroll, op. cit. (n.121) 41-3 for the value of *labor* in prose.

mind for Nepos' history, since Nepos will, like Livy, have wanted his history to be seen as the outcome of effort both in investigative and in stylistic effort. Yet let us not limit professions only to historians who write 'universal' histories. Josephus claims to have incurred expenses and pains in the composition of both his *Jewish War* and his *Jewish Antiquities*.[123] Witness too Tacitus' famous complaint in the *Annals*:

> I am not unaware that many of the things I have related and will relate seem perhaps insignificant and trivial to record. But no one is to compare our annals with the writings of those who composed the affairs of the Roman people long ago ... (2) they were recording in unrestricted movement, but our effort is narrow and without glory.[124]

Lucian uses πόνος in the sense of both artistic toil and the inquiry needed to establish the actions themselves. In the first passage, he says that 'the best writer has political understanding and the power of expression, and the latter may come from much practice, continuous toil, and imitation of writers of old'. We also find toil opposed to careless investigation, Lucian demanding that 'the deeds themselves must be gathered not at random but after judging often the same things with toil and painstakingly'.[125] This then is perhaps the best of both worlds, the belief that the historian needed to exert himself to discover what really happened, and to labour over the final creation, so that it might aspire to the high standard of one's predecessors.

We have found, then, a two-fold strain in the claims of effort emphasised by historians in their work: the one, going back to Herodotus and Thucydides via Theopompus assures the audience that the historian has undergone difficulties and undertaken travels in order to fulfil the demands of inquiry required by history. The other, evident in Theopompus and explicit in Isocrates, is an assurance that care – however we are to interpret this, but literary care is certainly an important part of it – has been expended over the history as an artistic work. When we recall the general reluctance of historians to use as a justification for a new history a finer stylistic treatment, or indeed to discuss the literary merits of their work,[126] this common claim of effort may serve as the

---

[123] Jos. *B. J.* 1.16; *A. J.* 1.9.
[124] Tac. *Ann.* IV.32.1–2: 'nobis in arto et inglorius labor'; cf. 61, 'aliorum meditatio et labor in posterum ualescit', with Martin and Woodman's commentary ad loc.
[125] Luc. *h.c.* 34 (συνεχεῖ τῷ πόνῳ); 47 (φιλοπόνως καὶ ταλαιπώρως).
[126] See above, pp. 116f.

acceptable substitute for an explicit statement that the historian has tried to write his history in an elevated or fine style.

Before leaving the topic, we should mention one other aspect of the notion of dangers undergone for a history. We have seen that it has its origins in the danger of travels made for investigation. But historians faced other dangers. Sallust, as we noted above, saw danger in writing history because the reader may attribute envy or malice to the historian if he writes with too much obvious partiality. And this was to become a more substantive danger under the Empire. Horace warns Asinius Pollio that the latter's history of the civil war is 'a work full of dangerous chance'.[127] The meaning here is two-fold: the characters in Pollio's history were the victims of dangerous chance, and the historian himself was at risk in narrating this period, because the topic was still painful in the telling and likely to upset those in power.[128] A similar 'danger' is implicitly referred to by Tacitus. The treatment of his own times, promised as a future undertaking in the preface of the *Histories*, is described as a 'richer and safer topic' (*uberiorem securioremque materiam*), and he means by 'safer' less dangerous for a writer to 'think what you want and say what you think' (*Hist.* 1.1.4). The close correlation of danger with professions of impartiality – the securer time is, after all, when you can indulge in the traditional free speech of the historian – suggests the difficulties which we noted above when one tries to write under autocratic regimes.[129] Ammianus at the outset of his Book XXVI says that he was going to avoid 'the dangers often attendant on truth' and mentions the procedure of older writers, such as Cicero, in publishing accounts of events after their deaths.[130] Ammianus is referring, however, not to free speech, but to the danger of inappropriate criticism from the ignorant, who will point to this or that omission.[131] Closer in spirit to the remarks above may be the opening of Book XXVIII, where Ammianus says that he was originally going to avoid an account of

---

[127] Hor. *Carm.* II.1.6: 'periculosae plenum opus aleae', with Nisbet and Hubbard's commentary ad loc.
[128] On Pollio's independence and harshness of judgement see Peter, *HRR* II.LXXXIV–V; Schanz-Hosius II.29–30.   [129] See Ch. II §2.
[130] Amm. XXVI.1.1: 'pericula ... ueritati saepe contigua'; on deferred publication, below, pp. 172f.
[131] Amm. XXVI.1.2; Matthews, *Roman Empire of Ammianus* 204–5 with n. 1 (where other opinions are surveyed).

Maximin's slaughter at Rome because of 'a justifiable dread', but will tell it now because of the better atmosphere of the present day.[132] In these passages, then, the particular 'danger' in writing history represents an evolution of the earlier (and largely Greek) concept of the historian who undergoes danger to benefit his audience, and seems instead designed to establish his impartiality and his freedom of speech. And that brings us to our next topic.

4. IMPARTIALITY

Of all the claims made by ancient historians, the promise to be impartial is far and away the most common. Indeed, as we saw above, the difficulties of investigation are always acknowledged by historians, but there is little explanation of what makes it difficult or how investigative problems have been resolved. Discussions of impartiality, on the other hand, abound; if we had to judge difficulty by the amount of ink spilled over the problems, we would conclude at first sight that the ancients thought it far more difficult to be unbiased than to find out what really, or even probably, happened. But this is not quite the whole story, because there is a close correlation between impartiality and the actual events of the history. Nevertheless, as all the historians bear witness, a freedom from bias was considered especially important for the historian. Naturally, the many men who wrote history when freedom was curtailed had a special interest in emphasising their impartiality, but it would be wrong to assume that this was an important virtue only under autocratic regimes. Rather, it was the universal tendency to take sides – to shade, however imperceptibly, into favour or censure – that the ancient historians saw as the consistent danger in writing history.[133] The solution could not be an abdication of judgement, even were that possible, because that would be alien to history's nature and purpose as imagined by many of the ancients: since history's utility lay partly in displaying proper and improper models of conduct, it was the historian's task to evaluate men and deeds.[134]

---

[132] Amm. XXVIII.1.2: 'ab hoc textu cruento gestorum exquisite narrando iustus me retraheret metus'.

[133] The danger is universal because the writing of history cannot be divorced from social and political uses and forces: see B. Lewis, *History: Remembered, Recovered, Invented* (Princeton 1975); J. H. Plumb, *The Death of the Past* (London and New York 1969).

[134] Not coincidentally, the promise to be impartial is a marked feature of the orators: see Weyman, *ALLG* 15 (1908) 278-9 for the passages.

Impartiality

Although the valuation did not need to be overt, it became common for the historian to speak, in his own person, words of praise or blame about the characters and events of his history.[135]

In this, as in all things, it is useful to glance at Homer. The Homeric narrator rarely speaks in his own person, and has been considered, in ancient times as well as modern, to be an 'objective' or fair-minded narrator, because of his obvious sympathy for Greeks and Trojans, and, more specifically, because of his reluctance to comment, in his own person as narrator, on the actions and motivations of his characters.[136] He is, in this sense, an unobtrusive narrator, but this is not, of course, the same as saying that he is an invisible or objective narrator. While it is true that Homer does not take sides openly, nevertheless there is evidence of intrusiveness of judgement in his narrative, and no reader of Homer is in doubt as to what constitutes good or noble or approved behaviour, and what constitutes its opposite.[137] Nor did the ancients think otherwise: Plutarch speaks of the advance discredit or recommendation that Homer gives in his poems, as for example, when he prefaces a speech by saying that the character 'spoke a sweet and clever word', or that one restrained someone 'with gentle words'. Conversely, Homer will point out discreditable behaviour, as when Achilleus' plans to dishonour Hector's corpse are labelled as 'evil deeds', or Achilleus taunts Agamemnon with 'grim words', or Pandarus is called a 'fool' for overtrusting to his archery.[138] Thus, if Homer be taken as a model, it might be expected that a more or less formal impartiality was expected in narrative, but that certain types of judgement might also be expressed.

An examination of remarks made by ancient historians indicates that

---

[135] See Fornara, *Nature* 105-20 for the movement towards explicit praise and blame. [136] See Introduction, pp. 3f.

[137] For the *Odyssey* see Booth, *Rhetoric of Fiction* 3-6; Gill, *CQ* 34 (1984) 151 n. 12 observes that the *Odyssey* 'is permeated with adjectives and adverbs which divide people into two camps', the wise and sensible, or the reckless and lawless.

[138] Plut. *aud. poet.* 4. See also de Jong, *Narrators and Focalizers* (15 ff.) who has a full discussion of such passages, a very useful summary of the objective/subjective controversy, and a conclusion that Homer is a far more intrusive narrator than is usually appreciated. One can argue that such narrative comment by Homer is not a question of moral application (see Griffin, *Homer on Life and Death* 85 n. 9), but Plutarch's comments suggest that the ancients saw it as approval or disapproval. Nor is this surprising when we consider the relation of narrator and character sketched above, §1.

they see impartiality as a fundamental component of historical truth, and that they oppose 'true' not to 'false', but to 'biased'.[139] For the Romans, at least, bias is presented as the great obstacle to truth, yet even among the Greeks, prejudice is high on the list of undesirable qualities, and its rejection is an essential element in establishing the historian's authority. In Lucian's essay, the issue of bias looms large: as opposed to inquiry, which is disposed of in a single paragraph (*h. c.* 47), impartiality receives treatment throughout the whole essay, from the opening criticisms of current writers on the Parthian Wars to the final image of the historian as a man who looks beyond present gratification or revenge towards the future, which will be his ultimate judge. For Lucian, bias and truth are clearly polar opposites.[140]

It remains important, nonetheless, to take the argument a few steps further. Why are they opposites? What is it about partiality – in particular, the desire to curry favour or redress past injuries – that makes it the opposite of truth? That answer, at least in Lucian's essay, is provided by a passage recounting a story of Alexander and the historian Aristobulus.[141] Lucian has just noted that even a flatterer does not always receive the favour he expects:

> Aristobulus described a single combat between Alexander and Porus, and read this particular passage to Alexander, thinking he would give great pleasure to the king by falsely attributing valorous actions to him and inventing deeds greater than the truth. Alexander took the book and, as they happened to be sailing on the Hydaspes river, threw the book straight into the water, saying, 'I should have done the same to you, Aristobulus, for fighting single combats on my behalf and slaying elephants with one javelin.'[142]

Aristobulus' flattery is discernible in two things: falsely attributing to the king valorous deeds that he had not performed (ἐπιψευδόμενος ἀριστείας τινὰς αὐτῷ), and inventing deeds greater than the ones he actually had done (ἀναπλάττων ἔργα μείζω τῆς ἀληθείας).[143] Even

---

[139] This has been convincingly demonstrated by Woodman, *RICH passim*, esp. ch. 2.   [140] Woodman, *RICH* 42–4, 68 nn. 257–8.
[141] The story is not likely to be true (see Homeyer, *Lukian* 198), but that is immaterial here.   [142] Luc. *h.c.* 12.
[143] On the different categories of historiographical lying see Wiseman, *L&F* 122–46; Aristobulus' lies come closest to Wiseman's fourth category, lying or exaggerating for dramatic effect with no concern whether true or not (132–8).

without the examples given by Lucian's 'Alexander' of single-handed battles and elephants brought low with one shot, it is clear from Lucian's language that Aristobulus' partiality, his desire to be in Alexander's good graces, caused him to invent some things and exaggerate others: Alexander did not fight a single combat with Porus, and elephants, though they fell, did not do so at one stroke.

Truth, then, is opposed to partiality because one who is not impartial will think nothing of inventing deeds to make his portrait, his argument, greater or more persuasive or more plausible. You cannot call Caligula a monster without saying what he actually did that made him a monster, and if your desire is to make someone a monster (or a hero) when the material is not to hand, then you have to make something up. Confirmation for this may be found as early as Aristotle's *Rhetoric*:

> First then it is necessary to grasp that on whatever thing one must speak or reason (whether it is political argument or anything else), one must have for this subject the facts (τὰ ὑπάρχοντα, lit. 'the things that already exist'). For if you had none, you would have nothing from which to make a conclusion... How could we praise the Athenians, if we did not have the sea battle at Salamis or the battle at Marathon or the actions of the children of Heracles or some other such thing? All speakers base their praise on facts that are noble or seem to be. Similarly, speakers blame from the opposite of this, examining whatever bad applies to them [sc. the Athenians] or seems to, such as that they subjected the Greeks or enslaved the Aeginetans and Potidaeans who had fought with them against the barbarian and performed valorous deeds, and other such things, if some fault exists. In the same way, those accusing and those defending themselves accuse and defend from the facts (ἐκ τῶν ὑπαρχόντων).[144]

Again, the relationship is clear: praise and blame must be based on what has happened. If we wish to praise or blame the Athenians, we have to point to the things that they actually did that urge us to our judgement. This is not to say that imaginative reconstruction (*inuentio* or εὕρησις) had no role in the writing of ancient history; but the ancients were able to distinguish the actual from the probable, even if they did not always follow it. Rhetorical amplification was acceptable to expand upon the 'hard core' of historical information,[145] but that is not what Lucian is

---

[144] Arist. *Rhet.* II.22, 1396a 4-23.
[145] See Woodman, *RICH* 87-9; 'hard core' is his phrase.

referring to in the story of Aristobulus, whose sin was to make up deeds (that is, to make up a hard core), not imaginatively reconstruct a deed that was done, the details of which were unknown. Towards the conclusion of the essay Lucian distinguishes the historian's task from that of the orator:

> For historians do not write in the same way as orators, but the things to be narrated already exist and will be spoken; for they have already happened. It is necessary only to arrange them and narrate them. Historians do not need to seek what to say but how to say it.[146]

Lucian here is explicitly denying the historian the right of making up the 'what to say', and granting him only the more limited tasks of arrangement and exposition.

The causes of bias, as the ancients saw them, were the benefits an historian enjoyed (or hoped he would) or the injuries he had received (or might receive); not surprisingly, historians who wrote under sole rulers are the ones most conscious of bias.[147] The ancients seem to have had a keen eye for detecting bias either way especially towards monarchs and tyrants. Theopompus is criticised by Polybius for his excessively hostile treatment of Philip and his court,[148] but the main figure here is Alexander and the writers who wrote adulatory or hostile histories of his deeds.[149] Strabo tells us that some of them even falsified geography to make Alexander's deeds and glory greater.[150] Plutarch says that Phylarchus is unreliable when he praises Cleomenes and criticises Aratus.[151] Hieronymus, so Pausanias thought, hated all kings except Antiochus and wrote in order to gratify him.[152] Timaeus is roundly censured by Polybius and Diodorus for telling lies about Agathocles, ignoring his successes, and attributing to him responsibility for every failure,

---

[146] Luc. *h. c.* 51; I follow the interpretation of Homeyer, *Lukian* 265–7, with references there.

[147] Luce, *CPh* 84 (1989) 19 and *passim*; as he points out, there is no evidence that the ancients saw anything other than personal benefits or injuries (as opposed to loyalty to a particular cause or belief) as the causes of bias. Even partisanship towards one's country was the result of the *beneficia* that a country gave to its citizens (19–21).   [148] Pol. VIII.11.1–4 = *FGrHist* 115 F 27.

[149] Fornara, *Nature* 64 sees the movement from impartiality as beginning with Callisthenes.   [150] Str. XI.7.4 = *FGrHist* 128 (Polycleitus) F 7.

[151] Plut. *Arat.* 38 (following Pol. II.47.4) = *FGrHist* 81 F 52.

[152] Paus. I.9.8 = *FGrHist* 154 T 11.

and Dionysius faults historians so enslaved to foreign kings that they wrote false histories of Rome to gratify them.[153] In the opposite extreme, Callias of Syracuse, having been taken up by Agathocles, never ceased praising his paymaster, however unjustly.[154] Polybius is accused by Posidonius of ingratiating himself with Tiberius Gracchus, by exaggerating the greatness of the settlements Gracchus captured in Spain, describing as 'cities' what were nothing more than 'forts'.[155]

In addition, both Greece and Rome were intensely competitive societies where envy (φθόνος, *inuidia*) was an expected and accepted motivation in those who strove for pre-eminence and glory.[156] Envy, after all, had its positive side in emulation. Some, of course, could not resist using history to exalt their ancestors' or their own achievements. At Rome, perhaps because of the close association between history and politics, it was only natural to assume that an historian who had himself been a participant would have difficulty in giving an account free of his own beliefs, preconceptions, and prejudices. The established oligarchy could take solace perhaps in the fact that history afforded a place where the retired politician 'fought again the old battles of Forum and Curia',[157] and shaped the tradition about himself and his rivals. Even more so could a new man such as Cato enter not only the ranks of the nobility but also the annals of history. Cato, however, seems to have overstepped the bounds by his intrusive and excessive self-laudation, another form of partiality towards which the ancients were particularly sensitive.[158] But other historians as well could be guilty of this type of glorification: Livy censures Licinius Macer for seeking unjustifiably to exalt his ancestors (VII.9.5). Nor were the nobility the only ones with a desire for glory: Tacitus, in describing the visit of Vitellius to the battle site at Bedriacum, accuses even the soldiers of exaggeration and falsification, and mixing false and true.[159] In sum, then, biased praise could come about from the desire to increase one's own or another's

---

[153] Pol. XII.15.1–10 = *FGrHist* 566 F 124b; Diod. XXI.17.1–3 = *FGrHist* 566 F 124d; D. Hal. *A.R.* 1.4.2–3.   [154] Diod. XXI.17.4 = *FGrHist* 564 T 3.
[155] *FGrHist* 87 F 51 = F 271 (E–K), with Walbank, *HCP* III.270.
[156] See Walcot, *Envy and the Greeks* 11–21. Dickie, *PLLS* 3 (1981) 183–5 notes that satirists always disavow *inuidia* as motivation, and stress instead the need for correction and the public good.
[157] Syme, *Ten Studies in Tacitus* 2, although this would have differed from historian to historian.   [158] See Ch. IV §1.
[159] Tac. *Hist.* II.70.3: 'iam tribuni praefectique, sua quisque facta extollentes, falsa uera aut maiora uero miscebant.'

glory, and for material gain or the desire for immortality. Excessive criticism and hostility could be the result of an attempt to gratify the victim's enemy, or (again) from the desire to increase one's own renown. In societies where one's own good name had to be won usually at others' expense, it was often necessary to bring one's opponent down.[160]

Read in this light, a profession of impartiality *was* a statement about the historian's inquiry – he was aware of the human tendency to invent or exaggerate – and the historian's character: he wished to be seen as competent to judge both men and deeds. Not all historians, however, explicitly state this. Herodotus must have considered that both his citation of numerous witnesses and the various versions he gave of events ensured that he could not be seen as partial. Thucydides likewise nowhere professes impartiality, but it can hardly be denied that his methodological statement read in its full context is meant to indicate that the historian has recognised and overcome the problem.[161] Polybius, however, is the first writer in whom we have explicit affirmations of impartiality, liberally sprinkled in his usual manner among general observations and precepts for would-be historians.[162] As a writer of contemporary history, Polybius needed to be especially sensitive to the charge of favouritism or hatred, and it is no coincidence that his most abject failure at impartiality comes when he fights old battles again in his treatment of the Aetolians.[163] In another section, where Polybius is defending Aristotle's account of the origins of the Epizephyrian Locrians against the attacks of Timaeus, Polybius says that he has paid many visits to the city of the Locrians and received favours and privileges from them, noting that he of all people ought to speak well of them because of his friendly relations with the people; and yet both in speech and writing he has affirmed Aristotle's version of their founding which is more discreditable to them.[164] Here Polybius paints himself as the truthful historian unswayed by loyalties or affections.[165] Nor is it coincidental that this remark occurs in a discussion of Timaeus' fault-finding, inaccuracy, and prejudice. Polybius by contrast, using a specific example, demonstrates his fundamental adherence to the principles of objectivity by underlining a special instance where it would have been tempting for him to alter the truth in order to repay a

---

[160] See Ch. V §1. [161] Thuc. I.22; see above, pp. 68f.
[162] See below, pp. 229ff. [163] See below, n. 206. [164] Pol. XII.5.1–5.
[165] Elsewhere he has remarked that history's function is not blame or praise but truth: VIII.8.3–9; X.21.8; XII.14.1–4.

benefit and to delight or gratify a portion of his readers. Diodorus, on the other hand, as a writer of non-contemporary history, had no need at the outset to aver impartiality, since in writing of the remote past he could not be seen as receiving any *beneficium*. He nevertheless tries to get his evenhandedness across by occasional observations on the partiality of his predecessors and invocations of his own freedom of speech.[166]

What obtained among the first Roman historians in this, as in so many matters, must remain obscure. If we believe that the early Roman historians were following the conventions of local history, then no profession of impartiality may have been given, as this seems not to have been common in local history.[167] Whether such Annalists as Claudius Quadrigarius, Valerias Antias, or Licinius Macer averred impartiality in their works cannot be known, but their follower Livy, perhaps significantly, did not. We know that a writer of contemporary history, C. Fannius, defended his change of party from *popularis* to optimate in his preface,[168] and Fannius does indeed seem to have presented impartial judgements in his work.[169] Cicero too suggests that impartiality was expected, and he notes that L. Lucceius, perhaps in his history, had spurned prejudice and embraced impartiality in a particularly striking way:

> ... that favour (*gratiam*) about which you wrote most beautifully in one of your prefaces, and which you demonstrated you could no more be moved by than Xenophon's Hercules could be moved by pleasure.[170]

We do not know whether it was the case that those who were not politicians or primarily politicians could make this claim more easily than those who had participated in the political life of the state. It is striking when Sallust says that his impartiality, which seems to exist as a direct result of his absence from politics, made him peculiarly qualified to write up Catiline's conspiracy. The abandonment of political life and the temptations of *cupido honoris*, *fama*, and *inuidia* have removed

---

[166] Diod. v.1.1–4 (on Timaeus); xxi.17.1–4 (on Timaeus and Callias of Syracuse).

[167] Jacoby, *Atthis* 71–9 and *passim* believed that political tendentiousness played rather a large role in (at least Athenian) local history, but this has been challenged: see Rhodes, *PoH* 73–81; Harding, *Androtion and the Atthis* 47–51.

[168] Fannius, *HRR* F 1 with Badian, in *Latin Historians* 14.

[169] Fornara, *Nature* 69–70.

[170] Cic. *Fam.* v.12.3; where this appeared is unknown, but the context of the letter suggests a history.

Sallust from the arena in which partiality most functions, and he presents his removal from that world as a specific proof that he can be impartial.[171] We do not know the full context of his similar profession of impartiality in the *Histories*, and whether he spoke there of a removal from public life as an advantage.[172] A profession of impartiality is lacking in the *Jugurtha*, and this absence is most likely to be explained by the fact that it was a non-contemporary history, and there could be no assumption that Sallust was writing for any gain to be expected.[173]

It is noteworthy that by Tacitus' time the historian will need to aver impartiality even for a non-contemporary history. The Greek and Roman historians of the Empire share a strong concern about bias because of the constant danger that the monarchic system (and a series of unstable Emperors) presented. The belief that all historians wrote out of fear or favour must have become deeply ingrained. Professions of impartiality in the Empire also become important because of the obvious need of an Emperor's favour for advancement. Tacitus' *Histories* presents an interesting case in point. We noted above that Tacitus did not wish to be seen as one of those ill-suited to history by his 'inscitia rei publicae ut alienae', and he thus mentioned his experience and social standing, which was, as often in the imperial era, dependent on the Emperor.[174] But since the ancients saw *beneficia* as a primary cause of bias, such a claim would alert his readers to the possibility or probability of bias. In other words, impartiality is somewhat more difficult for Tacitus to establish, since the method he used to assert his *dignitas* necessarily involved mention of those towards whom he would have some type of obligations. In a sense, the problems are only partially disposed of by his general profession of impartiality. So Tacitus added something more at the end of this section of the preface:

> I would not deny that my advancement was begun by Vespasian, increased by Titus, and carried farther by Domitian. But for those who have professed an uncorrupted trustworthiness, no one is to be described with affection or hatred. If I live long enough, I have reserved for my old age the principate of the deified Nerva and the imperial conquests of Trajan, a richer and safer topic, in the rare happiness of our times, when you can think what you want and say what you think.[175]

---

[171] Sall. *Cat.* 3.5–4.2, with Woodman, *RICH* 73–4.
[172] Sall. *Hist.* 1.6; below, pp. 246f.   [173] Luce, *CPh* 84 (1989) 28.
[174] Above, p. 143.   [175] Tac. *Hist.* 1.1.3–4.

One does not need to cast doubt on Tacitus' intention, when he wrote this preface, of writing in the future a history of his own time under Nerva and Trajan. He did not, of course, write this history (choosing instead the even more distant past) and we do not know why. Excessive concern with this fact, however, causes us to overlook the functional aspect of the final sentence of this first part of the preface. The *rara felicitas* of the present age praised here at the end brings us back to the opening of the preface and the historians who wrote *pari eloquentia ac libertate*.[176] In a kind of ring-composition, Tacitus strengthens here the generalised assertion of impartiality made in the previous sentence. He suggests that the age of Nerva and Trajan had again made possible the objectivity and impartiality of the historian. Coming after the vague 'incorruptam fidem', the very tangible 'ubi sentire quae uelis et quae sentias dicere licet' suggests a reality of *libertas* that the historian can once again achieve: Tacitus claims to live in a time when the historian is free to speak as he wishes.[177] Thus by moving between the general and the specific, by alternating positive with negative definition, Tacitus has adapted the Roman tradition about experience and impartiality in a novel and, for those writing under an Emperor, necessary way. In the later *Annals*, when Tacitus could not be suspected of specific favour or hatred,[178] he contented himself with a general assurance that he wrote impartially (1.1.3). In both works, however, Tacitus continues the trend that we have seen in Sallust, that depicts the difficulty of history as a spirit of independence and a freedom from bias, and sees the ideal historian as one not beholden to the interests of those in power. Tacitus' stronger and more extended defence was necessitated by what he wished to portray as the utter debasement of historiography between Livy and himself.[179]

[176] *Hist.* 1.1.1 'dum res populi Romani memorabantur, pari eloquentia ac libertate'; on *eloquentia* and *libertas* see Aubrion, *Rhétorique et histoire chez Tacite* 12-20.

[177] Assuming that this is mainly a literary device also eliminates the conflict between *Agr.* 3.3 (the promise of a *testimonium praesentium bonorum*) and the decision to write the *Histories* next. See also Woodman, *CQ* 25 (1975) 287-8; id., in *Contemporary History: Practice and Method* 162-3.

[178] Luce, *CPh* 84 (1989) 18 points out that Tacitus' denial in the *Annals*, even though not a contemporary history, is made because injury could have been done to his relatives or ancestors. Cf. *Ann.* IV.33.4 on the danger that even in a non-contemporary history, people may think you are covertly attacking them.

[179] For Tacitus and Livy, see below, pp. 252f. It is indicative of Tacitus' time that malicious talk was accepted as truth, whereas Sallust had said that when the historian criticises, the reader attributes it to the writer's *inuidia* or *maleuolentia* (*Cat.* 3.2); cf. Tac. *Agr.* 1.4.

We turn now to the Greeks of the early Empire. Josephus, although concerned with bias, has an interesting approach: at the outset of the *Jewish War* he castigates those who have brought forth false histories of the event 'either because of flattery towards the Romans or from hatred of the Jews' (*B. J.* 1.2). When he introduces himself as a participant, he recognises that these details may subject him to the charge of bias, and so he promises not to exaggerate the deeds of the Jews (1.9). He adds, however, that he will at times lament his country's fate, even though he knows this to be outside the realm of the historian's task, and he asks the indulgence of his audience for this 'transgression':

> I shall relate the deeds of both sides accurately, and I shall add remarks on the events to my narrative, giving my feelings leave to bewail the misfortunes of my country ... and if anyone should criticise our laments for our country's misfortunes, let pardon be given to a compassion contrary to the law of history ... and if one is too harsh a judge for pity, let him assign the deeds to the history, the laments to the writer.[180]

In Book v, in a striking passage, Josephus does indeed give free reign to his pity, addressing Jerusalem itself. This apostrophe is followed by the remark that 'emotions must be restrained according to the law of the work, since this is the occasion not for one's own lamentations, but for the narration of deeds'.[181] Each passage is a *captatio beneuolentiae* in which Josephus manages to express himself with full emotion, while at the same time indicating his knowledge of the genre's conventions.[182] In the earlier passage, the *captatio* is closely associated with Josephus' reflection that the Jews themselves were responsible for their misfortunes (1.10-12). This has the effect, of course, of showing a spirit of self-criticism that by its very frankness is meant to indicate to the reader an unprejudiced spirit. This attempt to portray objectivity is also supported elsewhere in the history by the very full criticism of historians of the Jewish War who have contradicted themselves by their flattery towards the Romans or hatred towards the Jews.[183] Something of

---

[180] Jos. *B. J.* 1.9-11. [181] Ibid. v.19-20.
[182] See Lindner, *Die Geschichtsauffassung des Flavius Josephus im Bellum Judaicum* 132-41 who notes the parallels with Jeremiah and the tradition of *Klagelieder* in the Hebrew Bible.
[183] Jos. *B. J.* 1.7-8; 13-16, the latter specifically against Greek historians whose mendacity is a favourite subject with Josephus (cf. *c. Ap.* 1.15-27.).

Josephus' spirit can be found in Polybius,[184] but most similar is Diodorus (basing himself on Polybius) lamenting over the destruction of Corinth by the Romans in 146 BC:

> Never, since deeds have been recorded by history, did such misfortunes hold Greece. Because of the magnitude of these sufferings, one could neither write nor read of this time without weeping.[185]

Or Velleius, lamenting over his country's fate in the civil wars:

> No one has even wept over the fortune of these times in a sufficiently worthy manner, much less expressed it in words.[186]

In the case of Arrian's *Anabasis*, it might be thought that the subject of Alexander would not need the same assurances against bias that one would give in a contemporary history. Yet at the outset Arrian claims – indeed almost as the primary virtue of his book – that his sources Ptolemy and Aristobulus are the most reliable witnesses because they wrote after Alexander's death and were thus free of the suspicion of having written from necessity (here instead of favouritism) or desire for gain (*Anab. proem.* 2), and suggests for his own book a similar freedom from bias. As we have seen in Tacitus, the motif is so strongly entrenched in the historiography of the Empire that it reveals itself even in non-contemporary history. It can be no accident, however, that it must especially be emphasised when one writes about a monarch.

Dio's examination of the difference between imperial and republican historiography also notes the presence of bias from early times (indeed, he considers it a normal part of all history that is written). He suggests that previously one could compare accounts of the same events and thus distinguish (and weed out) bias; in the Empire, by contrast, it is always thought that everything said or done results from what the current men in power want.[187] Dio's solution is to give the reports as he heard them, true or not, but to correct them from reading, hearsay, or autopsy. His frank recognition of an insuperable difficulty (for Dio does

---

[184] Attridge, *The Interpretation of Biblical History in the Antiquitates Judaicae of Flavius Josephus* 50 appositely compares Pol. XXXVIII. 4; cf. also Pol. XXXVIII. 1. 3 (ἐλεήσαι τις ἂν τοὺς "Ελληνας). At XXXVIII.4.1, Polybius excuses himself for writing in a more declamatory and ambitious manner, but there is no mention, at least in the preserved parts of his history, of weeping over his country's fate.   [185] Diod. XXXII.26.1.   [186] Vell. II.67.1.

[187] Dio, LIII.19.2–3; see above, p. 88.

seem to suggest that a multiplicity of reports leads to truth and without it this cannot be achieved) suggests his own method of avoiding the charge of bias: to correct report only where he has the means.[188]

Not all historians, of course, averred impartiality.[189] We have no evidence, for example, that Ctesias or Theopompus promised to be impartial, and Lucian's reference to Artaxerxes' physician who hopes to get a purple Median garment or necklace or Nisaean horse from his history suggests that Ctesias' bias was evident.[190] Ctesias' claim to authority, with its access to 'privileged' information, presupposes a different type of history: Ctesias wrote of the conflicts between a king and the Greek city-states, in which court intrigue was given a prominent role (justifiably or not). More importantly, he wrote with the purpose of presenting events from the Persian point of view, so that it was unnecessary to make a corresponding declaration about his sources from the Greek side. No pretence of impartiality seems to have been given, nor were the historical events themselves his exclusive concern. Ctesias promised accuracy but not necessarily impartiality of viewpoint.

The best example from surviving historians of an avoidance of professing impartiality is Livy, who in his preface frankly admits his *amor* towards his subject, while claiming the Romans to be a people greater and more pious than any of those before them. Later generations – admittedly, Roman – thought Livy to have been extremely fairminded. Seneca calls him 'by nature the most honest evaluator (*candidissimus aestimator*) of all great talents'.[191] His impartiality was thus of a different type from that expressed by Polybius, for Livy was impartial within an overall favourable treatment. Rome was the hero of Livy's history, and partiality for one's country was rarely

---

[188] Dio, LIII.19.6, where προσέσται μέντοι τι αὐτοῖς καὶ τῆς ἐμῆς δοξίας recalls Hdt. II.99.1 (cf. II.147.1), προσέσται δὲ αὐτοῖσί τι καὶ τῆς ἐμῆς ὄψιος, and suggests a similar procedure, an 'official' account with asides, expansions, corrections, and so forth.

[189] Syme's remark (*Tacitus* I.204), 'That he will be strictly impartial every Roman annalist proclaims at the outset', is surprising, since Livy, of course, does not do this.

[190] Luc. *h.c.* 39 (with Homeyer, *Lukian* ad loc.), where Ctesias is not named; he is immediately compared with Xenophon, a 'just historian' (δίκαιος συγγραφεύς).

[191] Sen. *Suas.* VI.22; cf. Tac. *Ann.* IV.34.3 with Martin and Woodman's commentary ad loc.

Impartiality

condemned.[192] No doubt it was acceptable if the historian did not justify his city's conduct on each and every occasion, or, if he did, it was of fundamentally less importance than the treatment he accorded individuals within the history. If, that is, he gave impartial evaluations of the characters in his history, this by itself meant that he was impartial, whereas an unremittingly favourable or hostile approach opened an historian, quite naturally, to the charge of bias, as we saw with Theopompus and Timaeus.[193] And for Polybius, it was the unremittingly favourable interpretation that Fabius and Philinus put on the events of the First Punic War that made their works suspect, though good enough in their way as a basis for Polybius' superior account. Livy, for all his partiality, could yet acknowledge the good qualities of Rome's greatest foe, Hannibal:

> And I hardly know whether he was more amazing in adversity than when successful, in as much as he was waging war so far from home, with varying fortune, with an army not of citizens but mixed from the runoff of all races who had no law or custom or common language, but different bearings, different clothing, arms, different rites and rituals, almost different gods. But he bound them by one bond, so that there was no dissension either among themselves or towards their leader.[194]

It is not a question here of a fundamentally favourable or hostile portrait – an historian can, after all, have his choices – but rather of the appearance that the historian has taken into consideration all of the evidence, and has not sought to suppress any of what Aristotle would call τὰ ὑπάρχοντα. We would especially like to know what Livy did when he came to Roman decline, which is only hinted at in the preface, for here he may have been compelled to make some sort of declaration of impartiality when treating civil war, much as Sallust had done. It is noteworthy that an 'impartiality' of praise and blame is visible in Livy's

---

[192] As Luce, *CPh* 84 (1989) 20 points out, only Lucian and Polybius make explicit claims that an historian must be impartial even towards his native city. Yet even Polybius allowed partiality towards one's country if it were done on the basis of the facts; and for Livy the facts surely confirmed that Rome was the greatest empire in history. The belief that the gods bring prosperity to men would have allowed the further inference that the Romans must have been the race most pleasing to the gods – at least while they rose as an empire.

[193] See above, p. 162; below, pp. 228ff.

[194] Livy, XXVIII.12.2-4. On the complexity (and contradiction) in Livy's portrait of Hannibal, see Walsh, *Livy* 103-5.

well-known evaluations of Cicero and Caesar,[195] and the charge that he was 'Pompeian' in sympathies, supposedly levelled against him by Augustus, suggests that he maintained his independence.[196]

There may have been more. Livy ceased publishing, though not writing, his history after Book CXX, and did not bring out Books CXXI–CXLII until, as he himself seems to have said, after the death of Augustus.[197] Whether or not he explained to the reader why he had withheld publication is not known. Since these books contained the deeds of Augustus, it may be that the historian explained his delay as the attempt to present an impartial portrait of the recently deceased Emperor, a portrait which was not, so far as we can tell, flattering or fawning.[198] A different type of deferred publication can be seen in Cicero's treatment of his *Expositio Consiliorum Suorum* which contained frank criticism of Caesar and Crassus. He gave this work to his son with the order to publish it only after Cicero was dead, no doubt so that it might seem more impartial than if Cicero was seen to gain something by it when alive.[199] A similar striving to present oneself as impartial must lie behind the elder Pliny, who in the preface of his *Natural History* says that his history, although completed, will not be published until after his death, 'lest my life be judged to have given anything to ambition'.[200] Here, of course, the suspicion is that Pliny's history was largely favourable towards its still living subjects, and his procedure will have been an attempt to cut the tie between partiality and *beneficia*: if he could receive no *beneficia* (as he could not, after death), there would be no suggestion that he wrote with any intention other than truth. It cannot, however, be said that this was a common solution to the problem of impartiality; among other reasons, the historian who delayed his work lost the chance of fame in his lifetime, and this, as we saw, was an important spur to the writing of history.[201] Or, more importantly

---

[195] Sen. *Suas.* VI.17 = Livy F 50 (Cicero); Sen. *N.Q.* V.18.4 = F 48 (Caesar).

[196] Tac. *Ann.* IV.34.3; on Livy's 'Pompeian' sympathies, Badian, in *Livius: Aspekte seines Werkes*, 11–12; cf. 27–8.

[197] Livy, *per.* CXXI, with the discussion of Badian, op. cit. (n.196) 23–8.

[198] Syme, *RP* I.433–9 saw Livy's treatment of the Augustan Age as largely favourable; so too Woodman, *RICH* 136–40 and many others; but cf. Badian, op. cit. (n.196) 19–23, 25–9 on Livy's *libertas*.

[199] Dio, XXXIX.10.1–3 (cf. 2, τῶν τῆς ἀκράτου παρρησίας ἐπικαρπιῶν νεωστὶ πεπειραμένος); Cic. *Att.* II.6.2; XIV.17.6; Amm. XXVI.1.2. On the work's nature see Rawson, *RCS* 408–15. [200] Pliny, *HRR* F 4 = *n. h. praef.* 20.

[201] See Ch. I §4.

[202] Jos. *Vita* 358–60. Not coincidentally, a similar belief impels modern scholars to

perhaps, if he waited until after the death of his subjects, he might encounter something like the criticism that Josephus levels against Justus of Tiberias: that by waiting until after the deaths of the participants to publish his account, he could not be confuted by contemporaries and participants.[202]

Even if an historian avers impartiality, he nevertheless knew the danger of praise and that his words might be interpreted as fawning or flattering. Thus historians will often make some form of truth claim just before praising a character. Herodotus justified his praise of the Athenians by a detailed argument meant to support his position; Polybius assures his reader that the praises of Aemilius Paullus' or Scipio Aemilianus' character are based on his own knowledge or other proofs; Velleius says he has not gone out of his way to praise the men who performed nobly in the events of AD 6–9 in Pannonia, and avers that 'among good men, a just frankness without mendacity is not a crime'; and Ammianus, admitting that his praise of Julian may border on panegyric, assures his readers that it is based on clear proofs.[203]

The historian, then, strove to display narrative impartiality. When Lucian ridicules a historian who began by calling the Parthian king 'the most disgusting and foullest Vologesus',[204] he was decrying just this lack. The ultimate model for the proper manner was Homer, the more immediate one Thucydides. In the former, as we have noted above, the narrator rarely gives explicit judgement about his characters, and he treats Greeks and Trojans with similar sympathy. So too in Thucydides, explicit praise or censure is rare, and there are but a handful of places where the narrator speaks in his own person on people or events.[205]

discount Cicero's *expositio* (Rawson, *RCS* 410).
[203] Hdt. VII.139; Pol. XXXI.22.1-11; 23-30; XXXVIII.21.3; Vell. II.116.5; Amm. XVI.1.2-3. The same claim of giving noble deeds their due is common among the encomiastic poets: see Dickie, *PLLS* 3 (1981) 183.
[204] Luc. *h.c.* 14: ὁ γὰρ μιαρώτατος καὶ κάκιστα ἀπολούμενος Οὐολόγεσος.
[205] The narrative impartiality of Thucydides is extraordinary, even if it is not absolute: one notes that even his judgements have less of the overt moral tone found in later historians. When he praises Pericles or rebukes Alcibiades, he does so not so much in terms of their personal character as of their public service. Elsewhere, he uses abstract language precisely as a distancing manoeuvre that keeps him from the necessity of allying his own feelings too closely with the narrator (see Parry, *The Language of Achilles and other Papers* 177-84). In general, because Thucydides sees history's utility largely in intellectual, not

After Thucydides, this narrative impartiality was, of course, affected by the insertion of judgements about character, but these too, as we saw, were expected to be fair, and they were, after all, mainly in digressions removed from the basic narrative. In the basic narrative, however, the narrator who was intrusive called attention to himself in a way that might reveal his prejudice. Given the audience's keen eye for anything that smacked of partiality, a less intrusive approach would have a greater chance of success.[206]

---

practical, terms (see Farrar, *Origins of Democratic Thinking* 126-37), and because his purpose is not to help his readers choose certain types of behaviour and avoid others, there is less need to ally himself with one side or the other. Since he believes himself to be indicating how things *are*, and how they are likely to be again, there is not the sense of history as a storehouse of moral *exempla*, from which the reader will choose those to emulate and those to avoid. In the major event that began the Peloponnesian War, the attack by Thebes on Plataea, Thucydides says only that the attack was a glaring violation of the peace, without judgement for or against (II.7.1: καὶ λελυμένων λαμπρῶς τῶν σπονδῶν). This would have been an obvious place for moralising, but Thucydides does nothing of the sort.

[206] One might add that certain types of 'ethnic' prejudice would not be seen as affecting the historian's impartiality. 'Punic faith' was probably not much of an indication of bias to a Roman. For some examples of other types see Pol. III.98.3 (Spaniards); XXVIII.14.1-4 (Cretans); Diod. 1.37.11 (Libyans); V.26.3 (Italians); 29.5 (Gauls); Sall. *Jug.* 46.3 (Numidians); Vell. II.118.1 (Germans); Jos. *A. J.* II.201 (Egyptians); Tac. *Hist.* III.47.2 and *Ann.* V.10.1 (Greeks); II.56.1 (Armenians). Cf. Livy, 1.53.4 where Tarquinius Superbus turns to deceit, 'minime arte Romana'. (Quite in another category is Polybius' treatment of the Aetolians, IV.3.1-3; 17.11; 62.1-4, et al., with its glaring lack of narrative impartiality.) Vice versa, foreigners are sometimes used to show the corruption of the historian's audience: see Trüdinger, *Die griechisch-römische Ethnographie* 133ff. On the tendency of both positive and negative characteristics of foreigners to 'migrate' and so form a common stock of motifs see Norden, *Die germanische Urgeschichte in Tacitus Germania* 42ff., esp. 56-9; A. Schroeder, *De ethnographiae antiquae locis quibusdam communibus observationes* (diss. Halle 1921).

IV
The historian's deeds

Up to this point our concern has been how the ancient historian justifies himself before his audience and attempts to portray himself as the proper person for the writing of history, that is, with his role as *narrator rerum*. The present chapter examines how he approaches his task when a participant in the very deeds he records, and how he reconciles the dual role of *actor* and *auctor rerum*. For in fact many historians of the ancient world had the opportunity to be both participant and rememberer.[1] The historian's formal method of presenting himself has received comparatively little attention, yet it is of interest not only because it tells us something of the way that men who wrote history in the ancient world approached the writing of their own deeds, but also what their concerns were in doing so. It is usually assumed that in order to give authority to his account, an historian who narrated his own deeds used the third person and maintained a show of formal impartiality. But a study of the surviving (and partially surviving) historians reveals a variety of approaches and methods, changing with time, the specific type of history written, and the individual intention of the historian himself.

I. PRAISE AND SELF-PRAISE

Aside from a single passage in Polybius,[2] no historian comments on the formal aspects of his presentation of himself in his work. There are, however, a few comments in Greek and Roman writers on the dangers inherent in speaking about oneself (περιαυτολογία), particularly in the matter of self-praise. The evidence is neither full nor

---

[1] Fornara, *Nature* 52–4 minimises the political role of the Greek historians, but see Chaniotis, *Historie und Historiker* 124–5, 382–8; Meissner, *Historiker* 215ff. for the political activity of numerous historians.

[2] Pol. XXXVI.12, quoted and discussed below, p. 189.

always consistent,³ and the attitude towards one's own praises seems to have changed slightly over time. It can hardly be denied that the commitment of one's deeds to a work of remembrance in itself entailed bestowing praise, even if it was not the desire of the author in the first instance to defend or praise his own achievements. And, as we saw above, praise and blame bring with them the danger of a charge of partiality. The model for successful self-praise was Demosthenes' *On the Crown* which had the reputation in antiquity as the best oration of the best orator, and was itself the subject of much imitation.⁴ Yet even before Demosthenes and the rhetorical codification of techniques, the difficulties of praising oneself (and even others) are everywhere evident in Greek literature, and a marked feature of Greek ethical belief.⁵ The Romans, who are usually seen as more tolerant of self-praise and the author's 'I' reveal, in fact, the same concerns as the Greeks, especially in the political world: for them too the least problematic and highest form of praise was praise from others.

Plutarch's tract on how to praise oneself and get away with it makes a useful starting-point, drawing (as it most likely does) on previous works, yet retaining the author's customary independence.⁶ Plutarch allows self-praise for the statesman not when it is done merely for love of praise, but 'when it brings some advantage to others or ourselves'. Although praise by others is best, one may praise oneself in certain circumstances, especially in defence,⁷ misfortune, or when wronged.

---

³ Most, *JHS* 109 (1989) 131 n. 87 speaks of a 'frequently discussed' topic, but cf. Radermacher, *RhM* 52 (1897) 423: 'die ... recht knappe rhetorische Literatur, die der Frage gewidmet ist'. The ancient sources are: Quint. XI.1.15-26; Plutarch's *On Self-Praise without Envy* (*de se ipso citra inuidiam laudando*); Hermog. *Meth.* 25, pp. 441-2 Rabe; Alexander, π. ῥήτορ. ἀφορμῶν, Spengel, *Rhet. Graeci* III.4.9-14 (only a promise to treat the topic); Aelius Arist. *Rhet.*, Spengel III.506.8-20; Gregory of Corinth, Walz, *Rhet. Graeci* VII.1298-1301. Unfortunately, none of the modern textbooks on rhetoric (Volkmann, Lausberg, Martin) has any material on this topic.
⁴ See F. Blass, *Die attische Beredsamkeit* III.1 (Leipzig ²1893) 436ff.
⁵ Walcot, *Envy and the Greeks, passim*; cf. Most, op. cit. (n.3) 125-33 for a refutation of earlier theories about the reserved nature of the Greeks towards praise.
⁶ See Radermacher, op. cit. (n.3) 419-24. On the structure of the work see H.-G. Ingenkamp, *Plutarchs Schriften über die Heilung der Seele* (Göttingen 1971) 62-9.
⁷ In the *Antidosis* (also an important text in the study of self-praise) Isocrates adopts the fiction of an *antidosis* in order to defend his actions and influence: see *Antid.* 6-8.

Yet even so, in praising oneself it is best to soften it with a variety of techniques.[8] There is a similar attitude displayed by Quintilian. When he comes to defend Cicero from the charge of excessive self-praise, he argues that Cicero extolled his political achievements rather than his oratory, and that this was justified because Cicero was defending himself against his own and the state's enemies. Praise for one's own eloquence, however, is distasteful, since there is the danger in this of exciting envy.[9] Yet the solution cannot be the false modesty whereby a rich man calls himself poor, or a noble refers to himself as undistinguished, because this is no less wearisome to the audience.[10] In sum, he sees praise as best when it is not self-praise.[11]

Although Cicero seems even by ancient standards to have indulged in excessive self-praise, he himself was aware at least of the problems inherent in so doing. In his letter of 55 BC to Lucceius, Cicero admits that he wants the *auctoritas* of Lucceius' *testimonium*, and feels it is of particular value since Lucceius has elsewhere proclaimed his devotion to truth; and, like Naevius' Hector, Cicero will rejoice not only in being praised while still alive, but in being praised by one who is himself praised (*Fam.* v.12.1). If Lucceius refuses, the alternative is not attractive:

> I shall be forced perhaps to do what some often censure (*quod non nulli saepe reprehendunt*): I myself shall write about myself, following the example to be sure of many and distinguished men. But I am sure you realise that there are problems in this type of composition: if there is anything to praise, writers must write more modestly about themselves, and if something is to be reprehended, they must pass over it. The result

---

[8] Plut. *de se ips.* 547F. Praise of oneself: 540C ff. (defence), 541A ff. (misfortune), 541C ff. (when wronged); praise by others the best: 539D (quoting Xen. *Mem.* II.1.31); techniques for mitigating self-praise: praise the audience too (542A–B), ascribe some success to chance or god (542E–F), use slight corrections or amendments (ἐπανορθώσεσι) to others' praise of you (543A–B), throw in some shortcomings (543F). Some of these techniques are discussed below, §3. Russell, in *Philosophia kai Eusebeia* 436 notes that self-disclosure is also acceptable as a teaching tool, when 'the moralist has to have the authority of his own life-style'.

[9] Quint. XI.1.17–18; he here recalls Isocrates and Sallust on the dangers of praising others: see above, pp. 152f. But Quintilian also notes (XI.1.16–17) that praise in itself alienates some people because it openly reveals differences in social status.

[10] Quint. XI.1.21 refers to the trick of feigning inability, finding it the most obnoxious type of boastfulness ('illa iactatio peruersa').

[11] Quint. XI.1.21–2: 'ab aliis ergo laudemur'.

is that it has, in fact, less trustworthiness, less authority, and many criticise it (*multi denique reprehendant*), saying that the heralds of athletic games are more honest, because these, after they have placed the crowns on the victors' heads and proclaimed their names in a loud voice, use a different herald when they themselves are given a crown at the games' end, lest they themselves should pronounce themselves victors in their own voice. This is what I want to avoid.[12]

The repetition of *reprehendere* shows what is uppermost in Cicero's mind, and his disregard of the *exemplum* of earlier distinguished men shows a recognition of the real world of Roman politics, and an unwillingness to idealise that is quite at odds with Tacitus' later remarks below. It is noteworthy that in this private letter Cicero recognises both the limited value of his praise of himself, and the correspondingly greater value of being praised by one of unblemished character. Quintilian notes that Cicero in his dialogues always made sure that any praises of himself were placed in the mouths of other characters.[13]

A letter from Pliny to Tacitus shows the persistence of the belief that self-praise is less effective than praise from another. In this letter Pliny sends an account of his action in the Senate to the historian for inclusion in his history, because he knows that it will be the more valuable if it is distinguished by Tacitus' testimony.[14] Nor must we be deceived by the opening of Tacitus' *Agricola* which, like Tacitus' other prefaces, is based on contrast, and seeks its effect by the juxtaposition of opposites:

> To hand down to posterity the deeds and characters of distinguished men, a custom of olden times, even our age, though caring little for its own affairs, has not abandoned, whenever some great and noble achievement has conquered and overcome the fault of small and great states alike, the ignorance of what is right, and jealousy. Among our ancestors, just as it was straightforward and more open to do things worthy of remembrance, so too the greater a man was, the more he was led to handing down a memory of his achievement without favour and ambition, and with the reward only of a good conscience. A good many indeed judged that to narrate their own life was confidence in their character rather than arrogance. Rutilius and Scaurus were neither disbelieved nor censured: for virtues are best appreciated in times in

---

[12] Cic. *Fam.* v.12.8–9.
[13] Quint. xi.1.21; cf. Cicero's remarks in *Orator* 104–6 where he speaks of himself in terms of what he *wants* to achieve, not what he *has* achieved.
[14] Pliny, *ep.* vii.33.3: 'si factum meum ... tuo ingenio tuo testimonio ornaueris'.

which they most easily bloom. But in the present, when I was intending to write the life of a man no longer alive, I had to seek permission, which I would not have had to do if I were intending to attack him: so harsh the times and inimical to virtues.[15]

The contrasts can hardly be clearer, the past more idealised, the present more condemned: on the one hand an earlier generation so devoted to virtue and so unthreatened by it that it found the accounts of men, *even when* they themselves wrote them, to be worthy of credibility (*fides*) and no occasion for disparagement; and, on the other hand, an age so ignorant of its own great men and so given over to jealousy that it finds cause for suspicion in the accounts of men *even when* others write them. The passage derives so much of its force from the paradox that in the old days even self-praise was believed and valued. But what we know of the competition among the nobility of Republican Rome hardly suggests so ideal a picture.[16]

To the extent that there is any modern discussion of the technique of treating one's deeds in one's own history, the concern is usually with issues of person, that is, whether the historian used the first person or the third person.[17] While issues of person are not unimportant, the distinction based on person alone tells us very little about the author's actual method when he narrates his own *res gestae*. If we distinguished simply by the use of person we would have in one group such disparate narrators as Thucydides, Xenophon, Caesar, and Josephus, while the other group would bring together Philochorus, Cato (probably), Velleius, Appian, Dio, and Ammianus. The usefulness of this type of distinction is limited: Thucydides appears as a character only briefly in his history, whereas Caesar is present throughout; Velleius and Ammianus are hardly the centre of their narratives, whereas Dio in his

---

[15] Tac. *Agr.* 1.1–4.
[16] There is danger in drawing historical conclusions from Tacitus' prefaces; the rhetoric here is used in a way similar to that of his historical works; in each case Tacitus defines himself by contrast and continuity with an earlier generation: see Leeman, in *Form und Sinn* 319, and below, pp. 250ff.
[17] The standard discussion is that of Norden, *Agnostos Theos* 311–27, although views of its inadequacy have been expressed: Momigliano, *Alien Wisdom* 57 n. 14; Fehling, in *Festschrift... H. Diller* 69 n. 1; Norden did not intend his work to be comprehensive, nor was his main concern history proper. There is a very useful discussion of the first-/third-person tradition in Mensching, *Caesars Bellum Gallicum: Eine Einführung* 43–9.

later books seems to have been. And what of Polybius who (as we shall see) belongs to both groups? Clearly, determination by use of first or third person will only take us so far, and cannot be the sole factor in a consideration of winning credibility for the narration of one's own actions. Perhaps more important is the distinction between person and perspective (or focalisation), between the questions 'who speaks?' and 'who sees?'.[18] Herodotus, for example, uses the first person fairly frequently throughout his whole work, but the perspective in Book II (or even Book IV, for that matter) is quite different from that of Books VI–IX.[19] Although tradition might dictate one or the other, it was not first or third person that the ancients observed, but rather proportion and praise. In this survey, then, we shall keep in mind not only issues of person, but also those of point of view, characterisation, perspective, and bias: for it is by a combination of all of these that the historian locates himself with reference to others in the larger framework of his history.

Since our discussion will treat both narrative histories and memoirs, we should here say something of the latter. The term 'memoirs' translates both ὑπομνήματα and *commentarii*, yet each of these words has a wider semantic range. The former can mean, among other things, 'lecture notes' or 'commentary'.[20] Polybius uses it in the sense both of 'memoirs' and 'histories',[21] while Lucian uses ὑπόμνημα to denote the 'preliminary sketch' that the historian should prepare before writing his fuller and more artistically adorned history.[22] The earliest memoirs in Greek were written by Demetrius of Phaleron and they treated his ten years of political rule at Athens (317–307 BC).[23] Memoirs were also written by King Pyrrhus of Epirus, King Ptolemy Euergetes II, and perhaps most famously Aratus of Sicyon, whom Polybius praised and from whose conclusion he began his own history of eastern affairs.[24]

---

[18] This important distinction is discussed by Génette, *Narrative Discourse* 164–9. See de Jong, *Narrators and Focalizers* 31ff. on focalisation.

[19] On the different perspective of Book II see Darbo-Peschanski, *Le discours du particulier* 112; Marincola, *Arethusa* 20 (1987) 121–37.

[20] See E. G. Turner, *Greek Papyri* (Oxford ²1980) 118–24; further bibliography at Momigliano, *Greek Biography* 90 n. 24.

[21] Pol. 1.1.1 (of his own history); IX.1.3; XII.25a.4, et al.; Walbank, *Polybius* 71 n. 20.

[22] Luc. *h. c.* 16; 48, with Avenarius, *LS* 85–104.

[23] See *FGrHist* 228, specifically called ὑπομνήματα at T 3b.

[24] *FGrHist* 229 (Pyrrhus, doubted by Jacoby, but cf. Momigliano, op. cit. (n.20) 89); 234 (Ptolemy, in twenty-four books!); and 231 (Aratus); see T 2a (Pol. I.3.1) for Polybius' starting-point.

The Latin term *commentarius* refers to anything that aids the memory,[25] and our earliest examples, the *commentarii* of Roman priests and magistrates, are completely unliterary.[26] A forerunner of Roman memoirs may have been the autobiographical letters written (in Greek) by Scipio Africanus and Scipio Nasica in the third and second centuries to Greek kings.[27] The form most relevant for our inquiry is the *commentarius de uita sua*, an account of a man's career (and at times entire life), which flourished at Rome and for which there is no Greek parallel.[28] The series of these *commentarii* begins with M. Aemilius Scaurus (writing probably after his censorship of 109 BC) and extends through the late Republic, when it is particularly popular, into the Empire: even emperors wrote their memoirs.[29]

Two points need to be made about memoirs. First, the distinguishing mark between memoirs and full-scale narrative history will almost certainly have been the perspective: in the former the memoirist, we must assume, was the focal point of the entire narrative, and events were told from his perspective and in so far as they affected his own actions.[30] This cannot be certain, since the only survivor of this genre is Caesar's *Commentarii* and, as we shall see, they may not have been typical. The second point is that these *commentarii* will have had different levels of stylistic adornment. It is usually assumed that these works served mainly as raw materials for narrative historians. Originally, indeed, they may have. As time went on, however, individuals would (as in any genre) experiment and modify, such that we should not automatically assume that every *commentarius* was simply a straightforward, unadorned account.[31] We have no evidence, for example, that Aemilius Scaurus thought of his *de uita sua* as merely a sketch to be worked up by some future (or contemporary) historian; the same is true for Rutilius

---

[25] A. von Premerstein, *RE* IV. 735-6.
[26] Bömer, *Hermes* 81 (1953) 210; Lewis, *ANRW* II. 34. 1, 663-8. The *commentarius* at Rome develops independently from ὑπομνήματα in Greece: Bömer, op. cit. 216-25.
[27] *FGrHist* 232, 233; Momigliano, op. cit. (n.20) 91-2 for possible Hellenistic precedents.   [28] Jacoby, *FGrHist Komm.* II. B. 639-40.
[29] Memoirs are attested for Augustus (Suet. *Aug.* 85.1), Tiberius (Suet. *Tib.* 61.1), Vespasian (Jos. *Vita* 342), Trajan (*HRR* F 1), Hadrian (*SHA Hadrian* 1.1), and Septimius Severus (Herodian, II.9.4).   [30] On focalisation see above, p. 179.
[31] Bömer, op. cit. (n.26) 234-8; cf. Ambaglio, *Athenaeum* 68 (1990) 503-8; some scholars continue to assume Lucian's definition of ὑπόμνημα as an unartistic sketch to be later elaborated by another; for the various shades see Rawson, *Intellectual Life* 227-9.

Rufus' five books *de uita sua*.³² Although it is usually assumed that Q. Lutatius Catulus' *liber de consulatu et de gestis suis* was sent to A. Furius Antias for the latter's epic poem *Annals*,³³ there is no ancient evidence for this, and Cicero, judging the book by the standards of high literature, says that it was written 'in the style of Xenophon'.³⁴ With Sulla the evidence is more complicated, but the dedication to Lucullus is not necessarily a determining factor in evaluating its genre.³⁵ Cicero himself provides another example: his *commentarius* on his consulship was so adorned with Isocrates' cosmetic box, he tells us, that Posidonius could not improve on it.³⁶ We can, then, assume that although a *commentarius* might at times be a sketch for some future historian, it could also be a full scale independent account, limited perhaps by its focus, but written with care and *ornatio*, and meant for the same audience, and with some of the same purposes, as a large-scale narrative history.

2. PERSON AND PERSPECTIVE

Thucydides is the model frequently held out as decisive,³⁷ but in this matter he seems to have exercised less influence than in all others, perhaps because his own participation was small and he made no attempt to exalt or magnify what he had done (as others did within a generation). His treatment of himself as a participant in events occurs in Book IV under the eighth year of the Peloponnesian War (424/3 BC) during Brasidas' rapid occupation of Thrace:

> Those [sc. in Amphipolis] opposed to betrayal [to the Spartan commander Brasidas], whose numbers were greater and prevented the

---

[32] Rutilius also wrote a history in Greek (*FGrHist* 815 T 4b; *HRR* FF 1–6) but its relation to the *de uita sua* is not clear.

[33] Peter, *HRR* I. CCLXIV-V, followed by H. Lucas, 'Die Annalen des Furius Antias', *Philologus* 92 (1937) 344–8; Bömer, op. cit. (n.26) 228; more cautiously, Schanz-Hosius I.206; Rawson, op. cit. (n.31) 228.

[34] Cic. *Brut.* 132 says of the *liber*: 'quem de consulatu et de rebus gestis suis conscriptum molli et Xenophonteo genere sermonis misit [i. e. 'dedicated', as A. E. Douglas in his commentary ad loc.] ad A. Furium poetam, familiarem suum'. The Greek author is clearly relevant here: no one suggests that the *Anabasis* was a sketch to be 'adorned' by others, or a piece to be integrated into a larger *Hellenica*.

[35] The work is referred to as πράξεις, *historia*, or *res gestae*; on its titulature see Bömer, op. cit. (n.26) 228–30. For dedications as an element in softening self-depiction see above Ch. I §3.   [36] Cic. *Att.* II.1.1–2.

[37] Norden, *Agnostos Theos* 317.

gates from being opened straightaway, send with Eukles the general, who had come from Athens to guard the place, to the other general in Thrace, Thucydides the son of Olorus (who wrote these things) who was at Thasos (this island is a colony of the Parians, distant from Amphipolis about a half day's sail) ordering him to bring help. And he, hearing these things, swiftly sailed with seven ships that happened to be present, wanting more than anything to get to Amphipolis before it gave in, but if not, to secure beforehand the town of Eion. Meanwhile Brasidas, fearing the help coming from Thasos, and learning that Thucydides had the right of working the gold mines in that part of Thrace and from this was among the most powerful of those on the mainland, hastened to seize the city ahead of them, if he could.[38]

Thucydides gives his name and patronymic in accord with his procedure elsewhere in introducing characters,[39] and then adds the brief phrase, 'who wrote these things', to avoid confusion and clarify the relationship between author and character.[40] The entire narrative of his actions is told in the third person, with his thoughts and intentions included like those of any other character. The knowledge which Brasidas obtains of Thucydides' influence in Thrace is told without comment by the author, as is his final arrival with the ships into Eion in the nick of time and a reference to his general ordering of affairs there. This concludes the presentation of his activities, and he disappears from the scene of action as quickly as he had entered it.[41] Issues of accuracy and honesty aside (both have been questioned),[42] we note that Thucydides' account of his activities is brief and within the narrative itself there is no overt justification or defence of his actions.[43] Nor does he intrude upon the narrative here the personal consequences – his exile

---

[38] Thuc. IV.104.4–105.1.   [39] See Griffith, *PCPhS* 187 (1961) 21–33.
[40] The reader already knew that an Athenian Thucydides wrote the history of the war (1.1.1), yet a previous Thucydides who was a commander and mentioned without patronymic at the end of the Pentekontaetia (1.117.2) could have caused confusion. See Hornblower, *CT* ad locc.   [41] See IV.105.1; 107.1.
[42] A full survey would be unprofitable here: see Gomme, *HCT* III.584–8; J. Classen and J. Steup, *Thukydides* (Berlin ⁵1919) I.xi–xvii.
[43] Westlake, *Essays on the Greek Historians* 123–37 suggests that Thucydides deliberately suppressed his reasons for being at Thasos. If there is distortion, of course, this is most likely the way it would be accomplished, not only for Thucydides but for other historians as well, since the ancients were far more attuned to what was put in (especially if it involves praise, cf. Plutarch on Ctesias, below) than able to see what had been left out.

from Athens – of his failure to safeguard Amphipolis. Since his exile has no consequences for the war, its mention is reserved for the place where it does have importance, on Thucydides' activities as an historian.[44] Thucydides' use of the third person is usually seen as a 'striving for objectivity',[45] yet he clarifies immediately that he is the author of the history in such a way as to leave no doubt of the relationship between narrator and character. Objectivity is of course a possibility; so too is imitation of Homer and his third-person narrative.[46] Most of all, if the associations inherent in the use of the first person revolved around display and advertisement,[47] it may be that Thucydides wanted to avoid such associations, and did not want his activity at Amphipolis to read like a travel report, nor to be classified with the work of a gossipy writer such as Ion of Chios who in his *Wanderings* also used the first person.[48] The model here would have to be Homer (who else for the narration of great deeds?) and his usual avoidance of overt comment within the narrative.[49] It was a question of perspective and focalisation: Thucydides' narrative of his own actions is written no differently from the rest of the history because the entire history is written by a practically omniscient narrator and the use of the first-person would have been inconsonant with this.[50] Scale is also important: Thucydides was hardly likely to arouse suspicion about his actions, because those actions form such a small part of the overall work: one could hardly conclude that he wrote his enormous history simply in order to justify in a few sentences his own actions at Amphipolis. It took the dogged Dionysius and his criticism by character[51] to suggest that Thucydides clearly bore a grudge against his city for his exile, and conveyed that malice into his history.[52]

---

[44] Thuc. v.26, on which see above, p. 133.
[45] So Norden, *Agnostos Theos* 317; cf. Gomme, *HCT* ad loc.
[46] On Thucydides and Homer, see the works cited at Introd. n. 23.
[47] See above, pp. 8f.
[48] Ion of Chios, *FGrHist* 392 F 6: Σοφοκλεῖ τῷ ποιητῇ ἐν Χίῳ συνήντησα, κτλ. [49] See above, p. 159.
[50] Whereas first-person emphasis as a special source (above, p. 80) only cemented this appearance.
[51] D. Hal. *Pomp.* 3 (II.374 Usher), almost alone in antiquity in criticising Thucydides; for the opposite belief about Thucydides' impartiality, compared to that of other historians, see Marcell. *Vita Thuc.* 26-7.
[52] Perhaps here is the place to note also that the four self-referential passages in Thucydides observe a careful distinction: the first person is used for statements of opinion, reasoning, inference, autopsy, and methodology, that is, anything that affected the history *qua* history. The third person, on the other hand, is used

Within a generation two very different works took advantage of Thucydides' procedure. Ctesias' *Persica*, a history of Persia from Ninus and Semiramis to Ctesias' own times, treated especially fully the years of Artaxerxes II, during which Ctesias himself was detained at the court and played a role in the events he described.[53] Plutarch, again with an eye towards self-praise, says that one must use Ctesias' history with caution; its reliability is suspect because Ctesias always finds a place for himself in the narrative.[54] We know from Xenophon that Ctesias described his treatment of the King's wound at the battle of Cunaxa, and from Photius and Plutarch that he figured very largely as an ambassador between the King and Evagoras, Conon, and Pharnabazus. He seems, moreover, to have had the full trust of Parysatis who used him as a special messenger between herself and Clearchus.[55] Since all of this activity fell within the last four books, Ctesias' presence must have been all the more obvious. (As we shall see, Polybius, when confronted with the same problem, showed himself aware of possible criticism and modified his procedure accordingly.) We do not know whether Ctesias used first or third person,[56] nor whether the narrative was marked by egregious

by Thucydides for formal openings and closings: the preface (1.1.1) serves as title page and introduction and is given in the third person (as is the ὁ αὐτὸς Θουκυδίδης of v.26.1) but the historian thereafter yields to the first person once he has introduced himself, whenever he gives opinions or explains methodology (1.1.3; 3.1; 3.2; 22.2), following the pattern set by Herodotus (*praef.*, 1.5.3). The first person is also used when Thucydides speaks as investigator or as one with superior knowledge: II.48.3 (the plague), VI.54.1 (Harmodius and Aristogeiton). The third person is also used when he is an historical character; *pace* Norden, *Agnostos Theos* 317, IV.104.4–105.1 is not an autoptic statement.

[53] Ctesias, *FGrHist* 688 F 5. On the arrangement of the work, Jacoby, *RE* XI.2, 2043. The first eight years of Artaxerxes II (405/4–398/7 BC) were treated in four books.

[54] *FGrHist* 688 T 7b (=Plut. *Artax.* 13): ἀεί τινας ἐν τῇ διηγήσει χώρας ἑαυτῷ δίδωσιν. Plutarch seems to have had a special aversion to using Ctesias' history: see Brown, *Historia* 27 (1978) 17.

[55] *FGrHist* 688 FF 21 (=Xen. *Anab.* 1.8.23–7); 27 §69; 28 (Clearchus); 30; cf. Eck, *REG* 103 (1990) 420–7.

[56] We have one fragment (F 68) with the first person: Κτησίου περὶ ἐλεβόρου· 'ἐπὶ τοῦ ἐμοῦ πατρὸς καὶ τοῦ ἐμοῦ πάππου ἰατρὸς οὐδεὶς ἐδίδου ἐλλέβορον, κτλ'. Jacoby places this under 'Medizinisches' and prints it in petite. Drews, *Greek Accounts of Eastern History* 194–5 n. 30 asks whether it may have come from the περὶ τῶν κατὰ τὴν Ἀσίαν φόρων as a section of the *Periodos*. I wonder, however, if it might not have appeared somewhere in the *Persica*: in F 14 §44 we find the remedies which Apollonides of Cos prescribed for harem ailments. Whatever the case, we cannot tell whether the passage is concerned with Ctesias as an historical actor.

apologetic. As his work centred around the Persian court, he was in a far more favourable position than Thucydides to put himself at or near the centre of the account. Yet however he portrayed himself, he shows an immediate appreciation and grasp of the possibilities opened up by Thucydides.

Nor was the lesson lost on Xenophon. His use of the third person is well known and Plutarch's explanation of his choice has been repeated by moderns:

> For Xenophon became his own historian, writing up the actions which he commanded and set in order, and ascribing them to Themistogenes of Syracuse, so that it would be more persuasive when he spoke about himself as if it were someone else, and he gave to someone else the renown for his writing.[57]

For Plutarch it is not the third person that is at issue here, but rather, as Plutarch himself notes, the use of the pseudonym Themistogenes,[58] and the resultant character that the praises of 'Xenophon' by this Themistogenes take on. Xenophon splits apart that relationship that Thucydides had guarded with the phrase 'who wrote these things', and even if the pseudonym were no more than a literary game, Xenophon must have known that some would not see through it. This account of himself, certainly panegyrical, would have 'seemed more reliable' because praise by another – that praise that Cicero wanted from Lucceius – did not carry the same stigma as self-praise.

The next two centuries are difficult to analyse, because of the loss of the major historians of those years, especially the Sicilian historians and the first-generation Alexander historians; in both groups were numbered active participants in the events they described. Of the former group, Philistus of Syracuse was present at the great battle in 413 between Athenians and Syracusans, was exiled in 386/5 by the tyrant Dionysius, and may have written his history in exile. We know that he

---

[57] Plu. *de glor. Athen.* 345E = *FGrHist* 108 T 3; cf. Momigliano, *Greek Biography* 57.
[58] Perhaps we should add 'if indeed Xenophon used this pseudonym', but Breitenbach, *RE* IX. A. 2, 646 is very convincing that all the evidence points back to Xenophon. See MacLaren, *TAPA* 65 (1934) 242 for other ancient texts supporting Plutarch. It is difficult to tell if this is the first literary forgery: see Speyer, *Die literarische Fälschung* 27-30.

was a character in his history.⁵⁹ Timonides of Leucas was a supporter of Dion and was made commander in a battle in which the latter was wounded.⁶⁰ Athanis of Syracuse was likewise a politician who wrote history and whose work dealt with the internal political struggles of Sicily.⁶¹ Even for Timaeus we can say very little: it is certain that he spoke of his father Andromachus and the founding of Tauromenium, and equally certain that he castigated his opponent Agathocles who banished him, but how he portrayed himself in all this is unknown.⁶²

No less uncertain is how the Alexander historians portrayed themselves. Since many of these histories were written by colleagues and assistants of Alexander himself, there were many opportunities for the historian to represent his own deeds. It was once believed that Ptolemy's history was a soldier's straightforward, unadorned and reliable account with a combination of first- and third-person narrative, but this view of Ptolemy has been questioned, and some have suggested both a political purpose to the history and a bias towards those who were his enemies.⁶³ Curtius' statement that Ptolemy was not reserved about his own renown⁶⁴ is tantalising but says nothing about the latter's narrative method. Also with Alexander was Aristobulus, who was entrusted with the restoration of the tomb of Cyrus, but how he himself told the story cannot be determined.⁶⁵ It should be added here that we fare no better on this topic with the historians of the Successors, many of

---

⁵⁹ See *FGrHist* 556 TT 3-4 (from Diodorus) and Jacoby *Komm.* ad loc. As Jacoby notes, F 59 shows that Philistus like Thucydides did not exaggerate his importance. Since he had a larger role than Thucydides he could not have quite the same reserve about himself. Jacoby's remark, however, that Philistus will have 'spoken of himself in his history in the third person like Thucydides, Xenophon, and others' (*Komm.* IIIb (Noten) 297 n. 1), while in itself not unlikely, is nevertheless based on no direct evidence.

⁶⁰ *FGrHist* 561 T 2; Jacoby, *Komm.* IIIb (Text) 521 notes that the information about Timonides must come from his own work. Our sole source of knowledge about him is Plutarch and it is uncertain whether he even wrote a formal history.

⁶¹ Theopompus (not always the best witness) called him a leader of the city (*FGrHist* 562 T 1).

⁶² Momigliano, *Terzo Contributo* 1.36 with n. 37; *FGrHist* 566 T 3a; FF 123, 124.

⁶³ Norden, *Agnostos Theos* 321; for the political nature and bias of the work, see Badian, *Studies in Greek and Roman History* 257-8; Errington, *CQ* 19 (1969) 233-42; Pearson, *Lost Histories* ch. VII; *contra*, Roisman, *CQ* 34 (1984) 373-85 who argues against the view that Ptolemy used his history for political purposes.

⁶⁴ Curtius, IX.5.21 (=*FGrHist* 138 F 26b): 'ipse scilicet gloriae suae non refragatus'. The phrase echoes Livy (XXXIV.15.9) on Cato: 'haud sane detractor laudum suarum'.   ⁶⁵ *FGrHist* 139 F 51.

whom were historical participants. Even so important a figure as Hieronymus must be largely resurrected from Diodorus who, however much he kept the substance of Hieronymus' autobiographical sections, did not keep the form.[66] All of these historians may have used their histories to defend their actions or, at the very least, to leave for posterity a positive impression of their own actions.[67]

With Polybius we are on rather firmer ground. Fifteen passages from his history survive in which the author is an historical character, but only ten are given in his own words.[68] All of the passages in which Polybius is a participator are preserved by the Constantinian Excerpts and it is well known that they sometimes preserve an author's *ipsissima uerba* but at other times alter the wording and presentation of the historical texts. Although the excerptors wished to give the individual passage in its essentials, they did not proceed with the same faithfulness as when copying a full text; they frequently omit material that they consider irrelevant to the topic, or they alter the beginnings and ends of excerpts to make the excerpts independently intelligible, or even at times simply summarise the historical circumstances.[69] They will also sometimes change a speech from direct to indirect discourse, and (most important for our purpose) change the first person into the third person

[66] For a reconstruction of Hieronymus' method see J. Hornblower, *Hieronymus of Cardia* 18-75; 107-79; 263-81.

[67] Badian, *YCS* 24 (1975) 147-70 has, for example, convincingly demonstrated that Nearchus in his *Periplous* presented himself in a favourable light vis-à-vis Alexander, without engaging in overt polemic or self-justification, and left an extremely favourable impression of himself on the historiographical tradition.

[68] I say 'from Polybius' history' to distinguish the passages preserved by the Constantinian excerptors from those passages found in later authors who are obviously drawing on Polybius' history but who have paraphrased or altered the passages for their own purposes. Thus I do not include in consideration here the following: xxxv.6.1-4, xxxviii.19 (both from Plutarch), and xxxix.2.1 (from Strabo). Also not considered is xxxix.5.4, which comes from a posthumous edition: see Walbank, *HCP* iii.735. I also do not consider here xxii.19.1 in which Polybius was present at a conversation between Philopoemen and Archon, because he does not portray himself there as a participator (Polybius was a young man at the time of the conversation and had most likely not yet begun his political career: Walbank, *HCP* iii.209), but rather as an eyewitness, and thus uses the first person.

[69] On the characteristics of the Constantinian Excerpts, see de Boor, *BZ* 1 (1892) 32-3; cf. Hunger, *Die hochsprachliche profane Literatur der Byzantiner* 1.244-6; Lemerle, *La première humanisme Byzantine* 267-300; for the danger of determining the scale and treatment of a history by its Constantinian fragments, see Thompson, in *The Greek Historians* 119-39.

to make the passage intelligible.[70] Despite this, an examination of the relevant passages before Book XXXVI show that Polybius consistently adhered to the third person and to narrative impartiality, even when he was an historical character.[71] Of particular interest is the account of the origins of his friendship with Scipio Aemilianus, a passage that is especially helpful in demonstrating the separation between Polybius the narrator (who speaks in the first person) and Polybius the historical character (who is always referred to in the third person). The narrator remarks, 'I made a promise in an earlier book to explain why the friendship of Scipio with Polybius [not 'me'] became so well known throughout Greece and Italy', and he then shifts to the third person maintaining this even for the personal dialogue between the two characters. At the end of the digression (which has included an appraisal of Scipio's character) the narrator reverts to the first person.[72]

In Book XXXVI this procedure changes. Polybius, now back in Achaea, is asked by the consul of 149, M'. Manilius, to go to Lilybaeum, presumably for his military skill in the coming war with Carthage. Polybius reached Corcyra and thinking (erroneously, it turned out) that the Carthaginians had surrendered, he returned to Achaea.[73] In this passage Polybius begins by referring to himself in the third person (Πολύβιον τὸν Μεγαλοπολίτην) and then shifts to first-person narration (ἡμεῖς δέ).[74] This is not simply variation or carelessness by the excerptor, as is shown by what follows:

> One ought not to be surprised if at one time we indicate ourselves by our proper name and at another time by general expressions such as 'after I said these things' or in turn 'when we agreed'. (2) For since we were involved to a great extent in the affairs that are going to be narrated after

---

[70] Millar, *Cassius Dio* 1-2 notes this for Dio. It is possible to check the excerptor's practice in Dio since it can be compared with Xiphilinus' epitome where Dio's original words are preserved. My examination of the parallel passages in Boissevain of Books LXVIII-LXX reveals that the excerptors retained Dio's first-person remarks.

[71] Pol. XXIV.6.1-7; XXVIII.3.7-9; 6.8-9; 7.8-13; 12.4-13.14; XXIX.23.1-25.7; XXXI.11.1-15.12; 23.1-29.12; XXXII.3.14; XXXVI.11.1-4.

[72] It is worthwhile to note that the excerptor preserved this alteration here, which gives us at least some confidence that he did so elsewhere. This account of Polybius' friendship with Scipio may be based on the meeting of Socrates and Alcibiades in the *Alcibiades Maior*: P. Friedländer, *Plato* (Princeton 1958) 1.323-32; *contra*, Walbank, *HCP* III.496.   [73] Walbank, *Polybius* 10.

[74] Pol. XXXVI.11.1-4.

these, it is necessary to vary the expressions about ourself, lest in putting forward our name constantly we give offence by repeating it, or again in saying on each occasion 'I' or 'by my effort' we should unwittingly fall into a style of presentation that is wearisome; (3) rather, by using all of these together and applying on every occasion that which is fitting to the occasion, we might avoid, to the extent that it is possible, the excessive offence of speaking about ourselves (διαφεύγωμεν τὸ λίαν ἐπαχθὲς τῆς περὶ αὐτῶν λαλιᾶς), (4) since such a manner of speaking is surprising, but yet is often necessary whenever it is not possible otherwise to explain clearly the matter at hand. (5) An assistance we have had by chance in this matter is that no one, up until our own times, has received the same proper name that we have, at least in so far as we know.[75]

This passage follows immediately after XXXVI.11.1-4 where the variation Πολύβιον-ἡμεῖς occurred.[76] This is significant, since it is Polybius' consistent procedure to place methodological statements throughout his history at the place where they are most relevant, especially when he is conscious of doing something new and anticipates the audience's surprise.[77] Here then is where Polybius' procedure changed. This means that before XXXVI.11 Polybius consistently said either 'I/we' or 'Poly-

---

[75] Pol. XXXVI.12.1-5; the only discussion I have found is that of Chodniček, *Neunzehnter Jahresbericht des K. K. Gymnasium. im 3. Bezirk in Wien* 28ff.
[76] Walbank, *HCP* III.671.
[77] A few examples: in Book I, after Polybius has given the starting-point of his work, he adds that he will also give some history anterior to the chronological limits he has set himself, since this earlier history is necessary for a proper understanding of the main subject. He tells his readers, therefore, not to be surprised (οὐ χρὴ θαυμάζειν, I.12.8) if he gives earlier bits of history in the further course of his work (ἐν τοῖς ἑξῆς, ibid.). In Book III he has a discussion of the causes of the First Punic War in which he distinguishes the war's beginnings, causes, and pretexts (III.6.1-7.3). He then explains why he has made so lengthy a digression and its relevance to the purposes of history (III.7.4). Also in Book III he defends himself for not treating geographical matters at individual points in his history (III.57.1-9): he did not, he says, wish to interrupt his narrative at each particular point and thereby distract the readers from their understanding of events by inserting irrelevant details. So they should not be surprised (οὐ χρὴ θαυμάζειν, III.57.6) if he avoids them here and in the future (ἐν τοῖς ἑξῆς, ibid.) since he has instead kept geographical remarks for the proper place and time (III.57.3). Although Polybius' work is full of such remarks (see also VI.2.1-4; VII.11.1-2; X.21.2-4; XI.1a.1; XXX.9.20-1; XXXVI.8.6; XXXVIII.4.1), these few passages suffice to show that Polybius places methodological statements at the point where he takes up or explains a new procedure or topic, or after the first instance of a new procedure. On Polybius' manner of digressing, see Ibendorff, *Untersuchungen zur darstellerischen Persönlichkeit des Polybios* 1-14, 20-2.

bius', but not both.[78] And unless we assume that the excerptor changed every first-person passage to third person, the logical conclusion is that before this, Polybius always used the third person.

The explanation for his new procedure is of interest. Polybius had early on said that the greatest spur to extending his history from its original limits was that he himself had been a participant (III.4.13). Thus it is the frequency of the historian's subsequent appearances in these later books that necessitates a stylistic change; it should be noted that nothing other than style is argued here. The author does not wish to be offensive in saying 'Polybius' again and again, nor tiresome in saying 'I' or 'me' constantly. There is no question of deceiving the reader, who will know on each occasion that 'I' and 'Polybius' refer to the same person. What seems rather to be at issue is the purely formal presentation expected of an historical character in a history,[79] since Polybius is aware that such a variation of first- and third-person reference is surprising (ἀπροσδεκτός).[80] Nor can it be mere coincidence when Polybius says that he is trying to avoid being burdensome or annoying (ἐπαχθής) when talking about himself, since these are the words used by the rhetoricians for the reaction of the audience to a speaker's self-praise.[81] The constant intrusion of the narrator cannot be eliminated but it can be mitigated, so Polybius suggests, by stylistic variation.

Both the position and content of the passage are good evidence,

---

[78] The passage offers evidence in addition that for Polybius no difference is to be assumed between first-person singular and plural, since 'after I said' and 'when we agreed' are offered as equivalent expressions. This is not the case with the later historians as we shall see below.

[79] The expressions 'after I said these things' and 'when we agreed' can only refer to the historian taking part in the action and not speaking in his persona as narrator. It would have been quite disingenuous for Polybius, who constantly interrupts the narrative with methodological pointers, to have suggested here that first-person intrusion by itself was burdensome to the reader.

[80] The word occurs only here in Polybius: A. Maurenbrecher, *Polybios-Lexicon* (Berlin, 1956–), s. v., who glosses the word as 'anstössig, befremdlich'.

[81] Demosth. *Cor.* 3: 'it is natural that all men hear slander and accusation with pleasure, but are annoyed with those who praise themselves' (τοῖς ἐπαινοῦσι δ' αὐτοὺς ἄχθεσθαι); cf. Hermogenes' title περὶ τοῦ ἀνεπαχθῶς ἑαυτὸν ἐπαίνειν; at v.49.4, Polybius had described Hermeias' praise of himself as 'burdensome' (φορτικῶς μὲν αὐτὸν ἐγκωμιάζων); more generally, Dionysius (*A. R.* 1.1.1) says that those who indulge in praises of themselves are ἐπαχθεῖς ... τοῖς ἀκούουσιν.

then, that the use of the third person for the author as participator was the accepted and expected procedure and that Polybius had previously followed it. It would be senseless (as well as insensitive to the great variety of people who wrote history between Xenophon and Polybius) to state categorically that this passage proves that every historian (be he a Ptolemy or a Hieronymus) referred to himself in the third person and in proportion[82] to the other deeds he narrated, but it does suggest that for Polybius, history (as opposed perhaps to memoirs or other genres) demanded the third person for all participants and a treatment commensurate in extent with the individual's participation and achievements. Polybius was aware that what followed was going to lose the perspective of history and become suspiciously like memoirs: indeed, the last few books do seem to have been quite different in character and orientation from the preceding universal history, since in their underlying treatment of the Romans, and in their expanded scale, Books XXXV to XXXIX break sharply with Books XXX to XXXIII.[83] The last five books view events from Rome's perspective, and the narrative is centred around Scipio and Polybius, treating (primarily) the events at which they (together and individually) were present.[84] Polybius is probably attempting to stave off the reproach that might accompany extended treatment of his own deeds within what purported to be a history. Whether anything more than literary artifice and audience expectations is at issue cannot be certain. For even if we accept that the later books were written by Polybius with an eye towards his own renown – and this is by no means certain – that aim could just as well have been achieved by the use of the third person. Nor can it be determined whether Aratus or the Romans (with their stronger tradition of *commentarii*) first suggested to Polybius the approach and orientation of the latter books. But it will be of use to look now at the Romans to see what can be determined of their methods in these matters, especially as the historian in early Rome had in all cases also been a participant.

[82] I say 'in proportion' because Polybius is clear that it is only his greater participation in the events that warrants a change in forms of self-reference. He had been mentioned frequently before Book XXXVI but this was only at individual incidents at different times, and his part had been small in a universal history.

[83] Walbank, *SP* 280–97; 325–43. Books XXX–XXXIII treated sixteen years from 168/7 to 153/2; books XXXV–XXXIX treated seven years, 152/1 to 146/5: Walbank, *SP* 334. For the different attitude towards Roman policy, ibid. 338–43.

[84] Ibid., esp. 343 with n. 147.

The limitations on our knowledge of the early Roman historians are by now well known, and our difficulty of saying anything certain on the topic of self-presentation is the same as on practically all the other aspects of these writers. Fabius Pictor was a character in his work,[85] but his method of narration cannot be recovered. More promising is a fragment of Cato's from a military narrative:

> On the following day, when the standards had been brought together and the front line had been made equal, we fought the legions of the enemy with infantry, cavalry, and auxiliaries.[86]

It is likely that Cato and his men are the subject of the verb here, and this gives two possibilities between which we cannot, unfortunately, decide: either that Cato was continuing in Latin the procedure that Fabius had used, or that Cato in deciding to write Latin history assumed a Latin audience and a viewpoint decidedly parochial, perhaps adapting the first-person style of the military commander's dispatch[87] to the needs of a large-scale narrative. It is also possible that Cato is here using 'we' in the way that later Roman historians do, to designate the Roman soldiers in battle with the enemy.[88] This tradition, which is not found among the

---

[85] *FGrHist* 809 F 20 = *HRR* F 24, in which Fabius uses a swallow to indicate the proper time for an escape from the Roman camp when the Ligurians were besieging it.

[86] Cato, *HRR* F 99 = Gellius, xv.9.5: 'Quippe M. Cato in quinta origine ita scripsit: Postridie signis conlatis aequo fronte peditatu, equitibus atque alis cum hostium legionibus pugnauimus.' This reading, from Hertz's 1883-5 *editio maior* of Gellius, is that given in Peter. In newer texts of Gellius (and in Chassignet's *Origines*), editors print *pugnauit* ('he [presumably the general; Cato did not give names of commanders in his history: below, n. 107] fought'). This reading appears in F (the oldest manuscript of Books IX-XX of Gellius), which is much preferred in newer editions. I have kept *pugnauimus* because F can be overvalued (see F. R. D. Goodyear, *CR* 21 (1971) 385-90; Holford-Strevens, *Aulus Gellius* 243-4), and, as there is no question of a *lectio difficilior* or of unanimous manuscript support, it seems to me that the sense is better served with *pugnauimus* since a plural makes more sense with 'cum hostium legionibus', and the entire sentence describes the arrangement and deployment of men in a military engagement. Certainty, however, is impossible. The events narrated in Cato's speech *de consulatu suo* (*ORF* 8 FF 21-49) were later narrated in the *Origines*; this narrative moves between first person singular and plural: see Norden, *Agnostos Theos* 319 with n. 1.

[87] The simple structure with verb at the end in the first person is indicative of this: see Fraenkel, *Kleine Beiträge* II.69-73 for examples.   [88] See App. V.

Greeks, even of the Empire, does have parallels with local history, where the narrator customarily uses the first person plural for the inhabitants of his state.[89] This procedure shows well the limited perspective of Roman historiography, and the assumption of a more intimate relationship between author and audience.

Not less significant in the *Origins* was Cato's decision to include his own speeches; the model here could be Xenophon's similar procedure in the *Anabasis*.[90] But what is of greater importance is that Cato seems to have used the technique in a decidedly political and polemical way. The speech for the Rhodians from Book v is preserved by Gellius,[91] but we lack the context: did Cato give another and opposing speech, how did he characterise himself and his opponent, how did he represent his effect on the Senate? This crucial gap in our knowledge also inhibits the drawing

---

[89] A few fragments from the Greek local historians who use the first person suggest a certain intimacy of audience, as is only to be expected. We have three verbatim quotations, at least two of which are unquestionably from local histories. The first, from Cleidemus' *Exegetikon* (perhaps not a local history), attempts to explain "Υης as a title of Dionysus by explaining that 'we [presumably 'we priests' but perhaps 'we Athenians'] offer sacrifices to Dionysus when it rains [ὕει]' (*FGrHist* 323 F 27). A fragment from Philochorus' *Atthis* is more informative, for this deals with the author's 'deeds': Philochorus reported the exile of the Athenians who were accused of subverting the democracy following the removal of Cassander's garrison at Athens in 307 BC, and in the course of doing so, he reports portents which occurred on the Acropolis and the subsequent consultation of the priests who were asked for their interpretation. Dionysius preserves Philochorus' actual words (328 F 67 = D. Hal. *Din.* 3 (II.260 Usher); cf. F 35a):

> on the Acropolis occurred the following portent: a bitch came into the temple of Athena Polias, and going into the Pandroseion lay down upon the altar of Herkeian Zeus, the one beneath the olive tree. Now it is a custom of the Athenians not to allow any dog onto the Acropolis. Around the same time a star was visible for some time in the heavens when the sun was out and the sky was clear. And when we were asked about the portent and the star's appearance, we said that it indicated a return of exiles, and that this would occur not by a revolution, but under the existing government. And this interpretation was correct.

This passage seems to be certain evidence that Philochorus narrated his own actions in his *Atthis* in the first person. Finally, the local historian of Thespiae, Aphrodisias-Euphemios, speaks of a local legend about the Argonauts as a 'λόγος παρ' ἡμῶν' (386 F 1).

[90] For Cato and Xenophon see Ch. V n. 150. It is likely too that the Alexander historians included their own speeches. Thus Astin, *Cato the Censor* 234 is perhaps wrong to say that Cato's inclusion of speeches was 'perhaps unique'; what might have been unique in Cato was the scale and focus.

[91] Gellius, VI.3.1–48 = *HRR* F 95 = *ORF* 8 FF 163–71.

of conclusions about Cato's narrative of his own actions, though we are certainly justified in accepting the view of antiquity that Cato praised himself fully and perhaps excessively in his history. Several passages, all from Plutarch's *Life* of Cato, present Cato in action in his history, and all show him in a favourable light, whether it be taking more than a city a day in Spain, refusing spoils after a battle, or almost singlehandedly bringing victory to the Romans.[92] Plutarch himself has to confess that Cato could not resist an opportunity to extol his own achievements.[93] So what may have been national prejudice towards Rome in Pictor's account of the First Punic War seems to have become for Cato personal *apologia*, though without the entire text of his work we are unable to judge the scale and focalisation. Was Cato the centre of the later books (V-VII), that is, did he become (like Xenophon in the *Anabasis* or Polybius in XXXV-XXXIX) more and more the main character, or was he an occasional character, forcefully drawn but not constantly present? He, more than anyone else, may have blurred the line between history and memoirs.[94]

We come now to the Romans and their *commentarii de uita sua* or *de rebus gestis*. M. Aemilius Scaurus seems to have written the first, but why Scaurus was motivated to write this work we do not know.[95] If it is the case that Cato's later books lost the wider perspective of more usual histories, it may be that Scaurus simply realised that one could write *de uita sua* without the accompanying framework of the *Origins* that Cato had had. In other words, if the *Origins* was a Roman history made up of one three-book narrative of non-contemporary history and one four-book account of contemporary history (more or less from Cato's point of view),[96] then Scaurus' work represents simply the jettisoning of the earlier history, an

---

[92] Cato, *HRR* F 129 (=Plut. *C. M.* 10) on his activities in Spain in 194; F 130 (=*C. M.* 14.1-2), on his service at Thermopylae in 191; see also *C. M.* 14.2-4, not printed by Peter who ends the fragment at 14.2, arbitrarily, in my opinion, since the speedy journey to Rome and the exaggerated welcome are part of the μεγα-λαυχία that Plutarch is referring to (14.1), and form a single piece with the previous narrative. (The second fragment is not included in Chassignet's edition because Plutarch does not mention the *Origines* by name here: see the criteria for inclusion in her edition at p. xxxv.) [93] Plut. *C. M.* 14.1.
[94] See Badian, in *Latin Historians* 9-10. C. Fannius, like Cato, included his own speeches in his history: Cic. *Brut.* 81.
[95] On Scaurus, see Schanz-Hosius 1.205-6; for suggestions why he wrote memoirs see Bates, *Memoirs and the Perception of History* 127 ff., esp. 131; cf. Lewis, *ANRW* II. 34. 1, 660-2.
[96] Badian, in *Latin Historians* 23 notes that Cato's and Fannius' histories had already shaded into political autobiography.

action that parallels the series of historical monographs that had just begun with Coelius Antipater. The distinction between memoirs and autobiographies, between apologetic and its absence, is not always easy to make, for the obvious reason that these works have perished, but also because the ancients themselves did not always make a strong distinction.[97] We can hardly doubt that Rutilius Rufus or Q. Lutatius Catulus defended their actions, overtly or implicitly in their memoirs. Nor is there any doubt that Sulla's work, whatever its title, treated his early years and his political career.[98] On the Greek side, Nicolaus of Damascus' *Life* treated his upbringing and contained a defence of his actions.[99] Nevertheless, it should not be simply assumed that political justification was always overt or the *raison d'être* of such works.[100]

Of all these works we know practically nothing of their narrative method. We need not doubt that since the author was at the centre, the element of self-display could be tolerated far more than in a history. We do, however, have a few verbatim fragments that show that the writers of works *de uita sua* used the first person. The evidence amounts to five, perhaps six, quotations in all, not overwhelming, but not altogether negligible given the wretched remains of pre-Sallustian historiography in general and hypomnematic literature specifically. The evidence, though not vast, is uniform, and there is no example before Caesar in which the writer of a *commentarius* uses the third person.[101] No doubt some of this might be the accident of survival; it may also simply have been the Roman tradition.[102]

---

[97] Momigliano, *Greek Biography* 89–90.

[98] Bömer, *Hermes* 81 (1953) 226–8 surveys the evidence for this.

[99] The fragments of Nicolaus' *Bios* in *FGrHist* 90 FF 131–9; on its character, Jacoby, *Komm.* II. C. 288–90. Bellemore, *Nicolaus: Life of Augustus* xvi thinks that Nicolaus wrote an account only of his upbringing (an ἀγωγή), and that the details of his political career were taken from the relevant sections of his *History*.

[100] Momigliano, op. cit. (n.97) 15 cautions that biographies rather than autobiographies may have been the place where praise could more easily be given and expected. Nor must we assume self-justification when the author's purpose may have been self-display: see below on Caesar.

[101] Scaurus, *HRR* F 6 (*ueni*); Rufus, F 9 = *FGrHist* 815 F 9 (*ueniebam*); F 14 (*me inuitum*); Sulla, F 3 (*me* and *nostri*, but perhaps from a speech); cf. Augustus, *HRR* FF 4 (*ludorum meorum* and *consecrauimus*); 24 (*nos uenimus*). Ptolemy Euergetes II also used the first person in his *Memoirs*: see *FGrHist* 234 FF 1; 6; 9–10.

[102] Maintained into the Empire, as one can see from Trajan's *Dacica*, *HRR* F 1: 'inde Berzobim, deinde Aizi processimus'. Given the evidence above, the first person plural here seems to be the Roman tradition (rather than an innovation of Trajan's, as Lewis, op. cit. (n.95) 638–9 n. 26 suggests).

Yet it is uncertain whether they form a proper model for Caesar's *commentarii*, for these are not about his life and upbringing, but are the records of the Gallic and civil wars.[103] It seems likely that for the former, at least, the original dispatches that Caesar sent from Gaul to the Senate were in the first person, and that Caesar used some of these dispatches, reworking them into his book and changing first to third person.[104] Yet since the evidence, scant as it is, suggests a consistency of procedure, it will not be presumptuous to suggest that Caesar's use of the third person was atypical and meant to be. Perhaps it was only a personal foible, as his remarks elsewhere suggest,[105] or perhaps it was literary emulation. As there is no evidence that it comes from earlier Roman writers, Xenophon's independent narrative of a military campaign may be the real model behind Caesar's *Gallic War* narrative.[106] For when we look at all the evidence from Roman historians (and memoirists before Caesar) we can state quite simply that no Roman historian ever refers to himself in the third person. The only possible exception might be Cato who, if he remained consistent in his omission of names for military commanders, would have referred to himself when a military commander in the third person as 'the general'.[107] But all the rest of the Romans, historians and memoirists alike, use the first person. And if we dismiss Cicero's remark that Caesar intended his *commentarii* as raw material for others (and this we are entitled to do[108]) we may suppose, instead,

---

[103] Fornara, *Nature* 181.
[104] Fraenkel, *Kleine Beiträge* II.69; for examples of an 'official' style alternating between first person singular and plural, see Norden, *Agnostos Theos* 318-20. Note that when the narrator speaks as narrator, he uses the first person, e.g. *B. G.* IV.17.1; v.6.1 ('de quo ante ab nobis dictum est'); 13.4. Norden, op. cit. 317 with n. 2 denies that Caesar ever uses the first person; he believed that the geographical passages were spurious, but this was not then and is not now generally accepted: see the older literature cited by Schanz-Hosius I.338.
[105] Adcock, *Caesar as a Man of Letters* 74-6 thinks it is perhaps 'a revealing mannerism', since Caesar seems even outside the *Commentarii* to have been fond of referring to himself in the third person. Cf. 'Caesar's wife', and Pollio's report at Pharsalus ('C. Caesar condemnatus essem', *HRR* F 2a); Adcock suggests that 'the constant use of his name in the *Commentarii* is not only a convention or a mask of objectiveness, but includes, as it were, the natural, almost automatic expression of his conscious preeminence' (76). [106] Fornara, *Nature* 181-2.
[107] Badian, in *Latin Historians* 8 points out that Cato's ban on names (Nepos, *Cato* 3.4) applied only to Roman and enemy commanders, not to other distinguished men. This leaves open the way that Cato in the latter part of his *Origins* referred to himself in domestic political life by name or with 'I'.
[108] Bömer, op. cit. (n.98) 239.

that Caesar intended a very finished piece, an *Anabasis* of a sort though influenced (of course) by Roman conventions. His use of the third person then suggests itself as an attempt to provide a definitive account, in the manner of an historian.[109]

Of the other historians at Rome, nothing can be said about the narration of their own actions. Livy had no political career, Sallust almost certainly did not reach the year of his tribuneship in the *Histories*,[110] and the contemporary portions of Tacitus' books of the same name have not survived. In moving on to the Empire we are aware of having lost an entire era, that of the late Republic and first years of the Empire, so that it is not possible to determine trends or conventions. A new order now existed for historians: the Emperor's eminence severely circumscribed the area and way in which men could narrate and extol their own achievement. Yet the historians of the Empire adapted remarkably well to the changed political conditions, and the death of political freedom did not take with it the practice of history.

In Velleius' summary history, the climax is the narrative of the Pannonian and Dalmatian wars fought by Tiberius in AD 6-9 in which Velleius took part. As with other imperial historians, the contemporary portions are not really a history of his times, but only an account of the events which he knew first hand and in which he participated.[111] There is a decidedly panegyrical tone in this narrative, but we have been prepared for it by Velleius' habit everywhere of praising or censuring.[112] Velleius uses the first person singular for himself, the first person plural for the Roman soldiers. No attempt is made at formal objectivity, and Velleius shows no hesitancy in presenting himself as allied and indebted to the Emperor.

Several Greek historians of the Empire maintain the Thucydidean use of the third person. This can be seen in Nicolaus' *History*, where his own actions are referred to in the third person,[113] and it is clearest of all

---

[109] See Eden, *Glotta* 40 (1962) 75-6 for Caesar's manipulation of audience expectations in a *commentarius*; see also Rüpke *Gymnasium* 99 (1992) 201-26 who argues that Caesar's works are war monographs, not memoirs or autobiography.   [110] Syme, *Sallust* 178.

[111] As pointed out above, pp. 91ff., a restricted circle of events is characteristic of much contemporary imperial historiography.

[112] See Woodman, *VP* 1.42-5.

[113] Assuming, that is, that Bellemore (above, n.99) is correct that passages referring to Nicolaus' career come from the *Histories*, not the *Life*: see *FGrHist* 90 FF 136-8.

in Josephus' *Jewish War*. Unlike Thucydides, however, Josephus allows a rather large place for his deeds, and portrays himself as a great general. Yet even he is careful not to become the dominant character or the focaliser: when he is on stage he makes sure that he is portrayed well, but after his capture in Book III he is no longer the main actor on the Jewish side, and the remaining four books give both the Roman and Jewish perspective, with Josephus' appearances limited to a few actions here and there.[114] From a later period we know that Dexippus, as a commander of Gallienus' forces against the Herulian invasions of Greece, portrayed his actions and even included his own speeches in his *Scythica*, using the third person.[115]

Dio shows a difference in perspective, although it is always possible that the fragmentary nature of the latter books of his history has skewed the original perspective of the history. Dio exceeds any previous historian in number and scale of preserved autobiographical participatory remarks.[116] As his work, like Polybius', is preserved in the later books only by excerpts and an epitome, the scale and proportion cannot always be determined. Since, however, many independent units are contained, we can examine the narration on a smaller scale. It is clear, for

---

[114] On the narrative perspective of the *Jewish War* see Rajak, *Josephus* 154ff. His appearances after his capture are at IV.623-9 (his liberation from chains); V.114; 261; 325-6 (is not taken in by Castor's ruse); 361-420 (urges surrender at Jerusalem; long speech of his recounting Jewish history beginning from Pharaoh!); 541-7 (hit by a stone but recovers); VI.93-117 (sent to speak to John); 365 (his constant entreaties and the abuse he received for them); VII.448 (implicated in the calumnies of Catullus). Since I am here concerned only with perspective, I emphasise the relative infrequency of his appearances after capture; for more on his self-presentation see below, §3.

[115] *FGrHist* 100 F 28; for discussion see Millar, *JRS* 59 (1969) 26-8; on the reduced focalisation of Dexippus' history see Ch. II n. 143.

[116] What we would want to know in particular is how fully Dio reported events at which he was not present. Dio states at LXXX.1.2 that his absence from Rome has hindered the fullness of the narrative to follow, and he may here betray his own reliance on the supply of materials at Rome that Diodorus had praised (above, p. 75). Yet if the interpretation given above (p. 92) of Dio's attitude in the latter books is correct, it may well be that the conflicts of Emperor and Senate played the dominant role. On Dio's own actions see: LXXII.18.1-21.3; LXXIII.1.4-5; 3.2; 8.1-5; 12.1-13.3; 16.1-17.4; LXXIV.1.3-2.3; 4.2-5.5; LXXV.4.1-7; LXXVI.1.2; 5.1; 6.3; 8.1-9.1; LXXVII.9.3-7; 17.1-18.4; LXXVIII.6.3; 37.5-38.2; LXXX.4.2-5.2. (Not included here are autoptic and methodological statements, incidental references to 'us Senators', and purely autobiographical passages (e.g. LXXVI.2.1).)

example, that much of the history was told from the point of view of the Senators (whom Dio always calls ἡμεῖς); clear too that many of the participatory remarks shade over into the autoptic where his presence as a Senator and participator is a guarantee of accuracy for an unusual or important action.[117] On the purely formal side we note that although his name ὁ Δίων occasionally appears in the narrative,[118] Dio always refers to his own actions with ἐγώ and ἡμεῖς. This is not the variation that Polybius envisioned, where the two words were used for himself interchangeably, for in Dio ἡμεῖς is always the narrator as a member of a group, either 'we consulars' or 'we Bithynians', or (most commonly) 'we Senators'.[119] Whether we must reckon with the influence of the more intimate tone of Roman historiography is not certain, but here seems highly probable.

Some passages in which Dio is a participant border on the anecdotal. When Commodus cuts off an ostrich's head and brandishes it at the Senators, Dio conceals his laughter, and persuades his colleagues to conceal theirs, by chewing on the laurel leaves of their crowns.[120] To be sure, the Senatorial perspective is a part of the larger heritage of Roman historiography, but Dio's accounts of the emperors and their relationship with the Senate is given supreme importance, and Dio's judgements on them and their reigns is in direct proportion to how well they treated the Senatorial class. An important consequence of this is the loss of formal objectivity, no less than in Velleius' case.[121] We are told, for example, that Pertinax treated the Senators (ἡμᾶς) generously and feasted them; Severus on the other hand made promises to 'us' which he ultimately did not keep, but gave 'us' his advisers full liberty to speak. Caracalla hated those of 'us' with education and showed his disregard for 'our' dignity by setting a eunuch over 'us'.[122]

Ammianus' narration of his own deeds is unique. Like Velleius he was a soldier in the army of an Emperor, but unlike the former he wrote a large-scale work in which his own participation in events was but one aspect. On the formal side, Ammianus, like Velleius, always uses the first

---

[117] See for example LXXV.4.3, and above, pp. 91f.
[118] Particularly when someone is addressing him: see LXXVIII.8.4.
[119] Dio, XLIII.46.5-6 (we consuls), LXIX.14.4 (we Bithynians; cf. LXXIV.11.2 where Priscus of Bithynia is described as πολίτης ἐμός).
[120] Dio, LXXII.21.1-2; as Dio realised (above, p. 91), this is not history.
[121] Millar, *Cassius Dio* 124ff. Naturally, emphasis is on the word 'formal'.
[122] Dio, LXXIII.3.4; LXXIV.2.1-2; LXXVI.17.1; LXXVII.11.2; 17.2-4.

person singular or plural, never the third person, and nowhere in the surviving text does his proper name appear – this too is in the tradition of Roman historiography. Distinctive in Ammianus, however, are long sections of narrative, sometimes of exciting escape. Even with the anecdotal passages of Dio considered, Ammianus' narratives of himself are unique.[123] Fortunately, in Ammianus we can see the scope and context of the remarks in a way we could not for Polybius and Dio. In some sense a mere numbering of the autobiographical passages in Ammianus will not give a sense of the extent of his activity, for we are dealing here not with brief and isolated extracts, but extended passages and in one case almost an entire Book (XIX).

He appears only briefly in Books XIV–XVI,[124] but beginning in Book XVIII he assumes a larger role. With Persia threatening war on the eastern border of the Empire, Ursicinus and his men went to Samosata (XVIII.4.7). Ursicinus was unexpectedly recalled to Rome, and Ammianus accompanied him as far as Thrace (6.5) when he was just as unexpectedly sent back to the East, and they returned to Nisibis to establish protective measures against a possible Persian assault (6.8). After fortifying Nisibis, they depart and the men find a young boy crying in the middle of the road whom they bring back to the city (6.9–10), an incident that becomes significant when Ammianus sees a tribune being pursued by the Persians. The tribune caught and killed, the Persians begin to pursue Ammianus himself, and what follows is the most exciting escape narrative in an ancient historian, told in the first person with a series of first-person verbs conveying the rapid movement.[125]

---

[123] Rosen, *Studien* 33: 'Es gibt wohl kaum eine Stelle in der antiken Historiographie, die diese Erzählung [sc. Ammianus' escape from Amida] an Dramatik übertrifft.' Cf. Matthews, in *History and Historians in Late Antiquity* 34 who compares it (not inappropriately) to a Hollywood screenplay.

[124] Amm. XIV.9.1 (himself attached to Ursicinus); 11.5 (journey to Mediolanum); XV.5.22–31 (journey to Cologne with Ursicinus to suppress the revolt of Silvanus); XVI.10.21 (assigned with Ursicinus to the East).

[125] Amm. XVIII.6.11–12: 'repetabam ... transirem ... demonstrabam ... ferebar'. Escape, of course, is a major theme in Xenophon's *Anabasis*, and there is perhaps an historiographical precedent for an escape narrative in the first person in a fragment from the last book of Appian's history (F 19):

> Once, when I was fleeing from the Jews during the war in Egypt [the Jewish revolt of AD 116 under Hadrian], and I was going through Arabia Petraea to the sea where a skiff was waiting to carry me across to Pelusium, an Arab was leading me on the road by night. As it was getting towards dawn, and I thought we were near the skiff, a raven croaked, and the Arab, very

Ammianus returns to his men and they move on to Amida; he resumes here the first person plural. There he is entrusted by Ursicinus with finding out the enemy's situation, and here he reverts to the first person, despite the presence of a centurion with him.[126]

The siege and fall of Amida take up most of Book XIX. Our concern here is not with Ammianus' narrative gifts (which are undeniable) but with the orientation of the account. The entire narrative is told from the point of view of Ammianus and the besieged inside the city: the fighting, the scouts sent to them by Ursicinus, the endurance of the plague, the restlessness and fearsomeness of the Gauls, and the Persians' entrance into the city are seen by the one

> troubled, said, 'we have wandered off course.' When the raven croaked again, he said, 'we have wandered very much off course.' I was bewildered and was looking to see whether some traveller would appear, but as it was still early morning, and the country was at war, I saw no one. A third time the Arab heard the bird, and then happily said, 'we have wandered to our advantage, and we are now on course.' And I had to smile if we should even now be on the wrong road, and I despaired, since, with enemies all around, it would not be possible to turn back towards the very people through whom I began my flight. And being at a loss, I gave myself up to the oracle, and went on. And as I was in this state, suddenly another river – very close to Pelusium – appeared, and a trireme bound for Pelusium. I boarded it and was saved. But the skiff, the one that awaited me on the other river, was captured by the Jews. So greatly did I enjoy the help of Fortune and so greatly did I marvel at the oracle.

The passage probably comes not from the narrative proper but rather from a digression, as seems clear both from the indefinite 'once' (ποτε) and from the end of the passage (not translated here) which is resumptive. The entire incident is presented, it seems, to vouch for the marvellous nature of Arabian divination; for explicit statements of autopsy as validation for marvels see above, pp. 82ff. Nevertheless, the attendant circumstances as narrated here are greater than needed simply for validation, and there is a significant resemblance, enough to suggest that escape narratives played a role in earlier Greek historiography, without, of course, positing a direct influence of Appian on Ammianus.

[126] Amm. XVIII.6.21: 'ad hunc (sc. Iouinianum) missus ego cum centurione quodam fidissimo', but then we find 'ueni...uisus...confessus...mittor'. The explanation must surely be that Ammianus is distinguishing himself from his fellow soldiers, for when Jovinianus gives him a guide to escort him to some cliffs for spying, Ammianus returns to the plural. There is little danger of confusion here, and we should note that Ammianus will vary the singular and plural, even when speaking about himself, so long as misunderstanding is unlikely: cf. XVIII.7.2: 'unde per loca itidem deserta et sola, magno necessitatis ducente solacio, celerius quam potui speraui *reuersi, confirmauimus* animos haesitantium, e.q.s.'; XVIII.8.12–13.

party.[127] Though entailing a certain loss of perspective, this manner of narration lends an excitement to the narrative, and there could be no doubt that the event itself was important and worthy of memory. But the passage that follows the fall of Amida is something different again. The Persians invade the city and butcher the inhabitants (XIX.8.4). Ammianus and two unarmed companions hide and escape at night into the desert (8.5-6); they then proceed to the tenth milestone where they stop because Ammianus' feet hurt.[128] A horse appears and they complete their escape. Being thirsty they searched for water and found a well, but its depth was too great to reach; having no ropes, they cut their garments into long strips, tied them together, attached to them one of the soldier's caps, and drew up the water; thence, making their way to the Euphrates, they saw some Persians pursuing Romans and, alarmed, changed their direction and returned (against all their expectations) to Antioch and safety (8.6-12).

There is, in fact, no participatory narrative in any other ancient historian comparable to this one. Unlike the siege of Amida, the escape of Ammianus himself serves no purpose (other than intrinsic interest) in the larger compass of the history,[129] and it is not surprising that scholars call attention to this incident. Yet an explanation (if only partial) seems at hand. We mentioned that Dio's work already shaded strongly to autobiography and memoirs, and this incident of Ammianus' could also be considered an extension into the territory of memoir. In addition, the narrative of exciting adventure and escape had become well known from the novel, and it is not so much a matter of importing one genre into another, as of applying some elements characteristic of one (very similar) genre to history, whether consciously or unconsciously.[130] In so doing Ammianus must have believed that his audience would find the account of interest in and of itself.

---

[127] See (all from Book XIX): 2.4; 2.13; 3.3; 4.1; 6.1-4; 8.1-4. A comparison with Thucydides' account of the siege of Plataea (II.71-8) is instructive, since there the viewpoints of the besiegers and the besieged are given.

[128] Perhaps an assertion of social status: see Ch. III n. 88.

[129] In the earlier personal incident where Ammianus returns a young boy to Nisibis, the importance of the incident is immediately apparent (XVIII.6.10-15).

[130] See the excellent discussion of the *Romanmotive* in Rosen, op. cit. (n. 123) 39-40, who compares Ammianus' narrative with those of Apuleius and Heliodorus. On the interaction of the novel and historiography see Schwartz, *Funf Vorträge über den griechischen Roman*; Hägg, *Novel in Antiquity* 111-14; Momigliano, *Sesto Contributo* 375.

Having had his moment (so to speak), Ammianus does not again play such a prominent part. The long narrative of Julian's eastern campaign (where the author reappears suddenly at XXIII.5.7)[131] is told from the perspective of the soldiers, and Ammianus is concerned once again to portray himself not as an individual historical actor, but simply as part of a larger group. In order to avoid the constant repetition of 'nos' he employs different expressions which give variety to the narrative and conceal the historian himself even more. The effect of the variation is to give a certain reliability and intimacy to the narrative, while moderating the presence of the narrator.[132] Clearly then, Ammianus' presentation of his own deeds in his history cannot be said to be disproportionate, even though the early narratives of his action approach memoirs, and he at least once flirts with irrelevancies. But the size of the work prevents imbalance. In the later accounts of Julian's campaigns he shows a sophisticated manner of presentation, altering expressions and perspectives, and sometimes shifting back and forth from first- to third-person narration, now including himself, now emphasising others.[133] The few early exceptions to his generally subdued profile do not seriously alter the fact that he retained elsewhere the wider perspective of 'great' historiography. And if he manages to tell us exactly how he and his companions drew water from a well, this does not seriously affect his claim to travel 'per negotiorum celsitudines' (XXVI.1.1).

If historians use the first person and writers of *commentarii* use the third, it will not be easy to establish tidy categories, especially when dealing with almost a thousand years of historiography. In place of

---

[131] It may be significant that Ammianus begins to use the first person again suddenly at XXIII.5.7, not having told us that he was now under Julian's command; the reader had not heard of his activities since XIX.8.12. This suggests that Ammianus may have mentioned in the preface that he served under Ursicinus and Julian; and it indicates as well that he need have said nothing about his activities after the preface and before XIV.9.1.

[132] In this part of the work, Ammianus never uses the first person singular; he uses first-person plural verbs at times (all references in this note are to Book XXIV): 1.5; 2.1-3; 4.31; 5.5; 7.7; 8.7; at other times he adopts the Roman convention of 'nostri' (4.7; 4.9; 5.8-9; cf. App. V) and still other times uses the third person plural (4.14; 4.23), or the collective *miles* with a singular verb (3.8-9; 4.11; 4.30; 6.15).

[133] A good example of his ability to distance himself from his comrades' disagreeable behaviour is XXIV.3.1-9 where the soldiers are disgruntled with Julian's modest donatives; it has parallels with Xenophon and Caesar, below, §3.

such categories, it may be preferable to sum up by genre the findings above.

In history proper (as opposed to memoirs), Thucydides set the course for the use of the third person and Xenophon's manipulation of it in the *Anabasis* (coupled with pseudonymous publication) showed its potential for giving the appearance of unbiased reporting. The next centuries are blank but when the tradition can again be traced we find Polybius adhering to it. In the last four books of his history, in accordance with his increased role, Polybius alternated between first and third person. Perhaps as the work became more like memoirs, Polybius adapted the style of that genre. Later, among the Greek historians of the Empire, we find a division. Josephus in the *Jewish War*, Nicolaus in his *History*, and Dexippus in his *Scythica* (all contemporary, or largely contemporary, histories) used the third person to refer to themselves and their deeds. Appian and Dio use the first person. Among the Romans, it can be stated simply that none of them, contemporary or non-contemporary, ever uses the third person for himself, substituting instead the first person singular and plural.

In hypomnematic literature, both Greek and Latin, the first person is used, and the focalisation is usually the writer himself. The exception is Caesar's use of the third person. What his purpose was in using the third person involves speculation, but it can be argued that he intended to follow Xenophon, and write an *Anabasis* of sorts. What we do see clearly, at any rate, is that memoirs or hypomnematic literature often impinge on, and merge with, histories. The last four books of Polybius may have been the first example, but their loss (where we would want the entire books in order to judge scale and orientation) precludes certainty. We see the mingling most clearly in the imperial historians Velleius, Dio, and Ammianus. The origins of this 'conflation' (if such it is, and not merely the influence of Rome all the way from Polybius to Dio) is an issue only if we insist on rigid classification. But here, no less than in other areas, the ancient historians were free to use the traditions they inherited, and instead of misappropriation and conflation, one can just as easily speak of flexibility, adaptation, and innovation.

3. STRATEGIES OF SELF-PRESENTATION

Three works survive in sufficient fullness for us to examine some techniques of self-presentation when the author records his own deeds:

Xenophon's *Anabasis*, Caesar's *Gallic War*, and Josephus' *Jewish War*.[134] Not surprisingly, perhaps, accusations of distortion and partiality have been brought against all these works, and my avoidance of entering these particular scholarly quarrels does not mean that I think them unimportant.[135] I wish rather to focus on some literary devices by which an author can shape his narrative in such a way as to mitigate his presence and achievement, since this seems to have been an important concern in antiquity: at the very least it must be conceded that ancient audiences listened differently when a man recorded his own achievements and when another did it for him. Some of these tactics appear codified in Plutarch and the rhetoricians, but there is no need to assume that these late writers invented them. As is usually the case with rhetoric, practice itself was codified, and there is evidence that certain means of diminishing the jealousy attendant on narrating one's own actions were already in existence in the Homeric poems.[136]

The Gods and fortune

Perhaps no aspect of ancient life is more difficult to assess than religious feeling and belief. A modern might well react with disbelief or disdain if

---

[134] It goes without saying that this brief survey is not meant to be exhaustive. I do not treat here Caesar's *Civil War*, since I agree with those who think it never received Caesar's final revisions: see J. M. Carter, *Caesar: Civil War Books I and II* (Warminster 1991) 16–21.

[135] On the political purpose of the *Anabasis* (which is usually seen related to the pseudonymous or anonymous publication), see Breitenbach, *RE* IX. A. 2, 1644–9; further, Nickel, *Xenophon* 38–43. For Caesar the bibliography is enormous and strongly bound up with his narrative method: Collins, *ANRW* I. 1, 922–66 is a useful starting-point; but scholars continue to emphasise Caesar's *déformation historique*: Rambaud, *L'Art de la déformation historique dans les Commentaires de César* before all others; cf. Mutschler, *Erzählstil und Propaganda in Caesars Kommentarien*; Richter, *Caesar als Darsteller seiner Taten*, esp. ch. IV; cf. Mensching, *Caesars Bellum Gallicum: Eine Einführung*, ch. III. Gelzer, *KS* II.207–35 seems to me to strike an excellent balance between the political and literary aspects of the work. In Josephus we have the possibility of comparing his account of the war in the *Jewish War* with that of the *Vita*, and there are many treatments: see Lindner, *Die Geschichtsauffassung des Flavius Josephus im Bellum Judaicum* 50–94 and, more comprehensively, Cohen, *Josephus in Galilee and Rome, passim*, esp. 232–42, where reference to earlier discussions will be found. The problem of these discrepancies has been de-emphasised by Rajak, *Josephus* 154 ff. who points out (i. a.) the difference in genre and the specific requirements of the war narrative.

[136] All the *topoi* here treated appear already in Demosthenes' *On the Crown*, and Plutarch takes numerous examples from Homer.

one claimed that one's success followed from the gods. Yet Plutarch, a believer in the gods if ever there was one, claims that if one must speak about oneself, it is more acceptable if one assigns a role to chance or to God, since (he argues) men prefer to be worsted by luck rather than by merit, because in luck they are not forced to see themselves as failures.[137] Whether such a purpose lies behind the employment of God and fortune in Xenophon, Caesar, Josephus, and others, or rather a real belief in the rightness of their cause, cannot, of course, be determined, but the appearance of fortune and the divine is so common that we should perhaps acknowledge a motif of divine aid, a motif that will naturally be of use in a war narrative by emphasising the justness of one's cause and at times the unjustness of one's opponents – and this motif, contrary to our expectations, diminishes rather than increases *inuidia* towards the main character.[138]

'And if you are a brave fighter, a god somehow gave that to you', says Agamemnon to Achilles at the beginning of the *Iliad* (1.178). The idea appears early and is not (certainly for historiography, at least) made less attractive by appearing in conjunction with great heroes: their dependence on the gods and their piety are part of their heroic outlook.[139] The historians could hardly gain admittance to the restricted ranks of Homeric heroes, but some echo of that heroism found expression in the emphasis on their own piety, their reliance on the gods, and the acknowledgement of their favours. It did Themistocles' reputation no harm when he admitted that it was first and foremost the gods and heroes of Greece who were responsible for her victory over Persia.[140] Thus there were epic and historiographic precedents.

The gods are a constant concern in the *Anabasis*, always in connection with Xenophon. At his formal introduction we find him consulting the oracle of Apollo (and in his enthusiasm asking the wrong question[141]) before he joined the expedition. At two important junctions in

---

[137] Plut. *de se ips.* 542E–F.
[138] Cf. King Pyrrhus, who in his memoirs attributed his failure to the anger of Persephone, whose shrine he had despoiled: *FGrHist* 229 F 1=D. Hal. *A. R.* xx.10.
[139] See Griffin, *Homer on Life and Death* 148–9 on the piety of Homeric heroes, and on the use of prayers and sacrifices to mark high points in the narrative.
[140] Hdt. VIII.109.3.
[141] One technique of effective self-praise is to admit to small faults while claiming large virtues (Plut. *de se ips.* 543F). Perhaps Xenophon here admits to a certain foolishness or lack of wisdom, while nevertheless calling attention to his piety.

his activities, a dream appears to him: when he decides to offer his services as a leader, and later when great despondency has taken the army and they cannot ford the river Kentrites.[142] He, like Homeric heroes, takes no important actions before offering sacrifice and consulting the omens. In his speech before the troops shortly after his selection, a soldier sneezes when Xenophon speaks the words 'with the gods'; in one dramatic passage Xenophon refuses to attack because the omens are unfavourable, even though the soldiers are starving; when some go out anyway they are destroyed; later, Xenophon refuses the sole command because of what the gods tell him, and even his decision to leave the army is presented as the advice of god.[143] 'We always begin with the gods', he says, and the success of the expedition is indeed seen to hinge not only on the justness of the Greeks' cause, but also on the punishment due to Tissaphernes and the opponents of the Greeks. Clearchus gives a strategically placed speech in which he reminds Tissaphernes to honour the gods – a point that Xenophon is careful to emphasise to the assembled troops. Even the later alliance with Seuthes is portrayed as pious since that ruler had been robbed of his ancestral lands; and he says he will recover them with the help of the gods and the Greeks.[144]

The gods do not play so large a role in Caesar's *Gallic War* and, aside from a few passages, no direct reference is made to their interests or wishes as humans could know them. One passage, however, is worth mentioning. In the first book, Caesar at his introduction portrays himself as remembering the army of L. Cassius which had been forced under the yoke (1.7.14), and only a few chapters later the defeat of the Tigurini by Caesar again recalls Cassius' army and equates Caesar's victory with the retribution due them, an action that came about 'either by chance or by the plan of the immortal gods' (1.12.6). The theme is

In the same way, Sallust in the *Catiline* concedes that he may have been ambitious, but his spirit was *insolens malarum artium*, and he wished only glory where others were motivated by jealousy (3.4–5); not coincidentally, ambition is described as very near to a virtue (11.1–2).

[142] *Anab.* III.1.4–10 (introduction and oracle of Apollo); I.11–14 (his dream); IV.3.8–13 (dream at the river, after which a fording place is reported by the soldiers). On the Homeric overtones of the first dream, see Rinner, *Philologus* 122 (1978) 144–9.

[143] *Anab.* III.2.8–9 (sneeze and vow to the gods); V.5.3 (bad omen); VI.4.13–19 (refusal to attack, though soldiers are starving); 4.23–6 (death of those under Neon who go out); VI.1.17–33 (refuses sole command); VII.6.44 (departure from the army). [144] VI.3.18 (16); II.5.3–7; III.1.21–2; VII.2.16–34, cf. 3.43.

reinforced immediately in Caesar's speech to the Helvetii which follows: here he cautions them against their insolence by reminding them that the gods grant temporary prosperity to the insolent, only to increase the pain of the punishment that will surely follow (1.14.5). Elsewhere there are but two mentions relevant here, the prayer of the standard bearer of the tenth legion when, in order to encourage his men, he leaps into the waters off Britain (IV.25.3); and Caesar's own encouragement to his troops that the disaster to Sabinus and Cotta, although caused by the rashness and fault of one in charge, had nevertheless been expiated by the favour of the immortal gods and the soldiers' own bravery (V.52.6).

What takes the place of the gods in Caesar is *fortuna*. Here Caesar had a precedent in Sulla who was so confident of his fortune that he claimed to have made his best decisions on the spur of the moment, to have followed the advice of dreams, and to have laid down his dictatorship without fear.[145] A more immediate example could be found in Pompey, whose *fortuna* was an important part of his success.[146] The role of fortune in warfare, so Caesar asserts, is great: in Caesar's own time the debate whether fortune or ability was more important was best resolved by claiming that a successful general needed both, and it is anyway unlikely that an ancient general would ever have claimed victory without acknowledging the importance of the gods. In a foreign war, citizens (if not each and every Senator) would certainly wish for their general to be fortune's favourite.[147] Naturally, the use of fortune can

---

[145] Plut. *Sulla* 6.8–10; 34.3–5; cf. 6.9: τῇ Τύχῃ τῆς ἀρετῆς πλέον ἔοικε νέμειν.

[146] See Weinstock, *Divus Julius* 113–14 with numerous references to the whole topic given there.

[147] Caes. *B. G.* VI.30.2; cf. 35.2; on the importance of a general possessing fortune and valour see Baldson, *JRS* 41 (1951) 3 with n. 38; cf. Kajanto, *ANRW* II. 17. 1, 537–8, who suggests that *fortuna* in Caesar means 'good luck' with no sense of personification. In looking at the *Gallic War* we must not import problems that we know from the later *Civil War*, where the *Kriegsschuldfrage* is all important and the battle is between fellow citizens: Caesar's use of *fortuna* in that work seems to have seriously misjudged the reaction of his audience, but there are, of course, other instances in his political career of his misjudgement of the limits of his fellow Romans' acceptance. Baldson, ibid. 1 n. 8 seems to quote Pliny, *n. h.* XXII.12 ('addat [sc. Sulla] ... superbum cognomen Felicem') out of context as evidence for a dislike of claiming fortune. The passage makes clear that Pliny is appalled because Sulla took the title after slaying fellow-citizens; on the difference in attitude between war with foreigners and that with citizens, see

have an apologetic purpose,[148] but let us not overlook its function in moderating the author's praise of himself. For if fortune is mistress in all things, she is as much so in victory as in defeat. Although there is brief mention of fortune in the early books, she only takes an important and emphasised role towards the end of the work. Ambiorix' escape from Minucius Basilus is ascribed to fortune, even though human activity also plays a role.[149] Far more dramatic is the role of Fortuna in the near disaster of Q. Cicero's neglect of Caesar's orders, where the narrator first calls attention to fortune's power (VI.35.2), and then emphasises how the incautious Cicero sends out troops to forage (36.2), and these are then met by the German cavalry who by chance (*casu*, 37.1) are just arriving there. The situation is dramatically narrated and the Roman soldiers are brought to the brink of terror when suddenly Caesar arrives on the scene.[150] The brisk 'quem timorem Caesaris aduentus sustulit' (41.4) is brilliantly understated, and the general then again warns of the power of fortune (42.1-2). That Caesar had no real belief in the power of his fortune is, of course, possible,[151] but not to be overlooked is the value that the appeal to fortune has in the narration of one's own deeds.

With Josephus we are back to the dreams sent by the gods, as found in Xenophon. Josephus frequently emphasises his power of prophecy, his knowledge, and his cleverness.[152] And allied to this in some way are

Collins, op. cit. (n.135) 923-6. Even so, it is interesting that *fortuna* is used far more often in the *Civil War* than in the *Gallic War*, as one can see from the list of passages in Rambaud, op. cit. (n.135) 257; for bibliography on Caesar's fortune, see Kajanto, ibid. 537 n. 85.

[148] See Rambaud, op. cit. (n.135) 261, 264 (his discussion is mainly confined to the B. C.); cf. Mensching, op. cit. (n.135) 97.

[149] Caes. B. G. VI.30.2-4; the human responsibility is not underplayed since the Gauls' natural custom of dwelling near woods and rivers (3) as well as the soldiers' bravery in keeping off the Romans while Ambiorix is escaping (4) are both mentioned.

[150] On Caesar's technique of varying viewpoint (focalisation), see Görler, *Poetica* 8 (1976) 95-119; he concludes (117-19) that the change of perspective is motivated by 'die Notwendigkeit, sein Vorgehen zu verteidigen'.

[151] W. Warde Fowler, 'Caesar's Concept of Fortuna', *CR* 17 (1903) 153-6, but he seems to me to minimise *B.G.* IV.26.5 ('hoc unum ad pristinam fortunam Caesari defuit') where *pristinam* suggests more than the momentary situation. It is, however, a support for my argument in the text above if Fowler is correct, since the motivation for including *fortuna* in the *B.G.* will not have been personal belief, and it could then be argued that Caesar is following historiographical or rhetorical precedent. But belief is difficult to demonstrate or deny.

[152] See *B. J.* II.573; 577; III.130; 135; 183; 358; 405-8 for his foreknowledge; for his craftiness, II.632-7 (ruse of the unmanned fleet); III.171-5; 176-89; 190-2; 222-8; 270ff.; 386-91.

the dreams and messages from God that motivate his actions. When he escapes as Jotapata falls, he was (he tells us) aided by divine assistance, and at the crisis of his fate he, like Xenophon, remembers his dreams and that he had been marked out to live – and he goes to the Roman general, he says, not as a traitor but as God's servant.[153] The Emperor Titus, as he looks on Josephus, reflects on the power of Fortune, and in pity persuades his father Vespasian to spare him; and the latter's power of prophecy is accepted when Vespasian verifies from others that Josephus had predicted the exact date of the taking of Jotapata and his own capture by the Romans. Later, when Josephus is freed from his chains, it is because Vespasian recalled that Josephus was a minister of the voice of God.[154]

The pretence of necessity

The rhetor Hermogenes allows as one method for self-praise the pretence of necessity (προσποίησις ἀνάγκης). We can add to this Plutarch's remarks that self-praise is justified when one is defending one's good name, or on trial, or in peril.[155] One remembers the fiction of a prosecution adopted by Isocrates in the *Antidosis* in order to give a defence of his life and character. So too do we find that Xenophon very often gives, as the justification for one of his speeches, the slanders that are being made against him, and these occasions are frequently portrayed in a dramatic manner, the climax coming when Xenophon himself speaks (usually last and longest) and persuades the soldiers (frequently to a man).[156] Since this pretence seems to be mostly a Greek concept,[157] there is nothing of this in the *Gallic War*, but it appears again in Josephus who, like Xenophon, uses the motivation of slanders against him as the occasion for his own defence, not so much in individual speeches, but rather in the composite portrait that emerges from his whole account.[158]

---

[153] *B. J.* III.341; 351–3.
[154] *B. J.* III.392–8; 405–8 (prediction of fall and capture); IV.623–9 (liberation). The notion of τύχη is problematic in Josephus: see Lindner, op. cit. (n.135) 85–94.   [155] Hermog. *Meth.* 25 (441.18 Rabe); Plut. *de se ips.* 541A.
[156] Xen. *Anab.* III.3.11–20; V.6.15–34 (he was compelled, ἠναγκάσθη, to rise, 27); 7.1–35; 8.1–26; VII.6.11–38; 7.20–47.
[157] Most, *JHS* 109 (1989) 114–33. Note how Dionysius says he is compelled to say something about himself in the preface, even though he is most unwilling (ἥκιστα βουλόμενος ἀναγκάζομαι περὶ ἐμαυτοῦ προειπεῖν, *A. R.* I.1.1).
[158] *B. J.* II.598–613; III.434–42; VI.365.

Commonness of action/praise of others

Under the term κοινότης λόγου the rhetors explain that instead of praising oneself alone, it is a good idea to praise oneself as part of a group, usually in a speech to the audience.[159] The technique is used to a certain degree by Xenophon but he is usually far more concerned to show himself as an ideal general urging, defending, inspiring, and saving his men. Perhaps his close connection to the gods allows him to assume this role. But in Caesar, on the other hand, the praise of the troops is everywhere, not – and such is the artistry of Caesar – so great as to disguise his own achievement, but strong enough so that he never seems to be acting alone, as we find Xenophon so often doing. So much of the discussion about 'Caesar' in the third person fails to notice that he is surrounded by a sea of 'nostri',[160] and the Roman convention here fosters a sense not only of intimacy but also of common achievement. This is further emphasised by Caesar's identification of himself and his actions with the *populus Romanus* as a unit: Ariovistus received his appellation of king and friend because of Caesar's and the Senate's generosity; it was the custom neither of the Roman people nor of Caesar to desert allies; although desirous of crossing the Rhine into the territory of the Sygambri, Caesar deems it worthy neither of his own dignity nor that of the Roman people to cross over in boats; when Caesar himself makes swift levies of troops he is careful to present it as an example of 'what the discipline and power of the Roman people could achieve'.[161] Although the technique can be a way of equating himself with the state, it serves a more important purpose in the narrative by diminishing the focus from the individual and emphasising instead the common effort.

So too the dispensing of praise in which Caesar is generous throughout. In the first book he takes care, before the battle with Ariovistus, to place legates and a quaestor in charge of the individual legions 'so that each man would have a witness of his virtues' (1.52.1), and his own work serves this same purpose. He often speaks of the *uirtus* or *studium singulare* of the troops and is not stingy with individual praise, singling out men as *uiri fortissimi*. Their failures are usually put down to fortune, or an excess of spirit, or (in a useful praise of himself) lack of a

---

[159] Hermog. *Meth.* 25 (441.17 Rabe).   [160] On this convention see App. V.
[161] Caes. *B. G.* 1.43.5; 45.1; IV.17.1; VI.1.4.

leader.[162] This generosity by the narrator convinces the audience that the praise of Caesar is not done at the expense of others, and therefore seems to have no ulterior aim.[163]

This same attitude can be seen from the other side in Velleius' history of his campaigns with Tiberius. Although taking obvious pride in his achievements Velleius does not emphasise his own glory. When he speaks of his participation, it is with studied deference, as when before narrating the campaigns of AD 4 he states that he assisted to the best of his *mediocritas*.[164] Later, in speaking of the same campaign in the following year, he is careful to praise the deeds of the entire army and to throw the emphasis onto its commander, Tiberius, rather than onto himself (II.106.1). He asserts his *mediocritas* again before narrating the revolt of Pannonia in AD 6 (III.3-4) and states the extent of his responsibility and participation as a *legatus Augusti* ordered by the *princeps* to escort a legion to Tiberius. There is evident pride in his account as he mentions that this gave him an honour equal to Senators, but it is also evident from the tone and manner of his narration that he portrays the honour as arising not from his own achievements but from being thought worthy of such a responsibility by the Emperor. Two final notes: at II.113.3 Velleius states that he was one of Tiberius' *legati* in charge of winter quarters at Illyricum when Tiberius was recalled to Rome (AD 7); at 121.3 he mentions that he participated in Tiberius' triumph at Rome (AD 11 or 12). In each case the pleasure of the historian at being involved in such deeds is evident and in neither case is any attempt made to speak at length about himself or to delineate his precise actions and responsibilities. Velleius' narrative style thus reflects the political realities of the era.[165]

---

[162] Praise of individual soldiers: II.25.1; IV.12.4; V.35.6-8; 37.5; 44; VI.38; 40; VII.47; 59.3-6; praise of the soldiers as a whole: IV.37.3; V.2.2; 8.4; VII.17.2-8 (their dignity and honour); 22.1; 50.1; cf. V.34.2: 'nostri, tametsi ab duce et a fortuna deserebantur, tamen omnem spem salutis in uirtute ponebant, e.q.s.'

[163] See Rambaud, op. cit. (n.135) 295-301 for the thesis that Caesar unfairly diminishes the achievements of his *legati*. But praise of his soldiers and legates was no threat to Caesar's own claim to glory.

[164] Vell. II.104.3: 'tum pro captu mediocritatis meae adiutor fui.' We have come a long way from Cato.

[165] Velleius' work is also important as an indication of trends to come, especially in its general tone of admiration and deference towards those in power: see Janson, *Latin Prose Prefaces* 124-7 for some later examples.

Praise in the mouth of others

In the *Antidosis* Isocrates brings on a young pupil who utters numerous praises of his teacher; Aristotle, who no doubt recognised the fiction for what is was, nevertheless considered Isocrates' technique an excellent way of bestowing praise on oneself.[166] The employment of a third-person narrative allows the author to place praise or admiration for his own actions into the mouth of another in a way that would be intolerable in a first-person account. We find, for example, Cheirisophus commending Xenophon both for his words and deeds, and saying that he wished he had many like him. In a later passage, when Xenophon is being slandered, he is defended by the soldiers who would prefer him to any other commander, and elsewhere he is characterised as having only the fault of being too friendly with the soldiers.[167] In Caesar, praise comes to him from the chiefs of Gaul (I.30.1-3); at other times the Aduatuci appeal in a speech to Caesar's *clementia* and *mansuetudo* which (we are told) they had heard of from others (II.31.3). Q. Cicero speaks to the Nervii of Caesar's *iustitia* (v.41.8). In a particularly bold example, Ariovistus boasts that if he put Caesar to death he would be much in favour with many nobles and leading men in Rome (I.44.12).[168]

Josephus makes very great use of this technique, especially at the climactic moment of the siege and fall of Jotapata. A messenger brings the report to Vespasian that if he should capture Josephus it would mean the capture of all Judaea since the man was reputed to be 'most sagacious' (III.143-4). When Josephus contemplates flight from the besieged city, he is implored by the people not to go, and here the narrator breaks in, giving as his opinion (ἔμοιγε δοκεῖν[169]) the belief that the people so acted because they were convinced that with Josephus present they would suffer nothing fearful; after the city is taken, Titus makes a search believing especially that the issue of the war rested on the capture of Josephus; Nicanor assures Josephus that his excellence makes him a source of wonder to the Romans; Josephus' bravery and intelligence are

---

[166] Arist. *Rhet.* III.17, 1418b 23-7.

[167] Xen. *Anab.* III.1.45 (Cheirisophus to Xenophon); VII.6.4; 5.10 (defended by soldiers).

[168] See also Cato, *HRR* F 130, where his commander Manius at Thermopylae says that neither he nor all the people of Rome could give Cato the recompense he deserves.

[169] *B.J.* III.202. Note the use of the first person when Josephus speaks as narrator.

mentioned by his fellows in hiding, and when he is finally brought out, the enemy recall his deeds and are struck by his change of fortune, to such an extent that they relent of their former anger.[170] Though applied with a heavy hand, Josephus' account here is following a standard procedure, and the claims are incredible (if they are incredible) because they are hardly backed up by the narrative: his actual deeds hardly warrant the superlative treatment; and he is further betrayed by his own account when it is seen that his capture in no way meant the taking of Judaea, since four books still remain after Josephus is taken prisoner. But the defence is that the narrator is proposing to give the viewpoints of others and, if pressed, can argue that he himself did not say the capture of Josephus meant the taking of Judaea, but only that Titus thought it did.[171] Deception, perhaps, but a type sanctioned by long use, and one to which an ancient audience may have been far less hostile.

Magnification of actions

Except for the openly partisan strain of Roman historiography ('our men fought brilliantly') the usual means of magnifying the greatness of one's achievements in a narrative is not direct praise but oblique references to one's opponents. In Xenophon this is done quite artfully: we are told of the king's unwillingness to allow the Greeks to return home, and of the impossibility of the journey through hostile countries; the greatness of the task is further emphasised by the soldier's despondency, as they are faced repeatedly with seemingly insurmountable difficulties: and within these great dangers and toils Xenophon again and again appears as the one who rescues his men.[172]

In the *Gallic War* a similar magnification of the enemy occurs. The Germans are so frightening that some of the soldiers feared even to look into their eyes; the Nervii fought while standing on piles of the corpses of their own comrades; the Gauls are enormous and have contempt for the small stature of 'our' men; the Germans are numbered at 430,000, the Gauls at one time surpassed all others in military courage; and at the

[170] Jos. *B. J.* III.193–202; 340; 347; 394–5.
[171] It is possible that Josephus' vigorous defence of the accuracy of his work in the *Vita* (361–3), in which he guarantees its reliability by appeal to the Emperor's approval, is meant to make these and similar characterisations believable. In any case, as Rajak, *Josephus* 155 points out, Josephus in making claims for a great war was obliged to show himself a great general.
[172] Xen. *Anab.* II.4.4 (the greatness of the task); cf. III.1.2–3; 1.26–32; 4.46–9; 5.1–6; IV.3.8–15; 4.12; 5.7–9; 5.15–21; V.2.8–27 (ἀθυμία and Xenophon's actions).

end, in the speech of Critognatus, the Gauls are portrayed as ready to fight with desperation and all their courage on behalf of their *libertas*.[173]

As frequently, Josephus is more explicit: at the outset of his work he has called it the greatest war of which we know or have report (1.1) and criticises the inconsistency of earlier writers who claimed that it was a great war, yet portrayed the Jews as worthless and easily conquered (7–8) – though Josephus will not exaggerate (9). The consequence is a dramatic narrative with great deeds and great virtues on both sides, even if the actions of the Jews are in the end more remarkable because although a small nation without great resources they withstood the onslaught of the world's most powerful empire. This is repeatedly emphasised in, for example, the contrast between the good order of the Romans and the dissensions of the Jews; the Herodotean enumeration of Vespasian's forces; the emphasis on the inventiveness and great courage of the besieged at Jotapata; and not least the siege at Masada.[174]

Such techniques as those briefly described above can be used by the writer of his own deeds as ways of lessening (for it is unlikely that he can completely eliminate) the reproach incurred when engaging in self-praise or self-display. The better writers use various techniques and use them more inconspicuously, but even the lesser writers can at times artfully praise themselves and get away with it. It was important, above all, to conceal any type of epideictic rhetoric, since this calls attention to itself in an unmistakeable way. And if we are to believe the few (and sometimes inconsistent) testimonia we have, the most important aspects of self-display were a solid basis for the praise, and an artful concealment of that same praise.

[173] *B. G.* I.39.1–7; II.27.3–5; IV.15.3; V.54.5; VII.77.1–16.
[174] Jos. *B. J.* II.577–82; III.115–26; 176–89; VII.280–406.

V
The 'lonely' historian: contrast and continuity

In an aside to his audience after narrating the revolt of the Theruingi and the slaughter of the Roman army under Lupicinus in AD 376, the 'lonely' historian[1] Ammianus Marcellinus asks the indulgence of his readers on a particularly difficult matter:

> And since after many events the narrative has reached this point, I earnestly entreat my readers (if I ever have any) not to demand of me a strictly accurate account of what happened or the exact number of the slain, which there was no way of finding out.[2]

The rather poignant parenthesis is consistent with the view that Ammianus presents elsewhere in his history of a public at Rome concerned only with the trivial biographies of emperors and caring more for the details of the private lives of the imperial household than with the grand sweep of *res gestae*.[3] The last antique historian is indeed a great one, and he may even have been as isolated as is sometimes suggested.[4] But in a larger sense, nearly every ancient historian seeks to portray himself as a lonely seeker of truth, as the only one who has somehow understood the historian's proper task, while his predecessors (as he will frequently remind us) failed in the effort, either because they were ignorant and ill-intentioned from the start, or, though men with the proper attitude and application, they did not yet embody all the

---

[1] So named by Momigliano, *Sesto Contributo* II.143-57.
[2] Amm. XXXI.5.10; cf. XIV.6.2.   [3] See below, n. 193.
[4] If Libanius' letter addressed to a Marcellinus were to the historian, it would be demonstrable that the persona of a lonely historian were deliberate. 'I hear that Rome herself has crowned your work', Libanius writes, 'and that her verdict is, that you have surpassed some and not fallen short of others' (*Ep.* 1063 Foerster). Although Matthews, *Roman Empire of Ammianus* 478-9 n. 1 still believes the historian is the addressee, strong arguments against the identification have been made by Fornara, *Historia* 41 (1992) 328-44; cf. G. Bowersock, *JRS* 80 (1990) 247-8 for the possible identity of Libanius' Marcellinus.

qualities necessary for a good historian, or live in a time that was suited to their abilities, or assay a task as grand as the one now placed before the reader. From Herodotus to Ammianus each historian is compelled to advance his own claims against those of others; and so nearly every historian is a 'lonely' historian, distinguishing himself from competitors, even if at the same time portraying himself as a continuator of some great and worthy predecessor. By such a process of contrast and continuity he seeks to mark out for himself a place in the historiographical tradition. He might engage in polemic with contemporaries or predecessors, and define certain aspects of his task in that way; he might single out for praise those historians whose tradition he claimed to be reviving or continuing. Not uncommonly, he might do both, and portray himself in contrast to some historians and as a continuator of others.

I. THE USES OF POLEMIC

'It's not enough to succeed. Others must fail.'[5]

One of the most distinctive aspects of ancient historiography is the liberal use of polemic against predecessors both named and unnamed. 'It would be unnecessary for me to point out to those better informed than me', says Josephus, 'in how many things Hellanicus disagrees with Acusilaus over genealogies; how often Acusilaus corrects Hesiod, or Ephorus reveals that Hellanicus is false in most of his statements; and that Timaeus reveals the mendacity of Ephorus, and later writers refute Timaeus, and everyone refutes Herodotus.'[6] Because polemic is an important aspect of self-definition by ancient historians in both traditions, it will be necessary first to say something of its origins and purpose, and why it was so useful a way of revealing as much about oneself as the object of attack.

The origins of polemic in Greek historiography are not difficult to find. As with inquiry, the guiding example was to be found among the early purveyors of wisdom and the natural scientists. Here, one after another, the writers define themselves by an explicit comparison with their predecessors, including chiefly the most important 'teacher'

---

[5] Gore Vidal, in G. Irvine, *Antipanegyric for Tom Driberg* 8 Dec. 1976, p. 2, quoted in *The Oxford Dictionary of Modern Quotations*, ed. Tony Augarde (Oxford 1991) 221.   [6] Jos. *c. Ap.* 1.16.

Homer. Hesiod covertly attacked Homer,[7] but beginning with Xenophanes, the attacks on predecessors become open and intense: not only is Homer 'in accordance with whom all have been taught' assailed, but Hesiod too. Heraclitus attacks Xenophanes by name, grouping him with Hesiod, Pythagoras, and Hecataeus as those with much learning but no intelligence; in another fragment he remarks that 'Homer deserves to be flung out of the contests, and also Archilochus.'[8]

The reason for this definition by contrast, and specifically by contrast with a perceived or actual predecessor, is perhaps to be found in the nature of oral society as a whole. Without a written text, it is more difficult to separate the known from the knower; in addition, oral societies have more face-to-face confrontations, so that a claim to truth cannot be separated from the arena in which that truth is debated or claimed.[9] If one is purveying a better way or a more accurate account, one must do so in relationship to what has already gone before. Homer as the pre-eminent teacher of Greece thus becomes the target of those who would seek to displace him. Nevertheless, we must be careful not to overemphasise this aspect of oral society, since not all oral or primarily oral societies are so agonistically toned.[10] The strong contrast between the medical writers of Middle Eastern and Asian civilisations (where innovation, although present, is not emphasised in terms of an individual authorial 'I') and those of Greece (where a whole series of scientific, philosophical, and medical writers announce themselves with awareness of and in contradistinction to their predecessors) makes it clear that we may be dealing with something quite individually Greek.[11]

Whatever the origins of polemic, its perpetuation was maintained by the study of rhetoric in education and the employment of imitation.

---

[7] Hes. *Theog.* 1-11 may be a swipe at Homer or Odysseus: see Bowie, *L&F* 20-1.

[8] Xenophanes, DK 21 B 10, 11; Heraclitus, DK 22 B 40, 42. See Lloyd, *Revolutions of Wisdom* 56-61 on Heraclitus' 'richly abusive fragments'.

[9] Ong, *Orality and Literacy* 43-4 emphasises knowledge within the context of struggle, and notes as well the boasting and tongue-lashings of characters in oral narratives. Yet Ong also sees (45-6) empathy, solidarity, and communal, not individual, identity as a feature of oral societies; and see next note.

[10] See the warnings of Thomas, *Literacy and Orality* 26-7, 104.

[11] Lloyd, *Revolutions of Wisdom* 50-61; id., *PCPhS* 40 (1994) 27-48. In historiography this approach may be seen in the emphatic 'I' of Herodotus' work, and the authorial display that one finds throughout his history: Lateiner, *Historical Method* 104 speaks of the 'ubiquity of argument and revisionism in the Histories'. On Herodotus' 'I', see above, pp. 7f.

Since an orator pleading his case does so against some opponent real or imagined, the orator is always set up against someone else.[12] The author of the *Rhetoric to Herennius* sums up the orator's two tasks succinctly: 'Our whole hope of victory and the whole method of persuasion rests on proof and refutation. For when we have set forth our arguments and have refuted those opposed to us, we have then completely accomplished the task of oratory.'[13] Not that this was considered the sole way of discovering the truth. In the *Gorgias*, Socrates explains to Polus that rhetorical refutation relies on producing many reputable witnesses, yet is worthless, since often many may give false witness against one true man.[14] Socrates contrasts this with his *elenchus*, 'the proper form of refutation' which has 'no resemblance' to rhetorical proof.[15]

Aristotle too is well aware of the tendency (which we all have, he says) to direct attacks towards others, not the matter itself.[16] Like Plato, Aristotle makes a distinction between dialectic and rhetoric, the former of which is a joint movement towards truth, the latter a competition in which one of two opponents must lose: 'he who would convert anyone to a different opinion should do so in a dialectical and not in a contentious manner ... for in arguments there is a common aim in view – except with mere contestants, for these cannot both reach the same goal.'[17] Since the study of rhetoric permeated all aspects of ancient life, the contentious tone of polemic was not unique to historiography; one of the medical writers advises that the ideal doctor should be 'harsh towards opposition',[18] not surprising when we consider that physicians competed before public audiences not only with other physicians but also with non-medical men who displayed their eloquence without any substantial knowledge of medicine.[19] Contention was an immediate

---

[12] On oratory's 'deep agonistic roots' see Ong, op. cit. (n.9) 111; in the eastern tradition, among the Indians and the Chinese, oppositions are minimised: ibid. and Lloyd, *PCPhS* 40 (1994) 27-48.   [13] [Cic.] *Herenn.* 1.18.

[14] Plato, *Gorg.* 471e-472c; for the appeal to numbers see App. IV §2.

[15] *Gorg.* 474a, 475e.   [16] Arist. *Cael.* 294b 6-11, with Lloyd, *MRE* 267.

[17] Arist. *Top.* 161a 32ff. Immediately before this (161a 23-4), Aristotle had noted that 'when people lose their tempers ... their argument becomes contentious, not dialectical'. Not coincidentally perhaps, historians are likened to athletes or combatants able or unable to 'endure the blows': see Wiseman, *CC* 27-9; for athletic metaphors in Polybius, Wunderer, *Polybios-Forschungen* III.55-9; see also Introd. n. 64.   [18] [Hipp.] *Decent.* 3.

[19] Lloyd, *Revolutions of Wisdom* 83-102. In the *Gorgias* (459a-b), Gorgias tells Socrates that in a competition the rhetorician would always defeat the real doctor. See also Polybius, above, p. 74.

consequence of competition, for if only one may win, it is just as effective if your opponent is seen to fail as it is for you yourself to triumph.

Imitation, too, could sanction polemic as a tool of instruction in two ways. First, the use of polemic by the early historians would naturally have served as a model for those who came after them. Second, the critical writings from antiquity mention that one way of teaching proper imitation was to point out what was wrong in certain works or authors. Quintilian, for example, suggests as a practical way of educating young students the demonstration by the teacher of what is faulty or poorly executed.[20] Lucian, in *How to Write History*, spends the entire first section detailing faults to be avoided when writing history.[21] And Plutarch tells of Ismenias the Theban, who would play well and then poorly, telling his students both how and how not to play the flute.[22] Finally, polemic could be used as a covert method of self-praise. As we saw above, the historian must be on his guard when praising himself. So an alternative is to denigrate one's opponent. Just as in panegyric, one might use criticism of others as a way of praising one's subject, so too in historiography, the denigration of one's predecessors was a useful means of advertising one's own skills and abilities, and could be used to suggest that one had avoided those things that made others inferior.[23]

Reference to predecessors by name becomes more and more a part of historiographical self-definition in the fourth century, as we can see even from the few fragments that survive. Polemic now becomes personal and more concerned with an individual's character.[24] The tone becomes pervasively hostile, and this too was sanctioned by rhetorical instruction: the refutation was the point in the speech when the orator sought, by expressing his own outrage, to raise his audience's emotion and put them into the same frame of mind:

[20] Quint. II.5.10-12; Clark, *Quart. Journ. Speech* 37 (1957) 16-18 notes its origin in Plato's *Phaedrus*.
[21] Luc. *h. c.* 7-32; M. D. Macleod, *Lucian* sees this first part as Lucian's main purpose, 'entertaining his audience with many of the tricks in his satirical repertoire in his rogues' gallery of historians' (284).
[22] Plut. *Demet.* 1.5-6, explaining why he wrote his monitory lives; alluding to what must have become a proverb, Eunapius (F 1) criticises Dexippus' chronology as 'how not to play the flute'.
[23] See Ramage, *ANRW* II. 33. 1, 640-5 for examples from panegyric and other genres.
[24] Schepens, *PoH* 40-1 with n. 3 points out that the criticism by the early historians is concerned with the substance, not the character, of their opponents. The same can be said for the early philosophers.

> The style will be fitting if it is expressive of emotion (παθητική) and character (ἠθική), and suitable to the matters at hand ... It is emotional if, when there is outrage, the language is that of an angry man ... The proper type of speech makes the matter persuasive. For the soul draws the false inference that the speaker speaks truly, because the audience feels the same on such matters; and so they think that the matter is as the speaker represents it, even when it is not; and the listener always shares the feeling of the one speaking emotionally.[25]

Since later writers confirm that an emotional or raised tone can affect the listeners' perception of right and wrong,[26] the way was open to the use of polemic.

Polybius adds further insight and a refinement on this topic. He suggests that criticism must be done in the proper spirit, a spirit of common benefit, not of individual achievement (reminiscent of Plato and Aristotle on dialectic). He distinguishes between good and fair critics and those who criticise in a spirit of rivalry, the latter group perhaps the one he has in mind when he avers that he does not, as some do, consider the faults of others to be virtues of his own.[27] Polybius knows too that it is easier to find fault with others than to behave faultlessly oneself, yet criticism, he says, remains necessary as a vehicle for discovering the truth.[28] An important distinction that Polybius emphasises again and again is that between intentional and unintentional falsehood in history. The latter, he says, is inevitable, given human nature and (for himself particularly) the vast amount of material to be included in his history; the proper response to this type of falsehood is pardon and generous correction.[29] Intentional falsehood, on the other hand, deserves censure and an implacable and harsh accuser.[30] Once detected, it poisons a whole history.[31]

---

[25] Arist. *Rhet.* III.7, 1408a 7-24. See further Gill, *CQ* 34 (1984) 156 on the 'pathetic' raising of emotions.   [26] Gill, op. cit. (n.25) 166 n. 99.

[27] On the good critic, see XVI.20.5-6; cf. VI.11.3-8, where Polybius distinguishes between those who criticise φιλοτιμώτερον ἢ δικαιότερον. For another's faults as one's own virtues, XVI.20.6; cf. Diod. XXVI.1.1-3.   [28] Pol. XII.25c.5.

[29] This is often stressed: XVI.20.8-9; XII.7.6; 12.4-5; XVI.14.7-8; XXIX.12.10-12.

[30] See XII.7.6; cf. 11.4 where Timaeus is worthy of implacable accusation; cf. 12.5. Deliberate lying may have its origins in partiality towards country or friends, or it may spring from a desire for gain, especially prominent in those who must write for a living: see Pol. XVI.14.7-8 where errors from ignorance (κατ' ἄγνοιαν) are opposed to the type of false writing (ψευδογραφία) that arises from loyalty to country or friends or from favour (ἢ πατρίδος ἕνεκεν ἢ φίλων ἢ χάριτος). If falsehood cannot be explained by these means, it may be attributed to a fault of character, such as bitterness (πικρία) or malice (κακοήθεια): Luce, *CPh* 84 (1989) 24-5.   [31] Pol. XII.25a.2.

The use of polemic by an historian was not, however, without danger. Since the historian's character was on display in the narrative, and he was expected to maintain a show of formal impartiality,[32] an excess of blame was no better than too much praise. Timaeus' performances in polemic, even allowing for the accidents of preservation and Polybius' less than candid evaluations, seem to have reached such a professional standard as to make all predecessors appear amateurs of the art. The man who had written against him at least two monographs (one of twelve books' length!) and nearly an entire book by another historian two generations later[33] must have aroused fierce passions, and there is every indication that his own work was written in a passionate spirit. This is not to say that he was not valued, or that his love of details and passion for inquiry (even if not of the Polybian type) went unappreciated. On the contrary, he must have been considered quite important if so many writers (not just historians) sought to overturn his influence. But his polemic was double-edged: successful, since even Polybius concedes that to many people Timaeus' fierce criticisms of others give to Timaeus' own history the appearance of accuracy and reliability;[34] ineffectual, since he became easier to dismiss precisely because his polemic was so ubiquitous.

It was for these reasons, then – its place in rhetoric, the desire to imitate past masters, its use as a less overt means of self-praise, its ability to challenge competitors – that polemic was and remained an important element for many in winning a place of honour in the historiographical tradition. As a general rule, the contemporary historian is less likely to use polemic than the non-contemporary historian, for the latter always has predecessors and must justify the bringing forward of a new treatment on an old theme.[35] Polybius is the obvious exception, but we must not let his excellence as a polemicist influence us too greatly; it is clear that he particularly relished such work, and saw it as a useful way of explaining his own attitude towards the writing of history. Aside from

---

[32] Above, pp. 158ff.
[33] Ister, *FGrHist* 334 F 59; 566 T 25; Polemon in twelve books (566 T 26; *FHG* III.108); and Polybius XII.
[34] Pol. XII.10.4; cf. 26d.4. See the similar remarks about Theopompus at VIII.11.2. Cf. Tac. *Ann.* XV.55.4, where an orator's confidence ('tanta uocis ac uultus securitate') gives the appearance of reliability; cf. Pliny *n. h. praef.* 30: 'qui obtrectatione alienae scientiae famam sibi aucupantur'; cf. Tac. *Hist.* I.1.2: 'malignitati falsa species libertatis inest'.   [35] See above, pp. 112ff.

him, however, it cannot be denied that the contemporary historians – Thucydides, Xenophon, Sallust in the *Catiline*, Velleius, Josephus in the *Jewish War*, Herodian, Dio in the contemporary portions, and Ammianus – do not use polemic as an element of self-definition in the way that the non-contemporary historians, such as Herodotus, Dionysius, and Arrian, do. This is not to say that it never happens. As seems clear from Josephus' *Life*, the rival history of the Jewish War by Justus of Tiberias attacked Josephus' already published work often (and perhaps by name), calling attention to the alleged bias of that account.[36] But on the whole it was non-contemporary history that proved the main arena in which polemic was practised. Even Polybius reserved some of his strongest criticisms for Theopompus and Timaeus, both of whom wrote before him.[37]

It should be noted, as well, that the extended polemic used by many Greek historians as an essential element of self-definition is not common among the Roman historians. This is not to say that the Roman historians do not engage in disputation, or that they do not criticise predecessors. One may find many examples of both, as we shall see. But they are less likely to engage in long disputations with individual predecessors and attempt to raise the emotions of the reader against some historian in the dock. Perhaps the only extended display-piece of a Greek type is Livy's treatment of how Alexander would have fared if he had attacked the Romans, a polemic directed against 'leuissimi ex Graecis'.[38] The passage is noteworthy because although it certainly displays Livy's abilities at disputation, the main object is not to show that Livy is superior to the Greeks who have written about Alexander, but that his theme – the Romans and their empire – is greater than any that the Greek historians can have attempted. It is certainly possible that Livy in magnifying his theme is exalting himself; but the difference between his polemical display and that of the Greeks is that Livy does not explicitly compare his methodology and performance to other named or unnamed historians.[39]

---

[36] Jos. *Vita* 336-44; 350. For a different approach to a similar problem see below n. 70.

[37] Although, as Schepens, *PoH* 41 notes, Polybius is the first to criticise historians whose subject matter was different from his own.

[38] Livy, IX.17-19. The Greeks attacked must include Timagenes (Jacoby, *Komm.* II. c. 223-4) and Metrodorus of Scepsis (Bowersock, *Augustus* 109 n. 2).

[39] See further Luce, *TAPA* 96 (1965) 218-29 with references to earlier discussions.

2. POLEMIC AND SELF-DEFINITION

Greek historiography begins in polemic:

> Hecataeus of Miletus speaks thus: I write what follows as it seems to me to be true; for the stories of the Greeks are varied, and, as is manifest to me, ludicrous.[40]

It would be invaluable to know how much Hecataeus used this confident and dogmatic tone throughout his work, and who the objects of his scorn were. In the *Genealogies* his main competitors would have been the poets and oral tradition, and one fragment, at least, suggests an assured and pointed tone:

> Aegyptus himself did not go to Argos but his children did. There were fifty, Hesiod says, but I say there were not even twenty.[41]

Hecataeus' successor and imitator Herodotus frequently engages in disputation with named and unnamed predecessors, ranging from brief expressions of disbelief to denial of epichoric tradition to full-scale display.[42] In the last, Herodotus compares the many and foolish tales of the Greeks with the reliable accounts of the priests of Memphis, Heliopolis, and Thebes, and this strikes a theme often repeated throughout the Egyptian *logos*.[43] There are the great polemical pieces on the flooding and sources of the Nile (where Herodotus attacks, though not by name, the accounts of many of the best-known thinkers and teachers in Greece) and on Heracles.[44] Then, having refuted geographers and mythographers, he not surprisingly comes to Homer and his account of the Trojan War.[45] As we saw above, Homer was an early target of the pre-Socratics who defined their own beliefs by contrast with the poet. Herodotus' refutation of Homer centres around the issues of reliability

---

[40] Hecataeus, *FGrHist* 1 F 1a.   [41] *FGrHist* 1 F 19.
[42] Lateiner, *Historical Method* 104–8 has an inventory of Herodotean polemic.
[43] Hdt. II.2.5: Ἕλληνες δὲ λέγουσι ἄλλα τε μάταια πολλά, an echo of Hecataeus' λόγοι πολλοί τε καὶ γελοῖοι; cf. 3.1. At II.143 Herodotus' most important predecessor, Hecataeus, is portrayed as comparing his own genealogy with that of the Egyptian priests at Thebes who opposed the poor Greek's 16 generations with their own 345. Scholars have viewed this passage differently, some seeing polemic, some not: see Lateiner, op. cit. (n.42) 94; West, *JHS* 111 (1991) 145–52 (disbelieving the historicity) sees it as a way for Herodotus to contrast pointedly the Greek and Egyptian traditions.
[44] Hdt. II.19–34 (Nile); 42–5 (Heracles).   [45] Hdt. II.112–20.

and probability; his own reconstruction of the *Iliad* legend is presented as both more accurate and more reasonable. The accuracy was to come from the priests (as it had throughout Book II), who in answer to Herodotus' inquiries, told him the whole story of Paris' arrival and detention in Egypt.[46] In this particular piece, Herodotus produces an astounding trump card: the evidence of a participant in the Trojan War. For the priests claimed that their version came from Menelaus himself, such that they had eyewitness testimony, whereas Homer himself made clear that he was of a later generation than that of the Trojan heroes.[47] Such a passage may symbolically represent the superiority of inquiry over inspiration, the triumph of history over poetry. The purpose of such disputation is both to show the superiority of Herodotus' account, and to call attention to himself as the shaper of the tradition, and as an active thinker in the tradition of the pre-Socratics and other sixth- and fifth-century intellectuals.[48] Unlike Polybius' later polemic, Herodotus' activity is not primarily meant to establish general principles, or to argue a certain approach towards the past (even if he thinks his own method superior); it is to establish the record of that past. Herodotus is not really a forerunner of later polemicists, since the appearance (whatever the reality) of Herodotus' disputation is that of disinterested knowledge.

The narrative manner of Thucydides moved away from display, and the narrator only rarely engages in overt polemic, as he does towards the end of the Archaeology, with unnamed poets and prose writers. One can see a profession of method in the author's comparison of himself with others. He calls attention to people's acceptance of what comes their way, rather than subjecting it to examination, and the historian draws the general conclusion from the specific: 'for most people, the search for truth is done without effort, and people prefer to be content with what is at hand' (1.20.3). This leads to summary criticism of poets and prose writers, the one adorning and amplifying, the other composing with a view towards pleasing an audience (1.21.1). Herodotus, though unnamed, is here the chief target,[49] and self-definition is accomplished by reference to others. When Thucydides later criticises Hellanicus' treatment of the history of Athens from the Persian to the Peloponnesian

---

[46] On the authority of priests, see above, pp. 108ff.
[47] That the narrator of the Homeric poems is from a later generation is evident from the invocation of the Muse at II.486: ἡμεῖς δὲ κλέος οἶον ἀκούομεν.
[48] On this milieu see above, pp. 7f. [49] See Introduction, n.100.

war, he merely characterises Hellanicus' work as brief and chronologically inaccurate (1.97.2), and then proceeds with his own account. No effort is expended on analysing or ridiculing Hellanicus, nor in exposing his errors, as Herodotus had done with Ionians and Hellenes. Even in perhaps his greatest display-piece, the digression in Book VI on the tyrannicides (a theme, it is noteworthy, from non-contemporary history), Thucydides merely asserts the superiority of his knowledge, before giving a version that is similar to his contemporary history in narrative manner.[50]

Nor is the mention of predecessors to be found in Xenophon. Indeed, the use of display would be destructive of the near anonymity this historian practised; what polemic there is, is covert, and acts by omission, not inclusion.[51] In contrast to this, Ctesias in his *Persica* distinguished his work by its consistent opposition to Herodotus:

> in his Books VII–XIII, he goes through the events of the reigns of Cyrus and Cambyses and the Magus, and of Darius and Xerxes, writing things opposite to Herodotus on nearly every matter, refuting him as a liar in many things and calling him a fable-monger (λογοποιός) as well ... And Ctesias says that for the majority of what he has recorded, he was himself an eyewitness or, where he was not, he learned of matters from the Persians themselves.[52]

The full quotation here, if Photius has preserved it accurately, reveals (not surprisingly) that Ctesias' self-definition occurred where he contrasted his predecessor's 'lies' with his own methodology, replacing the work of a 'fable-monger' with that of an eyewitness (αὐτόπτης) and an earwitness (αὐτήκοος).[53] His definition of himself seems to have been

---

[50] The digression is announced by Thucydides with an emphatic declaration: ἐγὼ ἐπὶ πλέον διηγησάμενος ἀποφανῶ (VI.54.1), and the first two chapters (54–5) concentrate on summation of the story and method. In 55, Thucydides is yet more emphatic: εἰδὼς μὲν ἀκοῇ ἀκριβέστερον ἄλλων ἰσχυρίζομαι (that Hippias was the eldest son). The use of the inspection of monuments (54.7, 55.1–2) is complemented by the argument from probability (55.1, εἰκός; 55.2: οὐδὲ ... ἀπεοικότως; 55.3 δοκεῖ μοι). Once this is done, however, the narrative of the events, 57–9, is without authorial interruption.

[51] On the 'déformation historique' of the *Hellenica* see Lévy, *PoH* 125–57 where earlier bibliography may also be found; on the *Anabasis* see Ch. IV n. 135.

[52] Ctesias, *FGrHist* 688 T 8.

[53] Jacoby, *RE* XI. 2, 2043ff. points out that Ctesias was quite dependent on Herodotus, and this too is as we might expect, given that self-criticism was never as thorough as criticism of others.

exclusively by contrast, unless we are to assume that his claim to be an eyewitness was an attempt to link himself to Thucydides and to contemporary history's superiority.[54]

As with Ctesias' condemnation of Herodotus, historians now attack other historians by name in their preface.[55] Dionysius tells us that both Anaximenes and Theopompus included polemic in their prefaces, and Duris in turn assailed Ephorus and Theopompus, again as a foil for defining his own approach.[56] How extensive and how bitter these attacks were cannot be determined, but everything we have seen so far does not suggest charitable admonition.[57] Nor do we know whether these historians who defined themselves in strong contrast to predecessors also claimed to follow certain models with whom they allied themselves. There seems little doubt that Theopompus was greatly influenced by Herodotus (he had made an epitome of his work[58]) both in the conception and organisation of his work, but explicit adherence is not attested.[59] Nor do we know whether Duris, in his famous remark against Ephorus and Theopompus, named predecessors whom he would follow.[60]

We have already mentioned the extensive polemic that was so much a part of Timaeus' history. He seems to have attacked predecessors on

---

[54] On this superiority, see Ch. II §1. We cannot say whether Dinon, who wrote a Persian history some years after Ctesias and differed from him in some details (*FGrHist* 690 FF 15-17), attacked his predecessor in his preface or elsewhere.

[55] Parke, *Hermathena* 67 (1946) 83-5 suggests that the early historians do not cite other prose writers (as opposed to poets) by name because they were not yet a part of the heritage of educated men.

[56] D. Hal. *A. R.* 1.1.1 = *FGrHist* 72 F 1 (Anaximenes); 115 F 24 (Theopompus); 76 F 1 (Duris).

[57] Indicative of the times is the action of Anaximenes who wrote a bitter invective against the Athenians, Lacedaemonians, and Thebans, imitating Theopompus' manner and signing Theopompus' name to it. Pausanias (VI.18.5 = *FGrHist* 72 T 6) says it went far in increasing people's hatred of Theopompus; for some doubts about the story see M. A. Flower, *Theopompus* 21-2.

[58] Theopompus, *FGrHist* 115 T 1, FF 1-4; Christ, *CQ* 43 (1993) 47-52 suggests that this epitome was not a separate work, but was included in the *Hellenica* as a kind of précis of earlier events.

[59] On Theopompus' indebtedness to Herodotus see Flower, op. cit. (n.57) 160-5.

[60] Duris, *FGrHist* 76 F 1. Photius presents the remark (Ἔφορος δὲ καὶ Θεόπομπος τῶν γενομένων πλεῖστον ἀπελείφθησαν·) as a direct quotation, and one might speculate that the initial δέ of the statement stands in opposition to an earlier μέν, in which other historians (Herodotus and Thucydides, perhaps?) were praised for their ability to use the proper style in historiography.

Polemic and self-definition

general and specific points.⁶¹ He called attention to his description of Athens' expedition to Sicily in a spirit of rivalry with Thucydides. For Philistus, he had nothing but scorn, correcting his language⁶² and ridiculing him mercilessly, as much for his politics as for his history.⁶³ He excoriated Callisthenes as a flatterer and a wonder-writer, going so far as to remark that his death at the hands of Alexander was a just punishment for his flatteries.⁶⁴ The historian Demochares was accused of impure acts, Ephorus of failing to defend history sufficiently against epideictic.⁶⁵ He similarly made general remarks about the value of history and truth in history. Nor did he limit himself to historians, but took on Plato, Aristotle, Theophrastus, and even Homer, not to mention the historical actors unlucky enough to be included in his work.⁶⁶ Although we cannot read Timaeus' own words, it is probable that his criticisms of other historians were an important way of expressing his own ideas on the writing of history (as Polybius was to do).⁶⁷ It is quite unlikely that Timaeus, given his attitude towards predecessors, aligned himself with anyone specifically by name. His approach seems rather to suggest that everyone before him had got it wrong, and that no one could approach him in writing about both past and present.

In no other surviving historian is polemic so widespread or so important a method of self-definition as in Polybius.⁶⁸ In his work we can see the conjunction of several trends: the spirit of criticism already evident in Hecataeus; the concern not only with an individual history, but with history as a genre, and its peculiar nature and purpose; the love

---

⁶¹ On Timaeus' polemic see Meister, *Historische Kritik* 10–27.
⁶² *FGrHist* 566 T 18 = Plut. *Nicias* 1. It cannot be certain from Plutarch's testimony that Timaeus explicitly asked his readers to compare his treatment with that of Thucydides and Philistus, but it is not unlikely, and the criticism of Philistus' language must have been explicit.   ⁶³ *FGrHist* 566 FF 113; 115; 154.
⁶⁴ *FGrHist* 566 F 155 = Pol. XII.12b.2.
⁶⁵ *FGrHist* 566 F 35 = Pol. XII.13–15 (Demochares); F 7 = Pol. XII.28–28a (Ephorus).
⁶⁶ His polemic frequently attacked character and social standing: Homer was a glutton, Aristotle a glutton and a gourmand, as well as the son of an apothecary: *FGrHist* 566 FF 152; 156.
⁶⁷ What purpose his polemic with non-historians served is uncertain; perhaps it was simply to undermine their authority on individual issues.
⁶⁸ There are many works on Polybian polemic: Meister, *Historische Kritik* is fundamental; see also Koerner, in *Polybios* 327–31; Walbank, *SP* 262–79; Petzold, *Studien zur Methode des Polybios, passim*; Lehmann, in *Polybe* 145–200; Mohm, *Untersuchungen zu den historiographischen Anschauungen des Polybios*; Schepens, *PoH* 39–61.

of display characteristic of epideictic[69] writing of all kinds; and the quarrelsomeness and pedantry begun in Alexandrian scholarship. In practice, he is a sensible and (on the whole) mild critic, despite the prevalent view of him as unfair and captious. Either his targets are unnamed[70] or some good qualities are conceded along with the criticisms.[71] Only at times does an historian provoke Polybius to indignation and ridicule, and these form the best-known polemics: with Phylarchus in Book II, Chaereas and Sosylus in III, Theopompus in VIII, Callisthenes and Timaeus in XII, and Postumius Albinus in XXXIX.[72] Polybius' criticisms of other historians, although copious and continuous, revolve around the same issues: the nature and superiority of universal history; the partiality of predecessors, especially the bitterness (πικρία) and slander (λοιδορία) of Theopompus and Timaeus; the use of the sensational and the dramatic; the proper spirit of inquiry; and the necessity of political experience.[73]

It is not coincidental that the attack on Timaeus contains the greatest number of methodological pronouncements by Polybius and gives us the fullest and best-rounded portrait of the historian's task,[74] for as we have seen, the historians do not speak in the abstract about their methodology, but explain what they pursue always in contrast to others. So as the portrait of Timaeus receives more and more brush strokes, a self-portrait of the artist himself emerges. Indeed, the extended refutation of Timaeus

[69] And with Polybius 'apodeictic' manner of narration as well: see Introd. n. 45.
[70] The majority of the unnamed historians are contemporary writers, usually of monographs. On the reasons for anonymity, Walbank, SP 269 suggests that an historian would not want to call attention to the existence of a rival work, 'especially if he had made more use of it than his criticisms might suggest'.
[71] So, for example, Fabius and Philinus are on the whole reliable; even Timaeus is granted a type of experience and labour in research.
[72] Three of these historians – Theopompus, Callisthenes, and Timaeus – treated a time that had nothing to do with Polybius' chosen theme. The criticism of Albinus, although full of ridicule, is based as much on his way of life as on his abilities as an historian, and no special methodological principles emerge from this criticism. Polybius had good reasons to despise Albinus: see Walbank, SP 268.
[73] Universal history: I.4.7-11; III.32; VIII.2; XXIX.12.1-2; cf. VII.7.6; partiality: I.14. 4-9; 15; VIII.9-11; XVI.14.6; 15; sensational and dramatic: II.17.6; II.56-61; III.38.1-3; 47.6-48.12; VII.7.6; X.2.5-6; XXXIII.21.1-2; inquiry: I.64.4; III.21.9-10; 26.1-2; experience: XII.25f.1-6.
[74] Sacks, Polybius 66-78 argues that this was exactly Polybius' purpose in writing XII, and that the object of his criticisms (Timaeus) was less important to him than the positive methodology that he wished to expound.

is the most distinctive piece of historiographical polemic to have survived from antiquity.[75] To catalogue Timaeus' failings did indeed take a great deal of time, for the list of his offences is long: poor (or no) inquiry; falsehood; lack of proportion; deficiency of judgment; inexperience; immoderateness; pedantry; love of paradox; ignorance; childishness; and excessive cavilling and fault-finding.[76] Some, especially the last, were not new with Polybius; others before had attacked Timaeus. Yet like Herodotus, Timaeus continued to be read, even if he never achieved the status of a model to be emulated,[77] and it is clear from Polybius' polemic that many held him to be an authority not easily refuted on the matters he treated.[78] Polybius might indeed say that he did not think another's faults to be his own virtues, but historians, like everyone, reveal themselves in their choice of friends and enemies.

The pervasively hostile tone could be justified on three counts. First, Polybius could claim that Timaeus was mendacious deliberately, not inadvertently, and thus deserved indignant censure: this claim was important for Polybius since throughout his history he had recommended generous correction and pardon for unintentional errors. Second, Timaeus himself had been a prodigious and wide-ranging polemicist – Polybius mentions this more often than anything else in Book XII – and it is therefore fair, given his defect of character (his πικρία), to treat him in exactly the same way.[79] Having stepped over the boundary of what was seemly, and having descended to foul language and slander, Timaeus had taken history's task to praise and blame beyond its acceptable limits. Third, as we noted above, rhetoric sanctioned the hostile tone for polemic, since one of polemic's primary goals was to raise the emotions and encourage a sense of outrage.

And yet Polybius must not, in his own criticism of Timaeus, become another Timaeus. This is almost certainly the reason why Polybius

---

[75] Plutarch's *On the Malice of Herodotus* is longer, but only about one-half of Polybius XII survives, and it is clear that the entire book was made up of polemic that had Timaeus at its centre: see Schepens, *PoH* 41 n. 6.

[76] Meister, *Historische Kritik* 3–49.

[77] On Timaeus' later influence and importance especially for Rome see Geffcken, *Timaios' Geographie des Westens* 177–85; cf. Momigliano, *Terzo Contributo* 1.50 n. 77; Meister, *SCI* 10 (1989/90) 55–65.

[78] Schepens, *PoH* 43–4 points out the difficulty attendant on one criticising in general and Timaeus in specific.

[79] See Boncquet, *Anc. Soc.* 13–14 (1982–3) 286–7 for the passages and for other ancient authors who accuse Timaeus of πικρία.

mentions Timaeus' love of cavilling and fault-finding no fewer than seventeen times in a sixty-page text. He constantly reminds the audience that the man in the dock deserves the treatment he is getting, and that the level of criticism is appropriate; every issue that can be brought up must be brought up, provided only that it does not smack of the pedantry and useless detail so characteristic of Timaeus himself. And the breadth of Timaeus' shortcomings is emphasised lest the criticisms seem to be disproportionate (as were Timaeus') and seem to pertain to individual points only. Anywhere one looks, Polybius might say, whether to geography, or foundation stories, or battles, or political events, or speeches, Timaeus' weaknesses are evident.

Lest Polybius himself acquire the reputation that Timaeus and Theopompus did for excessive fault-finding, not every historian comes in for passionate denunciation. Polybius claims to have written to Zeno in a cordial spirit to correct the latter's errors about Laconia, and he goes on to request from his readers the same generous correction for himself.[80] As an alternative to the type of indignant criticisms served to Timaeus, Theopompus, and all such deliberate liars, this incident with Zeno – who, unlike Timaeus (it is worthwhile to add), was in no way a competitor for the position of the authoritative historian of the West – demonstrates that Polybius is not to be confused with historians who criticise everyone out of malice, ill-will, or bitterness. For all his faults, Zeno was not, like Timaeus, fundamentally dishonest, and he thus deserves correction not censure.[81] The historian should show honourable conduct, and Polybius has occasion later to remark that he tells a story not to gloat but for the betterment of his readers.[82] Here is Polybius the historian who corrects others in the proper spirit, a task that he says serves the common good.[83] Once again, the paradeigmatic historian appears.[84]

[80] Pol. XVI.20.5–9; for a summary of different interpretations of Polybius' actions, Walbank, *Polybius* 54–5.

[81] Cf. Sacks, op. cit. (n. 74) 76–7 on the difference of treatment accorded Zeno and Timaeus.

[82] See II.61.1–6, where he requests the historian show honourable conduct, and, for the story not told to gloat, XXX.9.20–1.

[83] Like the other passages on this topic, it is, of course, a disguised *captatio beneuolentiae*. Diodorus too has similar remarks on generous correction (1.5.2), nor is it limited to historians; Strabo has a yet clearer call for indulgence, stating that as Ephorus gave way to Polybius and Polybius to Posidonius, Apollodorus and others, so too one should pardon and not think ill of him if he makes mistakes in borrowing historical material; for the reader should be content, he says, if 'we improve on others in a majority of cases' (X.3.5).   [84] See above, p. 136.

Polybius' contemporary Agatharchides opened Book v of his *On the Erythrean Sea* with a polemic against the style of writers who had cause to describe sufferings in their histories. It is in some sense no more than an extension of Polybius' criticism of Timaeus' inappropriate speeches; Agatharchides says that the style of a writer describing extreme misfortunes should not be too vivid, 'unless one assigns a reason appropriate to what is being described'.[85] Agatharchides' polemic, like Polybius', was also meant to serve a function within his work as a whole, for it preceded his account of the harsh life led by those who worked the Nubian gold mines of the Ptolemies (§§25–9), an account that Photius said could not be matched for its tragic description.[86] We may assume then that this polemic was a pre-emptive strike, informing the audience that since the historian is aware of the dangers of an excessively emotional portrayal in a history, the reader can have confidence in Agatharchides' description as based on an adequate understanding of causes, and not done merely for empty effect.

Diodorus too uses polemic to call attention to his own virtues. Aside from correction of individual incidents,[87] his most frequently named opponents are Herodotus and Timaeus.[88] Herodotus' main failing, as Diodorus reports it, is a fondness for myth and the marvellous. Although acknowledged as a 'curious inquirer and one skilled in history', he is faulted on the flood of the Nile, and for writing up tales and myths in his account of Egypt, a procedure that Diodorus contrasts with his own reliance in Egyptian matters on what is written by the priests in their holy books.[89] Later in Book x during his narration of the Persian Wars, Diodorus remarks that he corrects Herodotus 'not to criticise but to show how marvellous accounts prevail over true ones' (x.24.1). He criticises Timaeus three times by name, and once anonymously; although all the criticisms derive from Polybius, Diodorus has not followed him exactly, sometimes altering the charges for obvious reasons: unlike Polybius, Diodorus has no concern with the political experience that Polybius demanded of the historian and Timaeus lacked; we can

---

[85] Agatharchides, *Mar. Rubr.* §21 = *GGM* 1.119–22; cf. Pol. 11.56.13, where Phylarchus fails to arouse real pity because he does not properly explain causes and consequences.
[86] Phot. *Bibl.* 250, p. 447b = *GGM* 1.124–5 (§24).   [87] Diod. IV.56.7; V.23.1–4.
[88] How far Diodorus' polemic is based on the criticisms of Hecataeus of Abdera is uncertain: see Riemann, *Das herodoteische Geschichtswerk* 55–60.
[89] At 1.37.4 Herodotus is called ὁ πολυπράγμων ... καὶ πολλῆς ἱστορίας ἔμπειρος; for his account of Egypt see 1.69.7.

well imagine that the criticism of Timaeus for getting most of his history from books (whether or not it was true) would have been uncongenial to the author of an 'historical library'.[90] Even the Polybian criticisms retained by Diodorus seem to have been put to different use. Diodorus' contribution to the criticism of Timaeus is the (unusual) observation that Timaeus' well-known bitterness ruined the organisation of his history, presumably by long excurses on minor points.[91] Diodorus' criticism of Timaeus' story of the bull of Phalaris leads to a charge of invention, and to a Polybian distinction between intentional and unintentional falsehood, complete with the appropriate punishments recommended by Polybius; Timaeus is also reproved (as in Polybius) for his personal enmity towards Agathocles that caused him to write biased history.[92] Diodorus uses his polemic (whether borrowed or his own) to address a variety of historiographical issues: organisation; avoidance of 'unpurified' myth; the need to avoid 'tragic' presentation; and the need for impartiality.[93] Despite his sometimes haphazard use of polemic,[94] Diodorus has still used it to highlight those matters that he wishes the reader to see as his own contribution to the writing of history.[95]

Dionysius is different in his use of polemic. He saves his heavy fire in the preface for those who find fault with Fortune for giving the hegemony to Rome, and for historians so 'enslaved' to kings who hated Rome that they wrote unjust and flattering histories.[96] With these historians Dionysius' differences are the clearest. He also criticises certain of his predecessors for a lack of fullness in their accounts. Yet because he stakes much of his authority on the early historians of Rome, whom he will follow,[97] he cannot indulge in active polemic with them as a group or with their histories in their entirety. To convict them of numerous errors, or to ridicule them as Polybius did Timaeus, would undermine his own claim to be writing an accurate history based on epichoric records. His exposition and argument thus focus on details at

---

[90] See below, n. 131.   [91] Diod. v.1.1–4.   [92] Diod. XXI.17.1.
[93] Organisation: v.1.1–4; XVI.1.1–2; myth: 1.37.3; 69.7; v.23.2–4; x.24.1; tragic presentation: XIX.8.4; impartiality: XXI.17.1–4.
[94] See Meister, *Helikon* 13–14 (1973–4) 454–9 on Diodorus' polemic with the very authors he used.
[95] Occasionally, but rarely, individual historians are praised: Timaeus for the great attention he gave to chronology and Ephorus for his arrangement and language (v.1.3–4), two things Diodorus has claimed to be his special care in his work: 1.3.2; 3.4; 3.8 (chronology); XVI.1.1–3 (arrangement).
[96] D. Hal. *A. R.* 1.4.2–3.   [97] See below, pp. 244f.

occasional points throughout the narrative. In Book I, for example, he discusses the date of the foundation of Rome.[98] The point of this display by Dionysius seems to be both inclusivity – five major authors are cited – and superiority. Three of the early Roman historians are cited and two Greeks, not coincidentally the two who most had the claim to be considered the historian of the West, Timaeus and Polybius. Both Greeks are found wanting, and Dionysius' alliance with the Latin historian Cato is deliberate and in keeping with his promise to base his history on reliable Roman writers. At the same time, by including Fabius and Cincius (whom he does not follow), he shows himself to be conscientious towards the tradition without being a slave to everything written: he can exercise a critical faculty and a judicious scrutiny of what others have said, as well as demonstrating his proper understanding and mastery of chronology.[99] No generalised historiographic pronouncement occurs, only the display (and it is important) of the specific superiority to be found in Dionysius' history.

A similar but somewhat stronger display, which can certainly be considered polemic, is found in Book IV. This display also revolves around accurate calculation, in this case that of age: was it the sons or the grandsons of Tarquinius Priscus whom his wife entrusted to Servius Tullius upon Priscus' death?[100] Dionysius interrupts the narrative to give the reasons why he disagrees with Fabius and all the other historians who write that it was the sons of Priscus. He does this so that he will not be suspected of inventing; and he criticises the Roman historians for carelessness and laziness in their account because they did not examine the impossibilities and absurdities that would result if their interpretation were true. Here the use of probability and rationalisation are prominent, and these were especially important for Dionysius to display in writing a history of early Rome, since in all early history the tendency towards myth and improbability were greater than in contemporary history.[101] Dionysius' refutations, therefore, serve the larger purpose of demonstrating the method and approach that the historian has taken, and the care that he has given to the matters involved, even when they are very slight. They do not serve, as in Polybius, to articulate a larger theoretic for the writing of history; Dionysius is content to use the models and rules already in existence, wishing above all to show himself

---

[98] D. Hal. *A. R.* 1.72-5.   [99] See above, pp. 103ff.   [100] D. Hal. *A. R.* IV.6.7.
[101] See Ch. II §4.

a master of these, and a reliable practitioner of a pragmatic historiography. That he would attempt this on material that others would think intrinsically flawed is meant perhaps to display a superiority even to contemporary historians.

When we turn to the Roman tradition, we see a similar use of polemic as an element of self-definition. At the outset of Book IV of his *Origins*, where the history of his own time began, Cato distinguished what he would write from the Pontifical Chronicle. By criticising what was in this Chronicle – notices of famines and eclipses – he was no doubt highlighting the differences with his own work, which was presumably more detailed and more politically oriented; he may even have used this to cast suspicion on the early history of Rome and to justify his omission of early Roman history (which his predecessors had treated) and his beginning in the year 264.[102] Nor can he have had in mind only the Chronicle itself; he must also have intended to criticise earlier historians, such as Fabius Pictor, who had used this type of material in their histories.[103] Similarly, Sempronius Asellio found fault with annals, distinguishing them from the 'history' that he would write, which would give both the intentions of the historical actors and explanations of events. Annals were useless, since 'to write when a war began and ended, and who entered the city in triumph, and what was done in the war, without saying what the Senate decreed and what law was passed by the assembly or with what intentions things were done – this is telling stories to boys, not writing history.'[104]

In the rest of the Roman tradition, however, as represented by Sallust, Livy, Tacitus, and Ammianus we find a less epideictic or programmatic use of polemic, limited in the main to specific points of contrast, and a correspondingly greater concern with linking their works to illustrious predecessors, as a way of portraying themselves as heir to the tradition of Roman historiography. To this aspect we now turn.

---

[102] Cato, *HRR* F 77, with Frier, *Libri Annales* 275–6. On the difference between the Pontifical Chronicle and the *Annales Maximi* see Introd. n. 124. It is sometimes thought that Cato F 1 also refers to his predecessors, but this is less certain: see Schröder, *Das erste Buch der Origines* 50–1. [103] See Walbank, *SP* 97.
[104] Sempronius Asellio, *HRR* FF 1–2. These remarks echo Polybius: F 1 ~ Pol. XI.19a; F 2 ~ Pol. III.20.5.

3. CONTINUITY AND CULMINATION

Polemic highlights differences and separates an historian from his predecessors. Yet the dictates of imitation were based on aspiration towards realising an achievement similar to that of one of the masters of the genre: 'how Thucydides would have done it', to use Longinus' directive.[105] Even historians who used polemic might praise other historians and seek to ally themselves with predecessors they thought worthy of emulation. In so doing they make clear their own affinities and indicate how they wish to be seen. Sometimes, within this articulation, they suggest their superiority to an emulated model and portray themselves as the culmination of a tradition; and in this way distinguish themselves from all who have gone before.

The most obvious way of indicating a link with a predecessor is to begin one's history where he had left off. Thucydides' invention of contemporary history was regarded as a worthwhile and exceptional task, and no age after him ever lacked contemporary historians; even under the most difficult political conditions, men desired to leave a record of what they had known or seen or heard. Xenophon's *Hellenica* is the first instance of 'continuing' a predecessor, and this tradition has a long history in writers both Greek and Roman.[106] Xenophon must have wished his *Hellenica* to be seen as a continuation of Thucydides, for he links it up explicitly by the unusual beginning 'and after these things',[107] and he

---

[105] [Long.] *Subl.* 14.1; on imitation of a model, see Introd. §3.
[106] On the whole topic see Canfora, *Belfagor* 26 (1971) 653-70.
[107] Xen. *Hell.* 1.1.1 (μετὰ δὲ ταῦτα). Many ideas have been suggested to account for this work's unusual opening. The notion, once entertained, that a preface existed but has not survived (Engel, *De antiquorum epicorum didacticorum historicorum prooemiis* 45) has been occasionally revived (J. Hatzfeld, 'Le début des Hélleniques', *Mélanges offerts à A-M. Desrousseaux* (Paris 1937) 211-17, and Defosse, *Rev. Belge* 46 (1968) 18-22), but most scholars assume that the beginning in antiquity was as we have it. The *Hellenica* cannot really be said to have a 'virtual' preface (as does the more self-contained *Anabasis*: see Luc. *h. c.* 52), and although it is true that a reader, upon beginning it, would recognise it as a history of warfare between Athens and Sparta (Earl, *ANRW* I.2, 844), nevertheless it is still not clear to what affairs ταῦτα refers. Some suggest that Xenophon needed no preface because he was continuing Thucydides, but why this would be the case is not clear. Dillery, *Xenophon* 10-11 suggests that the author was trying to create something unique by attaching his work so close to Thucydides', whereas Krentz, *Xenophon: Hellenika* 86 suggests just the

imitates something of the narrative manner of his great predecessor.[108] This is not to say that his approach to history, however, is the same as Thucydides', for Xenophon stamped his work with his own concerns and methods. In other words, continuing a predecessor did not entail slavishly imitating him, nor even agreeing with him on the nature and purpose of history itself. Moreover, as is clear from the ending of the *Hellenica*, Xenophon himself envisions a continuator who will join up his work to Xenophon's own.[109] There were other continuators of Thucydides: Cratippus, the Oxyrhynchus historian, and Theopompus in his *Hellenica*.[110] The trend continued even after these writers: Diyllus of Athens began his history where Ephorus left off; Psaon of Plataea continued Diyllus; and Menodotus of Perinthus may have continued Psaon. Phylarchus continued Duris, or perhaps Hieronymus of Cardia.[111]

Nor does it have to be the case that an historian sets himself up as continuing only one predecessor: Polybius claims two, Aratus and Timaeus. Polybius will begin his account of eastern events with the 140th Olympiad, where Aratus of Sicyon ended his memoirs; for western actions, he will start at the 129th Olympiad, where Timaeus left

opposite, that lack of a formal preface is meant to distance himself from Thucydides. Canfora, op. cit. (n.106) 653–70 (cf. Dillery, op. cit. 10) suggests the epic cycle as a model for Xenophon's procedure as a continuator. Gray, *AJPh* 112 (1991) 202ff. has argued that Xenophon wanted to begin with the commencement of Spartan power over Greece at the end of the Peloponnesian War, but seeing Thucydides' history incomplete, believing in continuous history (as can be seen from his ending), and finding the other continuators who had already written unacceptable, he decided to give a summary account of the remaining seven years of the war. Inspiration for his decision must be found in Thucydides' brief treatment of the Pentekontaetia, by which he linked up his history with that of Herodotus (ibid. 207–8). For further discussion see Henry, *Greek Historical Writing* 1–54; Defosse, op. cit. The situation is complicated by the inconsistencies and omissions between the end of Thucydides and the beginning of the *Hellenica*: see L. Breitenbach, *Xenophons Hellenika* I² (Berlin 1884) 31ff.; Underhill, *A Commentary on the Hellenica of Xenophon* xvi–xvii.

[108] Although this should not be exaggerated: see Dover, *HCT* v.431–44; against the thesis that Xenophon edited Thucydides and used his papers, see Henry, op. cit. (n.107) 54–88.

[109] The τὰ δὲ μετὰ ταῦτα ἴσως ἄλλῳ μελήσει (VII.5.27) echoes the opening words; for discussion see Dillery, op. cit. (n.107) 11 with n. 18.

[110] Not all will have made their link explicit; Xenophon's work, for example, is clearly attached to something but the predecessor is not named. For a sketch of the Greek 'continuators' whom we know, see App. VI.

[111] See App. VI nn. 8–9.

off.[112] His continuation of the former has as its purpose an indication of political and historiographical solidarity with the type of history that Aratus wrote and whose standards Polybius will continue to maintain.[113] The case of Timaeus is more complicated: Polybius wishes to be seen, like his predecessor, as the historian of the West; in the course of the history, however, Polybius will make clear that he is much superior to Timaeus and far more deserving of the recognition given to his predecessor.[114]

Polybius also had his continuators: Posidonius wrote universal history from where his predecessor left off, and Strabo, two generations later, wrote up *Affairs after Polybius*.[115] As with Xenophon, we cannot posit that a claim to continue a predecessor meant a similar interest and orientation, and it is clear that Posidonius, for example, had far more catholic and cultural interests than Polybius. Continuation was, however, a way of laying claim to the importance and value of contemporary history and of indicating that one wished to be seen in a certain tradition. The trend continued well into the Empire. Herodian began his history where Chryserus had left off; and in the next century Eunapius began his history in AD 269/70, the year where Dexippus' *Historical Chronicle* had ended.[116] Indeed, it is remarkable that Eunapius praises Dexippus at length in his preface, and claims explicitly to be following his lead, even if he will not concern himself with the chronological problems so beloved by his predecessor.[117]

Among the Sicilian historians we find but one continuator, Athanis,

---

[112] Pol. I.3.1-2 (Aratus); I.5.1 (Timaeus).
[113] For Polybius and Aratus see Walbank, *Polybius* 77-9.
[114] Polybius praises Ephorus, the first to write universal history, as an indication of the tradition which he wishes to follow: v.33.2; xii.28.10. Yet Polybius also claims superiority to Ephorus because of both his predecessor's lack of experience (xii.25f), and the superiority of Polybius' own subject which, far more that Ephorus' work (which was limited to Greek affairs), can properly claim to be universal: 1.3.4, with Walbank, *Polybius* 67-8. Thus in a similar way Polybius follows and surpasses a respected predecessor.
[115] *FGrHist* 87 TT 1, 12b = TT 1, 1b (E-K); Strabo, 91 T 2, who (like Polybius) prefaced his work with a παρασκευή, in Strabo's case on events to the time of Alexander the Great (91 FF 1, 3).
[116] Chryserus' *Chronicle* went from the foundation of Rome to 180 (*FGrHist* 96 T 1), Herodian's history from 180 to 238. Herodian does not state in his history that he is continuing Chryserus, but the suggestion is attractive if, as is possible, both were imperial freedmen (see Ch. II n. 126).
[117] Dexippus, *FGrHist* 100 F 1; Eunapius F 1; its title was probably *History After Dexippus* (Blockley, *Fragmentary Classicising Historians* 1.2)

since the tradition here was for nearly every historian to treat Sicilian history from its origins. Philistus wrote *On Sicily* in seven books from earliest times to 406 BC, and *On Dionysius*, treating events from 406 to 367/6. When Athanis later wrote up the deeds of Dion of Syracuse, he joined his history to Philistus' by treating a period of seven years (368/7-362/1) between the end of Philistus' work (which broke off in the middle of Dionysius' reign) and the beginning of his own.[118] Noteworthy again is that Athanis in no way shared the political viewpoint of Philistus,[119] and his continuation cannot thus have been expected to entail an identification with his predecessor's beliefs.

The Romans too, like the Greeks, had a long tradition of continuators.[120] Even acknowledging that some of the links are tenuous, one may see nevertheless that the authors included all seem to have been primarily political historians who avoided for the most part the early and unreliable legends of Roman history. Because none of these works survives, it is difficult to tell whether the decision to join one's history to a predecessor's signalled an acceptance of the earlier historian's methods and aims. There seems fair certainty that Sallust in the *Histories* wished to be seen as the continuator of Sisenna, and Asinius Pollio, imitating the harsh style of Sallust, portrayed himself as continuing the outlook and disposition of his predecessor.[121] In the Empire, the elder Pliny's *History from the conclusion of Aufidius Bassus* shows homage to an honoured predecessor, and Ammianus' commencement 'from the principate of Nerva Caesar' is a clear link to the tradition of Tacitus, who had ended his *Histories* with the death of Domitian.[122]

Since we see that continuators among the Greeks, Sicilians, and Romans do not necessarily hold to their predecessors' beliefs and methods, we may well ask what the point of such claims was when one

---

[118] *FGrHist* 562 T 2.   [119] Jacoby, *FGrHist Komm.* IIIb (Text) 522.
[120] See App. VII.
[121] See Peter, *HRR* I.CCCXL (Sallust and Sisenna); Woodman, *RICH* 127-8 (Pollio and Sallust). For more on Sallust, below, pp. 246f.
[122] Syme, *Tacitus* I.288-9 on Pliny and Aufidius; on Ammianus and Tacitus, Matthews, *Roman Empire* 31-2 sees the date as of no more than 'formal significance' (32) and denies that Ammianus sought 'to evoke in any systematic way the substance or purpose of his predecessor's work' (ibid.). Perhaps so, but as we can see from Xenophon or Polybius, the continuation of a predecessor does not necessarily entail allegiance to his historiographical principles. More below, pp. 254ff.

had a different orientation and intent.[123] It could be to lay claim to a tradition; but far more likely, the element of emulation – which might easily be seen as arrogance or foolishness if one failed – is what is at issue here: for if you continue an author such as Ephorus or Livy or even Timaeus, who were seen as the definitive writers on their topics, you are inviting comparison with them, and claiming that your performance will rival theirs and likewise be 'definitive'. Both aspiration and emulation, linking one's work to a predecessor's is a way of making a claim, without overt advertisement of one's own abilities.

An historian may attempt to continue a predecessor, but he may also try to portray himself as the culmination of the historiographical tradition, as one can see clearly in Diodorus. In the preface he praises universal history and thus aligns himself with Ephorus, Polybius, and perhaps Posidonius (1.1.3). He contrasts his own work with that of previous universal historians: only a few, he says, have recorded events from earliest times down to their own day, and of them,

> most writers have written isolated wars of one nation or city. A few attempted to write universal histories (κοιναὶ πράξεις) beginning from the earliest times up to their own era; but some of these did not give the proper dates for these events, others omitted the deeds of the barbarians, and yet others renounced ancient mythical accounts, because of the difficulty of the task. Some did not fulfil the promise of their attempt because they were taken off by fate in mid-life. Of those who made an attempt at the task, no one brought their history further than Macedonian times; some ended with Philip, some with Alexander, some with the Diadochs or the Epigoni. And yet although many and great deeds have been accomplished after those events up to our own times, no historian has tried to treat them in one work, because of the greatness of the task.[124]

Three failings are specified: (i) the lack of proper dating; (ii) the omission of the deeds of non-Greeks; (iii) the omission of mythical material.

---

[123] I do not mean to discount the pragmatic reasons for not treating work already done by a predecessor. If an historian had a theme he liked, he naturally would not have wanted to write on what his predecessors had done. In that case, he need not even make reference to 'linking' his work with a predecessor's; he could simply have, like many historians, magnified his theme in isolation, without reference to others. I assume that if he made reference to a predecessor either in his title or text, he expected some reaction from this.

[124] Diod. 1.3.2–3.

(A fourth – failure to live long enough to complete the work – is not quite in the same category.) The presentation of the failures of his predecessors in this way allows Diodorus to distinguish himself from Ephorus (category iii), Polybius (ii and iii), and Posidonius (iii).[125] Such inclusiveness would have been difficult for any historian to obtain, and Diodorus has, of course, fashioned these shortcomings in such a way as to highlight his own work. Lastly, for any writer who may not have had any of the failings enumerated by Diodorus,[126] Diodorus mentions that no universal historian has carried his history beyond the Diadochs and the Epigoni, leaving all the glorious deeds after them and up to Diodorus' own time 'neglected', because of the magnitude of the task.[127] Here we have a good example of the attempt to make oneself unique *vis-à-vis* predecessors. A moment's reflection is sufficient to disprove this last remark, and the deeds from the middle of the third century to Diodorus' time could in no way be described as 'neglected'; far from it, they had been treated by (to name only two) Polybius and Posidonius. But these histories did not meet the previous requirements, and the statement, read in its context, is that 'no universal history that meets all of my above criteria goes beyond the Epigoni'. Diodorus argues that his work, unlike all previous ones, will be of the greatest benefit while at the same time offering the greatest ease. A single history will aid one in understanding numerous interrelated past events because it will be easy to follow, and 'a history of this sort must be considered greater than the others in the same way that the whole is more useful than the part and continuity more useful than discontinuity, and, again, as an exact knowledge of the date is more useful than ignorance of the period in which an action happened' (1.3.8). The 'bigger is better' argument presupposes that more is, in fact, more, and that if one could combine Ephorus and Polybius and Posidonius *and* the writers of individual monographs, one would have a unique

---

[125] Ephorus began with the return of the Heracleidae and thus avoided very early material (*FGrHist* 70 T 8). Polybius specifically left the mythical out of the realm of history. Posidonius began where Polybius left off (above, n. 115) and although he treated much material bordering on myth, he did not give the full and systematic treatment offered by Diodorus in Books I–V.

[126] Perhaps Zoilus and Anaximenes, both of whom began with theogonies (*FGrHist* 71 T 1, 72 T 14), and also Timagenes (88 F 2), though the latter as the writer of a work Περὶ Βασιλέων (F 1) may not have seemed a competitor for Diodorus. Alternatively, Theopompus would have fulfilled all of Diodorus' desiderata.   [127] Diod. 1.3.3.

and all-embracing history that would, by its very completeness, supersede all others. And so the position of Diodorus is secure: he comes at the end of a long tradition; through his effort and the ability to exploit the work of his predecessors, he has managed – like the reader of history whom he envisions in the preface – to benefit from their labours, producing in turn for his readers a superior work. He represents that 'optimistic' strain of belief in imitation, that the last in the line has the best position.[128]

This must also be the reason why Diodorus, beginning in Book XI, includes brief notices of the starting- and ending-points (sometimes with a summary of contents and the number of books) of the historians who treated the events he also is narrating.[129] Presumably, when the reader sees a continuous citation of historians, he is meant to conclude that the present historian is consistently basing his work on the authoritative historians whom he names. Diodorus wants his audience to think that he has throughout compared these different accounts and chosen from each what was best and most trustworthy.[130] As far as we can tell, this work is to be seen as a compilation or 'Library',[131] and as worthwhile precisely because Diodorus has chosen good sources. This is not to say, of course, that Diodorus necessarily has done this extensive sifting and collation,[132] only that he wants it to seem this way. He has taken a time-honoured tradition – basing a non-contemporary account on previous written sources – and made it into the foundation of his entire work: thus his praise in the preface of the vast supply of books available

---

[128] See above, p. 15.
[129] On Diodorus' literary citations, see Schwartz, *RE* V, 668–9 = *GG* 43–4. Diodorus mentions the starting- and/or ending-points of the following historians: Herodotus (XI.37.6); Thucydides (XII.37.2; XIII.42.5); Antiochus of Syracuse (XII.71.2); Xenophon (XIII.42.5; XV.89.3); Philistus (XIII.103.3; XV.89.3); Ctesias (XIV.46.6); Theopompus (XIII.42.5; XIV.84.7; XVI.3.8); Callisthenes (XIV.117.8; XVI.14.4); Hermeias (XV.37.3); Duris (XV.60.6); Anaximenes (XV.89.3); Athanis (XV.94.4); Dionysodorus (XV.95.4); Anaxis (ibid.); Demophilus (XVI.14.3); Diyllus (XVI.14.5; 76.6; XXI.5); Ephorus (XVI.76.5); Psaon (XXI.5); Menodotus (XXVI.4) Sosylus (ibid.). Philistus or Philinus is mentioned at XXIII.17, but in what context is unclear.
[130] As he does with the writers on Crete: above, p. 114.
[131] Schwartz, *RE* V, 663 = *GG* 35: 'Diodors Kompilation – ein Werk kann man das Buch nicht nennen'; he also points out that the title Βιβλιοθήκη is explicitly attested by Pliny, *n. h. praef.* 25; cf. J. Hornblower, *Hieronymus* 22–7.
[132] On Diodorus' use usually of a single source see Schwartz, *RE* V. 670ff. = *GG* 45ff.

at Rome is emphatic and functional.[133] His uniqueness, as he seems to wish us to see it, lies in the completeness of his work, its convenience, and its uniformity, for it goes without saying that a major contribution of Diodorus will have been his rewriting of his many sources in his own style, and in giving preference to those themes that he considers important. His claims of 'uniqueness' can thus best be summed up in terms of comprehensive compilation within the tradition of universal history, where Diodorus presents himself as coming last and thus able to offer more than his predecessors.[134]

A different type of relationship with predecessors, involving contrast, continuity and culmination, may be seen in Dionysius of Halicarnassus. Like Polybius, Posidonius, and even Diodorus,[135] he is a Greek explaining the Romans to his countrymen. His unique approach is to suggest that the true nature and character of Rome are still unknown, but that it may best become understood, paradoxically, by a study of Rome's early history, for her character was already visible then.[136] In making Rome's early history into the key for understanding the Rome of his own day, Dionysius can claim for himself new territory, untrodden by his predecessors. He names all those who might be seen as his predecessors and, thus, competitors: Hieronymus, Timaeus, Antigonus, Polybius, Silenus, Fabius Pictor, and Cincius Alimentus; and he then notes different shortcomings for the five Greeks and the two Romans who wrote in Greek. The former narrated but a few things about early Rome and even these were not accurately investigated, but were based on chance oral report;[137] the latter, as natives, could hardly be described in the same way,[138] and so their failing was to treat their

---

[133] This seems to me unmistakable based on 1.3.8 and 1.4.2–3. Schwartz, *RE* V, 663 = *GG* 35 makes clear that Diodorus' work is part of the encyclopedic tradition of the late Republic; Rawson, *Intellectual Life* 227 compares Diodorus' 'epitomising of earlier writers' with Brutus' résumés of Polybius and others.

[134] If this strikes us as disappointing, that is perhaps a reflection of our own preconceptions, not those of the age in which Diodorus lived. The attempt by Sacks, *Diodorus* to make Diodorus into an historian who made original contributions and gave shape and substance to his history seems to proceed from the assumption that Diodorus would not really want to be seen as a compiler. For criticisms of this approach, see C. W. Fornara, *CPh* 87 (1992) 383–8.   [135] For Diodorus and Rome see Sacks, op. cit. (n. 134) ch. V.

[136] D. Hal. *A. R.* 1.5.2.

[137] D. Hal. *A. R.* 1.6.1: ἐκ τῶν ἐπιτυχόντων ἀκουσμάτων. This is, of course, not true of Polybius' history in general, but Dionysius is referring to early Roman history.   [138] Because of the belief about epichoric sources: App. IV §4.

early history only summarily (1.6.2). None is described as hostile to Rome and so they are not in the same category as that earlier and anonymous group cited previously (4.2–3). Dionysius' criticism of all seven is brief and muted, no doubt because he does not wish to be seen in the censorious tradition that he had explicitly rejected at the opening of his history when he said he would not follow the procedure of Theopompus and Anaximenes by beginning with invective.[139] Thus none of these historians is accused of the more serious charges of slander, malice, or wilful abdication of the historian's duty. Moreover, since Dionysius was well aware that he could be suspected of inventing material from long ago, his solution was to ally himself firmly with the epichoric tradition of Rome.[140] He mentions his sojourn in Rome for precisely this reason, since it allowed him not only to converse, like Herodotus, with their most esteemed men (λογιώτατοι ἄνδρες)[141] but also to read those histories which the Romans themselves use. Just as he had named seven historians who were less than reliable, Dionysius now names seven writers whom he has followed: Cato, Fabius Maximus, Valerias Antias, Licinius Macer, Aelius, Gellius, and L. Calpurnius Piso Frugi.[142] But an important difference between Dionysius and Diodorus is that Dionysius explicitly states that these men's works served only as a basis for his own work.[143] Dionysius thus contrasts himself with his Greek-writing predecessors by emphasising his continuity with the Roman tradition, presenting himself, like Herodotus, Ctesias and others, as a Greek writing of foreign lands and basing his work on that land's native records.[144]

But he does not leave it there. He then takes a bolder step by asserting that his work, despite its sources and its 'local' appearance, is not to be taken as an *Atthis*, as nothing more than a bare chronicle, but rather

---

[139] D. Hal. *A. R.* 1.1.1.   [140] See above, pp. 234f.
[141] With Dionysius' phrase οἷς εἰς ὁμιλίαν ἦλθον (1.7.3), cf. Hdt. II.3.1: ἐλθὼν ἐς λόγους τοῖσι ἱρεῦσι.
[142] D. Hal. *A. R.* 1.7.3. The Fabius Maximus is Q. Fabius Maximus Servilianus, *cos.* 142 (Peter, *HRR* I.CLXXVII–VIII).
[143] Unlike Diodorus, Dionysius thus claims a specifically artistic achievement; note 1.7.3: ἀπ' ἐκείνων ὁρμώμενος τῶν πραγματειῶν (εἰσὶ δὲ ταῖς Ἑλληνικαῖς χρονογραφίαις ἐοικυῖαι), and cf. *Thuc.* 23 where these 'early' (for so Dionysius thought them) horographers are described as simple and lacking adornment. Not coincidentally it was Herodotus, says Dionysius, who gave artistic shape and adornment to what had been bare annals.
[144] On this motif, see above, pp. 107f.

as a fully fashioned history, one that will appeal, Dionysius says, to every type of historical reader, whether he be the one interested in political events, or is of a philosophic nature, or is simply one who enjoys reading history.[145] Since this is exactly the audience Dionysius envisions in his work *On the Ancient Orators*, it is clear that he sees his history as of a piece with his works of criticism, which in turn is closely allied with the Isocratean model of political and moral instruction.[146] Dionysius is thus laying claim to a grand Greek tradition, continuing the work of such masters as Herodotus[147] while at the same time using the example of Rome – a thing that truly had never been done before – in a thoroughly Greek way, aiming at a Greek audience, and addressing himself to peculiarly Greek issues and concerns. In keeping with the spirit of Dionysius' age, it is a classicising work, and seen in this light Dionysius' choice of the Greek writers whom he will supersede takes on an added meaning, for all of them are Hellenistic historians, writing in a style that Dionysius found repellent.[148] It may therefore be suggested that an additional line of contrast and continuity is to be seen in Dionysius' rejection of the Hellenistic aesthetic and his return to the proper models for historiography. In language, in subject matter, in attitude, and in method Dionysius' work bypasses an entire era of history writers and reconnects with the 'true' classical eloquence.

In the Roman tradition, it is difficult to trace strategies of continuity and contrast before Sallust. Cato, it has long been noted, opened his *Origins* with an echo of Xenophon's *Symposium*,[149] and although the reference is not accidental, whether it was meant to indicate any affiliation cannot be

---

[145] D. Hal. *A. R.* 1.8.3, and above, pp. 29f. [146] Gabba, *Dionysius* 79–80.

[147] In treating the most ancient myths, 'those which all historians before me have left aside, because they are difficult to find out without great application' (1.8.1, cf. above, pp. 121f.), Dionysius rescues from oblivion the early deeds of the Romans, and he is thus Herodotean investigator and bestower of glory: for idealising historiography see Fox, *JRS* 83 (1993) 31–2. It is clear too that Dionysius' choice of his 'noble' theme is modelled on Herodotus'; cf. *Pomp.* 3 (11.372 Usher): 'The first and practically the most necessary thing for all who write history is to select a subject noble and pleasing to readers.'

[148] Hieronymus and Polybius are also criticised in *On Literary Composition* (*Comp. Verb.* 4 (11.42 Usher)), because they neglected arrangement and were unconcerned with the beauty of language.

[149] Cato, *HRR* F 2 with Xen. *Symp.* 1.1.

determined.¹⁵⁰ Sempronius Asellio, in remarks we mentioned above, allied himself both with Cato's *Origins* and with Polybius' *Histories*,¹⁵¹ but it is difficult to say anything of the other early historians. The preface of Sallust's *Histories*, however, even in its fragmentary form, demonstrates well how a narrator might place himself within the tradition of his predecessors. Here Sallust refers to 'the abundance of most learned men' in whose company he now finds himself.¹⁵² He discussed his predecessors by name, singling out something valuable in each: Cato was praised for his brevity, Fannius for truth (1.4). He mentioned his immediate predecessor Sisenna,¹⁵³ perhaps reiterating what he had said in the *Jugurtha* about him, that he was praiseworthy in his accuracy but not as truthful towards some as he should have been.¹⁵⁴ If another fragment is rightly interpreted, Sallust may also have said that Cato in his long life composed many false things about good men.¹⁵⁵ This most likely was then followed by Sallust's promise (as in the *Jugurtha* and the *Catiline*) to be impartial (1.6). Sallust here has chosen various aspects of his predecessors to praise or criticise, and by so moving among them, sought to construct his own position in the tradition: he allied himself with Cato's style and brevity, with Sisenna's diligence and accuracy, and with Fannius' impartiality; and he distanced himself from Cato's rancorous use of history and from Sisenna's failure to speak as freely as the historian ought. By using his predecessors in this way, Sallust laid claim to several historiographic traditions, showing both continuity with his predecessors and contrast with their shortcomings.¹⁵⁶

---

[150] See Schröder, *Das erste Buch* 53–4; Cato's familiarity with Xenophon (cf. Cic. *Sen.* 59) makes it unlikely that this was accidental: Münscher, *Xenophon in der griechisch-römischen Literatur* 70–5. For Cato's Hellenism, see Gruen, *Culture and National Identity* 52–83.   [151] Above, n. 104.

[152] Sall. *Hist.* 1.3 'nos in tanta doctissimorum hominum copia', the model for Livy, below, n. 157.

[153] Assuming that it is he who is referred to as having 'recently written' (1.2): see Maurenbrecher ad loc.   [154] Sall. *Jug.* 95.3: 'parum ... libero ore'.

[155] Sall. *Hist.* 1.5: 'in quis longissimo aeuo plura de bonis falsa in deterius composuit', with Maurenbrecher's commentary. McGushin, *Sallust: Histories* II.55 relegates this to the fragments of uncertain reference and denies that it refers to Cato; see his survey of other possible candidates (217–18).

[156] A possible imitation of Sallust's procedure might be found in the early imperial historian Servilius Nonianus, who compared Sallust and Livy, saying that they 'were equal rather than similar' (*HRR* F 1). A. Klotz, *RE* II. A. 2 (1923) 1802 remarked, 'offenbar aus der Einleitung', but Syme, *Ten Studies in Tacitus* 102 is more cautious ('it might be a *dictum* only of the orator').

Although Livy's preface is heavily influenced by Sallust, no predecessors are named. He does, like Sallust, mention the vast crowd of writers on Roman history, but envisions the possibility of failing even to make the grade.[157] Though rare in an historian, this is standard rhetorical technique, the disavowal of ability and the diminution of expectations. The narrator presents himself as content even to be on the field with such great competitors. There is perhaps too not a little of that same irony with which the best speakers begin their speeches.[158] The real substance of Livy's self-definition comes in the remarks about his predecessors throughout his history. Although he gives a wealth of variant versions, frequently citing his predecessors by name, the two characteristics that stand out are a reliance on the earliest historians where possible, and a rejection of the invention and exaggeration of the later Annalists, especially those of the generation immediately preceding his. No doubt these latter were the ones whom he expected to replace, and his criticism of them is therefore more common and more wide-ranging. Like Dionysius, he surveys early history, and constantly reminds his audience of his own role in the reconstruction of the tradition. Although not in full-scale polemic, Livy nevertheless highlights his own virtues by criticism of the failings of others: Antias dares (*audet*) to give casualty numbers for the Romans in a battle in 464 BC; Piso omitted two sets of consuls either because he forgot or deliberately; Antias is again cited for exaggerations in his account of Hannibal's battle around Croton in 203; Coelius gives a complete exaggeration of Roman forces brought to Africa in 204; Antias is exposed as unreliable in comparison to Polybius, and elsewhere chastised for not having read Cato.[159] Although most Greek and Latin authors portrayed Scipio's voyage to Africa as unproblematic, Coelius Antipater gave a dramatic account with storms and shipwrecks; Antias gives the consul Villius in 199 a series of distinguished exploits, while all other writers say he did

---

[157] Livy, *praef*. 2-3: 'and if in so vast a crowd of writers (*in tanta scriptorum turba*) my own reputation should be obscure, I would console myself with the nobility and the greatness of those who will overshadow my name.' Moles, *PCPhS* 39 (1993) 145 notes the irony of Livy referring to his upper-class predecessors as a *turba*. Cf. above, pp. 140f.

[158] See Ch. IV n. 10. Livy had not yet made his mark on history (one assumes he had in oratory); once he did, he abandoned the pose: see F 58, quoted at Ch. I n. 95.

[159] Livy, III.5.12; IX.44.4; XXX.19.11; XXIX.25.3-4; XXXIII.10.8-10 (cf. XXXVI.19.11-12); XXXIX.43.1.

nothing of note;[160] Licinius Macer's praise of his own family makes his history unreliable; so too Cato's desire in his *Origins* always to emphasise himself means that the historian must be on guard.[161]

Livy portrays himself as hearkening back to an earlier tradition in his reliance on *ueteres auctores*, and, like Herodotus, who was at a loss where oral tradition was absent, so too Livy: the ancient authors do not give Lucretius as consul with Brutus and so Livy suggests 'nulla gesta res'; authors do not relate which consul was wounded in the attempt to capture Pometia in 502, so Livy will not either; nor will he assert as fact the revolt of the Antiates in 459 and Lucius Cornelius' supposed capture, although he finds it 'in a good many authors', because the 'writers of old' do not mention it. He can find, he says, no ancient authority for the manpower of the Volsci and Aequi; in another passage he will not interject his own opinion, since a source does not say it; and Livy rejects the story of the capture of Scipio's son that Antias had reported, because no other author gives it.[162] The purpose of these remarks is clear. Livy wants his readers to know that he is fully aware of the exaggerations and inventions of his predecessors, and so he seeks to distance himself from them by relying on the older authors who were eyewitnesses, and by showing himself aware of the way that actions become exaggerated over time.[163] Livy chooses suitable occasions to remind his readers that he is not involved in the wholesale invention of Roman history. This gravitation towards older and therefore reliable historians provides continuity with earlier masters, while the contrast – the uniqueness – is the care with which Livy has exceeded earlier authors, who (unlike him) exaggerated, invented, or displayed inadmissible bias.[164] It is not by chance that Livy's greatest criticisms are reserved for the historians of the previous generation,[165] while he allies himself with the older and more established historians from the past. His work is to be seen both in the tradition of continuity (with that earlier reliable tradition) and contrast (with his immediate predecessors). His work is also the culmination of that tradition because he subsumes and replaces the very historians on whom he based his own work. As with Diodorus, the one who comes last has the best position.

---

[160] Livy, XXIX.27.13–15; XXXII.6.5–8.
[161] Livy, VII.9.3–5 (cf. VIII.40.3–4); XXXIV.15.9.
[162] Livy, II.8.5; 17.3; III.23.7; VI.12.2–3; XXIX.14.9; XXXVII.48.1–7.
[163] Livy makes this explicit at XXII.7.4; cf. VIII.40.5; see also above, pp. 93f.
[164] On the importance of older authors see App. IV §1.
[165] The writer most frequently mentioned and criticised is Livy's immediate predecessor Valerius Antias; for the passages see Steele, *AJP* 25 (1904) 29–30.

Similar strategies of contrast and continuity are employed by Tacitus. In both the *Histories* and the *Annals*, he defines himself by remarks on his immediate and earlier predecessors. In the preface of the *Histories* (1.1.1) Tacitus explains his decision to begin in AD 69 by claiming that before this, Roman history was well treated. The earlier historians are here distinguished by their 'equal eloquence and freedom' (*pari eloquentia ac libertate*), whereas the latter generation is marked out by ignorance of statecraft, servility, and malice. The process of decline is seen as gradual (*primum ... mox*), justifying the author's decision to begin some years after Actium (ibid.). Similarly, in the preface of the *Annals*, there is a contrast between recent historians and those of the past. Here the decline of truthfulness in historiography is put earlier: although the deeds of the Roman people of old were commemorated by *clari scriptores*, and the age of Augustus did not lack its *decora ingenia*, nevertheless adulation (again) deterred them.[166] Already by Tiberius' time, fear or hatred were dominant.[167] Tacitus' affiliations are again made clear by the contrast between the great historians of the Republic, undeterred by fear or favour, and the more recent historians, not only inexperienced but partial and unreliable. Like Livy and unlike Sallust, Tacitus does not specify individuals in his preface, and he is concerned only to sketch in broad strokes what will eventually be filled out within the narrative.[168]

Tacitus' citation of predecessors by name is rare: in the *Histories* he names Vipstanus Messala as the source for an incident in which a son killed his father, and the same historian with Pliny the Elder for a detail in the siege of Cremona.[169] While not citing Cluvius Rufus as a source, he stigmatises his predecessor in the first book as eloquent and distinguished in peacetime, but unskilled in war; elsewhere, anonymous writers on the civil wars of AD 68–9 are criticised for their bias, and Tacitus gives an interpretation at odds with their favourable treatment.[170] Given the fragmentary state of the *Histories*, it is difficult to say whether such scant notices were usual throughout the book, or whether

---

[166] *Ann.* I.1.1–2.

[167] The discrepancy in the two prefaces about when exactly imperial historiography ceased to be reliable has occasioned much discussion: see Chilver, *Historical Commentary on Tacitus' Histories* 1.33–5 for a survey of opinions.

[168] Despite the anonymity, Tacitus constructed the preface of the *Histories* closely following Sallust's *Histories*: see Flach, *Philologus* 117 (1973) 76–86.

[169] Tac. *Hist.* III.25.2; 28.

[170] *Hist.* I.8.1 (Cluvius Rufus); II.100.2–101.1. There is also passing criticism of Greek writers at II.4.1.

the more common citation of anonymous authors was the rule.[171] In the *Annals* Pliny the Elder is criticised once openly, once tacitly,[172] while Tacitus reserves praise for Sallust and Servilius Nonianus.[173]

The most striking attitude displayed towards a predecessor, however, comes in Tacitus' portrayal of Cremutius Cordus, the historian of the republican civil wars and of Augustus, who is shown as an historical actor defending his work before the Senate. This presentation occurs immediately after the narrator's explicit comparison of his theme with those of his great republican predecessors, and so must be seen as closely related to it.[174] Tacitus claims that he cannot match them in subject, for they had enormous wars and great domestic political conflicts as their subjects; the imperial historian, by contrast, has only a gloomy catalogue of treason trials and deaths. The author seems to despair of true emulation with those earlier writers. Yet clearly this is emulation and a covert challenge to his predecessors: the lack of 'suitable' material makes Tacitus' task a *greater* challenge, and his achievement – a worthwhile history that will win for its subjects and its author immortality – is all the more admirable because achieved with a dearth of what was traditionally ennobling material. So the author equals, and in some ways exceeds, his predecessors.

It is with this background that Tacitus gives the speech of Cremutius. Tacitus was not the first to give in a history the speech of a fellow historian: Sallust had already done that in his *Histories* where the historian Licinius Macer, as tribune of the plebs in 73 BC, addresses the plebeian assembly.[175] As that earlier historian had called the plebs to *libertas*, so Cremutius' speech is a call to the Senate and a ringing defence of the historian's *libertas*.[176] The speech is not least notable for

---

[171] See R. H. Martin, *Tacitus* 190ff. Develin, *Antichthon* 17 (1983) 69ff. sees manipulation in nearly all of Tacitus' source citations.

[172] *Ann.* XIII.31.1 (with Koestermann, *Annalen* III.294); XV.53.3-4. Pliny is cited without comment or criticism at I.69.2 and XIII.20.2.

[173] Sallust is explicitly praised as an historian, *Ann.* III.30. 2 ('C. Sallustius, rerum Romanarum florentissimus auctor'); Servilius is praised in his obituary at XIV.19, where his historical works are mentioned; cf. Syme, *Ten Studies in Tacitus* 89, 101–2.

[174] *Ann.* IV.32.1–33.4. See Suerbaum, in *Politik und Literarische Kunst im Werk des Tacitus* 61–99 on the relationship between Cordus' speech and the historiographical remarks of the narrator that precede it.   [175] Sall. *Hist.* III.48.

[176] See Cancik-Lindemaier and Cancik, *AU* 29. 4 (1986) 16–35 on Cordus' speech as a defence of *libertas*.

Cremutius' invocation of earlier historians and the virtues for which they were praised. Livy is lauded for his impartiality, and Asinius Pollio and Messala Corvinus for their free speech and independence.[177] The line of predecessors in which Cremutius places himself can be seen as Tacitus' own attempt to be seen, via this character, as the continuator of that same line. The historian's trial is the manifestation of the danger that Tacitus himself had articulated when he said that an imperial historian must be careful because some will presume themselves portrayed when another's vice is depicted (*Ann.* IV.33.4). Yet the faith in the historian's task and ultimate success is emphasised in Tacitus' comments in his own person at the end of the speech, where he derides the foolishness of those who believe they can eliminate from the future the memory of their deeds; instead, these rulers bring dishonour to themselves and glory to the historians.[178]

It is to this tradition of free speech and incorruptibility that Tacitus is seeking to ally his work. It is a reinforcement of what he had portrayed in the prefaces, although there it had been done by denigrating his predecessors, even though it is clear that he (like Livy) used the very people he criticised.[179] It is not a matter of Tacitus being unjust to his predecessors.[180] Indeed, we note how briefly and how anonymously in each preface he treats the writers guilty of adulation or hatred. He could have followed the model of Sallust's *Histories* and named his predecessors, but he did not. For whatever reasons, he prefers the anonymity already seen in Livy's preface. If it is correct that Tacitus was going to use his predecessors for the most part, he may have had no wish to denigrate them or the substance of their work. Yet his concern is not truly with these immediate predecessors. The preface is an attempt to align himself with the great line of republican historians: thus he mentions in each preface the *magna ingenia* or the *clari scriptores* who once flourished at Rome, precisely in order to suggest that he himself, under different circumstances, and maybe against greater odds, will now continue that tradition. The prefaces highlight contrast with immediate predecessors, and more importantly a 'new' continuity with the great models of republican historiography. Tacitus' eyes are

---

[177] *Ann.* IV.34.3-4.   [178] *Ann.* IV.35.5.
[179] On Tacitus' sources, see Klingner, *Römische Geisteswelt* 483-503; Syme, *Tacitus* I.171-90; 271-303; id., *RP* III.1014-42; Wilkes, *CW* 65 (1971/2) 177-203; Goodyear, *Annals of Tacitus* I.25-8; Martin, op. cit. (n. 171) 189-213.
[180] As Leeman, in *Form und Sinn* 337, suggests.

not on Cluvius Rufus or Pliny the Elder or Fabius Rusticus: they are on Livy[181] and Pollio, and beyond them on Sallust all the way back to Cato.[182]

In Arrian's *Anabasis* we have one of the most sophisticated attempts at self-definition by continuity and contrast. Arrian allies himself immediately with Ptolemy and Aristobulus, laying claim to the first generation of Alexander historians and skipping over nearly all who had written of Alexander since.[183] Just as Livy and Tacitus had allied themselves with older writers, passing over their more recent predecessors, so Arrian hearkens back to the reliable contemporaries of Alexander. He then recalls Herodotus and Thucydides by inserting an extended preface designed to show his method.[184] When Alexander is at Troy, Arrian in a 'second preface', a masterpiece of self-definition,[185] echoes Herodotus and Thucydides,[186] and both emulates and vies with Xenophon: the emulation is in the choice of title – *Anabasis* – while the competition is in the comparison of his own subject with what Xenophon had chosen.[187] He bests Theopompus, who had claimed that 'Europe had never before produced a man like Philip' by saying that 'no other man has revealed so many or such great deeds in number or magnitude' as Alexander.[188] And like Theopompus, he asserts his primacy in the area of Greek literature: as Theopompus had said that he held first place in learning and culture, so Arrian states, 'I do not deem myself unworthy of the first place in

[181] It is fairly certain that Tacitus included Livy among 'republican' historians: so Goodyear, *Annals of Tacitus* 1.95, 96 n. 2; cf. Norden, *Ant. Kunstprosa* 1.234-7. But he is also the first of imperial historians, as Woodman, *VP* 1.37-40 points out.

[182] In the same way, Tacitus in the preface of the *Agricola* (1.1-4, quoted above, p. 178) hearkened back to Cato and the Republic, when praise of great men was permitted and freely encouraged.

[183] Arr. *Anab. praef.* 1; on the close identification of his work with Ptolemy's and Aristobulus' names see below, p. 275.   [184] Stadter, *ICS* 6 (1981) 157-71.

[185] For all aspects of this preface see Moles, *JHS* 105 (1985) 162-8; there are some supplementary observations in Marincola, *JHS* 109 (1989) 186-9 and Gray, *JHS* 110 (1990) 180-6.   [186] Moles, op. cit. (n.185) 163.

[187] Arr. *Anab.* 1.12.3, where Xenophon is twice named.

[188] Theopompus, *FGrHist* 115 F 27 ~ Arr. *Anab.* 1.12.4, with Marincola, op. cit. (n.185) 186; denied by Gray, op. cit. (n.185) 181 n. 6, who thinks that Theopompus' self-display would have been 'anathema' to Arrian; but the verbal echo is fairly strong, and Arrian's refusal to name himself, and his claim of first place in Greek letters (next note), argue that Theopompus is very much on his mind. Cf. Bosworth, *ANRW* II. 34. 1, 233 n. 40; id., *HCA* II.75.

Greek speech'.[189] In doing this, Arrian is promising at long last a literary achievement commensurate with that of Alexander's deeds. Ptolemy and Aristobulus, it must be assumed, will provide the base for this treatment, and in this respect Arrian seems to be reaching back beyond the 'inferior' treatments of Alexander by a later generation of historians to the more trustworthy eyewitnesses of the king's expedition.[190] Naturally, he wants his achievement to be seen in broad terms, both more accurate and more magnificent, and his two-fold approach allies him with reliable witnesses on the one hand, while on the other hand applying to his theme the manner of the masters – 'how Thucydides would have done it', precisely as Longinus had directed.[191]

The loss of Ammianus' preface, where an historian's relationship to his predecessors was usually most fully treated, has deprived us of the ability to see how he there presented himself. We may presume that he made his affinities clear, perhaps even naming predecessors whom he would emulate, and calling attention to the lack of a suitable history in Latin after the year AD 96, where Tacitus' *Histories* had ended.[192] He would be, in that sense, a 'continuator' of Tacitus; as we have seen above, however, this did not mean that his history need be similar to that of his predecessor: it meant that he wished to be seen as the practitioner of a serious history that had been practised long ago, and had by his time fallen (at least in Latin) into desuetude.[193] A 'link' with Tacitus in no way implies the same sort of history that Tacitus wrote,[194] and Ammianus' work is far differently oriented, not to say anything of the enormous changes that had taken place in the Roman world in the two centuries since Tacitus had written; in any case, the decision to join his work to that of Tacitus cannot have been a primary intention of

---

[189] Theopompus, *FGrHist* 115 F 25 (καὶ τούτους ἅμα αὐτῷ τὰ πρωτεῖα τῆς ἐν λόγοις παιδείας ἔχειν ἐν τοῖς "Ελλησιν) ~ Arr. *Anab*. 1.12.5 (οὐκ ἀπαξιῶ ἐμαυτὸν τῶν πρώτων ἐν τῇ φωνῇ τῇ Ἑλλάδι).

[190] Arr. *Anab. praef*. 2. By separating his source citations from his own claims of uniqueness, Arrian has avoided criticising Ptolemy and Aristobulus directly for stylistic shortcomings.

[191] Arrian in his other works presents himself similarly as the culmination of a tradition: see Marincola, op. cit. (n.185) 187 n. 20. For Longinus, above n. 105.

[192] Amm. xxxi.16.9: 'a principatu Caesaris Nervae exorsus'.

[193] See, for example, xxvi.1.1-2; xxviii.4.14; and on corrupt morals in general, xxviii.4.6-34.

[194] Tacitean influences on Ammianus are hardly to be found; see Matthews, *Roman Empire of Ammianus* 482-3 n. 45 (with the relevant bibliography cited); see also Sabbah, *La Méthode d'Ammien Marcellin* 101-11.

Ammianus' at the start, but only something done after he had begun his work.[195]

It is possible, nonetheless, to see Ammianus ally himself and vie with certain of his predecessors. As a Greek writing in Latin, he is heir to two traditions, and he calls forth models from both. In his description of Gaul he says that he will follow Timagenes, 'a Greek both in learning and language', a claim which is clearly meant to ally him with the Greek tradition of inquiry.[196] It is also possible that by invoking a man who was an outspoken critic of the powerful, Ammianus was laying claim to the historian's traditional freedom of speech.[197] Ammianus also cites Thucydides twice, calling him 'most distinguished';[198] Sallust is cited for a detail in the description of Gaul, and it seems clear that in language and outlook he was the premier Latin model for Ammianus.[199]

There is contrast as well: Ammianus clearly sets himself apart from those historians whom fear or niggling criticisms prevented from publishing their histories within their lifetime; by contrast Ammianus will not hesitate to speak the truth, nor fail through fear to place his work before the public and, so to speak, enter the arena where he will be judged.[200] Nor does he fear competition and rivalry with earlier historians: although Herodotus is cited on the building of the pyramids, another remark suggests a distancing from the earlier author. Ammianus, in describing his observation from a high position (as a spy) of the Persian king Sapor and attendant kings, with other leaders and all their innumerable soldiers filling the plains, asks how long 'storied Greece' (*Graecia fabulosa*) will continue to tell of the troops drawn up in Doriscus, a clear reference to Herodotus' story that Xerxes there numbered his millions of men.[201] A contrast is made between the

---

[195] The career of Julian must have been the spur to Ammianus' history: see Matthews, in *History and Historians in Late Antiquity* 30–41.

[196] Amm. xv.9.2 ('Timagenes, et diligentia Graecus et lingua'); see Sabbah, op. cit. (n.194) 27–9; Matthews, op. cit. (n.194) 464; id. in *History and Historians in Late Antiquity* 30–41, esp. 30–3.

[197] For Timagenes' outspokenness see Bowersock, *Augustus* 109–10; 125–6; Sordi, *ANRW* II. 30. 1, 795–6; Matthews, op. cit. (n.194) 552 n. 28 rather unfairly emphasises his boorishness, but cf. Bowersock, op. cit. 110.

[198] Amm. xix.4.4; xxiii.6.75 ('auctor amplissimus'); the praise of Timagenes and Thucydides may also be meant to contrast Ammianus' outlook with that of Tacitus who has much negative to say about the Greeks: see Syme, *Tacitus* II.511–19.

[199] Amm. xv.12.6; for Sallust and Ammianus see Matthews, op. cit. (n.194) 32.

[200] For the fear attendant on historians see above, pp. 157f.

[201] Amm. xviii.6.22–3; cf. Hdt. vii.59–60.

exaggerations so often later attributed to Herodotus and the present author's reliance on trustworthy evidence (*fidei testimonia*).[202] Although methodological, the passage also demonstrates emulation and rivalry, comparing Ammianus' own adventures with a canonical event from earlier Greek history.

Historical and historiographical emulation converge in Book XXIV. Here the Roman army is attacking the town of Pirisabora, and Ammianus details Julian's efforts in company with a band of soldiers to break down the walls of the town. Julian, despite heroic efforts, was forced finally to retreat, and was afterwards ashamed, 'because he had read that Scipio Aemilianus, with the historian Polybius and thirty soldiers, had undermined a gate of Carthage by a similar attack' (XXIV.2.16). The mention of the general and the historian is intended by Ammianus to draw attention to the similarity of his own account and participation, and perhaps is meant also as an endorsement of the type of historian desiderated by Polybius, one with both practical experience and a passion for inquiry.[203]

At his conclusion Ammianus identifies himself as 'a former soldier and a Greek',[204] by which he almost certainly is laying claim to the Polybian ideal. As a soldier, one not 'inexpertus belli',[205] he could claim a tradition through Velleius and Caesar among the Romans going all the way back to Xenophon, who had similarly, in the *Anabasis*, detailed his dramatic adventures of escape and battle.[206] And as a Greek, he is

---

[202] Sabbah, op. cit. (n.194) 66-7.
[203] On the similarities of these two incidents see Drexler, *Ammianstudien* 124-31; Sabbah, op. cit. (n.194) 98-9; for Polybius' emphasis on practical experience see above, pp. 71ff.   [204] Amm. XXXI.16.9: 'ut miles quondam et Graecus'.
[205] As Tacitus had said of Cluvius Rufus: see above, n. 170.
[206] Fornara, *Historia* 41 (1992) 329 calls his self-designation as *miles* 'a defining characteristic'; cf. 344; Matthews, op. cit. (n.194) 461 thinks that this is not a boast, noting that the writing of history in Ammianus' time was 'more characteristic of civilian, even aristocratic, pursuits than of the military profession', and noting as well that the soldiers in Ammianus' history are not portrayed with the literary culture and understanding needed for the writing of history. Such a view, however, fails to recognise both the tradition of soldier-historian and the way in which historiographical pronouncements can serve as challenges to the reader, while emphasising the modesty of the writer (important in imperial writers, as Janson, *Latin Prose Prefaces* 145-9 demonstrates). Ammianus' phrase 'pro uirium explicaui mensura' (XXXI.16.9) is no more apology than Livy's 'pro uirili parte' (*praef.* 3, with Moles, *PCPhS* 39 (1993) 146); like the earlier historian (also an outsider) Ammianus by diminution calls attention to what he has, in fact, actually achieved. It is true that, as Matthews points

appealing to the tradition of inquiry and learning[207] that distinguishes his work from its competitors, and (more importantly) that places him in a direct line with history's founders and best practitioners, to whom his work, like that of all the great historians, may be seen as both homage and challenge.[208]

> out (464), *auctoritas* counted more for Roman than Greek historians (see above, p. 130); but the designation of himself as *miles* can be seen as an attempt to ignore that tradition (which some Greek imperial historians had adopted: see above, pp. 144f.) and hearken back to the more purely Greek manner. For important studies of this passage, see the bibliography in Matthews, ibid. 551 n. 23.
>
> [207] This is especially seen in his scientific digressions where much technical material is paraded before the reader: see den Hengst, in *Cognitio Gestorum* 39–46.
>
> [208] Fornara, op. cit. (n.206) 420ff. argues that Ammianus' knowledge of and reference to the Greek historians are not substantial, whereas his imitation of Latin writers is 'deep and purposeful' (438). The most cited Latin author is Cicero, for as with his scientific digressions, so here too Ammianus appeals to the traditions of learning in the widest sense. On the importance of the designation as 'Greek' see Sabbah, op. cit. (n.194) 532–5; Matthews, op. cit. (n.194) 462–4.

Conclusion

Our study has concentrated on the explicit attempts by the ancient historians to convince the reader of their authority to narrate the deeds, and to portray themselves as believable narrators of those deeds. We have seen how the dictates of ancient literary criticism enjoined authors to work within a tradition, and to show their innovation within that tradition. As certain historians became accepted models for imitation, their concerns and approach dictated for those who followed the proper way to write history. As the earlier historians were 'authoritative', so their followers sought to imitate the manner by which those predecessors had constructed their own authority. It was in this way that authority and tradition were closely related, and so long as the belief in imitation held sway, there could be no authority outside of tradition.

In concluding, it may be useful to organise our results according to three categories. In the first we shall summarise our findings by topic, following the order of the chapters in the book. Then we shall compare the procedures of contemporary and non-contemporary historians. Finally, we shall look at some of the differences between Greek and Roman historians.

In presenting his work to the public, the ancient historian portrays it as something of great importance both in the doing and the telling. The contemporary historian, following Thucydides, emphasises that his particular period deserves special notice, because of the greatness of the deeds to be treated: superlatives of size and magnitude abound, and periods are described as overflowing with tumult, sufferings, and wars. Those who write of specific past events will claim that same greatness for their own period. If they have compiled a 'universal' history, whether of the Greek world, the Greco-Roman world, or just the Roman world, they will stress that their work surpasses those of their predecessors because of the number of worthwhile events that it contains. As a part of this presentation, it is not unusual for historians to say something of the way they came to write history. Yet even if they include details of their life, they present their history as motivated for the public good. In a few cases, where the poetic motif of dreams is borrowed, these are presented only as the incentive to write history, not as events that in any way dictated the form or methodology of history. Nor does the historian claim that he has written his history with a better style than his predecessors, since this would diminish the focus from the deeds themselves. This 'public' face that history was expected to wear also militated against the historian presenting his work for personal renown. Although it is clear from remarks made by ancient writers that glory and fame were expected and accepted motivations for writing history, the historian is careful within the history itself not to present his work as motivated by a desire for fame. Even Livy, who presents a personal side more than any other historian, promotes the public utility of the history before the reader. In this area, then, the historian's authority rested on presenting himself as having begun and intended his work in a public spirit.

Assertions of inquiry are one of the fundamental ways in which historians claim the authority to narrate deeds. The work is presented to the reader as the outcome of an examination of contemporaries or earlier authorities, who themselves are presented as eyewitnesses, or those who learned of events from eyewitnesses. The historian's faith in eyes and ears is rarely questioned, although after Polybius these sensory organs are expected to be used by one who is 'experienced', that is, a man of public affairs. The historian will usually emphasise his inquiry at the outset in the preface, and only rarely thereafter call attention to it. Explicit claims of inquiry and autopsy are employed as validation within the narrative itself only to vouch for marvels, unusual events, or high numbers, or to refute earlier or contemporary historians.

In a free society, remarks about the author's inquiry of participants usually served by themselves to guarantee the author's reliability. It might be necessary, however, especially in societies ruled autocratically, for the historian to locate himself close to the centre of power, although such a procedure ran the risk of impairing the audience's faith in his impartiality. A different approach was to write, according to one's limited perspective, the events about which one had certainty – whether this was a soldier's account of his campaigns or a Senator's 'memoirs' – and thereby avoid the need to narrate exclusively the political actions of kings or emperors. Where one confronted the actions at court directly, the use of rumour and report became almost an essential element in one's narration. Theopompus first seems to have exploited a contrast between surface and reality, and this attitude proved especially congenial for one attempting to 'get at' the truth beneath the façade: it was in its own way the historian's reaction to the more circumscribed field of inquiry in an autocracy.

Inquiry by itself, however, seems to have been insufficient for establishing the historian's authority. It was necessary to demonstrate as well that the historian had the proper character for his work. This could, of course, be conveyed simply by the manner of his narration. Yet most of the historians detailed their character for the reader, and did not leave the audience to infer it for themselves. The historian took care to demonstrate that he had the proper experience of men and affairs by sometimes detailing his political career. In Polybius, experience is elevated to an equal footing with inquiry, and both are portrayed as essential for the historian. For certain historians, their experience translates into an assertion of social status, by the mention of offices held. No less important than experience was the care that an historian gave to his work. Protestations of effort are very common, especially (as is to be expected) among the writers of large-scale works, such as universal histories. Some portray their efforts as the physical exertions of travel and inquiry. Others emphasise the reading and writing that went into the work, sometimes giving the exact number of years, so that the reader can be assured of the historian's seriousness of purpose, and of his belief that history is not a pastime but a task that requires many years of commitment. The assertion of care may also suggest the proper attention to literary effort, but this is not stated explicitly, since historians do not as a rule refer to this aspect of their work. Finally, and most importantly, the historian avers his impartiality. Prejudice, even more than faulty or inferior inquiry, was seen as the great enemy of truth in history, and so historians spend a great deal of effort trying to convince the reader that they have written without fear or favour. For the most part, they attempt to practise a narrative impartiality like that of Homer, but in some ways they are even more cautious. When praising, more so than when condemning, they show some circumspection and announce that their praise is based on proofs, which are then sometimes adduced.

Praise is also a strong concern when the ancient historian writes of his own deeds. Here he confronted the problem of writing an authoritative account of his own actions, and it is clear from a whole host of remarks by the ancients that this type of self-praise had serious drawbacks, and was, on the whole, less persuasive than praise from another. Xenophon solved the problem by using a pseudonym, which made the praises of 'Xenophon' in the *Anabasis* seem to be those of another. This was not, however, a widespread procedure. If he presented his deeds in a memoir (*commentarii* or ὑπομνήματα), it was expected that the writer himself was the focal point, and deeds were related in so far as they affected his own actions. If he was a participant in a larger history, however, the placing of himself front and centre might provoke the wary eye of an ancient reader, who seems to have been at all times very sensitive to the issue of self-praise. Ctesias and Cato, for example, are both censured for using every opportunity to put themselves in their histories. Nevertheless, whether in a memoir or a history, the writer used a series of techniques designed to lessen the dangers of self-praise, and he took care not to place too much emphasis on himself, or in any case not to do so directly.

Finally, the historian was aware that he was a practitioner in a genre with a tradition, and that he and his work must 'compete' against the works of contemporaries and predecessors. The prospect of successfully entering the hallowed ranks of the masters was seen differently at different times, but every historian was conscious that his readers would evaluate him by the standards of those commonly judged to be the best. In seeking to win a place for himself in the tradition, the historian frequently attempted to present himself as unique in some way, whether in his qualifications, his era, or his theme. He would, moreover, try to remove some authority from his predecessors by engaging in overt or subtle polemic with them. Excessive polemic ran the risk of branding the historian as bitter or malicious, but moderate polemic was seen as an effective tool for teaching and demonstration. If the historian pointed out how not to do something, readers could assume that he knew the proper way of doing it. Just as rhetoric was portrayed as a competition, so the writing of history also had winners and losers, and it was just as effective for your opponent – be he a predecessor or contemporary – to lose as it was for you to win. Yet it would be wrong to suggest that only polemic defines the place of the historian, for we see in many of them an explicit attempt to link their work to that of a respected predecessor. In some cases this takes the form of adapting previous ways of dealing with a subject to one's own work; in other cases, an historian presents himself as a follower of the best characteristics of those who have gone before;

sometimes he will suggest that his work is a culmination of a tradition; or, in a very common construction, he will portray his work as a rejection of a later tradition that has grown up around his subject, and as a link with an earlier and more reliable tradition. By the citation of various authors at occasional points in the narrative, he may indicate in which tradition he wishes to be seen and which he seeks to avoid. However he does this, he will try, above all, to make his work seem both homage and challenge to his predecessors, as both traditional and authoritative.

Although contemporary and non-contemporary historians frequently avail themselves of the same conventions, there are enough differences to make summation worthwhile. The first is in presentation of the work. Contemporary historians, as we mentioned above, emphasise the unique greatness of 'their' events. Non-contemporary historians may also do this (witness Sallust in the *Jugurtha* or Arrian in the *Anabasis*), but they are far more likely to assume the greatness of the events, and to present their work instead as in some way an improvement upon the record, whether this be by a more detailed, more accurate, fuller, or more impartial account. Authors of large-scale non-contemporary histories emphasise the greater number of deeds that their works contain and the consequently greater use that they will have. At certain points in the narrative, they will particularly emphasise one or another event, but the 'greatness' of their history is to be seen in its comprehensiveness.

A fundamental difference between contemporary and non-contemporary historians is not so much in their attitudes towards inquiry as in their presentation of it. As a rule, the contemporary historian avers his autopsy and inquiry at the outset of the work, and thereafter only very infrequently calls attention to it. In addition, his work has few variant versions in it. The whole is marked by a type of narrative assuredness: he presents himself as the establisher of the tradition, and is not in the main concerned to justify that account at every turn. On the other hand, the non-contemporary historian must portray himself as conversant with the entire relevant tradition. He is not in any way expected to go back and re-inquire into the events which he has chosen to narrate, but it was assumed that he would compare the accounts of his predecessors. This comparison might result in choices by the historian – attempts, for example, to weed out prejudice – but for many historians the mere recording of differences, without any attempt to decide them, was deemed sufficient. The historian was not expected in general to solve problems but rather only to note them. As opposed to the assured narrative of the contemporary historian, the non-contemporary historian, following in the tradition of Herodotus, portrays himself within the narrative as organiser and sifter, if not solver, of the tradition. He is far more likely to intrude into the narrative, and to place before his audience the difficulties of the tradition. Where he does choose, he can indicate something of his own knowledge and character. Not surprisingly, the choices, when they are made, follow rhetorical teaching, and can be reduced to a handful of conventions, despite the enormous number of variant versions recorded by ancient historians. The non-contemporary historian faced additional challenges, since his work might bring him into the realm of 'the mythical', a term that comprehends impossibilities, tall tales, and even stories magnified to suit an individual. Naturally, he 'rejected' myth, but his rejection consisted mostly of adopting a guarded narrative manner (fenced about with 'they say' or 'it is recorded') or of employing mild rationalisations when improbable stories were treated. He would thus not really reject myth so much as make it more presentable by giving it the proper look in a history.

As for issues of character, these are mostly the same for both types of writers, except that impartiality has a much greater place among contemporary historians. The reasons for being partial, as the ancients saw it, were expectations of rewards or attempts at revenge against those who had injured one. This was clearly more of a danger when one treated one's own time, for here the temptation to right wrongs would have been stronger. There was less chance that one turned to non-contemporary history out of partiality, and thus it was not as important to assert one's freedom from bias in narrating it. One might, however, even when writing about a monarch of long ago, still need to declare that one was impartial, since bias both for and against tended to be especially prevalent around autocrats. Moreover, there seems to be a trend as time goes on, since under the Empire historians now aver impartiality even for a non-contemporary history.

The attitude to predecessors will be different for a contemporary and a non-contemporary historian. In an important way, all historians had predecessors, since, as we mentioned above, one approached one's task with a consciousness of the tradition and those who were considered its masters. A contemporary historian, in making Thucydidean claims for his subject, was clearly asking to be seen in the light of his predecessor. But in a more practical sense, it is the non-contemporary historian who must place his work amidst all the other works that already exist on that topic. The production of another work on the same topic was itself a comment on previous treatments, suggesting that they were somehow inferior. If the author wrote on a much-treated topic, the challenge was all the greater. Nevertheless, the historian, as his audience would know, was basing his work, however 'improved', on those of his predecessors, and so he could not entirely destroy their authority. He must, rather, suggest an improvement in this or that area: he will present himself as more skilled, more experienced, less partial, and so forth. He does this, as a rule, at individual points in the narrative, sometimes naming his predecessors, sometimes merely referring anonymously to 'earlier writers'. The use of a name is less important than the suggestion of improvement. For it is in the tension between continuity and contrast that a non-contemporary historian must assert his authority: his predecessors do not need to be discounted so much as made to disappear.

Finally, a few words about the differences between Greek and Latin historiography. As has been clear, I hope, from this work, there are advantages to studying the traditions together. In certain matters, such as the presentation of their work or in their attitudes towards myth, they are clearly working in the same tradition. Nonetheless, there are some prominent differences in the way the historians in each tradition assert their authority.

First and foremost is in their narrative presence. As a rule, Roman historians are more reluctant to give details of themselves and to discourse on methodological problems within the text of their works, but this is not to say that they do not have the same concerns as the Greek historians. Rather, they reveal them in a different way, at occasional points in the narrative and often without calling attention to them. Our discussion of inquiry, for example, can use numerous explicit remarks by the Greek historians about the investigatory aspect of history. For the Romans, however, we must look at what they say impersonally throughout the text of their work, when they are looking at individual incidents or problems. Not surprisingly, this has led some to think that the Romans had no concern with inquiry, but it is rather the case that the Roman tradition, for whatever reason, did not parade the author's inquiry as an explicit element for winning credibility. The manner of conveying one's knowledge of the problems inherent in inquiry was to indicate it gradually throughout the work, in ways that would then be picked up by the audience.

Another difference is that whereas the Greek historians assert experience, the Roman historians tend to see that experience more specifically in terms of offices held or services to the state. It may be that since men of affairs first wrote history in Rome, it was only natural to emphasise one's public service. Certainly Cato will have been instrumental among the Romans in constructing an acceptable framework for winning authority, and he spoke in his *Origins* of his history as a work of his retirement. Sallust had to re-orient the focus, and to portray history as a suitable alternative to a public career, but even he was careful to make mention of his offices. Later on, it is possible to see Greeks of the Empire following the Roman lead, and speaking not of experience but of offices held. The mention of these, however, is largely ornamental, with no or little relevance for the composition of the history itself, and this seems to be a rare co-optation by the Greeks of a Roman convention.

Despite the opinion sometimes offered that the Greeks and the Romans had different levels of tolerance for self-praise, and consequently different views on the presentation of oneself in a history, our survey has found a remarkable uniformity in the tradition, and a concern among both Greeks and Romans with making an account of one's own deeds persuasive and authoritative. It is true that the memoir was more common among the Romans than among the Greeks, but so far as we can tell from the fragmentary remains of the tradition, it was not unusual for memoirs to be presented as finished pieces, and to be judged by the standards of large-scale history. Moreover, our examination of some techniques for mitigating the effects of self-praise have shown that they operate as much in a large-scale history as in a *commentarius*. We thus have no reason to think that self-praise was more tolerated in a memoir than in a history; what seems to have been tolerated and expected was that the focus would be on the individual. But this did not free him from the examining eyes of those who would look for evidence of bias in the treatment of his own deeds.

Both Greek and Roman historians indulge in polemic, but their approaches and methods are quite different. The Greeks are fond of extended polemic, individual passages where they pause from their narrative to place a rival historian in the dock and to raise the emotions of the reader against that historian. Sometimes they will construct a large portion of their own identity by criticism of their predecessors. This may be virulent or mild, but there is no hesitancy to be explicit. The Romans, on the other hand, confine polemic to individual points placed throughout the narrative, and sometimes mentioned only briefly and in passing. One does not find attempts at a prolonged raising of the emotions, although they may occasionally adopt the 'pathetic' tone that rhetoric sanctioned for refutation. More than the Greeks, however, the Romans seem to be concerned to define themselves as continuators of a tradition, and they try to portray their works as combining the best aspects of those predecessors recognised as the best. Their attempts to place themselves among the acknowledged masters are yet another way that all ancient historians seek authority in tradition.

Appendices

APPENDIX I

TABLE OF HISTORIANS

I give here a listing of the major historians mentioned in this book, together with their dates of birth and death, the events they treated, and (when known) the number of books in their histories. The reader should be aware that birth and death dates are in most cases approximations only (some are still strongly contested), as are quite frequently the exact beginning and ending points of individual works. Book divisions for the earliest historians are in many cases not the author's own, but they are nevertheless useful for estimating the comparative size of the work.

Historian	Title of work or topic	Periods treated	No. books
Hecataeus of Miletus (*fl.* late 6th and early 5th c. BC)	*Circuit of the Earth* *Genealogies (Histories ?)*	Gazeteer of Mediterranean coast Heroic genealogies	2 4
Charon of Lampsacus (*fl.* early 5th c. BC)	*Hellenica* *Persica*	Greek history Persian matters	4 2
Xanthus of Lydia (*fl.* 5th c. BC)	*Lydiaca*	Lydian matters	4
Herodotus of Halicarnassus (*c.* 484–420 BC)	*Histories*	560–479 BC	9
Hellanicus of Lesbos (*c.* 480–395 BC)	*Priestesses of Hera at Argos* *Atthis*	Chronological list Local history of Athens, early times – 404 BC	2
Antiochus of Syracuse (*fl.* late 5th c. BC)	*Sikelica* *On Italy*	Sicilian history, origins–424 BC Origins of Italian cities	9 1
Thucydides of Athens (before 454–after 404 BC)	*Histories*	Peloponnesian War, 431–411 BC (incomplete)	8
Philistus of Syracuse (*c.* 430–356 BC)	*On Sicily* *On Dionysius*	Origins–406 BC 406–367/6 BC	7 4

Appendix 1

Historian	Title of work or topic	Periods treated	No. books
Oxyrhynchus Historian	?*Histories*	Greek history, 412–386 (?) BC	
Xenophon of Athens (*c.* 430–*c.* 360 BC)	*Hellenica* *Anabasis*	Greek history, 411–362 BC Expedition and return of Greek mercenaries, 401–399 BC	7 7
Cratippus of Athens (*fl.* late 5th/early 4th c. BC)	*Hellenica* (?)	Greek history, 411–395/4 (?) BC	
Ctesias of Cnidus (*fl.* late 5th/early 4th c. BC)	*Persica* *Indica*	Assyrian, Persian history, early times–397 BC Indian ethnography	23 1
Athanis of Syracuse (*fl.* mid/late 4th c. BC)	*Deeds of Dion*	Sicilian history, 362/1–336 BC	13
Theopompus of Chios (*c.* 378?–after 320 BC)	*Epitome of Herodotus* *Hellenica* *Philippica* ('Affairs around Philip')	Greek history, 411–395/4 BC Greek and Macedonian history, 359–336 BC	2 12 58
Ephorus of Cyme (*c.* 405–330 BC)	*Histories*	Greek and non-Greek history, 1069/8–341/0 BC	30
Callisthenes of Olynthus (*c.* 370–327 BC)	*Hellenica* *Deeds of Alexander*	Greek history, 386–356 BC 336–329 (?) BC	10
Ptolemy I, Soter (*c.* 367–282 BC)	*Deeds of Alexander* (?)	Alexander's accession, 336–death, 323 BC	
Aristobulus (360s–270s BC)	*Deeds of Alexander* (?)	Alexander's accession, 336–death, 323 BC	
Duris of Samos (*c.* 340–*c.* 260 BC)	*Histories*	Greek history, 370/69–281/0 BC	at least 23
Hecataeus of Abdera (*fl.* 300 BC)	*Aegyptiaca*	Egyptian origins, history, and culture	
Berossus of Babylon (*fl.* 290 BC)	*Babyloniaca*	Babylonian origins, history, and culture	3
Manetho (*fl. c.* 280 BC)	*Aegyptiaca*	Egyptian origins, history, and culture to 342	3
Hieronymus of Cardia (*c.* 364–*c.* 260 BC)	*History of the Successors*	Alexander's Successors, 323–272 (?) BC	
Timaeus of Tauromenium (*c.* 350–after 260 BC)	*(?Sicilian) Histories* *Wars of Pyrrhus* *Olympic Victors*	Sicilian history, early times–289/8 BC Conflicts of Pyrrhus and Rome, ending 264/3 BC Chronological work	38

Table of historians

Historian	Title of work or topic	Periods treated	No. books
Phylarchus of Athens (*fl.* mid/late 3rd c. BC)	*Histories*	Greek history, 272-220 BC	28
Q. Fabius Pictor (*fl.* mid/late 3rd c. BC)	*History of Rome* (in Greek)	Origins-?	
Philinus of Acragas (*fl.* mid/late 3rd c. BC)	?	First Punic War, 264-241 BC	
Polybius of Megalopolis (200-after 118 BC)	*Histories*	264 (Greek affairs from 220) -146 BC	40
	The Numantine War	Roman activity in Spain (?), ending 133 BC	
M. Porcius Cato (234-149 BC)	*Origins*	Origins of Rome and Italian city-states; events from *c.* 264-149 BC	7
Sempronius Asellio (*c.* 160-*c.* 90 BC)	*Histories* (?)	Roman history, 146-91 BC	at least 14
Posidonius of Apamea (*c.* 135-51/50 BC)	*Histories*	Universal history, 146-86 (?) BC	52
L. Cornelius Sisenna (*c.* 118-67 BC)	*Histories* (?)	Roman history, 91-79 BC	more than 13
Sallust (86-34 BC)	*Catilinarian Conspiracy (War?)*	64-62 BC	1
	War with Jugurtha	116-107 BC	1
	Histories	78-67 (?) BC	5
Diodorus of Sicily (died after 36 BC)	*Historical Library*	Universal history, early times-60 BC	40
Pompeius Trogus (*fl.* late 1st c. BC)	*Philippic Histories*	Universal history, early times-20 BC	44
Dionysius of Halicarnassus (*fl.* late 1st c. BC)	*Roman Antiquities*	Rome, origins-264 BC	20
Livy (59 BC-AD 17)	*From the Founding of the City*	Rome, origins-9 BC	142
Nicolaus of Damascus (*c.* 64 BC-before AD 6)	*Histories*	Universal history, beginning with Assyrian empire-4 BC	144
Velleius Paterculus (*c.* 20/19 BC-?)	*Roman History* (?)	Early history (?)-AD 29	2
Q. Curtius Rufus (*fl.* mid/late 1st c. AD)	*History of Alexander*	Alexander's accession, 336-death, 323 BC	10

Appendix 1

Historian	Title of work or topic	Periods treated	No. books
Josephus (AD 37/8–after 100)	*On the Jewish War*	Roman involvement with Judaea, c. 170 BC–AD 70	7
	Jewish Antiquities	Early history to the Jewish War	20
Tacitus (AD 55/6–after 118)	*Histories*	Roman history, AD 69–96	14
	Annals	Roman history, AD 14–68	16
Appian (before AD 100–c. 165)	*Roman History*	Roman history by area to AD 117	24
Arrian (c. AD 86–after 170 (?))	*Anabasis of Alexander*	Deeds of Alexander, accession to death, 336–323 BC	7
	Events after Alexander	Alexander's successors, 323–319 BC	10
	Bithyniaca	Local history of Bithynia	8
	Parthica	Rome's wars with Parthia, Crassus to Trajan	17
Cassius Dio (AD 164 or 165–after 229)	*Roman History*	Origins–AD 229	80
Herodian (c. AD 180–?)	*Histories*	Roman history, AD 180–238	8
Dexippus of Athens (c. AD 210–?)	*Historical Chronicles*	Early history–AD 269/70	12
	Events after Alexander	Alexander's successors, 323–321 BC	4
	Scythica	Rome's wars with the Goths, AD 238–74	3
Ammianus Marcellinus (c. AD 330–c. 395)	*Res Gestae*	Roman history, AD 96–378	31

APPENDIX II

NAME AND NATIONALITY

Imitation of predecessors may occur in many ways; I discuss briefly here one of those ways, the manner of an historian in the formal introduction of himself to the audience.

Hesiod, of course, is the first poet to name himself in his work.[1] In a similar way Theognis, although beginning with one (or several) prefaces to the gods, inserted his name into the text as what he calls a 'seal' (σφραγίς). The nature of this seal has been much discussed, some seeing it as a mark of poetic pride, others as an attempt to guarantee the authentic character of the text itself.[2] Both in fact may be present. Of the other lyric, elegiac, and iambic poets we can single out Alcman, Phocylides, Demodocus, Solon, and Susarion as those who name themselves in their poems, yet we must also recognise that such a procedure need imply neither *Dichterstolz* nor the presence of the author as a character in the text itself.[3]

Both pride and presence in the text can first be unmistakably seen in the philosophers, who as a group exert the strongest influence on the early historians. Here names are used with evident pride and as an emphasis on the originality of the work. The author introduces himself as a speaker as we can see, e.g., in Alcmaeon: 'Alcmaeon of Croton, the son of Peirithos, spoke the following to Brotinos and Leon and Bathyllos.'[4] His persona is that of a

[1] Hes. *Theog.* 22-4: αἵ νυ ποθ' Ἡσίοδον καλὴν ἐδίδαξαν ἀοιδήν.
[2] Theognis, 22-3: Θεύγνιδός ἐστιν ἔπη | τοῦ Μεγαρέως. πάντας δὲ κατ' ἀνθρώπους ὀνομαστός. On the prefaces see West, *Hesiod: Theogony* 55; on Theognis' seal, Kranz, *Studien zur antiken Literatur und ihrem Fortwirken* 42-3.
[3] Alcman F 39 (*PMG* 39); Phocylides FF 8, 10, 11, 14; Demodocus, F 2; Solon, F 33 (a particularly excellent warning for knowing the context of such a procedure); Susarion, F 1 (his genuineness defended, West, *Studies in Greek Elegy and Iambus* 183 ff.). Warning against *Dichterstolz*: Kranz, op. cit. (n.2) 29; against presence in the text, Fehling, in *Festschrift... Diller* 66. For the various types of 'I' in poetry, see the survey and discussion of Slings, *The Poet's I in Archaic Greek Lyric* 1-30.
[4] DK 24 B 1: Ἀλκμαίων Κρωτωνιήτης τάδε ἔλεξε Πειρίθου υἱὸς Βροτίνῳ καὶ Λέοντι καὶ Βαθύλλῳ.

teacher, and he gives his city and his patronymic. The numerous parallels with the literature of the Orient and the Hebrew Bible show that early Greek philosophers borrowed this means of introduction from the East,[5] and these writers see themselves as bringing the 'true' interpretation of the world. This furnishes the best link with the first historiographical preface we possess, that of Hecataeus in the *Genealogies*:

Ἑκαταῖος Μιλήσιος ὧδε μυθεῖται· τάδε γράφω, ὥς μοι δοκεῖ ἀληθέα εἶναι. οἱ γὰρ Ἑλλήνων λόγοι πολλοί τε καὶ γελοῖοι, ὡς ἐμοὶ φαίνονται, εἰσίν.[6]

Unlike Alcmaeon, Hecataeus offers the name of his country instead of, not (as in Alcmaeon) in addition to, a patronymic: Hecataeus assumes his audience is pan-Hellenic, as one would expect for a work whose intention was to establish the record in chronology for Hellas. The procedure is imitated, of course, by Herodotus (Ἡροδότου Ἁλικαρνησσέος ἱστορίης ἀπόδεξις)[7] and Thucydides (Θουκυδίδης Ἀθηναῖος ξυνέγραψε, 1.1.1), both of whom, like Hecataeus, eschew patronymic. Yet we cannot assume that this was a rule; we do not know how Pherecydes or Hellanicus or other early writers referred to themselves, whether with patronymic or nationality or both. In the opening of his *On Italy*, Antiochus introduces himself as 'Antiochus, son of Xenophanes'.[8] Perhaps he expected his work to have simply local interest, but unfortunately we have too few examples to be cer-

---

[5] Fehling, op. cit. (n.3) 65ff. He interestingly notes that this convention is not to be found in the historical books of the Bible: 'Sie kennen kein Ich im text, und keine Nennung des Verfassers... Kurz, sie haben sozusagen keine Verfasser' (68). See esp. his parallels between Hebrew and Greek beginnings, 69-71. The actual words of the openings of philosophical works are preserved only for Alcmaeon, on the basis of whom they are supplied for others: ⟨Ἡράκλειτος Βλόσωνος Ἐφέσιος τάδε λέγει⟩ and ⟨Ἴων Χῖος τάδε λέγει⟩ (Fehling is insufficiently cautious with these). M. L. West, *Early Greek Philosophy and the Orient* (Oxford 1971) 9 assumes that Pherecydes' book began ⟨Φερεκύδης Σύριος τάδε ἔλεξε Βάβυος υἱός⟩. On the matter of early book openings, see W. Burkert, *Lore and Science in Ancient Pythagoreanism* (Cambridge, Mass. 1972) 252 with n. 68; Schmalzriedt, *ΠΕΡΙ ΦΥΣΙΟΣ. Zur Frühgeschichte der Buchtitel*. See also L. Koenen, 'Der erste Satz bei Heraklit und Herodot', *ZPE* 97 (1993) 95-6 for the connection between Heraclitus, Hecataeus, and Herodotus.

[6] *FGrHist* 1 F 1a.

[7] Hdt. *praef.*; Fehling's claim, op. cit (n.3) 74 that Herodotus' ἱστορίης ἀπόδεξις corresponds to 'Schau', 'Sprüche', or 'Wort' in the Hebrew Bible is not convincing.

[8] *FGrHist* 555 F 2: ʼΑντίοχος Ξενοφάνεος τάδε ξυνέγραψε, κτλ. (Von Fritz, *Griechische Geschichtsschreibung* 1.508 mistranslates as 'Antiochos of Syracuse'.)

tain. Ctesias in the *Indica* may have introduced himself as 'Ctesias, son of Ctesiarchus, of Cnidus',[9] so that we should leave open the possibility that an author might present himself differently in different works.[10]

It is usually assumed that the introduction of the book title made unnecessary the author's name and nationality.[11] We are unable to trace this in any detail because of the fragmentary remains of the histories between Xenophon and Polybius. Xenophon maintained anonymity and in both *Hellenica* and *Anabasis* plunged *in medias res*: Lucian says that this 'virtual' preface was much imitated in antiquity.[12] Neither Polybius nor Diodorus introduces himself in the text, their prefaces being concerned to magnify their theme and its importance.[13]

The Roman historians never use a formal introduction of themselves by name into the text, but they show an interest in both their own and others' homelands. Velleius faults Homer for failing to include the name of his country in his work; and Pompeius Trogus says that he would be an ungrateful citizen if, when he had treated affairs of all other people, he remained silent only about his own country.[14] This suggests that both of these historians, at least, had something to say about their origins within their history.

A somewhat different convention is evident among the Greek historians of the early Empire. Here we find the author formally introducing himself by name at the end of an extended and self-contained preface. After giving the disposition and purpose of his work, Dionysius concludes the preface with:

---

[9] If Luc. *v. h.* 1.3 (Κτησίας Κτησιάρχου Κνίδιος) is meant as a parody; see Fehling, op. cit. (n.3) 65 n. 5.

[10] Jacoby, *Abhandlungen* 120-1 (cf. *FGrHist* IIIb (Text) 2; (Noten) 2-3) infers with some probability that when the biographical testimonia lack patronymic, it is unlikely that the author gave it. He also suggests (*Abhandlungen* 196 n. 73; cf. *FGrHist Komm.* IIIa. 2) that Charon may have spoken of himself as 'son of Pythokles' in the *Persica*, as 'Lampsacenus' in the Ὧροι. And since the Suda gives several patronymics for Hellanicus, Jacoby assumes that that author gave only his nationality.

[11] Schmalzriedt, op. cit. (n.5) 26-7, 31 points out that tragedies had titles because of their number, while prose authors only saw fit to give titles when there was the necessity of referring to one work among many.

[12] Luc. *h. c.* 52; on the many imitators, ibid. 23. He is referring to the *Anabasis*; this does not apply, I think, to the *Hellenica*, which presents special problems: see Ch. V n. 107.

[13] For Polybius named as an historical character see above, pp. 188ff. I assume that 1.42.1, which contains Diodorus' name in the third person, is an interpolation: see Burton, *Diodorus Siculus* 141.

[14] Vell. 1.7.1; Trogus F 161 = Justin, XLIII.1.1-2. Kraus, *Livy: Ab Urbe Condita Book VI* 1 notes that Livy hints at his northern origins by narrating Antenor's foundation of his home town Padua (1.2-3) before that of Rome.

'And I, who have put together this account, am Dionysius, son of Alexander, of Halicarnassus.'[15] Josephus introduces himself as well in the preface of the *Jewish War* with, 'I am Josephus, son of Matthias, [Hebrew by race,] from Jerusalem'.[16] Appian has a rather more self-conscious introduction that emphasises his renown:

> Who I am who have written these things, many know and I myself have indicated, but to speak more clearly, I am Appian of Alexandria.[17]

Arrian, on the other hand, plays with convention:

> As for who I am who make this judgement in my favour, I do not need to write my name, for it is not unknown among men, nor what my country is, nor my family, nor any office I held in my native country.[18]

Not unreasonably, the similarities of the latter two has suggested imitation or parody.[19] It may be wrong, however, to focus exclusively on these two authors since there is evidence that several writers of the time discussed name and nationality, often with an eye towards Homer.[20] Arrian's anonymity is here meant to recall Homer's, since the poet has just been suggested by Alexander's visit to the tomb of Achilles and his praise of Achilles' chronicler Homer.[21] In a more explicit introduction, Kephalion said he would not reveal his γένος and πατρίς just as Homer had not revealed his; conversely, Lucian records a preface in which an historian, in praising his πατρίς Miletus, claimed to have done better than Homer, who made no mention of

---

[15] D. Hal. *A. R.* 1.8.4: ὁ δὲ συντάξας αὐτὴν Διονύσιός εἰμι Ἀλεξάνδρου Ἁλικαρνασεύς.

[16] Jos. *B. J.* 1.3: ἐγὼ ... Ἰώσηπος Ματθίου παῖς, [γένει Ἑβραῖος] ἐξ Ἱεροσολύμων.

[17] App. *praef.* 62: τίς δὲ ὢν ταῦτα συνέγραψα, πολλοὶ μὲν ἴσασι καὶ αὐτὸς προέφηνα, σαφέστερον δ' εἰπεῖν, Ἀππιανὸς Ἀλεξανδρεύς, κτλ. Gray, *JHS* 110 (1990) 181 n. 6 thinks Appian's delay in naming himself displays some reserve.

[18] *Anab.* 1.12.5: ὅστις δὲ ὢν ταῦτα ὑπὲρ ἐμαυτοῦ γιγνώσκω, τὸ μὲν ὄνομα οὐδὲν δέομαι ἀναγράψαι, οὐδὲ γὰρ οὐδὲ ἄγνωστον ἐς ἀνθρώπους ἐστίν, οὐδὲ πατρίδα ἥτις μοί ἐστιν οὐδὲ γένος τὸ ἐμόν, οὐδὲ εἰ δή τινα ἀρχὴν ἐν τῇ ἐμαυτοῦ ἦρξα. Arrian considers Alexander at Troy the real beginning of his work: see Moles, *JHS* 105 (1985) 167; Marincola, *JHS* 109 (1989) 187-8.

[19] Discussion in Stadter, *Arrian* 64-5; Bosworth, *HCA* 1.106-7; id., *Arrian to Alexander* 33 n. 86.

[20] Marincola, op. cit. (n.18) 188; to the passages there add Apion, *FGrHist* 616 F 15, who claimed to have learned the country and parents of Homer, but would not divulge it; see also Velleius on Homer, above, n. 14.

[21] Moles, op. cit. (n.18) 164 n. 13.

his country.²² Like Homer, Arrian wishes the deeds to be considered foremost, but unlike Homer his anonymity calls attention to itself, and in this sense Arrian's self-display remains well within (and plays upon) the historiographical tradition. One suspects too that something more is at stake when we look at the actual opening of the *Anabasis*:

> Ptolemy, son of Lagus, and Aristobulus, son of Aristobulus – whatever these two say in common about Alexander the son of Philip, these things I have written as entirely true.²³

The form of the names in the nominative hearkens back to the early historiographical openings and these explicitly named sources stand in stark contrast to the narrator's anonymity. For Arrian's original audience, however, we must assume that there was, of course, not confusion, but rather admiration for the clever exploitation of an old convention.

Finally, we should note the mechanical imitators castigated by Lucian, many of whom gave their names merely in imitation of Herodotus and Thucydides: an imitator of Thucydides began, like him, with name and nationality (Κρεπερήιος Καλπουρνιανός Πομπηϊουπολίτης), and three others, in probable imitation of Herodotus, began, like him, with their names (and sometimes nationality) in the genitive case: Antiochianus, the victor in the games of Apollo (Ἀντιοχιανοῦ τοῦ Ἀπόλλωνος ἱερονίκου), Demetrius of Sagalassus (Δημητρίου Σαγαλασέως), and Callimorphus, the physician (Καλλιμόρφου ἰατροῦ).²⁴ If these are genuine,²⁵ they are also evidence that in the Empire, among Greek writers at least, it was not uncommon to find the historian still introducing himself and beginning his work with his name.²⁶ But this mindless imitation reveals that no new conventions were being utilised, and suggests the exhaustion of what, after all, hardly lent itself to much creative imitation.

---

²² *FGrHist* 93 T 2; 205 F 1 (=Luc. *h. c.* 14).
²³ Arr. *Anab. praef.* 1: Πτολεμαῖος ὁ Λάγου καὶ Ἀριστόβουλος ὁ Ἀριστοβούλου ὅσα μὲν ταὐτὰ ἄμφω περὶ Ἀλεξάνδρου τοῦ Φιλίππου συνέγραψαν, ταῦτα ἐγὼ ὡς πάντῃ ἀληθῆ ἀναγράφω. I have tried to get across in the translation the effect of putting Ptolemy's and Aristobulus' names in the nominative at the beginning of the work.
²⁴ Luc. *h. c.* 15 (=*FGrHist* 208 F 1); 30 (=207 F 1); 32 (=209 F 1); 16 (=210 F 1).
²⁵ See Introd. n. 5.
²⁶ The citation Δημητρίου Σαγαλλασέως Πάρθικα (32), however, looks like a title.

APPENDIX III

ISOCRATES ON AUTOPSY AND INQUIRY?

Two passages of Isocrates are sometimes cited to argue that the orator inverted the usual preference of eyes over ears, and in doing so encouraged the writing of non-contemporary over contemporary history. In the former (*Paneg.* 7–10), Isocrates' exhortations not to avoid what has been said before but rather to attempt to say it better than has previously been said is seen both as a rejection of contemporary history that relies on eyewitness accounts, and a preference for non-contemporary history whose main goal is stylistic excellence and a lack of concern with accuracy.[1] This view is then supported by the second passage (*Panath.* 149–50) where Isocrates says that all men have greater knowledge 'from hearsay rather than from sight', διὰ τῆς ἀκοῆς ἢ τῆς ὄψεως.[2] It would indeed require a great orator to demonstrate that ears are more trustworthy than eyes, and an examination of the full context of each passage shows that Isocrates in fact said nothing of the sort.

(i) *Paneg.* 7–10: Isocrates has announced at the beginning of this work that he will give his counsels on the war against the Persians and on domestic concord; he knows it is a much-worked theme, but he hopes to treat it differently (and, of course, better). He reminds his audience that since there is still time for action, the theme remains appropriate for discussion:

> In addition, if it were possible to reveal the same actions in only one way, one could suppose that it is superfluous for one speaking the same as those [sc. who have already spoken] to annoy the audience again. But since words have such a nature that it is possible to discourse on the same things in many ways, and make great things lowly or give size to small things, or to go through the things of old in a new way or to speak about things that have recently happened in an old style, so one must not avoid those topics on which others have spoken, but one must try to speak better than they. For past deeds we hold in common, but the use of these

---

[1] Scheller, *De hell. hist. conscr. arte* 65ff.; Peter, *GL* II.190; id., *Wahrheit* 180–3; Avenarius, *LS* 81–3.   [2] Avenarius, *LS* 82.

at the proper time and the consideration of what is appropriate for each
and the good arrangement of words belongs to those who think rightly.
And I think that both the other arts and philosophic rhetoric would make
the greatest advance if one marvelled at and honoured not the ones who
first began these works, but the ones who made each of them their best,
and not the ones who want to speak about those things that no one has
ever spoken about before, but those who know how to speak in a way
that no one else can.

Isocrates' supposed 'programmatic' remarks come in a traditional praise of
the powers of oratory,[3] which can, by changing its focus, bring new aspects
of old problems to light. One could perhaps take this passage as a plea for
the striving of stylistic excellence, but the context makes clear that speaking 'in a way no one has before' has just as much to do with the *content* of
the advice which will be based on the *proper use* of the exempla which history provides.[4] Isocrates does indeed go on to vaunt his own powers
(11-14), but this does not change the fact[5] that in the present passage he is
not divorcing style and content, and it is clear that the excellence of his
speech is a result of the excellence of his advice, that is, its content. It is
certainly not to be denied that the attitude here enunciated could be
removed from its context and used to justify a new treatment of noncontemporary history. But it is a slender peg on which to hang an historiographical manifesto.

(ii) *Panath.* 149-50: This interesting passage comes as a digression that
is itself a comment on the narrative just given by the orator of great deeds in
Athenian history. Isocrates has been speaking on early Athenian history (he
gives his reasons for going so far back in §120), starting from before a time
when words such as oligarchy and democracy even existed (119), then treating certain aspects of the early king Theseus (126ff.), and his followers
(130-3), and after a brief interruption (134-8) returning to the democracy
and its excellences. Then Isocrates continues:

[3] Cf. Plato, *Phaedr.* 267a6-b2: 'Shall we leave Tisias and Gorgias alone, who saw
probabilities as more valuable than truth and who seem to make small things
great and great things small by the power of words and new things old and their
opposite new and who discovered both the conciseness of words and boundless measures about everything?'

[4] In §4 Isocrates has said that the finest speeches are those which concern the
greatest things and bring the greatest benefit to the audience. See next note.

[5] If anything it confirms it, since Isocrates later says that he deserves scorn if he
does not measure up to his theme (14); and cf. *ad fin.* where he encourages others to give speeches of substance that make a difference in the lives of those who
hear them (188-9).

> Some perhaps might say – since nothing prevents me from interrupting my speech – that I am unusual in daring to say that I know accurately about affairs at which I was not present when they occurred. But I think I am doing nothing illogical. For if I alone trusted to the traditions and records about things of long ago which have come down to us from that time, then reasonably I would be censured. But as it is, even many intelligent men would seem to have the same experience as I. And apart from this, if I were put to the test and proof, I could demonstrate that all men have greater knowledge from oral tradition than from autopsy and know greater and finer deeds having heard them from others rather than from events at which they themselves happened to be present.

Read in context it is clear that this passage is not an inversion of the traditional relationship between eyes and ears. Isocrates first claims as one of the proofs for his accurate knowledge of the past the fact that tradition has recorded it.[6] He then claims that he could show that all men have greater knowledge from report, since all people have heard about greater and nobler deeds than have actually been present and witnessed them. Isocrates is saying no more than that men rarely witness great deeds, and that their main source of information about them is not their own experience but tradition, however they receive this. This is especially true, of course, when the deeds are very ancient. Note what the Athenians in Thucydides say when about to rehearse their deeds to the Spartans:

> As for events of long ago, what can we say about things for which the traditions [lit., hearings] of stories are witnesses rather than the eyesight of the listeners?[7]

Comparisons with oral or largely oral societies show that the ears are seen as the chief means of receiving traditions. Oral societies are aural to an extent not easily comprehensible to literate societies.[8] In neither of these passages is Isocrates concerned with the comparison of *certainties* (and this is the main point) between past and present or oral report and eyewitness participation.

That Isocrates had important views on the uses of history[9] and that his ideas had consequences for historiography should not be doubted; but that

---

[6] On this see above, pp. 105f.
[7] Thuc. 1.73.2: καὶ τὰ μὲν παλαιὰ τί δεῖ λέγειν, ὧν ἀκοαὶ μᾶλλον λόγων μάρτυρες ἢ ὄψις τῶν ἀκουσομένων; On this difficult passage see Schepens, *Anc. Soc.* 6 (1975) 262 with reff. there.
[8] Ong, *Orality and Literacy* 71-4.
[9] G. Schmitz-Kahlmann, *Das Beispiel der Geschichte im politischen Denken des Isocrates* (Leipzig 1939).

he favoured as more exact and more reliable the past rather than the present or ears more than eyes is not to be accepted.[10]

[10] Schepens, in *Historiographia Antiqua* 101 rejects the Peter/Avenarius interpretation, referring to his dissertation *Het belang van de autopsie in de historische methode van de Griekse geschiedschrijvers van Herodotos tot Polybius* (Leuven 1974) 267-9, 297-301.

APPENDIX IV

VARIANT VERSIONS

An examination of how historians choose from among variant versions sheds some light on the methodology assumed in writing non-contemporary history. As we noted at the outset, the historian differs from the Homeric narrator by his lack of omniscience. Unlike the poet, the historian does not know all, nor does he pretend on each occasion to be able to explain motivation or cause. We may term this entire phenomenon 'narrative uncertainty', and it can be as brief as a few words ('either willingly or unwillingly'), or as lengthy as a full digression and refutation. In the latter cases, one can sometimes find methodological pronouncements. The material will repay a full study, and I present here only an overview of those occasions when the historian explicitly cites two (or more) versions and ascribes them either to unnamed authorities ('some say', 'others believe', 'there are some who write') or to named sources whom he is (presumably) following in part or *in toto*, and then chooses one over the other.[1] This type gives insight into an historian's methodology.[2] In those cases where an

---

[1] I do not include here the types of narrative uncertainty that revolve around the motives of individuals. An example of this type would be Herodotus' statement that Megacles' daughter told her mother of Peisistratus' unusual sexual habits, 'either being asked by her mother or not' (1.61.2). On this type of variant, for example, especially prominent in Herodotus, it is impossible to believe that there were two traditions about Megacles' daughter, one holding that she had told her mother because asked, another that she had done so unbidden. S. West, *CR* 39 (1989) 190 holds these types of narrative uncertainty to be storytellers' devices: 'They inspire confidence in the narrator's conscientiousness, so that we are disposed to accept what he says on matters of more substance where he admits to no such uncertainty.' Another type is the placing of a natural explanation side by side with a mythical or marvellous one: in the *Hellenica* Xenophon explains the surprising attack by the Spartans against the Thebans in this way: 'it is possible that the hand of heaven (τὸ θεῖον) is responsible, and it is possible to say that no one could stand against desperate men' (VII.5.12).

[2] It goes without saying that the variant versions that an historian explicitly cites are not necessarily all the variant versions in his sources. This can be demonstrated without difficulty in the numerous places where we know of a different version in a source that an historian claims to have used, but which is

1. APPEAL TO EYEWITNESSES / CONTEMPORARIES / OLDEST HISTORIANS

Eyewitness testimony was considered always the best form of knowledge in ancient historiography, and little uncertainty about its value is ever expressed.[3] It is therefore not surprising that writers of non-contemporary history will frequently call attention to their reliance on contemporary eyewitnesses. When they express their opinions about their choice, they suggest that exaggeration or error creeps in over time, as people pass stories on from one to another.[4] Following this, Livy chooses Fabius Pictor rather than Piso on the cost of Tarquinius' temple, 'because he is the older writer'; Fabius is likewise Livy's choice of authority for the Second Punic War because he was a contemporary of the event.[5] Although there is no agreement about the year or the consuls when a dictator was first appointed at Rome, Livy states that he finds the name of T. Larcius 'among the oldest writers' (II.18.4-7). Conversely, Livy hesitates to record a revolt of the Antiates in 459 BC, because there is no mention of it in the older writers.[6] A particularly effective use of the reliance on contemporaries is in Arrian's account of Alexander's assault on the town of the Malii. Arrian notes that some recorded Ptolemy to have mounted the wall with Alexander and protected him, thus receiving the name 'Saviour'. He counters this with the evidence of Ptolemy himself, who says that he was not present there but

---

not recorded by the historian using that source. To name just two: Livy would have us believe that he followed Polybius but at XXII.5 and 52 he gives versions at variance with Polybius' accounts (III.84 and 97, respectively), without any acknowledgement of the discrepancy. Nor shall we here consider the problems that historians make when they haphazardly or uncritically combine versions from two or more sources, without resolving the basic conflicts.

[3] See Ch. II §1.

[4] See above, pp. 93f. An additional reason for accepting these older sources may be found in rhetorical teachings, where distinctions between ancient and modern witnesses were noted and the use of each was discussed. Aristotle in the *Rhetoric* (1.15, 1375b 26-76a 17) distinguishes between the two: 'Of witnesses there are two sorts, ancient and recent.... By ancient I mean the poets and other well-known persons whose judgements are clear ... ancient ones are the most persuasive; for they are incorruptible.'

[5] Livy, 1.55.8-9; XXII.7.4; cf. Pol. III.9.1-5 where he notes, in the course of refuting Pictor, that many give credence to the man because he was a Roman Senator and a contemporary.   [6] Livy, III.23.7; cf. XXIX.14.9.

commanding his own troops. He calls this the greatest error of historians who have written about this, and explains the necessity of his digression because many false stories have arisen from this episode, and he must therefore encourage care in historians.[7]

2. APPEAL TO THE NUMBERS ('MOST WRITERS')

'The proof of truth', said Josephus (*c. Ap.* 1.26), 'is universal agreement.' Barring this, the ancients seem to have thought that one was closer to truth the more witnesses one could produce: more was better.[8] But for the historians, it remained if not the truth, then a reliable approach to it. Livy follows the majority of authors who said that the Horatii were Albans; in the plebeian secession of 494 BC their place of withdrawal is given either as the Mons Sacer or the Aventine, but the former is the more common account (*frequentior fama*); and at the battle of the Ticinus when Scipio is wounded, the majority of writers say that his son, not a Ligurian slave, saved him. Diodorus says that 'a majority of writers agree' that the many-bodied creatures of Egypt were destroyed by Zeus and Osiris; and Tacitus, in describing the death of Drusus, says that he will follow the majority of authors.[9]

3. APPEAL TO THE MORE PERSUASIVE/ PROBABLE/BELIEVABLE

This is a common appeal among the historians, although (or perhaps because) its meaning is not always easy to explain. It seems most frequently to indicate a rationalised or de-mythologised version, or perhaps one lacking in exaggeration or histrionics, but in most cases it is impossible to tell because the rival version or versions are suppressed. There is reason to believe that some type of reckoning based on probability (τὸ εἰκός, *probabile*) underlies the 'more persuasive' or 'more reliable' accounts, but the historian here asks the audience to rely on his judgement and good sense for the version that he produces. So Antiochus of Syracuse announced that his

---

[7] Arr. *Anab.* VI.11.8; his words are echoed by Quintus Curtius, IX.5.21.

[8] It is precisely this appeal to the numbers that Plato tries to refute in his examination of Polus in the *Gorgias*, where he refers to a refutation 'orator-fashion' that relies on the accumulation of witnesses; see Lloyd, *MRE* 101-2 with references to Plato given there. See also Ch. V n. 14.

[9] Livy, 1.24.1; 11.32.2-3; XXI.46.7-10: ('quod et plures tradidere auctores et fama obtinuit'); Diod. 1.26.8; Tac. *Ann.* IV.10.1; cf. *Hist.* 11.50 (death of Otho): 'uulgatis traditisque demere fidem non ausim'.

history of Italy was composed of 'the most persuasive and clearest matters from ancient accounts'. Diodorus in several places claims that he is relying on a more persuasive account: of Sesoösis he will narrate 'the most persuasive events and those that agree with the evidence still in existence'; when he writes of Crete, he will follow 'the more persuasive accounts', especially relying on 'those who are most trustworthy.'[10] Elsewhere Diodorus contrasts a 'more persuasive' account with a 'mythical' account, and sometimes chooses the former.[11] Similarly, Dionysius distinguishes a more persuasive account of the condemnation of Sp. Cassius by the people from a less persuasive account in which Cassius is condemned by his father; so too with two versions of the death of Sp. Maelius.[12] Claiming to follow 'those authors more worthy to be believed', Livy denies that the Samnites betrayed Neapolis to the Romans in 326 BC.[13] Tacitus, in a passage just mentioned above, says that in giving the death of Drusus he has followed the things given by the majority and the most trustworthy (*plurimis maximaeque fidei*) writers. Appian claims that although many different things have been written about the battle of Pharsalus, he will write up 'the most persuasive matters' (τὰ πιθανώτατα). And Ammianus, in his account of the Nile's sources, says that he will follow the writers who, he thinks, are close to the truth.[14]

4. NATIVE TRADITION (APPEAL TO THE ἐπιχώριοι OR *INCOLAE*)

The reliance on native sources is an important aspect of Herodotus' history, and it is not unlikely that he was here inheriting a tradition already present in Hecataeus.[15] It has a long history in ancient historiography and in other genres as well.[16] Thucydides at one point in his preface suggests that the inhabitants of a land are no better than others in discovering the truth, but his manner of expressing it indicates that the usual assumption was that the

---

[10] Antiochus, *FGrHist* 555 F 2 = D. Hal. *A. R.* 1.12.3, quoted above, Ch. II n. 181; Diod. 1.53.1 (Sesoösis); v.80.4 (Crete).

[11] Diod. IV.6.1-3 (no choice); v.56.3-4; on Diodorus and myth see above, pp. 119ff.   [12] D. Hal. *A. R.* VIII.79.1 (Cassius); XII.4.2 (Maelius).

[13] Livy, VIII.26.5-6: 'cum auctoribus hoc dedi quibus dignius credi est'.

[14] Tac. *Ann.* IV.10.1; App. *B. Civ.* II.70 ; Amm. XXII.15.3.

[15] Jacoby, *RE* VII. 2. 2740 says of the appeal to the *epichorioi*: 'eine Eigenheit nicht etwa der Περίοδος gewesen ist, sondern auch der Γενεαλογίαι'. Verdin, *Anc. Soc.* 1 (1970) 190-1 notes that Herodotus usually follows native sources.

[16] See Verdin, op. cit. (n.15) 186-200 for a full treatment; Fehling, *Herodotus and his 'Sources'* 162-4 gives many examples of what he considers false epichoric source citations in later writers.

natives were the best informed of all about their history.[17] Thucydides himself uses the *topos*, however, when he finds it convenient, especially in his digression on Sicily.[18] The validity of epichoric traditions was proverbial, and the testimony of the natives is frequently invoked to suggest a superior source.[19] Timaeus, who was much given to epichoric traditions, described the appearance of the Penates in Lavinium and claimed to have learned of them from the *epichorioi*.[20] Polybius in two passages relies on his meetings with the natives: in the first, he brings forth as a superior testimony on the character of Hannibal the opinions of the Carthaginians themselves, 'for the natives know not only the way the wind blows, as the proverb has it, but also the characters of their countrymen better than anyone else'.[21] Another passage gives additional reasons why one should trust native traditions. In his defence of Aristotle's account of the origins of the Epizephyrian Locrians, Polybius says (XII.5.5) that he knows that Aristotle's account about the colony is the account that they have received 'from their fathers' (ἡ φήμη παρὰ πατέρων). This notion has an obvious appeal and one of wide use.[22] It is evident from the local historians and from Thucydides' comment mentioned above that the ancients believed that the most reliable reports about a certain land were to be found in that land itself, a tradition that Dionysius follows when he says that he will write his history from 'those writers whom the Romans themselves approve'.[23] It would indeed be invaluable to have Cato's *Origins*, for in the second and third book of that work he was faced with the same problem that Herodotus had, of classifying and preserving epichoric oral tradition.[24] One of the fragments indi-

---

[17] Thuc. I.20.1, criticising the Athenians: 'For people accept accounts from one another of what has gone before, even if it is their native tradition, without testing them.' The words, 'even if it is their native tradition' (καὶ ἦν ἐπιχώρια σφίσιν ᾖ), suggest that his audience assumed ἐπιχώριοι to be better informed of their own history.

[18] Citation of local sources: I.9.2 (but note the qualification as οἱ τὰ σαφέστατα Πελοποννησίων μνήμῃ παρὰ τῶν πρότερον δεδεγμένοι); VI.2.2. On the sources for Sicily, Dover, *HCT* IV.198-202 (with references) has made it very likely that Thucydides used Antiochus of Syracuse for the early history of Sicily.

[19] This is not to say that it really was native tradition, since often the Greeks attributed to natives a Hellenised version of their early history: see Bickerman, *CPh* 47 (1952) 75-6.

[20] *FGrHist* 566 F 59; on Timaeus' industry in this matter see Pol. XII.27a.3.

[21] Pol. IX.25.3; but he then tempers this with the testimony of Masinissa, whom he claims to have spoken 'more accurately' (ἀκριβέστερον, 25.4).

[22] Cf. Hdt. II.143, where the office of priest at Thebes is handed down from father to son.

[23] D. Hal. *A. R.* I.7.3: οἱ πρὸς αὐτῶν ἐπαινούμενοι Ῥωμαίων.

[24] Nepos, *Cato* 3.3 praised Cato for his industry in this matter.

cates he may have given traditions in the Herodotean manner;[25] just as interesting, however, is his remark on the Ligurians, where he says, 'they themselves are unlettered and lie about their origins, and barely remember the truth'.[26] The passage suggests that if a nation did not know its own origins, nothing could be done. On the other hand, as we can see from Polybius' refutation of Timaeus over the Epizephyrian Locrians, problems arose when there were conflicting epichoric traditions about the same areas, especially if, as was the case there, both versions were probable. Here, the historian would have to rely on other appeals, or admit that the truth was completely unknown.[27]

5. APPEAL TO CHARACTER

As seen in Chapter III §1, character is of fundamental importance in asserting the historian's authority. Where historians make a choice which is based on the character of their source, they will appeal to that source's social standing or effort, or impartiality, adding sometimes that the usual reasons for mendacity were absent. Again, this is good rhetorical practice which both Greeks and Romans employed. Diodorus, for example, will not recount certain Egyptian matters, 'because there is no accurate account nor is any writer who attests to them worthy of belief'. Conversely, he can state that the Sicels are indigenous because it has been recorded by the most distinguished historians, and that there are nine, not three, Muses, as has been recorded by the most illustrious writers. Livy casts doubt on Licinius Macer and calls his testimony 'of less weight' (*leuior*) because of the praise he habitually gives his family.[28] The clearest appeal to character is found in the beginning of the *Anabasis* where Arrian cites Ptolemy as a reliable witness not only because he accompanied Alexander, but also 'because in as much as he was a king, it would have been more shameful for him to lie than for another'.[29] Elsewhere Arrian commends his work on

---

[25] Cato, *HRR* F 71; on the background to this fragment see Chassignet, *Caton* 33a n. 5. [26] *HRR* F 31; cf. *HRR* F 32.

[27] For a rejection of epichoric tradition (rare after Herodotus) see Posidonius, *FGrHist* 87 F 53 = F 246 (E-K) with Kidd, *Commentary* II.846-51.

[28] Diod. 1.29.6; V.2.4; IV.7.1; Livy, VI.9.3-5.

[29] Arr. *Anab. praef.* 1-2; Pédech, *Compagnons* 237 believes that Ptolemy put his title as 'king' in his history; it is possible of course, but Arrian's interpretation of these men's histories should not be retrojected onto Ptolemy and Aristobulus themselves: see Bosworth, *HCA*, ad loc. The dates of publication are unknown (for a recent attempt, see Pédech ibid. 234-7).

India by saying that he has followed 'two estimable men, Megasthenes and Eratosthenes'.[30]

In sum, then, the various methods by which ancient historians choose different versions cannot be said to establish an historical methodology. Rather, sources are chosen (when they are chosen) because of rhetorical criteria – reliability, numbers, 'persuasiveness', the character of the writer. Nevertheless, the selection of certain sources by a historian is an important element in his own credibility, for it is by selecting, criticising, and improving his predecessors that he makes his own abilities and character manifest to the reader.[31]

[30] Arr. *Anab.* v.5.1: Μεγασθένης τε καὶ Ἐρατοσθένης, δοκίμω ἄνδρε.
[31] On predecessors and the historian's characterisation of himself, see Ch. V §2-3.

APPENDIX V

THE ROMAN CONVENTION OF 'NOS' AND 'NOSTRI'

It is characteristic of the Roman historians to use the first-person plural frequently when referring to the Roman state or to Roman soldiers in battle. Cato may have been the first to do this, since one fragment of the *Origins* speaks of 'our commander'.[1] By Sallust's time, the convention is already fully developed. He speaks of 'our ancestors', 'our state', 'our army', and he refers to Romans in battle as 'our men', 'our forces' or simply 'nostri'.[2] Caesar as well in the *Gallic War* refers to 'our men'.[3]

Sallust does not use this convention, however, in the *Catiline*,[4] nor do the Romans use this designation when writing about civil war, where it might seem manifestly inappropriate.[5] A striking exception is Caesar, who even in the *Civil War* uses 'nostri' – but as a reference to his own men, not the Roman soldiers of his enemies.[6] This must have been a bold step, and, if not pure arrogance, may perhaps be taken as another indication that the work lacked his *ultima manus*.[7] Of Caesar's continuators the authors of the *Alexandrian War* and the *Spanish War* use 'nostri' of Caesar's men, the author of the *African War* does not.[8]

Velleius too speaks of Roman soldiers in the first person plural, the more appropriately in that he himself was a soldier and participant;[9] but he also follows the convention where he is not involved, referring to 'our empire' and 'our slaughter' by Ariminius.[10] Tacitus is also fond of this

---

[1] Cato, *HRR* F 82: 'imperator noster, si quis extra ordinem depugnatum init, ei multam facit.' To be safe, we should allow that it may come from a speech; for another possible example see Ch. IV n. 86.

[2] Sall. *Jug.* 4.5; 19.7; 29.7; 38.7; 43.5; 50.6; 101.6 et al.; *Hist.* III.96; IV.36.

[3] See above, pp. 212f.

[4] In the *Catiline* one finds only 'nostri maiores' (12.3).

[5] Tacitus in the *Histories* does not use it in the narration of civil wars, only foreign ones. See n. 11 below.

[6] See *B. Civ.* 1.18.2; 22.1; 40.6, et al. Note 1.43-7 (siege of Ilerda) where *nostri* is contrasted with *Afraniani* (esp. 46.4-5)   [7] See Ch. IV n. 134.

[8] See (e.g.) *Bell. Alex.* 10.1; *Bell. Hisp.* 11.1. On the authors of these works, possibly Caesar's own men, see Schanz-Hosius I.344-5.   [9] Vell. II.107; 112; 114.

[10] Vell. II.109.1; 105.1; cf. 118.2.

convention, and uses it both in the *Histories* (when battles with foreigners are narrated) and the *Annals*.[11] A fragment of Granius Licinianus refers to 'our soldiers',[12] and Ammianus continues the tradition, using it both for himself as a member of the soldiery and as a common expression for Roman troops in general.[13]

It is perhaps surprising that this convention is not found in Livy, who frankly confesses his love for Rome and his intention to treat her events exclusively.[14] Livy, it is true, speaks of 'our age' witnessing the closing of Janus' temple, and of stratagems used by 'our and foreign commanders'; he notes that 'we Romans' have never been beaten and never will be, provided 'we live' with the love of peace and civil harmony.[15] But he does not employ the convention of 'nos' or 'nostri' when narrating battles or embassies, and he nowhere refers in his own person to Roman soldiers as 'our men'.[16]

There is nothing like this in the Greek historians. Among the writers of local history there was certainly a more intimate tone,[17] but whether this extended to narratives of battles cannot be known. Josephus, for example, in the *Jewish Antiquities* frequently refers to the Jews in the first person plural.[18] But in his narratives of battles, he refers to them always in the third person. Here, of course, since Josephus has written his work for non-Jews, he cannot assume that same intimacy of audience as a Roman historian, writing for a Roman audience, could.[19]

[11] See (out of many) Tac. *Hist.* I.2.1; III.45.2; IV.13.1; 18.3; 20.3; 23.1, et al.; note that Tacitus can refer to an earlier time as 'ciuili inter nos bello' (v.9.1); *Ann.* I.55.1; II.45.2; IV.48.1; VI.31.1; XIII.37.1.

[12] Gran. Lic. XXXV.68: 'milites nostri castra capiunt, e.q.s.'

[13] Amm. XXVII.2.6; XXVIII.5.4; XXIX.2.16; XXX.2.1, et al.

[14] Livy, *praef.* 11; IX.17.1 (probably ironic).

[15] Livy, I.19.3; VII.14.6; IX.19.15; 19.17.

[16] At XXV.19.11 we find 'nostri duces' but this is in indirect discourse; at XXV.39.15 the pursued Romans are referred to as 'nostros' but he is here quoting Piso; and at XXX.26.9 'nobis' is part of the quotation of Ennius. Leeman, *Orationis Ratio* I.196, in noting Livy's avoidance of this Roman convention, suggests that the historian is 'rather ... a loyal admirer than a part and a product' of Roman history. See also above, pp. 140f. for Livy as outsider. [17] See Ch IV n. 89.

[18] Jos. *A. J.* I.4; 158; III.143; 318, et al; cf. *B.J.* 1.9-11, quoted above, p. 168.

[19] I should note also Amm. XXIX.2.16, 'noster Hypatius' of the city and praetorian prefect. See also Dio, LXXII.3.3, where he refers to 'our Dacia', and LXXX.4.1, where the Roman soldiers are referred to as τὰ στρατιωτικὰ ἡμῖν (but this is not a battle).

APPENDIX VI

GREEK CONTINUATORS

Dates in parentheses are the beginning and ending points of the history.

Mainland Greece	Sicily and the West

Herodotus
(560–479)
|
Thucydides[1]
(479–411)

Xenophon   Cratippus[2]   Theopompus[3]   Hellenica   Philistus[4]
(411–362) (411–?394)   (411–394)   Oxyrhynchia   (origins–367/6)
                                         (411–?) |
                         Ephorus[5]   Athanis[6]
                         (1069–341/0)   (362/1–336)
                         |
Duris of Samos   Diyllus[7]
(370/69–?281)   (357/6–297/6)
| |
                         Psaon of Plataea[8]
                         (297/6–?)
Phylarchus[9]
(272–220)
                         Aratus[10]   Timaeus
                         (?251–221)   (early times–264)

                         Polybius[11]
                         (264/3–146/5 or 145/4)

                    Posidonius[12]   Strabo[13]
                    (146–70s?)   (145/4–31?)

Chryserus[14]
(753 BC–AD 180)
|
Herodian   Dexippus, *Chronike Historia*
(AD 180–238)   (early times?–AD 269/70)
                                        |
                                        Eunapius
                                        (AD 269/70–404)

1. Thucydides joined his work to Herodotus' by his narrative of the Pentekontaetia (I.89-117): see Canfora, *Belfagor* 26 (1971) 662; Jacoby, *Abhandlungen* 39 with n.66.
2. *FGrHist* 64 TT 1-2; Schwartz and Jacoby thought Cratippus to be a Hellenistic writer (see Jacoby, *Abhandlungen* 322-33, esp. 326ff.), but cf. Breitenbach, *RE* Suppl. XII. 414-418 for counter-arguments; Bruce, *Historical Commentary on the Hellenica Oxyrhynchia* 22-7 leans towards Cratippus as the author of the *Hellenica Oxyrhynchia*; see also Meister, *Griechische Geschichtsschreibung* 65-8; P. Harding, 'The Authorship of the Hellenica Oxyrhynchia' *AHB* 1 (1987) 101-4.
3. The *Hellenica* is here being referred to; Theopompus' *Philippica* reveals a different orientation, but not a different belief in the value of continuous history; rather, in the latter the events are arranged around an individual: this was a new type of organisation; but it represents a return to the unity of theme that Herodotus and Thucydides had practised.
4. He wrote *On Sicily* in seven books from earliest times to 406, and *On Dionysius [I]* in four books to 367/6.
5. Ephorus' son Demophilus completed his father's work, bringing it to the year 341/0: *FGrHist* 70 T 9a with Jacoby, *Komm.* II. C. 28-9.
6. *FGrHist* 562 T 2. Before beginning his topic proper, he completed Philistus' history by treating a period of seven years (τὸν ἄγραφον χρόνον) left out by his predecessor.
7. *FGrHist* 73 T 2. Diyllus treated the years 357/6-341/0 in his first σύνταξις, continuing Ephorus in his second; R. Drews, 'Ephorus and History Written κατὰ γένος', *AJP* 84 (1963) 244-55 at 255 n. 3 considers it absurd that Diyllus' second *syntaxis* should continue Ephorus' and not Diyllus' own work; he suggests that Ephorus had described Macedonian and Persian affairs for 356-340, but not Greek and Sicilian affairs. Diyllus' first *syntaxis* then treated Greece and Sicily for 356-340; and his second *syntaxis* covered Greek and non-Greek affairs from 340-296.
8. *FGrHist* 78 T 1. Psaon may have been continued by Menodotus of Perinthus (Jacoby *Komm.* II. C. 143). Lorenz, *Untersuchungen z. Geschichtswerk des Polybios* 85-6 n. 85 claimed that he continued Phylarchus.
9. Jacoby (*Komm.* II. C. 133) thinks it more likely that Phylarchus continued Duris rather than Hieronymus.
10. The earliest datable fragment is for the year 251. On the beginning and ending point of Aratus' *Memoirs* see Jacoby, *Komm.* II. B. 654, who points out that Aratus would have treated his upbringing and the previous history of the Achaean League before beginning the contemporary portions of his work.
11. Pol. 1.5.1=*FGrHist* 566 T 6a; Pol. 1.3.1=*FGrHist* 231 T 2a.
12. *FGrHist* 87 TT 1, 12b=TT 1, 1b (E-K).
13. *FGrHist* 91 F 1. Strabo's Τὰ μετὰ Πολύβιον only began properly in Book V, Books I-IV being a summary of early Greek history to the year 145/4.
14. *FGrHist* 96; he was a freedman of Marcus Aurelius.

APPENDIX VII

ROMAN CONTINUATORS

Dates in parentheses are the beginning and ending points of the history.

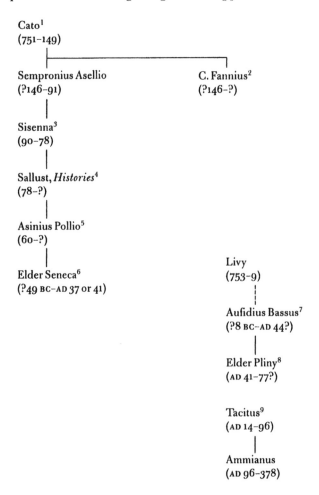

Cato[1]
(751–149)

Sempronius Asellio   C. Fannius[2]
(?146–91)   (?146–?)

Sisenna[3]
(90–78)

Sallust, *Histories*[4]
(78–?)

Asinius Pollio[5]
(60–?)

Elder Seneca[6]   Livy
(?49 BC–AD 37 or 41)   (753–9)

                               Aufidius Bassus[7]
                               (?8 BC–AD 44?)

                               Elder Pliny[8]
                               (AD 41–77?)

                               Tacitus[9]
                               (AD 14–96)

                               Ammianus
                               (AD 96–378)

[1] Cato died in 149; he mentions the prosecution of Servius Galba in the same year (*HRR* F 109).

² Beginning and ending points of Fannius' history are unknown, but he was considered an authority for the 130s and 120s. He may have treated early Roman history.
³ Sisenna began with the Social War of 90, and perhaps ended with Sulla's death in 78. Book I treated early Roman history summarily; see Schanz-Hosius I.325.
⁴ It is uncertain when Sallust's *Histories* ended; the latest datable fragment comes from the year 67.
⁵ The beginning point of Pollio's history is guaranteed by Horace, *Carm.* II.1.1-4; it is unclear when his history ended since his topic, the civil wars, is ambiguous. He narrated the death of Cicero (43) and the battle of Philippi (42): Peter, *HRR* II.LXXXVIIff. Nisbet-Hubbard, *Commentary on Horace Odes II*, 8 favour 42 as the closing date, Woodman, *RICH* 127-8 suggests that his work extended into the 30s.
⁶ Seneca's *Historiae* began, says his son, 'ab initio bellorum ciuilium' (*HRR* F 1); some have taken this to mean the arrival of Caesar in Italy in 59 (as in Livy), some believe this means the death of Tiberius Gracchus in 133 (as Appian); see Peter, *HRR* II.CXVIII-VIIII.
⁷ Bassus wrote a *German Wars* as well as *Histories*. The various views on the beginning and ending of the latter are summarised by Syme, *Tacitus* II.697-9; I follow here his suggestion that Aufidius may have begun in 8 in order to join his work to Livy's; there is, however, no explicit evidence for this. Syme (ibid.) also suggests an ending around AD 44 or 47.
⁸ He is explicitly attested as having entitled his work *a fine Aufidi Bassi* (Pliny, *ep.* III.5.6).
⁹ These dates combine the *Annals* (14-68) and the *Histories* (69-96).

Bibliography

Adcock, F., *Caesar as a Man of Letters* (Cambridge 1961).
Alföldy, G., 'Herodians Person', *Anc. Soc.* 2 (1971) 204-33.
Alonso-Núñez, J. M., 'An Augustan World History: The *Historicae Philippicae* of Pompeius Trogus', *G&R* 34 (1987) 56-72.
— 'The Emergence of Universal Historiography from the 4th to the 2nd centuries BC', in *Purposes of History. Studies in Greek Historiography from the 4th to the 2nd centuries BC*, edd. H. Verdin, G. Schepens, and E. deKeyser (*Studia Hellenistica* 30; Leuven 1990) 173-92.
— ed., *Geschichtsbild und Geschichtsdenken im Altertum* (Darmstadt 1991).
Ambaglio, D., *L'Opera Storiografica di Ellanico di Lesbo* (Pisa 1980).
— 'Fra hypomnemata e storiografia', *Athenaeum* 68 (1990) 503-8.
Anderson, G., *The Second Sophistic. A Cultural Phenomenon in the Roman Empire* (London and New York 1993).
Andrei, O., *A. Claudius Charax di Pergamo* (Bologna 1984).
Armayor, O. K., 'Herodotus' Influence on Manethon and the Implications for Egyptology', *CB* 61 (1985) 7-10.
Astin, A. E., *Cato the Censor* (Oxford 1979).
Atkinson, J. E., *A Commentary on Q. Curtius Rufus' Historiae Alexandri Magni Books 3 and 4* (Amsterdam 1980).
Attridge, H. W., *The Interpretation of Biblical History in the Antiquitates Judaicae of Flavius Josephus* (Missoula 1976).
Aubrion, E., *Rhétorique et histoire chez Tacite* (Metz 1985).
Avenarius, G., *Lukians Schrift zur Geschichtsschreibung* (Meisenheim am Glan 1956).
Ax, W., 'Die Geschichtsschreibung bei Quintilian' in id., ed., *Memoria Rerum Veterum. Neue Beiträge zur antiken Historiographie und Alten Geschichte. Festschrift für Carl Joachim Classen z. 60. Geburtstag* (Stuttgart 1990) 133-55.
Badian, E., *Studies in Greek and Roman History* (Oxford 1964).
— 'The Early Historians', in *Latin Historians*, ed. T. A. Dorey (London 1966) 1-38.
— 'Nearchus the Cretan', *YCS* 24 (1975) 147-70.
— 'Livy and Augustus', in *Livius: Aspekte seines Werkes*, ed. W. Schuller (Konstanz 1993) 9-38.

Baldson, J. P. V. D., 'Sulla Felix', *JRS* 41 (1951) 1-10.
'Some Questions about Historical Writing in the Second Century BC', *CQ* n. s. 3 (1953) 158-64.
Barber, E. L., *The Historian Ephorus* (Cambridge 1935).
Barnes, T. D., 'The Composition of Cassius Dio's *Roman History*', *Phoenix* 38 (1984) 240-55.
'Literary Convention, Nostalgia and Reality in Ammianus Marcellinus', in *Reading the Past in Late Antiquity*, edd. G. Clarke et al. (Rushcutters Bay, Australia 1990) 59-92.
Barwick, K., 'Die Gliederung der Narratio in der rhetorischen Theorie und ihre Bedeutung für die Geschichte des antiken Romans', *Hermes* 63 (1928) 261-87.
Bates, R. L., *Memoirs and the Perception of History in the Roman Republic* (diss. Univ. of Pennsylvania 1983).
Bellemore, J., *Nicolaus of Damascus: Life of Augustus* (Bristol 1984).
Beltrametti, A., *Erodoto. Una storia governata dal discorso. Il racconto morale come forma della memoria* (Florence 1987).
Bering-Staschewski, R., *Römische Zeitgeschichte bei Cassius Dio* (Bochum 1981).
Bickerman, E., 'Origenes Gentium', *CPh* 47 (1952) 65-81.
Bigwood, J. M., 'Ctesias' *Indica* and Photius', *Phoenix* 43 (1989) 302-16.
Bloch, H., 'Studies in the Historical Literature of the Fourth Century BC', *HSCP* Suppl. 1 (1940) 303-76.
Blockley, R. C., *The Fragmentary Classicising Historians of the Later Roman Empire: Eunapius, Olympiodorus, Priscus and Malchus*, 2 vols. (Liverpool 1981-3).
Boedeker, D., 'Simonides on Plataea: Narrative Elegy, Mythodic History', *ZPE* 107 (1995) 217-29.
Bömer, F., 'Der Commentarius', *Hermes* 81 (1953) 210-50.
Bompaire, J., *Lucien écrivain* (Paris 1958).
Boncquet, J., 'Polybius on the Critical Evaluation of Historians', *Anc. Soc.* 13-14 (1982-3) 277-91.
Bonner, S. F., *The Literary Treatises of Dionysius of Halicarnassus* (Cambridge 1939).
Roman Declamation in the Late Republic and Early Empire (Liverpool 1949).
Education in Ancient Rome (London and Berkeley 1977).
Boor, C. de, 'Römische Kaisergeschichte in byzantinischer Fassung', *BZ* 1 (1892) 13-33.
Booth, W., *The Rhetoric of Fiction* (Chicago ^{2}1983).
Bosworth, A. B., *A Historical Commentary on Arrian's History of Alexander* (Oxford 1980-).
From Arrian to Alexander (Oxford 1988).
'Arrian and Rome: The Minor Works', *ANRW* II. 34. 1 (1993) 226-75.
Bowersock, G., *Augustus and the Greek World* (Oxford 1965).
Greek Sophists in the Roman Empire (Oxford 1969).

Bowie, E. L., 'Greeks and their Past in the Second Sophistic', in *Studies in Ancient Society*, ed. M. I. Finley (London and Boston 1974) 166-209; orig. in *Past and Present* 46 (1970) 3-41.

'Lies, Fiction and Slander in Early Greek Poetry', in *Lies and Fiction in the Ancient World*, edd. C. Gill and T. P. Wiseman (Exeter and Austin, Tex. 1993) 1-37.

'The Readership of Greek Novels in the Ancient World', in *The Search for the Ancient Novel*, ed. J. Tatum (Baltimore and London 1994) 435-59.

Breebaart, A. B., *Enige historiografische aspecten van Arrianus' Anabasis Alexandri* (Leiden 1960).

Breitenbach, H., *Historiographische Anschauungsformen Xenophons* (Freiburg i. d. Schweiz 1950).

'Xenophon von Athen', *RE* IX. A. 2 (1967) 1569-2052.

'Hellenika Oxyrhynchia', *RE* Suppl. XII (1970) 383-426.

Bremmer, J. and Horsfall, N., edd., *Roman Myth and Mythography* (London 1987).

Briscoe, J., *A Commentary on Livy XXXI-XXXIII* (Oxford 1973; repr. with addenda 1989).

Brodersen, K., 'Appian und sein Werk', *ANRW* II. 34. 1 (1993) 339-63.

Brown, T. S., *Timaeus of Tauromenium* (Berkeley 1958).

'Suggestions for a Vita of Ctesias of Cnidus', *Historia* 27 (1978) 1-19.

Bruce, I. A. F., *A Historical Commentary on the Hellenica Oxyrhynchia* (Cambridge 1967).

Brunt, P. A., 'Cicero and Historiography', in *Studies in Greek History and Thought* (Oxford 1993) 181-209; orig. in *ΦΙΛΙΑΣ ΧΑΡΙΝ. Miscellanea di Studi Classici in onore di Eugenio Manni* (Rome 1980) 1.311-40.

'On Historical Fragments and Epitomes', *CQ* n. s. 30 (1980) 477-94.

Bucher, G., 'The *Annales Maximi* in the Light of Roman Methods of Keeping Records', *AJAH* 12 (1987 [1995]) 2-61.

Bung, P., *Quintus Fabius Pictor, der erste römische Annalist* (diss. Cologne 1950).

Burstein, S., *The Babyloniaca of Berossus* (Malibu, Calif. 1978).

Agatharchides of Cnidus: On the Erythraean Sea (London 1989).

Burton, A., *Diodorus Siculus. Book I. A Commentary* (Leiden 1972).

Cairns, F., *Generic Composition in Greek and Roman Poetry* (Edinburgh 1972).

Cameron, A., 'Introduction: The Writing of History', in ead., ed., *History as Text* (London and Chapel Hill 1989) 1-10.

Cancik-Lindemaier, H. and Cancik, H., 'Zensur und Gedächtnis: Zu Tacitus, *Annales* IV. 32-38', *AU* 29. 4 (1986) 16-35.

Canfora, L., 'Il ciclo storico', *Belfagor* 26 (1971) 653-70.

'Le but de l'historiographie selon Diodore', in *Purposes of History. Studies in Greek Historiography from the 4th to the 2nd centuries BC*, edd. H. Verdin, G. Schepens, and E. deKeyser (*Studia Hellenistica* 30; Leuven 1990) 313-22.

Caplan, H., *[Cicero] ad C. Herennium* (London and Cambridge, Mass. 1954).

Cawkwell, G., 'Introduction' to *Xenophon: The Persian Expedition* (Harmondsworth 1972) 9-48.
  'Introduction' to *Xenophon: A History of My Times (Hellenica)* (Harmondsworth 1979) 7-46.
Champlin, E., *Fronto and Antonine Rome* (Cambridge, Mass. 1980).
Chaniotis, A., *Historie und Historiker in der griechischen Inschriften. Epigraphische Beiträge zur griechischen Historiographie* (Wiesbaden 1988).
Chassignet, M., *Caton: Les Origines* (Paris 1986).
Chilver, G. E. F., *A Historical Commentary on Tacitus' Histories I and II* (Oxford 1979).
  A Historical Commentary on Tacitus' Histories IV and V, completed and revised by G. B. Townend (Oxford 1985).
Chodniček, J., 'Über die Gründe der theoretischen Excurse und Bemerkungen des Polybius', in *Neunzehnter Jahresbericht des K. K. Gymnasium. im 3. Bezirk in Wien* (Vienna 1888).
Christ, M. R., 'Theopompus and Herodotus: A Reassessment', *CQ* n. s. 43 (1993) 47-52.
Clark, D. L., 'Imitation: Theory and Practice in Roman Rhetoric', *Quart. Journ. Speech* 37 (1951) 11-22.
Cohen, S. J. D., *Josephus in Galilee and Rome. His Vita and Development as a Historian* (Leiden 1979).
Collins, J. H., 'Caesar as a Political Propagandist', *ANRW* I. 1 (1972) 922-66.
Connor, W. R., 'History without Heroes. Theopompus' Treatment of Philip of Macedon', *GRBS* 8 (1967) 133-54.
  Thucydides (Princeton 1984).
  'Narrative Discourse in Thucydides', in *The Greek Historians: Literature and History. Papers Presented to A. E. Raubitschek*, ed. M. H. Jameson (Saratoga, Calif. 1985) 1-17.
Cornell, T. J., 'The historical tradition of early Rome', in *Past Perspectives. Studies in Greek and Roman Historical Writing*, edd. I. S. Moxon, J. D. Smart, and A. J. Woodman (Cambridge 1986) 67-86.
Cova, P., *I principia historiae e le idee storiografiche di Frontone* (Naples 1970).
D'Alton, J. F., *Roman Literary Theory and Criticism* (New York 1931).
Darbo-Peschanski, C., *Le discours du particulier* (Paris 1987).
Davidson, J., 'The Gaze of Polybius' *Histories*', *JRS* 81 (1991) 10-24.
Defosse, P., 'A propos du début insolite des "Helléniques"', *Rev. Belge* 46 (1968) 5-24.
Dessau, H., 'Die Vorrede des Livius' in id., ed., *Festschrift . . . Otto Hirschfeld* (Berlin 1903) 461-6.
Develin, R., 'Tacitus and the techniques of insidious suggestion', *Antichthon* 17 (1983) 64-95.
Dewald, C., 'Narrative Surface and Authorial Voice in Herodotus' *Histories*', *Arethusa* 20 (1987) 147-70.

Dickie, M. W., 'The Disavowal of *invidia* in Roman Iamb and Satire', *PLLS* 3 (1981) 183-208.
Dihle, A., 'The Conception of India in Hellenistic and Roman Literature', *PCPhS* n.s. 10 (1964) 15-23.
Dillery, J., *Xenophon and the History of his Times* (London and New York 1995).
Dodds, E. R., *Pagan and Christian in an Age of Anxiety* (Cambridge 1965).
Dover, K. J., *Thucydides* (*Greece and Rome* New Surveys in the Classics, No. 7; Oxford 1973).
Dowden, K., 'Apuleius and the Art of Narration', *CQ* n.s. 32 (1982) 419-35.
'The Roman Audience of *The Golden Ass*', in *The Search for the Ancient Novel*, ed. J. Tatum (Baltimore and London 1994) 419-34.
Drews, R., *The Greek Accounts of Eastern History* (Cambridge, Mass. 1973).
Drexler, H., *Ammianstudien* (Hildesheim and New York 1974).
DuQuesnay, I. M., 'Vergil's First Eclogue', *PLLS* 3 (1981) 29-182.
Earl, D. C., *The Political Thought of Sallust* (Cambridge 1961).
'Prologue Form in Ancient Historiography', *ANRW* I. 2 (1972) 842-56.
Eck, B., 'Sur la vie de Ctésias', *REG* 103 (1990) 409-34.
Edelstein, L. and Kidd, I. G., *Posidonius I. The Fragments* (Cambridge ²1989).
Eden, P. T., 'Caesar's Style: Inheritance versus Intelligence', *Glotta* 40 (1962) 74-117.
Egermann, F., *Die Proömien zu den Werken des Sallust* (Vienna and Leipzig 1932).
Ek, S., *Herodotismen in der Archäologie des Dionys von Halikarnass* (Lund 1942).
'Eine Stiltendenz in der Römischen Archäologie des Dionysios von Halikarnass', *Eranos* 43 (1945) 198-214.
Else, G., *Aristotle's Poetics: The Argument* (Cambridge, Mass. and Leiden 1957).
Engel, G., *De antiquorum epicorum didacticorum historicorum prooemiis* (diss. Marburg 1910).
Erbse, H., *Studien zum Verständnis Herodots* (Berlin and New York 1992).
Errington, R. M., 'Bias in Ptolemy's History of Alexander', *CQ* n. s. 19 (1969) 233-42.
Evans, J. A. S., *Herodotus. Explorer of the Past* (Princeton 1991).
Fantham, E., 'Imitation and Evolution: The Discussion of Rhetorical Imitation in Cicero *De Oratore* 2. 87-97 and some Related Problems of Ciceronian Theory', *CPh* 73 (1978) 1-16.
'Imitation and Decline: Rhetorical Theory and Practice in the First Century after Christ', *CPh* 73 (1978) 102-16.
Farrar, C., *The Origins of Democratic Thinking* (Cambridge 1988).
Fehling, D., 'Zur Funktion und Formgeschichte des Proömiums in der älteren griechischen Prosa', in ΔΩPHMA: *Festschrift... H. Diller* (Athens 1975) 61-75.
Herodotus and his 'Sources', translated by J. G. Howie (Leeds 1989); revised and expanded edition of *Die Quellenangaben bei Herodot. Studien zur Erzählkunst Herodots* (Berlin and New York 1971).

Flach, D., 'Die Vorrede zu Sallusts Historien in neuer Rekonstruktion', *Philologus* 117 (1973) 76-86.
Flory, S., 'Who Read Herodotus' *Histories*?', *AJPh* 101 (1980) 12-28.
'The Meaning of τὸ μὴ μυθῶδες (1.22.4) and the Usefulness of Thucydides' History', *CJ* 85 (1990) 193-208.
Flower, H. I., '*Fabulae Praetextae* in Context: When Were Plays on Contemporary Subjects Performed in Republican Rome?', *CQ* 45 (1995) 170-90.
Flower, M. A., *Theopompus of Chios. History and Rhetoric in the Fourth Century BC* (Oxford 1994).
Fornara, C. W., *Herodotus. An Interpretative Essay* (Oxford 1971).
The Nature of History in Ancient Greece and Rome (Berkeley, London, and Los Angeles 1983).
'Studies in Ammianus Marcellinus. I. The Letter of Libanius and Ammianus' Connection with Antioch', *Historia* 41 (1992) 328-44.
'Studies in Ammianus Marcellinus. II. Ammianus' Knowledge and Use of Greek and Latin Literature', *Historia* 41 (1992) 420-38.
Fox, M., 'History and Rhetoric in Dionysius of Halicarnassus', *JRS* 83 (1993) 31-47.
Fraenkel, E., 'Ein Form römischer Kriegsbulletin', in *Kleine Beiträge zur klassischen Philologie* (Rome 1964) II.69-73; orig. in *Eranos* 54 (1956) 189-94.
Horace (Oxford 1957).
Fraser, P., *Ptolemaic Alexandria*, 3 vols. (Oxford 1972).
Frier, B. W., *Libri Annales Pontificum Maximorum: The Origins of the Annalistic Tradition* (Rome 1979).
Fritz, K. von, *Die griechische Geschichtsschreibung*, 2 vols. (Berlin and New York 1967).
Funaioli, G., 'Livius im Plane seines Werkes', *Die Antike* 19 (1943) 214-30.
Furneaux, H., ed., *The Annals of Tacitus*, 2 vols. (Oxford 1896, ^{2}1907).
Gabba, E., 'Storici greci dell'impero romano da Augusto ai Severi', *RSI* 71 (1959) 361-81.
'True History and False History in Classical Antiquity', *JRS* 71 (1981) 50-62.
'The Historians and Augustus', in *Caesar Augustus: Seven Aspects*, edd. F. Millar and E. Segal (Oxford 1984) 61-88.
Dionysius and the History of Archaic Rome (Berkeley and Los Angeles 1991).
Geffcken, J., *Timaios' Geographie des Westens* (Berlin 1892).
Gelzer, M., 'Römische Politik bei Fabius Pictor', in *Kleine Schriften* III.51-92; orig. in *Hermes* 68 (1933) 129-66.
'Der Anfang römischer Geschichtsschreibung', in *Kleine Schriften* III.92-103; orig. in *Hermes* 69 (1934) 46-55.
'Nochmals über den Anfang römischer Geschichtsschreibung', in *Kleine Schriften* III.104-10; orig. in *Hermes* 82 (1954) 342-8.
'Die pragmatische Geschichtsschreibung des Polybios', in *Kleine Schriften* III.155-60; orig. in *Festschrift für C. Weickert* (Berlin 1955) 87-91.

'Über die Arbeitsweise des Polybios', in *Kleine Schriften* III.161-90; orig. in *SHAW Phil-hist. Kl.* Abh. 3 (Heidelberg 1956).
'Caesar als Historiker' in *Kleine Schriften* II.307-35.
Kleine Schriften, 3 vols., edd. H. Strasburger and C. Meier (Wiesbaden 1964).
Genette, G., *Narrative Discourse* (Ithaca 1980).
Georgiadou, A. and Larmour, D., 'Lucian and Historiography: "De Historia Conscribenda" and "Verae Historiae"', *ANRW* II. 34. 2 (1994) 1448-508.
Gill, C., 'The *Ethos/Pathos* Distinction in Rhetorical and Literary Criticism', *CQ* n. s. 34 (1984) 149-66.
Gill, C. and Wiseman, T. P., edd., *Lies and Fiction in the Ancient World* (Exeter and Austin, Tex. 1993).
Ginsburg, J., *Tradition and Theme in the Annals of Tacitus* (New York 1981).
'*In maiores certamina*: Past and Present in the *Annals*', in *Tacitus and the Tacitean Tradition*, edd. T. J. Luce and A. J. Woodman (Princeton 1993) 86-103.
Görler, W., 'Die Veränderung des Erzählerstandpunktes in Caesars Bellum Gallicum', *Poetica* 8 (1976) 95-119.
Gold, B. K., *Literary Patronage in Greece and Rome* (Chapel Hill and London 1987).
Gomme, A. W., Andrewes, A. and Dover, K. J., *A Historical Commentary on Thucydides*, 5 vols. (Oxford 1941-79).
Goodyear, F. R. D., *The Annals of Tacitus I: Annals 1.1-54* (Cambridge 1972).
Tacitus (Greece and Rome New Surveys in the Classics, No. 4; Oxford ²1979).
The Annals of Tacitus II: Annals 1.55-81 and Annals 2 (Cambridge 1981).
'On the Character and Text of Justin's Compilation of Trogus', in *Papers on Latin Literature* (London 1992) 210-23; orig. in *PACA* 16 (1982) 1-24.
Gossman, L., *Between History and Literature* (Cambridge, Mass. 1990).
Gould, J., *Herodotus* (London 1989).
Grant, M., *Greek and Roman Historians: Information and Misinformation* (London and New York 1995).
Gray, V., 'Mimesis in Greek Historical Writing, *AJPh* 108 (1987) 467-86.
The Character of Xenophon's Hellenica (London and Baltimore 1989).
'The Moral Interpretation of Arrian's *Anabasis*', *JHS* 110 (1990) 180-6.
'Continuous History and Xenophon, *Hellenica*', *AJPh* 112 (1991) 201-28.
Griffin, J., *Homer on Life and Death* (Oxford 1980).
'Die Ursprünge der Historien Herodots', in *Memoria Rerum Veterum. Neue Beiträge zur antiken Historiographie und Alten Geschichte. Festschrift für Carl Joachim Classen z. 60. Geburtstag*, ed. W. Ax (Stuttgart 1990) 51-82.
Griffith, G. T., 'Some Habits of Thucydides when introducing Persons', *PCPhS* 187 (1961) 21-33.
Gruen, E., *Culture and National Identity in Republican Rome* (Ithaca 1992).
Hägg, T., *Narrative Technique in Ancient Greek Romances* (Lund 1971).
The Novel in Antiquity (London and Berkeley 1983).

Halbfas, F., *Theorie und Praxis in der Geschichtsschreibung bei Dionys von Halikarnass* (diss. Münster 1910).
Halliwell, S., *Aristotle's Poetics* (London and Chapel Hill 1986).
Hamilton, J. R., *Plutarch: Alexander. A Commentary* (Oxford 1969).
Hansen, M. H., 'The Battle Exhortation in Ancient Historiography: Fact or Fiction', *Historia* 42 (1993) 161-80.
Harding, P., *Androtion and the Atthis* (Oxford 1994).
Harris, W., *Ancient Literacy* (Cambridge, Mass. 1990).
Havelock, E., *Preface to Plato* (New Haven 1964).
Heldmann, K., *Antike Theorien über Entwicklung und Verfall der Redekunst* (Munich 1982).
Hengst, D. den, 'The Scientific Digressions in Ammianus' Res Gestae', in *Cognitio Gestorum. The Historiographic Art of Ammianus Marcellinus*, edd. J. den Boeft, D. den Hengst, and H. C. Teitler (Amsterdam et al. 1992) 39-46.
Henry, W. P., *Greek Historical Writing. A Historiographical Essay Based on Xenophon's Hellenica* (Chicago 1967).
Herkommer, E., *Die topoi in den Proömien der römischen Geschichtswerke* (Tübingen 1968).
Hermann, W., *Die Historien des Coelius Antipater* (Meisenheim am Glan 1979).
Herzog, R., ed., *Restauration und Erneuerung. Die lateinische Literatur von 284 bis 374 n. Chr.* (Munich 1989).
Heubeck, A., West, S. and Hainsworth, J. B., *A Commentary on the Odyssey I. Introduction and Books I-VIII* (Oxford 1988).
Heuss, A., 'Alexander der Grosse und die politische Ideologie des Altertums', *A&A* 4 (1954) 65-104.
Holford-Strevens, L., *Aulus Gellius* (London 1988; Chapel Hill 1989).
Homeyer, H., *Lukian: wie man Geschichte schreiben soll* (Munich 1965).
Hornblower, J., *Hieronymus of Cardia* (Oxford 1981).
Hornblower, S., *Thucydides* (London and Baltimore 1987).
  A Commentary on Thucydides (Oxford 1991-).
  'Introduction' in id., ed., *Greek Historiography* 1-72.
  'Narratology and Narrative Technique in Thucydides' in id., ed., *Greek Historiography* 131-66.
  ed., *Greek Historiography* (Oxford 1994).
  'The Fourth-Century and Hellenistic Reception of Thucydides', *JHS* 115 (1995) 47-68.
Howald, E., *Vom Geist antiker Geschichtsschreibung* (Munich and Berlin 1944).
Hüber, L., 'Herodots Homerverständnis', in *Synusia: Festgabe . . . W. Schadewaldt*, edd. H. Flashar and K. Gaiser (Pfullingen 1965) 29-52.
Humphreys, S. C., 'Social Relations on Stage: Witnesses in Classical Athens', *History and Anthropology* 1 (1985) 313-69.
Hunger, H., *Die hochsprachliche profane Literatur der Byzantiner*, vol. 1 (Munich 1978).

Hunter, V., *Past and Process in Herodotus and Thucydides* (Princeton 1982).
Hurst, A., 'Un critique grec dans la Rome d'Auguste: Denys d'Halicarnasse', *ANRW* II. 30. 1 (1982) 839-65.
Huxley, G. L., 'Aristotle as Antiquary', *GRBS* 14 (1973) 271-86.
   Herodotus and the Epic (Athens 1989).
Ibendorff, E., *Untersuchungen zur darstellerischen Persönlichkeit des Polybios* (Rostock 1930).
Isnardi, M., 'Τέχνη e ἦθος nella metodologia storiografica di Polibio', *SCO* 3 (1955) 102-10.
Jacoby, F., *Die Fragmente der griechischen Historiker* (Berlin and Leiden 1922-56; Leiden 1994-).
   'Über die Entwicklung der griechischen Historiographie und den Plan einer neuen Sammlung der griechischen Historikerfragmente', in *Abhandlungen* 16-72; orig. in *Klio* 9 (1909) 80-123.
   'Hekataios (3) von Milet', *RE* VII.2 (1912) 2667-750.
   'Hekataios (4) aus Abdera', *RE* VII.2 (1912) 2750-69.
   'Herodotos', *RE* Suppl. II (1913) 205-520.
   'Kephalion', *RE* XI.1 (1921) 191-2.
   'Ktesias', *RE* XI.2 (1922) 2032-73.
   Atthis. The Local Chronicles of Ancient Athens (Oxford 1949).
   Abhandlungen zur griechischen Geschichtsschreibung, ed. H. Bloch (Leiden 1956).
Jal, P., 'Pline et l'historiographie latine', *Helmantica* 38 (1987) 171-86.
Janson, T., *Latin Prose Prefaces. Studies in Literary Conventions* (Stockholm 1964).
Jones, C. P., *Culture and Society in Lucian* (Cambridge, Mass. 1986).
Jong, I. J. F. de, *Narrators and Focalizers. The Presentation of the Story in the Iliad* (Amsterdam 1987).
   'The Subjective Style in Odysseus' Wanderings', *CQ* n. s. 42 (1992) 1-11.
Kajanto, L., 'Fortuna', *ANRW* II. 17. 1 (1981) 502-58.
Kaster, R. A., *Suetonius: De Grammaticis et Rhetoribus* (Oxford 1995).
Keitel, E., 'Homeric Antecedents to the *Cohortatio* in the Ancient Historians', *CW* 80 (1986/7) 153-72.
Kennedy, G., *The Art of Persuasion in Greece* (Princeton 1963).
   The Art of Rhetoric in the Roman World (Princeton 1972).
   Greek Rhetoric under Christian Emperors (Princeton 1983).
Kidd, I. G., *Poseidonius II. Commentary* (Cambridge 1989).
   'Posidonius as Philosopher-Historian' in *Philosophia Togata,* edd. M. Griffin and J. Barnes (Oxford 1989) 38-50.
Kindstrand, J. F., *Homer in der zweiten Sophistik* (Uppsala 1973).
Kirk, G. S., *The Iliad: A Commentary. I. Books I-IV* (Cambridge 1985).
Klingner, F., 'Tacitus und die Geschichtsschreiber des 1. Jahrhunderts n. Chr.', in *Römische Geisteswelt* (Munich ^{5}1965) 483-503; orig. in *MH* 15 (1958) 194-206.

Koerner, R., 'Polybios als Kritiker früherer Historiker', *WZ Jena* 6 (1956/57) 547-8; summary in *Polybios*, edd. N. Stiewe and K. Holzberg, 327-31.
Koestermann, E., *Tacitus. Annalen*, 4 vols. (Heidelberg 1963-8).
Kohl, R., *De scholasticarum declamationum argumentis ex historia petitis* (Paderborn 1915).
Kranz, W., *Studien zur antiken Literatur und ihrem Fortwirken* (Heidelberg 1967).
Kraus, C. S., *Livy: Ab Urbe Condita. Book VI* (Cambridge 1994).
Krentz, P., *Xenophon: Hellenika I-II.3.10* (Warminster 1989).
Krischer, T., 'Herodots Prooemium', *Hermes* 93 (1965) 159-67.
Kroll, W., *Studien zum Verständnis der römischen Literatur* (Stuttgart 1924).
  'Rhetorik', *RE* Suppl. VII (1940) 1039-138.
Kuhrt, A., 'Berossus' Babyloniaka and Seleucid Rule in Babylonia', in ead. and S. Sherwin-White, edd., *Hellenism in the East* (London and Berkeley 1987) 32-56.
Laistner, M. L. W., *The Greater Roman Historians* (Berkeley 1947).
Lanata, G., *Poetica Pre-Platonica* (Florence 1963).
La Penna, A., 'Storiografia di Senatori e storiografia di letterati', in *Aspetti del pensiero storico classico* (Turin 1978) 43-104.
Lateiner, D., 'The Empirical Element in the Methods of Early Greek Medical Writers and Herodotus: A Shared Epistemological Response', *Antichthon* 20 (1986) 1-20.
  The Historical Method of Herodotus (Toronto 1989).
Lausberg, H., *Handbuch der literarischen Rhetorik*, 2 vols. (Munich ²1973).
Lebek, W., *Verba Prisca. Die Anfänge des Archaisierens in der lateinischen Beredsamkeit und Geschichtsschreibung* (Göttingen 1970).
Leeman, A. D., *A Systematical Bibliography to Sallust (1879-1950)* (Leiden 1952).
  Orationis Ratio. The Stylistic Theories and Practice of the Roman Orators, Historians and Philosophers, 2 vols. (Amsterdam 1963).
  'Structure and Meaning in the Prologues of Tacitus', in *Form und Sinn. Studien zur römischen Literatur (1954-1984)* (Frankfurt am Main et al. 1985) 317-48; orig in *YCS* 23 (1973) 169-208.
Lefkowitz, M., 'The First Person in Pindar', in *First-Person Fictions* 1-71; orig. in *HSCP* 67 (1963) 177-253.
  'The Poet as Hero', in *First-Person Fictions* 111-26; orig. in *CQ* n.s. 28 (1978) 459-69.
  The Lives of the Greek Poets (Baltimore and London 1981).
  'The Poet as Athlete', in *First-Person Fictions* 161-8; orig. in *SIFC* 3rd ser. 2 (1984) 5-12.
  First-Person Fictions. Pindar's Poetic 'I' (Oxford 1992).
Lehmann, G. A., 'Polybios und die ältere und zeitgenössische griechische Geschichtsschreibung: einige Bemerkungen', in *Polybe* (Entretiens Hardt 20; Geneva 1973) 145-200; discussion, 201-5.

Lemerle, P., *La première humanisme Byzantine* (Paris 1971).
Lévy, E., 'L'art de la déformation historique dans les *Hélleniques* de Xenophon', in *Purposes of History. Studies in Greek Historiography from the 4th to the 2nd centuries BC*, edd. H. Verdin, G. Schepens, and E. deKeyser (*Studia Hellenistica* 30; Leuven 1990) 125-57.
Lewis, R. G., 'Imperial Autobiography, Augustus to Hadrian', *ANRW* II. 34. 1 (1993) 629-706.
Lieberich, H., *Studien zu den Proömien in der griechischen und byzantinischen Geschichtsschreibung. I. Teil, Die griechischen Geschichtsschreiber* (Munich 1898).
Lindner, H., *Die Geschichtsauffassung des Flavius Josephus im Bellum Judaicum* (Leiden 1972).
Lloyd, G. E. R., *Polarity and Analogy. Two Types of Argumentation in Early Greek Thought* (Cambridge 1966).
— *Magic, Reason and Experience. Studies in the Origin and Development of Greek Science* (Cambridge 1979).
— *The Revolutions of Wisdom* (Berkeley and Los Angeles 1987).
— 'Adversaries and Authorities', *PCPhS* n. s. 40 (1994) 27-48.
Loraux, N., '*Ponos*. Sur quelques difficultés de la peine comme nom de travail', *AION* (Arch.) 4 (1982) 171-92.
— *The Invention of Athens. The Funeral Oration in the Classical City* (Cambridge, Mass. and London 1986) Eng. tr. by A. Sheridan of *L'invention d'Athènes. Histoire de l'oraison funèbre dans la 'cité classique'* (Paris 1981).
Lorenz, K., *Untersuchungen zum Geschichtswerk des Polybios* (Stuttgart 1931).
Lucas, D. W., *Aristotle: Poetics* (Oxford 1968).
Luce, T. J., 'The Dating of Livy's First Decade', *TAPA* 96 (1965) 209-40.
— *Livy: The Composition of his History* (Princeton 1977).
— 'Tacitus' Conception of Historical Change', in *Past Perspectives. Studies in Greek and Roman Historical Writing*, edd. I. S. Moxon, J. D. Smart, and A. J. Woodman (Cambridge 1986) 143-57.
— 'Ancient Views on the Causes of Bias in Historical Writing', *CPh* 84 (1989) 16-31.
— 'Livy, Augustus and the Forum Augustus' in *Between Republic and Empire*, edd. K. Raaflaub and M. Toher (Berkeley 1990) 123-38.
— 'Tacitus on "History's Highest Function": *praecipuum munus annalium*', *ANRW* II. 33. 4 (1991) 2904-27.
MacLaren, M., 'Xenophon and Themistogenes', *TAPA* 65 (1934) 240-7.
Macleod, C., 'Thucydides on Faction (3.82-83)' in *Collected Essays* (Oxford 1983) 123-39; orig. in *PCPhS* n.s. 25 (1979) 52-68.
Macleod, M. D., *Lucian: A Selection* (Warminster 1991).
Maehler, H., *Die Auffassung des Dichterberufs im frühen Griechentum bis zur Zeit Pindars* (Göttingen 1963).
Malitz, J., *Die Historien des Poseidonios* (Munich 1983).
— 'Das Interesse an der Geschichte. Die griechischen Historiker und ihr

Publikum', in *Purposes of History. Studies in Greek Historiography from the 4th to the 2nd centuries BC*, edd. H. Verdin, G. Schepens, and E. deKeyser (*Studia Hellenistica* 30; Leuven 1990) 323-49.

Marincola, J., 'Herodotean Narrative and the Narrator's Presence', *Arethusa* 20 (1987) 121-37.

'Some Suggestions on the Proem and "Second Preface" of Arrian's *Anabasis*', *JHS* 109 (1989) 186-9.

'Plutarch's Refutation of Herodotus', *AncW* 20 (1994) 191-203.

Marrou, H. I., *Histoire de l'Education dans l'Antiquité*, 2 vols. (Paris [7]1975).

Marshall, A. J., 'Library Resources and Creative Writing at Rome', *Phoenix* 30 (1976) 252-64.

Martin, J., *Antike Rhetorik: Technik und Method* (Munich 1974).

Martin, R. H., *Tacitus* (Berkeley and London 1981).

Martin, R. H. and Woodman, A. J., edd., *Tacitus: Annals IV* (Cambridge 1989).

Matthews, J., 'Ammianus' Historical Evolution', in *History and Historians in Late Antiquity*, edd. B. Croke and A. Emmett (Sydney and London 1983) 30-41.

The Roman Empire of Ammianus (London and Baltimore 1989).

Mazzarino, S., *Il pensiero storico classico* (Bari [2]1966).

McDonald, A. H., 'The Style of Livy', *JRS* 47 (1957) 155-72.

McGushin, P., *Sallust: The Histories*, 2 vols. (Oxford 1992-4).

McKeon, R., 'Literary Criticism and the Concept of Imitation in Antiquity', in *Critics and Criticism*, ed. R. S. Crane (Chicago 1952) 147-75; orig. in *MPh* 34 (1936-7) 1-35.

Meissner, B., 'Πραγματικὴ ἱστορία: Polybius über den Zweck pragmatischer Geschichtsschreibung', *Saeculum* 37 (1986) 313-51.

Historiker zwischen Polis und Koenigshof. Studien zur Stellung der Geschichtsschreiber in der griechischen Gesellschaft in spätklassischer und hellenistischer Zeit (Göttingen 1992).

Meister, K., 'Absurde Polemik bei Diodor', *Helikon* 13-14 (1973-4) 454-9.

Historische Kritik bei Polybios (Wiesbaden 1975).

'The Role of Timaeus in Greek Historiography', *SCI* 10 (1989/90) 55-65.

Die griechische Geschichtsschreibung (Berlin 1990).

Mendels, D., 'Preliminary Thoughts on "Creative History" in the Hellenistic Near East in the 3rd and 2nd centuries BCE', *SCI* 10 (1989/90) 78-86.

'The Polemical Character of Manetho's *Aegyptiaca*', in *Purposes of History. Studies in Greek Historiography from the 4th to the 2nd centuries BC*, edd. H. Verdin, G. Schepens, and E. deKeyser (*Studia Hellenistica* 30; Leuven 1990) 91-110.

Mensching, E., *Caesars Bellum Gallicum: Eine Einführung* (Frankfurt/Main 1988).

Mette, H. J., 'Die "Kleinen" griechischen Historiker heute', *Lustrum* 21 (1978) 5-43; 'Nachtrag', ibid. 22 (1979-80) 107-8; 'Ergänzungun ... bis zum Jahre 1984', ibid. 27 (1985) 33-8.

Millar, F., *A Study of Cassius Dio* (Oxford 1964).
'P. Herennius Dexippus: The Greek World and the Third-Century Invasions', *JRS* 59 (1969) 2-29.
Misch, G., *Geschichte der Autobiographie* 1.1 *Das Antike* (Bern³ 1949).
Mohm, S., *Untersuchungen zu den historiographischen Anschauungen des Polybios* (diss. Saarbrücken 1977).
Moles, J. L., 'The Interpretation of the "Second Preface" in Arrian's *Anabasis*', *JHS* 105 (1985) 162-8.
'Truth and Untruth in Herodotus and Thucydides', in *Lies and Fiction in the Ancient World*, edd. C. Gill and T. P. Wiseman (Exeter and Austin, Tex. 1993) 88-121.
'Livy's Preface', *PCPhS* n.s. 39 (1993) 141-68.
Momigliano, A., 'Ancient History and the Antiquarian', in *Contributo alla Storia degli Studi Classici* (Rome 1955) 67-106; in English in *Studies in Historiography* (London and New York 1966) 1-39; orig. in *JWCI* 13 (1950) 285-315.
'The Place of Herodotus in the History of Historiography', in *Secondo contributo alla Storia degli studi classici e del mondo antico* (Rome 1960) 29-44; orig. in *History* 43 (1958) 1-13.
'Atene nel III Secolo a. C. e la Scoperta di Roma', in *Terzo contributo alla Storia degli studi classici e del mondo antico* (Rome 1966) 1.23-53; in English in *Essays* 37-66; orig. in *RSI* 71 (1959) 529-56.
The Development of Greek Biography (Cambridge, Mass. 1971).
'Tradition and the Classical Historian', in *Quinto Contributo alla Storia degli studi classici e del mondo antico* (Rome 1975) 13-31; also in *Essays* 161-77; orig. in *H&T* 11 (1972) 279-93.
'The Lonely Historian Ammianus Marcellinus', in *Sesto Contributo* II. 143-57; orig. in *ANSP* ser. 3, 4 (1974) 1393-407.
Alien Wisdom. The Limits of Hellenization (Cambridge 1975).
Essays in Ancient and Modern Historiography (Oxford 1977).
'The Historians of the Classical World and their Audiences: Some Suggestions', in *Sesto Contributo* 361-76; orig. in *ANSP* ser. 3, 8 (1978) 59-75.
Sesto contributo alla storia degli studi classici e del mondo antico (Rome 1980).
The Classical Foundations of Modern Historiography (Berkeley, Los Angeles, and London 1990).
Most, G. W., 'The Stranger's Stratagem: Self-disclosure and Self-sufficiency in Greek Culture', *JHS* 109 (1989) 114-33.
Müller, D., 'Herodot – Vater des Empirismus? Mensch und Erkenntnis im Denken Herodots', in *Gnomosyne: Festschrift für Walter Marg* (Munich 1981) 299-318.
Münscher, K., *Xenophon in der griechisch-römischen Literatur* (Leipzig 1920).
Murray, O., 'Hecataeus of Abdera and Pharaonic Kingship', *JEA* 56 (1970) 141-71.

'Herodotus and Hellenistic Culture', *CQ* n. s. 22 (1972) 200-13.

'Herodotus and Oral History', in *Achaemenid History. Proceedings of the Groningen Achaemenid History Workshop* II. *The Greek Sources*, ed. H. Sancisi-Weerdenburg and A. Kuhrt (Leiden 1987) 93-115.

Murray, P., 'Poetic Inspiration in Early Greece', *JHS* 101 (1981) 87-100.

Mutschler, F.-H., *Erzählstil und Propaganda in Caesars Kommentarien* (Heidelberg 1975).

Nenci, G., 'Il Motivo dell' Autopsia nella Storiografia Greca', *SCO* 3 (1955) 14-46.

Nickel, R., *Xenophon* (Darmstadt 1979).

Nicolai, R., *La storiografia nell'educazione antica* (Pisa 1992).

Nisbet, R. G. M. and Hubbard, M., *A Commentary on Horace: Odes Book II* (Oxford 1978).

Nissen, H., *Kritische Untersuchungen über die Quellen der vierten und fünften Dekade des Livius* (Berlin 1863).

Nock, A. D., 'Poseidonius', in *Essays on Religion and the Ancient World*, ed. Z. Stewart (Oxford 1972) II.853-76; orig. in *JRS* 49 (1959) 1-15.

Norden, E., *Agnostos Theos. Untersuchungen zur Formen-Geschichte religiöser Rede* (Leipzig and Berlin 1913).

Die germanische Urgeschichte in Tacitus Germania (Leipzig and Berlin ^{3}1923).

Die antike Kunstprosa, 2 vols. (Berlin ^{5}1958).

Ogilvie, R. M., 'Livy, Licinius Macer, and the *Libri Lintei*', *JRS* 48 (1958) 40-6.

A Commentary on Livy, Books I-V (Oxford 1965; repr. with addenda 1970).

Ong, W. J., *Orality and Literacy* (London 1972).

Paassen, Chr. van, *The Classical Tradition of Geography* (Groningen 1957).

Parke, H. W., 'Citation and Recitation: A Convention in Early Greek Historians', *Hermathena* 67 (1946) 80-91.

Parry, A., 'Thucydides' Use of Abstract Language', in *The Language of Achilles* 177-84; orig. in *YCS* 45 (1970) 3-20.

'Thucydides' Historical Perspective', in *The Language of Achilles* 286-300; orig. in *YCS* 22 (1972) 47-61.

The Language of Achilles and other Papers (Oxford 1989).

Paul, G. M., '*Urbs capta*: Sketch of an Ancient Literary Motif', *Phoenix* 36 (1982) 144-55.

A Historical Commentary on Sallust's Bellum Jugurthinum (Leeds 1984).

Pauw, D. A., 'Impersonal Expressions and Unidentified Spokesmen in Greek and Roman Historiography and Biography', *ActClass* 23 (1980) 83-95.

Pearson, L., *Early Ionian Historians* (Oxford 1939).

The Local Historians of Attica (Philadelphia 1942).

The Lost Histories of Alexander the Great (New York and London 1960).

The Greek Historians of the West. Timaeus and his Predecessors (Atlanta 1987).

Pédech, P., *La méthode historique de Polybe* (Paris 1964).

Historiens Compagnons d' Alexandre: Callisthène - Onésicrite - Néarque - Ptolémée (Paris 1984).
Pelling, C. B. R., 'Truth and Fiction in Plutarch's *Lives*', in *Antonine Literature*, ed. D. A. Russell (Oxford 1990) 19-51.
Peter, H., *Historicorum Romanorum Reliquiae* (Stuttgart ²1914; 1906).
Die geschichtliche Literatur über die römische Kaiserzeit bis Theodosius I, 2 vols. (Leipzig 1897).
Wahrheit und Kunst. Geschichtsschreibung und Plagiat im klassischen Altertum (Leipzig and Berlin 1911).
Petzold, K.-E., *Studien zur Methode des Polybios und zu ihrer historischen Auswertung* (Munich 1969).
'Zur Geschichte der römischen Annalistik', in *Livius: Aspekte seines Werkes*, ed. W. Schuller (Konstanz 1993) 151-88.
Pfister, F., 'Isokrates und die spätere Gliederung der *narratio*', *Hermes* 68 (1933) 457-60.
Piérart, M., 'L'historien ancien face aux mythes et aux légendes', *LEC* 51 (1983) 47-62, 105-15.
Potter, D. S., *Prophecy and History in the Third Century: A Historical Commentary on the Thirteenth Sibylline Oracle* (Oxford 1990).
Premerstein, A. von, 'Commentarii', *RE* IV.1 (1900) 726-59.
Pritchett, W. K., *Dionysius of Halicarnassus: On Thucydides* (Berkeley 1975).
Raaflaub, K. A. and Toher, M., edd., *Between Republic and Empire. Interpretations of Augustus and his Principate* (Berkeley, Los Angeles, and London 1990).
Radermacher, L., 'Studien zur Geschichte der griechischen Rhetorik', *RhM* 52 (1897) 412-24.
'Kanon', *RE* X. 2 (1919) 1873-8.
Rahn, P. J., 'Xenophon's Developing Historiography', *TAPA* 102 (1971) 497-508.
Rajak, T., *Josephus. The Historian and his Society* (London 1983).
Ramage, E., 'Juvenal and the Establishment: Denigration of Predecessors in the "Satires"', *ANRW* II. 33. 1 (1989) 640-707.
Rambaud, M., *L'Art de la déformation historique dans les Commentaires de César* (Paris ²1966).
Rasmussen, H., ed., *Caesar* (Wege der Forschung 43; Darmstadt 1967).
Rawson, E., 'Prodigy Lists and the Use of the Annales Maximi', in *Roman Culture and Society* 1-15; orig. in *CQ* n.s. 21 (1971) 158-69.
'The First Latin Annalists', in *Roman Culture and Society* 245-71; orig. in *Latomus* 35 (1976) 689-717.
'L. Cornelius Sisenna and the Early First Century BC', in *Roman Culture and Society* 363-88; orig. in *CQ* n.s. 29 (1979) 327-46.
'History, Historiography, and Cicero's *Expositio Consiliorum Suorum*', in *Roman Culture and Society* 408-15; orig. in *LCM* 7.8 (1982) 121-4.
Intellectual Life in the Late Roman Republic (London and Baltimore 1985).

'The Antiquarian Tradition: Spoils and Representations of Foreign Armour', in *Roman Culture and Society* 582-98; orig. in *Staat und Staatlichkeit in der frühen römischen Republik*, ed. W. Eder (Stuttgart 1990) 157-73.
Roman Culture and Society. Collected Papers (Oxford 1991).
Reardon, B. P., *Courants littéraires grecs des IIe et IIIe siècles après J.-C.* (Paris 1971).
Renehan, R., 'A Traditional Pattern of Imitation in Sallust and his Sources', *CPh* 71 (1976) 97-105.
Rhodes, P. J., 'The Atthidographers' in *Purposes of History. Studies in Greek Historiography from the 4th to the 2nd centuries BC*, edd. H. Verdin, G. Schepens, and E. deKeyser (*Studia Hellenistica* 30; Leuven 1990) 73-81.
Richter, W., *Caesar als Darsteller seiner Taten: Eine Einführung* (Heidelberg 1977).
Riemann, K.-A., *Das herodoteische Geschichtswerk in der Antike* (diss. Munich 1967).
Rinner, W., 'Zur Darstellungsweise bei Xenophon, Anabasis III 1-2', *Philologus* 122 (1978) 144-9.
Robinson, P., 'Why do we believe Thucydides? A Comment on W. R. Connor's "Narrative Discourse in Thucydides"', in *The Greek Historians: Literature and History. Papers Presented to A. E. Raubitschek*, ed. M. H. Jameson (Saratoga, Calif. 1985) 19-23.
Roisman, J., 'Ptolemy and His Rivals in his History of Alexander', *CQ* 34 (1984) 373-85.
Romm, J., *The Edges of the Earth in Ancient Thought: Geography, Exploration and Fiction* (Princeton 1992).
Rosen, K., *Studien zur Darstellungskunst und Glaubwürdigkeit des Ammianus Marcellinus* (Bonn 1970).
'Politische Ziele in der frühen hellenistischen Geschichtsschreibung', *Hermes* 107 (1979) 460-77.
Rubin, Z., *Civil War Propaganda and Historiography* (Brussels 1980).
Ruch, M., 'Tite-Live, Histoire Romaine. Points de vue sur la Préface', *Didactica Classica Gandensia* 7 (1967) 74-80.
Rüpke, J., 'Wer las Caesars bella als commentarii?' *Gymnasium* 99 (1992) 201-26.
Russell, D. A., *Longinus: On the Sublime* (Oxford 1964).
'De Imitatione', in *Creative Imitation and Latin Literature*, edd. D. West and A. J. Woodman (Cambridge 1979) 1-16.
Criticism in Antiquity (London 1981).
Greek Declamation (Cambridge 1983).
'Self-disclosure in Plutarch and Horace', in *Philosophia kai Eusebeia. Festschrift . . . A. Dihle*, edd. G. Most, H. Petersmann, and A. Ritter (Göttingen 1993) 426-37.
Russell, D. A. and Winterbottom, M., *Ancient Literary Criticism* (Oxford 1972).

Ryberg, I. S., 'Tacitus' art of innuendo', *TAPA* 73 (1942) 383-404.
Sabbah, G., *La Méthode d'Ammien Marcellin. Recherches sur la Construction du discours historique dans les Res Gestae* (Paris 1978).
Sacks, K., *Polybius on the Writing of History* (Berkeley 1981).
'Historiography in the Rhetorical Works of Dionysius of Halicarnassus', *Athenaeum* 61 (1983) 65-87.
Diodorus Siculus and the First Century BC (Princeton 1990).
Sallmann, K., 'Der Traum des Historikers: Zu den "Bella Germaniae" des Plinius und zur julisch-claudischen Geschichtsschreibung', *ANRW* II. 32. 1 (1984) 578-601.
Scanlon, L., *Narrative, Authority, and Power: The Medieval Exemplum and the Chaucerian Tradition* (Cambridge 1994).
Schanz, M., Hosius, C., and Krüger, G., *Geschichte der römischen Literatur*, 4 vols. (Munich 1914-35).
Scheller, P., *De hellenistica historiae conscribendae arte* (diss. Leipzig 1911).
Schepens, G., 'Ephore sur la Valeur de l'Autopsie (*FGrHist* 70 F 110 = Polybe XII 27.7)', *Anc. Soc.* 1 (1970) 163-82.
'Arrian's View of his Task as Alexander-Historian', *Anc. Soc.* 2 (1971) 254-68.
'The Bipartite and Tripartite Divisions of History in Polybius (XII 25e & 27)', *Anc. Soc.* 5 (1974) 277-87.
'"Ἔμφασις und ἐνάργεια in Polybios' Geschichtstheorie', *RSA* 5 (1975) 185-200.
'Some Aspects of Source Theory in Greek Historiography', *Anc. Soc.* 6 (1975) 257-74.
'Historiographical Problems in Ephorus' in *Historiographia Antiqua. Commentationes... in honorem W. Peremans* (Leuven 1977) 95-118.
L' 'Autopsie' dans la Méthode des historiens grecs du Ve siècle avant J.-C. (Brussels 1980).
'Les rois ptolémaïque et l'historiographie. Réflexions sur la transformation de l'histoire politique', in *Egypt and the Hellenistic World*, edd. E. Van 't Dack, P. Van Dessel, and W. Van Gucht (*Studia Hellenistica* 27; Leuven 1983) 351-68.
'Polemic and Methodology in Polybius' Book XII', in *Purposes of History. Studies in Greek Historiography from the 4th to the 2nd centuries BC*, edd. H. Verdin, G. Schepens, and E. deKeyser (*Studia Hellenistica* 30; Leuven 1990) 39-61.
Schmalzriedt, E., ΠΕΡΙ ΦΥΣΙΟΣ. *Zur Frühgeschichte der Buchtitel* (Munich 1970).
Schreckenberg, H., *Die Flavius-Josephus Tradition in Antike und Mittelalter* (Leiden 1972).
Schröder, W. A., *M. Porcius Cato. Das Erste Buch der Origines* (Meisenheim am Glan 1971).
Schultze, C., 'Dionysius of Halicarnassus and his Audience', in *Past*

Perspectives. Studies in Greek and Roman Historical Writing, edd. I. S. Moxon, J. D. Smart, and A. J. Woodman (Cambridge 1986) 121–41.

Schwartz, E., 'Appianus', in *Griechische Geschichtschreiber* 361–93; orig. in *RE* II (1985) 216–37.

'Cassius Dio', in *Griechische Geschichtschreiber* 394–450; orig. in *RE* III (1899) 1684–1722.

'Diodorus' in *Griechische Geschichtschreiber* 35–97; orig. in *RE* V.1 (1903) 663–704.

'Dionysius von Halicarnassus', in *Griechische Geschichtschreiber* 319–60; orig. in *RE* V.1 (1903) 934–61.

Funf Vorträge über den griechischen Roman (Berlin ²1943).

Griechische Geschichtschreiber (Leipzig 1959).

Scobie, A., 'Storytellers, Storytelling and the Novel in Greco-Roman Antiquity', *RhM* 122 (1979) 229–59.

Seel, O., *Die Praefatio des Pompeius Trogus*, Erlangen Forschungen 3 (Erlangen 1955).

Shatzman, I., 'Tacitean rumours', *Latomus* 33 (1974) 549–78.

Sherwin-White, S. and Kuhrt, A., edd., *From Samarkhand to Sardis: New Perspectives on the Seleucid Empire* (London and Berkeley 1983).

Shrimpton, G. S., *Theopompus the Historian* (Montreal 1991).

Shutt, R. J. H., *Studies in Josephus* (London 1961).

Skutsch, O., *The Annals of Quintus Ennius* (Oxford 1985).

Slings, S. R., 'Poet's Call and Poet's Status in Archaic Greece and Other Oral Cultures', *LF* 112 (1989) 72–80.

'The I in Personal Archaic Lyric: an Introduction', in id., ed., *The Poet's I in Archaic Greek Lyric* (Amsterdam 1990) 1–30.

Smart, J. D., 'Thucydides and Hellanicus' in *Past Perspectives. Studies in Greek and Roman Historical Writing*, edd. I. S. Moxon, J. D. Smart, and A. J. Woodman (Cambridge 1986) 19–35.

Snell, B., *Die Entdeckung des Geistes* (Göttingen ⁴1975).

Sordi, M., 'Timagene di Alessandria: uno storico ellenocentrico e filobarbaro', *ANRW* II. 30. 1 (1982) 775–97.

Spawforth, A., 'Symbol of Unity? The Persian-Wars Tradition in the Roman Empire', in *Greek Historiography*, ed. S. Hornblower (Oxford 1994) 233–47.

Speyer, W., *Die literarische Fälschung im heidnischen und christlichen Altertum* (Munich 1971).

Stadter, P., 'Flavius Arrianus: The New Xenophon', *GRBS* 8 (1967) 155–61.

Arrian of Nicomedia (Chapel Hill 1980).

'Arrian's Extended Preface', *ICS* 6 (1981) 157–71.

Starr, R. J., 'The Scope and Genre of Velleius' History', *CQ* n.s. 31 (1981) 162–74.

'The Circulation of Literary Texts in the Ancient World', *CQ* n. s. 37 (1987) 213–23.

Steele, R. B., 'The Historical Attitude of Livy', *AJPh* 25 (1904) 15-44.
Stein, F.-J., *Dexippus et Herodianus quatenus Thucydidem secuti sint* (diss. Bonn 1957).
Steinmetz, P., *Untersuchungen zur römischen Literatur des zweiten Jahrhunderts nach Christi Geburt* (Wiesbaden 1982).
Stephens, S. A., 'Who Read Ancient Novels?', in *The Search for the Ancient Novel*, ed. J. Tatum (Baltimore and London 1994) 405-18.
Stevenson, R. B., 'Lies and Inventions in Deinon's Persica', in *Achaemenid History. Proceedings of the Groningen Achaemenid History Workshop* II. *The Greek Sources*, edd. H. Sancisi-Weerdenburg and A. Kuhrt (Leiden 1987) 27-35.
Stiewe, K. and Holzberg, N., edd., *Polybios* (Darmstadt 1982).
Strasburger, H., *Homer und die Geschichtsschreibung*, in *Studien zur alten Geschichte*, 2 vols. (Hildesheim and New York 1982) II.1057-97; orig. in *SHAW* 1 (Heidelberg 1972).
Strebel, H. G., *Wertung und Wirkung des thukydideischen Geschichtswerkes in der griechisch-römischen Literatur* (diss. Munich 1935).
Strobel, K., 'Zeitgeschichte unter den Antoninen: Die Historiker des Partherkrieges des Lucius Verus', *ANRW* II. 34. 2 (1994) 1316-60.
Suerbaum, W., *Untersuchungen zur Selbstdarstellung älterer römischer Dichter* (Hildesheim 1968).
'Der Historiker und die Freiheit des Wortes: Die Rede des Cremutius Cordus bei Tacitus, *Ann.* 4, 34/35' in *Politik und Literarische Kunst im Werk des Tacitus*, ed. G. Radke (Stuttgart 1971) 61-99.
Syme, R., 'The Senator as Historian' in *Ten Studies in Tacitus* 1-10; orig. in *Histoire et Historiens dans l' Antiquité Classique* (Entretiens Hardt 4; Geneva 1958) 187-201.
'Obituaries in Tacitus', in *Ten Studies in Tacitus* 79-90; orig. in *AJPh* 79 (1958) 18-31.
Tacitus, 2 vols. (Oxford 1958).
'Livy and Augustus' in *Roman Papers*, ed. E. Badian (Oxford 1979) I.400-54; orig. in *HSCP* 64 (1959) 27-87.
Sallust (Berkeley 1964).
'The Historian Servilius Nonianus' in *Ten Studies in Tacitus* 91-109; orig. in *Hermes* 92 (1964) 408-24.
Ten Studies in Tacitus (Oxford 1970).
Emperors and Biography. Studies in the Historia Augusta (Oxford 1971).
'How Tacitus Wrote *Annals* I-III', in *Roman Papers*, ed. A. R. Birley (Oxford 1984) III.1014-42; orig. in *Historiographa Antiqua. Commentationes... in honorem W. Peremans* (Leuven 1977) 231-63.
Thomas, R., *Oral Tradition and Written Record in Classical Athens* (Cambridge 1989).
Literacy and Orality in Ancient Greece (Cambridge 1992).

'Performance and Written Publication in Herodotus and the Sophistic Generation', in *Vermittlung und Tradierung von Wissen in der griechischen Kultur*, edd. W. Kullmann and J. Althoff (Tübingen 1993) 225-44.

Thompson, W. E., 'Fragments of the Preserved Historians – Especially Polybius', in *The Greek Historians: Literature and History. Papers Presented to A. E. Raubitschek*, ed. M. H. Jameson (Saratoga, Calif. 1985) 119-39.

Timpe, D., 'Le Origini di Catone e la storiografia latina', *AAPat* 83 (1970-1) 1-33.

'Fabius Pictor und die Anfänge der römischen Geschichtsschreibung', *ANRW* I. 2 (1972) 928-69.

'Erwägungen zur jüngeren Annalistik', *A&A* 25 (1979) 97-119.

'Mündlichkeit und Schriftlichkeit als Basis der frührömischen Überlieferung', in *Vergangenheit in mündlicher Überlieferung*, edd. J. von Ungern-Sternberg and H. Reinau (Stuttgart 1988) 266-86.

Todd, S. C., 'The Purpose of Evidence in Athenian Courts', in *Nomos: Essays in Athenian Law, Politics and Society*, edd. P. Millett, P. Cartledge, and S. Todd (Cambridge 1990) 19-39.

Toher, M., 'On the Use of Nicolaus' Historical Fragments', *CA* 8 (1989) 159-72.

'Augustus and the Evolution of Roman Historiography', in *Between Republic and Empire*, edd. K. Raaflaub and M. Toher (Berkeley 1990) 139-54.

Toye, D. L., 'Dionysius of Halicarnassus on the First Greek Historians', *AJPh* 116 (1995) 279-302.

Trüdinger, K., *Studien zur griechisch-römischen Ethnographie* (Basel 1918).

Underhill, G. E., *A Commentary on the Hellenica of Xenophon* (Oxford 1900; repr. with Oxford text of E. C. Marchant, 1906).

Ungern-Sternberg, J. von, 'Überlegungen zur frühen römischen Überlieferung', in *Vergangenheit in mündlicher Überlieferung*, edd. J. von Ungern-Sternberg and H. Reinau (Stuttgart 1988) 237-65.

Usher, S., 'The Style of Dionysius of Halicarnassus in the "Antiquitates Romanae"', *ANRW* II. 30. 1 (1982) 817-38.

Van 't Dack, E., Van Dessel, P. and Van Gucht, W., edd. *Egypt and the Hellenistic World. Proceedings of the International Colloquium Leuven, 24-26 May 1982* (*Studia Hellenistica* 27; Leuven 1983).

Vercruysse, M., 'A la recherche du mensonge et de la vérité: La fonction des passages méthodologiques chez Polybe', in *Purposes of History. Studies in Greek Historiography from the 4th to the 2nd centuries BC*, edd. H. Verdin, G. Schepens, and E. deKeyser (*Studia Hellenistica* 30; Leuven 1990) 17-38.

Verdin, H., 'L'importance des recherches sur la méthode critique des historiens grecs et latins', *Stud. Hell.* 16 (1968) 289-308.

'Notes sur l'attitude des historiens grecs à l'égard de la tradition locale', *Anc. Soc.* 1 (1970) 183-200.

De historisch-kritische Methods van Herodotus (Brussels 1971).

'La fonction de l'histoire selon Denys d'Halicarnasse', *Anc. Soc.* 5 (1974) 289-307.

'Les remarques critiques d'Hérodote et de Thucydide sur la poésie en tant que source historique', in *Historigraphia Antiqua. Commentationes... in honorem W. Peremans* (Leuven 1977) 53-76.

'Agatharchide et la tradition du discours politique dans l'historiographie grecque', in *Egypt and the Hellenistic World*, edd. E. Van 't Dack, P. Van Dessel, and W. Van Gucht (*Studia Hellenistica* 27; Leuven 1983) 407-20.

'Agatharchide de Cnide et les Fictions des Poètes', in *Purposes of History. Studies in Greek Historiography from the 4th to the 2nd centuries BC*, edd. H. Verdin, G. Schepens, and E. deKeyser (*Studia Hellenistica* 30; Leuven 1990) 1-15.

Verdin, H., Schepens, G. and deKeyser, E., edd., *Purposes of History. Studies in Greek Historiography from the 4th to the 2nd centuries BC* (*Studia Hellenistica* 30; Leuven 1990).

Veyne, P., *Did the Greeks Believe in their Myths?* (Chicago 1988).

Volkmann, R., *Die Rhetorik der Griechen und Römer in systematischer Übersicht* (Leipzig ²1885; repr. Hildesheim 1963).

Vretska, K., *Sallust. De Catilinae Coniuratione*, 2 vols. (Heidelberg 1976).

Walbank, F. W., 'Polybius, Philinus and the First Punic War', in *Selected Papers* 77-98; orig. in *CQ* 39 (1945) 1-18.

'Tragic History: A Reconsideration', *BICS* 2 (1955) 4-14.

A Historical Commentary on Polybius, 3 vols. (Oxford 1957-78).

'History and Tragedy', in *Selected Papers* 224-41; orig. in *Historia* 9 (1960) 216-34.

'Polemic in Polybius', in *Selected Papers* 262-79; orig. in *JRS* 52 (1962) 1-12.

'The Historians of Greek Sicily', *Kokalos* 14-15 (1968-9) 476-98.

Polybius (Berkeley and London 1972).

'Polybius between Greece and Rome', in *Selected Papers* 280-97; orig. in *Polybe* (Entretiens Hardt 20; Geneva 1974) 1-31.

'Polybius' Last Ten Books', in *Selected Papers* 325-43; orig. in *Historiographia Antiqua. Commentationes in honorem . . . W. Peremans* (Leuven 1977) 139-62.

Selected Papers. Studies in Greek and Roman History and Historiography (Cambridge 1985).

'Timaeus' View of the Past', *SCI* 10 (1989/90) 41-54.

'Profit or Amusement: Some Thoughts on the Motives of Hellenistic Historians', in *Purposes of History. Studies in Greek Historiography from the 4th to the 2nd centuries BC*, edd. H. Verdin, G. Schepens, and E. deKeyser (*Studia Hellenistica* 30; Leuven 1990) 253-66.

Walcot, P., *Envy and the Greeks* (Warminster 1978).

Walker, B., *The Annals of Tacitus: A Study in the Writing of History* (Manchester 1952).

Walsh, P. G., *Livy: His Historical Aims and Methods* (Cambridge 1961).

Wardman, A., 'Myth in Greek Historiography', *Historia* 9 (1960) 403-13.

Weinstock, S., *Divus Julius* (Oxford 1971).

Wellesley, K., *Cornelius Tacitus: The Histories Book III* (Sydney 1972).
West, D. and Woodman, A. J., edd., *Creative Imitation and Latin Literature* (Cambridge 1979).
West, M. L., *Hesiod: Theogony* (Oxford 1966).
  Studies in Greek Elegy and Iambus (Berlin and New York 1971).
  Hesiod: Works and Days (Oxford 1979).
West, S., 'Herodotus' Portrait of Hecataeus', *JHS* 111 (1991) 144-60.
Westlake, H. D., 'Thucydides and the Fall of Amphipolis', in *Essays on the Greek Historians and Greek History* (Manchester 1969) 123-37; orig. in *Hermes* 90 (1962) 276-87.
Weyman, C., '*Sine ira et studio*', *ALLG* 15 (1908) 278-9.
Wheeldon, M. J., '"True Stories": the Reception of Historiography in Antiquity', in *History as Text*, ed. A. Cameron (London and Chapel Hill 1989) 33-63.
White, H., 'The Burden of History', in *Tropics of Discourse. Essays in Cultural Criticism* (Baltimore and London 1978) 27-50.
  'The Question of Narrative in Contemporary Historical Theory', in *The Content of the Form. Narrative Discourse and Historical Representation* (Baltimore and London 1987) 26-57.
Whitehead, D., 'Tacitus and the Loaded Alternative', *Latomus* 38 (1979) 474-95.
Whittaker, C. R., *Herodian*, 2 vols. (Cambridge, Mass. and London, 1969, 1970).
Wilkes, J., 'Julio-Claudian Historians', *CW* 65 (1971/2) 177-203.
Will, W., 'Die griechische Geschichtsschreiber des 4. Jahrhunderts: Eine Zusammenfassung', in *Geschichtsbild und Geschichtsdenken im Altertum*, ed. J. M. Alonso-Núñez (Darmstadt 1991) 113-35.
Wiseman, T. P., 'Legendary Genealogies in late-Republican Rome', in *Roman Studies* 207-18; orig. in *G&R* 21 (1974) 153-64.
  Clio's Cosmetics: Three Studies in Greco-Roman Literature (Leicester 1969).
  'Practice and Theory in Roman Historiography', in *Roman Studies* 244-61; orig. in *History* 66 (1981) 375-93.
  'Lying Historians: Seven Types of Mendacity' in *Lies and Fiction in the Ancient World*, edd. C. Gill and T. P. Wiseman (Exeter and Austin, Tex. 1993) 122-46.
  'Monuments and the Roman Annalists', in *Historiography and Imagination* 37-48; originally in *Past Perspectives. Studies in Greek and Roman Historical Writing*, edd. I. S. Moxon, J. D. Smart, and A. J. Woodman (Cambridge 1986) 87-100.
  'The Origins of Roman Historiography', in *Historiography and Imagination* 1-22.
  Roman Studies. Literary and Historical (Liverpool 1987).
  Historiography and Imagination. Eight Essays on Roman Culture (Exeter 1994).

Woodman, A. J., 'Sallustian Influence in Velleius Paterculus', in *Hommages à M. Renard* (Brussels 1968) 1.785-99.
'Questions of Date, Genre and Style in Velleius: Some Literary Answers', *CQ* n. s. 25 (1975) 272-306.
Velleius Paterculus. The Tiberian Narrative (2.94-131) (Cambridge 1977).
'Self-Imitation and the Substance of History', in *Creative Imitation and Latin Literature*, edd. D. West and A. J. Woodman (Cambridge 1979) 143-55.
Velleius Paterculus. The Caesarian and Augustan Narrative (2.41-93) (Cambridge 1983).
'Reading the Ancient Historians', *Omnibus* 5 (1983) 24-7.
Rhetoric in Classical Historiography (London, Sydney, and Portland 1988).
'Contemporary History in the Classical World', in *Contemporary History: Practice and Method*, ed. A. Seldon (Oxford 1988) 149-64.
'The Preface to Tacitus' *Annals*: More Sallust?', *CQ* n. s. 42 (1992) 567-8.
'*Praecipuum munus annalium*: The Construction, Convention and Context of Tacitus, *Annals* 3.65.1', *MH* 52 (1995) 111-26.
Wunderer, C., *Polybios-Forschungen. Beiträge zur Sprach- und Kultur-Geschichte* II. *Zitate und geflügelte Worte bei Polybios*; III. *Gleichnisse und Metaphern bei Polybios* (Leipzig 1901, 1909; repr. Darmstadt 1969).
Zegers, N., *Wesen und Ursprung der tragischen Geschichtsschreibung* (diss. Cologne 1959).

Index locorum

AELIUS ARISTIDES
Orat. 36. 108 = *FGrHist* 665 F 68   109 n.237
Rhetorica, 506.8-20 (Spengel)   176 n.3
AEMILIUS SCAURUS
F 6   196 n.101
AGATHARCHIDES OF CNIDUS
de Mare Rubro, §21   233 n.85
§24   233 n.86
§§25-9   233
§110   59 n.102; 149 n.96
ALCMAEON
B 1   271 n.4
ALCMAN
F 39   271 n.3
ALEXANDER
π. ῥήτορ. ἀφορμ. 4.9-14 (Spengel)   176 n.3
AMELESAGORAS, *FGrHist* 330
T 2   51 n.67
AMMIANUS MARCELLINUS
XIV.4.6   85 n.109
XIV.6.2   217 n.2
XIV.9.1   201 n.124, 204 n.131
XIV.11.5   201 n.124
XV.1.1   79 n.79, 80 n.83
XV.5.22-31   201 n.124
XV.9.2   255 n.196
XV.12.6   255 n.199
XVI.1.2   39 n.17
XVI.1.2-3   173 n.203
XVI.10.21   201 n.124
XVII.1.14   39 n.17
XVII.4.6   102 n.199
XVIII.4.7   201
XVIII.6.5   201
XVIII.6.8   201
XVIII.6.9-10   201
XVIII.6.10-15   203 n.129
XVIII.6.11-12   201 n.125

XVIII.6.21   202 n.126
XVIII.6.22-3   255 n.200
XVIII.6.23   125 n.319
XVIII.7.2   202 n.126
XVIII.8.12-13   202 n.126
XIX.2.4   203 n.127
XIX.2.13   203 n.127
XIX.3.3   203 n.127
XIX.4.1   203 n.127
XIX.4.4   255 n.198
XIX.6.1-4   203 n.127
XIX.8.1-4   203 n.127
XIX.8.4   203
XIX.8.5-6   203
XIX.8.6   147 n.88
XIX.8.6-12   203
XIX.8.12   204 n.131
XXII.8.1   85 n.109
XXII.15.3   283 n.14
XXIII.5.7   204, 204 n.131
XXIII.6.21   85 n.109
XXIII.6.30   85 n.109
XXIII.6.75   255 n.198
XXIV.1.5   204 n.132
XXIV.2.1-3   204 n.132
XXIV.2.16   256
XXIV.3.1-9   204 n.133
XXIV.3.8-9   204 n.132
XXIV.4.7   204 n.132
XXIV.4.9   204 n.132
XXIV.4.11   204 n.132
XXIV.4.14   204 n.132
XXIV.4.23   204 n.132
XXIV.4.30   204 n.132
XXIV.4.31   204 n.132
XXIV.5.5   204 n.132
XXIV.5.8-9   204 n.132
XXIV.6.15   204 n.132
XXIV.7.7   204 n.132
XXIV.8.7   204 n.132

Index locorum

XXVI.1.1   92 n.140, 157 n.130, 204
XXVI.1.1-2   32 n.160, 254 n.193
XXVI.1.2   157 n.131, 172 n.199
XXVI.10.19   83 n.97
XXVII.2.6   288 n.13
XXVII.4.2   85 n.109
XXVIII.1.2   158 n.132
XXVIII.4.6-34   254 n.193
XXVIII.4.14   254 n.193
XXVIII.5.4   288 n.13
XXIX.1.24   79 n.79, 82 n.90
XXIX.2.16   288 n.13, 288 n.19
XXX.2.1   288 n.13
XXX.4.4   81 n.90
XXXI.5.10   32 n.160, 217 n.2
XXXI.7.16   81 n.90
XXXI.16.9   254 n.192, 256 n.204, 256 n.206
ANAXAGORAS
  B 21   66 n.14
  B 21a   66 n.14
ANAXIMENES OF LAMPSACUS, *FGrHist* 72
  T 6   228 n.57
  T 14   242 n.126
  F 1   228 n.56
ANONONYMOUS HISTORIAN OF CORINTH, *FGrHist* 204
  F 1   80 n.83
ANONYMOUS HISTORIAN OF LUCIUS VERUS, *FGrHist* 203
  F 5   80 n.83
ANONYMOUS HISTORIAN OF MILETUS, *FGrHist* 205
  F 1   275 n.22
ANTIOCHIANUS, *FGrHist* 207
  F 1   149 n.90, 275 n.24
ANTIOCHUS OF SYRACUSE, *FGrHist* 555
  F 2   100 n.181, 272 n.8, 283 n.10
ANTISTHENES OF RHODES, *FGrHist* 508
  T 1   80 n.83
APHRODISIAS OF THESPIAE, *FGrHist* 386
  F 1   194 n.89
APION OF OASIS, *FGrHist* 616
  F 5   109 n.235
  F 12   109 n.235
  F 15   274 n.20
APOLLODORUS OF ATHENS, *FGrHist* 244
  T 2   55 n.82
APPIAN
  praef. 1.15   42
  praef. 18   42 n.25
  praef. 26   42 n.25, 145 n.77
  praef. 29-42   42

praef. 39   145 n.77
praef. 45-52   47 n.46
praef. 46-8   145
praef. 62   145 n.78; 274 n.17
Illyrica 16   89 n.123
Syriaca 207   30 n.149
B. Civ. 1.24   30 n.149, 151 n.105
  11.70   283n.14
F 19   201 n.125
ARATUS OF SICYON, *FGrHist* 231
  T 2a   180 n.24, 290 n.11
ARISTOBULUS, *FGrHist* 139
  T 6   80 n.83
  T 8   59 n.101
  F 1   87 n.117
  F 20   82 n.92
  F 35   82 n.92
  F 38   82 n.92
  F 41   82 n.92, 82 n.93
  F 42   82 n.92
  F 51   187 n.65
  F 54   82 n.92, 82 n.93
ARISTOTHEOS, *FGrHist* 835
  T 1   21 n.98
ARISTOTLE
  Anal. Pr. 46a 4ff.   74 n.51
  de Caelo 294b 6-11   220 n.16
  Hist. Anim. 566a 6-8   74 n.50
    573a 10-16   74 n.50
    574b 15-19   74 n.50
  Poet. 3, 1448a 19-25   6 n.22
  Rhet. 1.2, 1356a 4-8   129 n.2
    1.2, 1356a 8-13   129
    1.8, 1366a 8-16   129
    1.15, 1375a 22-b25   105 n.216
    1.15, 1375b 26-76a17   281 n.4
    1.15, 1376a 33-b30   105 n.216
    11.1, 1377b 20-8   129 n.3
    11.1, 1378a 6-8   130
    11.22, 1396a 4-23   161 n.144
    III.7, 1408a 7-24   222 n.25
    III.16, 1417b 7-8   133 n.21
    III.17, 1418b 23-7   214 n.166
  Topica 161a 23-4   220 n.17
    161a 32ff   220 n.17
[ARISTOTLE]
  Rhet. ad Alex. 38.2   130 n.6
ARISTOXENUS
  Harm. 1.6   113 n.256
ARRIAN OF NICOMEDIA
  Anabasis
    praef. 1   117 n.279, 253 n.183, 275 n.23

ARRIAN OF NICOMEDIA (cont.)
  Anabasis (cont.)
    praef. 1-2   285 n.29
    praef. 2   115 n.265, 169, 254 n.190
    I.12.2   113 n.257, 116 n.278
    I.12.3   253 n.187
    I.12.4   36 n.7, 253 n.188
    I.12.5   146 n.81, 254 n.189, 274 n.18
    IV.10.1-2   59 n.101
    V.1.2   120 n.295
    V.5.1   286 n.30
    VI.11.8   282 n.7
    VII.18.5   82 n.93
    VII.27.3   107 n.227
    VII.30.3   43 n.28
  Bithyniaca, FGrHist 156
    T 4a   111 n.250
    F 14   53 n.75
ASINIUS POLLIO
  F 2a   197 n.105
  F 4   116 n.275
ATHANIS, FGrHist 562
  T 1   187 n.61
  T 2   240 n.118, 290 n.6
AUGUSTUS
  F 4   196 n.101
  F 24   196 n.101

BEROSSUS, FGrHist 680
  T 1   110 n.241
  T 2   53 n.74
  F 1   110 n.242
  F 1b(1)   110 n.241
BION, FGrHist 332
  T 3   110 n.244

CAESAR
  Bellum Ciuile
    I.18.2   287 n.6
    I.22.1   287 n.6
    I.40.6   287 n.6
    I.43-7   287 n.6
    I.46.4-5   287 n.6
  Bellum Gallicum
    I.7.14   208
    I.12.6   208
    I.14.5   209
    I.30.1-3   214
    I.39.1-7   216 n.173
    I.43.5   212 n.161
    I.44.12   214
    I.45.1   212 n.161

I.50.4   79 n.75
I.52.1   212
II.10.1   79 n.76
II.11.2   79 n.76
II.15.3   79 n.77
II.16.1   79 n.75
II.17.2   79 n.75
II.25.1   213 n.162
II.27.3-5   216 n.173
II.31.3   214
II.32.4   79 n.78
IV.12.4   213 n.162
IV.15.3   216 n.173
IV.17.1   197 n.104, 212 n.161
IV.19.1   79 n.76
IV.25.3   209
IV.26.5   210 n.151
IV.37.3   213 n.162
V.2.2   213 n.162
V.6.1   197 n.104
V.6.7   79 n.78
V.8.4   213 n.162
V.8.6   79 n.75
V.13.4   197 n.104
V.18.4   79 n.75, 79 n.76
V.34.2   213 n.162
V.35.6-8   213 n.162
V.37.5   213 n.162
V.41.8   214
V.44   213 n.162
V.52.4   79 n.75, 79 n.77
V.52.6   209
V.54.5   216 n.173
V.57.2   79 n.76
VI.1.4   212 n.161
VI.30.2   209 n.147
VI.30.2-4   210 n.149
VI.35.2   209 n.147, 210
VI.36.2   210
VI.37.1   210
VI.38   213 n.162
VI.40   213 n.162
VI.41.4   210
VI.42.1-2   210
VII.17.2-8   213 n.162
VII.18.1   79 n.75
VII.22.1   213 n.162
VII.39.3   79 n.76
VII.44.2   79 n.76
VII.47   213 n.162
VII.50.1   213 n.162
VII.54.1   79 n.76

Index locorum

VII.59.3-6   213 n.162
VII.72.1   79 n.76
VII.77.1-16   216 n.173
[CAESAR]
  Bell. Alex. 10.1   287 n.8
  Bell. Alex. 11.1   287 n.8
CALLIAS OF SYRACUSE, *FGrHist* 564
  T 3   163 n.154
CALLIMORPHUS, *FGrHist* 210
  F 1   90 n.133, 275 n.24
  FF 1-2   148 n.90
CALLISTHENES OF OLYNTHUS, *FGrHist* 124
  F 12   84 n.102
  F 12(a)   80 n.83
CASSIUS HEMINA
  F 28   102 n.196
CATO
  Origines, F 1   137 n.44, 236 n.102
    F 2   45 n.37, 78 n.68, 137 n.44, 139, 246 n.149
    F 3   137 n.44
    F 31   285 n.26
    F 32   285 n.26
    F 71   285 n.25
    F 77   236 n.102
    F 82   287 n.1
    F 95 = *ORF* FF 163-71   194 n.91
    F 99   193 n.86
    F 109   291 n.1
    F 118   101 n.186
    F 129   195 n.92
    F 130   195 n.92, 214 n.168
  de cons. suo FF 21-49   193 n.86
  de sumptu suo F 173   130 n.8
CATULLUS
  1.3-7   155 n.120
CENSORINUS
  de die natali 21.1-2   124 n.312
CHAIREMON OF ALEXANDRIA, *FGrHist* 618
  T 6   110 n.240
  F 2   110 n.240
  F 6   110 n.240
CHARAX OF PERGAMUM, *FGrHist* 103
  T 1   112 n.251
CHRYSERUS, *FGrHist* 96
  T 1   89 n.126, 239 n.116
CICERO
  ad Atticum 11.1   54 n.79
    11.1.1   55 n.81
    11.1.1-2   182 n.35
    11.6.2   172 n.199
    XIV.17.6   172 n.199

Brutus 7-9   45 n.34
  13   55 n.82
  81   195 n.94
  112   54 n.79
  132   54 n.79, 182 n.34
  262   10 n.42
de Div. 1.56   48 n.54
  1.59   48 n.54
  11.62   54 n.79
ad Fam. V.12.1   177
  V.12.3   165 n.170
  V.12.8-9   178 n.12
de Finibus V.52   28 n.135
de Inv. 1.97   130 n.7
de Opt. Gen. 15   151 n.105
de Orat. 11.115   130
  11.182   130
Orator 100-1   15 n.67
  104-6   178 n.13
  120   151 n.105
de Rep. 1.7-8   45 n.34
de Sen. 21   102 n.195
  59   247 n.150
Topica, 75   50 n.62
  77   50 n.62
Tusc. Disp. 1.1   45 n.34
[CICERO]
  Rhet. ad Herenn. 1.8.12-13   118 n.287
    1.18   220 n.13
    11.47   35 n.2
    IV.63   130 n.9
CINCIUS ALIMENTUS, *FGrHist* 810
  F 5   78 n.67, 137 n.43
  F 5(3)   80 n.83, 81 n.86
  F 5(5)   80 n.83, 81 n.86
CLAUDIUS QUADRIGARIUS
  F 79   55 n.83
CLEIDEMUS OF ATHENS, *FGrHist* 323
  F 14   111 n.248
  F 27   194 n.89
COELIUS ANTIPATER
  F 1   55 n.83
  F 2   116 n.273
  F 29   116 n.273
  F 50   83 n.95
COTTA
  F 1   83 n.99
CRATERUS, *FGrHist* 342
  T 1   104 n.208, 290 n.2
  T 2   290 n.2
CREPEREIUS CALPURNIANUS, *FGrHist* 209
  F 1   275 n.24

CTESIAS OF CNIDUS, *FGrHist* 688
  T 3   87 n.115, 134 n.27
  T 7b   185 n.54
  T 8   80 n.83, 87 n.115, 227 n.52
  F 5   107 n.229, 134 n.27, 185 n.53
  F 14 §44   185 n.56
  F 21   185 n.55
  F 27 §69   185 n.55
  F 28   185 n.55
  F 30   185 n.55
  F 45 §51   82 n.91
  F 45b 82 n.91
  F 45dβ 82 n.91
  F 68   185 n.56
Q. CURTIUS RUFUS
  V.6.9   106 n.226
  IX.1.34   106 n.225
  IX.5.21   187 n.64, 282 n.7
  X.10.11   106 n.225

Q. DELLIUS, *FGrHist* 197
  F 1   80 n.83
DEMETRIUS
  de Eloc. 113   15 n.70
DEMETRIUS OF PHALERON, *FGrHist* 228
  T 3b   180 n.23
DEMETRIUS OF SAGALLASUS, *FGrHist* 209
  F 1   275 n.24
DEMOCRITUS
  B 11   66 n.15
  B 125   66 n.15
  B 299   66 n.15
DEMODOCUS
  F 2   271 n.3
DEMOSTHENES
  de Corona 3   191 n.81
DEXIPPUS OF ATHENS, *FGrHist* 100
  T 3   90 n.133
  F 1   239 n.117
  F 28   199 n.115
DINON, *FGrHist* 690
  FF 15–17   228 n.54
DIO CASSIUS
  I.1.2   106 n.221
  XXXIX.10.1–3   172 n.199
  XLIII.46.5–6   200 n.119
  XLIX.36.4   81 n.89, 147 n.85
  LIII.19   88
  LIII.19.2–3   169 n.187
  LIII.19.6   89 n.124, 170 n.188
  LIV.15.1–4   89 n.124
  LXVI.1.4   49 n.56

  LXVII.18.2   83 n.96
  LXVIII.27.2–3   83 n.96
  LXIX.1.2–3   81 n.89, 147 n.86
  LXIX.14.4   200 n.119
  LXXII.3.3   288 n.19
  LXXII.4.2   91 n.137
  LXXII.18.1–21.3   199 n.116
  LXXII.18.3–4   91 n.136
  LXXII.18.4   80 n.83
  LXXII.19.1   92 n.139
  LXXII.21.1–2   200 n.120
  LXXII.22.6   49
  LXXII.23   38
  LXXII.23.1   49 n.56
  LXXII.23.2–5   49 n.57
  LXXII.23.5   152 n.106
  LXXIII.1.4–5   199 n.116
  LXXIII.3.2   199 n.116
  LXXIII.3.4   200 n.122
  LXXIII.8.1–5   199 n.116
  LXXIII.12.1–13.3   199 n.116
  LXXIII.16.1–17.4   199 n.116
  LXXIV.1.3–2.3   199 n.116
  LXXIV.2.1–2   200 n.122
  LXXIV.4.2–5.5   199 n.116
  LXXIV.11.2   200 n.119
  LXXV.4.1–7   199 n.116
  LXXV.4.3   200 n.117
  LXXVI.1.2   199 n.116
  LXXVI.2.1   199 n.116
  LXXVI.5.1   199 n.116
  LXXVI.6.3   199 n.116
  LXXVI.8.1–9.1   199 n.116
  LXXVI.17.1   200 n.122
  LXXVII.11.2   200 n.122
  LXXVII.17.1–18.4   199 n.116
  LXXVII.17.2–4   200 n.122
  LXXVII.9.3–7   199 n.116
  LXXVIII.6.3   199 n.116
  LXXVIII.8.4   83 n.96, 200 n.118
  LXXVIII.10.1–2   50 n.59
  LXXVIII.37.5–38.2   199 n.116
  LXXX.1.2   199 n.116
  LXXX.4.1   288 n.19
  LXXX.4.2–5.2   199 n.116
  LXXX.5.3   50 n.61
DIO CHRYSOSTOM
  Orat. 18.10   135 n.30
DIODORUS
  I.1.1   59, 151 n.105
  I.1.1–4.5   46 n.42
  I.1.4   46 n.42

Index locorum

I.1.4–5	43 n.28
I.1.5	25 n.123, 59
I.2.2	46 n.42
I.2.4	46 n.42, 150 n.97
I.2.4–3.1	59 n.103
I.2.8	121 n.298
I.3.1	46 n.42, 150 n.100
I.3.2	234 n.95
I.3.2–3	114 n.260, 241 n.124
I.3.3	242 n.127
I.3.4	234 n.95
I.3.5–8	106 n.221
I.3.6	150 n.98
I.3.8	234 n.95, 242, 244 n.133
I.4.1	46 n.42, 150 n.98, 152 n.106
I.4.2–3	244 n.133
I.4.3–5	75 n.55
I.4.6	119
I.5.2	232 n.83
I.9.5	103 n.202
I.11.1–29.6	121 n.299
I.26.8	282 n.9
I.29.6	285 n.28
I.36.4–5	151 n.102
I.37.3	234 n.93
I.37.4	233 n.89
I.37.11	174 n.206
I.42.1	273 n.13
I.46.7	109 n.234
I.46.8	109 n.234
I.53.1	283 n.10
I.69.7	121 n.297, 233 n.89, 234 n.93
I.83.9	109 n.234
I.96.2–98.9	121 n.299
III.11.3	108 n.233
IV.1.1–4	120 n.292
IV.6.1–3	283 n.11
IV.7.1	285 n.28
IV.8.3	120 n.293
IV.8.4	120 n.294
IV.56.17	233 n.87
V.1.1–4	165 n.166, 234 n.91, 234 n.93
V.1.3–4	234 n.95
V.2.4	285 n.28
V.23.1–4	233 n.87
V.23.2–4	234 n.93
V.26.3	174 n.206
V.29.5	174 n.206
V.56.3–4	283 n.11
V.80.4	114 n.261, 283 n.10
X.24.1	121 n.297, 233, 234 n.93
XI.37.6	243 n.129
XII.37.2	243 n.129
XII.71.2	243 n.129
XIII.42.5	243 n.129
XIII.82.6	101 n.192
XIII.103.3	243 n.129
XIV.46.6	243 n.129
XIV.84.7	243 n.129
XIV.117.8	243 n.129
XV.1.3	151 n.102
XV.37.3	243 n.129
XV.48.1–4	41 n.22
XV.60.6	243 n.129
XV.89.3	243 n.129
XV.94.4	243 n.129
XVI.1.1–2	234 n.93
XVI.1.1–3	234 n.95
XVI.3.8	243 n.129
XVI.14.3	243 n.129
XVI.14.4	243 n.129
XVI.14.5	243 n.129
XVI.76.5	243 n.129
XVI.76.6	243 n.129
XVII.46.2	86 n.111
XVII.52.6	109 n.234
XVII.56.4	151 n.102
XVII.94.1	151 n.102
XIX.8.4	234 n.93
XX.72.2	41 n.22
XXI.5	243 n.129
XXI.17.1	234 n.92
XXI.17.1–3	163 n.153
XXI.17.1–4	165 n.166, 234 n.93
XXI.17.4	163 n.154
XXVI.1.1–3	222 n.27
XXVI.4	243 n.129
XXXII.26.1	169 n.185
XXXVII.1.1–6	41
XL.8	59 n.104

DIONYSIUS OF HALICARNASSUS

Antiquitates Romanae, I.1.1   60 n.105, 191 n.81, 211 n.157, 228 n.56, 245 n.139

I.1.2	43 n.28, 132 n.17
I.1.4	153 n.113
I.2.1	43 n.28
I.2.2	121 n.300
I.3.1–5	42
I.4.1	42, 96 n.164
I.4.1–2	46 n.43
I.4.2	113 n.257, 113 n.258
I.4.2–3	163 n.153, 234 n.96, 245
I.4.3	31 n.154
I.5.2	244 n.136

DIONYSIUS OF HALICARNASSUS (cont.)
Antiquitates Romanae (cont.)
1.5.3   43
1.5.4-6.3   113 n.258
1.6.1   244 n.137
1.6.2   77 n.62, 245
1.6.4   43 n.28
1.6.5   53 n.75, 132 n.17
1.7.1-2   113 n.258
1.7.2   152 n.106
1.7.3   245, nn.141-3, 284 n.23
1.8.1   121 n.301, 246 n.147
1.8.3   30 n.145, 30 n.146, 246 n.145
1.8.4   274 n.15
1.12.3   283 n.10
1.32.2   101 n.190, 102 n.194
1.36.1   122 n.305
1.36.2   122 n.306
1.37.2   101 n.190, 102 n.194
1.39-40   123 n.307
1.39.1   123 n.307
1.41-2   123 n.307
1.42.1-4   123 n.308
1.42.4   123 n.309
1.45.4   113 n.258
1.55.1   115 n.272
1.68.1-2   101 n.190, 115 n.272
1.72-5   235 n.98
II.20.1-2   123 n.310
II.23.5   101 n.190, 115 n.272
IV.6.7   235 n.100
VII.72.12   101 n.190
VII.72.18   101 n.190, 115 n.272
VIII.79.1   283 n.12
IX.53.6   16 n.72
XI.1.4   30 n.147
XII.4.2   283 n.12
XX.10   207 n.138
de Comp. Verb. 4 (II.42 Usher)   246 n.148
25 (II.224 Usher)   152 n.108
de Dinarch. 3 (II.260 Usher)   194 n.89
7 (II.268-70 Usher)   13 n.57
de Lys. 8   129 n.5
ad Pomp. 3 (II.372 Usher)   246 n.147
3 (II.372-6 Usher)   47 n.45
3 (II.374 Usher)   15 n.65, 184 n.51
3 (II.380-2 Usher)   18 n.87, 132 n.18
6 (II.386-96 Usher)   132 n.18
6 (II.392-4 Usher)   121 n.297
6 (II.392-6 Usher)   43 n.28
6 (II.392 Usher)   87 n.114, 149 n.93
6 (II.394-6 Usher)   95 n.158, 135 n.31

6 (II.396-8 Usher)   118 n.286
de Thuc. 5   7 n.29, 51 n.67, 99 n.178, 120 n.296
5-6   122 n.303
6   15 n.65, 153 n.113
7   122 n.304
9   17 n.81
23   7 n.26, 245 n.143
50-1   30 n.144
[DIONYSIUS]
Ars Rhet. 19 (II.373 Us.-Raderm.)   14 n.59
DIONYSIUS OF MILETUS, FGrHist 687
F 1   101 n.190
DIYLLUS OF ATHENS, FGrHist 73
T 2   290 n.7
DURIS OF SAMOS, FGrHist 76
F 1   117 n.280, 228 n.56, 228 n.60

EMPEDOCLES
B 3   4 n.16
B 4   4 n.16
ENNIUS
Ann.1.3   48 n.54
EPHORUS, FGrHist 70
T 8   242 n.125
T 9a   290 n.5
F 9   70 n.32, 97 n.169
F 31b   97 n.170
F 105   103 n.202
F 110   70 n.134
F 111   152 n.109
F 122   97 n.170
F 149   97 n.171
F 199   97 n.170
EPICHARMUS
B 12   65 n.13
EUNAPIUS
F 1   221 n.22, 239 n.117
EURIPIDES
Suppl. 846-56   68 n.27
EUTROPIUS
10.16   79 n.79
EUTYCHIANUS OF CAPPADOCIA, FGrHist 226
F 1   80 n.83, 90 n.133

FABIUS PICTOR, FGrHist 809
T 2   80 n.83
T 6a   77 n.64
F 4   77 n.66
F 15   138 n.47
F 19b   83 n.99
F 20   193 n.85

Index locorum

FANNIUS
  F 1   165 n.168
  F 4   81 n.86
FRONTO
  ad Verum I.2.1   90 n.132
           I.2.2   36 n.8

GELLIUS
  VI.3.1-48   194 n.91
  XV.9.5   193 n.86
GRANIUS LIGINIANUS
  XXXV.68   288 n.12
GREGORY OF CORINTH
  Walz, *Rhet. Graeci*, VII.1298-1301   176 n.3

HECATAEUS OF ABDERA, *FGrHist* 264
  F 2   108 n.232
  F 25   109 n.234
HECATAEUS OF MILETUS, *FGrHist* 1
  T 12a   67 n.18
  T 21   65 n.11
  F 1a   5 n.19, 225 n.40, 272 n.6
  F 19   225 n.41
  F 20   101 n.190
  F 300   107 n.230
HELIODORUS, *AETHIOPICA*
  II.28 = *FGrHist* 665 F 60(c)   109 n.237
HERACLITUS
  B 35   65 n.10
  B 40   65 n.11, 219 n.8
  B 42   219 n.8
  B 55   65 n.10
  B 101a   65 n.10
  B 107   65 n.13
  B 129   65 n.12
HERMOGENES
  Meth. 25   176 n.3, 211 n.154, 212 n.159
HERODIAN
  I.1.4-5   38
  I.2.5   80 n.83, 147 n.84
  II.9.4   181 n.29
  II.15.6-7   92 n.142
  III.7.8   39
HERODOTUS
  praef.   8, 41, 48, 185 n.52, 272 n.7
  I.5.3   185 n.52
  I.8.2   67 n.23
  I.49   103 n.205
  I.61.2   280 n.1
  I.106.2   112 n.254
  I.184   112 n.254
  II.2.5   225 n.43
  II.3.1   108 n.231, 110 n.239, 225 n.43, 245 n.141
  II.19-34   225 n.43
  II.23   118 n.285
  II.42-5   225 n.44
  II.45.1   118 n.285
  II.73.1   102 n.194
  II.99-146   101 n.190
  II.99.1   170 n.188
  II.112-20   225 n.45
  II.143   225 n.43, 284 n.22
  II.143.1   107 n.230
  II.147.1   170 n.188
  II.156.2   102 n.194
  III.98-105   112 n.255
  III.115.2   148 n.91
  IV.44   67 n.20, 112 n.255
  V.59   101 n.190
  VI.137.1   99 n.179
  VII.20.2-21.1   34
  VII.59-60   255 n.200
  VII.60.1   103 n.205
  VII.139   173 n.203
  VIII.109.3   207 n.140
  VIII.128.1   103 n.205
  VIII.133   103 n.205
HESIOD
  Theog. 1-11   219 n.7
         22-4   271 n.1
         22-32   4 n.14
HIERONYMUS OF CARDIA, *FGrHist* 154
  T 2   88 n.120
  T 7   80 n.83
  T 11   162 n.152
  F 8   88 n.120
HIPPIAS OF ELIS, *FGrHist* 6
  T 3   20 n.96
(HIPPOCRATES)
  Decent. 3   220 n.18
A. HIRTIUS
  ap. Caes. *Bell. Gall.* VIII .*praef.*8   78 n.74
HOMER
  Il. I.1-7   3 n.8
      I.78   207
      II.484-93   3 n.8, 64 n.3
      II.486   226 n.47
      II.761-2   3 n.8
      XI.163-4   50 n.61
      XI.218-20   3 n.8
      XIV.508-9   3 n.8
      XVI.112-3   3 n.8
  Od. 11.92-5   64 n.6

HOMER (cont.)
  Od. (cont.)
    III.186-7   64 n.6
    VIII.487-91   63 n.1
    XII.389-90   4 n.13
    XVI.470   64 n.7
    XIX.173   15 n.70
    XXII.347-9   4 n.10
HORACE
  Carm. II.1.1-4   292 n.5
    II.1.6   157 n.127
    II.20   57 n.92
    III.30.1-6   57 n.92

ION OF CHIOS, FGrHist 392
  F 6   184 n.48
ISOCRATES
  Antidosis 6-8   176 n.7
    9   87 n.117
  Panath. 1   118 n.287
    8   152 n.107
    11   44 n.33
    119   277
    120   277
    126 ff.   277
    130-3   277
    134-8   277
    149-50   276-8
  Paneg. 4   277 n.4
    7-10   276-7
    11-14   277
    13   152 n.111
    13-14   152 n.107
    14   277 n.5
    188-9   277 n.5
ISTER, FGrHist 334
  F 59   223 n.33

JOSEPHUS
  Antiq. Jud. 1. 2   60 n.106, 112 n.253
    1.4   60 n.107, 111 n.246, 288 n.18
    1.8-9   52 n.69
    1.9   52 n.70, 156 n.123
    1.12   113 n.258
    1.26   111 n.246
    1.158   288 n.18
    II.201   174 n.206
    III.143   288 n.18
    III.318   288 n.18
  Bell Jud. 1. 1   38, 216
    1.2   115 n.265, 168
    1.3   80 n.83, 90 n.131, 145 n.74, 274 n.16

1.4   38 n.13
1.4-5   38
1.7-8   168 n.183, 216
1.9   168, 216
1.9-11   168 n.180, 288 n.18
1.10   90 n.131
1.10-12   168
1.11   38 n.13
1.13-16   168 n.183
1.16   156 n.123
1.18   90 n.131
II.573   210 n.152
II.577   210 n.152
II.577-82   216 n.174
II.598-613   211 n.158
II.632-7   210 n.152
III.115-26   216 n.174
III.130   210 n.152
III.135   210 n.152
III.143-4   214
III.171-5   210 n.152
III.176-89   210 n.152, 216 n.174
III.183   210 n.152
III.190-2   210 n.152
III.193-202   215 n.170
III.202   214 n.169
III.222-8   210 n.152
III.270ff.   210 n.152
III.340   215 n.170
III.341   211 n.153
III.347   215 n.170
III.351-3   211 n.153
III.358   210 n.152
III.386-91   210 n.152
III.392-8   211 n.154
III.394-5   215 n.170
III.399-408   49 n.56
III.405-8   210 n.152, 211 n.154
III.434-42   211 n.158
IV.623-9   199 n.114, 211 n.154
V.19-20   168 n.181
V.114   199 n.114
V.261   199 n.114
V.325-6   199 n.114
V.361-420   199 n.114
V.541-7   199 n.114
VI.93-117   199 n.114
VI.365   199 n.114, 211 n.158
VII.280-406   216 n.174
VII.448   199 n.114
c. Ap. 1. 8-10   103 n.200
  1.15-27   168 n.183

1.16	218 n.6
1.19-23	103 n.200
1.24-5	60 n.106
1.26	282
1.54	111 n.246
1.55	80 n.83
Vita 1	145 n.76
336-44	224 n.36
350	224 n.36
358-60	173 n.202
361-2	90 n.128
361-3	215 n.171
363-6	90 n.129
366	90 n.130
367	90 n.128

JUSTIN
praef. 1   61 n.111, 137 n.40, 142 n.61
praef. 2   155 n.118
praef. 4   155 n.118
XLIII.1.1-2   142 n.62, 273 n.14
XLIII.5.11-12   141 n.60

KEPHALION, *FGrHist* 93
T 2   114 n.263, 275 n.22
F 1b   114 n.263

KRITON, *FGrHist* 200
T 2   80 n.83, 90 n.133
T 3   148 n.90
F 1   83 n.99

LACTANTIUS
Inst. 1.6.7   55 n.82

LIBANIUS
Epist. 1063   217 n.4

LICINIUS MUCIANUS
FF 7, 10, 12, 13, 18, 20, 24   82 n.91

LIVY
praef. 1   140 n.56, 153 n.115
praef. 2   112 n.253, 140 n.53
praef. 2-3   248 n.157
praef. 3   5 n.21, 61, 140 n.54, 256 n.206
praef. 4   45, 96 n.164
praef. 4-5   153 n.115
praef. 5   45 n.38
praef. 6   124 n.311
praef. 9-10   46
praef. 10   43 n.28
praef. 11   288 n.14
praef. 13   153 n.115
1.2-3   273 n.14
1.19.3   288 n.15
1.24.1   282 n.9
1.53.4   174 n.206
1.54.4   151 n.102
1.55.8-9   281 n.5
II.8.5   249 n.162
II.10.11   124 n.313
II.17.3   249 n.162
II.18.4-7   281
II.32.2-3   282 n.9
III.5.12   248 n.159
III.23.7   249 n.162, 281 n.6
III.56.3   10 n.42
V.15.12   131 n.12
V.21.8-9   120 n.296, 124 n.313
V.32.7   131 n.12
V.42.3   86 n.111
VI.1.2   103 n.201
VI.9.3-5   285 n.28
VI.12.2-3   249 n.162
VI.20.10   131 n.12
VII.9.3-5   249 n.161
VII.9.5   163
VII.14.6   288 n.15
VII.29.1-2   154
VIII.26.5-6   283 n.13
VIII.40.3-4   249 n.161
VIII.40.5   249 n.163
IX.17-19   224 n.38
IX.17.1   288 n.14
IX.19.15   288 n.15
IX.19.17   288 n.15
IX.44.4   248 n.159
X.24.4   10 n.42
XXI.1.1-2   42
XXI.1.2   40 n.20
XXI.32.7   94 n.153
XXI.38.3   78 n.67
XXI.38.3-5   137 n.43
XXI.46.7-10   282 n.9
XXII.5   281 n.2
XXII.7.4   249 n.163, 281 n.5
XXII.52   281 n.2
XXV.19.11   288 n.16
XXV.39.15   288 n.16
XXVII.12.2-4   171 n.194
XXVIII.24.1   93 n.148
XXVIII.46.16   102 n.193
XXIX.1.4   151 n.102
XXIX.14.9   249 n.162, 281 n.6
XXIX.25.3-4   248 n.159
XXIX.27.13-15   249 n.160
XXX.19.11   248 n.159
XXX.26.9   288 n.16

LIVY (cont.)
  XXXI.1.1   154 n.117
  XXXI.1.1-5   42 n.24, 154
  XXXII.6.5-8   249 n.160
  XXXIII.10.8-10   248 n.159
  XXXIV.15.9   187 n.64, 249 n.161
  XXXVI.19.11-12   248 n.159
  XXXVII.48.1-7   249 n.162
  XXXVIII.56.3-4   102 n.198
  XXXIX.43.1   248 n.159
  per.CXXI   172 n.197
  F 48   172 n.195
  F 50   172 n.195
  F 58   46 n.39, 57 n.95, 248 n.158
[LONGINUS]
  de Sublim. 1.3   57 n.93
    4.2   152 n.108
    13.2-14.1   13 n.57
    14.1   237 n.105
LUCIAN
  Quom. hist. conscr. 7-32   221 n.21
    8   10 n.42, 126 n.321
    10   126 n.322
    12   160 n.142
    14   173 n.204, 275 n.22
    15   12 n.51, 13 n.58, 275 n.24
    16   10 n.42, 148 n.90, 180 n.22, 275 n.24
    18   13 n.58
    18-21   90 n.133
    23   273 n.12
    29   66 n.16, 67 n.23
    30   148 n.90, 275 n.24
    32   275 n.24, 275 n.26
    34   156 n.125
    34-54   13 n.58
    39   170 n.190
    42   126 n.324
    47   75, 156 n.125, 160
    48   180 n.22
    51   162 n.146
    52   237 n.107, 273 n.12
    60   126 n.325
  Herodotus 1   61 n.112
  Varia Historia 1.3   273 n.9
    1.4   66 n.16

MAGNOS OF CARRHAE, FGrHist 225
  T 1   80 n.83, 90 n.133
MANETHO, FGrHist 609
  T 7a   110 n.239
  T 11b   53 n.74
  T 11c   53 n.74
  F 1   110 n.239

  F 10   110 n.239
  F 25   110 n.239
MARCELLINUS
  Vita Thuc. 26-7   184 n.51
    35-7   15 n.65
MARCUS AURELIUS
  Med. 1.17.9   50 n.63
MENANDER RHETOR
  390.4-6 (Russell-Winterbottom)   50 n.62
MIMNERMUS
  F 13   4 n.15, 8 n.31
MNESIPTOLEMUS OF CYME, FGrHist 164
  T 1   88 n.120
  T 2   24 n.117
  T 3   24 n.117

NAEVIUS
  Bell. Poen. F 2   137 n.42
NEPOS
  Cato 3.3   284 n.24
    3.4   197 n.105
  Chronicles, F 7   155 n.120
NICOLAUS OF DAMASCUS, FGrHist 90
  F 44 §7   107 n.230
  FF 131-9   196 n.99
  F 135   30 n.148, 52 n.68, 155 n.119
  FF 136-8   198 n.113

OLYMPOS, FGrHist 198
  F 1   80 n.83, 88 n.121

PARMENIDES
  B 1   4 n.16
PAUSANIAS
  I 9.8   162 n.152
  I 15.1-3   20 n.94
  VI 18.5   228 n.57
PHILIP OF PERGAMUM, FGrHist 95
  F 1   43 n.28, 151 n.105
PHILISTUS OF SYRACUSE, FGrHist 556
  T 3   187 n.59
  T 4   187 n.59
  F 56   80 n.83
  F 59   187 n.59
PHILOCHORUS, FGrHist 328
  F 35a   194 n.89
  F 67   111 n.249, 194 n.89
PHOCYLIDES
  FF 8, 10, 11, 14   271 n.3
PHOTIUS
  Bibl. 84   29 n.138
    250   233 n.86

Index locorum

PHYLARCHUS, *FGrHist* 81
  F 52   162 n.151
PLATO
  epist. 7.324b–326b   44 n.33
  Gorg. 459a–b   220 n.19
    471e–472c   220 n.14
    474a   220 n.15
    475e   220 n.15
  Hipp. Mai. 285d   20 n.96
  Phaedrus 267a6–b2   277 n.3
  Rep. III. 392d–394d   6 n.22
    X 599a–b   60 n.109
    X 599b5–7   60 n.109
PLINY THE ELDER
  Historiae, F 4   172 n.200
  Hist. Nat. praef. 16   57 n.95
    praef. 20   172 n.200
    praef. 25   243 n.131
    praef. 30   223 n.34
PLINY THE YOUNGER
  epist. III. 5.3   48 n.53
    III.5.4   47 n.47
    III.5.6   292 n.8
    V 8.1–2   62 n.114
    V 8.12   105 n.220
    VII 33.3   178 n.14
PLUTARCH
  Alex. 1.2   92 n.140
  Ant. 82.3–5   88 n.121
  Arat. 38   162 n.151
  Artax. 13   185 n.55
  aud. poet. 4   159 n.138
  Brut. 4   29 n.138
    48   83 n.95
  Cat. Mai. 10   195 n.92
    14.1   195 n.93
    14.1–2   195 n.92
    14.2–4   195 n.92
    20.7   55 n.84
  Comp. Dem. et Cic. 3.1   54 n.79
  Demetr. 1.5–6   221 n.22
  de se ips. 539D   177 n.8
    54E–F   207 n.137
    543F   207 n.141
    540C ff.   177 n.8
    541A   221 n.155
    541A ff.   177 n.8
    541C ff.   177 n.8
    542A–B   177 n.8
    542E–F   177 n.8
    543A–B   177 n.8
    543F   177 n.8
    547F   177 n.8

  de glor. Ath. 345E   186 n.57
    345E–F   58 n.97
  de Herod. Malig. 854F   118 n.285
    855C–D   118 n.286
  Lucull. 1.4   54 n.79
  Nicias 1   229 n.62
  Phocion 5   131 n.13
  Pomp. 76.7   88 n.121
  Sulla 6.8–10   209 n.145
    6.9   209 n.145
    34.3–5   209 n.145
POLYBIUS
  I.1.1   11 n.47, 180 n.21
  I.1.2   25 n.120, 43 n.28, 151 n.105
  I.1.3   241
  I.1.5   37
  I.2.2–7   37
  I.3.1   180 n.24, 290 n.11
  I.3.1–2   239 n.112
  I.3.4   239 n.114
  I.4.1–11   47 n.46
  I.4.5   37
  I.4.7   37 n.12
  I.4.7–11   230 n.73
  I.4.8–11   37
  I.5.1   239 n.112, 290 n.11
  I.12.8   190 n.77
  I.12.8–9   99 n.177
  I.14   98 n.175
  I.14.1–9   115 n.265
  I.14.2   77 n.64
  I.14.4–9   230 n.73
  I.15   230 n.73
  I.64.4   230 n.73
  II.16.13–15   120 n.296
  II.17.6   230 n.73
  II.40.4   98 n.175
  II.47.4   162 n.151
  II.56   24 n.118
  II.56–61   230 n.73
  II.56.3   153 n.113
  II.56.13   233 n.85
  II.61.1–6   232 n.82
  II.62.2   136 n.38
  III.4.13   78 n.68, 80 n.83, 136 n.34
  III.6.1–7.3   190 n.77
  III.7.4   190 n.77
  III.7.4–7   99 n.177
  III.9.1–5   281 n.5
  III.20.5   236 n.104
  III.21.9–10   230 n.73
  III.26.1–2   230 n.73
  III.32   230 n.73

POLYBIUS (cont.)
III.33.17-18   102 n.193
III.36.1-6   83 n.100
III.38.1-3   230 n.73
III.47.6-48.12   230 n.73
III.48   115 n.271
III.57.1-9   190 n.77
III.57.2-59.8   83 n.100
III.57.3   190 n.77
III.57.6   190 n.77
III.58-9   127 n.327
III.59   84 n.102
III.59.7   149 n.95, 151 n.105
III.64.11   131 n.11
III.84   281 n.2
III.91.7   127 n.328
III.97   281 n.2
III.98.3   174 n.206
IV.2.1-3   98 n.174
IV.2.2   136 n. 34
IV.3.1-3   174 n.206
IV.17.11   174 n.206
IV.62.1-4   174 n.206
V.33.1   37 n.11
V.33.2   239 n.114
V.49.4   191 n.81
VI.2.1-4   190 n.77
VI.11.3-8   222 n.27
VII.7.6   230 n.73
VII.11.1   11 n.46
VII.11.1-2   190 n.77
VIII.2   230 n.73
VIII.8.3-9   164 n.165
VIII.8.7   131 n.14
VIII.9-11   230 n.73
VIII.10.9   151 n.102
VIII.11.1-4   162 n.148
VIII.11.2   223 n.34
VIII.13.3-4   37 n.10
VIII.36.2-3   131 n.11
IX.1.2-5   24 n.118
IX.1.3   180 n.21
IX.2.1-3   98
IX.2.5   43 n.28
IX.12-20   136 n.37
IX.20.4   136 n.37
IX.25   116 n.271
IX.25.3   284 n.21
IX.25.4   284 n.21
X.2.5-6   230 n.73
X.11.4   75 n.53
X.21.2-4   190 n.77

X.21.8   164 n.165
X.45.6   136 n.37
XI.1a.1   190 n.77
XI.10.4-5   131 n.11
XI.19a   236 n.104
XII.4c.3   98 n.175
XII.4c.4-5   76 n.57
XII.5.1-5   99 n.176, 164 n.164
XII.5.3   151 n.102
XII.5.5   284
XII.7.6   222 n.29, 222 n.30
XII.10.4   223 n.34
XII.11.4   222 n.30
XII.12.4-5   222 n.29
XII.12.5   222 n.30
XII.12b.2   229 n.64
XII.13-15   229 n.65
XII.14.1-4   164 n.165
XII.15.1-10   163 n.153
XII.22.6   71 n.39
XII.24-26e   132 n.19
XII.25a.2   222 n.31
XII.25a.4   180 n.21
XII.25c.5   222 n.28
XII.25d.1-25e.7   104 n.209
XII.25d.2-7   74 n.49
XII.25e.1-7   83 n.100
XII.25e.1-25h.4   72 n.42
XII.25f   239 n.114
XII.25f.1   106 n.221
XII.25f.1-6   230 n.73
XII.25f.1-7   72 n.40
XII.25g-25i   145 n.73
XII.25g-25i.9   136 n.38
XII.25g.1-28a.10   98 n.173
XII.25g.1-3   73 n.46
XII.26d.3-27.6   72 n.43
XII.26d.4   223 n.34
XII.27.1   65 n.10
XII.27.4-6   151 n.102
XII.27.7   70 n.34
XII.27.8-9   73 n.45
XII.27a.3   284 n.20
XII.28-28a   229 n.65
XII.28.3-5   153 n.113
XII.28.10   239 n.114
XII.28a.3   149 n.94
XII.28a.8-10   73 n.47
XVI.14.3   59 n.102
XVI.14.6   230 n.73
XVI.14.7-8   222 n.29, 222 n.30
XVI.15   230 n.73

Index locorum 329

XVI.17.10-11   80 n.82
XVI.20.5-6   222 n.27
XVI.20.5-9   232 n.80
XVI.20.6   222 n.27
XVI.20.8-9   222 n.29
XVIII.46.14   151 n.102
XX.12.8   75 n.53
XXI.38.1-7   82 n.94
XXII.19   81 n.85
XXII.19.1   188 n.68
XXIV.6.1-7   189 n.71
XXVIII.3.7-9   189 n.71
XXVIII.6.8-9   189 n.71
XXVIII.7.8-13   189 n.71
XXVIII.12.4-13.14   189 n.71
XXVIII.13.5   151 n.102
XXVIII.14.1-4   174 n.206
XXIX.5.1-3   136 n.34
XXIX.5.1-9.13   81 n.85, 86 n.113
XXIX.5.3   86 n.113
XXIX.8.10   86 n.113
XXIX.12.1-2   230 n.73
XXIX.12.10-12   222 n.29
XXIX.23.1-25.7   189 n.71
XXX.9.20-1   190 n.77, 232 n.82
XXXI.11.1-15.12   189 n.71
XXXI.22.1-11   173 n.203
XXXI.23-30   173 n.203
XXXI.23.1-29.12   189 n.71
XXXI.30.1   25 n.122
XXXII.3.14   189 n.71
XXXIII.21.1-2   230 n.73
XXXIV.2.9-10   119 n.290
XXXIV.4.1   119 n.290
XXXIV.5.2-9   84 n.102
XXXIV.10.6-7   84 n.102
XXXV.6.1-4   188 n.68
XXXVI.8.6   190 n.77
XXXVI.11.1-4   189 n.71, 189 n.74
XXXVI.12   175 n.2
XXXVI.12.1-5   190 n.75
XXXVIII.1.3   169 n.184
XXXVIII.4   169 n.184
XXXVIII.4.1   169 n.184, 190 n.77
XXXVIII.6   118 n.286
XXXVIII.19   188 n.68
XXXVIII.21.1   82 n.94
XXXVIII.21.3   173 n.203
XXXIX.2.1   188 n.68
XXXIX.5.4   188 n.68

POLEMON
FHG III.108   104 n.208, 223 n.33

POLYCLEITUS OF LARISSA, *FGrHist* 128
F 7   162 n.150
POMPEIUS TROGUS
F 14a   155 n.118
F 161   273 n.14
F 165   141 n.60
POSEIDONIUS, *FGrHist* 169
F 1   80 n.83
POSIDONIUS, *FGrHist* 87
T 1=T 1 Edelstein-Kidd   239 n.115, 290 n.12
T 12b=T 1b EK   239 n.115, 290 n.12
F 37=F 255 EK   88 n.121
F 51=F 271 EK   163 n.155
F 53=F 246 EK   84 n.103, 285 n.27
F 55=F 274 EK   85 n.105
F 58a=F 269 EK   85 n.105
F 66=F 244 EK   84 n.103
F 73=F 245 EK   84 n.103
POSTUMIUS ALBINUS, *FGrHist* 812
TT 1-7   137 n.43
PRAXAGORAS OF ATHENS, *FGrHist* 219
T 1 (§8)   37 n.9
PSAON OF PLATAEA, *FGrHist* 78
T 1   290 n.8
PTOLEMAIOS OF MENDES, *FGrHist* 611
T 1   110 n.240
PTOLEMY I, SOTER, *FGrHist* 138
T 1   80 n.83
F 26b   187 n.64
PTOLEMY VIII, EUERGETES II, *FGrHist* 234
FF 1, 6, 9-10   196 n.101
PYRRHUS OF EPIRUS, *FGrHist* 229
F 1   207 n.138

QUINTILIAN
II.4.2   118 n.287
II.5.10-12   221 n.20
III.8.9   78 n.70
X.1.31   61 n.112
X.1.74   135 n.30
X.2.1   13 n.55
X.2.4-8   15 n.68
X.2.12   13 n.57
X.2.17   17 n.76
X.2.27-8   14 n.60
XI.1.15-26   176 n.3
XI.1.16-17   177 n.9
XI.1.17-18   177 n.9
XI.1.21   177 n.10, 178 n.13
XI.1.21-2   177 n.11
XII.1.8   57 n.93

RUTILIUS RUFUS, *FGrHist* 815
T 4b   182 n.32
FF 1-6   182 n.32
F 9   196 n.101
F 14   196 n.101

SALLUST
Cat. 1.6   44
2.9   60 n.108
3.1   44
3.1-2   60
3.2   152 n.110, 167 n.179
3.3-5   44
3.4-5   208 n.141
3.5-4.2   166 n.171
4.1   44 n.32, 45 n.36
4.2   44
4.4   39 n.18
8.5   60 n.109
10.2   151 n.102
11.1-2   208 n.141
12.3   287 n.4
36.4-37.1   39
48.9   81 n.86
52.10-11   16 n.71
61.1-6   40
Historiae, 1.2   247 n.153
I.3   60 n.110, 247 n.152
I.4   247
I.5   247 n.155
I.6   166 n.172, 247
II.98   151 n.102
III.48   251 n.175
III.96   287 n.2
IV.36   287 n.2
Jugurtha, 4.1-7   43 n.28
4.3   44 n.32, 139, 152 n.112
4.3-4   139
4.5   287 n.2
4.5-8   139
5.1   40
5.2   40
17.7   85 n.107, 105 n.217
19.7   287 n.2
29.7   287 n.2
38.7   287 n.2
43.5   287 n.2
46.3   174 n.206
50.6   287 n.2
85.31   10 n.42
95.3   247 n.154
101.6   287 n.2

SCHOLIA
Od. δ 447=*FGrHist* 665 F 60(b)   109 n.237
SCRIPTORES HISTORIAE AUGUSTAE
Hadr. 1.1   181 n.29
16.1-6   19 n.89
Tac. 10.3   32 n.159
SCYLAX OF CARYANDA, *FGrHist* 709
T 3   67 n.20, 112 n.255
SEMPRONIUS ASELLIO
F 1   138 n.49, 236 n.104
F 2   43 n.28, 138 n.49, 236 n.104
F 6   78 n.69, 80 n.83, 138 n.49
SENECA THE ELDER
Contr. II.1.33   50 n.62
Hist. F 1   292 n.6
Nat. Quaes. V.18.4   172 n.195
Suas. VI.17   172 n.195
VI.22   170 n.191
SENECA THE YOUNGER
*Apoc.*1.2   5 n.20
ep. 79.6   15 n.69
114.1   132 n.16
SERVILIUS NONIANUS
F 1   247 n.156
SEXTUS EMPIRICUS
adv. Math. I.263-4   118 n.287
SIDONIUS APOLLINARIS
epist. IV.3.2   56 n.91
SILENUS OF CALEACTE, *FGrHist* 175
T 2   80 n.83
SIMONIDES
F 11.21   8 n.31
SOLON
F 13.1-2   4 n.15
F 33   271 n.3
F 36.3-5   4 n.15
SOSYLUS OF LACEDAEMON, *FGrHist* 176
T 1   80 n.83
STOBAEUS
Florilegium III.12.14   65 n.9
STRABO
Geograph. VIII.1.1   84 n.101
X.3.5   232 n.83
X.4.17   97 n.171
XI.7.4   162 n.150
XV.1.61   82 n.93
Historiae, *FGrHist* 91
T 2   239 n.115
F 1   239 n.115, 290 n.13
F 2   43 n.28
F 3   239 n.115

Index locorum

SUETONIUS
  Aug. 85.1   181 n.29
  diu. Iul. 56.4   116 n.275
  gramm. 3.1-2   55 n.86
    10   28 n.138
SULLA
  F 3   196 n.101
SUSARION
  F 1   271 n.3

TACITUS
  Agricola, 1.1-4   179 n.15, 253 n.182
    1.4   167 n.179
    3.3   167 n.177
  Annales, 1.1.1-2   250 n.166
    1.1.2   115 n.265
    1.5.3   95 n.160
    1.55.1   288 n.11
    1.61.2   81 n.90
    1.69.2   251 n.172
    II.24.4   94 n.151
    II.39.3   94 n.152, 94 n.154
    II.45.2   288 n.11
    II.56.1   174 n.206
    II.60.3-4   109 n.236
    II.73.4   94 n.150
    II.82.1   94 n.151
    II.88.3   113 n.257
    III.16.1   116 n.276
    III.19.2   94 n.153
    III.30.2   251 n.173
    III.44.1   94 n.151
    III.65.1-2   31 n.152
    IV.10.1   282 n.9, 283 n.14
    IV.32.1-2   156 n.124
    IV.32.1-33.4   251 n.174
    IV.32.2   91 n.134, 93 n.145
    IV.32.2-33.2   43 n.28
    IV.33.4   167 n.178, 252
    IV.34.3   170 n.191, 172 n.196
    IV.34.3-4   252 n.177
    IV.35.5   252 n.178
    IV.48.1   288 n.11
    IV.53.2   116 n.276
    IV.61   156 n.124
    V.10.1   174 n.206
    VI.7.5   113 n.257
    VI.28.6   125 n.317
    VI.31.1   288 n.11
    XI.11.1   81 n.88, 144 n.72
    XI.11.3   125 n.318
    XIII.20.2   251 n.172

    XIII.31.1   251 n.172
    XIII.37.1   288 n.11
    XIV.19   251 n.173
    XIV.58.3   94 n.152
    XV.53.3-4   251 n.172
    XV.55.4   223 n.34
  Dialogus, 10.1   57 n.93
  Historiae, 1.1.1   143 n.68, 167 n.176, 250
    1.1.2   223 n.34
    1.1.3   143 n.68, 167
    1.1.3-4   166 n.175
    1.1.4   157
    1.2.1   38, 288 n.11
    1.2.2-3   38
    1.8.1   250 n.170
    1.29.1   94 n.150
    1.34.2   94 n.152
    1.41.2   94 n.150
    1.90.3   94 n.152
    II.4.1   250 n.170
    II.42.1   95 n.160
    II.46.1   93 n.147
    II.50   282 n.9
    II.50.2   125 n.315
    II.70.3   94 n.149, 163 n.159
    II.83.1   94 n.151
    II.90.2   94 n.152
    II.100.2-101.1   250 n.170
    III.25.2   250 n.169
    III.28   250 n.169
    III.45.2   288 n.11
    III.47.2   174 n.206
    III.54.1   94 n.154
    III.61.2   94 n.149
    IV.6.1   57 n.94
    IV.13.1   288 n.11
    IV.18.3   288 n.11
    IV.20.3   288 n.11
    IV.23.1   288 n.11
    IV.50.1   93 n.146
    V.9.1   288 n.11
THEMISTOGENES OF SYRACUSE, *FGrHist* 108
  T 3   186 n.57
THEOGNIS
  1-18   4 n.15
  22-3   271 n.2
  769«72   4 n.15
THEOPHANES OF MYTILENE, *FGrHist* 188
  T 2   80 n.83
THEOPOMPUS, *FGrHist* 115
  T 1   228 n.58

THEOPOMPUS (cont.)
T 19   37 n.10, 132 n.19
T 20a 80 n.83, 87 n.114, 149 n.93
T 21   135 n.30
T 25   132 n.19
T 28b 132 n.19
T 45   135 n.30
FF 1–4 228 n.58
F 24   228 n.56
F 25   58 n.98, 80 n.83, 135 n.29, 254 n.189
F 27   36 n.6, 162 n.148, 253 n.188
F 154 105 n.218
F 342 73 n.45, 133 n.22
F 381 121 n.299

THUCYDIDES
I.1.1   38 n.13, 133, 182 n.40, 185 n.52
I.1.3   70 n.33, 96 n.166, 185 n.52
I.2–19 68
I.3.1   185 n.52
I.3.2   185 n.52
I.9.2   284 n.18
I.10.1–3 68 n.25
I.20.1 70 n.33, 96 n.166, 97, 148 n.91, 284 n.17
I.20.3 97, 226
I.20.3–21.1 21 n.100
I.21.1 97, 226
I.22   164 n.161
I.22.1–3 80 n.83
I.22.2 68, 153 n.113, 185 n.52
I.22.2–3 67 n.22
I.22.3 69, 88, n.122, 133, 148 n.91
I.22.4 12 n.51, 21 n.101, 21, 58 n.98, 96 n.166
I.23.1–2 35
I.23.1–4 40 n.20
I.23.6 67 n.24
I.33.2 151 n.102
I.70.8 151 n.102
I73.2   70 n.33, 278 n.7
I.89–117 290 n.1
I.97.2 113 n.256, 114 n.259, 115 n.269, 227
I.117.2 183 n.40
II.7.1 174 n.205
II.8.3 36 n.4
II.11.1 36 n.4
II.20.2 36 n.4
II.35.2 152 n.111
II.47.3 36 n.4
II.48.3 80 n.84, 185 n.52
II.64.3 36 n.4
II.71–8 203 n.127

II.77.4 36 n.4
II.94.1 36 n.4
III.82.4–7 16 n.71
III.98.4 36 n.4
IV.40.1 36 n.4
IV.64.3 15 n.70
IV.104.4 80 n.84
IV.104.4–105.1 183 n.38, 185 n.52
IV.105.1 183 n.41
IV.107.1 183 n.41
V.14.3 36 n.4
V.23–4 104 n.210
V.26   133, 184 n.44
V.26.1 134 n.26, 185 n.52
V.26.2–3 134 n.23
V.26.3 134 n.25
V.26.4 134 n.25, 134 n.26
V.26.5 133, 134 n.23, 134 n.25
V.47   104 n.210
V.60.3 36 n.4
V.64.2 36 n.4
V.74.2 36 n.4
VI.2.2 284 n.18
VI.16.6 151 n.102
VI.31.1 36 n.4
VI.31.6 36 n.4
VI.54–5 227 n.50
VI.54.1 115 n.270, 185 n.52, 227 n.50
VI.54.7 101 n.191, 227 n.50
VI.55   227 n.50
VI.55.1 227 n.50
VI.55.1–2 227 n.50
VI.55.2 227 n.50
VI.55.3 227 n.50
VI.57–9 227 n.50
VII.30.3 36 n.4
VII.44.1 69
VII.66.2 36 n.4
VII.70.2 36 n.4
VII.71.2 36 n.4
VII.71.7 36 n.4
VII.85.4 36 n.4
VII.86.5 36 n.4
VII.87.5 36 n.4
VII.87.6 36 n.4
VIII.41.2 36 n.4
VIII.68.2 36 n.4
VIII.96.1 36 n.4
VIII.106.1 36 n.4

TIMAEUS OF TAUROMENIUM, *FGrHist* 566
T 3a   187 n.62
T 6a   290 n.11

Index locorum

TT 16-19   132 n.19
T 18   229 n.62
T 25   223 n.33
T 26   223 n.33
F 7   149 n.94, 229 n.65
F 12   105 n.219
F 26   101 n.192
F 34   71 n.38
F 35   229 n.65
F 59   284 n.20
F 113   229 n.63
F 115   229 n.63
F 123   187 n.62
F 124   187 n.62
F 124b   163 n.153
F 124d   163 n.153
F 152   229 n.65
F 154   229 n.63
F 155   229 n.64
F 156   229 n.65
TIMAGENES OF ALEXANDRIA, *FGrHist* 88
F 1   242 n.126
F 2   242 n.126
TIMONIDES OF LEUCAS, *FGrHist* 561
T 2   187 n.60
F 2   80 n.83
TRAJAN
Dacica F 1   181 n.29, 196 n.102

VELLEIUS PATERCULUS
I.7.1   142 n.62, 273 n.14
II.16.2   143 n.65
II.67.1   169 n.186
II 69.5   143 n.65
II.76.1   143 n.65
II.79.1   151 n.102
II.101.2-3   79 n.79, 81 n.87
II.101.3   83 n.99
II.104.3   213 n.164
II.104.4   79 n.79
II.105.1   287 n.10
II.106.1   213
II.106.1-2   36 n.8
II.107   287 n.9
II.109.1   287 n.10
II.111.3-4   213
II.112   287 n.9
II.113.3   213
II.114   287 n.9
II.115.5   173 n.203
II.118.1   174 n.206
II.118.2   287 n.10

II.121.3   142 n.64, 213
II.122.2   151 n.102
II.124.3-4   142 n.64
VIRGIL
Aen. IV.188   93 n.146
IV.190   93 n.146
VOLUMNIUS
F 1   83 n.95

XANTHUS OF LYDIA, *FGrHist* 765
T 5   7 n.28
XENOPHANES
B 10   219 n.8
B 11   219 n.8
XENOPHON
Anabasis, II.4.4   215 n.172
II.5.3-7   208 n.144
III.1.2-3   215 n.172
III.1.4-10   208 n.142
III.1.11-14   208 n.142
III.1.12   150 n.102
III.1.21-2   208 n.144
III.1.26-32   215 n.172
III.1.45   214 n.167
III.2.8-9   208 n.143
III.3.11-20   211 n.156
III.4.46-9   215 n.172
III.5.1-6   215 n.172
IV.3.8-13   208 n.142
IV.3.8-15   215 n.172
IV.4.12   215 n.172
IV.5.7-9   215 n.172
IV.15.15-21   215 n.172
V.2.8-27   215 n.172
V.5.3   208 n.143
V.6.15-34   211 n.156
V.6.27   211 n.156
V.7.1-35   211 n.156
V.8.1-26   211 n.156
VI.3.18 (16)   208 n.144
VI.4.13-19   208 n.143
VI.4.23-6   208 n.143
VII.2.16-34   208 n.144
VII.3.43   208 n.144
VII.5.10   214 n.167
VII.6.4   214 n.167
VII.6.11-38   211 n.156
VII.6.44   208 n.143
VII.7.20-47   211 n.156
Hellenica, I.1.1   237 n.107
II.3.56   10 n.43
III.2.7   10 n.41

333

XENOPHON (*cont.*)
  Hellenica (*cont.*)
    III.5.12   151 n.102
    IV.3.2   69 n.31
    IV.3.16   10 n.43
    IV.8.1   10 n.43
    V.1.4   151 n.102
    VI.2.32   10 n.43
    VI.2.39   10 n.43
    VII.2.1   10 n.43
    VII.5.12   280 n.1
    VII.5.27   36 n.5, 237 n.109
  Memorab. II.1.31   177 n.8
  Symp. 1.1   246 n.149

ZENO OF RHODES, *FGrHist* 523
  T 3   80 n.83
ZOILUS OF AMPHIPOLIS, *FGrHist* 71
  T 1   242 n.126

Index of Greek words

ἀγώνισμα, 21
ἀδύνατα, 125
ἀκρίβεια / ἀκριβής, 21 n.100, 68, 70, 77 n.62, 114 n.262, 115 n.269, 115 n.270, 120, 121
ἀναγινώσκοντες, 25
ἀνθρώπινον, τό, 22
ἀορασία, 72
ἀπειρία, 71
ἀρχαιολογία, 119
αὔξησις, 34
αὐτοπάθεια, 72

δαιμόνιον, τό, 49, 50
διαγωγή, 30
διάθεσις, 18

εἰκάζειν, 97
εἰκός, 282
ἐμπειρία, 70 n.34
ἔμφασις, 72
ἐπαχθής, 190-1
ἐπιστήμη, 75
ἐπιχώριοι, 283
εὐεργέτης, 46

ἠθοποιΐα, 129

ἱερογραμματεύς, 110
ἱστορία, 118

κακοζηλία, 13 n.58
κίνδυνος, 153-4
κλέος, 35
κοινότης λόγου, 212
κτῆμα, 21
κτίσεις, 100

μαρτύριον, 97
μαρτύς, 104
μυθογράφοι, 127
μυθολογίαι, 119
μῦθος / τὸ μυθῶδες, 117-27, *passim*

ὄψις, 67

παίδεια, 148 n.90, 254 n.189
παλαιά, τά, 70, 96 n.166, 97 n.169
πάρεργον, 46, 149
παρέργως, 153
παρρησία, 86
περιαυτολογία, 175
περιττός, 24
πλάσμα, 118
πολιτικός, 24, 30
πολυμαθίη, 65
πολυπράγμων, 24
πόνος, 150-1, 154 n.117, 156
προσποίησις ἀνάγκης, 211

σαφῶς / τὸ σαφές, 69, 96 n.196, 117, 121
σημεῖον, 97
σκοπεῖν, 97
σφραγίς, 271

τεκμήριον, 97
τύχη, 23

φθόνος, 163
φιλαναγινώσκοντες, 25
φιλήκοος, 24
φιλομαθοῦντες, 24
φιλόσοφοι, 30

ψυχαγωγία, 121 n.297

General index

Well-known figures are listed under their common English name (e.g., 'Cicero', not 'Tullius'), lesser knowns under their family name (e.g., 'Valerius', not 'Antias').

accuracy (ἀκρίβεια/τὸ ἀκριβές), 21 n.100, 70, 77 n.62, 120, 121; as a justification for rewriting a history, 115–16; claimed by Thucydides as his guiding principle, 68; defined as fullness of accounts, 114; not verifiable in myth, 127
actors, historians likened to, by Plutarch, 58
Acusilaus of Argos, 218
adornment, opposed to truth, 55
Aelius Aristides, 176 n.3; and Egyptian priests, 109; given literary assistance by his dreams, 50
Aelius Stilo, L., first Roman grammarian, dedicatee of Coelius Antipater's history, 55
Aelius Tubero, Q., mentioned by Dionysius as a source for early Roman history, 245
Aemilius Paullus, praised by Polybius, 173
Aemilius Scaurus, M., 178; dedicates his work, 54; inaugurates series of *commentarii de uita sua*, 181; possible reasons for writing a *commentarius*, 195–6; use of first person, 196 n.101
Aeneid, 123
Aeschylus, 16 n.73
Agatharchides, 87 n.117, 150; effort too great for him to complete his history, 149; his *On the Erythrean Sea* a history, not a geography, 2 n.3; on fame and toil, 59, 149; polemic with sensationalistic writers, 233; 'tragic' account of the Nubian gold mines, 233
Agathocles, tyrant of Sicily, censured by Timaeus, 162; praised by Callias, 163
Agrippina, the Younger, her *Memoirs* cited by Tacitus, 116
Alcmaeon, introduces himself in text, 271
Alcman, names himself in text, 271
Alexander the Great, 22, 87, 113; and

Callisthenes, 59; as a focus for biased accounts, 162; chastises Aristobulus for his partiality, 126, 160–1; deeds exaggerated by authors, 162; employs historians, 24; subject of Curtius Rufus' history, 32 n.155; subject of histories in Second Sophistic, 31
Alexander the Great, historians of, 36; as participants, 187; emphasised proximity to Alexander as basis for their account, 87; likely to have included their own speeches in their histories, 194 n.90
Amelesagoras, as divinely inspired historian, 51 n.67; date and genuineness, 51 n.67
Ammianus Marcellinus 1, 2, 5, 6, 11, 12, 32, 77, 90, 96, 205, 236, 283, 291; and the addressee of Libanius' letter, 217 n.4; assumes small audience for his history, 217; history not dedicated, 54; justifies praise of Julian by proofs, 173; magnifies achievements of Julian, 39; on danger of writing contemporary history, 158; on inappropriate criticism of his work, 157; scolds sensationalistic accounts, 32; wants to avoid dangers, 157

attitude towards myth, 125; autopsy of Scythia, 81; chides 'Graecia fabulosa', 125; cites experiences in East as source, 81; claims of autopsy and inquiry, 80 n.83; correction of predecessors by autopsy, 85; describes and quotes from obelisks in Egypt, 102; gives detailed account, while claiming to have forgotten exact details, 81–2 n.90; interest in geography and ethnography, 85; vouches for *terrores* by his own autopsy, 83

activities at Nisibis, 201; as participant in Julian's eastern campaign, 204; escape in the

aftermath of Amida's fall, 203; escape
narratives, 201; focalisation of history
maintained, 179, 200, 204; mentions role as
participant to guarantee authority, 79;
narrative of his own actions, 10 n. 39, 200-4;
narrative of siege and fall of Amida, 202-3;
narrative perspective, 202; pursuit by the
Persians, 201-2; use of Roman first person
plural convention, 288; varies use of
singular and plural, 200, 202 n.126, 204
n.132
  as continuator of Tacitus, 240, 254; cites
Sallust, 255; contrasts himself with
contemporaries, 255; criticises Herodotus'
exaggerations, 255; differences with Tacitus,
254-5; heir to two traditions, 255;
identification as 'Greek', 102 n.199, 257;
identification as *ingenuus*, 147-8;
identification as soldier, 256 with n.206;
imitates Cicero, 16 n.73; in tradition of
soldier-historian, 147; knowledge of Latin
writers, 257 n.208; lost preface of, 254;
models his style on Sallust, 255; possibly
imitates Thucydides, 81-2 n.90; praises
Thucydides, 255; praises Timagenes, 255;
recalls Polybius and Scipio Aemilianus, 256;
scientific digressions of, 257 n.207
amplificatio: *see* magnification
Anaxagoras, on sense perception, 65-6
Anaximenes, 242 n.126; included polemic in
his preface, 228; pseudonymous work
imitating Theopompus, 228 n.57; work
mentioned by Diodorus, 243 n.129
Anaxis, his work mentioned by Diodorus, 243
n.129
Annales Maximi, 15; possibly published by P.
Mucius Scaevola *c*. 130 BC, 26 n.124;
separate from Pontifical Chronicle, 26 n.124
annalistic form, as an element of imitation,
17-18
Annalists, Roman, 27, 116 n.277, 136, 141 n.58,
165; extent of their invention, 27 n.132; term
to distinguish writers of year-by-year
histories, 27 n.131
Annals, of A. Furius Antias: *see* Furius Antias;
of Ennius: *see* Ennius; of the Pontifex
Maximus: *see Annales Maximi*; of Varro: *see*
Varro
Anonymous historian of Corinth, his claim of
autopsy and inquiry, 80 n.83
Anonymous historian of L. Verus, 90 n.133; his
claim of autopsy and inquiry, 80 n.83

Anonymous historian of Miletus, claims to
have bested Homer, 274-5
Antias: *see* Valerius Antias
antidosis, fiction adopted by Isocrates for self-
praise, 176 n.7, 214
Antigonus, mentioned by Dionysius as
predecessor, 244
Antiochianus, 148; mechanical imitator of
Herodotus, 275
Antiochus I, Soter, Berossus' history dedicated
to him, 53
Antiochus III, the Great, 88; rewards
historian, 24 n.117
Antiochus of Syracuse, 282; collector of
accounts, 100; introduces himself with
patronymic, 272; source for Thucydides,
284 n.18; work mentioned by Diodorus, 243
n.129
antiquarians, their use of documents, 104
Antisthenes of Rhodes, his claim of autopsy
and inquiry, 80 n.83; praised by Polybius, 59
Aphrodisias-Euphemios, local historian of
Thespiae, 194 n.89
Apion of Oasis, betters Herodotus, 109; claims
autopsy, 109 n.235; sees Homer's shade, 274
n.20; uses priests for validation, 109
apodeictic method, of Polybius, 10 with n. 45
Apollodorus of Athens, 232 n.83; as model for
later historians, 55 n.82; dedicates his
Chronicle to Attalus II, 55
Appian, 44, 179, 283; amplification of his
history, 42; and Arrian's preface, 146-7, 274;
and history's pleasure, 30; and history's
utility, 30; does not mention qualifications,
145; emphasises his unique approach, 47;
escape narrative a precedent for Ammianus',
202 n.125; introduction of himself, 274;
mentions honours and social status, 145-6;
narrative of his own actions, 201 n.125;
undoes Polybius' concept of universal
history, 47 n.46; use of first person, 201
n.125, 205
Aratus of Sicyon, 289; continued by Polybius,
98, 180, 238; his *Memoirs* praised by
Polybius, 180; structure of his memoirs, 290
n.10; valued by Polybius as eyewitness and
participant, 98 n.175
archaism, and imitation, 18-19
Archilochus, 19
archives: *see* documents
argumentum, classified by rhetoricians as
similar to truth, 118

Aristeas, 51 n.67
Aristobulus of Cassandreia, historian of Alexander, chastised by Alexander for his partiality, 160-1; claim of autopsy and inquiry, 80 n.83; claims autopsy of Brachmanes' meeting with Alexander, 82; fondness for marvels, 82; gives his age in the preface, 87; his book thrown into the river by Alexander, 126; in Arrian's *Anabasis*, 275; narrative of his own actions, 187; notes wonders he saw in Asia, 84; praised by Arrian for absence of bias, 114, 169; reports prophecy of Peithagoras about Alexander, 82
Aristophanes, 23 n.110
Aristotheos of Troezen, 21 n.98
Aristotle, 105, 281 n.4; and Egyptian priests, 109; attacked by Timaeus, 105, 229; defended by Polybius, 164; different attitude towards character from his followers, 130; distinction between dialectic and rhetoric, 220; documents and constitutions collected by his school, 104; on atechnic and entechnic proofs, 128-9; on elements of character that contribute to persuasion, 130; on indirect construction of character, 129; on need for experience in inquiry, 74; on persuasion from character, 128-9; on polemic with individuals, 220; on raising the emotions in speech, 222; on technique of self-praise in the mouth of others, 214
Aristoxenus, 113 n.256
arrangement, as an aspect of imitation, 17
Arrian of Nicomedia, 31 n.154, 48, 224, 281, 285; as dispenser of praise, 18; as emulator and imitator of Xenophon, 18 n.86; boasts of his literary ability, 253-4; desires to show himself knowledgeable about the tradition, 107; vies with Theopompus, 253
  Anabasis, 18; ambiguous opening of, 275; and Appian's preface, 146-7, 274; anonymity in preface, 146-7, 274-5; as culmination of tradition, 254 n.191; as imitation of Xenophon's *Anabasis*, 17; assertion of irrelevance of offices, 146-7; claim that Alexander's deeds never worthily treated, 116; criticism of Callisthenes, 59; imitation of Herodotus, 17, 253; imitation of Thucydides, 17, 253; inclusion of myth, 120 n.295; magnification of Alexander in, 36; praise of Ptolemy and Aristobulus, 114, 169, 253-4, 275; promise of worthy treatment of Alexander's deeds, 254; records more than he believes, 107; second preface of, 253-4; superior in style and content, 116-17; self-definition in, 253-4
  Bithynian History, dedicated to his homeland, 53; author introduces himself as priest, 111
Artemidorus, his dreams, 50
Asclepiades, his classification of narratives by subject matter, 118
Asinius Pollio, 197 n.105, 291; as model for Tacitus, 253; continues Sallust, 240; faults Caesar for inaccuracy, 116; free speech praised by Cremutius Cordus, 252; independence of, 157 n.128; possible closing date for his history, 292 n.5; warned by Horace of the danger of writing contemporary history, 157
Ateius Philologus, L., compiles *Breuiarium* for Sallust, 28 n.138
Athanis (Athanas) of Syracuse, 289; and narrative of his own actions, 187; joins his history to Philistus', 240, 290 n.6; sole Sicilian continuator, 239; work mentioned by Diodorus, 243 n.129
Athenians, criticised by Thucydides for ignorance of their own history, 115
athlete, historian as, 220 n.17; *see also* competition
Attalus II, Apollodorus' *Chronicle* dedicated to him, 55
Atthis, style of, rejected by Dionysius, 245
Atticism, 18
Atticus, T. Pomponius, his labour praised by Cicero, 151 n.105; his *Liber Annalis*, 28; its dedication to Cicero, 55
attitude (διάθεσις, *dispositio*), 18
auctoritas, of the individual, as authenticating device, 12 n.49; its importance for the Romans, 130, 137-8, 257 n.206
audience, and 'down-marketing', 28-9; for Greek historiography constant, 33; for history in antiquity, 19-33; for the novel, 23 n.113; for 'tragic' history, 23; mass, in late Republic, 28; *see also under individual historians*
Aufidius Bassus, 144 n.69, 291; continued by Pliny the Elder, 240, 292 n.8; possibly joined his *Histories* to Livy's, 292 n.7; possibly omitted Drusus Nero from his history, 48 n.52
Augustus, and the new order at Rome, 143; calls Livy 'Pompeian', 172; his forum, 20; his

Memoirs, 181 n.29; their dedication, 54; uses the first person, 196 n.101

Aurelius, Marcus, thanks gods for dreams, 50

authority, achieved by constant assurance in Herodotus, 8; achieved by narrative homogeneity, 9; 'artificial', by author's comments, 6; historiographical, 1, 3-12, 258-66, and *passim*; implicitly asserted by Romans, 11, and *passim*; importance of style in, 10 n.42; literary, 1; of epic poets, 3-4; of lyric poets, 4

autopsy (eyewitness), 63-86, 281; and disbelief, 86 n.111; appeal to, by non-contemporary historians, 281-2; as one method to knowledge among the pre-Socratics, 65; as superior to report in the *Odyssey*, 64; as unreliable, 66; in the Roman historians, 77; insufficient alone for knowledge, 65; its value questioned by Thucydides, 67-8; needing verification, 68; needs experience to guide it, according to Polybius, 72-4; not devalued by Isocrates, 276-9; one of the three parts of history, according to Polybius, 72; superior to literary sources, 72

explicit remarks of, 80-6; as authenticating device in forgeries, 83; as validation for high numbers, 83; as validation for marvels, 82-3; as validation for special source, 80-1; in geography and ethnography, 83-5; in Mimnermus, 4; not invoked by an historian for matters in his native country, 101 n.190; only occasionally inserted into the narrative by the historians, 79-80

Baebius Macer, Q., 47

benefactor, historian as, 46, 149-51

beneficia, see benefits

benefit, of history: *see* utility

benefits, enjoyed by the historian, acknowledged by certain historians, 141-4; as cause for partiality, 144 n.70, 162

Berossus, 24, 111 n.246; date of his work, 110 n.241; dedicates *Babyloniaca* to Antiochus Soter, 53; introduces himself as priest of Baal, 110; perhaps writes to reverse policies of Seleucus I, 53 n.74

biographer, unknown, of the Roman emperors, 32 n.158

biography, 2; differs from history by its greater interest in details, 92 n.140; replaces narrative history among the Romans in the Empire, 32

breuiarium, 32; distinguished from epitome, 28 n.138; of Eutropius, 29 n.138; of Festus, 29 n.138; of Florus, 29 n.138; of Granius Licinianus, 29 n.138

Breuiarium rerum omnium Romanarum, compiled by L. Ateius Philologus for Sallust, 28 n.138

Brutus, M., epitomises Polybius, 29 n.138

Cacus, mythical figure, rationalised by Dionysius, 123

Caesar, C. Iulius, 143; criticised by Asinius Pollio for inaccuracy, 116; criticised by Cicero in his *Expositio*, 172; dedicatee of Varro's *Antiquitates*, 55; Livy's assessment of, 170-1; use of Roman first person plural convention, 287

his *commentarii*, as war monographs, 197-8; careful to cite sources in, 79; citation of prisoners and deserters as sources, 79; magnification of opponents in, 215-16; meant as definitive account, 198; narrative validated by autopsy and inquiry, 79; political purpose of, 206 n.135; portrayal of Caesar as representative of the Roman state in, 212; possible precedent for genre in Xenophon's *Anabasis*, 197-8, 205; praise of the troops in, 212-13; praised by others in the work, 214; precedent for use of *fortuna* in Pompey, 209; in Sulla, 209; present throughout his history, 179; probably not typical of the genre, 181; techniques of self-presentation in, 206-16 *passim*; use of first person for narrator, 197 n.104; use of fortune in, 209-10; use of gods in, 208-9; use of third person in, 197

Callias, accused by Diodorus of partiality, 165 n.166; praises Agathocles, 163

Callimorphus, physician writing history, 90 n.133, 148; echoes Theopompus' remarks on learning, 148 n.90; imitates Herodotus' opening, 275

Callisthenes, and myth, 120; and partiality, 162 n.149; attacked by Timaeus, 229; claim of autopsy and inquiry, 80 n.83; claims Alexander's fame depends on him, 59; criticised by Polybius, 230; on the Nile's flood, 84; ridiculed by Polybius for his naïveté in military matters, 71; work mentioned by Diodorus, 243 n.129

Calpurnius Piso Frugi, L., 27, 281; attacked by Livy, 248; cited by Dionysius as a source for early Roman history, 245; interest in monuments, 102
canon, of historians, 18–19
Cassius Hemina, first Annalist, 27; possible polemic with 'armchair' historians, 102 n.196; use of monuments, 102
Cato, M. Porcius, the Elder, 17, 30, 136, 179, 187 n.61, 291; as model for Tacitus, 253; defines history as an occupation for leisure time, 45; importance of *auctoritas* in his speeches, 130 n.8; important in establishing the Roman historian's persona, 137–8; influence on Sallust, 45, 139; mentioned by Dionysius as his source for early Roman history, 245; perhaps used praise songs as source for his early history, 100–1; possibly criticised in Sallust's *Histories*, 247; praised by Sallust in *Histories*, 247; praised history, 137; Sempronius Asellio allies with, 247; shown in a favourable light in his history, 195; use of first and third person in *de consulatu suo*, 193 n.86; use of Roman first person plural convention, 287; writes history for his son, 55 n.84
  Origins (*Origines*), based in part on author's participation, 78; excessive self-laudation in, 163, 195; inclusion of Cato's speeches in, 194; interest in geography, 85 n.110; later books shade into autobiography, 195 n.96; narrative of author's actions in, 193–5; not dedicated, 55; omission of names of commanders in, 197; opening echo of Xenophon, 246–7; perspective of the later books unknown, 194–5; polemic with Pontifical Chronicle, 236; possible adaptation of dispatch style in, 193; possible attack on Fabius, 236; praise of author by others in, 214 n.168; probable use of the first person, 193–4; self-praise criticised by Livy, 249; use of local tradition as source in Books II and III, 101, 284–5; use of tombstones as sources in, according to Cicero, 102; widens audience for Roman history, 27; written in Latin, 27; written in retirement, 137
Cato, M. Porcius, the Younger, 16 n.71
Catullus, C. Valerius, and Nepos' *Chronicle*, 155–6; assimilates dual notion of effort, 155
Catulus, Q. Lutatius, 196; *liber de consulatu* dedicated to A. Furius Antias, 54, 182; requests that style be improved, 55; style judged by Cicero, 182
Chaereas, criticised by Polybius, 230
Chairemon, identifies himself as sacred scribe, 110
Chaldaeans, possessors of an ancient and reliable history, 103
character, appeal to, as a way of resolving variant versions, 285–6; as an element of historiographic authority, 6, 128–74 *passim*, 260; discussed by Cicero, 130; importance in everyday life as an element for winning credibility, 131; in oratory, 128–30; interest in by historians, 92; more important in Roman rhetoric than in Greek, 130; not much discussed in Roman rhetoric, 130; of historian judged from his history, 132; of the narrator on display in a history, 131–2, 223; of person delivering a speech, 130; of Tacitus as read from his work, 132 n.16; of Thucydides, as read from his work, 132 n.16
Charax of Pergamum, 112 n.251
Charon of Lampsacus, possible different methods of introduction in his histories, 273 n.10
Christianity, changes audience for history, 33
chronicles, 2, 53 n.73
Chronicles, of Nepos: *see* Nepos
chronography, as genre of historiography, defined, 2
Chryserus, freedman of Marcus Aurelius, 89 n.126, 148, 289; his work possibly continued by Herodian, 239
Cicero, M. Tullius, 15, 81, 100, 102, 116, 130 n.7; asks that style be improved, 55; believes in incremental progress, 15 n.67; cited by Ammianus, 257 n.208; claims stylistic excellence for his memoir, 55 n.81, 182; compares Lucceius to Hercules, 165; dedicates his work on his consulship, 54; defended by Quintilian, 177; deferred publication of his *Expositio Consiliorum Suorum*, 172, 173 n.202; dream of Marius, 48; echoes of, in Ammianus, 16 n.73; echoes of, in Sallust, 16 n.73; expects historian to be impartial, 165; Livy's assessment of, 170–1; method of self-praise in his dialogues, 178; on Caesar's *Commentarii*, 197; on Catulus' memoir, 182; on labour and benefit, 151 n.105; on the problems of self-praise, 177–8; on use of dreams, 50 n.62;

General index

portrays exile as beneficial, 45 n.34; praises Atticus' labour, 151 n.105; praises history's universal appeal, 28; wants the *auctoritas* of Lucceius for his actions, 177, 186

Cincius Alimentus, L., bases contemporary history on his own autopsy, 77–8, 80 n.83; his inquiry of Hannibal, 81, 137; mentioned by Dionysius as predecessor, 244; treated the early history of Rome only summarily, 245

civil war, as subject of magnification, 38–40

Claudius Quadrigarius, 28, 165; dedicates his history, 55–6; possible dedicatee his patron, 56 n.89

Cleidemus, 111, 194 n.89

Cleitarchus, and the validation of his history, 88 n.119

Cluvius Rufus, 253; stigmatised by Tacitus, 250

Coelius Antipater, L., 85 n.110, 196; bases his account of Second Punic War on reliable predecessors, 116; criticised by Livy, 248; dedicates his work to L. Aelius Stilo, 55; hears C. Gracchus tell of his dream about his brother, 83; imitated by Sallust, 17; inaugurates historical monograph in Latin, 55; introduces dedication into Roman historiography, 55; provides alternative account of Marcellus' death, 116; work known for its literary polish, 55; writes historical monograph, 17

Commodus, 49; Dio's recording of his activities, 91–2

common people, unable to discern truth, 94

commonness of action, as a way of mitigating self-praise, 212–13

competition, with past writers, 14; as a spur to literary creativity, 14; *see also* athlete

Constantinian Excerpts, their procedure and limitations, 188–9

continuation, as homage to a predecessor, 237; common in Greek and Roman historians, 237–41; does not necessarily imply similar ideas or beliefs about history, 238–40; first done by Xenophon, 237

continuators, 17; Greek, 237–9; Roman, 240; Sicilian, 239–40

correction, of predecessors, Diodorus on, 232 n.83; Polybius on, 232 n.82; Strabo on, 232 n.83; *see also* polemic

Cotta, L. Aurelius, validates marvel by autopsy, 83

Crassus, M. Licinius, as source for Sallust, 81; criticised by Cicero in his *Expositio*, 172

Craterus, his collection of decrees, 104

Cratippus, 36, 289; continues Thucydides, 238; possible author of *Hellenica Oxyrhynchia*, 290 n.2

Cremutius Cordus, portrayed by Tacitus as defending historian's free speech, 251–2; praises earlier historians Livy, Asinius Pollio, and Messala Corvinus, 252; used by Tacitus to indicate his own historiographical aims, 252

Crepereius Calpurnianus, 13 n. 58; his error in imitation, 12; mechanically imitates Thucydides, 12, 275

Ctesias of Cnidus 89, 111 n.246, 112, 118 n.285, 183 n.43, 245; claims of autopsy and inquiry, 80 n.83; claims superiority as eyewitness, 228; dependence on Herodotus, 227 n.53; example not much followed, 89; polemic with Herodotus, 227; portrayed his activities in his work, 185; possible differences with Dinon, 228 n.54; possible method of introducing himself, 273; validates his account by his experience as prisoner of Artaxerxes, 134; by his presence at court, 87; by his role as participant, 87, 134; work mentioned by Diodorus, 243 n.129; wrote up events from the Persian point of view, 170

Indica, marvellous account, 22; disbelieved by audience, 82

Periodos, 185 n.56

Persica, as a preview of court histories, 22 n.106; based on royal records, 107; criticised by Lucian for partiality, 170; filled with self-praise, 185; no evidence of claim of impartiality in, 170; perhaps featured prominent position of author in later books, 185–6; shades into romance, 22; unknown whether author used first or third person, 185

Curtius Rufus, Q., chooses Alexander as subject, 32 n.155; date, 32 n.155; does not separate tradition into its component parts, 106; on Ptolemy's self-praise, 187; reports more than he believes, 106

danger, and benefit to the reader, 150–1; and impartiality, 157; as subject matter of history, 150–1 n.102; conjunction with toils, 150–1 n.102; of writing contemporary history, 32;

danger (*cont.*)
  of writing history, 149-51; of writing history under an autocratic regime, 157-8; origins as a motif in historiography, 150-1
dedications, 53-7; as an element for mitigating self-praise, 54; as 'justification' for author to tell his life story, 54-5; common in autobiographies and memoirs, 54-5; common in minor genres, 53; in Greek local history, 53-4; in Hellenistic historiography, 53; in narrative histories, 55-6; in Roman historiography, 54-6; in scholarly works, 55; more common in Roman than in Greek historiography, 54; possible conflict of with impartiality, 54, 57
Dellius, Q., access to Cleopatra the validation for his account, 88; his claim of autopsy and inquiry, 80 n.83
Demetrius of Phaleron, his *Memoirs*, 180
Demetrius of Sagallasus, mechanical imitator of Herodotus, 275
Demochares, ridiculed by Timaeus, 229
democracy, and historiography, 22, 86
Democritus, on sense perception, 66; on travel and inquiry, 66 n.15
Demodocus, iambic poet, names himself in text, 271
Demodocus, singer in the *Odyssey*, praised by Odysseus, 63
Demophilus, son of Ephorus, completes his father's history, 290 n.5; his work mentioned by Diodorus, 243 n.129
Demosthenes 13, 15, 191 n.81, 206 n.136; his *On the Crown* the model for successful self-praise, 176
Dexippus, of Athens, 32, 90 n.133, 289; chronology criticised by Eunapius, 221 n.22; continued by Eunapius, 239; imitates Thucydides, 17; includes his own speeches in his *Scythica*, 199; narrative of his own deeds, 199; praised by Eunapius, 239; reduced scope of his history, 92-3; use of the third person, 199, 205
Diadochs: *see* Successors of Alexander
dialectic, 220, 222
dignitas: *see* status, social
digressions, 11, 118 with n.286
Dinon, his differences with Ctesias, 228 n.54
Dio Cassius, 32, 44, 146, 201, 224, 288 n.19; adapts contemporary history to the changed circumstances of his time, 92; and the effort of reading earlier sources, 106; attitude to Severus, 49; audience the Senatorial order, 31, 91-2; cites his experience among the Pannonians for his account of them, 81; claims of autopsy and inquiry, 80 n.83; claims to have read all relevant material about Rome, 106; combines poetic and historiographic motifs, 51; compares himself to Hector, 50-1; conclusion of his history, 50; dreams, 47 n.50, 48-51; encouraged by Severus to write history, 49-50; gives exact number of years working on his history, 151-2; gives 'official' versions of events, supplemented by his own knowledge or opinions, 89; invokes his father as source, 81; line between inquiry and social status not always clear, 147; magnification of theme in, 38; mentions his father, 147; mentions offices he held, 147; narrative of his own actions, 10 n.39, 199-200; narrative of Senatorial actions, 200; on bias in history, 169; on oracles, 83; on the difficulties of inquiry in the Empire, 88-9; possibly influenced by Josephus' portrayal of himself, 49 n.56; predicts Severus' accession to power, 49; reasons for recording events, 91; reduced scope of his history, 92-3; seems to have been the centre of his narrative in the later books, 179-80, 199; solution to the problem of bias, 169-70; use of the first person, 200, 205; use of the third person, 200; use of ἡμεῖς for various groups, 200; work shading to autobiography, 203, 205
Diocles of Peparethos, source for Fabius Pictor, 77
Diodorus of Sicily, 18, 34, 40, 48, 141 n.59, 155, 199 n.116, 222 n.27, 244, 249, 282, 283, 285; account dependent on Hecataeus of Abdera, 108; allies himself with Ephorus, Polybius, and Posidonius, 241; amplification of his history, 41; of the Marsic War, 41; and Heracles, 149-50; audience of, 25; cites the beginning- and ending-points of his predecessors, 243; claims access to Egyptian records, 108; claims to have spent thirty years on his history, 151-2; claims to have travelled widely for his history, 75; comes at the end of the tradition, 243; contrasts his work with previous universal historians, 241-2; criticises Herodotus' use of myth, 121 n.297; criticises Timaeus for partiality, 162, 234; for poor organization, 234; does not

General index

introduce himself in text, 273; explains difficulties of using myth, 119-20; includes myth in his history, 119; justifies use of myth in history, 119-20; laments Corinth's destruction, 169; name in the text an interpolation, 273 n.13; on benefit to the reader from historian's efforts, 151; on correction of predecessors, 150; on early records, 103; on effort expended on his history, 150; on fame of his own history, 59 n.104; on generous correction, 232 n.83; on historian's fame, 59; on interpreting myth, 120; on partiality of his predecessors, 165; polemic with Herodotus, 233; polemic with Herodotus possibly dependent on Hecataeus of Abdera, 233 n.88; polemic with Timaeus, 233-4; praises Ephorus, 234 n.95; praises supply of books at Rome, 75; praises Timaeus, 234 n.95; praises universal history, 46, 241; purpose of citations of predecessors, 243-4; purpose of including myth, 121; sees 'accuracy' as fullness, 114; sees his work as a 'Library', 243; sees his work as combination of all his predecessors, 243; sees his work's benefit in its completeness, 114, 244; statements of autopsy, 108-9 n.234; suggests superiority is the number of accounts, 114; surpasses his predecessors, 242-3; uses different narrative manner for myth, 121; work of a combination of types, 26

Dionysius of Halicarnassus, 3, 7, 18, 19 n.89, 40, 44, 48, 127, 141 n.59, 224, 228, 248, 283; amplification of theme, 42-3; and self-praise, 191 n.81; appeals to native tradition, 284; as dispenser of praise, 18; asserts effort necessary, 46, 153 n.113; audience of, 30, 246; chooses early Rome as subject, 46; claims his work not a local history, 245-6; claims twenty-two years of work on his history, 151-2; comes close to dedicating his history to Rome, 53 n.75; 'compelled' to speak of himself, 211 n.157; contrasts mythic with historical account, 122-3; converses with renowned Romans, 245; definition of myth in, 122; does not dwell on his own praise, 60; envisions three classes of readers, 30; explains benefit of myth, 123 n.310; follows Isocratean model of instruction, 246; formal introduction of himself in text, 273-4; includes myth in his role as collector of traditions, 123; lays claim to Greek classical tradition, 246; on foundation of Rome, 235; on myth in early historians, 122; panegyrical nature of his work, 56, 245; presents himself as a Greek writing of foreign lands, 245; promises to display a favourable attitude, 132; rationalises myth, 122-3; rejects Hellenistic writers and aesthetic, 246; rejects myth, 121; sees accuracy as fullness, 114; six-book epitome of his work, 29 n.138; unique approach of his work, 244; uses autopsy for Roman monuments, 101 n.190

accuses Thucydides of holding a grudge towards Athens, 184; allies himself with Cato, 235; allies himself with epichoric sources, 234, 245; claims Thucydides could have chosen better theme, 47 n.45; criticises historians writing for foreign kings, 163; criticises Polybius' account of the Pallanteum, 102; faults predecessors for incompleteness, 113, 234; his polemic unlike Polybius', 235; imitated by Josephus' *Jewish Antiquities*, 17; imitates Herodotus, 16 n.74, 123, 246 n.147; imitates Thucydides, 16 n.72, 123; names seven Greek predecessors, 244; names seven Roman predecessors he will follow, 245; on Herodotus' character, 132; on Philistus' character, 132; on Theopompus' ability to detect hidden causes, 95; on Theopompus' character, 132; on Thucydides' character, 132; on Xenophon' character, 132; polemic with Cincius, 235; with early historians on the grandsons of Tarquinius Priscus, 235-6; with Fabius, 235; with Polybius, 235; with previous historians of Rome, 234; with Timaeus, 235; praises Theopompus, 153; praises Thucydides for rejecting myth, 122; purpose of refutations, 235; reads characters of historians from their writings, 132; sees Herodotus as competitor with predecessors, 14-15; sees Herodotus as culmination of tradition, 7 n.29; sees Thucydides as innovator from Hellanicus and Herodotus, 15; sees Thucydides as writing for all people, 30; shortcomings of his predecessors, 244-5; uses autopsy to correct predecessors, 115

Dionysius of Miletus, criticised by Herodotus, 101 n.190

Dionysodorus, his work mentioned by Diodorus, 243 n.129

dispositio: *see* attitude
Diyllus of Athens, 289; arrangement of his work, 290 n.7; continues Ephorus, 238, 290 n.7; is continued by Psaon, 238; work mentioned by Diodorus, 243 n.129
documents, and archives, 103-4, 107; causes of their rarity in historians, 104-5; collected by Aristotle and his school, 103-4; by Craterus, 104; by Polemon, 104; come to replace oral testimony in Athenian courts, 104; common in antiquarians, 104; importance discounted by Polybius, 104; no evidence of them for the Greeks' and Romans' earliest history, 99; not fundamentally different from other types of evidence, 105; not prohibited in narrative, 104 n.211; not used much by ancient historians, 103; of limited use in a narrative, 104; of particular interest to Timaeus, 104; reliability based on the character of the witness, 104; subject to refutation, 105; *see also* inscriptions
dreams, as legitimating devices in rhetoric, 50; as motivations to writing history, 47-51
Drusus Nero, advises Pliny the Elder to write of the German wars, 47-8; possibly left out of Aufidius Bassus' history, 48 n.52
Duris of Samos, 3, 19, 289; assails Ephorus and Theopompus in his preface, 228; criticises Theopompus' epideictic style, 117 n.280, 135 n.30; possibly continued by Phylarchus, 238, 290 n.9; work mentioned by Diodorus, 243 n.129

ears, less trustworthy than eyes, 65, 67
effort, as a component of inquiry, 72; as claim to authority, 148-57 *passim*, 260; as equivalent to claiming a finer style, 156-7; conjunction with danger, 150-1 n.102; essential in compiling evidence, according to Polybius, 72; in Agatharchides, 149; in Diodorus, 149; in historians writing large-scale works, 154-5; in Livy, 153-4; in Polybius, 149; in Sallust, 153; in the writing of history, 148; in Theopompus, 148-9; in Timaeus, 149; literary, 152-7; practical, 148-57; rewarded by fame, 149-50; two types of, 148; two types of, in Lucian, 156
Egyptians, possessors of the most ancient and reliable history, 103
elenchus, 220
Empedocles, invokes Muse, 4
Emperor, Roman, as a focus for imperial historiography, 92; as writer of memoirs, 181; effect of his taste, 19
Empire, Roman, difficulties of inquiry in, 88-9
empiricists, in medicine, 74
encomium, not to be introduced into history, 126
Ennius, Q., 288 n.16; claims to be both poet and historian, 26; dream of Homer, 48; scope of his *Annals*, 26; writes historical epic *Annals*, 26
envy (φθόνος, *inuidia*), as an element in partiality, 163; common in Greek and Roman society, 163; disavowed by satirists, 163
Epaphroditus, encourages Josephus to write history, 52; his identity, 52 n.69
Ephorus, 3, 23 n.109, 40, 120, 151 n.103, 218, 232 n.83, 241, 289; and myth, 120; attacked by Duris, 228; by Timaeus, 229; began his history with return of the Heracleidae, 242 n.125; combines contemporary and non-contemporary history, 96; continued by Diyllus, 238, 290 n.7; discusses genre of history, 70 n.32; elaborates methodology for contemporary and non-contemporary history, 69-71, 97; first to praise universal history, 37; includes geography in history, 83; notes that societies sometimes change customs, 97; on effort required by history, 152; on reliability of written records, 103; praised by Diodorus, 241; praised by Polybius, 239 n.114; praised by Strabo for his accounts of the foundations of cities, 97; ridiculed by Polybius for his inexperience, 71-2; sees presence at events as guarantee of reliability, 70; surpassed by Diodorus, 242; surpassed by Polybius, 239 n.114; universal history of, 23; work completed by his son Demophilus, 290 n.5; work mentioned by Diodorus, 243 n.129
Epicharmus, connects sense perception and wisdom, 65 n.13
epichorioi: *see* natives
Epimenides, 51 n.67
Epipolae, battle narrated by Thucydides, 69
epitome, 2, 32; distinguished from *breuiarium*, 28 n.138; of Dionysius, 29 n.138; of Herodotus, by Theopompus, 22 n.108, 228; of Polybius, by Brutus, 29 n.138; of Trogus, by Justin, 29 n.138
Eratosthenes, divided eras into unknown, mythic, and historical, 124 n.312; praised by Arrian as reliable, 285-6

'ethnic' prejudice, 174 n.206
ethnography, 53 n.73; as genre of historiography, defined, 2; claims of autopsy in, 83-5
Eudoxus, and Egyptian priests, 109
Euhemerus, his reliability praised by Polybius, 84 n.102
Eumaeus, character in the *Odyssey*, equates seeing with knowing, 64
Eunapius, 32, 289; continues Dexippus, 239; criticises Dexippus' chronology, 221 n.22; not concerned with chronology, 239; praises Dexippus, 239
Euripides, questions the value of autopsy reports, 68
Eutropius, 29, 32 n.158; mentions role as participant to guarantee authority, 79
Eutychianos of Cappadocia, 90 n.133; his claim of autopsy and inquiry, 80 n.83
exempla, 31, 46
expense, by Theopompus in putting together his *Philippica*, 87, 149; by Timaeus in researching his narrative of the Tyrians, 149
experience, as means of establishing historian's authority, 133-48 *passim*; as one of the three parts of history, according to Polybius, 72; essential for the historian, according to Polybius, 71-5; in Polybius, 136; its absence lessens the value of history, 72; its importance in medicine, 74; its lack in Timaeus, 71; its relationship to inquiry according to Polybius, 72-4; its relationship to inquiry, according to Aristotle, 74; personal (αὐτοπάθεια), needed for a vivid account, 72; praised by Theopompus, 72-3; Roman more political, 136-7, 265
Expositio Consiliorum Suorum: see Cicero
eyes, more trustworthy than ears, 65, 67; *see also* autopsy
eyewitness, *see* autopsy

Fabius Maximus Servilianus, Q., mentioned by Dionysius as a source for early Roman history, 245
Fabius Pictor, Q., 98, 136-7, 195, 281; as character in his history, 193; as priest, 138; audience of, 26-7; bases contemporary portion on his own autopsy, 77; claim of autopsy and inquiry, 80 n.83; criticised by Polybius for partiality towards Rome, 77, 114, 171; different views of his activity, 100 n.185; first Roman historian, 26; follows Diocles of Peparethos on the founding of Rome, 77-8; history translated into Latin, 27 n.129; mentioned by Dionysius as predecessor, 244; possibly attacked by Cato in *Origins*, 236; possibly used Philinus for Carthaginian viewpoint, 77; purpose in writing history, 137 n.41; treated early history of Rome summarily, 245; used oral tradition for his account of early Rome, 100; uses Greek conventions, 138; validates high numbers by claim of autopsy, 83
Fabius Rusticus, 253
fabula, 120 n.296; classified by rhetoricians as untrue and unlike truth, 118
fabula praetexta, as historical source, 27 n.128
facts, as the basis for praise and blame according to Aristotle, 161; invented on account of partiality, 160-1
falsehood, difference between intentional and unintentional, 222
family tradition, 20, 26; as source for non-contemporary history, 99
Fannius, C., 291; his autopsy of Tiberius Gracchus, 81; impartiality, 165; includes his speeches in his history, 195 n.94; praised by Sallust in *Histories*, 247; work shades into autobiography, 195 n.96
Favorinus, 51 n.64
fear, as a motive for falsification, 94; *see also* danger
Festus, 29 n.138, 32 n.158
first person: *see* person
flattery, its use chided by Lucian, 125-6; *see also* partiality
Florus, 29
focalisation, 180
Fortune (Τύχη, *Fortuna*), 49; as a way of mitigating self-praise, 206-11; growing importance in fourth century historiography, 23; in Caesar's works, 209-10; in Sulla's *Memoirs*, 209; praised by Polybius, 37
fortune, reversals of, 23, 25; used by early historians, 120 n.296, 122
Forum of Augustus, 20
foundings, of cities, as subject for historians, 100
freedmen, imperial, as historians, 89 n.126, 148
freedom of speech, the historian's, 86, 157; circumscribed by autocratic regimes, 86; defended by Cremutius Cordus, 251
friends, as motivators for writing history, 52-7

Fronto, his history of Lucius Verus, 32; pressured by Verus, 36 n.8; promised letters and memoranda for his history by Verus, 90 n.132

Furius Antias, A., author of epic poem, *Annals*, 182; dedicatee of Q. Lutatius Catulus' memoir, 182

Galen, his father's dream, 51 n.64

Gellius, Cn. 27; mentioned by Dionysius as his source for early Roman history, 245

genealogy, 20; as genre of historiography, 1

genres, of historiography, 1

geography, 2, 24; claims of autopsy and, 83-5; falsified in order to flatter Alexander, 162; not of great interest to Romans writing history, 85

glory, as motivation for writing history, 57-62 *passim*, 172; not usually claimed in writing history, 61-2, 259

gods, use of, as a way of mitigating self-praise, 206-11

Gracchus, C., dedicates his autobiography, 54; dream of his brother, 48

Gracchus, Ti., 81, 163; appears to his brother in a dream, 48

Granius Licinianus, 29; use of Roman first person plural convention, 288

Greece, as a Roman province, 29

Hadrian, his *Memoirs*, 181 n.29

Hannibal, his character assessed by Livy, 171

hard core, of deeds, already in existence for the historian, 162; as a basis for elaboration, 161

hatred: *see* partiality

Hebrew Bible, its possible influence on Greek prefaces, 272 with n.5

Hecataeus of Abdera, 108 n.233; and Herodotus, 108; claims access to Egyptian priestly records, 108; date of his work, 110 n.241; possible source for Diodorus' polemic with Herodotus, 233 n.88; source for Diodorus' account of Egypt, 108

Hecataeus of Miletus, 7, 229; and the prefaces of philosophers, 271-2; attacked by Herodotus, 101 n.190; audience of, 20, 272; before the priests at Thebes, 107 n.230, 225 n.43; called a 'far-wandering man', 67; criticised by Heraclitus, 65, 219; first historian, 7 n. 26; his history cited by Herodotus, 99 n.179; may have used priestly records, 107; means of validation, 5, 225; methodology unknown, 66-7; polemic with Hesiod, 225; polemic with predecessors, 225; preface, 5, 225, 272; preface imitated by Herodotus and Thucydides, 272; probable reliance on native tradition, 283; promises greater accuracy, 115

Hector, as model for Dio, 50-1

Heliodorus, and Egyptian priests, 109

Hellanicus of Lesbos, 15, 218; *Attic History* probably based on oral tradition, 100; criticised by Thucydides, 226-7; criticised for incompleteness, 113; for brevity, 114; for chronological inaccuracy, 115; not known how he referred to himself in his works, 272

Hellenica Oxyrhynchia: *see* Oxyrhynchus historian

Heracles (Hercules), accounts of him both historical and mythical, 122-3; and Lucceius, 150 n.101, 165; and Nicolaus of Damascus, 150 n.101, 155; and Trogus, 154-5; as model for historian, 46, 59, 150, 155; his deeds not to be judged by human standards, 120; Herodotus' display piece on, 225

Heraclitus, 272 n.5; attacks Archilochus, 219; Hecataeus, 219; Hesiod, 219; Homer, 219; Pythagoras, 219; Xenophanes, 219; criticises early Greek thinkers, 65, 219; on insufficiency of sense perception, 65; on value of sense perception, 65

Hercules: *see* Heracles

Hermagoras, set aside place in the speech to construct speaker's character, 130

Hermeias, his work mentioned by Diodorus, 243 n.129

Hermocrates, 51 n.64

Hermogenes, on the pretence of necessity for self-praise, 211

Herod Agrippa (M. Iulius Agrippa II), approves Josephus' history, 90; provides Josephus with material for his history, 90

Herod the Great, encouraged by Nicolaus to study history, 30; encourages Nicolaus to write history, 52

Herodian 32, 48, 146, 224, 289; begins where Chryserus left off, 239; claim of autopsy and inquiry, 80 n.83, 92; imitates Thucydides, 17; magnification of his theme, 38; magnification of Severus, 39; on offices held, 147; possibly an imperial freedman, 89 n.126; reduced scope of his history, 92-3

Herodotus of Halicarnassus, 1, 5-7, 12, 13 n.58, 16-18, 20-2, 37, 43, 45, 51, 63, 69, 86, 91, 95,

101, 120-2, 133-4, 156, 218, 224, 227, 231, 245, 289, 290 n.3; amplification, 34-5; *Assyrian History*, 112 n.254; audience of, 20; different focalisation in Books II and IV, 180; different from his Ionian predecessors, 20; dispenser of praise, 18; display of inquiry, 8, 100, 272 n.7; does not aver impartiality, 164; echoes of Homer in his preface, 35 n.2; imitates Hecataeus of Miletus, 225 n.43, 272; includes ethnography and geography in his work, 83 n.100; influenced by Ionian rationalism, 7; intrusive narrator, 7, 219 n.11; justifies praise of the Athenians, 173; model for stylistic imitation, 16 n.74; monumentality of his work, 20; on Heracles, 225; on the moving island of Chemmis, 102; on the Trojan War, 225-6; polemic not programmatic, 226; polemic with predecessors, 225-6; polemic with Homer, 225-6; possible model in Telemachus in *Odyssey*, 64 n.6; preface, 8, 48; recitations at Olympia, 20 n.92, 61 n.112; refers only once to effort, 148; rival and imitator of Homer, 14; similar to medical writers, 8 n.33; universality of treatment, 20, 41

account of Egypt as more accurate than his predecessors', 115; account of Egypt based on priests, 108; at a loss where oral tradition is lacking, 103 n.205; cites Hecataeus' history, 99 n.179; difference in citation of foreign and Greek monuments, 101 n.190; emphasises process of research, 9; hierarchy of epistemological factors, 96; history presented as a compilation of oral traditions, 99-100; methodology, 8-9, 67; on myth, 118 n.285; reliance on native tradition, 283

and Hecataeus of Abdera, 108; and Manetho, 110; character judged as fair by Dionysius, 132; 'continued' by Thucydides, 290 n.1; criticised by Ctesias, 227-8; criticised by Plutarch, 118 n.285, 132, 231 n.75; epitomised by Theopompus, 22 n.108, 228; exaggerations criticised by Ammianus, 255-6; influence on Dionysius, 16 n.74, 246 n.147; influence on Theopompus, 228; influences Thucydides in alternation of person in preface, 185 n.52; recalled in Arrian's *Anabasis*, 253; work mentioned by Diodorus, 243 n.129

Hesiod, 218; attacked by Xenophanes, 219; by Heraclitus, 65, 219; attacks Homer, 219;

dream of, 48; first poet to name himself, 271; instructed and visited by Muses, 4, 51

Hieronymus of Cardia, 192, 290 n.9, claim of autopsy and inquiry, 80 n.83; criticised for his partiality by Pausanias, 162; literary style criticised, 246 n.148; mentioned by Dionysius as predecessor, 244; narrative of his own actions, 188; participation with Antigonus a method of validation, 88; possibly continued by Phylarchus, 238

Hipparchus, 84

Hippias of Elis, 20

Hirtius, A., acknowledges that he was not present at events, 78; apologises for completing Caesar's work, 78

historia, classified by rhetoricians as true, 118

historian, as athlete, 220 n.17; as benefactor, 46; as culmination of his predecessors, 15 n.69, 241-6; as narrator partakes in glory of deeds, 58; as participant in his history, 175-216 *passim*; avoids oaths to profess truth, 5; avoids professions of inspiration, 5; honoured for his history, 24; 'lonely' persona of, 217-18; not a profession in antiquity, 19; political activity of, 175; relation to power, 1 n.1; summation of his claims to authority, 262-4

historians
  Greek, *passim*; and inquiry, 66-88; and polemic, 218-19; differ from Romans in asserting authority, 5-6 and *passim*; summary of conventions in, 264-6
  Roman, *passim*; differ from Greeks in asserting authority, 5-6 and *passim*; do not introduce themselves in text, 273; early means of asserting authority unknown, 11; possible adoption of Greek conventions, 137; summary of conventions in, 264-6
  Sicilian, as continuators, 239-40; as participants, 186-7

historiography, avoids dedications, 54; benefit of, 11 n.47, 25, 30, 59; classification of genres in, 1-2; contemporary the dominant form, 77; court, 22 n.106, 86-9; divided by Polybius into three parts, 72; 'great', 53 n.73; idealising, 246 n.147; influenced by democracy, 86 n.112; interest in character, 92; mirrors political changes in fourth century 22-3; practised by many with different approaches, 3; pragmatic, 24; 'rhetorical', 2-3; 'tragic',

historiography (*cont.*)
> 23, 24 n.118; under autocratic regimes, 86–95; written for the subject's glory, 62
>
> contemporary, methodology, 66–86; more sparing of polemic, 224; summary of conventions in, 262–4
>
> Greek, concern with classical history, 31; continuity of, 32; of the Empire, 30–3; summary of its differences with Roman, 264–6; use of polemic in self-definition, 224
>
> imperial, absent in Latin between Tacitus and Ammianus, 32, 217; concern with bias, 166–70; restricted focus, 32, 86–95
>
> local (horography), 24, 53; and priests, 111–12; genre of historiography, defined, 2; its lack of concern with impartiality, 165; use of the first person in, 194 n.89
>
> non-contemporary, based on consultation of the previous written tradition, 105–6; inconsistent attitude of the ancients toward, 96–9; justifications for writing it, 112–17; methodology and presuppositions, 95–117, *passim*; not preferred by Isocrates, 276–9; preferred as a way to avoid the charge of bias, 96 n.163; summary of conventions in, 262–4; traditions already established in essence, 106
>
> Roman, comparatively late in developing, 26; effect of Annalists on, 27; non-existent between Tacitus and Ammianus, 32; of the Empire, 32; openly partisan, 215; province of the upper class, 27; rare use of polemic, 224; summary of its differences with Greek, 264–6

history: genre of historiography, defined, 2; pragmatic, 24; rhetorical, 2–3; tragic, 23, 24 n.118; universal, praised by Diodorus, 46, 241; by Polybius, 37

Homer, 13, 51, 109 n.235, 206 n.136, 207; anonymity of, 274–5; anonymity imitated by Arrian, 274–5; by Kephalion, 274; attacked by Heraclitus, 219; by Hesiod, 219; by pre-Socratics, 219; by Timaeus, 229; by Xenophanes, 219; faulted by Velleius for failing to record his country, 273; geography of, 119 n.290; Herodotus' polemic with, 225–6; influences historiographical narrative, 6; influences Thucydides in use of the third person, 184; narrative authority from the Muses, 63–4; narrative impartiality, 159, 173; narrator part of a later generation, 226 n.47; narrator unobtrusive, 159; occasional intrusion of judgement, 159; piety of his heroes, 207; praised by Plutarch for his advance evaluation, 159; quoted by Polybius, 82 n.94; refers to his activity as narrator, 3 n. 8; surpassed by anonymous historian, 274–5; Thucydides' rivalry with, 15 n.65

Odyssey, epistemological hierarchy of, 64; evaluations of individuals in, 159 n.137; interest in knowledge, 64; narrator more aware of poetic authority, 3; *see also* Odysseus

Horace, 57; warns Asinius Pollio of the danger of writing contemporary history, 157

horography: *see* historiography, local

imitation (μίμησις), of predecessors, 13 n.53, 237; and competition, 14; and innovation, 14; by adapting context, 15–16; divided by Dionysius into natural and learned, 13 n.57; essential to proper literary creation, 12; excessive or bad (κακοζηλία), 13 n.58; generic, 17; historiographical, 15; insufficient by itself for success, 13 n.57; leading to improvement, 15; not a literal copying, 13; of arrangement, 17–18; of attitude, 18; of book numbers, 18; of dialect, 16; of non-historians, 16 n.73; of poets, 16 n.73; of spirit, 13–14; of type of history, 17; of typical or recurring incidents, 17; of words devoid of context, 16 n.72; self-imitation, 18 n.86; use of polemic as a teaching tool in, 221; verbal, 15–17

impartiality, and political advancement by Emperor, 166; as claim to authority by historians, 158–74, 260; as not suppressing any of the facts, 171; averred by Polybius, 164; coexists with narrator's judgment, 159; common claim in oratory, 158 n.134; common for non-contemporary history in the Empire, 166; common whenever subject is autocrats, 162–3; expected in an historian, 160, 223; in imperial historians, 168–73; in Lucian, 160; more important among contemporary historians, 263; most discussed topic by ancient historians, 158; narrative, in Homer, 159; not at issue in chronicles and epitomes, 55; not averred by all historians, 164, 170; not common claim in local history, 165; not common claim in non-contemporary history before the Empire,

General index

166; not explicitly claimed by Herodotus or Thucydides, 164; possibly compromised by dedications, 54; relationship to inquiry, 160-4; relationship to the historian's judgement of individuals, 158-9; seen as the greatest challenge, 158; *see also* partiality
injury, as cause for partiality, 162
innovation, and imitation, 14
inquiry, as authenticating device, 5; as claim to authority, 63-127 *passim*, 259-60; difficult to know its extent among the early Roman historians, 77; difficulty of, under autocratic regimes, 88-9, 259-60; display of, in Herodotus, 8, 100; importance in observation, according to Aristotle, 74; in contemporary historiography, 262-3; in Homer, 63-4; in non-contemporary historiography, 262-3; in philosophers, 64-6; not much discussed by historians after Polybius, 75; not to be doubted as important in establishing Roman historian's authority, 78; of little importance in Lucian, 160; of natives, as basis for ethnographical material, 83-5; referred to only indirectly by Roman historians, 77; relationship to experience, 72-4; relationship to impartiality, 160-4; use of explicit remarks of, 80-6
inscriptions, commonplace by the end of the fifth century in Athens, 103; in Thucydides, 104; *see also* documents
introduction, of the author in the text, as an aspect of imitation, 271-5
invention, of deeds, not permitted by Lucian, 162; rhetorical, 161
inuidia: *see* envy
Ion of Chios, his *Wanderings*, 184; possible opening of his work, 272 n.5
Ionian rationalism, 7
Ionic dialect, as element of imitation of Herodotus or early writers, 16
Ismenias the Theban, 221
Isocrates, 55 n.81, 87 n.117, 134, 152, 156, 177 n.9, 182; adopts fiction of *antidosis* to defend himself, 176 n.7, 214; classifies narratives by subject matter, 118 n.287; influence on Sallust, 44; model for historians' claims of literary effort, 152; on autopsy and inquiry, 276-9; 'patron' of rhetorical historiography, 3; praise of himself in the mouth of his pupil, 214; praises his own literary ability, 152; spends ten years on *Panegyricus*, 152

Ister, his book against Timaeus, 223 n.33
Iulius Hyginus, C., freedman of Augustus, 89 n.126
ius imaginum, 27

Jeremiah, Book of (Hebrew Bible), 168 n.182
Josephus, 40, 48, 53 n.71, 60, 109 n.238, 179, 282; attacked by Justus of Tiberias, 224; claims historians write for glory, 60; claims of autopsy and inquiry, 80 n.83; claims truth, not glory, his aim, 60; compares written with oral tradition, 103; criticises Justus for deferred publication of his *Jewish War*, 173; identifies himself as priest, 111; imitates Dionysius, 17 n.79; laments his country's fate, 168; on polemic of Greek historians amongst themselves, 218; possibly influences Dio's portrayal of himself, 49 n.56; use of first person plural, 288
  Jewish Antiquities, 18, 60; as imitation of Dionysius' *Roman Antiquities*, 17; encouragement of Epaphroditus in, 52-3; more complete than its predecessors, 113
  Jewish War, 52; amplification of theme, 38; appeals to Emperor for validation of his history, 215 n.171; assertion of reliability in, 215 n.171; castigation of previous biased histories of Jewish rebellion, 115, 168; claim of impartiality, 168; conflicts with account given in the *Life*, 206 n.135; dreams in, 211; effort in composition, 156; emphasis on author's power of prophecy in, 210; experience of author as participant, 90, 145; focalisation of his account, 199; identification of author as priest in, 145; imitates Thucydidean monograph 17; introduction of author, 274; magnification of actions in, 216; no mention of special sources in, 90; political purpose of, 206 n.135; praise of author by others in, 214-15; techniques of self-presentation in, 206-16 *passim*; use of third person for author's deeds, 199, 205
  Life, access of author to power in, 90; conflicts with account in *Jewish War*, 206 n.135
judgements, expected to be fair, 174; expected to be based on the facts, 161-2; *see also* partiality *and* impartiality
Julian, 90; his deeds magnified by Ammianus, 39; praised by Ammianus, 173

Justin, 137 n.40; assumes Trogus wrote for glory or the novelty of the work, 61; compares his *otium* with Trogus' *labor*, 155 n.118; compares Trogus to Hercules, 154–5; his epitome of Pompeius Trogus, 29 n.138; his preface and Trogus', 142 n.61

Justus of Tiberias, 90; attacks Josephus' *Jewish War*, 224; criticised by Josephus for deferring publication of his work, 173

Kephalion, 18; cites historians and accounts he uses in his history, 114; imitates Homer's anonymity, 275

Kriton, 90 n.133, 148 n.98; his claim of autopsy and inquiry, 80 n.83; validates splendour of Trajan's triumph by autopsy, 83

labour: *see* effort
lamentations, by historians over their country's fate, 168–9
laudatio funebris, 27
Libanius, his letter to Marcellinus, 217 n.4
Liber Annalis, of Atticus: *see* Atticus
libertas: *see* freedom of speech
Libri Lintei, of Licinius Macer, as superior source, 116
Licinius Macer, C., 28, 124 n.314, 165; criticised by Livy, 163, 248–9; mentioned by Dionysius as his source for early Roman history, 245; portrayed by Sallust in his *Histories*, 251; uses linen books (*libri lintei*) to assert superiority, 116
Licinius Mucianus, his book on natural curiosities, 82 n.91
literacy, in antiquity, 23
Livius Andronicus, 15
Livy, 3, 5, 19, 20, 29, 40, 44, 48, 77, 102 n.193, 120 n.296, 187 n.61, 198, 236, 241, 250, 281–3, 285, 291; amplification, 41–2; and his fame, 46, 57, 61, 140; and Padua, 273 n.14; and Roman first person plural convention, 288; apolitical, 12 n.49, 29, 140; as outsider, 140; avoids question of his qualifications, 140; combination of assured and diffident narrator, 12 n.49; disavows ability in preface, 140–1, 248; does not dedicate his history, 54; emphasises moral component of history, 29; emphasises the effort of his task, 140, 153–4; hesitant towards his renown in the preface, 61; last Annalist, 27 n.131; member of the municipal aristocracy, 28 n.134; on Alexander and Rome, 224;

portrays character as important element of persuasion, 131; portrays history as personal pleasure, 45–6, 61, 140; preface meant for the early books, 78; reasons for writing non-contemporary history, 112

and Varro's division of eras, 124; as Herodotean investigator, 11; attitude towards myth, 124; careful narrative manner when telling myths, 124; compares myth to the theatre, 124; does not use autopsy for Roman monuments, 101 n.190; juxtaposes natural and supernatural explanation, 124; poor on geography, 85; reliability achieved by fullness of material, 114; sole statement of autopsy, 102 n.198

assessment of Augustan principate, 172; called 'Pompeian' by Augustus, 172; confesses his love of country, 170; delayed publication of his later books, 172; does not aver impartiality, 165, 170; impartial within an overall favourable framework, 170; impartially assesses Caesar, 171–2; impartially assesses Cicero, 171–2; impartially assesses Hannibal, 171; seen by later Romans as impartial evaluator of men and deeds, 170–1

as model for Tacitus, 253; attacks Annalists, 248–9; attitude towards his predecessors, 140, 248–9; avoids bias of predecessors, 249; avoids exaggerations of predecessors, 248–9; avoids later inventions of predecessors, 249; criticises Licinius Macer for excessive praise of his family, 163; his impartiality praised by Cremutius Cordus, 252; influenced by Sallust's prefaces, 140, 141 n.58, 248; most often attacks Antias, 249 n.165; polemic with Greek historians, 224; relies on earliest historians, 248–9; Servilius Nonianus on, 247 n.156

Longinus, 254; encourages imitation of the masters, 13, 237

Lucceius, L., asked by Cicero for monograph on his consulship, 177, 186; compared with Hercules by Cicero, 165; rejects partiality, 165

Lucian, 2, 16, 51 n.164, 148, 275; and impartiality, 160; date of his *How to Write History*, 2 n.5; distinguishes between poetry and history, 125–6; does not allow partiality for one's city, 171 n.192; his ideas compared with Thucydides', 76; implies Ctesias is

partial, 170; on autopsy and inquiry, 75-6; on effort in writing history, 156; on faults of historians, 221; on flattery in history, 125-6; praises Xenophon for impartiality, 170 n.190; ridicules lack of narrative impartiality, 173; satirised historians in, 2 n.5; sees difficulty of inquiry primarily influenced by flattery, 76
Lucius Verus, 90; and Fronto's history, 32; pressures Fronto, 36 n.8; promises Fronto letters and memoranda for Fronto's history of his wars, 90 n.132
Lucullus, dedicatee of Sulla's *Memoirs*, 182
Lysias, as master of character delineation, 129

magnification (αὔξησις, *amplificatio*), in universal historians, 37, 40-2; in writers of individual rulers, 36-7; in writers of monographs, 39-40; of deeds, 258-9; of opponents, as a method of self-praise, 215-16; of theme, 34-43; originally developed for epideictic, 35 n.2
Magnos of Carrhae, 90 n.133; his claim of autopsy and inquiry, 80 n.83
majority, of witnesses, appeal to, as a way of resolving variant versions, 282; derided by Plato, 282 n.8
malice, accepted as truth, 167 n.169; arising from the reader's jealousy, 167 n.169
Manetho, 24; and Herodotus, 110; announces himself as priest, 109-10; dedicates history to Ptolemy II, 53; his date, 110 n.241
Marathon, 20
Marius, C., appears to Cicero in a dream, 48
Marius Maximus, 32 n.158
Marsic War, its amplification by Diodorus, 41
marvels, validated by autopsy, 80, 82-3
Maximus of Tyre, 51 n.67; praises value of dreams, 50
medical writers, Polybius and, 76; their use of display, 8; their use of polemic, 8, 220
medicine, divided, like history, into three parts, 76; its importance for Polybius, 74; need for experience in, 74-5
mediocritas, 57, 213
Megasthenes, 110 n.241; his account of India, 112 n.255; reliable source for Arrian, 285-6
Melesagoras: *see* Amelesagoras
memoirs, 2; as term for ὑπομνήματα and *commentarii*, 180; different levels of stylistic adornment in, 181-2; difficult to separate from autobiography, 196; distinguishing mark is perspective, 181; level of apologetic difficult to gauge, 196; not always sketch to be worked up by later writers, 181-2; self-praise in, 265
Greek (ὑπομνήματα), as 'preliminary sketch', 180, 181 n.31; earliest written by Demetrius of Phaleron, 180; other writers of, 180; range of meanings of the term, 180; use of the first person in, 196 n.101, 205
Roman (*commentarii*), Caesar's work probably not typical of the genre, 181, 197-8; common at Rome, 181; develop independently from Greek ὑπομνήματα, 181 n.26; earliest examples of, 181, 195-6; possible forerunners of, 181; range of meanings of the term, 181; unliterary character, 181; use of the first person in, 196, 205
memory, influences report of actions, 69
Menander, 23 n.110; and the character of the speaker, 131 n.13
Menander Rhetor, and the use of dreams, 50 n.62
Menodotus of Perinthus, possible continuator of Psaon, 238; work mentioned by Diodorus, 243 n.129
Messala Corvinus, his free speech praised by Cremutius Cordus, 252
Metrodorus of Scepsis, 224 n.38
Micon, his painting of Marathon in the Painted Stoa, 20
mimesis (μίμησις), two meanings of the term, 12 n.52; as narrative representation, 6; as imitation of previous writers: *see* imitation
Mimnermus, appeals to eyewitnesses, 4; invokes Muse in his *History of Smyrna*, 8 n.31
Mnesiptolemus, 24 n.117; closely allied with Antiochus, 88
monarchy, its influence on historiography, 22, 86-95, 166
monograph, historical, 2; form imitated, 17
monuments, as source for history, 20; as source for non-contemporary history, 99, 101-3; in Herodotus' account of Egypt, 101; rare use by Thucydides, 101; used by Ammianus, 102; by Cato, 102; by Dionysius, 102; by Polybius, 101-2; by Roman Annalists, 102; by Timaeus, 101
Mucius Scaevola, P., possibly publishes *Annales Maximi c.* 130 BC, 26 n.124

Muses, as inspiration for composition, 61; as 'present and knowing all things', 64; invoked as authorising, 3, 63-4; invoked by Empedocles, 4; by historical poets, 8 n.31; by Homer before enumeration, 3 n.8; by lyric poets, 4; visit and instruct Hesiod, 4
myth, and Thucydides, 117-18; appropriate in digressions, 118; as local story, often exaggerative, 127; benefit of its inclusion in history, 120, 123 n.310; compared to the theatre, 120, 124; dual meaning in Lucian, 125-6; in Herodotus, 118 n. 285; in history, 117-27 *passim*; in Latin historians, 123-5; in Livy, 124; inappropriate to history's pragmatic task, 127; included but not endorsed by the historian, 118; its rejection a claim to authority, 123; linked to praise and encomia in Lucian, 126; not to be judged by human standards, 120; rationalised, 118, 282-3; 'tamed' by Thucydides, 119; treated carefully after Thucydides, 118
mythographers, chided by Polybius, 127
mythography, as genre of historiography, defined, 1

Naevius, C., 177; his *Bellum Poenicum* first Roman historical work, 26; its date, 26 n.125; refers to his military experience, 137
name, use of, as an element of imitation, 271-5; not equivalent to presence in the text, 271
narrative, historical, and epic, 6-7; and traditional story-telling, 7; divided according to narrator, 6 n.22; divided according to subject matter, 6 n.22, 118-19; earliest types unknown, 7; employs 'artificial' authority, 6; homogeneity as an element of authority, 9; influenced by Homer, 6; needs to be felicitously presented, 79-80; not constantly interrupted by remarks on autopsy and inquiry, 79-80; uses *mimesis*, 6
narrator
  historical, 5-12 and *passim*; and the narrative of his own deeds, 179-216; compared to actor by Plutarch, 58; less intrusive in Roman historiography, 11, 264-5; more strongly pronounced in Greek historiography, 264; partakes in glory of deeds narrated, 58
  epic, 3, 159, 173; rarely intrudes in the narrative, 3, 7; *see also* Homer

nationality, of the historian in introducing himself, 271-5
natives, 105 n.219; appeal to, as a way of resolving variant versions, 283-4; belief in their validity, 283-4; *see also* tradition, local
Naucrates, 135
Nearchus of Crete, 84; and the narrative of his own actions, 188 n.67
necessity, as a motive for self-praise, 211
negotium, 45, 78 n.68, 139, 141 n.58
Nepos, Cornelius, and Catullus' dedicatory poem, 155-6; audience for his work, 29; his *Chronicles*, 28; his *Lives*, 28
Nestor, offers Telemachus benefit of his inquiry, 64
Nicolaus of Damascus, 29, 30 n.148, 107 n.230; and history's benefit, 30; compares himself to Heracles, 155; encouraged by Herod to write history, 52; his *Life*, 196; narrative of his own actions, 198; uses third person, 198, 205
notatio, 130 n.9
novel, its audience, 23 n.13; its narratives of escape possible influence on historiography, 203
number, of books, as an element of imitation 18
numbers, appeal to, as a way of resolving variant versions, 108 n.233

Odysseus, anticipates methods of validation for contemporary history, 63; cites 'source', 4 n. 13; model for Diodorus of man of experience, 149; not an omniscient narrator, 4; praises Demodocus for his song, 63
Odyssey: *see* Homer
oligarchy, and historiography, 22
Olympos, his access to Cleopatra as validation for his account of her, 88; his claim of autopsy and inquiry, 80 n.83
Onesicritus, 84
oral society, its features, 219; polemic in, 219
oral tradition, 26; attacked by Hecataeus of Miletus, 225; compared with written tradition by Josephus, 103; Isocrates on, 276-9; use for non-contemporary history, 99-101
orators, as a source for history, 20; different relationship to material from that of historians, 162
Origins: *see* Cato the Elder
ornatio, 182
otium, and the writing of history, 137-9

Oxyrhynchus historian, 10 n.43, 36, 289; continues Thucydides, 238; imitates arrangement of Thucydides, 17; possibly Cratippus, 290 n.2

pains: *see* effort
Palatine library, as reflecting the Emperor's taste, 18-19
panegyric, 27, 221; as a source for history, 20; *see also laudatio funebris*
Parmenides, invokes δαίμονες, 4
partiality, against other nations, 174 n.206; and inquiry, in Lucian, 76; arising from love of country or friends, 222 n.30; as a motive for invention or exaggeration of deeds, 94, 160-1; inferred from one's treatment of individuals, 171; inferred when historian has access to ruling power, 89; its causes, 162-3; not allowed toward one's native country by Lucian or Polybius, 171 n.192; of informants, 69; of predecessors, as a justification for re-writing a history, 114-15; opposed to truth, 160; permitted towards one's country, 170-1; towards foreigners, 174 n.206; *see also* impartiality
participation, in military campaigns, as basis for historical account, 90-1; *see also* experience
patronage, its importance for inquiry, 89
patronus, 130
Pausanias, 111, 162, 228 n.57
Pergamum, 18
Pericles, his funeral oration, 152
Persian Wars, as historical subject in Second Sophistic, 31
person
  first and third, in narrative of one's own actions, 179-205; limit of this distinction, 179-80; use of less importance than element of praise, 180
  first, use of, by Ammianus, 200-4; by Dio, 199-200; by early philosophers, 5; by Herodotus, 8; by medical writers, 8; by Polybius, 10-11, 190-2; by Thucydides, 9, 134 n.26; first-person plural, Roman convention of, 193, 287-8; in memoirs, 195-6, 204-5; more pronounced in Livy than in other Roman historians, 11-12; rare after Thucydides, 10; used by Greek local historians, 194 n.89
  third, use of, 205; by Caesar, 196-8; by Dexippus, 199; by Josephus, 199; by Thucydides, 134 n.26; in earlier part of Polybius, 188-9; never by Roman historian for himself, 197
perspective: *see* focalisation
persuasion, by character, 129-30
Phemius, bard in the *Odyssey*, claims instruction and inspiration, 3
Pherecydes, of Athens, 100; not known how he introduced himself, 272
Pherecydes, of Syros, his book opening, 272 n.5
Philinus of Acragas, 77, 98; partiality criticised by Polybius, 114, 171; possible source for Fabius, 77; possibly mentioned by Diodorus, 243 n.129
Philip of Macedon, and Theopompus, 87
Philip of Pergamum, emphasises effort, 151
Philistus of Syracuse, 289; claim of autopsy and inquiry, 80 n.83; continued by Athanis, 240; judged a flatterer by Dionysius, 132; may have written his history in exile, 187; narrative of his own actions, 186-7; ridiculed by Timaeus, 229; work mentioned by Diodorus, 243 n.129
Philochorus, 179; as priest, 111; narration of his own actions, 194 n.89
philosophers, emphasise their own knowledge, 4-5; engage in polemic, 5, 218-19; question value of sense-perception, 64-6; see themselves as bringing truth to audience, 272; use Muse as authenticating, 4; use of display by, 8; use of their name in text, 271
Phlegon of Tralles, freedman of Hadrian, 89 n.126, 148
Phocylides, names himself in text, 271
Phoenicians, possessors of an ancient and reliable history, 103
Phylarchus, 289; continues Duris or Hieronymus, 238, 290 n.9; criticised by Polybius, 24 n.118, 153 n.113, 230, 233 n.85; unreliable towards Cleomenes and Aratus, 162
Pindar, Thucydides' rivalry with, 15 n.65
Plato, 13, 15, 16 n.73, 61 n.113, 277 n.3; attacked by Timaeus, 229; derides refutation using appeal to numbers, 282 n.8; influence on Sallust, 44, 60 n.109; on philosophical and rhetorical proof (*elenchus*), 220; states that argument must follow *logos*, 9
Pliny the Elder, 49, 50, 62, 114 n.264, 144 n.69, 223 n.34, 253, 291; and Sulla's title *felix*, 209 n.147; defers publication of his history to guarantee impartiality, 172; expresses

Pliny the Elder (*cont.*)
surprise at Livy, 57; joins his history to Aufidius Bassus', 240, 292 n.8; mentioned by Tacitus, 250-1; motivated by dream of Drusus Nero to write of German wars, 47-8; scope of his *German Wars*, 47

Pliny the Younger, desires to write history, 62; gives bibliography of his uncle's writings, 47; on difference between contemporary and non-contemporary historiography, 105; requests Tacitus' testimony for his own actions, 178; sees history as a vehicle for the historian's immortality, 62

Plutarch, 77, 183 n.43, 188 n.68, 206; compares historians to actors, 58; criticises Phylarchus' partiality, 162; his *Political Precepts*, 29 n.142; his work, *On Praising Oneself without Envy*, 176-7; on Cato's excessive self-praise, 195; on self-praise using the gods and fortune, 207; on use of negative examples in teaching, 221; on Xenophon's use of pseudonym Themistogenes, 186; polemic with Herodotus, 118 n.285, 231 n.75; praises Homer's use of advance evaluation, 159; sees character as more important than eloquence, 131; sees historians as sharing in their subject's renown, 58; sees myth and praises as suitable for digressions in history, 118 n.285; suspicious of Ctesias' *Persica*, 185

poets, and fame, 57; different means of validation from that of historians, 3-5

polemic, as covert self-praise, 221; as teaching tool, 221-2; aspect of an oral society, 219; aspect of imitation, 221; authenticating device by early historians, 5; by early philosophers and sophists, 5, 8, 218-19; by medical writers 8, 220; becomes more personal in the fourth century, 221; distinctive feature of ancient historiography, 218; element for winning authority, 261; more common in Greek than Roman historians, 224, 265-6; more common in non-contemporary history, 223-4; not widespread in Middle Eastern and Asian societies, 219; peculiarly Greek, 219; rare in contemporary history, 224; Timaeus' renown in, 223; tone of, 221-2; use in rhetoric, 219-20

Polemo, 51 n.64

Polemon, his book against Timaeus, 223 n.33; his collection of inscriptions, 104

Polybius 2, 18, 21, 23 n.114, 25, 34, 42, 45, 48, 59, 70, 106, 146, 170, 175, 199, 201, 205, 220 n.19, 233, 240 n.122, 244, 284, 289; apodeictic method of, 10 with n. 45, 136; audience of, 24-5; claims his history as 'pragmatic', 24; concern with the genre of history, 229, 230 n.73; does not introduce himself by name in text, 273; envisions three groups of readers, 24; fond of comparisons with medicine, 74 n.49; interest in practical matters, 136; intrusive narrator, 10; on narrative in history, 80; places methodological statements where most relevant, 190; portrays his experiences as paradeigmatic for future historians, 11 n.44, 136, 232; praises universal history, 37; writes biography, 19; writes work on military tactics, 19

avoided myth in his work, 242 n.125; bases account on native information, 115; cites theory and eyewitness evidence in geographical book, 84 n.102; claim of autopsy and inquiry, 80 n.83; defends Aristotle on the Epizephyrian Locrians, 98-9, 284; distinguishes between myth-writers and historians, 127; gives no methodology for the writing of non-contemporary historiography, 98; importance of geography in history, 83 n.100; included geography in history, 83; justifies inclusion of non-contemporary history in his work, 99; on difficulties of inquiry, 71-5; on discovering matters from a secret meeting, 86 n.113; on myth, 119; on mythical geography, 119 n.290; on questioning of witnesses, 76 n.57; re-writes First Punic War, 98; underlines special source, 80; uses monuments for non-contemporary historiography, 101-2; vouches for character of Chimara by mention of his meeting with her, 82; vouches for character of Scipio by his presence at events, 82

avers his own impartiality, 164; claims bias of Fabius and Philinus necessitates re-writing of First Punic War, 114; distinguishes between intentional and unintentional falsehood, 222; does not allow partiality towards one's city, 171 n.192; excuses himself for writing in a declamatory manner, 169 n.184; expresses pity for the Greeks, 169 n.184; failure to be impartial in his narrative of the Aetolians, 164, 174 n.206; generous correction of Zeno, 232; justifies praise of Scipio Aemilianus and Aemilius Paulus, 173; on dangers and hardships undergone for his history, 149; on historian's efforts, 151; on importance of character, 131; requests the historian show honourable conduct, 232, n.82; requires political experience of the historian, 145 changes use of first and third person for his own actions in Book XXXVI, 189; later books lose focalisation of history, 192, 195; maintains formal distance between himself as narrator and character, 189; narrative of his friendship with Scipio Aemilianus, 189; narrative of his own actions, 188-92; no difference between his use of first-person singular and plural, 191 n.78; participation a reason for extending his history, 191; possibly influenced by Aratus, 192; possibly influenced by Romans, 192; reasons for his change of person in narrative of his own actions, 189-91, 205; uses both first and third person, 180, 191; uses third person for his own activities before Book XXXVI, 189, 205; wishes to avoid excessive self-praise, 191

Book XII directed against Timaeus, 223-4, 230-2; breadth of his criticism against Timaeus, 231-2; claims superiority to Timaeus, 239; continues Aratus, 98, 180, 238; continues Timaeus, 238; contrasts his impartiality with Timaeus' bias, 164; criticises Callisthenes, 230; criticises Chaereas and Sosylus, 230; criticises Phylarchus, 24 n.118, 230; for insufficient effort, 153 n.113; criticises Postumius Albinus, 230 with n.72; criticises Pytheas' reliability, 84 n.102; criticises Theopompus, 224, 230-2; for hostility to Philip, 162; criticises Timaeus for account of the Epizephyrian Locrians, 98-9; for bitterness of character, 231; for deliberate falsehood, 231; for excessive polemic, 231; for hostility to Agathocles, 162; for lack of effort, 153; for lack of experience, 71; for love of cavilling and fault-finding, 232; for slander, 231; on effect of Timaeus' polemic, 223; on Euhemerus' reliability, 84 n.102; on Fabius Pictor's bias, 171; on Philinus' bias, 171; on purpose of criticism, 222; praises Aratus, 180, 239; praises Ephorus, 239 n.114;

purpose of polemic, 226; rejects orientation of Theopompus, 37; use of polemic, 229-30

cited by Ammianus, 256; continued by Posidonius, 239; by Strabo, 239; criticised by Posidonius for bias towards Tiberius Gracchus, 163; criticisms of Timaeus echoed by later historians, 233-4; epitomised by Brutus, 29 n.138; his ideal embraced by Ammianus, 256; literary style criticised, 246 n.148; mentioned by Dionysius as predecessor, 244; praised by Diodorus, 241; remarks on history echoed by Sempronius Asellio, 236 n.104; surpassed by Diodorus, 242

Pompeius Trogus, 61, 143, 146; epitomised by Justin, 29 n.138; imitates Theopompus' *Philippica*, 17; Justin's preface not a reliable guide to his history, 142 n.61; mentions his ancestors' achievements and advancements, 141; purpose and sources, 142 n.61; treated his own country, 142, 273; unknown how he portrayed himself in preface, 142

Pompey, and his *fortuna*, 209

Pontifex Maximus, his chronicle: *see* Pontifical Chronicle

Pontifical Chronicle (*tabula apud pontificem*), 26, 100; attacked by Cato, 236; by Sempronius Asellio, 236; separate from *Annales Maximi*, 26 n.124

portents, their use in Roman historiography, 125

Poseidonius (historian of Perseus), his claim of autopsy and inquiry, 80 n.83

Posidonius of Apamea, 151 n.104, 232 n.83, 244, 289; and Cicero's memoir, 182; continuator of Polybius, 239; criticises Polybius for partiality towards Ti. Gracchus, 163; influence on Sallust, 44 n.33; possibly praised by Diodorus, 241; source for Diodorus' account of the Marsic War, 41 n.22; surpassed by Diodorus, 242; treatment of myth, 242 n.125; use of autopsy in ethnographical excursions, 85; use of geography in history, 84; with Marius at his death, 88

Postumius Albinus, A., criticised by Polybius, 230

pragmatic history, 27

praise, and partiality, 176; and self-praise, 260-1; as component of historiography, 6; in encomiastic poets, 173 n.203; must be based

praise, and partiality (*cont.*)
    on facts, according to Aristotle, 161; of
    oneself by others, as a way of mitigating self-
    praise, 214–15; of others, as mitigating self-
    praise, 212–13; often preceded by a truth
    claim, 173; *see also* partiality
Praxagoras of Athens, magnifies Constantine's
    virtues, 37 n.9
pre-Socratics: *see* philosophers
predecessors, as models to be followed and
    bested, 115–16, 241–57 *passim*; as sources for
    a non-contemporary history, 99; attitudes
    towards, 263–4; their incompetence a reason
    for re-writing history, 43 n.29
preface, as place for establishing the
    historian's character, 133; virtual, used by
    Xenophon, 237 n.107, 273 n.12
prejudice: *see* partiality
priests, as basis for Herodotus' account of
    Egypt, 108, 225–6; as sources, 90 n.127;
    cited for special information, 108–9;
    Egyptian, 108–10; Greek, and local history,
    111–12; historians as, 109–12; Josephus'
    mention of, as a mark of social status, 145;
    primary means of validation for Egyptian
    matters, 109
probability, appeal to, as a way of resolving
    variant versions, 282–3
proofs, atechnic, 128; entechnic, 128–9
Psaon of Plataea, 289; continues Diyllus, 238;
    possibly continued by Menodotus, 238, 290
    n.8; work mentioned by Diodorus, 243
    n.129
Ptolemaios, priest of Mendes, 110
Ptolemy I (Soter), historian of Alexander, 192;
    character of his history, 187; claim of
    autopsy and inquiry, 80 n.83; in Arrian's
    Anabasis, 275; not reserved about his own
    renown, 187; praised by Arrian for absence
    of bias, 114, 169; reliability as 'king', 285
Ptolemy II (Philadelphus), Manetho's history
    dedicated to him, 53
Ptolemy VIII (Euergetes II), his *Memoirs*, 180;
    uses the first person, 196 n.101
publication, deferred, as a guarantee of
    veracity, 172–3; criticised as a way to avoid
    refutation, 173; not often chosen by
    historians, 172–3
Pyrrhus, of Epirus, 207 n.138; his *Memoirs*,
    180
Pythagoras, criticised by Heraclitus, 65, 219
Pytheas, his reliability questioned by Polybius,
    84 n.102

Quintilian, avers possibility of improving on
    predecessors, 15; defends Cicero, 177; his
    On the Causes of Corrupted Eloquence, 15
    n.69; on Cicero's techniques of self-praise,
    178; on native ability and imitation, 13 n.57;
    on self-praise, 177; on teaching from bad
    examples, 221; praises imitation, 13; sees
    renown as important spur to literary
    achievement, 57, 61 n.112

readings (of histories): *see* recitations
reality, contrasted with surface appearance,16
    n.71; in Tacitus, 94–5; in Theopompus, 95;
    in Thucydides, 67–8
recitations, of historical works, 20–1; by
    Aristotheos, 21 n.98; by Herodotus at
    Olympia, 20 n.92, 61 n.112; in Rome, 28;
    public, 24
refutation, of laws, 105; of written testimony,
    105; part of a speech used for raising the
    emotions, 221–2; *see also* polemic
'remembrancers', 99 n.179
renown: *see* glory
representation: *see* mimesis
rhetoric, importance of character in, 6, 128–30;
    polemic in, 219–21
Rhetoric to Alexander, emphasises importance
    of character of speaker, 130; on the orator's
    task, 220
Rhetoric to Herennius, on the orator's task,
    220; unconcerned with character, 130
Rome, opposition to, by Greek historians, 31
    n.154,
rumour (*fama*), its effect on truth, 93–4
Rutilius Rufus, P., 178, 196; his *de uita sua*,
    181–2; its relationship to his history in
    Greek, 182 n.32; uses the first person, 196
    n.101

Sallust, 44, 46, 92, 157, 177 n.9, 198, 224, 236,
    246, 250; attempts to forge a new persona,
    78; *Breuiarium* compiled for his use, 28
    n.138; concern with relation between history
    and public life, 138–9; concern with *uirtus*,
    44; connects impartiality with removal from
    public life, 165–6; de-emphasises political
    experience, 139–40; defends himself from
    the charge of *inertia*, 139, 152; does not
    dedicate his histories, 54; emphasises moral
    component of history, 29; explains how he
    came to history, 44–5; follows monograph
    form of Antipater, 17; imitation of
    Thucydides, 16 n.71; influenced by

Isocrates, 44; influenced by Plato, 44, 60 n.109, 140; justifies his abandonment of the state, 139; on historian's glory, 60; persona influenced by Cato, 45; possibly influenced by Posidonius, 44 n.33; prefaces atypical, 78; revises Cato's contrast of *otium* and *negotium*, 139; sees difficulty of history in adequate artistic expression, 152; sees difficulty of history in disbelief of audience, 152; use of archaic style, 16-17; use of Roman first person plural convention, 287 as model for Tacitus, 253; continued by Asinius Pollio, 240; imitators castigated by Quintilian, 17; model for Ammianus, 255; praised by Tacitus, 251; Servilius Nonianus on, 247 n.156; style imitated by many, 17

Catiline, 11, 16 n.71, 77; claim of impartiality in, 165; citation of Crassus as source, 81; magnification of subject, 39-40; self-praise in, 208 n.141

Histories, 45 n.37, 291; claim of impartiality in, 166, 247; continuation of Sisenna, 240; lays claim to several historiographic traditions, 247; mention of Sisenna, 247; portrayal of author in an abundance of learned men, 60 n.110; portrayal of Licinius Macer in, 251; possible criticism of Cato, 247; praise of Cato, 247; praise of Fannius, 247; strategies of alliance in, 247

Jugurtha, amplification of subject, 40; disclaimer of responsibility for African sources, 85, 105; importance of suffering in, 40 n.20

Scipio Aemilianus, P. Cornelius, narrative of his friendship with Polybius, 189; praised by Polybius, 173

Scipio Africanus, P. Cornelius, his autobiographical letter, 181

Scipio Nasica, P. Cornelius, his autobiographical letter, 181

scribe, sacred (ἱερογραμματεύς), 110

scriptor rerum, as Ennius' characterisation of himself, 26 n.126

Scylax of Caryanda, 67; possible predecessor of Ctesias on India, 112 n.255

Second Sophistic, 31-2; and Alexander, 32 n.155

self-defence, as motivation for inventing things, 94; spur to partiality, 163; *see also* self-praise

self-praise, 175-9; acceptable in certain situations, 176-7; and polemic, 221; as reason for inventing things, 93-4; as spur to partiality, 163; attitude of ancients towards, 176-7; dangers of, 54; in a memoir, 265; more likely to be caught by an ancient reader than distortion by omission, 183 n.43; never as good as praise by others, 176-8; should avoid epideictic style, 216; techniques for mitigating it, 177, 207 n.141

Sempronius Asellio, 291; allies with Cato and Polybius, 247; based his history on his participation, 78; claim of autopsy and inquiry, 80 n.83; defends history against annals, 138, 236; echoes Polybius, 236 n.104; possible use of experience, 138

Senatorial history, under the Empire, 91, 93

Seneca the Elder, 291; beginning point of his history uncertain, 292 n.6; expresses belief in improvement by imitation, 15; on use of dreams, 50 n.62; praises Livy's impartiality, 170

Servilius Nonianus, 144 n.69; compares Sallust and Livy, 247 n.156; praised by Tacitus, 251

Severus, Septimius, advises Dio to write history, 49-50; amplification of his deeds by Herodian, 39; attitude of Dio towards, 49; his *Memoirs*, 181 n.29

Silenus of Caleacte, his claim of autopsy and inquiry, 80 n.83; mentioned by Dionysius as predecessor, 244

Simonides, invokes Muse in his *Battle of Plataea*, 8 n.31

Sisenna, L. Cornelius, 291; continued by Sallust in the *Histories*, 240; criticised by Sallust in *Jugurtha*, 247; mentioned by Sallust in *Histories*, 247; structure of his history, 292 n.3

Solon, 4; names himself in text, 271

sophists: *see* philosophers

Sosylus of Lacedaemon, criticised by Polybius, 230; his claim of autopsy and inquiry, 80 n.83; work mentioned by Diodorus, 243 n.129

sources, for contemporary history, 66-79; for non-contemporary history, 95-112; literary, as a component of writing history, 72; method of resolution when they differ, 280-6

status, social, adopted by Greeks of the Empire as authenticating device, 144-6; as element in claiming authority, 141-7; mocked by Arrian, 146-7; of speaker as authenticating, 6; used by Romans, 141-4

Strabo, 162, 188 n.68, 289; audience of, 30; continues Polybius' history, 239; on generous correction, 232 n.83; on geographical excurses, 83; praises Ephorus, 97; structure of his *Affairs after Polybius*, 290 n.13
style, and authority, 10 n. 42; insufficient as justification for re-writing history, 116-17; simple or plain, as a mark of reliability, 10 n. 42, 55
Successors of Alexander (Diadochs), 24, 87; historians of, 88; historians of, as participants, 187-8; use of history by, 24 n.115
Suetonius, 32 n.158
Sulla, L. Cornelius, 196; asks that style be improved, 55; dedicates his work to Lucullus, 54, 182; title of his work uncertain, 182 n.35; use of fortune, 209; uses the first person, 196 n.101
Susarion, names himself in text, 271

tabula apud pontificem: see Pontifical Chronicle
Tacitus, Cornelius, 2, 11, 32, 40, 92, 142, 148, 169, 198, 223 n.34, 224, 236, 282-3, 291; addresses Senatorial order, 31; as a member of distinguished company of Senator-historians, 144; asked by Pliny to write up Pliny's actions, 178; asserts his impartiality, 144; asserts historian's freedom of speech, 167; careful in the matter of self-praise, 144 n.72; character of the man read from his work, 132 n.16; concern with *uirtus*, 31; critical disposition of, 18; disapproval of mention of *beneficia* by predecessors, 143; does not dedicate his histories, 54; idealises the past, 179; imitates himself, 18 n.86; mention of *beneficia* received, 143-4; mentions his offices and experience, 81, 144, 166; on philosophers and fame, 57; on poets and fame, 57; on self-praise, 178-9; records Senatorial opinions, 31; representative of different approach to imperial historiography, 93; use of Roman first person plural convention, 287; writings other than history, 19
  appears to reject myth, 124-5; claims to treat material passed over by others, 113, 116; dependent on books for his geographical knowledge, 85; invokes elders as superior source, 116; on difficulties of inquiry, 93-4; on exaggeration by the soldiers, 163; remarks on rumour and truth, 93-4; use of conflict between surface and reality, 95; use of Egyptian priests, 109; use of myth in his history, 125; use of variant versions, 94-5
  allies himself with great republican writers, 252-3; cites *Memoirs* of the Younger Agrippina, 116; criticises Greek writers, 250; criticises immediate predecessors, 115, 250-1; criticism of writers on the civil wars, 250; derides those who seek to suppress history, 252; does not name predecessors in preface, 250; on decline of imperial historiography, 167, 250; portrayal of Cremutius Cordus, 251-2; praises earlier historians, 250; praises Sallust, 251; praises Servilius Nonianus, 251; pretends to disavow comparison with republican predecessors, 251; rarely cites predecessors by name, 250-1
  continued by Ammianus, 240, 254; differences with Ammianus, 254-5; neglect of his work in the third century, 32
  Agricola, its genre, 2 n.3; promise to write of present times in, 167 n.177; preface of, 178-9
  Annals, as an inglorious task, 156; claim of impartiality in, 167; inquiry in, 93-5; poverty of the subject, 91 n.134, 251
  Histories, 77; claim of impartiality in, 166; inquiry in, 93-5; magnification of subject, 38; on danger of contemporary history, 157; promise to write of present freedom in, 166-7; reservation of safer topic for author's old age, 157
Tacitus, the emperor, 32
Telemachus, 64; as model for Herodotus, 64 n.6
temple records, 107
Thales, on eyes and ears, 65
theatre, compared to myth, 120, 124
Themistocles, 207
Themistogenes of Syracuse, as pseudonym of Xenophon, 186
Theodectes, 135
Theognis, his name in the text, 271; his seal (σφραγίς), 271; invokes elders for authority, 4; invokes gods, 4
Theophanes, accompanies Pompey, 88; claim of autopsy and inquiry, 80 n.83
Theopompus, 29, 37, 48, 152 n.108, 156, 171, 187 n.61, 223 n.34, 289; ability to detect unseen causes, 95; and myth, 120, 121 n.297, n.299; claim of autopsy and inquiry, 80

n.83; claims first place in literary ability, 58, 135; compares himself with contemporaries, 135; critical disposition of, 18; epideictic style of, 135-6; expended great effort, according to Dionysius, 148-9; incurs great expense, according to Dionysius, 87; no evidence that he claimed impartiality, 170; on his oratorical excellence, 58; on his own renown, 58; praises practical experience, 73, 133; progression of works, 22; travels for his history, 87; uses documents to question Peace of Callias, 105

Arrian's competition with, 253-4; attacked by Duris in his preface, 135, 228; criticised by Polybius, 37 n.10, 162, 230, 232; criticism of characters in his history, 135; criticism of predecessors, 135; included polemic in his preface, 228; indebted to Herodotus, 228; judged as exacting by Dionysius, 132; likened to orator by ancient critics, 135 n.30; polemic with the Athenians, 105; possibly a victim of Anaximenes' pseudography, 228 n.57; praised by Dionysius for his efforts, 153; remarks on education echoed by Callimorphus, 148 n.90; work mentioned by Diodorus, 243 n.129

Epitome of Herodotus, 22 n. 108, 208
Hellenica, 22, 36, 58; continues Thucydides, 238
Philippica, 22; different orientation of, 36, 290 n.3; importance of rhetorical ability in, 136; magnification of Philip's deeds in, 36; title imitated by Pompeius Trogus, 17
third person: *see* person
Thucydides, 2, 13, 17-18, 23, 37, 38, 40, 43, 48, 73, 74, 86, 91, 95, 98, 106, 120, 152, 156, 186, 198, 224, 228, 278, 280, 290 n.3; alternation of person in preface follows pattern of Herodotus, 185 n.52; amplification, 35-6; and effort, 148, 150; as unintrusive narrator, 8, 173; audience of, 21; avoids treating non-Greek world, 35 n.3; character read from his work, 132 n.16; extended preface as element of authority, 9; fashions narrative different from Herodotus', 9-10; on experience, 133-4; on Peloponnesian War as one war, 134; sees his work as permanent possession, 21, 58

concerned with underlying realities, 67; contrasts myth with clarity, 117; criticises mythic element in his predecessors, 117-18; disowns myth in his history, 117; documents of little use in his narrative of Sicily, 104; does not suggest autopsy superior to inquiry, 67-8; emphasis on reasoning and analysis, 9; emphasises result of research over process, 9; includes peace treaties in his work, 101; inconsistent in his attitude towards the past, 96-7; invokes autopsy on the plague, 80; makes ἀκρίβεια the guiding principle, 68; methodology in the Archaeology, 97, 106 n.224; methodology of, 67-8; narrative based on eyewitness and reports, 67; on contemporary and non-contemporary events, 70 n.33; on difficulty of reconstructing battles, 69; on unreliability of native tradition, 283-4; remarks on autopsy and inquiry compared with Lucian's, 76; removes substructure of inquiry from his history, 69; sees autopsy as influenced by memory and prejudice, 69; sets precedent for use of explicit statements of autopsy and inquiry, 80; use of abstract language to maintain narrative impartiality, 173-4 n.205; uses evidence of monuments in Harmodius and Aristogeiton digression, 101

a character in his history, 179; avoids associations inherent in first person, 184; distinguishes between narrative of his deeds and his role as narrator, 183-4; does not overtly justify his actions within the narrative, 183; justification of his actions at Amphipolis, 183-4; narrative of his own actions, 182-4; not decisive model for historian's narration of his own deeds, 182; on his exile, 184; use of his name and patronymic, 183; use of third person influenced by Homer, 184; use of first person when speaking as investigator, 184-5 n.52; use of third person, 184-5 n.52, 205

'continues' Herodotus, 290 n.1; criticises performance pieces, 21; imitation of Homer, 15 n.70; models preface on Hecataeus of Miletus, 272; on Herodotus, 9 n.34, 185 n.52; narrative manner in polemic, 227 n.50; polemic with Hellanicus, 113-14, 226-7; polemic with poets and prose writers, 21 n.100, 226; rival of Homer, 14; rival of Pindar, 15; sparing use of polemic, 226-7; use of Antiochus of Syracuse, 284 n.18

attacked by Dionysius as holding a grudge against Athens, 184; character judged as harsh by Dionysius, 132; cited by Ammianus, 255; continuators of, 237-8; description of civil war imitated by later

Thucydides (cont.)
historians, 16 nn.71-2; by Sallust, 16 n.71; his impartiality praised by later writers, 184 n.51; his war monograph imitated, 17; model for narrative impartiality, 173; model for stylistic imitation, 16 n.74; praised by Dionysius for rejecting myth, 122; recalled by Arrian, 253; Timaeus' rivalry with, 229; work mentioned by Diodorus, 243 n.129
Thucydides, Athenian commander, 183 n.40
Tiberius, his *Memoirs*, 181 n.29
Timaeus of Tauromenium, 70, 75, 171, 218, 233, 241, 284-5, 289; banished by Agathocles, 187; competitor with Polybius as historian of the West, 231; exiled from Sicily, 71; father Andromachus, 187; importance of, 223, 231; methodology for contemporary history unknown, 71; narrative of his own actions, 187; on expense and difficulty of his research, 149; on founding of Tauromenium, 187; possibly relies on eyewitnesses and participants, 71; relies on monuments and inscriptions for non-contemporary history, 71, 101; uses documents to refute Aristotle's account of Epizephyrian Locrians, 105
  attacks Aristotle, 229; Callisthenes, 229; Demochares, 229; Ephorus, 229; Homer, 229; Philistus, 229; Plato, 229; Theophrastus, 229; bitterness (πικρία) of, 223, 231 n.79; castigated Agathocles, 187; continued by Polybius, 238; criticised by Diodorus, 165 n.166; for lying about Agathocles, 162; criticised by Polybius, 230-2; for bitterness of character, 231; for deliberate falsehood, 231; for excessive polemic, 231; for lacking experience, 71, 72 n.40; for love of cavilling and fault-finding, 232; for lying about Agathocles, 162; for prejudice, 164; for relying too greatly on books, 72; for slander, 231; criticised for maliciousness, 132; criticisms make his own history seem reliable, 223; excess of polemic, 223; mentioned by Dionysius as predecessor, 244; probably did not align himself with predecessors, 229; works written against him, 223
Timagenes, 224 n.38; his outspokenness, 255 n.197; praised by Ammianus, 255
Timonides, his claim of autopsy and inquiry, 80 n.83; narrative of his own actions, 187; uncertain whether he wrote a history, 187 n.60

titles, book, 272 n.5, 273; imitation of, 17
Titus, approves Josephus' history, 90
toils: *see* effort
tombstones, used by Cato as historical source, according to Cicero, 102
topoi, historiographical, *passim*; innovation in, 14 n.61; summary of, 258-62
tradition
  historiographical, appeal to, as element of winning authority, 12-19; as shaper of historiographical authority, *passim*; conservative throughout antiquity, 12; winning a place in, 261
  local, and myth, 122-3; as source for non-contemporary history, 99; importance for Antiochus' work on Italy, 100; importance for Cato's *Origins*, 101; manufactured by Greeks, 108 n.232, 284 n.19; *see also* natives
  written, and priests, 108-112; as basis for new treatment of old theme, 103; compared with oral tradition by Josephus, 103; distinction between privileged and non-privileged, 107; not abandoned by later historians, 106; seen by the ancients as valuable, 103; used by historians of non-Greek lands, 107
Trajan, 90; his *Memoirs*, 181 n.29; uses first person, 196 n.102
'translation', of native histories, as a favourite device for forgers, 110 n.244; presented by historians to a Greek audience, 110
travellers' reports, 67
Trogus: *see* Pompeius Trogus
truth, and falsehood seeming like truth, 4; backed up by oaths or bargains, 4; guaranteed by Muse, 3; opposed to bias, 160-1

universal history, 2; of Velleius, 29 n.141; praised by Diodorus, 46, 241; by Polybius, 37
utility, of history, 25, 43 n.28; changes in fourth century, 22-3

Valerius Antias, 28, 165; attacked by Livy, 248-9; member of the municipal aristocracy, 28 n.134; mentioned by Dionysius as his source for early Roman history, 245
variant versions, 280-6; chosen according to rhetorical criteria, 286; importance for historiographical methodology, 280-1; in Tacitus, 94-5; more common in non-

contemporary than contemporary history, 107 n.228; not always cited by historians, 280 n.2; not resolved by the ancient historian, 107; not the same as narrative uncertainty, 280 n.1; result of the lack of written records, according to Josephus, 103; technique for avoiding omniscience, 94

Varro, M. Terentius, 104 n.212; dedicates his *Antiquitates* to Julius Caesar, 55; distinguishes mythic, obscure, and historic eras, 124; his *Annals*, 28

Velleius Paterculus, 29, 77, 90, 142–3, 146, 224; dedicated his work probably to M. Vinicius, 55 n.82; emphasises autopsy of summit conference between Romans and Parthians, 81; faults Homer for failing to record his country, 273; genre of his work, 2 n.3, 29 n.141; justifies praise of men in Pannonian campaign, 173; laments his country's fate in civil wars, 169; magnification of Tiberius' deeds, 36; mentions his ancestors, 142–3; mentions role as participant to guarantee authority, 79; modesty in presentation of his own achievements, 213; narrative of his own actions, 198; not the centre of his narrative, 179; panegyrical nature of his history, 56; possible use of dedication, 56; praise of others, 213; reasons for mentioning his family, 143; use of first person, 198, 205; use of Roman first person plural convention, 287; validates splendour of Tiberius' triumph by autopsy, 83

Vespasian, his *Memoirs*, 181 n.29; approves Josephus' history, 90

Vinicius, M., addressee and possibly dedicatee of Velleius' history, 55–6

Vipstanus Messala, mentioned by Tacitus, 250

Virgil, 14 n.62

uirtus, 44, 212

vividity (ἔμφασις), in narrative, needs personal experience, 72

Vologesus, described in too biased a manner, 173

Volumnius, P., vouches for marvel at the battle of Philippi, 83

witnesses, difference between ancient and modern, according to Aristotle, 281 n.4

Xanthus of Lydia, as spur to Herodotus, 7; his date contested, 7 n.28; may have used royal records, 107 with n.230

Xenophanes, attacks Homer, 219; criticised by Heraclitus, 65, 219

Xenophon, 29, 150–1 n.102, 179, 182, 192, 195, 224, 240 n.122, 280 n.1, 289; believes eyewitnesses to be most reliable, 69; complains of history's restrictions, 22; does not elaborate methodology, 69; does not mention his experience, 134; extreme application of Thucydidean narrator, 10, 273; historian of his own deeds, 58; interest in character and morality, 21–2; not the editor of Thucydides' work, 238 n.107; not the ἐγώ of Thucydides v.26.4, 134 n.26; reliability of, 10; writes biography and philosophy, 19

Arrian's competition with, 253; Arrian's imitation of, 18 n.86, 253; character judged as pious by Dionysius, 132; model for soldier-historian, 91, 256 n.206; model for stylistic imitation, 16 n.74; possible influence on Caesar, 197, 205; praised by Lucian for impartiality, 170 n.190; use of polemic covert, 227; work mentioned by Diodorus, 243 n.129

Anabasis, 18; difficult to place in a single genre, 2 n.3; escape theme in, 201 n.125; imitated by Arrian's *Anabasis*, 17; magnification of opponents in, 215; political purpose of, 206 n.135; portrayal of Xenophon as ideal general in, 212; portrayal of Xenophon's piety in, 207–8; praise of Xenophon by others in, 214–15; techniques of self-presentation in, 206–15 *passim*; use and purpose of pseudonym Themistogenes, 186, 205; use of gods in, 207–8; use of third person in, 186; virtual preface of, 237 n.107, 273 n.12; defense of Xenophon from slander in, 211

Hellenica, 'continues' Thucydides, 237–8; does not have a virtual preface, 237 n.107; does not use traditional amplification of subject, 36; envisions its own continuation, 238; omission of Xenophon's name in, 10 n.41; unusual opening of, 237–8 n.107

years, exact numbers of, spent on a history, 151–2

Zeno of Rhodes, corrected by Polybius, 232; his claim of autopsy and inquiry, 80 n.83; praised by Polybius, 59

Zoilus of Amphipolis, 244 n.126

Ingram Content Group UK Ltd.
Milton Keynes UK
UKHW011944050723
424637UK00001B/11